RHS GARDEN FINDER 2006-2007

EDITOR: CHARLES QUEST-RITSON

THINK
BOOKS

THINK
BOOKS

A Think Book

First published in Great Britain in 2006 by
Think Publishing
The Pall Mall Deposit
124-128 Barlby Road, London W10 6BL
www.think-books.com

Published in association with
Royal Horticultural Society
80 Vincent Square London SW1P 2PE
www.rhs.org.uk

Distributed in the United States and Canada by:
Sterling Publishing Co., Inc.
387 Park Avenue South, New York, NY 10016-8810

Managing Editors: Emma Jones and Simon Maughan
Sub Editors: Rica Dearman and Kelly Walker
Designer: Lou Millward

Text layouts by Cooling Brown
Maps produced by JP Map Graphics

ISBN-10: 1-84525-018-4
ISBN-13: 978-1-84525-018-8

Printed and bound in Italy by Grafica Veneta S.p.A.

Main cover image: Julia Pigula/flowerphotos.com
Additional images: Front cover, left to right: RHS Garden Harlow Carr, Scampston Hall, Levens Hall.
Back cover, from top: Borde Hill Garden, Chatsworth, Wakehurst Place, Chatsworth,
Abbotsbury Sub-Tropical Gardens. Spine: The National Botanic Garden of Wales.

CONTENTS

KEY TO SYMBOLS
P Parking available   ⬠ Dogs permitted
WC Toilet facilities   ♿ Access for the disabled
✿ Plants for sale   🎁 Gift Shop
✕ Restaurant   ☕ Light refreshments

RHS, THE UK'S LEADING GARDENING CHARITY

The RHS believes that horticulture and gardening enrich people's lives. We are committed to bringing the personal and social benefits of growing plants to a diverse audience of all ages, to enhance understanding and appreciation of cultivated plants, and to provide contact with the natural world.

We believe that good practice in horticulture and gardening in both private and public spaces is a vital component of healthy sustainable communities and the creation of long-term environmental improvements

The RHS has four gardens around the UK: Wisley in Surrey, Hyde Hall in Essex, Rosemoor in Devon and Harlow Carr in North Yorkshire. It runs the best flower shows in the world and is a world leader in horticultural science and libraries. The RHS runs education and outreach programmes across the UK to help people realise their potential.

Its charitable activities include:
- Promoting biodiversity and creating wildlife habitats at its gardens;
- Creating hands-on opportunities for children to grow plants and learn about the natural environment;
- Encouraging sustainable horticulture and environmental care;

- Providing expert gardening advice;
- Running the RHS Award of Garden Merit scheme to help gardeners choose plants that perform well;
- Undertaking scientific research into issues affecting gardeners;
- Educating and training gardeners of all levels and experience;
- Maintaining the Lindley Library, the finest horticultural library in the world.

The RHS receives no government grants and for every pound received from members' subscriptions, needs to raise more than twice as much again to fund its charitable work.

It also relies on donations and sponsorship to supplement income from its garden operations, flower shows, shops and plant centres.

JOIN NOW & SAVE 10%

PLUS
FREE £5 SEED
VOUCHER
WHEN YOU JOIN BY
DIRECT DEBIT

Join the Royal Horticultural Society

- **FREE** entry with a guest to all four inspirational RHS Gardens
- **FREE** access to over 130 RHS recommended gardens*
- **FLOWER SHOWS:** privileged entry and reduced rate tickets to RHS flower shows Chelsea, Hampton Court Palace and the RHS Flower Show at Tatton Park, alongside eight London shows
- **FREE** monthly magazine, *The Garden* (*RRP £4.25*), delivered to your doorstep
- **FREE** invaluable support and advice from our expert gardeners and much more...

Take advantage of the 10% saving and pay only £~~42~~ £37.80 when you join today. **Call 0845 130 4646** quoting ref 2183 or join online at www.rhs.org.uk

Terms & Conditions: The offer is valid until 31-10-06 and cannot be used in conjunction with any other offer or membership transaction. This offer relates to RHS Individual membership only.
*Some throughout the opening season, some at selected periods.

The RHS, the UK's leading gardening charity

INDEX OF GARDENS FREE TO MEMBERS OF THE RHS

For gardens that are open to RHS members at selected times of year only in your county, please visit www.rhs.org.uk/rhsgardenfinder/gardenfinder.asp

REjuvenate

Discover a land rich in history, laced with quiet lanes linking quaint villages surrounded by beautiful countryside. With historic woodlands, rolling wheatfields dotted with poppies and windmills, estuaries and coastal villages, it's the ideal location for rejuvenation.

Why not visit one of the many gardens and historic houses for a relaxing day out?

Please call 0845 600 73 73 or visit our website www.realessex.co.uk and request your complete pack on Essex including our garden guide.

RealEssex

DELIVERED BY **ex|dra**
ESSEX DEVELOPMENT &
REGENERATION AGENCY

"The inchbald is one of the top garden design courses and consistently produces high calibre students" Andy Sturgeon, garden designer

novelty rose 2006
'Hot Chocolate'

Rose of the Year 2006
& Novelty Rose 2006,
available now from rose growers
& garden centres countrywide

rose of the year 2006
'Champagne Moment'

SPECIAL OFFER!

If you love walking, join the Ramblers... for 20% less

WHETHER YOU'RE A SEASONED WALKER OR SOMEONE WANTING TO MAKE MORE OF YOUR LEISURE TIME, JOINING THE RAMBLERS WILL ENABLE YOU TO EXPLORE THE GREAT OUTDOORS AND GET THE MOST OUT OF WALKING.

AS A MEMBER YOU WILL BENEFIT FROM:

Walking opportunities we have over 450 local groups just waiting to welcome you on their walks
Discretionary discounts in many outdoor stores including 10% off at both Millets and Blacks
walk BRITAIN guide, full of information and accommodation listings (rrp. £5.99 but FREE to members)
Quarterly magazine, walk Access to our extensive Ordnance Survey map library

Photo: Richard Mann

JOIN US TODAY AND CLAIM YOUR 20% DISCOUNT

Single membership £19.20 (normally £24)
Joint membership (two adults at the same address) £25.60 (normally £32)

TO JOIN, GO TO
www.ramblers.org.uk/offer
and use code RHSB
or call 020 7339 8500.

THE CHARITY WORKING FOR WALKERS

The Ramblers

www.ramblers.org.uk

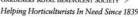

INTRODUCTION

Welcome to the new edition of the *RHS Garden Finder 2006*. This is a companion volume to the *RHS Plant Finder*. The *RHS Plant Finder* tells you where to find the right nurseries for plants; the *RHS Garden Finder 2006* will tell you where to see the same plants growing in gardens which are open to the public. This is all the more important now that membership of the Royal Horticultural Society brings free access for its members to more than 150 gardens up and down the United Kingdom and abroad.

The aim of this book is to supply sufficient detail to enable readers to decide if and when to plan a visit. The list is not exhaustive. It offers a selection of the different types of garden which are open to the public: ancient and modern, large and small, public and private. We welcome suggestions for additions, deletions or alterations to entries (please email us at questritson@aol.com). All major gardens which are open regularly are listed as a matter of course. These include many gardens of the National Trust and the National Trust for Scotland as well as botanic and public gardens and those attached to stately homes. But many gardens do not open to visitors regularly: the National Gardens Scheme lists over 3,000. In this book you will find a selection of these gardens which open only once a year or by appointment. Some guides would omit them on the grounds that it is not worthwhile to give publicity to gardens which so few people can visit but, if a good garden is seldom open, it is all the more important to know when the opportunity to see it will arise. This book also concentrates upon gardens with plants: some of the great historic gardens of the 18th century have comparatively

brief descriptions, because their landscapes are rather short on horticultural content. On the other hand, some of the best gardens for plants are those which have large 'living collections' for teaching purposes – botanic gardens, and those attached to horticultural colleges. They are among the most interesting for garden-lovers to visit.

Nurseries

Because this book is plant-led, it also includes about 150 leading nurseries. Almost all have a demonstration garden attached to them, just as most gardens have a nursery or plant stall. This is a recent development – it started about 25 years ago – but is now quite normal: visitors to a nursery like to see plants growing in a garden before making their purchases, and visitors to a garden like the opportunity to buy some of the plants they have seen there. It would not be right to exclude the inspirational series of model gardens at Bridgemere in Cheshire, Barnsdale in Leicestershire or the National Garden Exhibition Centre in Co. Wicklow just because they are attached to a commercial enterprise that sells plants.

How to use this book

Gardens are listed by county or region (for Scotland), and then alphabetically by name. The order is England, Scotland, Wales, Channel Islands, Northern Ireland and the Republic of Ireland. In general, we have stuck to the familiar 1974 counties of England and Wales and to the Scottish regional divisions. There are three exceptions: the county of Avon has been redistributed between Gloucestershire and Somerset,

Cleveland has been included with North Yorkshire, and Humberside has been split between Lincolnshire and the East Riding of Yorkshire. We have also divided Hereford and Worcester into its two component parts again. We have been careful to ensure, so far as possible, that gardens are listed in the county or region in which they actually lie, which is not always the county or region their postal addresses suggest, or where their owners believe themselves to live. Thus the Savill Garden lies in Surrey, even though most of Windsor Great Park is in Berkshire, and the gardens at Burford House near Tenbury Wells are neither in Herefordshire nor in Worcestershire, but across the border in Shropshire. To find out about a specific garden, turn to the index at the back: it should take you straight to the page you need.

Practical details

Our source for practical information about directions, opening times, admission charges, parking, lavatories, disabled facilities and refreshments has been the owners or their staff, backed up by our own enquiries where appropriate. The accuracy of these details is not guaranteed, but is believed to be correct at the time of going to press. We rely to a great extent on information which has been submitted to us by third parties. Not everyone who was approached has replied – or replied in time – and this explains some gaps. We very much regret having to drop a number of important gardens which have failed to reply to our requests for a 2006 update. A paperless version of the book is online as part of the Royal Horticultural Society's website (www.rhs.org.uk) and updates will be made as and when they are available. Inclusion in this book or on the Society's website, or exclusion from either of them, should not be construed as a recommendation or condemnation. And,

though this book carries the Royal Horticultural Society's endorsement, its comments and opinions are the editor's, and his alone.

Contacting gardens

In order to assist readers with special needs, or those hoping to arrange a group visit by special appointment, we list the telephone and fax numbers to which enquiries should be directed. In many cases this is the private telephone line of the owners: readers are urged to respect their privacy. If telephone and fax numbers have been omitted, this is because the owners prefer to receive such requests by letter.

Websites

There has been a great increase recently in the number of gardens and nurseries with dedicated internet sites. Many are beautifully designed and extremely informative. They help to attract visitors, especially groups from gardening clubs and tour operators. Please remember that website addresses change frequently and inexplicably. We have checked all the hundreds in this book during the autumn of 2005 and have only included those which are up and running and seem to us to offer useful information. Many websites are of excellent quality: some of the nursery sites permit online ordering. Others exist only as registered names: we have omitted them.

Visiting times

Many gardens are attached to other attractions – most typically, a house which is also open to the public. The visiting times we have given relate only to the garden. Please remember that most gardens have a last admission time. Typically it will be 30 or 45 minutes before they close, but it can be much longer. Remember, too, that a pre-booked group can often make a visit at a time or season when the garden is not open to individual visitors.

Prices

As with times, so with prices. The admission prices we have given relate only to the garden. If the house or some other attraction is open at the same time, a supplement may be payable. Some owners insist on you buying a full ticket, notably the Tussauds Group at Alton Towers and Warwick Castle, though most are more reasonable. It is true that some gardens may seem rather expensive but, generally speaking, the market rules of supply and demand apply and you get what you pay for. And it should be said that for every garden which is over-priced there are ten inspirational plantsman's gardens, run by their owners on a strictly non-commercial basis, where you can be certain of wonderful flowers, good design and a genuine welcome.

Many gardens offer special rates to groups and, if details are not given, it may be worth asking whether a reduction is available and what minimum number is acceptable. Please remember, however, that not all gardens permit parties: popular gardens which already suffer from wear and tear may not welcome increased visitor numbers. Special rates for families are sometimes available, especially at larger gardens attached to stately homes, where the garden is only one of many entertainments offered to the visitor. There are endless permutations on the numbers of adults and/or children which constitute a 'family' and the age at which a child becomes an adult and has to pay the full entry price. Season tickets are sometimes available, and good value for people who live near a large garden or stately home.

Entrance fees vary, and a few owners have told us that they may increase fees in the middle of the season. Some have a high season for a month or so – like Exbury in Hampshire and Leonardslee in West Sussex in spring. Others have a special day of the week or open days for charity when the entrance fee is higher. A few owners had not yet fixed their 2006 times or admission charges by the time we went to press and we have therefore indicated that the times or prices quoted are for 2005. All entrance fees are, in any event, liable to be changed: visitors would do well to take more money than they think they will need. Some gardens have honesty boxes, and it is also important to take lots of change, so that you are not forced to choose between paying too much and paying too little.

It is worth remembering that National Trust members are usually admitted free to Trust properties. Readers are strongly recommended to join the National Trust in any event: its portfolio of blue chip gardens is so comprehensive that no garden tour is complete without a visit to one or more of its properties.

Facilities

This guide uses a variety of symbols to show whether a garden has such facilities as public conveniences or plants for sale. We have indicated whether parking is available: this may be at the garden itself or on a public road very close to it. Parking may be at some distance from the house. At Saltram, in Devon, it is 500 yards (457m) away, and this is by no means exceptional. You can, however, expect better parking facilities at a popular property which offers a wide range of entertainments than at a small plantsman's garden in a country lane.

It is often a condition of admission that no photograph taken within the garden may be sold or used for public reproduction without the consent of the property owner. Some forbid photography altogether. Corporate owners like the National Trust or English Heritage do not welcome dogs at their properties, except guide dogs. Some restrict dogs to particular areas of a property, like the car park, or the woods and parkland rather than the garden proper. Private owners are generally better disposed, though visitors should remember to keep their dogs on leads. A few owners – like the Howards at Castle Howard – go out of their way to say that dogs are actually welcome, but not all have shaded areas for parking.

Disabled visitors

We have generally indicated which gardens are suitable for disabled people, though it is important to stress that access may only be partial. Often an area around the house or entrance is accessible for people in wheelchairs, but the more remote parts of the garden are quite unsuitable. It is best to ring before your visit to check. The same is true of other disabled facilities. We have not specified the nature of those facilities, but in most cases they include lavatories and ramps which are suitable for the wheelchair-bound. It is best to enquire in advance of a visit if particular items of special equipment are required. The National Trust is especially good at adapting its properties to accommodate the needs of disabled visitors.

Size of gardens

We have asked owners to indicate the size of their garden and the number of people who work in it. Taken together, these two statistics help to suggest how intensively a garden is worked and how long you need to allow for your visit. The number of gardeners must be interpreted flexibly. Some owners have told us how many paid gardeners they employ: others have included their own contributions and based their figure on how much time they and their family give to the garden.

The NCCPG

Four common abbreviations are used freely throughout the text: RHS for the Royal Horticultural Society, NGS for the National Gardens Scheme, SGS for Scotland's Gardens Scheme, and NCCPG for the National Council for the Conservation of Plants and Gardens. We have noted the NCCPG National Collections which are held at the gardens and nurseries we list, and we have supplied a separate index of them towards the end of the book. Not all genera are the subject of a National Collection: there are still some horticulturally important groups of plants which have not yet been seriously collected and studied under the auspices of the NCCPG. Other genera have been split into a number of different collections. This is particularly necessary in the case of such a large genus as *Rhododendron* or those, like *Euphorbia*, which require a great variety of growing conditions. Moreover, the NCCPG has wisely introduced a system of duplicate collections to insure against the risks which face every collection of rare plants. The need to maintain duplicate collections and split large genera explains why certain names occur several times in the list of National Collections towards the end of the book. The list of National Collections on the NCCPG website (www.nccpg.com) is updated fairly regularly.

Champion trees

For most gardens, we give a brief list of features. These include general information like 'good collection of trees' and more specific facts like 'tallest *Quercus cerris* in the UK'. Occasionally we have added some features which are not strictly plants, but do add enormously to the character of a garden. Information about outsize trees is taken principally from the records kept by that excellent organisation the Tree Register of the British Isles (see www.tree-register.org). There are two ways of measuring trees: height and girth. Sometimes the tallest specimen will also have the thickest trunk – but not always. Both the tallest and the biggest can claim to be the champion tree, and we have sometimes made this distinction when noting record-breakers in gardens. Tree measurements can never be fully up to date: some records have not been verified since the great gales of 1987 and 1990.

2005

Many garden-owners regarded 2005 as a fairly good year for visitors and are hopeful for 2006. There is a noticeable increase in the number of gardeners which the owners of large gardens employ. However, there are also signs that garden-visiting is meeting stiff competition for visitors' time and money. Fewer gardens opened for the National Gardens Scheme in 2005 than in 2004. Some owners of large gardens that are regularly open to the public have responded by putting up their entry prices by substantially more than the rate of inflation, which may not prove a wise policy in the long term. Others are extending their open season – one major garden told us that two thirds of their visitors now come when the snowdrops are in flower. One way to remain solvent, and make it worthwhile to remain open to visitors, is to cram the calendar with events of every kind, but this changes the nature of a visit for garden-lovers. Two very

important gardens in the Welsh marches, Hodnet Hall and Bryan's Ground, have decided not to open again in 2006. For many such gardens the cost of employing extra staff to offer refreshments, and maintain plant sales and gift shops is uneconomical. Even with these facilities, which members of the public expect and should increase their spending, a large garden needs at least 40,000 visitors a year to remain profitably open throughout the season.

Acknowledgments

The editor is very grateful to the many people who have helped in the compilation of this work. First and foremost he thanks all the garden-owners, nurseries, horticulturists, colleges, societies and everyone else who has responded to his requests for information. He is greatly indebted to them, and regrets that it is not always possible to give each the personal attention which is their due. Particular thanks go to the staff in the regional offices of the National Trust. Special thanks are also due to Ian Buckley, Brent Elliott, Ali Higgs, Geoff Hodge, Caroline Houlden, Simon Maughan and others at the Royal Horticultural Society. The editor also acknowledges the considerable input of others who have worked on this project: John Hodgson, David Lamb, Peter Cooling and our colleagues at Think Publishing. Finally thanks are due for their endeavours to Brigid and Madeline Quest-Ritson and Christopher and Katharine Blair.

Charles Quest-Ritson, Editor,
The RHS Garden Finder, P.O. Box 673, Salisbury, Wiltshire. SP3 4BU.
questritson@aol.com

GARDENS
TO
VISIT

ENGLAND

The purpose of this short introduction is to highlight some of the considerations that apply to gardens in England, but not to those in other parts of the UK or abroad. The first point to make is that gardens and gardening are essentially an English phenomenon. England has always taken the lead in horticultural matters within the British Isles, and gardening is still – to some extent – one of our most important cultural, artistic and scientific exports. Within England there are differences of garden emphasis and style between regions. Alpine gardening has many followers in the north of England; Cornish gardens tend to be rhododendron woodland gardens; the smart designers tend to practise in and around London. Gardening is probably at its strongest as a national pursuit in the south-east of the country, where more than half the Royal Horticultural Society's members live. But there are good gardens of every kind open to the public in every part of the country. In fact they are also fairly evenly distributed throughout England, except perhaps for the east Midlands, which has fewer good gardens than its rich agriculture might suggest. Gardens and garden-making depend as much upon social and economic circumstances as upon soil and climate.

A word about the grading of historic gardens is needed. During the 1980s, English Heritage's predecessors compiled a register of gardens and parks of special historic interest. The aim was to draw attention to the nation's heritage, so that designed landscapes were not overlooked, for example in plans for new development. There are three gradings, each of which assesses the historic layout, features and architectural ornaments. Grade I parks and gardens are 'of exceptional interest'; Grade II* parks and gardens are 'of great quality'. Grade II parks and gardens are 'of special interest'. These gradings reflect the importance of a particular garden or park and compare it with others in England as a whole. The register is in 46 parts, one for each of the 1974 English counties, and copies are available from English Heritage. The information they contain about the individual gardens is very comprehensive. It covers the site, area, dates and designers of key surviving elements, surviving features of the garden or park, and other interesting aspects such as historic associations.

The best source of reference for plants and nurseries is the annual publication *RHS Plant Finder*. It shows where the main concentrations of nurseries are – in Surrey, for example – and where there are few, like northern Cornwall. It lists only a handful of garden centres, which is a pity because most people buy their plants at local garden centres rather than specialist nurseries. There is no publication which tells you where to find a good garden centre, though the Garden Centre Association does have a very helpful searchable website (www.gca.org.uk). The advantage of buying from one of its 150 members is that all are subject to annual inspections by an independent auditor and must satisfy stringent standards to remain members.

The starting point for garden visiting English gardens must be the 'Yellow Book' which the National Gardens Scheme publishes annually in February under the full title *Gardens of England & Wales Open to the Public*. The Yellow Book is a best-seller. Its sales immediately after publication exceed 5,000 copies per week, three times the success rate of its nearest rival among best-selling paperback reference books. It is wonderfully comprehensive and totally undiscriminating. The owners write their own garden entries, with the result that a really good garden may come across as self-deprecatingly boring, while an exciting description can often lead to disappointment. Beware of self-publicists: you can usually spot the hype. The Yellow Book lists over 3,000 gardens and is the single most important guide to visiting gardens in England and Wales, and the least expensive. Copies of *Gardens of England & Wales Open to the Public* in 2006 will be available as from the end of February 2006.

Members of the RHS enjoy free entry to many gardens throughout England. Some are free throughout the year:

others for only a month or so. It is important that members should note carefully when they may expect free entry and when they may not. In most gardens the privilege applies only to members of the RHS, not to any guests who accompany them. Nevertheless, it is an impressive list and a major benefit of membership. The list has grown considerably in recent years, and the Royal Horticultural Society hopes to expand it yet further.

In addition to its Free Access gardens, the Royal Horticultural Society has a system of running lectures at a number of nurseries and garden centres in England, most of which are listed in this book, with a note of how to find out further details. The Society's own *Members' Handbook 2006* and website (www.rhs.org.uk) give full details of these and of the many lectures, demonstrations, workshops, garden walks and other events held at RHS Partner Colleges.

BEDFORDSHIRE

Both the Grade I gardens in Bedfordshire – Woburn Abbey and Wrest Park – are open to the public. Few of its other important gardens remain open to visitors, though every garden-visitor should seek out the gloriously eccentric Swiss Garden (Grade II*). The headquarters of the Royal Society for the Protection of Birds, The Lodge at Sandy, is also rated as a Grade II garden and open daily throughout the year. Shuttleworth College at Old Warden is now a RHS Partner College, but Bedfordshire is otherwise horticulturally underdeveloped. It is not over-endowed with arboreta, though Woburn has a fine collection of trees: there are a number of record-breakers there, as well as at Swiss Garden, Toddington Manor and Wrest Park. Surprisingly few private gardens open for the National Gardens Scheme and the county has no National Collections. There are few nurseries, too: best known is Blom's Bulbs at Melchbourne, close to the border with Northamptonshire, but it is not open to visitors. One para-horticultural curiosity worth seeing is the 'Tree Cathedral' near Whipsnade Zoo.

THE MANOR HOUSE
Church Road, Stevington, Bedford MK43 7QB

Tel: 01234 822064
www.kathybrownsgarden.homestead.com
Location 5 miles north-west of Bedford, off A428.
Opening hours 2 pm – 6 pm; 28 May & 30 July. Plus 6 pm – 9 pm on 21 June for NGS. And groups at other times by appointment.
Admission fee Adults £3.50; Children free.

P WC ⅏ ✿ ⬭

This is a very interesting newish garden – the owners moved here in 1991 and have designed and planted it with a sense of style that is contemporary rather than nostalgic. Kathy Brown is a garden-writer and cookery-writer, and these interests have overlapped in such titles as *The Edible Flower Garden* (1999). But she has also written books about container gardening, bulbs and cottage gardening – all of which have to some extent been worked out in the garden here. She is very good on structure: the French garden is an essay in formal design. It starts right outside the house, with a terrace that has a *gâteau* of tiles and stone at its centre: box cones and gravelled parterres lead down to a circular fountain. Planting is another of her skills: the containers are exuberantly filled with all kinds of unconventional material including long-term succulents and other exotics. Elsewhere are masses of bulbs, some for spring and many for summer display. Ninety late-flowering clematis extend the season alongside rambling and climbing roses. Gazebos, pergolas, a parterre leading to a wildflower meadow with a prairie planting of grasses at the centre, a cottage garden and a wisteria walk are among the many other features. The latest designs are a grass garden inspired by Barbara Hepworth's 'Green Caves' and a topiary garden which was influenced by Mark Rothko. Definitely a garden to see now and return to in future, as it develops.

🌿 good modern design; bulbs; old roses; clematis; wildflower meadow; containers; succulents; grasses; cream teas.

Owned by Simon & Kathy Brown
Number of gardeners owners only
Size 1.8ha (4½ acres)

SWISS GARDEN
Old Warden, Biggleswade SG18 9EA

Tel: 01767 627666
www.shuttleworth.org
Location 1½ miles west of Biggleswade.
Opening hours 10 am - 5 pm (4 pm from November to March); daily; all year. Closed Christmas week.
Admission fee Adults £4; Concessions £3.

🅿 🚾 ♿ 🌱 🎁 ✕ ☕

The Swiss Cottage in the Swiss garden was built in the 1820s for Lord Ongley – the guidebooks call it 'an outstanding example of the Swiss picturesque' – but most of the rustic, Gothic, landscape garden we see today was largely developed by the Shuttleworth family in the 1870s. It is a remarkable relic: a picturesque pleasure ground of winding paths and sinuous waterways, little cast-iron bridges and romantic huts, Pulhamite rockwork and thatched curiosities, quaint kiosks and soaring ironwork arches, gullies and ferneries, vast conifers and cheerful rhododendrons, and an early grotto-glasshouse (note the small panes of glass) planted as a fernery. In short – most enjoyable to visit.

picturesque landscape; rhododendrons; Pulhamite grotto; fernery; Swiss Cottage; publications and souvenirs shop; restaurant at nearby Shuttleworth Collection.

Owned by Bedfordshire County Council as lessee
Number of gardeners 1
Size 3.6ha (9 acres)
English Heritage Grade II*

TODDINGTON MANOR
Toddington LU5 6HJ

Tel: 01525 872576 **Fax:** 01525 874555
www.toddingtonmanor.co.uk
Location M1, Jct 12; first right in village; house just past 30 mph sign.

Opening hours 11 am - 5 pm; 29 May (plus ten other gardens in village). Pre-booked group visits welcome from June to mid-July.
Admission fee Adults £3.50; Children free.

🅿 🔊 🚾 ♿ 🌱

This garden is now in its prime, and has all been made by the owners since 1979 around some magnificent old trees. It has some excellent features, notably a lime avenue which leads into a cherry walk, and a wonderfully high standard of maintenance. The walled garden has long beds of delphiniums and peonies and a fine garden of herbs (culinary, medicinal and insect-repelling), while the double herbaceous border has been extended and is now 100m long and 6m wide. There is also a good modern rose garden of white and yellow floribundas interplanted with philadelphus. Further away from the house are a wild garden and three small ponds: visiting children may borrow nets to go dipping.

woodland walks; roses (mainly old-fashioned); herbs; mature conifers; good herbaceous borders; largest *Tilia* 'Petiolaris' in the British Isles.

Owned by Sir Neville & Lady Bowman-Shaw
Number of gardeners 2
Size 2.4ha (6 acres), plus 8ha (20 acres) of woodland

WOBURN ABBEY
Woburn MK17 9WA

Tel: 01525 290333 **Fax:** 01525 290271
www.discoverwoburn.co.uk
Location 1½ miles from Woburn on A4012.
Opening hours 10 am - 4 pm; daily; 24 March to 2 October.
Admission fee Park: £3 per car.

🅿 🚾 ♿ 🌱 🎁 ☕

Woburn may not have the reputation of being a gardeners' garden, but Humphry Repton, who designed the park, considered it one of his finest achievements. The deer park is home to ten different types of deer: one is the Muntjac deer from China, some of which escaped during World War II and have spread through much of England. Nearer the house are a pinetum and a quercetum (a collection of oaks), cedars, redwoods, huge swamp cypresses and such rarities as mature specimens of the hardy 'rubber tree' *Eucommia ulmoides* and *Acer triflorum*. Elsewhere are lily ponds, fritillaries, wild orchids and masses of naturalised *Narcissus* – more than 100 daffodil cultivars. The private gardens are simple and formal, mainly 19th-century and Italianate, but they include a circular hornbeam maze with a Chinese pavilion at its centre, herbaceous borders, a rose garden, a camellia house, and lots of good statues.

mature conifers; fine collection of trees; deer park; tallest *Zelkova sinica* (17m) in the British Isles; two shops; lunches & teas.

Owned by The Duke of Bedford
Number of gardeners 6
Size 16.8ha (42 acres)
English Heritage Grade I

WREST PARK
Silsoe MK45 4HS

Tel: 01525 860152 (weekends)
www.english-heritage.org.uk
Location ¾ mile east of Silsoe.
Opening hours 10 am - 6 pm (5 pm in October); Saturdays & Sundays; April to October.
Admission fee Adults £4.50; Concessions £3.40; Children £2.30; Family £11.30.

The 'English Versailles' is dominated by a graceful long canal which runs down to the classical domed pavilion built by Thomas Archer in 1710. Capability Brown came here later, but worked around the earlier design. The house came later still, in the 1830s. Many historic garden buildings have survived, some from as far back as the 1730s and others from the 19th century, including the orangery, the Mithraic altar, the bowling-green house and the Chinese temple and bridge. In the walled garden and around the house are a rose garden, bedding displays and glasshouses. In the park are handsome specimen trees, including a fine example of the purple-leaved birch (*Betula pendula* 'Purpurea').

grand parterres; long vistas; largest pink chestnut (*Aesculus* x *carnea*) in the British Isles; gift shop; light refreshments.

Owned by English Heritage
Size 36ha (90 acres)
English Heritage Grade I

BERKSHIRE

Even in its attenuated post-1974 shape, Berkshire is well provided with good gardens. Few of its great historic gardens and landscapes are open to the public, though Berkshire's only Grade I landscape, Windsor Great Park, is, of course, open all the time, while Inkpen House and Lutyens's masterpiece Folly Farm (both Grade II*) open for the National Gardens Scheme. There are good specimen trees in Windsor Great Park and the grounds of Eton College. Nurseries are less common than garden centres: Henry Street Garden Centre at Arborfield is one of the more individual ones, with a special line in roses. Berkshire has comparatively few National Collections, though the Crown Estates have no fewer than nine of them at the Savill Gardens and Valley Gardens, just over the border into Surrey.

ENGLEFIELD HOUSE
Englefield, Theale, Reading RG7 5EN

Tel: 0118 930 2221 **Fax:** 0118 930 3226
www.englefield.co.uk
Location On A340, 1 mile from M4, Jct 12.
Opening hours 10 am – 6 pm; Mondays; all year. Plus Tuesdays – Thursdays from 1 April to 1 November.
Admission fee Adults £3; Children free.
🅿 ♿

The garden at Englefield descends dramatically from the hill above the house through open woodland where mature native trees like oak and beech are mixed with Victorian conifers. The underplanting was begun in 1936 with advice from Wallace & Barr and has continued ever since. Here are collections of camellias, rhododendrons, eucryphias, acers, magnolias, cornus, davidias, azaleas (many of them the nearly extinct Ghent varieties) and other unusual trees and shrubs. A grotto has lately been built at the top of the stream, lined with a mosaic of pine cones. There are drifts of daffodils and other spring and summer bulbs and wonderful autumn colour. Grey stone balustrades and wide staircases, built in 1860, enclose the lower terraces where there are formal plantings, mixed borders, roses, topiary, wide lawns, water features and small enclosed areas (some lately paved and pebbled). A children's garden with hidden jets of water from four small statues is fun for younger visitors. A walled kitchen garden has recently been restored to produce many varieties of fruit, vegetables, herbs and flowers. The garden is enclosed by a deer park, with magnificent views over the lake and surrounding countryside.

🌿 woodland garden; roses (mainly old-fashioned); rhododendrons & azaleas; daffodils; good herbaceous borders; deer park.

Owned by Sir William & Lady Benyon
Number of gardeners 3
Size 3.6ha (9 acres)
English Heritage Grade II

FOXGROVE
Skinners Green, Enborne, Newbury RG14 6RE

Tel: 01635 40554
Location On western edge of Skinners Green.
Opening hours 10 am – 4 pm; 18 February, for snowdrops. Groups welcome by appointment. sat after fen show.
Admission fee Adults £2; Children free.
🅿 📶 🌿 ☕

Foxgrove is a plantsman's garden, linked to Louise Peters's nursery next door: Audrey Vockins is her aunt. Bulbs, alpines and herbaceous plants are Audrey's great interest. The hellebores, crocuses and snowdrops give a great display in early spring. There are good shrubs (including more than 50 daphnes), roses and handsome small trees, too. Louise's nursery (a RHS Partner Nursery) is open from 10 am to 5 pm from Wednesday to Sunday but closed in August. It carries an interesting range of hardy and cottage garden plants, including several new *Saxifraga* cultivars from the Czech Republic. Its speciality is snowdrops, which are sold by mail order 'in the green'. Other specialities – worth visiting the nursery to see – are hellebores, grasses and penstemons, and some newly planted herbaceous borders. There will be four RHS Special Events at Foxgrove in 2006; details from 020 7821 3408.

snowdrops; good herbaceous borders; primulas; spring bulbs; cyclamen & colchicums in autumn; bluebells; bank garden; tea & cakes.

Owned by Miss Audrey Vockins
Size 0.8ha (2 acres)

FROGMORE GARDENS
The Home Park, Windsor Castle, Windsor SL4 2JG

Tel: 020 7766 7305 **Fax:** 020 7930 9625
www.royalcollection.org.uk
Location Via the Long Walk from Park Street, Windsor.
Opening hours 10 am – 5.30 pm (last admissions 4 pm); 16 to 18 May and 26 to 28 August.
Admission fee £3.50 in May (garden only). Adults £5.50; Children £3.50 in August (includes house).

Frogmore was for many years a royal residence: most of the house dates from the reign of George III. The grounds were first laid out in 1793, when the lake was excavated and the spoil used to create a series of mounds and banks. The many garden buildings include a Gothic temple, an Indian kiosk, a tea-house, the Duchess of Kent's mausoleum and the Royal Mausoleum where Queen Victoria and Prince Albert lie. Nearby, but closed to visitors, is a cemetery where many members of the royal family have been interred since the middle of the 19th century. During the 1920s and 1930s, the gardens were extensively developed by the planting of ornamental trees and shrubs, underplanted by bulbs. The May openings are less expensive than the August ones, because the price for the latter includes a visit to the house. The house may also be visited in May, but there is a separate charge for it then.

historic landscape & buildings.

Owned by H.M. The Queen
Number of gardeners 5
Size 14ha (35 acres)
English Heritage Grade II*

THE LIVING RAINFOREST
Hampstead Norreys, Thatcham RG18 0TN

Tel: 01635 202444 **Fax:** 01635 202440
www.livingrainforest.org
Location Signed from M4, Jct 13. From A34 southbound, follow signs to East Ilsey, then Hampstead Norreys.
Opening hours 10 am – 5.15 pm; daily; all year. Closed 25 & 26 December.
Admission fee Adults £5.65; Concessions £4.95; Children £3.65. (Prices under review.)

The Living Rainforest consists of two large landscaped glasshouses, computer-set to create two different rainforest climates. Each has a thickly planted collection of exotic plants of every kind, many of them rare or endangered. There is a particularly

THE HARRIS GARDEN

University of Reading, School of Plant Sciences, Whiteknights, Reading RG6 6AS

Tel: 0118 378 8072 **Fax:** 0118 378 8160
www.plantsci.rdg.ac.uk/harrisgarden
Location On A327, 1 mile south-east of Reading.
Opening hours 2 pm – 6 pm; 9 April, 14 May, 11 June, 9 July, 13 August, 10 September & 8 October (closes at 5 pm).
Admission fee Adults £3; Children free.

P WC & ※ ☞

The Harris Garden was begun as recently as 1988, though it occupies what was once part of a famous landscape garden created by the 4th Duke of Marlborough (while still Marquess of Blandford) between 1798 and 1817. The idea was to develop a garden as an adjunct to the teaching of horticulture, landscape and botany by the School of Plant Sciences at the University. It is very much a gardener's garden, full of horticultural interest. Annuals, for example, are grown both in traditional drifts of individual plants, and in experimental mixtures. There is a 'jungle garden' of plants grown solely for spectacular sub-tropical effects. The winter garden concentrates upon plants whose flowers, bark or form give particular pleasure in the dark months of the year. The orchard is not a fruit garden, but a collection of ornamental crab apples underplanted with wildflowers and bulbs which flower from January to early June. There is a large heather garden, where plants are in turn interplanted with dwarf conifers; it is designed to lead naturally to a wildflower meadow. The walled garden has been developed as a traditional kitchen garden, with fruit trained on the walls, vegetables, herbs and flowers. The formal gardens include an area where Gertrude Jekyll's famous flower border at Munstead Wood has been reproduced to illustrate her ideas on colour planting – Richard Bisgrove is the great expert on Jekyll's planting style and one of the team behind the Harris Garden. But there is much more to see, including the woodland garden, a golden garden, a cherry bowl (flowering cherries around a circular clearing with bulbs which flower at the same time), a stream- and pond-garden, an autumn foliage bed and a splendid mixed border nearly 130m long. The garden is well supported by a Friends organisation – details are available from the Hon. Secretary at www.friendsoftheharrisgarden.org.uk

✿ sub-tropical plants; roses (mainly old-fashioned); plantsman's collection of plants; herbs; plants under glass; good herbaceous borders; fine collection of trees; Mediterranean shrubs; hardy annuals; heathers; primula dell; water garden; teas.

Owned by The University of Reading
Number of gardeners 2
Size 5ha (12½ acres)
NCCPG National Collections *Iris* (species)

fine and near-comprehensive collection of tropical aroids, including the epiphytic *Anthurium warocqueanum* from Colombia and the terrestrial A. *watermaliense* from Costa Rica. The flowering plants are wonderful in winter when the tropical orchids flower, and in spring when the jade vine (*Strongylodon macrobotrys*) flowers for several months – it has even set seed here. Later, in the summer, *Victoria amazonica* becomes one of the great attractions when it fills one of the pools. But the Living Rainforest is fascinating whatever the season or the weather outside, and there are tropical monkeys, butterflies and birds, too.

tropical plants from the Amazon basin and around the world; gift shop; refreshments.

Owned by The Living Rainforest
Number of gardeners 2
Size 1,860 sq m (20,000 sq ft) under glass

OLD RECTORY
Burghfield RG3 3TH

Tel: 0118 983 3200
Location Right at Hatch Gate Inn & first entrance on right.
Opening hours For NGS. Groups at other times by appointment.
Admission fee Adults £2.50; Children free; Groups £3.
P WC & 🌳 ▭
This highly acclaimed garden was designed by Ralph Merton and planted by Esther Merton, a first-rate plantswoman who knew exactly what she wanted to achieve. She had a very good eye for plants, and collected them herself all over the world, as well as exchanging gifts with her gardening friends throughout Britain. Her legacy includes wonderful roses, lush summer pots, quantities of spring bulbs (some of them rare), tiny alpines and unusual hellebores – all of them extremely well grown. The *tour de force* is a double

herbaceous border where plants build up their impact through repetition, backed by yew hedges which get taller towards the end, to cheat the perspective. It leads to a pool framed by dense plantings of strong foliage – ferns, hostas, maples. But the planting continues, and last year (2005) saw a new Mediterranean border and a 'heritage kitchen garden' for growing vegetables from the HDRA Heritage Seed Library.

snowdrops; rock garden; plantsman's collection of plants; good late herbaceous borders; stone troughs; exotic displays in tubs; hellebores; lilies; teas.

Owned by A.R. Merton
Number of gardeners 2
Size 1.8ha (4½ acres)

OLD RECTORY
Farnborough, Wantage OX12 8NX

Tel: 01488 638298 **Fax:** 01488 638091
Location In Farnborough village, opposite church.
Opening hours 2 pm – 5.30 pm; 23 April, 14 May & 25 June. And by written appointment (£5, which includes tea, coffee & cakes, in aid of Farnborough Church).
Admission fee Adults £2.50. For NGS.
P WC & 🌳
This excellent garden has been made by the owners on a high, cold, windy site since 1965. Lots of hedges and thick planting were the keys to survival, but the effect now is of shelter and luxuriance. There are splendid double herbaceous borders, clever colour plantings, a collection of small-flowered clematis, a kitchen garden, a *boule* garden and an expanding arboretum (191 trees so far).
roses (mainly old-fashioned & climbers); good herbaceous borders.

Owned by Mr & Mrs Michael Todhunter
Number of gardeners 1½
Size 2.4ha (6 acres)

BUCKINGHAMSHIRE

Buckinghamshire is wonderfully stocked with large estates and grand, historic gardens. All three Grade I landscapes – Cliveden, Stowe and West Wycombe Park – are regularly open to the public, as are the two Rothschild gardens at Ascott and Waddesdon. These estates also have many fine trees. The National Gardens Scheme is active in the county, and lists over 80 gardens to visit, often in village clusters. Dorneywood Garden at Burnham is particularly worth seeing on its all-too-rare openings for the National Gardens Scheme. There are, however, comparatively few National Collections in the county.

ASCOTT
Wing, Leighton Buzzard LU7 0PS

Tel: 01296 688242 **Fax:** 01296 681904
www.nationaltrust.org.uk
Location ½ mile east of Wing.
Opening hours House & garden: 2 pm - 6 pm; Tuesday - Sunday; 14 March to 30 April & 1 to 31 August. Tuesday - Thursday; 2 May to 27 July. Garden only: 1 May & 28 August for NGS.
Admission fee Garden only: Adults £4; Children £2.
P WC & ❦

Ascott is an opulent late-Victorian extravaganza. It was largely planned by Leopold de Rothschild and planted with trees and shrubs supplied by the famous Chelsea nurseryman Sir Harry Veitch. The Dutch garden, the Madeira walk, the Venus garden and the topiary sundial date from this period (c.1880-1920) and include two fountains by Thomas Waldo Story. The topiary sundial is famous: its Roman numerals are planted in box and the gnomon at the centre is made of golden yew grafted onto green Irish yew. The motto – in Latin – reads 'Light and shade by turn, but love always'. Much in these old gardens has been restored, remade and replanted in recent years. The bedding in the Dutch garden changes its plants and colours twice a year. The 'long walk' to the lily pond now has a serpentine shape created by beech hedges and the old fern garden has been replanted as a box parterre and is now known as the sunken garden. And there is a 'planet topiary garden', built to resemble the astrological symbols of the 12 planets and showing their position in the sky at the very moment Sir Evelyn and Lady de Rothschild were each born. But there are fine old trees, and new plantings, too, including a young collection of modern magnolias and groups of *Davidia involucrata*, *Aesculus indica* and *Juglans nigra*, and good spring bulbs, too.

🌿 woodland garden; topiary; mature conifers; good herbaceous borders; spring bulbs; Dutch garden; tallest *Cedrus atlantica* 'Aurea' in the British Isles.

Owned by The National Trust
English Heritage Grade II*

BLOSSOMS
Cobblers Hill, Great Missenden HP16 9PW

Tel & Fax: 01494 863140
Location 2½ miles north-west of Great Missenden by Rignall Road, signed Butlers Cross, to Kings Lane about 1 mile on right, then to top of Cobblers Hill. Right at yellow stone marker and right after 50 yards.
Opening hours By appointment only.
Admission fee £2 for National Gardens Scheme.
P & ⌾

The origins of this fascinating plantsman's garden go back to 1925 when a previous owner started to plant up a four-acre field and an acre of beech wood filled with bluebells. Dr and Mrs Hytten have lived here since 1975 and have benefited from the substantial windbreaks planted in the 1920s and 1930s. Having once been open – there is still a fine view of the Misbourne Valley – Blossoms is essentially a woodland garden now, with an established apple orchard and some lusty specimen trees including a liquidambar and a fern-leaved beech *Fagus sylvatica* 'Aspleniifolia'. The Hyttens have thickened up the woodland themselves and made good collections of maples, eucalyptus and willows, together with some more unusual trees, such as *Tetradium daniellii*, *Davidia* and *Metasequoia*. Add on a herbaceous border, shrub borders (including some interesting new shade-lovers), a scree garden, a rock garden, a rare collection of herbaceous plants, a cutting garden, a number of very large climbing roses, a small lake, smaller ponds, patios and statues (mostly wood-carvings) – and the scale and variety of the owners' achievement will be apparent. The owners say that spring and autumn are the best seasons, but like all good plantsman's gardens there is lots of interest throughout the year.

a plantsman's collection of good plants; woodland walks; trees, ponds & wooden sculptures; rock garden; good herbaceous borders; teas by arrangement.

Owned by Dr & Mrs Frank Hytten
Number of gardeners owners only
Size 2ha (5 acres)

CHENIES MANOR
Chenies, Rickmansworth WD3 6ER

Tel & Fax: 01494 762888
Location Centre of Chenies village.
Opening hours 2 pm - 5 pm; Wednesdays, Thursdays & Bank Holidays; April to October. Plus special plant sale on 16 July from 10 am to 5 pm (£4.50).

Admission fee Gardens only: £3.50. (Under review.)

The richly planted gardens at Chenies Manor are full of variety but designed to complement the Elizabethan house. Their most spectacular period is spring – April and early May – when 300 different cultivars of tulip come into flower in and around the sunken garden, modelled on Hampton Court. All come from Bloms and all are clearly labelled: each is grown in groups of 10 to 50 bulbs and offers a wonderful opportunity to learn about tulips. Later comes the summer bedding, interspersed with herbaceous plantings – red dahlias with white forms of *Campanula latiloba*, for example. And there are colour borders everywhere: a very easy but effective one mixes *Alchemilla mollis* with catmint and *Sisyrinchium striatum*. Add in a physic garden for herbs, a grass labyrinth, a yew maze, a kitchen garden, and some beautiful old lawns and yew hedges, and you have a garden of great harmony.

bulbs; topiary; herbs; fruit; physic garden; award-winning maze; tea, coffee, home-made cakes.

Owned by Mrs A. MacLeod Matthews
Number of gardeners 1, plus family
Size 1.8ha (4½ acres)
English Heritage Grade II*

CLIVEDEN
Taplow, Maidenhead SL6 0JA

Tel: 01628 605069 **Fax:** 01628 669461
www.nationaltrust.org.uk
Location 2 miles north of Taplow, M4, Jct 7.
Opening hours 11 am - 6 pm (4 pm from 30 October); daily; 15 March to 22 December.
Admission fee Grounds: Adults £7.50; Children £3.70; Family £18.70.

Cliveden is a vast (and very important) landscape garden, filled with whatever money could buy: balustrading from the

Villa Borghese in Rome, the dramatic 'Fountain of Love' and a huge parterre below the house. The best of all is the Arcadian ilex wood. Allow lots of time to visit this garden of wonders.

 woodland garden; snowdrops; roses (mainly modern); fruit; good herbaceous borders; bluebells; good autumn colour; tallest *Juglans cinerea* (24m) in the British Isles; National Trust shop; light refreshments & meals.

Owned by The National Trust
Number of gardeners 9
Size 64ha (160 acres)
NCCPG National Collections *Catalpa*
English Heritage Grade I

HARTWELL HOUSE
Oxford Road, Aylesbury HP17 8NL

Tel: 01296 747444 **Fax:** 01296 747450
www.hartwell-house.com
Location 2 miles from Aylesbury, on A418 towards Oxford.
Opening hours For guests of the hotel.
Admission fee Free to patrons.

The gardens at Hartwell House were laid out early in the 18th century, in the formal style. When they were landscaped by Richard Woods (a follower of Capability Brown), most of the garden buildings were retained, in particular a Gothic tower and pavilion by James Gibbs. The modern gardens are especially fine in springtime, with hosts of snowdrops, daffodils, winter aconites, primroses and anemones. In the orchard old varieties of apples are grown, while the walls of the former kitchen garden support apricot, peach, pear and plum trees – the same cultivars as were originally planted in 1868. Flowers for the house and fresh herbs for the kitchen are grown in Hartwell's gardens. Last year (2005) saw the reopening of the restored Sir William Lee folly bridge. Most restoration is

planned for this year, notably the Lady Elizabeth Lee garden. There will be two RHS Special Events at Hartwell House in 2006; details from 020 7821 3408.

hotel, restaurant & spa.

Owned by Historic House Hotels Ltd
Number of gardeners 3
Size 36ha (90 acres)
English Heritage Grade II*

HUGHENDEN MANOR
High Wycombe HP14 4LA

Tel: 01494 755573 **Fax:** 01494 474284
www.nationaltrust.org.uk
Location 1½ miles north of High Wycombe.
Opening hours 11 am - 5 pm; Wednesday - Sunday plus Bank Holidays, 1 March to 5 November. Plus 2, 3, 9, 10, 16 & 17 December.
Admission fee Garden only: £2.50; Children £1.80. Park & woodland: free.

Hughenden is not a great garden, but interesting for its association with Disraeli. The garden was made by his wife in the 1860s and has a classic gardenesque planting of specimen trees on the North Lawn and a more Italianate design on the southern side. The National Trust has restored it, using photographs taken in 1881, so that the parterres are once again planted with Victorian annuals and bedding.

good herbaceous borders; 61 old apple varieties; rolling parkland; formal Victorian parterres with bright bedding out as in Disraeli's day; National Trust shop; stableyard restaurant.

Owned by The National Trust
English Heritage Grade II

LOWER ICKNIELD FARM

Lower Icknield Way, Great Kimble,
Aylesbury HP17 9TX

Tel & Fax: 01844 343436
Location On B4009 between Great Kimble &
Longwick.
Opening hours 9 am – 5 pm; daily; all year.
Closed from Christmas to New Year.
Admission fee Free.

The display garden attached to Lower
Icknield Farm Nurseries is best from July to
September. The structure comes from
hardy perennials and grasses, but
supplemented by tender perennials and
annuals. These include *Argyranthemum*
(they used to have a National Collection)
and tender salvias – mainly the Mexican
species like *S. greggii* and the *S. x jamensis*
hybrids. All the plants they sell are raised
on the nursery – none is brought in – and
they sell no sundries apart from their own
brand of growing compost. Plants are what
they raise, and there is a succession of half-
hardy patio and house plants for sale
throughout the year, as well as hardy
bedding and a good range of unusual
hardy perennials.

good display garden; salvias;
argyranthemums.

Owned by Mr & Mrs J. Baldwin
Number of gardeners 1
Size 2ha (5 acres)

THE MANOR HOUSE

Bledlow, Princes Risborough HP27 9PB

Tel: 020 7584 4243 **Fax:** 020 7823 1476
Location Off B4009.
Opening hours 2 pm – 6 pm; 7 May & 18 June for
NGS. And by appointment.
Admission fee £4.50.

This is one of the greatest gardens of our
times: beautifully planted and well
maintained, it has all been made on thin
chalk soil since 1969. There are four parts:
first, the garden 'proper' round the house,
enclosed by hedges of beech, hornbeam or
yew. Best is the armillary garden, an
exercise in topiary with the sphere at its
centre, surrounded by four cubes of yew,
smaller hedges and labels of box. Next
comes the walled garden with a gazebo in
the centre whose eight trellised posts are
planted with rambling roses. The central
grass walk is lined with apple trees trained
as spheres around a wire globe: they rise
from parterre boxes of teucrium, each
planted with a different herb – sage,
chives, Greek oregano and so on. The
third part of the garden is quite different –
2½ acres of sculpture garden, started in
1991 and already remarkably mature. The
land has been contoured to maximise the
movement of the surface, and give
contrasts of height and depth. Its fluid
modern design is a great foil to the formal
gardens around the house. The presiding
spirit is a life-size gorilla by Michael
Cooper. The fourth part of the garden is
different again – four acres of water
garden, started in 1979 on the site of three
old watercress beds. The 13 springs which
issue from its sides are the headwaters of
the River Lyde, a tributary of the Thames.
The steep valley sides are thickly planted
with shrubs and herbaceous plants. A
wooden walkway, Japanese in style, takes
you round the edge of the lakes at the
bottom. The muddy banks are planted
with candelabra primroses, gunneras,
hostas and astilbes. Unlike the rest of the
garden, this part is open daily (and free)
from dawn to dusk.

good herbaceous borders; sculptures;
new water feature by William Pye.

Owned by Lord & Lady Carrington
Number of gardeners 3
Size 3.6ha (9 acres)

STOWE LANDSCAPE GARDENS

Stowe, Buckingham MK18 5EH

Tel: 01280 822850 **Fax:** 01280 822437
www.nationaltrust.org.uk
Location 3 miles north-west of Buckingham.
Opening hours 10.30 am – 5.30 pm (last
admissions 4 pm); Wednesday – Sunday & Bank
Holiday Mondays; 1 March to 29 October. 10.30 am
– 4 pm; Saturdays & Sundays; 4 November to
25 February 2007. Closed 27 May, 24 & 25
December. Garden may close in bad weather.
Admission fee Adults £6; Children £3; Family £15.

This mega-landscape is considered by some
the most important in the history of
gardens. William Kent designed the
Temple of Venus (1731), the Shell Bridge
(1733), and the highly original Temple of
British Worthies (1734) which has statues
of Alfred the Great, the Black Prince,
Queen Elizabeth, John Milton and 12
further historic persons – Stowe was a
highly fashionable garden with a strong
political message. Capability Brown laid
out the Grecian Valley in the 1740s: it was
while he was head gardener at Stowe that
he developed his skill in simplifying formal
gardens and creating the distinctive curves
and contours which we now recognise as
an essential feature of the English
landscape garden. The National Trust has
undertaken extensive restoration and
renovation since it took over in 1989. Go
if you have not been already, and go again
if you have. Stomp round slowly, and
contemplate the history and symbolism of
each feature. Read the National Trust's
excellent guide and then go round again,
this year, next year, every year, and
commune with the *genius loci*.

tallest *Fraxinus angustifolia* var.
lentiscifolia (24m) and largest **x**
Crataemespilus grandiflora (9m) in the British
Isles; National Trust shop; tea-room.

Owned by The National Trust
English Heritage Grade I

TURN END

Townside, Haddenham, Aylesbury
HP17 8BG

Tel: 01844 291383/291817
Location Turn at Rising Sun in Haddenham, then
300 yards on left. Park in street.
Opening hours Groups of 10+ by appointment.
Admission fee On application.

Peter Aldington was once a young
architect, much influenced by Le Corbusier
and James Stirling. In 1963 he and his wife
bought this plot and built their house – a
modern architectural classic, much
photographed, cited, visited and copied
(and now listed). Aldington believed that
his job as an architect was to make
connections and create forms which
enclosed spaces for people to use and enjoy.
He then set out to apply the same
principles to his garden, drawing upon his
love of textures and materials to design and
plant it. The garden, like the house,
became one of the most acclaimed to be
made in the latter half of the 20th century.
Over the years Aldington was able to
increase its size by small additions. It still
covers less than one acre, but never was
space so ingeniously used to create an
illusion of size. A brilliant series of
enclosed gardens, sunken or raised, sunny
or shady, each different and yet
harmonious, contrasts with lawns, borders
and glades. The story is told in *A Garden
& Three Houses* by Jane Brown (Garden
Art Press, 1999): the Aldingtons still have
a few copies for sale.

brilliant design - a series of spaces;
rock garden; a plantsman's collection
of plants; ferns; grasses.

Owned by Mr & Mrs Peter Aldington
Number of gardeners 1
Size 0.4ha (1 acre)

WADDESDON MANOR
Aylesbury HP18 0JH

Tel: 01296 653226 **Fax:** 01296 653212
www.waddesdon.org.uk
Location A41 Bicester & Aylesbury; 20 miles from Oxford.
Opening hours 10 am – 5 pm; Saturdays & Sundays; 7 January to 26 March. Wednesday – Sunday & Bank Holiday Mondays; 29 March to 23 December.
Admission fee Grounds only: Adults £5; Children £2.50. RHS members free in March, September & October.

P wc & ¥ ❀ ♿

The garden at Waddesdon was laid out in the 1870s and 1880s for Baron Ferdinand de Rothschild by the French landscape designer Elie Lainé. This involved levelling the crown of a hill, planting it with mature trees and creating the drives, banks and formal gardens which were essential to the design. The result is one of the finest Victorian gardens in Britain, which has been meticulously restored since 1990 by Lord Rothschild, working in conjunction with the National Trust. A grand park, splendid formal gardens, a rococo aviary and extravagant bedding are the first fruits of his work. Formal bedding in the parterres is a Waddesdon speciality. There will be two RHS Special Events at Waddesdon in 2006; details from 020 7821 3408.

daffodils; good herbaceous borders; magnificent bedding; spring walk with 80,000 crocuses; gift & wine shop; tea-room; restaurant.

Owned by The National Trust
Number of gardeners 8 full-time, 2 part-time, plus interns & students
Size 66ha (165 acres)
English Heritage Grade II*

WEST WYCOMBE PARK
West Wycombe HP14 3AJ

Tel: 01494 513569/755573
www.nationaltrust.org.uk
Location West end of West Wycombe on A40.
Opening hours 2 pm – 6 pm; Sunday – Thursday; April to August.
Admission fee Adults £3; Children £1.50.

P wc & ¥

This park, with a lake in the shape of a swan, was made by Sir Francis Dashwood between 1735 and 1782, in a rococo style that was modified by later generations. It has been well restored and embellished by modern additions, including three modern eye-catchers designed by Quinlan Terry.
Owned by The National Trust
English Heritage Grade I

CAMBRIDGESHIRE

Cambridgeshire has a good number of historic gardens. Though only Wimpole Hall is rated as Grade I, there is a great cluster of Grade II* and Grade II landscapes in Cambridge itself: these include the University Botanic Garden and the following colleges – Christ's, Emmanuel, King's, Queen's, St John's and Trinity (including Trinity Hall). The Backs are also rated Grade I – and is one of the few places in the country where the strange but beautiful parasite *Lathraea clandestina* has naturalised (RHS Garden Wisley is another). The University Botanic Garden has by far the most exciting and comprehensive collection of plants in the county, especially for those trees that grow particularly well in the dry climate: many are the tallest of their kind in the British Isles. The National Gardens Scheme is well supported in Cambridgeshire, and has quite a number of villages where several smaller gardens open together. In Cambridge itself, several colleges open for the National Gardens Scheme, including Clare, Emmanuel, King's and Trinity. The county is thinly supplied by nurseries and garden centres, but Monksilver Nursery is a magnet for keen plantsmen and of international importance as a source of rare plants. Cambridgeshire has its fair share of National Collections – here again the lead is set by the University Botanic Garden with no fewer than nine National Collections from *Alchemilla* to *Tulipa*.

ABBOTS RIPTON HALL
Abbots Ripton PE28 2PQ

Tel: 01487 773555 **Fax:** 01487 773545
Location Off B1090.
Opening hours 2 pm – 5 pm; 21 May, 25 June, 9 & 23 July & 6 August, for NGS and various local charities. Groups of 12+ by appointment.
Admission fee Adults £3; Children (under 16) £2.
P **WC** **&** **※** **D**
Humphrey Waterfield, Lanning Roper and Jim Russell all worked here, and few garden owners have had as many gardening friends as Lord De Ramsey's parents, who made and remade this garden over more than 50 years. The result is a garden of stylish individuality – as witness the Gothic trellis work and the bobbles of yellow philadelphus – but also of great unity. The present Lady De Ramsey has retained the unity of style while replanting many of the borders. In early summer it can fairly claim to be the most beautiful garden in England. irises; grey border; Chinese bridge; trellis work; splendid herbaceous borders; tallest *Pyrus pyraster* (12m) in the British Isles; new arboretum of rare oaks; teas.

Owned by Lord De Ramsey
Number of gardeners 1, plus 2 part-time
Size 3.2ha (8 acres)
English Heritage Grade II

ANGLESEY ABBEY
Lode CB5 9EJ

Tel: 01223 810080 **Fax:** 01223 810088
www.angleseyabbey.org
Location Off B1102, signed from A14.
Opening hours 10.30 am – 5.30 pm (last admissions 4.30 pm); Wednesday – Sunday & Bank Holiday Mondays; 22 March to 29 October. Plus Tuesdays in local school holidays. Winter Garden: Wednesday – Sunday; 4 January to 19 March & 1 November to 22 December, then from 30 December to 25 March 2007.
Admission fee Gardens: Adults £4.30, but £3.60 in winter.
P **WC** **&** **※** **❀** **D**

Though not begun until 1926, the grounds at Anglesey already deserve to be famous, for they are the grandest made in England during the 20th century. Majestic avenues and 35 acres of fine turf are the stuff of them: visit Anglesey when the horse-chestnuts are out and tulips glow among cowslips in the wildflower meadows. Large formal gardens, carved out of the flat site by yew hedges, house the 1st Lord Fairhaven's collection of classical and renaissance sculpture. The winter garden bursts with snowdrops and aconites, coloured stems and glistening evergreens. Then there are smaller gardens, said to be more intimate, where thousands of dahlias and hyacinths hit the eye: glorious or vainglorious, Anglesey has no match.

snowdrops; good herbaceous borders; landscaping on the grandest scale; long avenues of trees; dahlias; cyclamen; good autumn colour; winter walk; National Trust shop; licensed restaurant & picnic area.

Owned by The National Trust
Number of gardeners 6
Size 39ha (98 acres)
English Heritage Grade II*

CLARE COLLEGE FELLOWS' GARDEN
Clare College, Trinity Lane, Cambridge CB2 1TL

Tel: 01223 333200 **Fax:** 01223 333219
www.clare.cam.ac.uk
Location Enter from Clare Old Court off Trinity Lane, or from Queens Road.
Opening hours 10.30 am – 4.30 pm; daily; April to September.
Admission fee £2.50.
&

Two acres of views and vistas, walks and Hidcote-style enclosures filled with exquisite spring bulbs, spectacular hot-colour borders dating from the 1950s and herbaceous borders. The Fellows' Garden was largely laid out from 1947 onwards by Professor Nevill

Willmer, who died in 2001 aged 98. The features include a newly replanted (2003) pond garden, a scent garden, a new Victorian-style sub-tropical garden and fine examples of taxodiums, metasequoias and *Tilia* 'Petiolaris'. Willmer was extremely skilful in his manipulation of perspective and colour. Elizabeth Banks Associates have recently set out a ten-year plan to restore some of the original features which have been lost over the years.
Owned by The Master & Fellows
Number of gardeners 2
Size 0.8ha (2 acres)
English Heritage Grade II*

CROSSING HOUSE GARDEN
Meldreth Road, Shepreth, Royston SG8 6PS

Tel: 01763 261071
Location 8 miles south of Cambridge off A10.
Opening hours Dawn – dusk; daily; all year.
Admission fee Free.
P WC &

One of the wonders of modern gardening, the Crossing House celebrates the achievements of its makers since 1959, on an unpropitious site right beside the main railway line to Cambridge. Box-edged beds separated by granite paths contain thousands and thousands of different plants, densely planted in the cottage style. Shrubs, herbaceous plants, alpines and bulbs are planted in the same beds, to maximise the effect at all seasons. Peat beds, arches, topiary, a pool and raised beds are some of the features which add variety to the most intensely and intensively planted small garden in England. And every few minutes a London express whizzes past.

plantsman's collection of plants.

Owned by Mr & Mrs D.G. Fuller and Mr J. Marlar
Number of gardeners owners only
Size 0.1ha (¾ acre)

CAMBRIDGE UNIVERSITY BOTANIC GARDEN

Bateman Street, Cambridge CB2 1JF

Tel: 01223 336265 **Fax:** 01223 336278
www.botanic.cam.ac.uk
Location Entrance on Bateman Street, 1 mile to south of city centre & 5 mins from railway station.
Opening hours 10 am – 4 pm in winter (5 pm in spring & autumn, 6 pm in summer); daily, except 24 December to 2 January.
Admission fee Adults £3.50; OAPs £3; Children free.

P WC & ☘ ⬭

This exceptionally attractive botanic garden is essential visiting for any garden-lover who does not already know it. It has so many good and interesting features that you could spend all day here and not be bored. Cambridge's is also one of the most beautiful and best-maintained botanic gardens in the country. The limestone rock garden is one of its major attractions, where the plantings are arranged geographically. It overlooks the small lake whose surface is covered by water lilies. Late spring is the time to see the nearby woodland garden. Here are fine tree specimens, including *Dipteronia sinensis*, *Tetracentron sinense* and the hardy paw-paw *Asimina triloba*, and a dawn redwood (*Metasequoia glyptostroboides*) grown from the original introduction of seed into the UK in 1948. Along the sides of the little stream which runs through the wood are candelabra primulas, astilbes, irises and a bed of the giant horse tail *Equisetum telmateia*. Late spring is also the time to see the horse-chestnuts in flower, the Persian lilacs and the National Collections of shrubby *Lonicera* and *Ribes*. The garden has a very good collection of peony species, which are in some places interplanted with its hardy geraniums: perhaps one reason why the garden is so attractive is that its National Collections are of supreme horticultural value. The garden also maintains two acres of (mainly herbaceous) systematic beds, a feature which was created by the first curator Andrew Murray in 1845. It contains some 1,600 species, belonging to 98 families and growing in 157 beds: it is both historically important and beautiful in its design. Everywhere, too, are wonderful trees: was there ever a tree more beautiful than the type specimen of *Quercus* 'Warburgii'? The winter garden, planted in 1978, is the best in England, and draws on stems, leaves, bark and flowers to create its unique beauty. The superb series of linked glasshouses are a blessed sanctuary to horticulturally smart undergraduates during the cold months of an East Anglian winter, but every aspect of the garden's existence is educationally aware.

good herbaceous borders; important rock garden; species roses; dry garden; genetics garden; British wild plants; winter garden; tallest *Catalpa* x *erubescens* 'Purpurea' (11m) in the British Isles (and 21 other record trees); shop in summer months; light refreshments.

Owned by University of Cambridge
Number of gardeners 18
Size 16ha (40 acres)
NCCPG National Collections *Alchemilla*; *Bergenia* (species & primary hybrids); *Fritillaria* (European species); *Geranium* (species & primary hybrids); *Lonicera* (shrubby species & primary hybrids); *Ribes* (species & primary hybrids); *Ruscus*; *Saxifraga* (European species); *Tulipa* (species & primary hybrids)
English Heritage Grade II*

DOCWRA'S MANOR
Shepreth, Royston SG8 6PS

Tel: 01763 261557/260677
www.docwrasmanorgarden.co.uk
Location Off A10 to Shepreth, 5 miles north-east of Royston.
Opening hours 10 am – 4 pm; Wednesdays & Fridays; all year. 2 pm – 5 pm; first Sunday of month; April to October. For NGS: 14 May. And by appointment.
Admission fee Adults £4; Children free.

🅿 🆆 ♿ 🌱 ⌂

This is very much a plantsman's garden, whose lush profusion defies the dry, cold, alkaline site. Docwra's Manor is a series of small gardens – walled, wild, paved and so on – each brimming with interesting plants and good combinations. There is a sense of abundance, whatever the season. Interesting seedlings are encouraged and nurtured. Everything you see has been made by Mrs Raven since she and her late husband bought the house in 1954. Do read John Raven's charming and erudite *The Botanist's Garden*, available from Mrs Raven by post for £10 and one of the classics of 20th-century garden-writing.

🌿 plantsman's collection of plants; good herbaceous borders; Mediterranean plants; teas for NGS opening.

Owned by Mrs John Raven
Number of gardeners 1
Size 1ha (2½ acres)

ELSWORTH HERBS
Avenue Farm Cottage, 31 Smith Street, Elsworth, Cambridge CB3 8HY

Tel & Fax: 01954 267414
Location Smith Street runs through the middle of Elsworth; garden is towards the western end.
Opening hours By appointment.
Admission fee Free.

🅿 🌱

This is an excellent example of a small boutique nursery attached to a National Collection – in this case two of them, *Artemisia* and *Nerium oleander*. Its range is wide – over 50 oleanders, for example, which is twice as many as anyone else – but the owners do not carry large stocks, so they are happy to propagate to order. The list of *Artemisia* species is quite unique – a triumph of plantsmanship.

Owned by Dr J.D. & J.M. Twibell
Number of gardeners owners only
Size 0.3ha (¾ acre)
NCCPG National Collections *Artemisia; Nerium oleander*

ELTON HALL
Peterborough PE8 6SH

Tel: 01832 280468 **Fax:** 01832 280584
Location A605, 8 miles west of Peterborough.
Opening hours 2 pm – 5 pm; Wednesdays; June to August. Also Thursdays & Sundays in July & August, 29 & 30 May & 28 August. Parties by appointment.
Admission fee Garden only: Adults £4; Children free. RHS members free (only at some times).

🅿 🆆 ♿ 🌱 🌰 ⌂

The house is a castellated extravaganza. The Victorian and Edwardian gardens have been energetically restored in recent years which makes Elton highly visitable. The high spots are the parterre, sunken garden, rose garden and new millennium orangery. Best in June and July.

🌿 roses (mainly old-fashioned); good herbaceous borders; fine collection of trees; handsome hedges; good colour plantings; plant centre on site; tea-room.

Owned by Sir William Proby Bt.
Number of gardeners 2½
Size 10.3ha (26 acres)
English Heritage Grade II*

HARDWICKE HOUSE
High Ditch Road, Fen Ditton, Cambridge
CB5 8TF

Tel & Fax: 01223 292246
Location ½ mile east of village.
Opening hours By appointment only
Admission fee Adults £3; Children 50p.

This is an excellent plantsman's garden
with an emphasis on herbaceous plants,
roses and bulbs. The owner has a particular
interest in Asia Minor, as witness an area
devoted to Turkish plants and bulbs. The
aquilegias are good, too.
plantsman's collection of plants; good
herbaceous borders; bulbs.

Owned by John Drake
Number of gardeners owner only
Size 0.8ha (2 acres)
NCCPG National Collections *Aquilegia*

MONKSILVER NURSERY
Oakington Road, Cottenham CB4 8TW

Tel: 01954 251555 **Fax:** 01223 502887
Location North of Cambridge: between Oakington
& Cottenham.
Opening hours 10 am – 4 pm; Friday – Saturday;
March to June, & October. Special open day: 11 am
– 4 pm; 23 September.
Admission fee Free.

This remarkable nursery is deservedly
fashionable and now has an excellent
display area. Monksilver specialises in
finding and rescuing really rare plants. They
say that their areas of speciality include
Anthemis, *Arum*, *Astrantia*, *Aster*, bulbs,
Euphorbia, ferns, *Galanthus*, grasses and
sedges, *Hemerocallis* species, herbaceous
perennials, *Lamium*, *Lathyrus*, *Monarda*,
Pink Sheet plants ('pink sheets' are
NCCPG search lists), *Pulmonaria*,
Ranunculus ficaria, *Sedum*, *Solidago*, *Vinca*,
rare shrubs and trees, variegated and wild
collected plants. But the truth is that they
list hundreds of other plants which are
equally interesting. Many nurseries claim to
have 'rare and unusual' plants: in the case
of Monksilver, the boast is consistently
true. A fifth of the catalogue changes each
year.
Owned by Alan Leslie & Joe Sharman

NETHERHALL MANOR
Tanners Lane, Soham, Ely CB7 5AB

Tel: 01353 720269
Location In middle of Soham: turn right off the
main road into Tanners Lane.
Opening hours 2 pm – 5 pm; 27 March, 1 May, 7 &
14 August.
Admission fee Adults £2.

This is an unusual garden, worth seeing for
its individual collections of genera and
plant groups which offer something of
interest at every season. Many came from
Timothy Clark's great-grandmother, who
was a herbalist. The hellebores are good in
spring and include many seedlings given by
Helen Ballard. Elsewhere are the seldom-
seen *Helleborus* 'Günther Jürgl' (one of the
first of the upright-facing, double cultivars),
H. 'Circe' (long thought to be extinct, but
saved by Nancy Lindsay) and a small
collection of Eric Smith's selections,
including *H.* 'Sirius' which Timothy Clark
considers still the best yellow. Other
goodies include: *Primula auricula* 'Duke of
Edinburgh'; the double-flowered sweet
rocket *Hesperis matronalis* 'Flore Pleno',
which was reintroduced from meristems
collected in this garden; *Fritillaria imperialis*
'Foremost'; *Hyacinthus* 'Prince Albert
Victor'; and the collection of 19th-century
Pelargonium cultivars, including 'Turtle's
Surprise', and 'Sophie Dumaresque'.
Calceolarias, heliotropes and florists' tulips
are other specialities (look out for T.
'Cardinal Manning', 'Lincolnshire' and
'Bacchus', all extremely rare). Some of the
garden's progeny are now finding their way
into the *RHS Plant Finder*, including

Heliotropium arborescens 'Netherhall White' and *Chrysanthemum* 'Netherhall Moonlight'. The one-acre garden is immaculately maintained – its lawns are completely weedless – and includes a neat kitchen garden area.

a great plantsman's garden; hyacinths; Victorian pelargoniums; florists' tulips; teas in aid of charity.

Owned by Timothy Clark
Number of gardeners 1 part-time
Size 0.4ha (1 acre)

PECKOVER HOUSE & GARDEN
North Brink, Wisbech PE13 1JR

Tel & Fax: 01945 583463
www.peckoverhouse.co.uk
Location Signed from Wisbech.
Opening hours 12 noon – 5 pm; Tuesdays, Wednesdays, Saturdays & Sundays; 2 May to 5 November. Plus weekends only from 25 March to 30 April, Good Friday & Bank Holiday Mondays. And Mondays from 31 July to 1 September. Wisbech Rose Fair: 29 & 30 June.
Admission fee Adults £3.

Peckover is an exceptionally fine example of a walled town garden, dating principally from the 19th century, complete with monkey puzzle, fernery and spotted laurel shrubberies. It has good herbaceous borders, Victorian bedding schemes, over 70 different roses, summerhouses and pool gardens. Three of the orange trees in the conservatory are 300 years old.

Victorian shrubberies; orangery; fernery; good bedding; herbaceous borders; gift shop; restaurant.

Owned by The National Trust
Number of gardeners 1½
Size 0.8ha (2 acres)
English Heritage Grade II

WIMPOLE HALL
Arrington, Royston SG8 0BW

Tel: 01223 207257 **Fax:** 01223 207838
www.wimpole.org
Location 8 miles south-west of Cambridge on A603.
Opening hours 10.30 am – 5 pm; daily, except Thursdays & Fridays (but open Good Friday); 18 March to 1 November. Open on Thursdays from 22 July to 31 August. 11 am – 4 pm; daily, except Thursdays & Fridays; 1 to 15 March and 4 November to 20 December. Park open all year.
Admission fee Garden: Adults £3; Children £1.50. Park: free.

Wimpole is an important classical 18th-century landscape where Bridgeman, Brown and Repton have all left their mark. It has a fine 19th-century collection of trees in and around the park, and grand Victorian parterres, where 72 flower beds are arranged as eight Union Jack patterns and brightly arrayed with 24,000 bedding plants. There is a lot of new horticultural interest in the old two-acre kitchen garden, where fruit and vegetables are grown on a big scale to supply the National Trust restaurant, and flowers are grown for traditional decoration. An improving garden.

woodland garden; daffodils; Chinese bridge; parterre; traditional greenhouses in walled garden; National Trust shop; restaurant & tea-room.

Owned by The National Trust
Number of gardeners 3
NCCPG National Collections *Juglans*
English Heritage Grade I

CHESHIRE

Cheshire has a fair number of important historic landscapes, including Adlington Hall, Arley Hall, Eaton Hall, Lyme Park and Tatton Park, but none is important enough to be accorded Grade I status by English Heritage. Nevertheless, Cheshire has a good reputation for gardens and gardening: it is a prosperous county, with sandy soils and plenty of rainfall. This makes it a good area for nurseries and garden centres; probably the best known are Bridgemere Nurseries and Stapeley Water Gardens, both at Bridgemere, where the International Water Lily Society also has its base. Collinwood Nurseries at Mottram St Andrew is one of the leading growers of chrysanthemums, with an exceptionally comprehensive list of cultivars. Other specialist nurseries are Caddick's Clematis Nursery at Thelwall and the two rose nurseries C. & K. Jones at Tarvin and Fryer's Roses at Knutsford. The National Gardens Scheme lists a fair number of middle-sized gardens: azaleas and rhododendrons are particularly popular. Reaseheath College near Nantwich is a RHS Partner College.

ADLINGTON HALL
Macclesfield SK10 4LF

Tel: 01625 829206 **Fax:** 01625 828756
www.adlingtonhall.com
Location 5 miles north of Macclesfield off A523.
Opening hours 2 pm – 5 pm; Wednesdays; June to August. Also throughout the year by prior appointment on weekdays for groups of 20 or more: telephone the guide on 01625 820875.
Admission fee Adults £6; Children £3; Groups (20+) £5.50. RHS members free.
🅿 🚾 ♿ 🌱 ⛫

It is good to see this important historic garden regularly open to the public again, and to know that the owner is adding her own improvements in another part of the estate. These include a maturing maze, a rose garden, a parterre and the 'Father Tiber' water garden. Many of the historical features have been restored: some are still awaiting their turn. One of the oldest is an avenue of yews planted in 1660. An ancient avenue of lime trees, planted in 1688 to celebrate the accession of William and Mary, leads to a woodland wilderness with follies. These include a shell cottage (1750s), a temple to Diana, a Chinese bridge and a hermitage.

historic landscape; ancient lime avenue; woodland garden; tea-room.

Owned by Mrs C.J.C. Legh
Number of gardeners 4
English Heritage Grade II*

ARLEY HALL
Great Budworth, Northwich CW9 6NA

Tel: 01565 777353 **Fax:** 01565 777465
www.arleyhallandgardens.com
Location 5 miles west of Knutsford.
Opening hours 11 am – 5 pm; Tuesday – Sunday & Bank Holidays; 2 April to 2 October. Plus weekends in October.
Admission fee Adults £5; OAPs £4.50; Children £2. RHS members free, except during special events.
🅿 🚐 🚾 ♿ 🌱 🪴 ⛫

Arley has pleached limes, red *Primula florindae*, clipped ilex cylinders (10m high), pretty shrub roses and a magnificent collection of rhododendrons, azaleas and rare trees and shrubs. But its claim to fame is the double herbaceous border, backed and buttressed by yew hedges, perhaps the oldest and certainly still one of the best in

England. The arboretum has been built by Lord Ashbrook over the last 30 years and is underplanted with rhododendrons, azaleas and flowering shrubs. This year (2006) over 6,000 spring bulbs have been planted in the woodland walk by Arley staff and members of The Friends of Arley. There will be two RHS Special Events at Arley Hall in 2006; details from 020 7821 3408.

topiary; avenues; two walled gardens; roses (mainly old-fashioned); good herbaceous borders; HHA/Christie's Garden of the Year in 1987; shop; nursery; lunches & light refreshments.

Owned by Viscount Ashbrook
Number of gardeners 4
Size 5ha (12½ acres)
English Heritage Grade II*

BLUEBELL COTTAGE GARDENS & LODGE LANE NURSERY
Lodge Lane, Dutton, Warrington
WA4 4HP

Tel: 01928 713718
www.lodgelanenursery.co.uk
Location Turn off A533 midway between Runcorn & Northwich.
Opening hours Nursery: 10 am – 5 pm; Wednesday – Sunday & Bank Holidays; mid-March to mid-September. Garden: 10 am – 5 pm; Friday Sunday & Bank Holidays; May to August.
Admission fee Adults £3; Children free. RHS members free. Nursery free at all times.

Lodge Lane Nursery sells more than 2,000 different herbaceous plants: it is particularly strong on penstemons, but there are big collections of achilleas, alliums, asters, campanulas, digitalis, euphorbias, geraniums, nepeta, salvias and ornamental grasses, too. Bluebell Cottage Gardens are the nursery's show gardens, well worth a visit in their own right. The gardens have been developed as a series of smaller gardens within the garden. Each

has a different theme: among them are the herb garden, the yellow garden, the 'healing' garden and the scree bed. Large island beds are used to display herbaceous plants: the owners believe that there is nothing to beat them for colour (and sheer garden value) from early to late summer. The wildflower meadow has three acres of native flowers among the grasses, including perennial cornflowers, scabious, yarrows, red clover and meadow cranesbill. At the far side of the meadow are three more acres of native woodland, carpeted with bluebells in May. Nine RHS Special Events will take place at Bluebell Cottage Gardens during 2006; details from 020 7821 3408.

wildflower meadow; 3,000 different plants.

Owned by Jack & Anne Stewart
Number of gardeners 4 part-time
Size 0.6ha (1½ acres), plus meadow & woodland
NCCPG National Collections Inula

BRIDGEMERE GARDEN WORLD
Bridgemere, Nantwich CW5 7QB

Tel: 01270 521100 **Fax:** 01270 520215
Location M6, Jct 15 & 16: follow signs.
Opening hours 9 am – 7 pm (6 pm in winter); daily; all year, except 25 & 26 December.
Admission fee Free.

More than twenty immaculate show gardens in different styles are the attraction of Bridgemere. They are intended to give you ideas on design and planting for your own garden. There is a very wide range of interesting plants for sale, too – Bridgemere propagates its own stock. A new arboretum opens in 2007, and the narrow-gauge railway which takes you there is already in place. Definitely worth a visit, whatever the season.

woodland garden; roses (ancient & modern); rock garden; plantsman's collection of plants; herbs; plants under glass;

fruit; good herbaceous borders; several shops, as well as the famous garden centre; restaurant & coffee shop.

Owned by J. Ravenscroft
Number of gardeners 3
Size 2.4ha (6 acres)

CAPESTHORNE HALL
Siddington, Macclesfield SK11 9JY

Tel: 01625 861221 **Fax:** 01625 861619
www.capesthorne.com
Location A34, 3 miles south of Alderley Edge.
Opening hours 12 noon - 5 pm; Wednesdays, Sundays & Bank Holidays; April to October.
Admission fee Adults £4; OAPs £3; Children £2.

Ⓟ ⓌⒸ ♿ ▯

There are lots of interesting things to see at Capesthorne Hall, provided you are prepared to explore the grounds and find them. Fine trees are certainly a feature: the Victorian arboretum contains some very vigorous wellingtonias and chestnuts, supplemented by recent plantings over the last 50 years. Vernon Russell-Smith designed the formal lakeside gardens in the 1960s: mixed borders of shrub roses and herbaceous plants. Along the rhododendron walk is a splendid mixture of hardy hybrids interspersed with *Rhododendron ponticum* and the sweet-scented *Rhododendron luteum*. They flourish under a canopy of tall English oaks and wild cherries. Here, too, are two cork trees, *Quercus suber*. By the time you have discovered the rose arbour, the avenue of American hawthorns, the ice house and the golden glade (planted to commemorate the golden wedding of Sir Walter and Lady Bromley-Davenport in 1983), you will have some measure of just how much the garden has to offer.

🌿 woodland garden; fine collection of trees; historic park; tea-room.

Owned by Sir W.A. Bromley-Davenport
Number of gardeners 2

CHOLMONDELEY CASTLE GARDENS
Malpas SY14 8AH

Tel: 01829 720383 **Fax:** 01829 720877
Location Off A49 Tarporley to Whitchurch road.
Opening hours 11.30 am - 5 pm; Wednesdays, Thursdays, Sundays & Bank Holidays; 2 April to 28 September.
Admission fee Adults £4; Children £1.50. RHS members free in June.

Ⓟ ⓌⒸ ♿ 🌺 🐛 ▯

The gardens below this handsome early 19th-century castle set in rolling parkland have been redeveloped since the 1960s with horticultural advice from Jim Russell. The new plantings have been well integrated into the classical landscape and have added an entirely new horticultural dimension to the landscape. The exquisite temple garden, curling the whole way around a small lake, is breathtakingly beautiful. Highly recommended.

🌿 woodland garden; rock garden; good herbaceous borders; fine collection of trees; azaleas & rhododendrons; gift shop; tea-room; light lunches & home-made teas.

Owned by The Marchioness of Cholmondeley
English Heritage Grade II

DORFOLD HALL
Nantwich CW5 8LD

Tel: 01270 625245 **Fax:** 01270 628723
Location 1 mile west of Nantwich on A534.
Opening hours 2 pm - 5 pm; Tuesdays & Bank Holiday Mondays; April to October. Also 2 pm - 5.30 pm on 21 May for NGS.
Admission fee House & gardens: Adults £5; Children £3. NGS day: Adults £5; Children £2.50.

Ⓟ ⬦

William Andrews Nesfield designed the formal approach but the main reason for visiting the gardens at Dorfold Hall is the new woodland garden of rhododendrons and other shrubs, leading down to a stream where *Primula pulverulenta* has naturalised in its thousands. Recent additions include summer herbaceous borders and an orchard walk. Do not miss the incredible hulk of an ancient Spanish chestnut in the stableyard.

spring woodland garden; camellias; magnolias; rhododendrons & azaleas; daffodils & bluebells; good summer herbaceous borders.

Owned by R.C. Roundell
Number of gardeners 2
Size 7.2ha (18 acres)
English Heritage Grade II

DUNGE VALLEY HIDDEN GARDENS
Windgather Rocks, Kettleshulme, High Peak SK23 7RF

Tel & Fax: 01663 733787
www.dungevalley.co.uk
Location 1 mile south of Kettleshulme village: follow brown tourist signs and turn down a minor road towards Goyt Valley.
Opening hours 10.30 am – 5 pm; Thursday – Sunday; March to August. Plus Tuesdays & Wednesdays in May. Open on Bank Holiday Mondays.
Admission fee Adults £3; Children £1.

These hidden gardens 300m up in the Pennines are a surprise and a delight: few are so high, and fewer still so full of colour. It is not only the number of plants which gives such pleasure, but the surprise of finding so many that one might suppose too tender – embothriums, desfontainia and mahonias, for example. But there are also fine rhododendrons, old-fashioned roses and flowering borders in an almost Himalayan setting. The nursery has one of the largest selections of rhododendrons for sale in northern England.

rhododendrons & azaleas; roses; hardy trees & shrubs; tea-room; lunches & light refreshments.

Owned by David & Elizabeth Ketley
Number of gardeners 2
Size 2.6ha (7 acres)

GRANADA ARBORETUM
Jodrell Bank, Macclesfield SK11 9DL

Tel: 01477 571339 **Fax:** 01477 571695
www.manchester.ac.uk/jodrellbank/viscen
Location On A535 between Holmes Chapel & Chelford.
Opening hours 10.30 am – 4.30 pm; daily; mid-March to 29 October. 10.30 am – 3 pm; Tuesday – Friday; November to mid-March. 11 am – 4 pm on Saturdays & Sundays during Cheshire school holidays.
Admission fee Adults £1.50; Children £1.

The Granada Arboretum at Jodrell Bank was founded by Sir Bernard Lovell in 1971 with funding from the Granada Foundation. This wonderful arboretum specialises in alders, birches, crab apples, maples and *Sorbus*. Long straight rides lead spaciously into the distance. The plantings are young and vigorous, the groupings imaginative. A huge radio telescope dominates the site: an awesome presence.

shop; café.

Owned by Manchester University
Number of gardeners 2
Size 14ha (35 acres)
NCCPG National Collections *Malus; Sorbus*

HARE HILL GARDEN
Garden Lodge, Over Alderley, Macclesfield SK10 4QB

Tel: 01625 828981
www.nationaltrust.org.uk
Location Between Alderley Edge & Prestbury.
Opening hours 10 am – 5 pm (last admissions one hour before closing); Wednesdays, Thursdays, Saturdays, Sundays & Bank Holiday Mondays; 5 April to 29 October. Open daily from

8 to 28 May for rhododendrons & azaleas.
Admission fee Adults £2.70; Children £1.25.
Parking £1.50 (refunded on admission).

P WC &

Hare Hill is a woodland garden, thickly
planted with trees and underplanted with
rhododendrons, azaleas and shrubs by Jim
Russell in the 1960s. In the middle is a
walled garden which has been developed as
a flower garden with a pergola, arbour and
tender plants against the walls. Planting
continues with new cultivars. Perhaps best
in May, there are still some rhododendrons
to flower with the roses in July.

woodland garden; rock garden;
plantsman's collection of plants; good
herbaceous borders.

Owned by The National Trust
Number of gardeners 1½
Size 4ha (10 acres)

LITTLE MORETON HALL
Congleton CW12 4SD

Tel: 01260 272018
www.nationaltrust.org.uk
Location 4 miles south of Congleton on A34.
Opening hours 11.30 am – 5 pm (or dusk, if
earlier – 4 pm until 25 March); Wednesday –
Sunday & Bank Holiday Mondays; 1 March to 5
November. 11.30 am – 4 pm; Saturdays & Sundays;
11 November to 17 December.
Admission fee Adults £5.50; Children £2.80;
Family £13. Parking £5 (refunded on admission).

P WC & 🌱 ▯

Little Moreton Hall is the handsomest
timber-framed house in England – an icon
of domestic Tudor architecture. When the
National Trust asked Graham Stuart
Thomas to design and plant a suitable
period garden, he specified box-edged
borders with yew topiary and gravel
infilling – and very fine they are, too. A
speciality has been made of old varieties of
fruit, vegetables and herbs around the knot
garden. Peaceful, charming and orderly.

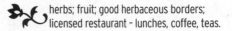
herbs; fruit; good herbaceous borders;
licensed restaurant – lunches, coffee, teas.

Owned by The National Trust
Number of gardeners 1
Size 0.4ha (1 acre)
English Heritage Grade I

LYME PARK
Disley SK12 2NX

Tel: 01663 762023 **Fax:** 01663 765035
www.nationaltrust.org.uk
Location 6½ miles south-east of Stockport on
A6, just west of Disley.
Opening hours 11 am – 5 pm (1 pm – 5 pm on
Wednesdays & Thursdays); daily; 25 March to 31
October. 12 noon – 3 pm; Saturdays & Sundays; 4
to 24 March and 4 November to 17 December.
Admission fee Garden only: Adults £3.50;
Children £2. Plus £4.50 for car (National Trust
members free).

P WC & 🌱 ▦ ▯

There is much of horticultural interest at
Lyme, as well as the razzmatazz of a country
park: traditional bedding out, two
enormous camellias in the conservatory,
and a Jekyll-type herbaceous border by
Graham Stuart Thomas where the colours
run from orange to deepest purple. Best of
all is the sunken Dutch garden whose
looping box and ivy parterres contain the
most extravagant bedding displays. The
National Trust has now assumed full
control of the garden and restored the
structure in line with the original Lewis
Wyatt design. Lyme Park featured as
Pemberley in the BBC's *Pride & Prejudice*.

roses (mainly old-fashioned); good
herbaceous borders; spring bulbs;
bedding out; orangery by Wyatt; Dutch garden;
shop; restaurant & coffee shop (April to October).

Owned by The National Trust
Number of gardeners 4
Size 6.7ha (17 acres)
English Heritage Grade II*

MELLORS GARDEN

Hough Hole House, Rainow, Macclesfield
SK10 5UW

Tel: 01625 573251 **Fax:** 01625 572389
Location In Sugar Lane.
Opening hours 2 pm - 5 pm; 29 May & 28 August.
And by appointment.
Admission fee £1.50.

P WC ⊘

This remarkable small garden was laid out
in the 19th century as an allegory of
Christian's journey in *Pilgrim's Progress* and
originally planted only with plants that are
mentioned in the Bible. Features represent
such places as the Wall of Salvation, the
Cave of the Holy Sepulchre, Vanity Fayre,
the Dark River, the Delectable Mountains,
Doubting Castle and the Celestial City. A
spiritual and historical experience more
than a horticultural one.

refreshments by arrangement.

Owned by Mr & Mrs A. Rigby
Size 0.8ha (2 acres)

NORTON PRIORY MUSEUM & GARDENS

Tudor Road, Runcorn WA7 1SX

Tel: 01928 569895
Location Well signed locally.
Opening hours 12 noon - 5 pm (6 pm on
weekends & Bank Holidays); daily; March to
October.
Admission fee Adults £4.75; OAPs £3.45; Family
£12.50.

P WC & ✿ ⚫ ⊘

The old walled garden at Norton Priory
has a new layout modelled on 18th-century
precedents and intended to instruct and
please visitors. A cottage garden border, a
medicinal herb garden and an orchard rub
shoulders with colour borders, kitchen
gardens and a scented garden. Beyond are
16 acres of woodland garden with Georgian
summerhouses and glades by the stream.

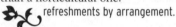 roses (ancient & modern); rock garden;
herbs; fruit; good herbaceous borders;
current holder of Sandford Award; garden
produce shop; refreshments at museum site.

Owned by Norton Priory Museum Trust (Halton
Borough Council)
Number of gardeners 2
Size 15ha (38 acres)
NCCPG National Collections *Cydonia oblonga*

PEOVER HALL

Over Peover, Knutsford WA16 9HW

Tel: 01565 830395 **Fax:** 01565 830241
Location 3 miles south of Knutsford.
Opening hours 2 pm - 5 pm; Mondays &
Thursdays; April to October. And for NGS.
Admission fee Adults £3; Children £2.

P WC & ⊘

First a classic 18th-century parkland, then
an Edwardian overlay of formal gardens –
yew hedges and brick paths. Now Peover
has modern plantings, too – borders in
colour combinations, a herb garden, and a
rhododendron dell in the woods.

topiary; roses (mainly old-fashioned);
herbs; walled garden; landscaped park;
rhododendrons; tea-room (Mondays only).

Owned by R. Brooks Ltd.
Number of gardeners 3
Size 6.4ha (16 acres)
English Heritage Grade II

THE QUINTA

Swettenham Village, Congleton
CW12 2LD

Tel: 01477 537698
www.tattongardensociety.co.uk
Location Access through garden of Swettenham
Arms pub.
Opening hours 9 am - dusk; daily; all year,
except 25 December. For NGS: May & 10
September.
Admission fee Adults £2.50. RHS members free.

NESS BOTANIC GARDENS
Neston CH64 4AY

Tel: 0151 353 0123 **Fax:** 0151 353 1004
www.nessgardens.org.uk
Location Signed off A540, Chester to Hoylake.
Opening hours 9.30 am – 4 pm (5 pm from March to October); daily; all year. Closed 25 December.
Admission fee Adults £4.70; Concessions £4.30. £3.70 from November to January.

🅿 ⓦⓒ ♿ ✲ ◉ ⌂

Ness was the creation of a Liverpool cotton merchant, Arthur Bulley, who laid out the garden in 1898 and started to plant it with new species from abroad. He was particularly interested in Himalayan and Chinese plants: he believed that many could become established in cultivation in Britain and he therefore sponsored such plant collectors as George Forrest and Frank Kingdon Ward. It is to Bulley that we owe such plants as *Gentiana sino-ornata* and *Pieris formosa* var. *forrestii*, and it was at Ness that many Chinese plants were first grown in Europe – notably the candelabra primulas. Ness was presented to the University of Liverpool by Bulley's daughter in 1948 and has continued to develop as a public amenity, a tourist attraction and a teaching garden, while still retaining the 'feel' of a private garden. It is beautifully laid out in a sequence of incidents: both its design and plantings have continued to improve year by year. The main features are as follows: a laburnum arch; a herb garden; a rhododendron border (long and deep) underplanted with many lilies; an excellent heather garden; sandstone terraces where tender plants like *Ribes speciosum* flourish; a rock garden with an enormous range of different environments, south-facing and north-facing, limestone and sandstone, sunny, shaded and damp; a water garden; a camellia collection; an arboretum; a *Sorbus* collection, soon to be recognised by the NCCPG as a National Collection; herbaceous borders; and glasshouses with arid displays including the crown of thorns (*Euphorbia milii*).

As with all botanic gardens, there is no end of things to see whatever the season, and your visit can be as short or as long as it suits. In practice, however, Ness is one of those gardens where you tend to spend much longer than you intended. A £2m development plan will be completed early in 2006 with the construction of a new visitor centre. The Friends of Ness are very active and the website, too, is very comprehensive.

🌿 roses (mainly old-fashioned); mature conifers; fine collection of trees; 30m laburnum arch; camellia walk; notable collections of *Sorbus, Betula, Salix* & *Cotoneaster*; tallest *Alnus cremastogyne* (3.3m) in the British Isles; gift shop; plant nursery; café.

Owned by The University of Liverpool
Number of gardeners 11
Size 26ha (65 acres)
English Heritage Grade II

🅿 🆆𝒸 ♿

The Quinta Arboretum was created by Sir
Bernard Lovell, originator of the Jodrell
Bank Radio Telescope, and is now owned
by the Tatton Garden Society, of which he
is President. The garden features more than
10,000 trees and shrubs (2,000 taxa), with
a 5ha (12.4 acres) wild wood (owned by
Cheshire Wildlife Trust), flower-rich
meadows and beautiful views over the
River Dane meanders. The Royal Botanic
Garden Edinburgh has sponsored a
collection of endangered conifers. Also of
merit are collections of *Quercus* species and
Hebe cultivars, each with 100+ taxa.

 nice young arboretum; wildflowers;
woodland garden.

Owned by The Tatton Park Garden Society
Size 11ha (28 acres)
NCCPG National Collections *Fraxinus*; *Pinus*

REASEHEATH COLLEGE
Nantwich CW5 6DF

Tel: 01270 625131 **Fax:** 01270 625665
www.reaseheath.ac.uk
Location 1 mile north of Nantwich on A51.
Opening hours 2 pm – 4 pm; Wednesdays; 17 & 24
May. College open day: 11 am – 5 pm; 14 May.
Guided tours for groups at other times.
Admission fee Donation to NGS.

🅿 🆆𝒸 ♿ �<u></u> 🌑 🗗

Reaseheath has been thoroughly replanted
recently: there is an enormous amount to
enjoy and learn here. Highlights include a
woodland garden, a model fruit garden, a
lake, a gravel garden, good bedding on the
formal terraces and splendid mixed borders.
woodland garden; rhododendrons &
azaleas; good herbaceous borders; fine
collection of trees; heather garden; formal
bedding; Reaseheath Garden Centre, open daily,
all year; shop & coffee lounge.

Owned by Reaseheath College
Number of gardeners 2
Size 12ha (30 acres)

RODE HALL
Church Lane, Scholar Green, Stoke on
Trent ST7 3QP

Tel: 01270 882961 **Fax:** 01270 882962
www.rodehall.co.uk
Location 5 miles south-west of Congleton
between A34 & A50.
Opening hours 2 pm – 5 pm; Tuesday – Thursday
& Bank Holiday Mondays; 1 April to 30 September.
Plus 12 noon – 4 pm; daily except Mondays; 4 to
26 February, for snowdrops.
Admission fee Garden only: Adults £3; OAPs
£2.50. RHS members free.

🅿 ⬌ 🆆𝒸 🌑 🍴 🗗

Stand on the terraces at Rode Hall and
take in the prospect: William Andrews
Nesfield's 1860s rose garden and Humphry
Repton's landscape beyond. The 'pool' is
nearly a mile long and 150 yards (137m)
wide. But horticulture is also here in
abundance: take the boathouse walk past
the old stew pond (pretty marginals and a
waterfall) to the wildflower garden
(terraced rock garden – early 19th-century
– *very* early for this sort of garden) where
snowdrops, sarcococcas, hellebores (lots),
ferns, primroses and soldanellas flourish in
the lee of rhododendrons. Note the
splendid Loderi crosses, which smell of
sugared almonds and extend the flowering
season into early June. Admire Professor
Pratt's scented azaleas (would that more
people knew and grew them) and note how
the plantings of rhododendron species are
being extended into the adjacent Old
Wood. Then visit the walled kitchen
garden (about two acres) and see the rows
of decorative vegetables set between
cornflowers, poppies, marigolds and flowers
for drying. Espaliered fruit trees cover the
walls between 4m abutilons: Cheshire has a
mild climate. Look inside the greenhouses
and see the many geraniums with scented
leaves. And ponder the industry of the
head gardener, Kelvin Archer, who grows
over 40 cultivars of gooseberry here and
holds the world record for the largest
gooseberry fruit.

woodland garden; topiary; snowdrops; roses (mainly old-fashioned); fruit; mature conifers; ice house; rhododendrons; grotto; laburnum walk; fully functional two-acre walled kitchen garden; garden produce; cream teas; light lunches in February.

Owned by Sir Richard Baker Wilbraham
Number of gardeners 2
Size 2.4ha (6 acres)
English Heritage Grade II

STAPELEY WATER GARDENS
London Road, Stapeley, Nantwich CW5 7LH

Tel: 01270 623868 **Fax:** 01270 624919
www.stapeleywg.com
Location A51, 1 mile south of Nantwich.
Opening hours Water Garden & Garden Centre: 9 am (10 am on Sundays) - 6 pm (5 pm in winter, 4 pm on Sundays & 8 pm on summer Wednesdays); daily; all year, except Easter Sunday & Christmas Day. The Palms Tropical Oasis: 10 am - 6 pm (5 pm in winter); daily; all year, except Christmas Day.
Admission fee The Palms Tropical Oasis: Adults £4.45; OAPs £3.95; Children £2.60.

P WC & ❦ ✿ ✕ ▽

Part entertainment, part nursery and part display garden, the Palms Tropical Oasis is worth a visit in its own right. A long rectangular pool in the Moorish style is flanked by tall palms, strelitzias and other showy tropical flowers. The display gardens outside are fascinating all through the year, especially the water gardens where all the water lilies grow.

plants under glass; collection of hardy water lilies; *Victoria regia*, the giant water lily; major nursery & garden centre; cafeteria & terrace restaurant.

Owned by Stapeley Water Gardens Ltd
NCCPG National Collections *Nymphaea*

TATTON PARK
Knutsford WA16 6QN

Tel: 01625 534400 **Fax:** 01625 534403
www.tattonpark.org.uk
Location Off M6, Jct 19 & M56, Jct 7 - well signed.
Opening hours 10 am - 6 pm; Tuesday - Sunday & Bank Holiday Mondays; all year, but open 11 am - 4 pm from 3 October to 23 March 2007.
Admission fee Not yet known as we went to press. RHS members free. car-parking charges apply.

P WC & ❦ ✿ ✕ ▽

Humphry Repton laid out the parkland at Tatton. Joseph Paxton designed both the formal Italian garden and the exquisite fernery, claimed as the finest in the UK. Later came a Japanese garden (restored for the Japanese festival in 2001) and Shinto temple (1910), such follies as the African hut, and the mass plantings of rhododendrons and azaleas. Work on restoring the walled garden and its glasshouses continues apace. Tatton Park is wonderfully well organised for visitors, and gets better every year. Be prepared for a long and absorbing visit. The RHS Flower Show at Tatton Park will take place from 19 to 23 July 2006 (tickets from 0870 906 3811).

good herbaceous borders; fine collection of trees; rhododendrons & azaleas in May; biggest *Quercus* x *schochiana* in the British Isles; current holder of Sandford Award; Europa Nostra award for restored orangery & fernery; shop (closed Mondays); restaurant (closed Mondays in winter).

Owned by The National Trust (managed by Cheshire County Council)
Number of gardeners 13
Size 20ha (50 acres)
NCCPG National Collections *Adiantum*
English Heritage Grade II*

CORNWALL

Many of the great historic gardens of Cornwall are also the most interesting horticulturally. Mount Edgcumbe and Tresco are both rated Grade I gardens of national importance, while Caerhays Castle, Lanhydrock, Tregrehan and Trewithen are Grade II* and Antony, Carclew, Chyverton, Cotehele, Glendurgan, Heligan, Lamellen, Pencarrow, Penjerrick, St Michael's Mount, Trebah, Trelissick and Trengwainton are all Grade II. It is a proud list, unmatched by any other county, and evidence of how the big estates have always dominated the gardening scene in Cornwall. The county still has its own horticultural organisation, the Cornwall Garden Society: its spring show is a showcase for camellias and rhododendrons. About 80 gardens open every year for the Cornwall Festival of Spring Gardens which runs from mid-March to the end of May: details from the Cornwall Tourist Board on 01872 322900. Almost all the gardens have fine collections of trees, too: those at Trebah, Tregrehan and Trewithen are particularly noted for the age and size of their specimens, while the woodlands of Caerhays contain an exceptional number of well-grown rarities. A new type of Cornish garden has, however, been emerging over the last 25 years, where the owners have taken advantage of the climate to grow a very wide range of newer plants: Pine Lodge, Lamorran and Bosvigo are good examples and will doubtless be followed by others. The county's National Collections reflect the opportunities which the mild climate makes possible: among them are *Escallonia* at Duchy College (a RHS Partner College), *Azara* at Trelissick, *Grevillea* at Pine Lodge and *Acacia* at Tresco. Finest of all is the National Collection of *Dahlia* at Varfell Farm at Long Rock, just off the A30, where some 2,000 species and cultivars can be seen by prior appointment (further details from dahlias@wgltd.co.uk). Cornish nurseries cater well for the local market: the Duchy of Cornwall Nursery at Lostwithiel has the largest stock of all, while tender exotica are the speciality of Trevena Cross Garden Centre near Helston and Lower Kenneggy Nurseries near Penzance. Best known is Burncoose & South Down Nurseries, a regular winner of Gold Medals for its spectacular displays of flowering trees and shrubs at RHS shows throughout the year.

ANTONY
Torpoint PL11 2QA

Tel: 01752 812191 **Fax:** 01752 815724
www.nationaltrust.org.uk
Location 5 miles west of Plymouth; 2 miles north-west of Torpoint.
Opening hours 1.30 pm - 5.30 pm (last admissions 4.45 pm); Tuesday - Thursday & Bank Holiday Mondays; 4 April to 31 October. Plus Sundays from June to August.
Admission fee Adults £2.80; Children £1.40. Combined ticket with Antony Woodland Garden: Adults £4.60; Children £2.20.

P WC ♿ ❦ ● ↻

Antony has been an historic and important garden for centuries – and every generation has left its mark. Its classic late 18th-century landscape is superb, though there is considerable debate as to whether Humphry Repton designed it or the Pole-Carews (as they were then called) listened to Repton's advice but followed little of it. The yew walk with its lead statues of a shepherd and his shepherdess and the huge Burmese temple bell, flanked by stone lanterns, date from the 19th century. Much of the horticultural interest was created by Sir John Carew Pole in the middle of the 20th century – masses of bulbs, the lime tree avenues, over 600 early *Hemerocallis* hybrids from the USA, a 9.2m loquat tree (*Eriobotrya japonica*) against the house, the vast cork oak (*Quercus suber*) (another record-breaker), the venerable old 'Black Walnut' (*Juglans nigra*) on the main lawn and the beautiful spring-flowering *Magnolia denudata*. The position is superb – an elevated promontory above the Tamar estuary, just across Plymouth Sound from Devon. Sir Richard and Lady Carew Pole, who now live at Antony, have continued to intensify and extend this plantsman's garden: more spring-flowering trees and shrubs have been planted, alongside the creation of gardens for summer and autumn interest. The summer garden is particularly effective: hybrid musk roses are underplanted with lilies, irises, phlox and peonies and its walls are covered in clematis, climbing roses, lemon-scented verbena and *Cytisus battandieri*. But there is much to see at every season – the magnolia walk in spring, the knot garden, the terraces in high summer with giant catmint (*Nepeta* 'Six Hills Giant') mingling with the floribunda rose 'Iceberg' and free-standing fig trees *Ficus carica* 'White Marseilles' in autumn. And it is a large garden, so you need to allow a lot of time to do it justice.

🌿 mature conifers; good herbaceous borders; magnolias; yew hedges; tallest Japanese loquat *Eriobotrya japonica* (9.2m) in the British Isles (and two other tree records); National Trust shop; tea-room.

Owned by The National Trust
Number of gardeners 3, plus 2 trainees
Size 14ha (35 acres)
NCCPG National Collections *Hemerocallis*
English Heritage Grade II

ANTONY WOODLAND GARDEN
Antony House, Torpoint PL11 2QA

Tel: 01752 812191 **Fax:** 01752 815724
Location 5 miles west of Plymouth; 2 miles north-west of Torpoint.
Opening hours 11 am - 5.30 pm; daily, except Mondays & Fridays (but open on Bank Holidays); 1 March to 31 October.
Admission fee Adults £4; Accompanied Children free.

P WC ↻

This is the 'Cornish' part of the grounds at Antony, still controlled by the Carew Pole family rather than the National Trust. It is a garden of considerable botanical interest divided into two main areas. First comes the Wilderness, a wooded area to the north-west of the house which runs down to the banks of the River Lynher. Three vistas frame the house from the river: Humphry Repton's influence is clearly apparent here. The Wilderness has been planted with trees and shrubs like Japanese maples, a tunnel of *Camellia* x *williamsii* 'Donation' and *Camellia japonica* 'Lady de Saumarez', *Magnolia obovata*, rhododendron species and hybrids including the strongly scented 'Loderi' and *R. griffithianum*. There is a conifer dell with giant redwoods *Sequoiadendron giganteum*, *Cryptomeria japonica* and *Taxus baccata* 'Dovastoniana' and three ponds cascading down a valley to the salt pans and the Bath House pond. The second area is Westdown, where the planting consists mainly of camellias of considerable variety (including the National Collection of *Camellia japonica*) interspersed with Asiatic magnolias and rhododendron species, thriving in the deep valley. The magnolias include specimens of 'Charles Raffill', *M. dawsoniana*, and *M. campbellii* subsp. *mollicomata* 'Lanarth'. The two areas are joined by the Garden Field where ornamental trees have been underplanted with flowering shrubs and daffodils. A path through deep-scented shrubs and birches completes the link along the river's edge. The Carew Poles have also commissioned several pieces of contemporary sculpture for the garden and the wider estate.

woodland garden; plantsman's collection of plants; mature conifers; camellias; magnolias; rhododendrons & azaleas; tea-room as for Antony (q.v.).

Owned by The Carew Pole Garden Trust
Number of gardeners 1
Size 26ha (65 acres)
NCCPG National Collections *Camellia japonica*

THE BARBARA HEPWORTH MUSEUM & SCULPTURE GARDEN
2 Barnoon Hill, St Ives TR26 1AD

Tel: 01736 796226 **Fax:** 01736 794480
www.tate.org.uk/stives/hepworth
Location In town centre.
Opening hours 10 am – 5.30 pm; daily; March to October. 10 am – 4.30 pm; Tuesday – Sunday; November to March. Last admissions 30 mins before closing. Closed 24 to 26 December.
Admission fee Adults £4.50; Concessions £2.25. Free to over-60s and under-18s.

Dame Barbara Hepworth's studio and garden have been run by the Tate Gallery since 1980. Hepworth died in 1975, and asked (in her will) that Trewyn studios and the sub-tropical garden should become a permanent setting to exhibit her works. Visiting them gives you a remarkable insight into one of the 20th century's most important sculptors and the garden which was an essential part of her creative process.

 shop.

Owned by Tate Gallery & Hepworth Estate
Number of gardeners 2
Size 0.2ha (½ acre)
English Heritage Grade II

BOSAHAN
Manaccan, Helston TR12 6JL

Tel: 01326 231351 **Fax:** 01326 231497
www.gardensofcornwall.com
Location Off Manaccan to St Anthony road; or uphill from Treath & first left.
Opening hours 11 am – 4.30 pm; Monday – Friday. Charity day: 1 pm – 5.30 pm on 29 April.
Admission fee Adults £4; OAPs £3; Disabled £2; Children £1.50.

Bosahan dates from the 19th century but is being restored and revived by Christine Graham-Vivian, who is a garden designer. It has two atmospheric valleys of large tree ferns, rhododendrons, magnolias, azaleas, palms, conifers, camellias and southern hemisphere plants, leading down to the Helford River. Down by the large pond are good plantings of bog plants and marginals. Bosahan is said to have been one of the inspirations for Daphne du Maurier's novel *Rebecca*.

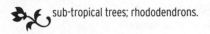 sub-tropical trees; rhododendrons.

Owned by Mr & Mrs R.J. Graham-Vivian
Number of gardeners 1
Size 4ha (10 acres)

BOSVIGO
Bosvigo Lane, Truro TR1 3NH

Tel & Fax: 01872 275774
www.bosvigo.com
Location Turn off A390 at Highertown, just west of Sainsbury's roundabout, then 500 yards down Dobbs Lane.
Opening hours 11 am – 6 pm; Thursdays & Fridays; 3 March to 30 September.
Admission fee Adults £3.50; Children (5-15) £1.

Not a typical Cornish garden, the emphasis at Bosvigo is upon herbaceous plants, chosen for their individual qualities and planted in fine colour combinations. The woodland garden is more traditional, and underplanted with snowdrops, hellebores, wood anemones, erythroniums and epimediums, but the rest of the garden is at its best in summer and keeps well into the autumn. Over the last 25 years or so, Wendy and Michael Perry have created a series of small walled or hedged garden 'rooms' around the mainly Georgian house. Each has its own colour theme: the walled garden heaves with polite blues, mauves and pinks while another is mainly of gold and white. Reds and oranges co-exist in a 'hot' garden which, according to Patrick Taylor in the *Daily Telegraph*, 'will blow your socks off'. Many of the plants are rare, and some are sold in the small specialist nursery.

woodland garden; plantsman's collection of plants; good herbaceous borders; unusual perennials; Victorian conservatory; colour borders; excellent small herbaceous nursery.

Owned by Wendy & Michael Perry
Number of gardeners owners only
Size 0.8ha (2 acres)

BURNCOOSE GARDENS & NURSERIES
Gwennap, Redruth TR16 6BJ

Tel: 01209 860316 **Fax:** 01209 860011
www.burncoose.co.uk
Location Directly on A393 Redruth to Falmouth road between villages of Lanner & Ponsanooth.
Opening hours 8.30 am (11 am on Sundays) – 5 pm; daily, except 25 December; all year.
Admission fee Gardens: Adults £2; Children free. Nursery: free.

Burncoose Nurseries specialise in rare and unusual plants: they list over 3,500 different ones – mainly ornamental trees and shrubs – which makes them one of the best for sheer choice in all Europe. Their real specialities are camellias, rhododendrons, magnolias and conservatory plants. Burncoose has won 19 gold medals at the last 25 Chelsea Flower Shows and numerous gold medals at Hampton Court, Tatton Park and other shows. The garden is a woodland garden, carpeted with bluebells, primroses, snowdrops and wild violets in spring. Two monkey puzzles *Araucaria araucana* are over 30m (100ft) high and a *Eucryphia* x *nymansensis* reaches 13m (40ft). Most of the ornamental plants have been planted since 1900 and the older ones have been matched in recent years by substantial additions. There will be three RHS Special Events at Burncoose Nurseries in 2006; details from 020 7821 3408.

woodland garden; rhododendrons & azaleas; plantsman's collection of plants; camellias; bluebells; magnolias; rare trees & shrubs; important nursery (major RHS gold medal winner); teas & light refreshments.

Owned by Charles Williams
Number of gardeners 1
Size 12ha (30 acres)

CARCLEW GARDENS
Perran-ar-Worthal, Truro TR3 7PB

Tel: 07747 111477
Location A39 east at Perran-ar-Worthal; 1 mile to garden.
Opening hours 2 pm – 5.30 pm; 16 April; for NGS. And at any time by written appointment.
Admission fee Adults £3.50; Children 50p.

P WC

Carclew's garden first opened to the public in 1927 and has continued to do so for charity every year since then. It was once the greatest rhododendron garden in the South-West: some of the oldest rhododendrons were grown from Sir Joseph Hooker's Himalayan collections nearly 150 years ago. The many fine trees include a large ginkgo and a form of *Quercus* x *hispanica* which is *not* 'Lucombeana'. The Chopes have been busy replanting and restoring the garden: the waterfall has recently been repaired.

woodland garden; roses (mainly modern); rhododendrons; tallest *Pseudolarix amabilis* (23m) in the British Isles.

Owned by The Chope family
Number of gardeners 1
English Heritage Grade II

CARWINION
Mawnan Smith, Falmouth TR11 5JA

Tel: 01326 250258 **Fax:** 01326 250903
www.carwinion.com
Location From Mawnan Smith, turn left at Red Lion pub, 500 yards up hill on right.
Opening hours 10 am – 5.30 pm; daily, or by appointment; all year.
Admission fee Adults £3.50; Children free.

P WC

Twelve acres of Cornish jungle, exotically thick with vast rhododendrons, camellias, *Trachycarpus fortunei*, drimys, gunneras, lysichitons, ferns, hellebores and the largest collection of bamboos in the South-West.

woodland garden; sub-tropical plants; mature conifers; nearly 200 different bamboos; gunneras; bluebells; teas in summer.

Owned by Anthony Rogers
Number of gardeners 1
Size 4.8ha (12 acres)

CHYVERTON
Zelah, Truro TR4 9HD

Tel: 01872 540324 **Fax:** 01872 540648
Location 1 mile south-west of Zelah on A30.
Opening hours By appointment from March to May; magnoliaphiles at any time by appointment.
Admission fee Adults £6; Children (under 16) free. Visits are personally conducted.

P WC

Chyverton started out as a Georgian landscape garden. Later owners planted a pinetum in the 1830s and the first rhododendrons in 1890. The horticultural plantings have, however, been very much extended since the 1920s, initially with some advice from Sir Harold Hillier (his first ever advisory visit), but latterly by the owners themselves. Nigel Holman is a distinguished plantsman: Hugh Johnson calls his garden 'a magic jungle'. Magnolias are a particular interest: there are over 150 cultivars and several Chyverton seedlings now bear cultivar names. Many other established plants have also been grown from seed, including plants collected by Nigel Holman in China. But there is much more to interest the plantsman. A lanky red-stemmed hedge of *Luma apiculata* below the house is outstanding. The planting continues – no sprays or trimmed edges – and is now accompanied by the placement of statues in suitable sites.

woodland garden; plantsman's collection of plants; mature conifers; magnolias, including four record-breakers; nothofagus; tallest *Rhododendron* 'Cornish Red' (16m) in the British isles.

Owned by Nigel Holman
Number of gardeners 1
Size 50ha (125 acres)
English Heritage Grade II

CAERHAYS CASTLE GARDENS
Gorran, St Austell PL26 6LY

Tel: 01872 501310 **Fax:** 01872 501870
www.caerhays.co.uk
Location Between Mevagissey & Portloe.
Opening hours 10 am – 5 pm; daily; 13 February
to 31 May.
Admission fee Adults £5.50; Children (5-16)
£2.50. RHS members free from 13 February to 12
March.

P ⟿ WC 🌿 🐛 ⟁

Caerhays has belonged to the Williams family since 1853, but it was not until the young J.C. Williams took over the estate in the 1890s that they began to develop the gardens. It seems that the original inspiration came from a RHS daffodil conference: it sparked JCW's lifelong interest in hybridising. By 1903 he was sponsoring E.H. Wilson's collections in China and this was followed by a partnership with George Forrest. Of the many plants that these expeditions introduced, Caerhays is best known for its magnolias, but JCW is also remembered as a great hybridiser of rhododendrons and camellias. *Camellia* x *williamsii* was named for him: some of the original plants still flourish at Caerhays, including 'J.C. Williams', 'Mary Christian' and 'Saint Ewe'. The present owner, and his son Charles Williams, have been no less involved in conserving and improving the remarkable plant collections at Caerhays. They make a point of trying to accommodate rare and unusual plants, whose cultural requirements take precedence over the niceties of garden design. And the Williams are still involved in wide-scale plantings – especially since

the garden suffered serious damage in the 1990 great gale. Magnolias remain a major interest and almost all the new forms and cultivars coming out of Australia, USA and New Zealand have been added to the garden and have grown away well. One of the joys of Caerhays is to stumble upon magnificent old specimens deep in its 100 acres of woodland. Among the many rare trees are fine specimens of *Laurus azorica*, *Lithocarpus cleistocarpus*, *Lithocarpus henryi*; magnolias like M. *delavayi*, M. *nitida*, M. *robusta* and M. *salicifolia*; and such oaks as *Quercus acuta*, Q. *crassifolia*, Q. *glauca*, Q. *ilicifolia*, Q. *lamellosa*, Q. *lanata*, Q. *lodicosa*, Q. *oxyodon* and Q. *phillyreoides*. Almost all these species are known to few of us: this litany of names is a measure of the importance of Caerhays. There is much to discover, so you should allow plenty of time. And see the website – very informative. There will be seven RHS Special Events at Caerhays in 2006; details from 020 7821 3408.

🌿 woodland garden; plantsman's collection of plants; mature conifers; fine collection of trees; camellias; magnolias; rhododendrons; tallest specimen of *Emmenopterys henryi* (17m) in the British Isles, and 37 other record-breaking trees (including eight *Acer* species); gift shop; tea-room & beach shop/café in car park.

Owned by F.J. Williams CBE
Number of gardeners 4
Size 24ha (60 acres)
NCCPG National Collections *Magnolia*
English Heritage Grade II*

COTEHELE
St Dominick, Saltash PL12 6TA

Tel: 01579 351346 **Fax:** 01579 351222
www.nationaltrust.org.uk
Location 14 miles from Plymouth via Saltash.
Opening hours 10.30 am – dusk; daily; all year.
Admission fee Adults £4.80; Children £2.40.

P WC & ✻ ● ⊡

Broad Victorian terraces below the house
support many tender climbers such as
Jasminum mesnyi, while the beds beneath
have wallflowers and roses. Down the
wooded valley are camellias,
rhododendrons and shade-loving plants
which thrive in an ancient woodland, kept
damp by a small stream. The National
Trust has undertaken much gentle
restoration and renewal in recent years.
woodland garden; topiary; roses
(mainly modern); daffodils; fine
collection of trees; palms; ferns; pretty dovecote;
National Trust gift shop; restaurant (18 March to
31 October).

Owned by The National Trust
Number of gardeners 3, plus 2 students
Size 5.6ha (14 acres)
English Heritage Grade II

DUCHY OF CORNWALL NURSERY
Cott Road, Lostwithiel PL22 0HW

Tel: 01208 872668 **Fax:** 01208 872835
www.duchyofcornwallnursery.co.uk
Location 1½ miles off A390 at Lostwithiel.
Opening hours 9 am – 5 pm; Monday – Saturday.
10 am – 5 pm; Sundays. Closed Bank Holidays.

P WC & ✻ ⊡

The Duchy of Cornwall Nursery stocks an
extensive general range of all types of
plants, and will interest even the most
discriminating plantsman. Its policy does
not compromise on quality: it offers the
cultivars which it considers the best. These
range from reliable old favourites to rare
and recent cultivars. It was recently

described as resembling 'a series of
specialist nurseries in one nursery' because
of the depth and breadth of its range. It is
especially good on hardy fuchsias, and
hopes that its collection will one day be
recognised by the NCCPG. It is also one of
the few nurseries which still supply bare-
rooted stock in winter.

 tea-room.

THE EDEN PROJECT
Bodelva, St Austell PL24 2SG

Tel: 01726 811911 **Fax:** 01726 811912
www.edenproject.com
Location Signed from A30, A390 & A391.
Opening hours 10 am – 6 pm (4.30 pm from
November to March. Last admissions 1½ hours
before closing); daily; all year, except 24 & 25
December.
Admission fee Adults £13.80; OAPs £10; Children
£5.

P WC & ✻ ● ⊡

The promoters of this imaginative project
hope to provide visitors with an
understanding of the world of plants, and
their importance to human welfare. The
area under glass is described as being the
size of 30 football pitches. One of the
gigantic conservatories – all made in a
disused clay-pit near St Austell – is
landscaped as a rainforest. The others
represent Mediterranean, South African
and Californian climate-zones. Staples like
cocoa, coffee, bananas and rubber are
grown alongside plants used in paper, wine,
scent and brewing. Outside are collections
of camellias, lavender, sunflowers and
hemp, and one million spring bulbs. There
is plenty of hype, too, but visitors all speak
enthusiastically of the experience.
giant glasshouses; exotic plants; gift
shop; several cafés and restaurants.

Owned by The Eden Trust
Number of gardeners 30, plus support staff
Size 14.7ha (37 acres)

GLENDURGAN
Mawnan Smith, Falmouth TR11 5JZ

Tel: 01326 250906 **Fax:** 01872 865808
www.nationaltrust.org.uk
Location 1 mile west of Mawnan Smith, close to
Trebah.
Opening hours 10.30 am - 5.30 pm (last
admissions 4.30 pm); Tuesday - Saturday & Bank
Holiday Mondays; 11 February to 28 October.
Closed Good Friday.
Admission fee Adults £5; Children £2.50.
🅿 🆆 🌱 🐞 🗗

Glendurgan is a steep, sub-tropical valley
garden on the Helford River with a good
collection of old rhododendrons and
camellias. It also boasts an extraordinary
1830s maze of clipped cherry laurel,
recently restored and best seen from the
new viewing platform above. Indeed, the
whole garden is almost best when viewed
from the top – but the temptation to
wander down and into it is irresistible.
🌱 woodland garden; sub-tropical plants;
mature conifers; laurel maze; wildflowers;
huge tulip tree; tallest *Eucryphia lucida* (13m) in the
British Isles; small shop; tea-room.

Owned by The National Trust
Number of gardeners 3, plus 1 trainee
Size 14ha (35 acres)
English Heritage Grade II

HEADLAND
Polruan-by-Fowey PL23 1PW

Tel: 01726 870243
www.headlandgarden.co.uk
Location Find Polruan: go to bottom of Fore Street,
along West Street, left up Battery Lane to end.
Opening hours 2 pm - 6 pm; Thursdays; May to
September.
Admission fee Adults £2.50; Children £1.
🆆 🗗

A cliff garden with 500 steps, the sea on
three sides and a sandy beach, Headland is a
lesson in what will tolerate salt-laden winds:
eucalyptus, acacias, foxgloves and junipers,
but especially cacti and succulents – agaves,
aloes, echeverias, sedums, lampranthus and
crassulas. The design and the variety of the
planting make it seem much larger than its
1¼ acres and there are many stone seats
tucked in between the rocky outcrops.
🌱 cacti & succulents; salt-spray resistant
plants; cream teas in garden.

Owned by Jean Hill
Size 0.5ha (1¼ acres)

HELIGAN GARDENS
Pentewan, St Austell PL26 6EN

Tel: 01726 845100 **Fax:** 01726 845101
www.heligan.com
Location St Austell to Mevagissey road; follow
brown tourist signs.
Opening hours 10 am - 6 pm (5 pm from
November to February); daily; all year, except 24
& 25 December.
Admission fee Adults £7.50; OAPs £7;
Children £4.
🅿 🆆 ♿ 🌱 🐞 🗗

Heligan calls itself 'The Lost Gardens of
Heligan' but its 200 acres have been
spectacularly rescued since 1990 from a
jungle of neglect. The owners emphasise
that it is 'definitely not just another pretty
garden' but best described as a whole series
of gardens within a garden. Its productive
kitchen gardens – there are five walled
gardens – are of particular interest: they
contain over 300 cultivars of fruits, herbs
and vegetables, some of them no longer
commercially available – there is a strong
emphasis on heritage varieties. Many of the
working buildings are once again carrying
out their original functions – fruit stores,
tool and potting sheds, pineapple pits,
peach, vine and melon houses, manure-
heated frames and the bachelor gardeners'
bothies. Elsewhere is an Italian garden, a
Sundial garden, a New Zealand garden,
and the alpine ravine. Newly recovered
features emerge with incredible speed:
recent restorations include the 22-acre lost

'jungle' valley with a large collection of Tasmanian tree ferns and 60 bamboo cultivars. Behind all this modern activity is a 19th-century plantsman's jungle, with conifers and palms as the background for camellias, tree ferns and rhododendrons dating from the Hooker expeditions of 1849-50. The enthusiasm of the restorers is infectious and their achievements are already substantial. The owners are brilliant at getting financial support and publicity – with the result that the gardens can get very crowded.

woodland garden; sub-tropical plants; rock garden; rhododendrons & azaleas; beautiful ferny gully; splendid kitchen garden; farm shop; licensed restaurant; tea-rooms.

Owned by Heligan Gardens Ltd
Number of gardeners 25
Size 80ha (200 acres)
English Heritage Grade II

KEN CARO
Bicton, Liskeard PL14 5RF

Tel: 01579 362446
Location Signed from A390, midway between Callington & Liskeard.
Opening hours 10 am – 6 pm; Sunday – Friday; 26 February to 29 September.
Admission fee Adults £3.50; Children £1.

Ken Caro was started in 1970 as two acres of intensely planted formal gardens in different styles, and extended in 1993 by taking in a further two acres. It is very much a plantsman's garden with good herbaceous plants and shrubs, not at all a traditional Cornish garden. All-round colour is important here, and so are the panoramic views. The owners are flower-arrangers: look for architectural plants and original combinations.

plantsman's collection of plants; mature conifers; good herbaceous borders; tea/coffee.

Owned by Mr & Mrs K.R. Willcock
Number of gardeners 2
Size 1.8ha (4½ acres)

LAMORRAN HOUSE
Upper Castle Road, St Mawes TR2 5BZ

Tel: 01326 270800 **Fax:** 01326 270801
www.lamorrangardens.co.uk
Location ½ mile from village centre.
Opening hours 10 am – 5 pm; Wednesdays & Fridays; April to September.
Admission fee Adults £5; Children free. Groups £4.50.

The garden at Lamorran has been almost entirely made since 1980, on a steep site above Falmouth Bay. It is tightly designed in the Italian style, but also full of unusual plants – an English Mediterranean garden in Cornwall, say the owners, or a mainland Tresco, though it is closest to the great English garden at La Mortola on the Italian Riviera. Their latest ventures are a new walled garden and a bank planted with cacti and succulents. They have also greatly increased the number of cyatheas in the garden. But tender rhododendrons from Asia are yet another interest, and plants from Australia, too. The collection of unusual plants is simply amazing: very adventurous. The planting is guided by a desire to experiment with hardiness and tempered by the aesthetic demands of the whole garden. So the garden is not a *botanic* collection, but an extremely good *horticultural* one, and the plants are chosen and placed for their decorative merit and their contribution to the whole.

sub-tropical plants; plantsman's collection of plants matched to a firm design; good herbaceous borders; fine collection of trees; extensive plantings of Australian & South African plants; over 25 different palms.

Owned by Mr & Mrs Robert Dudley-Cooke
Number of gardeners 2
Size 1.8ha (4½ acres)

LANHYDROCK
Bodmin PL30 5AD

Tel: 01208 265950 **Fax:** 01208 265959
www.nationaltrust.org.uk
Location 2½ miles south-east of Bodmin.
Opening hours 10 am - 6 pm (dusk, if sooner);
daily; all year.
Admission fee Garden only: Adults £5; Children
£2.50.

Lanhydrock is a grand mansion, mainly
19th-century, with one of the best formal
gardens in Cornwall – clipped yews, box
parterres and bedding out, as well as large
herbaceous borders. The woodlands behind
are impressive for their size and colourful
rhododendrons in spring. But it is the
magnolias which impress the visitor most:
140 different species and cultivars.
woodland garden; topiary; good
herbaceous borders; bluebells;
Victorian parterres; spring bulbs; National Trust
shop; restaurant.

Owned by The National Trust
Number of gardeners 5
Size 12.3ha (31 acres)
English Heritage Grade II*

MOUNT EDGCUMBE GARDENS
Cremyll, Torpoint PL10 1HZ

Tel: 01752 822236 **Fax:** 01752 822199
www.mountedgcumbe.gov.uk
Location At end of B3247 in south-east Cornwall,
or by ferry from Plymouth.
Opening hours Formal gardens & park: dawn -
dusk; daily; all year. House & Earl's Garden: 11 am
- 4.30 pm; Sunday - Thursday; April to
September. Guided tours for groups by
appointment.
Admission fee Formal gardens & park: free.
House & Earl's Garden: Adults £4.50; OAPs £3.50;
Children £2.25.

A long, stately grass drive runs down from

the house to Plymouth Sound, through oak
woods interplanted with large ornamental
trees. The formal gardens are right down
on the waterside, protected by a clipped
ilex hedge 10m high. There are no less
than ten acres of gardens here, including
an Italian garden (made in the 1790s), a
French garden (Regency), a modern
American garden, a New Zealand garden
complete with geyser, a Jubilee garden, the
18th-century Thomson's Seat, an orangery
with newly acquired orange trees, and the
fern dell with ivies and tree ferns. The two-
acre Earl's Garden has a 400-year-old lime
tree and a Victorian shell seat among the
herbaceous borders, summerhouses and
statues. Allow plenty of time to do justice
to these majestic pleasure gardens.
sub-tropical plants; plants under glass;
daffodils; good herbaceous borders;
fine collection of trees; summer bedding; deer
park; formal gardens; fern dell; genuine Victorian
rose garden; tallest cork oak *Quercus suber* (26m)
in the British Isles; gift and book shops; tea-room;
orangery; restaurant in formal gardens.

Owned by Cornwall County Council & Plymouth
City Council
Number of gardeners 4
Size 4ha (10 acres), plus 320-ha (800-acre) park
NCCPG National Collections *Camellia*
English Heritage Grade I

PENCARROW
Washaway, Bodmin PL30 3AG

Tel: 01208 841369 **Fax:** 01208 841722
www.pencarrow.co.uk
Location 4 miles north-west of Bodmin - signed
off A389 at Washaway.
Opening hours 9.30 am - 5.30 pm; daily; 1 March
to 31 October. For NGS: 10 April.
Admission fee Adults £4; Children £1. Groups
welcome by appointment (discounts usually
available).

The mile-long drive at Pencarrow leads to
an avenue of rhododendrons and rare

conifers before you eventually come to the pretty Anglo-Palladian house. On one side are the outlines of an Italian garden, complete with fountain, laid out in the 1830s, and next to it a great granite rock garden where vast jagged boulders from Bodmin Moor lie strewn among the trees and shrubs. Pencarrow is famous for its conifers: an ancestor planted one of every known variety in the mid-19th century and the survivors are so venerable that the great Alan Mitchell wrote a guide to them. The monkey puzzle *Araucaria araucana* acquired its nickname when a visitor to Pencarrow, Charles Austen, remarked to his host, after some thought, 'that tree would puzzle a monkey'. Since about 1970 the owners have steadily retrieved the garden from the state of dereliction in which it was left at the end of World War II and added a further 200 or so conifers. Recent plantings have involved the addition of over 700 of the best modern rhododendrons, 70 camellias and many other broadleaved trees and shrubs. It is good to see the fortunes of such a distinguished garden revived.

important collection of mature conifers; Italian garden; rhododendrons; camellias; great granite Victorian rock garden; blue hydrangeas; ice house; monkey puzzle avenue; craft shop; light lunches & cream teas.

Owned by The Trustees of the Molesworth-St Aubyn Family
Number of gardeners 3
Size 20ha (50 acres)
English Heritage Grade II

PENJERRICK
Budock Water, Falmouth TR11 5ED

Tel: 01872 870105
www.penjerrickgarden.co.uk
Location 3 miles south-west of Falmouth, entrance at junction of lanes opposite Penmorvah Manor Hotel.

Opening hours 1.30 pm – 4.30 pm; Wednesdays, Fridays & Sundays; March to September.
Admission fee Adults £2.50; Children £1.

The garden at Penjerrick was begun by the Fox family in the mid-19th century. It is a great plantsman's garden, famous in particular for its Barclayi and Penjerrick hybrid rhododendrons. Some of the original plants still survive in the peaceful woodland garden, thick with exotics: tender plants thrive in the lush, sheltered valley. The garden is recovering well from a period of neglect: it sums up all that was best about private Cornish gardens 100 years ago. Take your gumboots, and prepare for a fascinating walk.

woodland garden; rhododendrons; camellias; tree ferns; ponds & bamboos.

Owned by Mrs Rachel Morin
Number of gardeners ½
Size 4ha (10 acres)
English Heritage Grade II

PINE LODGE GARDENS & NURSERY
Holmbush, St Austell PL25 3RQ

Tel: 01726 73500 **Fax:** 01726 77370
www.pine-lodge.co.uk
Location East of St Austell between Holmbush & Tregrehan.
Opening hours 10 am – 6 pm; daily; all year, except 24 to 26 December.
Admission fee Adults £5.50; Children £3.

This modern 30-acre garden is quite unlike the typical Cornish garden. It has several distinct styles and contains over 6,000 different plants, all of which are labelled. In addition to the rhododendrons, magnolias and camellias so familiar in Cornish gardens there are Mediterranean and southern-hemisphere plants grown for year-round interest, herbaceous borders, a fernery, a formal garden, a Japanese garden, a woodland walk and shrubberies. The water features include a large wildlife pond, an ornamental pond, a lake with breeding black swans and an island, and marsh gardens. Trees are a particular interest: Pine Lodge has an acer glade, a young four-acre pinetum, and an arboretum. The wildflower meadow is planted with over 7,000 bulbs and flowers. The pace of the garden's development is very exciting and the owners' appetite for new plants grows even stronger every year. This year (2006) sees a new one-hectare (2½-acre) winter garden.

woodland garden; good herbaceous borders; Japanese garden; good water features; lots of interesting plants; garden nursery with plants from wild-collected seed; tea-room.

Owned by Mr & Mrs Raymond Clemo
Number of gardeners 4
Size 12ha (30 acres)
NCCPG National Collections *Grevillea*

PINSLA GARDEN & NURSERY
Cardinham, Bodmin PL30 4AY

Tel: 01208 821339
Location Follow brown tourist signs from Cardinham village.
Opening hours 10 am – 6 pm; daily; March to October.
Admission fee Adults £2.50; Children free. Nursery free.

Winding paths, granite boulders, unusual textures and a stone circle in the meadow: these, and the sculptures, are some of the garden features designed to 'arouse your emotions and feed your soul' at Pinsla. But there are also fine herbaceous borders, naturalistic plantings, shade-plantings and alpine beds – and a nursery with a good choice of herbaceous and alpine plants, ferns, bamboos and succulents.

good nursery; teas.

Owned by Mark & Claire Woodbine

Number of gardeners 1½
Size 0.6ha (1½ acres)

ST MICHAEL'S MOUNT
Marazion TR17 0EF

Tel: 01736 710507 **Fax:** 01736 719930
www.stmichaelsmount.co.uk &
www.nationaltrust.org
Location 1 mile south of Marazion.
Opening hours Garden: 10.30 am – 5.30 pm; Monday – Friday (weather & tide permitting); May & June. Plus Thursdays & Fridays from July to October.
Admission fee Adults £3.

St Michael's Mount is a triumph for man's ingenuity in the face of Atlantic gales, salt spray and bare rock – with sand for garden soil. Careful experiment over the generations has enabled the owners to plant a remarkable garden of plants which resist the elements: *Luma apiculata*, Rugosa roses, correas, nerines, Hottentot figs and naturalised agapanthus. On the north side, a sparse wood of sycamores and pines gives protection to camellias, azaleas and hydrangeas. Nigel Nicolson called it 'the largest and loveliest rock garden in England'. There is nothing rare about the plants: the wonder is that they grow at all.

sub-tropical plants; natural rock garden; wild narcissus; naturalised kniphofias and agapanthus; National Trust shop; National Trust refreshments.

Owned by James St Aubyn & The National Trust
Number of gardeners 4
Size 4ha (10 acres)
English Heritage Grade II

TREBAH GARDEN TRUST
Mawnan Smith, Falmouth TR11 5JZ

Tel: 01326 252200 **Fax:** 01326 250781
www.trebah-garden.co.uk
Location 4 miles south-west of Falmouth, signed

from Treliever roundabout at A39/A394 junction, through Mawnan Smith to garden.
Opening hours 10.30 am - 5 pm (last admissions); daily; all year.
Admission fee Adults £5.80; OAPs £5.30; Children (5-15) & Disabled Visitors £2; Children (under 5) free. RHS members free from November to March. Half price from November to mid-February.

P ⇔ WC ♿ ✿ ▦ ♿

Trebah has been vigorously restored and improved since the Hibberts bought it in 1980. The view from the top is magical – a beautiful, secret, wooded valley which runs right down to the Helford estuary. A new Monet-style bridge provides a focal point at the bottom. A stream cascades over waterfalls, through two acres of blue and white hydrangeas, and spills out over the beach. Vast trees, natural and exotic, line the steep sides, while the central point is held by a group of elegant tall palms. Glades of huge sub-tropical tree ferns mingle with giant gunneras, puyas and echiums, while along the sides and overhead is the rolling canopy of 100-year-old rhododendrons. A paradise for plantsmen, Trebah is also popular with children, whose curiosity is aroused by trails, quizzes and educational games. It is a garden for all people and for all seasons – open every day of the year.

🌿 woodland garden; sub-tropical plants; plantsman's collection of plants; fine collection of trees; massed hydrangeas; lilies and candelabra primulas; extensive new plantings of palms & succulents at the top of the garden; tallest hardy palm *Trachycarpus fortunei* (15m) in the British Isles and three other tree records; plants for sale; private beach on Helford River; café; shop.

Owned by The Trebah Garden Trust
Number of gardeners 4, plus volunteers & students
Size 10ha (25 acres)
English Heritage Grade II

TREGREHAN
Par PL24 2SJ

Tel: 01726 812438 **Fax:** 01726 814389
www.tregrehan.org
Location 1 mile west of St Blazey on A390.
Opening hours 10.30 am - 5 pm; Wednesday - Sunday, except Easter Sunday; mid-March to mid-June. 2 pm - 5 pm; Wednesdays mid-June to end of August.
Admission fee Adults £4; Children free.

P WC ♿ ✿ ♿

An old Cornish garden whose 20 acres of woodland date back 200 years and include a fine range of Victorian conservatories, tall conifers and vast, venerable rhododendrons. Tregrehan is best known for the camellias bred here by the late Gillian Carlyon, especially 'Jenefer Carlyon' which won her the Cory Cup from the RHS. But Tom Hudson's collections in warm temperate regions have also made a big impact on the garden which, under his guidance, has become an important living genebank of known-source plants. His recently planted South-East Asia garden is open only to groups, by prior appointment.

🌿 woodland garden; camellias; pinetum; walled garden; sunken garden; phytogeographic planting; teas.

Owned by T.C. Hudson
Number of gardeners 2
Size 8ha (20 acres)
English Heritage Grade II*

TRELISSICK GARDEN
Feock, Truro TR3 6QL

Tel: 01872 862090 **Fax:** 01872 865808
www.nationaltrust.org.uk
Location A39 off main Truro to Falmouth road. Or summer ferry from Falmouth, St Mawes & Truro.
Opening hours 10.30 am - 5.30 pm; daily; 11 February to 29 October. 11 am - 4 pm; daily; 30 October to 23 December. 11 am - 4 pm; 23 to 31 December & 2 January to 9 February 2007.
Admission fee Adults £5.50; Children £2.75.

⊡ ⓌⒸ ♿ ❀ 🌑 ⬭

Once famous as 'the fruit garden of Cornwall' – there is a newly planted (2003) Cornish apple orchard – and still maintained by the National Trust, Trelissick is particularly colourful in August and September when the hydrangeas are in full flower. There are over 100 cultivars, some in a special walk. But venerable conifers and tender plants are also features: *Erythrina crista-galli*, cannas and hedychiums are among the many good things that over-winter outside, not to mention daffodils, rhododendrons and camellias in spring.

⚬⚬ woodland garden; plantsman's collection of plants; mature conifers; aromatic plant garden; fig garden; hydrangeas; tallest tree fern *Dicksonia antarctica* (6m) in the British Isles; National Trust shop; refreshments.

Owned by The National Trust
Number of gardeners 4
Size 10ha (25 acres)
NCCPG National Collections *Azara, Photinia*
English Heritage Grade II

TRENGWAINTON GARDEN
Madron, Penzance TR20 8RZ

Tel: 01736 363148 **Fax:** 01736 367762
www.nationaltrust.org.uk
Location 2 miles north-west of Penzance, ½ mile west of Heamoor.
Opening hours 10 am – 5 pm (5.30 pm from April to September); Sunday – Thursday & Good Friday; 12 February to 29 October.
Admission fee Adults £5; Children £2.50.
⊡ ⚬ ⓌⒸ ♿ ❀ 🌑 ⬭

Trengwainton has one of the best collections of tender plants on the Cornish mainland, all thanks to the Bolitho family who started planting seriously only in 1925. Much came from original seed from such collectors as Kingdon Ward: some rhododendrons flowered here for the first time in the British Isles, among them *R. macabeanum*, *R. elliottii* and *R. taggianum*.

The plants in many Cornish gardens are past their best. Not so at Trengwainton, where many are in their prime. It is a garden to wander through slowly, giving yourself as much time as you need to enjoy its riches.

⚬⚬ woodland garden; sub-tropical plants; roses (mainly old-fashioned); lilies; acacias; *Myosotidium hortensia*; tree ferns; tallest *Xanthoceras sorbifolium* (7m) in the British Isles (and two record trees); National Trust shop; tea-room.

Owned by The National Trust
Number of gardeners 4
English Heritage Grade II

TRERICE
Kestle Mill, Newquay TR8 4PG

Tel: 01637 875404 **Fax:** 01637 879300
www.nationaltrust.org.uk
Location 3 miles south-east of Newquay; turn right off A3058 at Kestle Mill.
Opening hours 10.30 am – 5 pm; daily, except Saturdays; 26 March to 29 October.
Admission fee Adults £2; Children £1.
⊡ ⓌⒸ ♿ ❀ 🌑 ✕ ⬭

A perfect West Country manor house with pretty Dutch gables, Trerice is unusual among Cornish gardens. It is small and comparatively formal: the design and herbaceous plantings are its best points. It is not surrounded by swirling rhododendron woodland. There is a perfect harmony between the Elizabethan architecture and the gardens. Somewhat anomalously, it boasts the largest collection of mid-Victorian to current-day lawn mowers in the country. They are both interesting and fun to visit.

⚬⚬ colour borders; good collection of apple trees; lawn mower museum; National Trust shop; restaurant.

Owned by The National Trust
Number of gardeners 1
Size 5.6ha (14 acres)

TRESCO ABBEY
Isles of Scilly TR24 0PU

Tel & Fax: 01720 424105
www.tresco.co.uk
Location Direct helicopter flight from Penzance, or boat from St Mary's.
Opening hours 10 am – 4 pm; daily; all year.
Admission fee Adults £8.50; Children free. (Under review.)

⊲⊳ 🚾 ♿ 🌱 📷 ☐

The sub-tropical gardens on Tresco are unique in the British Isles. They were first designed and planted by Augustus Smith in 1834: his successors have been equally passionate in their search for tender plants that will grow outside on Tresco's south-facing terraces as nowhere else in Britain. The collection is especially strong in plants from South Africa, Australia and New Zealand but, even though any account of Tresco reads like a list of plants, it is still very much an ornamental garden which strives for horticultural effect. The oldest specimens include Canary Island palms, a large number of aeoniums from both the Canary Islands and Madeira, agaves from America and puyas from Chile. Since the great gale of 1990, the gardens have been extensively replanted, with hundreds of exotic plants from Kew, all protected by extensive new shelter belts. No matter what time of the year, there is always a lot of colour and much of interest: proteas and acacias in winter; the shrubby foxglove (*Isoplexis sceptrum*); mesembryanthemums and agapanthus in summer. There is also a shady area where tree ferns and *Musschia wollastonii* flourish. Many people come here year after year to admire the displays of plants which cannot be seen elsewhere in Britain. The standards of maintenance are exemplary. The heliport has now been moved further away from the garden, which improves the visitor's enjoyment enormously.
🌿 sub-tropical plants; plantsman's collection of plants; mature conifers; cacti; succulents; South African, Australian and New Zealand plants; tallest *Luma apiculata*

(20m), *Metrosideros excelsa* (20m) and *Cordyline australis* (15m) in the British Isles; gift shop; licensed café.

Owned by Robert Dorrien Smith
Number of gardeners 5, plus 3 students
Size 6.7ha (17 acres)
NCCPG National Collections *Acacia*
English Heritage Grade I

TREVARNO GARDENS & NATIONAL MUSEUM OF GARDENING
Helston TR13 0RU

Tel: 01326 574274 **Fax:** 01326 574282
www.trevarno.co.uk
Location 3 miles west of Helston, signed from junction of A394 & B3302.
Opening hours 10.30 am – 5 pm; daily; all year, except 25 & 26 December.
Admission fee Adults £5.15; OAPs £4.45; Children £1.95. RHS members free.

🅿 🚾 ♿ 🌱 📷 ☐

Trevarno is an interesting new project – an old estate which has been restored and developed since 1997 and which promises to become one of the great gardens of Cornwall again. The old woodland gardens have been cleared, the lake dredged, the 19th-century Italian garden restored and the fountain conservatory refurnished. Work continues: there are plans for a series of stylishly themed gardens dedicated to the flora of different parts of the world. Meanwhile the National Museum of Gardening has a vast and fascinating collection of old garden tools and horticultural equipment of every sort; it alone is worth a long journey to see. There will be 11 RHS Special Events at Trevarno in 2006; details from 020 7821 3408.
🌿 garden restoration; museum of gardening; shop; refreshments.

Owned by M. Sagin
Number of gardeners 4
Size 12ha (30 acres)

TREWIDDEN GARDENS
Penzance TR20 8TT

Tel: 01736 363021 **Fax:** 01736 368142
Location Off A30, 2 miles west of Penzance.
Opening hours 10.30 am - 4.30 pm; Wednesday -
Sunday, & Bank Holiday Mondays; 15 February to
1 October.
Admission fee Adults £4; Children free.

The gardens at Trewidden have only been
regularly open to the public since 2002,
and there is much to see. It is essentially a
springtime garden, perhaps at its best
towards the end of March, but there is
plenty of colour and interest in every
season – which is why the garden is now
open right through to October. The
camellia collection is one of the largest
(300+ cvs.) while the tree fern dell claims
to have more dicksonias than any other
garden in the northern hemisphere, some
of them 150+ years old. Rare specimens
include a venerable jelly palm *Butia
capitata*, Chilean nut trees *Gevuina avellana*
and the garden's own magnolia 'Trewidden
Belle'.

broadest *Metasequoia
glyptostroboides* in the UK; unusual
plants for sale; light refreshments.

Owned by Alverne Bolitho
Number of gardeners 2
Size 4.8ha (12 acres)

TREWITHEN
Grampound Road, Truro TR2 4DD

Tel: 01726 883647 **Fax:** 01726 882301
www.trewithengardens.co.uk
Location A390 between Probus & Grampound.
Opening hours 10 am - 4.30 pm; Monday -
Saturday (& Sundays February to May); February
to September.
Admission fee Adults £5; Children £1. Adults
£4.50 (& RHS members free) from July to
September.

Trewithen's setting is magnificent. Instead
of the steep terraces of most Cornish
gardens, there is a spacious flat lawn that
stretches for 200 yards (183m) into the
distance, with gentle banks of
rhododendrons, magnolias and rare shrubs
on all sides. It sets the tone for the garden's
grandeur, which was largely the work of
George Johnstone in the early years of the
20th century. Johnstone was a great
plantsman. He subscribed to plant-hunting
expeditions, such as those of Frank
Kingdon Ward. Note how he used laurel
hedges to divide up the woodland and give
structure to the garden. He also had an eye
for placing plants to advantage. As a
breeder, he gave us *Rhododendron* 'Alison
Johnstone', *Ceanothus arboreus* 'Trewithen
Blue' and *Camellia saluensis* 'Trewithen
White'. The Michelin Guide gives
Trewithen its top award of three stars –
vaut le voyage!

woodland garden; rhododendrons &
azaleas; plantsman's collection of
plants; camellias; good herbaceous borders; fine
collection of trees; magnolias; quarry garden;
cyclamen; tallest *Magnolia campbellii* subsp.
mollicomata (19m) in the British Isles and 16
more record-breaking tree species; excellent
nursery & garden shop; tea-room with light
refreshments.

Owned by A.M.J. Galsworthy
Number of gardeners 4
Size 12ha (30 acres)
English Heritage Grade II*

CUMBRIA

Cumbria came into being in 1974, an amalgam of the old counties of Cumberland, Westmorland and the northern part of Lancashire. Gardening in Cumbria is dominated by the Lake District: both Wordsworth's garden at Rydal Mount and Ruskin's at Brantwood are open to visitors. There are good historic gardens of the grander sort, too. Though few in number, almost all the most important are open to the public: Levens is rated Grade I, while Dalemain, Holker, Muncaster and Sizergh are all Grade II*. Cumbria's acid soils and the highest rainfall in England are very favourable to the growth of conifers: many of the older gardens have fine specimens of *Abies*, *Picea* and *Pinus*, while Muncaster also offers an extensive collection of *Nothofagus*

species. The National Gardens Scheme is active in the county, and particularly successful in persuading garden-owners in and around the Lake District to open for charity. Cumbria has comparatively few nurseries, but the ones we list below are exceptionally good. The county has its fair share of National Collections, with clusters of genera at three of the larger gardens: *Halesia*, *Pterostyrax*, *Styrax*, *Sinojackia* and other *Styracaceae* at Holker; *Astilbe*, *Hydrangea* and *Polystichum* at Holehird; and *Asplenium scolopendrium*, *Cystopteris*, *Dryopteris*, and *Osmunda* at Sizergh. Cumbria Campus at Newton Rigg near Penrith is a RHS Partner College, with lectures, demonstrations and garden walks throughout the year. Visit this useful website: *www.visitcumbria.com*.

ACORN BANK GARDEN
Acorn Bank, Temple Sowerby, Penrith CA10 1SP

Tel: 01768 361893/366826 **Fax:** 01768 366824
www.nationaltrust.org.uk
Location North of Temple Sowerby, 6 miles east of Penrith on A66.
Opening hours 10 am - 5 pm; Wednesday – Sunday, & Bank Holiday Mondays; 25 March to 29 October.
Admission fee Adults £3.20; Children £1.60.
🅿 wc ♿ � ⬛ ⬦

Acorn Bank claims to have the largest collection (250 cvs.) of culinary and medicinal plants in the North: it was redesigned and replanted in 2002-2003. The garden is especially worthwhile in spring when thousands and thousands of daffodils fill the woodland slopes, and the fruit trees flower in the old walled garden.

Best of all is the huge quince tree in the herb garden, a wondrous sight in flower or fruit.

🌿 woodland garden; roses (mainly old-fashioned); herbs; fruit; good herbaceous borders; spring bulbs; woodland walk past mill; National Trust shop; tea-room.

Owned by The National Trust
Number of gardeners 1
Size 1ha (2½ acres)

BRANTWOOD
Coniston LA21 8AD

Tel: 01539 441396 **Fax:** 01539 441263
www.brantwood.org.uk
Location East side of Coniston Water, 2½ miles from Coniston, 4 miles from Hawkshead.
Opening hours 11 am - 5.30 pm; daily; mid-

March to mid-November. 11 am - 4.30 pm; Wednesday - Sunday; rest of year.
Admission fee Adults £3.75; Children £1.

P ◁ WC ぐ ♥ ♣ ✕ ▯

This woodland garden was laid out by John Ruskin from 1871 to 1886 but somewhat altered and neglected after his death in 1900. Working with the natural materials of the site, Ruskin developed a series of experimental gardens within the ancient woodland and on the high moorland behind. When the Brantwood Trust began the task of reclamation, it decided to restore the garden as it was in Ruskin's lifetime, and to expand it as a modern re-interpretation of his ideas – thereby continuing his work and addressing contemporary issues. The Victorian 'viewing terrace' has been restored, and Ruskin's 'zig-zaggy garden' is now looking young again. Ascending from the Purgatory of the car park, visitors reach Paradise through the levels inspired by Dante's *Divine Comedy*. Here, too, are a Ruskin-style collection of British herbs in a Gothic walk. The idea is to 'explore cultural history through human reaction to plants'. So Brantwood is a garden which offers thought-provoking ideas for everyone. Below Ruskin's 'living laboratory', exotic ornamental plantings frame wonderful views across Coniston Water. There is a regular passenger ferry service from Coniston Boat-buildings: the steam yacht *Gondola* also calls from May to October.

rhododendrons & azaleas; daffodils; bluebells; cottage garden; extensive native fern collection; bookshop & craft gallery; plants for sale; meals, light refreshments & drinks all day.

Owned by The Brantwood Trust
Number of gardeners 2
Size 10ha (25 acres)

DALEMAIN
Penrith CA11 0HB

Tel: 017684 86450 **Fax:** 017684 86223
www.dalemain.com
Location M6, Jct 40, A66, A592, between Penrith & Ullswater.
Opening hours 10.30 am - 5 pm; Sunday - Thursday; 26 March to 29 October. 11 am - 4 pm; Sunday - Thursday; rest of year. Closed Christmas and January.
Admission fee Gardens only: £4. RHS members free from 5 April to 3 May. NGS days: 30 April & 3 September.

P WC ぐ ♥ ♣ ▯

Dalemain has belonged to the Hasell family since 1679. The history of the garden starts, however, with a 16th-century terrace, of which very few remain anywhere in the British Isles. Then comes a kitchen garden with fruit trees planted 250 years ago, though the overall 'feel' of Dalemain is Edwardian. Most of the plantings are modern, including the formal knot garden and the long and richly planted herbaceous border which overlooks the park and the Lakeland Fells. The mixed borders and roses are dreamily English, particularly the Rose Walk, which boasts more than 100 old-fashioned roses. Nearby is the wild garden with drifts of meconopsis and martagon lilies in late spring, though it is fair to say that this is a garden which looks good at all seasons. Plants are well labelled and well grown.

woodland garden; roses (mainly old-fashioned); herbs; meconopsis; old flower and fruit varieties; good herbaceous and mixed borders; biggest *Abies cephalonica* in the British Isles; gift shop; morning coffee, light lunches, afternoon teas.

Owned by Robert Hasell-McCosh
Number of gardeners 2
Size 2ha (5 acres)
English Heritage Grade II*

GRAYTHWAITE HALL
Ulverston, Hawkshead LA12 8BA

Tel: 01539 531248 **Fax:** 01539 530060
www.visitcumbria.com/sl/grayhall.htm
Location Between Newby Bridge & Hawkshead.
Opening hours 10 am – 6 pm; daily; April to
August.
Admission fee Adults £3; Children £1.
P ◁ WC

Graythwaite shows Thomas Mawson on
home ground and at his best. Formal
gardens in the Arts & Crafts style by the
house drop down to sweeping lawns;
beyond the stream is a woodland of
rhododendrons and azaleas. The yew
topiary is good – some castellated and
some with a mixture of green and gold
cultivars.
topiary; roses (ancient & modern);
rock garden; fine collection of trees.

Owned by Myles Sandys
Number of gardeners 1
Size 4.8ha (12 acres)

HARTSIDE NURSERY GARDEN
Alston CA9 3BL

Tel & Fax: 01434 381372
Location ¼ mile south-west of Alston on A686
to Penrith.
Opening hours 11.30 am – 4.30 pm; Monday –
Friday. 12.30 pm – 4 pm; Saturdays & Sundays. 11
March to 31 October. Other months by
appointment.
P

This high-level nursery (over 300m, or
1,000 ft) specialises in alpines, particularly
in primulas (lots of interesting forms of
Primula gracilipes, for example), autumn-
flowering gentians, dwarf shrubs, conifers
and hardy ferns: all are home-grown in
the cold North Pennines. The display
gardens are maintained in a relaxed style
and worth a visit: there is lots to admire.

HOLEHIRD GARDENS
Lakeland Horticultural Society, Patterdale
Road, Windermere LA23 1NP

Tel: 01539 446008
www.holehirdgardens.org.uk
Location 1 mile north of Windermere town, off
A592.
Opening hours Dawn – dusk; daily; all year.
Wardens usually on hand to give advice from
Easter to October. Groups strictly by
arrangement.
Admission fee Free, but suggested donation of
£3.
P WC ♿

Holehird is a demonstration and trial
garden, maintained entirely by members of
the Lakeland Horticultural Society. The
society's aim is to 'promote and develop the
science, practice and art of horticulture,
particularly with regard to the conditions
prevailing in the Lake District'. In practice
this means an exposed site with neutral-to-
acid soil conditions in a cool, wet climate.
The gardens have recently been extended to
about ten acres. The old walled garden has a
splendid herbaceous border. Elsewhere are
an extensive rock and scree garden and an
expansive area of woodland as well as the
formal gardens in front of the mansion. The
interesting thing for visitors is to see what
flourishes: alpines, rhododendrons and
azaleas, camellias, magnolias, heathers, bulbs
(especially snowflakes, cyclamen and wild
daffodils), gentians, hostas, meconopsis,
ferns and much, much more at every time of
the year. The flowering of the National
Collection of astilbes in July and August
coincides with the first hydrangeas, which
then continue into October. Some of the
oldest plantings date back to the original
owners in the 19th century. There will be
an RHS Special Event at Holehird Gardens
in 2006; details from 020 7821 3408.
woodland garden; rock garden; herbs;
plants under glass; heathers; roses;
hostas; ferns; Victorian garden; walled garden;
spring bulbs; rhododendrons & azaleas.

Owned by The Lakeland Horticultural Society
Number of gardeners about 70 volunteers
Size 4ha (10 acres)
NCCPG National Collections *Astilbe*, *Hydrangea*, *Polystichum*

HOLKER HALL
Cark-in-Cartmel, Grange-over-Sands
LA11 7PL

Tel: 01539 558328 **Fax:** 01539 558378
www.holker-hall.co.uk
Location M6, Jct 36; follow brown tourist signs.
Opening hours 10.30 am – 5.30 pm (last admissions 5 pm); Sunday – Friday; 26 March to 29 October.
Admission fee Adults £5.70; OAPs & Students £5; Children £3. RHS members free (only at some times).

The 19th-century formal gardens below the house are scrumptiously planted as herbaceous borders, the first of many imaginative modern designs and plantings throughout this extensive garden. The woodland has foxgloves, rhododendrons and splendid trees: Joseph Paxton supplied a monkey puzzle and Lord George Cavendish the cedars grown from seeds he brought back from the Holy Land. The Gulf Stream enables many exotic trees and shrubs to flourish and flower which might not otherwise be hardy in this northerly climate.

formal & woodland gardens; roses (ancient & modern); rhododendrons; fine limestone cascade & fountain; HHA/Christie's Garden of the Year in 1991; tallest *Ilex latifolia* (15m) in the British Isles (and two other tree records); food hall; gift shop; cafeteria (licensed).

Owned by Lord Cavendish of Furness
Number of gardeners 6
Size 10ha (25 acres)
NCCPG National Collections *Styracaceae* (incl. *Halesia*, *Pterostyrax*, *Styrax*, *Sinojackia*)
English Heritage Grade II*

HUTTON-IN-THE-FOREST
Penrith CA11 9TH

Tel: 01768 484449 **Fax:** 01768 484571
www.hutton-in-the-forest.co.uk
Location 3 miles from Exit 41 of M6 on B5305, 6 miles north-west of Penrith.
Opening hours 11 am – 5 pm; daily, except Saturdays; April to October. Specialist Plant Fair: 14 May. Charity open days: 4 June, 9 July & 20 August. House open: 11 am – 4.30 pm; Wednesdays, Thursdays, Sundays & Bank Holiday Mondays; 12 April to 1 October.
Admission fee Gardens only: Adults £3.50; Children £1.

The charm of Hutton-in-the-Forest derives from its many architectural, gardening and landscape styles which span 400 years but come together as an historic and romantic whole. The pale pink sandstone house is old, handsomely sited and built onto a mediaeval pele tower. Salvin refashioned it in the 19th century and Gilpin restored the terraces at about the same time: the fine topiary is a little later. Beyond the terraces is a woodland garden where large conifers are underplanted by billowing rhododendrons. A woodland walk with 65 different tree species surrounds the property. The walled garden, once a kitchen garden dating from the 1730s, is now the main flower garden: a double herbaceous border runs from end to end, backed by thick yew hedges. This is a very traditional garden of great serenity.

woodland walk; herbaceous borders in the walled garden; terraces with topiary; 17th-century dovecote; refreshments when house open.

Owned by Lord & Lady Inglewood
Number of gardeners 1
Size 4.4ha (11 acres)
English Heritage Grade II

LARCH COTTAGE NURSERIES
Melkinthorpe, Penrith CA10 2DR

Tel: 01931 712404 **Fax:** 01931 712727
www.larchcottagenurseries.com
Location 4 miles south of Penrith, just off A6.
Opening hours 10 am - 5.30 pm (dusk in winter); daily; all year, except over Christmas.
Admission fee Free.

P WC & ❀ ❀ ☕

This nursery garden has one of the longest list of plants in the north of England, including many items which are not available from anyone else. Within the walls are a smart restaurant in the Tuscan style, and a neat Japanese-style garden. But the plants deserve a long visit to study.

Japanese garden; unusual plants; nursery; restaurant.

Owned by Peter Stott
Number of gardeners 8, plus seasonal staff
Size 2ha (5 acres)

LEVENS HALL
Kendal LA8 0PD

Tel: 01539 560321 **Fax:** 01539 560669
www.levenshall.co.uk
Location 5 miles south of Kendal on A6.
Opening hours 10 am - 5 pm; Sunday - Thursday; 12 April to 13 October.
Admission fee Adults £6; Children £3.

P WC & ❀ ❀ ✕ ☕

Levens means topiary: huge overgrown chunks of box and yew. Some is said to be left over from a simple formal parterre laid out in 1694 and supplemented by golden yews in the 19th century. Some is more recent – successive generations have been good about replacing plants and restoring the garden when necessary. The arbours and high yew hedges, some of them crenellated, are spangled with *Tropaeolum speciosum* and the parterres planted annually with 15,000 plants, which makes Levens one of the best places to study the expensive art of bedding out. Well maintained.

topiary; spring & summer bedding; new fountain garden; HHA/Christie's Garden of the Year in 1994; gift shop and plant centre; light lunches & teas.

Owned by C.H. Bagot
Number of gardeners 5
Size 4ha (10 acres)
English Heritage Grade I

MUNCASTER CASTLE
Ravenglass CA18 1RQ

Tel: 01229 717614 **Fax:** 01229 717010
www.muncaster.co.uk
Location A595, 1 mile east of Ravenglass on west coast of Cumbria.
Opening hours 10.30 am - 6 pm; daily; all year. Closed January.
Admission fee Adults £6.50; Children £4.50. RHS members free from July to November.

P ⬳ WC & ❀ ❀ ✕ ☕

Visit Muncaster in May, when the rhododendrons are at their peak. Many are grown from the original seed introduced by such plant hunters as Forrest and Kingdon Ward in the 1920s and 1930s. The owners have made an excellent job of identifying and labelling them: some have turned out to be the tallest of their kind in England. The castle was revamped by Salvin in the 1860s: stand on its wonderful long curved terrace (*very* long – half a mile) above the steep slopes and soak up the intensely romantic landscape of the Lakeland hills around. Ruskin called it 'the gateway to Paradise'. There will be an RHS Special Event at Muncaster in 2006; details from 020 7821 3408.

woodland garden; mature conifers; camellias; maples; masses of new plantings; bluebells; tallest *Nothofagus obliqua* (31m) in the British Isles; two gift shops; snacks & full meals.

Owned by Mrs P.R. Gordon-Duff-Pennington
Number of gardeners 4, plus some part-time help
Size 31ha (77 acres)
English Heritage Grade II*

RYDAL MOUNT
Ambleside LA22 9LU

Tel: 01539 433002 **Fax:** 01539 431738
www.rydalmount.co.uk
Location 1½ miles north of Ambleside on A591, turn up Rydal Hill.
Opening hours 9.30 am – 5 pm; daily; March to October. 10 am – 4 pm; daily, except Tuesdays; November to February. Closed 8 to 31 January.
Admission fee Adults £2.50. Guided garden tours with poetry reading, by arrangement, £5.50.
P ⌀ WC

Kept very much as it was in the poet's day, the garden at Rydal Mount is a memorial to William Wordsworth. He believed that a garden should be informal in its design, harmonise with the country and keep its views open. Lake Windermere and Rydal Water are the backdrop; the gardens include fell-sided terraces, herbaceous borders, rock pools and an ancient Norse mound. The rhododendrons and bluebells are spectacular in season – and the daffodils.

daffodils; bluebells; trees; rhododendrons.

Owned by Rydal Mount Trust (Wordsworth Family)
Number of gardeners 1
Size 1.6ha (4 acres)
English Heritage Grade II

SIZERGH CASTLE
Kendal LA8 8AE

Tel & Fax: 01539 560951
www.nationaltrust.org.uk
Location 3½ miles south of Kendal.
Opening hours 12.30 pm – 5.30 pm; Sunday – Thursday; 2 April to 29 October. Plus some winter openings.

Admission fee Garden only: Adult £4; Children £2.
P WC ♿ ♣ ✿ ◗

One of the best National Trust gardens, Sizergh has lots of interest from wild daffodils and alpines in April to hydrangeas and a hot half-hardy border in September – *Beschorneria yuccoides* and *Buddleja colvilei*. Best of all is the 1920s rock garden, made of local limestone, and home to an important (and beautiful) collection of ferns – over 100 hardy species and cultivars. Some of the 60 dwarf conifers have grown to a remarkable size.

good herbaceous borders; wildflower meadow; tender plants; National Trust shop; tea-room.

Owned by The National Trust
Number of gardeners 2
Size 6.4ha (16 acres)
NCCPG National Collections *Asplenium scolopendrium; Cystopteris; Dryopteris; Osmunda*
English Heritage Grade II*

WINDERWATH GARDENS
Winderwath, Temple Sowerby, Penrith CA10 2AG

Tel & Fax: 01768 88250
Location On A66, 5 miles east of Penrith.
Opening hours 10 am – 4 pm, Monday – Friday; 10 am – 12 noon, Saturdays; March to October. For NGS: 1 pm – 4 pm 11 June.
Admission fee Adults £2.50; Children free.
P WC ✿ ♣

The structure of the garden at Winderwath dates back to about 1900; the wellingtonia, cut-leaf beech and cedar date from this time. The present owner has planted extensive herbaceous beds, alpines and Himalayan species.

plants for sale.

Owned by Jane Pollock
Number of gardeners 2
Size 2ha (5 acres)

DERBYSHIRE

Derbyshire has no fewer than five historic gardens that are listed as Grade I: Chatsworth, Haddon, Hardwick, Kedleston and Melbourne. All are regularly open to the public. The National Gardens Scheme is very active in the county, with a good number of medium-sized and small gardens listed in the Yellow Book. Nevertheless, it is the larger gardens on old estates that offer the most horticultural interest. Much of Derbyshire is high and cold in winter, yet it also has some excellent nurseries and garden centres. Bluebell Nursery & Arboretum, right in the south of the county, has one of the most exciting collections of trees and shrubs in the British Isles. And Abbey Brook Cactus Nursery in Matlock, which is celebrating its golden jubilee in 2006, has for long been the UK's leading specialist nursery for cacti and succulents. Its six National Collections of *Conophytum, Echinopsis, Gymnocalycium, Haworthia, Lithops* and *Mammillaria* are unmatched by any other collection holder. Begonias and gladioli are popular in Derbyshire, and fine displays are often seen at local flower shows. Derby College at Broomfield Hall is a RHS Partner College with a wide range of workshops and lectures throughout the year: details from 01332 836600.

ABBEY BROOK CACTUS NURSERY
Bakewell Road, Matlock DE4 2QJ

Tel: 01629 580306 **Fax:** 01629 558552
www.abbeybrookcacti.com
Location On A6, 2 miles north of Matlock.
Opening hours 1 pm – 4 pm; Wednesday – Friday. 1 pm – 5 pm; Saturdays, Sundays & Bank Holiday Mondays. Closed January, plus 25 & 26 December.
Admission fee Free.
P [wc] ☘ ⌀

2006 is Abbey Brook's golden anniversary; the UK's leading cactus nursery was founded in 1956. It is now 90 per cent wholesale and with 1,000,000 plants in stock, but the retail list is still remarkable – it offers over 2,000 cultivars, and has at least the same number again among its stock plants. The nursery is worth a visit at any time of the year – so is the website, which offers a full-colour catalogue. Cactus buffs need no introduction to Abbey Brook, but the nursery is also extremely interesting for those whose gardening interests are quite different. It displays the wonder and beauty of these plants in such a way that you cannot help responding to them – and their extraordinary diversity. There are three special open weekends for the NCCPG this year: 11 & 12 March, 27 & 28 May, and 15 & 16 July 2006. And look out for the golden anniversary exhibit in the NCCPG pavilion at the Hampton Court show. ❧ restaurant/café.

Owned by Brian Fearn
Number of gardeners 4
Size 0.15ha (⅓ acre) of glass
NCCPG National Collections *Conophytum, Echinopsis* hybrids; *Gymnocalycium, Haworthia, Lithops, Mammillaria*

BLUEBELL ARBORETUM & NURSERY
Annwell Lane, Smisby, Ashby-de-la-Zouch LE65 2TA

Tel: 01530 413700 **Fax:** 01530 417600
www.bluebellnursery.co.uk
Location 200 yards south of Smisby Church. Follow brown tourist signs to arboretum.

Opening hours 9 am – 5 pm (4 pm from November to February); Monday – Saturday; all year. 10.30 am – 4.30 pm; Sundays; March to October (NB closed on Sundays from November to February). Closed on Easter Sunday and from 24 December to 4 January.
Admission fee Adults £2.50; Children free. RHS members free.

P WC ✿ ♣

Bluebell Arboretum & Nursery has been a stalwart supporter of RHS shows for some years now and has won many medals for its displays of rare trees and shrubs. The six-acre arboretum has expanded every year since it was first planted in 1992 and is already remarkably mature, but the owners are keen to emphasise that 'you should not expect to find a Westonbirt, Wisley or Wakehurst' yet. Nevertheless, it is a most interesting place to visit, with a fluid design and two ponds. The tallest trees are birches, alders and some tearaway balsam poplars from Sissinghurst which have already reached 15m. Most visitors are intrigued by the many cultivars of dogwoods (*Cornus alternifolia* 'Argentea' is especially fine), maples (look out for *Acer tegmentosum*) and beech (*Fagus sylvestris*). Particular successes include *Morus alba* 'Pendula', *Juglans nigra* 'Laciniata' and *Magnolia* 'Vulcan'. Other highlights are fine specimens of *Quercus castaneifolia* 'Green Spire' and the very rare *Quercus rhysophylla* from Mexico, and the largest collection of deciduous hollies *Ilex verticillata* in Europe. The website allows on-line ordering: the nursery sells many more plants than those listed in its excellent catalogue. Three RHS Special Events will take place at Bluebell Arboretum & Nursery during 2006; details from 020 7821 3408.

🌿 fine collection of trees & shrubs; important tree & shrub nursery.

Owned by Mr & Mrs Robert Vernon
Size 2ha (5 acres)

CALKE ABBEY
Ticknall DE73 1LE

Tel: 01332 863822 **Fax:** 01332 865272
www.nationaltrust.org.uk
Location 10 miles south of Derby on A514 in village of Ticknall.
Opening hours 11 am – 5 pm; Saturday – Wednesday; 18 March to 29 October. Daily from 29 June to 1 September.
Admission fee Adults £4.20; Children £2.10.

P ⬦ WC & ♣ ▷

The 'sleeping beauty' house is matched by a deliberate air of fading glory in its garden. In the walled garden is a fine collection of old garden buildings, including a peach house, orangery, stove house and ice house. The flower garden is planted in the 19th-century 'patchwork' style and includes the only surviving Auricula Theatre, originally built to display the perfection of these beautiful 'florist's' plants. The traditional summer bedding is very well done. The drive runs along a magnificent avenue of ancient limes.

🌿 vegetables; fruit; good herbaceous borders; dahlias; good Victorian-style bedding; deer park; horse-chestnut trees; local varieties of apples & soft fruit; National Trust gift shop; licensed restaurant.

Owned by The National Trust
Number of gardeners 3½
Size 4ha (10 acres)
English Heritage Grade II*

DAM FARM HOUSE
Ednaston, Ashbourne DE6 3BA

Tel: 01335 360291
Location Turn off A52 to Bradley, opposite Ednaston Lane end.
Opening hours Visitors & parties by arrangement (telephone or letter) from April to October.
Admission fee Adults £3.50; Children free.

P WC & ✿

CHATSWORTH
Bakewell DE45 1PP

Tel: 01246 582204 **Fax:** 01246 583536
www.chatsworth.org
Location 8 miles north of Matlock off B6012.
Opening hours 11 am (10.30 am from June to August) – 6 pm (last admissions 5 pm); daily; 15 March to 20 December.
Admission fee Adults £6; OAPs £4.50; Children £2.75; Family £14.50.

🅿 ⏸ 🚾 ♿ 🌸 ✕ 🏳

Chatsworth sits near the bottom of a high valley on the edge of the Peak District surrounded by over 1,000 acres of beautiful landscaped park – the work of Capability Brown. Into this naturalistic setting successive Dukes of Devonshire have inserted formal designs, flower gardens and magnificent garden buildings. Despite their piecemeal history, the gardens at Chatsworth all come together as a single ornament for the house. They have been open to the public for nearly 200 years. The glory days of Chatsworth's garden were the 1830s and 1840s when Sir Joseph Paxton and the 'bachelor Duke' built the Emperor fountain, the rock garden (huge boulders surrounded by conifers), the arboretum, the pinetum and the 'conservative wall', which was intended to keep the heat and ripen fruit trees. The present Dowager Duchess has been responsible for some stylish additions such as the serpentine hedges which lead from the Victorian ring pond to a bust of the 6th Duke. Perhaps the best-known features at Chatsworth today are the Great Cascade, built in about 1700 and unique in England, and the Canal, dug at the same time as a formal sheet of water to set off the southern façade of the house. But there is much of horticultural interest too: a tulip tree avenue, the bamboo walk, Victorian yews of different hues, the rose garden, the cottage garden, the kitchen garden, a new 'sensory' garden, the blue-and-white and the orange borders and record trees like *Pinus peuce*. Chatsworth has also long been famous for its camellias and glasshouse grapes, both of which have won many prizes at RHS shows. But perhaps the greatest joy of Chatsworth is the sense, which still pervades the entire estate, that it is a private garden in which every visitor feels that he is a welcome guest.

🌿 woodland garden; topiary; roses (mainly modern); rock garden; rhododendrons & azaleas; fine collection of trees; pinetum; maze; tulip tree avenue; millennium planting of 100 oaks in 50 different varieties; tallest *Pinus strobus* (42m) in the British Isles; plants for sale in stableyard; licensed self-service restaurant.

Owned by Chatsworth House Trust
Number of gardeners 21
Size 42ha (105 acres)
English Heritage Grade I

Mrs Player (born a Loder) has made this outstanding garden on a greenfield site since 1980. The design is firm, and the planting exuberant. Clipped hedges enclose a series of separate gardens which flow into each other, but in contrast to the firm design, the planting belongs to the cottage garden tradition. There is a formal garden by the house which ends in a delicate white wire gazebo. The borders are richly planted with the best of modern plants – *Cercis canadensis* 'Forest Pansy', for example, and *Viburnum sargentii* 'Onondaga'. Clematis are a favourite and there is a surprisingly large number of plants which one might suppose too tender for Derbyshire – cistus, ceanothus and penstemons. Recent additions include a number of magnolias and a collection of *Cornus kousa* and *C. florida* forms and hybrids. This garden is now in its prime: the trees are semi-mature and the plants have lost none of their youthful vigour. Rare plants abound and are always being added, but it is their treatment which makes the garden such an exciting place to visit and learn from: their planting, training and cultivation are a model for our times.

roses (mainly old-fashioned); fine collection of trees; scree garden; young arboretum.

Owned by Mrs Jean Player
Number of gardeners part-time help
Size 1.2ha (3 acres)

ELVASTON CASTLE
Borrowash Road, Elvaston DE72 3EP

Tel: 01332 571342 **Fax:** 01332 758751
Location 5 miles south-east of Derby. Signed from A6 & A52.
Opening hours Dawn – dusk (Old English Garden: 9 am – 5 pm, but 4 pm in winter); daily; all year.
Admission fee Gardens: free. Car park: 80p midweek, £1.40 weekends.

This is an historic garden, famous for its spectacular lumpy, yew topiary. It has good rhododendrons in the park, and magnificent conifers. It was saved from oblivion by Derbyshire County Council some 25 years ago. The parterres were replaced and the walled garden replanted with fine double herbaceous borders, good seasonal bedding and dahlias, and renamed the Old English Garden. The castle is now subject to a controversial plan to turn it into a hotel.

topiary; roses (mainly old-fashioned); good herbaceous borders; gift shop; restaurant open all year 11 am – 3.30 pm, closed Mondays.

Owned by Derbyshire County Council
Number of gardeners 6
English Heritage Grade II*

HADDON HALL
Bakewell DE45 1LA

Tel: 01629 812855 **Fax:** 01629 814379
www.haddonhall.co.uk
Location 1½ miles south of Bakewell on A6.
Opening hours 12 noon – 4.30 pm; daily; 1 May to 30 September. Plus Saturday – Monday in April & October (Easter opening Friday – Tuesday).
Admission fee House & garden: Adults £7.75; OAPs £6.75; Children £4.

Haddon Hall is a substantial house which dates mainly from about 1600. The gardens, however, are less than 100 years old, having been laid out by the 9th Duchess of Rutland in the 1910s and 1920s along the much older terraces. The Duchess planted formal features like yew trees to add to the structure, but her great passion was for roses, and it is for these most beautiful of flowers that the garden is now known. The collection is a good one and, though it lacks any real rarities, it is kept up-to-date by the addition of all the best repeat-flowering cultivars, which means that there is a good selection of modern roses among the older ramblers and noisettes. The hybrid teas include the bright crimson 'Royal William' and pink 'Paul Shirville' and among the floribundas are yellow 'Arthur Bell' and the dark red 'The Times' rose. But shrub roses and wild rose species are also well represented. There are 60 different cultivars of delphinium in the herbaceous borders, which are supplemented by tender perennials and annuals, hardy and half-hardy. In June and July there is no more beautiful and romantic garden in England.

topiary; good herbaceous borders; roses of every kind; clematis; delphiniums; coffee, lunch, afternoon teas.

Owned by Lord Edward Manners
Number of gardeners 2
English Heritage Grade I

HARDWICK HALL
Doe Lea, Chesterfield S44 5QJ

Tel: 01246 850430 **Fax:** 01246 858424
www.nationaltrust.org.uk
Location Signed from M1, Jct 29.
Opening hours Gardens: 11 am - 5.30 pm; Wednesday - Sunday; 25 March to 29 October.
Admission fee Garden only: Adults £4; Children £2; Family £10.

P WC & ☐

The formal gardens at Hardwick are of special interest to those with a sense of history: tall hedges of hornbeam and yew, spacious and simple. In the 'Elizabethan' (actually 1970s) herb garden, thyme and chamomile, lavender, laurel and rue are supplemented by seasonal bedding and dahlias. Elsewhere are old fruit trees, a nut garden, a mulberry avenue, old roses and modern borders in the Jekyll style.

good herbaceous borders; daffodils; fine hedges; mulberry walk; hollies; refreshments Wed/Thurs/Sat/Sun when Hall is open.

Owned by The National Trust
Number of gardeners 3
Size 3.6ha (9 acres)
English Heritage Grade I

KEDLESTON HALL
Derby DE22 5JH

Tel: 01332 842191 **Fax:** 01332 844059
www.nationaltrust.org.uk
Location 5 miles north-west of Derby, signed at A38/A52 roundabout.
Opening hours 10 am - 6 pm; daily; 11 March to 29 October.
Admission fee Park & garden only: Adults £3.10; Children £1.55.

P WC & ♣ ☐

Kedleston is an important historic garden. The 18th-century landscaped park runs down to a long lake. The house is matched by a Robert Adam summerhouse in the circular garden: impressive and important. Lord Curzon moved it to its present position at the side of the lawns. The park has some splendid trees, most notably a fern-leaved beech (*Fagus sylvatica* 'Aspleniifolia').

roses (mainly modern); rhododendrons & azaleas; handsome Adam orangery; National Trust shop; lunches & teas.

Owned by The National Trust
Number of gardeners 2½
Size 7ha (17½ acres)
English Heritage Grade I

LEA GARDENS
Lea, Matlock DE4 5GH

Tel: 01629 534380 **Fax:** 01629 534260
Location 3 miles south-east of Matlock.
Opening hours 10 am - 5.30 pm; daily; 20 March
to 30 June.
Admission fee Adults £3.50; Children 50p;
Season ticket £6; wheelchair-bound free.

P ⟡ WC ❦ ⟡

These rhododendron gardens were
started in 1935 by John Marsden-Smedley
who was so inspired by his visits to
Bodnant and Exbury that he decided to
plant his own rhododendron collection.
He was then aged 68: by the time he died
aged 92 in 1959, the garden contained
some 350 cultivars of rhododendron and
azalea. Since that time, it has belonged to
the Tye family, who have continued to
maintain and develop it. The standard of
maintenance is extremely high and it is
one of the most beautiful gardens to visit
in season. Much is on a steep slope and
some of the paths are narrow, but an
energetic pusher should be able to
negotiate a wheelchair around most of
the garden: the principal areas are fairly
open. There are large numbers of modern,
low-growing rhododendron and azalea
hybrids underplanted with naturalised
bluebells. Little attempt has been made to
segregate the colours but the plants are
graded for height, so you stand on a path
and look at a mass of rhododendrons of
every imaginable hue rising from knee
level right back to huge giants far behind.
There have been some interesting
interplantings with other plants in recent
years – ornamental trees, especially
conifers, and herbaceous plants like
gunneras, celmisias, *Dactylorhiza foliosa*
and *Meconopsis betonicifolia*. It should
also be said that the garden is extremely
well organised for visitors to enjoy
themselves.

🌿 rhododendrons & azaleas; tea & coffee
shop.

Owned by Mr & Mrs J. Tye
Number of gardeners 3
Size 1.8ha (4½ acres)

MELBOURNE HALL
Melbourne DE73 8EN

Tel: 01332 862502 **Fax:** 01332 862263
www.melbournehall.com
Location 8 miles south of Derby.
Opening hours 1.30 pm - 5.30 pm; Wednesdays,
Saturdays, Sundays & Bank Holiday Mondays;
April to September. Plus 2 pm - 4.30 pm daily in
August (but closed 7, 14 & 21 August).
Admission fee Adults £3.50; OAPs £2.50.

P WC ♿ ⬥ ⟡

Melbourne is a near-perfect example of an
early 18th-century garden, influenced by
Le Nôtre. Terraces, circular *bassins*,
palisades of limes, intersecting *allées*, lumpy
old hedges and the famous yew tunnel will
all fire the visitor's imagination. The lead
statues (from Jan van Nost's foundry in
Piccadilly in about 1710) are unique: so is
the large urn known as the Four Seasons,
which was originally cast for Queen Anne.

🌿 rococo design; turf terracing; grand
avenues; shop; refreshments.

Owned by Lord Ralph Kerr
Number of gardeners 2
English Heritage Grade I

RENISHAW HALL
Renishaw Park, Sheffield S21 3WB

Tel: 01246 432310 **Fax:** 01246 430760
www.sitwell.co.uk
Location 2½ miles from M1, Jct 30.
Opening hours 10.30 am - 4.30 pm; Thursday -
Sunday & Bank Holiday Mondays; 24 March to 2
October.
Admission fee Adults £5; Concessions £4.20. RHS
members free.

P WC ♿ ❦ ✕ ⟡

The gardens at Renishaw were laid out in
around 1900 by Sir George Sitwell,

grandfather of the present owner. Sir George was an expert on Italian gardens and his book *On the Making of Gardens* (1909) is a gardening classic. He applied the principles of Italian renaissance gardens to the garden he made at Renishaw: symmetry, proportion, scale and shadow. What we see today are yew hedges, pools, fountains, grass and statues – a garden which would not be out of place in Tuscany or the Veneto. The plantings are modern, mainly herbaceous, and colour-schemed, but kept within pastel shades to emphasise the line of the formal garden. The soft colours of old-fashioned roses are perfect: Renishaw has three separate rose gardens with over 1,000 roses. In the woodland garden and against the walls of the kitchen garden, tender plants thrive that seldom survive in Derbyshire – *Acacia dealbata*, *Cytisus battandieri* and fremontias.

Renishaw is also worth visiting in the spring, when daffodils fill the lime avenue: they were first planted in 1680 on the advice of no lesser authority than John Evelyn. They are followed by the flowering of the bluebell wood with rhododendrons, camellias and magnolias. In the recently restored orangery, the National Collection of yuccas is displayed against an Arizona landscape.

Italian garden; yew walks & pyramids; clematis; woodland walks; roses (ancient & modern); good herbaceous borders; daffodils; café.

Owned by Sir Reresby Sitwell
Number of gardeners 4
Size 2.8ha (7 acres) of formal gardens, plus woodlands
NCCPG National Collections *Yucca*
English Heritage Grade II*

DEVON

No county has such an abundance of good gardens and nurseries as Devon: Devonians maintain that it is the best place in the world for gardening with plants. Rich soils ('Devon acres') and high rainfall make for excellent growth, but the county's microclimates are immensely variable, from the cold, windswept uplands of Dartmoor to valleys along the southern coast that are virtually frost-free. The Royal Horticultural Society's West Country flagship at Rosemoor shows what can be done to develop a major horticultural garden in a very short span. And there is no private garden in England to match the lifetime achievements of the late Dr Smart at Marwood Hill, now well maintained by his nephew. Devon has some fine general nurseries and garden centres, like Hill House near Ashburton, but surely no county ever had such an abundance of specialist nurseries. Their specialities include hostas (Roger and Ann Bowden near Okehampton), rare perennials (Carol Klein's Glebe Cottage Plants), violets (Devon Violet Nursery at Rattery), rare trees (Thornhayes Nursery near Cullompton) and penstemons (Shirley Reynolds at Seaton). Devon has 51 National Collection holders, more than any other county, including many tender genera like *Azara* and *Agapanthus*. There are comparatively few top-class historic gardens and – such as they are – they tend to date from the 19th century like Bicton. Nevertheless, the history of Devon gardens is extremely well documented and the Devon Gardens Trust has a large and vigorous membership. Bicton, Killerton and Endsleigh have splendid collections of old trees: in Edwardian times the avenue of monkey puzzles (*Araucaria araucana*) at Bicton was one of the wonders of English horticulture. Bicton College of Agriculture is a RHS Partner College. The National Gardens Scheme also does exceptionally well in Devon, with more gardens open for its charities than anywhere else in the South-West. Deep, narrow lanes and inadequate signage are problems for garden-visitors. Nevertheless, Devon remains a county of horticultural superlatives.

ARLINGTON COURT
Arlington, Barnstaple EX31 4LP

Tel: 01271 850296 **Fax:** 01271 851108
www.nationaltrust.org.uk
Location 8 miles north of Barnstaple on A39.
Opening hours 10.30 am - 5 pm; Sunday - Friday; 26 March to 29 October. Plus 10.30 am - 5 pm Saturdays; July & August.
Admission fee Gardens only: Adults £5, but £2.60 on Saturdays in July & August.

P ⬥ WC ⬥ ✿ ✿ ⬥

Arlington offers mature parkland on a level site in front of a fine Georgian house. It has a pretty Victorian formal garden: herbaceous borders and basket beds on three grass terraces, around a handsome conservatory. In the walled garden, recently part-restored, 19th-century fruit and vegetables grow alongside local cultivars.

🌿 mature conifers; huge old rhododendrons; National Trust shop; tea-room.

Owned by The National Trust
Number of gardeners 2
Size 12ha (30 acres)
English Heritage Grade II

BICTON PARK GARDENS
East Budleigh, Budleigh Salterton EX9 7BJ

Tel: 01395 568465 **Fax:** 01395 568374
www.bictongardens.co.uk
Location On B3178 between Budleigh Salterton &
Newton Poppleford.
Opening hours 10 am - 6 pm (5 pm in winter); daily,
except Christmas Day.
Admission fee Adults £5.95; OAPs £4.95; Children
£4.95; Dogs £1. RHS members free in January,
February & November.

P ｗｃ ♿ ☀ ⚘ ◻

There is lots to see at Bicton, including the
Italian garden, American garden,
Mediterranean garden and stream garden, as
well as the classical orangery, three walled
gardens, the (recently restored) hermitage,
and the finest pre-Paxton palm house, built
from 18,000 tiny panes of glass. The trees are
important and impressive: they include 25
champions. There are collections of dwarf
conifers, roses (ancient and modern) and
ferns. Colour comes from fine camellias,
magnolias, azaleas and rhododendrons. A
rugged *Wisteria sinensis* is thought to be
Britain's oldest at over 180 years. And there
is a narrow-gauge railway to chug you
through the pinetum and lakeside areas.
woodland garden; roses (ancient &
modern); plantsman's collection of plants;
plants under glass; mature conifers; good
herbaceous borders; fine collection of trees; tallest
Grecian fir *Abies cephalonica* (41m) ever recorded in
the British Isles; garden shop; restaurant.

Owned by Simon & Valerie Lister
Number of gardeners 6
Size 25ha (63 acres)
English Heritage Grade I

ANN & ROGER BOWDEN
Hostas, Sticklepath, Okehampton
EX20 2NL

Tel: 01837 840481 **Fax:** 01837 840482
www.hostas-uk.com
Location Near Okehampton, in centre of
Sticklepath, near turning signed 'Skaigh'.
Opening hours By appointment only. Garden
open for NGS: 10.30 am - 5 pm; 6 & 7 May, 3 & 4
June, 1 & 2 July.
Admission fee Adults £2; Children free.

P ｗｃ ☀

Ann and Roger Bowden know everything
there is to know about hostas: they are the
UK's leading ambassadors for these useful
and easy-to-grow beauties. They sell them
from a handsome catalogue with excellent
photographs. Prices are fair and range from
£3 for basic species to £15 for the latest
imported hybrids. But the choice is
magnificent: some 400 different hostas, of
which a large number are new or reintroduced. Their garden at Cleave House
in Sticklepath (NB there are two
Sticklepaths in Devon – this is the
Okehampton one) has been developed
over the last 30 years with mixed plantings
for year-round interest. But the display
beds for their National Collection of
hostas are here, too – an incredible 1,000
cultivars.

Owned by Mr & Mrs Roger Bowden
Number of gardeners 1
Size 0.4ha (1 acre)
NCCPG National Collections *Hosta* (modern
hybrids)

BUCKLAND ABBEY
Yelverton PL20 6EY

Tel: 01822 853607 **Fax:** 01822 855448
www.nationaltrust.org.uk
Location Signed from A386 at Yelverton.
Opening hours 2 pm - 5 pm; Saturdays &
Sundays; 18 February to 19 March. 10.30 am -
5.30 pm; Friday - Wednesday; 25 March to 29
October. 2 pm - 5 pm; Saturdays & Sundays; 4 to
26 November. 11 am - 5 pm; Saturdays & Sundays;
2 to 17 December.
Admission fee Adults £3.70; Children £1.80. Free
in winter.

P ⬧ ｗｃ ♿ ☀ ⚘ ◻

Originally a Cistercian abbey, then the
house of Sir Francis Drake, the main

interest for garden-lovers is the charming herb garden along the side of the Great Barn. It has over 50 different culinary and medicinal herbs. The new Elizabethan garden has topiary bushes, Tudor-style plantings and a flowery mead with a small orchard of old fruit cultivars.

herbs; current holder of Sandford Award; National Trust shop; refreshments.

Owned by The National Trust
Number of gardeners 1½
Size 1.2ha (3 acres)

BURROW FARM GARDENS
Dalwood, Axminster EX13 7ET

Tel: 01404 831285 **Fax:** 01404 831445
www.burrowfarmgardens.co.uk
Location Turn north off A35 at Taunton Cross: follow brown tourist signs for ½ mile.
Opening hours 10 am – 7 pm; daily; April to September.
Admission fee Adults £4; Children 50p.

There are nearly ten acres of plantsmanship at Burrow Farm Gardens, and long views over the sweeping hills. A formal pergola walk is lined with shrubs and climbing roses, while the woodland garden is underplanted with rhododendrons, azaleas and interesting herbaceous plants. The candelabra primulas have naturalised all through the bog garden. And the garden is still growing – both in its size and in the intensity of its planting. A recent addition was the rill garden, lined with luxuriantly colour-themed plantings of shrubs and unusual herbaceous plants.

plantsman's collection of plants; woodland garden; nursery; morning coffee, light lunches, teas.

Owned by Mr & Mrs J. Benger
Number of gardeners 2
Size 4ha (10 acres)

CASTLE DROGO
Drewsteignton EX6 6PB

Tel: 01647 433306 **Fax:** 01647 433186
www.nationaltrust.org.uk
Location Drewsteignton village: signs from A30 & A382.
Opening hours 10.30 am – 4.30 pm; 4, 5, 11 & 12 March. 10.30 am – 5.30 pm; daily; 18 March to 29 October. 10.30 am – 4.30 pm; daily; 30 October to 5 November. 11 am – 4 pm; Friday – Sunday; 6 November to 17 December.
Admission fee Adults £4.50; Children £2.50.

This is a major 1920s garden, made to match the last castle built in Britain – a granite vanity which was one of Lutyens's most remarkable works. The gardens, too, are grand and grandiose and, up on the edge of Dartmoor, the highest gardens owned by the National Trust. They are mainly within a large enclosed area, tightly hedged against the wind by thick, clipped yew. The design, by George Dillistone, is formal and terraced with granite steps and walls. Both the rose garden (planted with hybrid teas and floribundas) and the vast and vivid herbaceous borders are a contrast with the austere castle on its windy bluff. Weather-beaten, lichen-heavy Japanese cherries, rhododendrons and acers survive in the woodland spring garden on the slopes below.

woodland garden; roses (ancient & modern); rock garden; good herbaceous borders; National Trust shop; self-service tea-rooms.

Owned by The National Trust
Number of gardeners 2½
Size 5ha (12½ acres)
English Heritage Grade II*

CLOVELLY COURT
Clovelly, Bideford EX39 5SZ

Tel: 01237 431200 **Fax:** 01237 431205
www.clovelly.co.uk
Location Signed in village; next to Parish Church of All Saints.

Opening hours 10 am – 4 pm; daily; March to October.
Admission fee Adults £1.50; Children free. RHS members free in March & October.

P WC & ✿

The main thing to see at Clovelly Court is the range of five Victorian fruit houses against the south-facing side of the walled kitchen garden. They even have their original manual levers. Peaches and apricots are the main fruits under glass but others, notably apples and pears, have been trained outside as espaliers, fans and cordons. The working kitchen garden is organically run and supplies local businesses. It is unusual to see 19th-century domestic industry on such a scale today – well worth a quick visit. And the setting of parkland and Bideford Bay is very fine.
Owned by The Hon. John Rous
Number of gardeners 1, plus 3 part-timers
Size 0.6ha (1½ acres)

COLETON FISHACRE GARDEN
Coleton, Kingswear, Dartmouth TQ6 0EQ

Tel: 01803 752466 **Fax:** 01803 753017
www.nationaltrust.org.uk
Location 3 miles from Kingswear off Lower-Ferry Road.
Opening hours 11 am – 5 pm; Saturdays & Sundays; 4 to 26 March. 10.30 am – 5 pm; Wednesday – Sunday & Bank Holiday Mondays; 29 March to 29 October.
Admission fee Adults £5.40; Children £2.70.

P WC & ✿ 🏛

The Lutyens-style house at Coleton Fishacre was built by Oswald Milne for Sir Rupert and Lady Dorothy D'Oyly Carte in 1925. Rare bulbs flourish in the warm terraces which surround it. The woodland garden, thickly planted with rhododendrons, azaleas and camellias, spills down a secret valley to the sea. A stream runs down the valley, dammed to make small pools along the way, where damp-loving perennials luxuriate. Almost frost-free, the range and size of southern hemisphere trees and shrubs is astounding. ✿ woodland garden; sub-tropical plants; plantsman's collection of plants; good herbaceous borders; rhododendrons; rare trees; tallest *Catalpa bungei* in the British Isles (and two other record trees); interesting new plantings in the 'Holiwell' area; visitor reception area & tea-room.

Owned by The National Trust
Number of gardeners 3
Size 10ha (25 acres)
English Heritage Grade II

DARTINGTON HALL
Dartington, Totnes TQ9 6EL

Tel & Fax: 01803 862367
www.dartingtonhall.org.uk
Location 2 miles north-west of Totnes.
Opening hours Dawn – dusk; daily; all year. Groups by prior appointment only. And for NGS.
Admission fee Donation (£2 suggested).

P WC & ✿ ☕

Dartington is one of the best examples of grand mid-20th-century gardening in England: it was restored and improved with American money at a time when few Englishmen could afford to spend on such a scale. Some famous designers are associated with it: Beatrix Farrand designed the courtyard and influenced the woodland plantings. Percy Cane built the long staircase and opened up some of the long vistas. Henry Moore deposited a reclining woman. The scale is magnificent, and wholly appropriate to the house and landscape. The grassy 'tiltyard', planted with Irish yews known as the 'twelve apostles', is now considered iconic. The gardens are very well maintained and full of horticultural interest, but the detail is never allowed to obscure the greater scheme of it. Dartington also has fine mature trees and some interesting modern additions like the quietly contemplative Japanese garden.

🌿 woodland garden; topiary; magnolias; rhododendrons; camellias; dry-landscape Japanese garden; refreshments.

Owned by Dartington Hall Trust
Number of gardeners 4
Size 11.1ha (28 acres)
English Heritage Grade II*

DOCTON MILL
Lymebridge, Hartland, Bideford EX39 6EA

Tel & Fax: 01237 441369
www.doctonmill.co.uk
Location Follow brown tourist signs from A39.
Opening hours 10 am - 6 pm; daily; March to October.
Admission fee Adults £4; OAPs £3.75; Children (under 16) £1. RHS members free on Saturdays.

P ⌖ WC 🌻 ♿

Docton has a working water mill, a natural bluebell woodland (into which shrubs like rhododendrons have been planted over the last 20 years), an old orchard, and several distinct areas of herbaceous and shrub plantings. The daffodils in spring are spectacular. The new owners have made many improvements. First they planted up a small field with magnolias (25 cultivars) and flowering shrubs. Then they built and filled a large new glasshouse. But there is also a fine bog garden (candelabra primulas in late spring) and a collection of old roses underplanted with herbaceous and ground-cover plants. And the emphasis now is upon planting for summer show, especially in July and August.

🌿 apple orchards; daffodils; some young magnolias; light refreshments & cream teas.

Owned by Mr & Mrs J. Borrett
Number of gardeners 3
Size 3.4ha (8½ acres)

ESCOT
Ottery St Mary, Exeter EX11 1LU

Tel: 01404 822188 **Fax:** 01404 822903
www.escot-devon.co.uk
Location Signed from A30 at Fairmile.
Opening hours 10 am - 6 pm (5 pm from November to March); daily; all year. Closed 25 & 26 December.
Admission fee Adults £5.50; OAPs & Children £4 (under threes free). Reduced rates from November to March.

P ⌖ WC 🌻 ✕ ♿

Escot is a elegant Regency house, with distant views to East Hill: Capability Brown advised on the prospect. The walled garden has a pretty collection of climbing roses, and a few old shrub roses, too. The woodlands around the house are full of good Victorian rhododendrons, a hardy fernery, some good 19th-century trees (holm oaks, purple beech, cedar and wellingtonias) and good new plantings. Great efforts have been made to make Escot fun for the young – not just animals, fish and birds, but also trails, a maze by Adrian Fisher, a collection of upside-down trees and a cork oak hung with bottles by Ivan Hicks. It is fairly wild and roughly maintained, and is not a place for sensitive horticulturists, but brilliant for children.

🌿 snowdrops; rhododendrons & azaleas; mature conifers; bluebells; water-plants for sale; home-cooked lunches & cream teas.

Owned by John-Michael Kennaway
Number of gardeners 1
Size 10ha (25 acres)

EXETER UNIVERSITY GARDENS
Exeter EX4 4PX

Tel: 01392 263059 **Fax:** 01392 264547
www.ex.ac.uk/admin/be/grounds1969
Location 1 mile north of city centre: gardens throughout main campus.
Opening hours Dawn - dusk; daily; all year.
Admission fee Free.

P ⌖

THE GARDEN HOUSE
Buckland Monachorum, Yelverton PL20 7LQ

Tel: 01822 854769 **Fax:** 01822 855358
www.thegardenhouse.org.uk
Location Signed off A386 on Plymouth side of Yelverton.
Opening hours 10.30 am - 5 pm; daily; March to October.
Admission fee Adults £5; OAPs £4.50; Children £1.

🅿 �🆆🅲 ♿ 🏵 ⬤ ⟁

The Garden House was first developed by the late Lionel Fortescue, a retired Eton 'beak', between 1945 and 1981. The setting is awesome: a ruined ecclesiastical site on the edge of Dartmoor, with stupendous views. Fortescue was responsible for much of the design and planting as we still see it in the walled garden. He was a great plantsman and insisted upon growing only the best forms and cultivars. He also believed that plants should be well fed and firmly controlled: they still flourish on the treatment and Fortescue's plantings have continued to fulfil their early promise. Over the 25 years between 1978 and 2003, the Garden House was improved in quite a different way under the guidance of the curator Keith Wiley. He developed six acres of interconnected gardens, each dedicated to a single theme. The South African garden is intended to replicate the spring flowering of the South African veldt: it is probably best in July and August. Nearby is the quarry garden where natural outcrops have been covered with such plants as rock roses and creeping thymes around a series of ponds fed by a waterfall. The cottage garden is a wildflower meadow where the native campions and ox-eye daisies are joined by such plants as *Alchemilla mollis* and astrantias. There is a maple glade underplanted with thousands of naturalised crocuses in March, followed by azaleas in April and May. And the autumn colour is spectacular. Elsewhere are a lime avenue, a spring garden, a herbaceous bed, a wisteria bridge and a bulb meadow. But this is a garden in an active state of evolution, full of new features and stimulation at every time of the year. In 2003 Keith Wiley handed over to the present head gardener Matt Bishop, who is an authority on snowdrops; there are snowdrop walks to see his collection in January and February.

🌿 plantsman's collection of plants; good herbaceous borders; alpine bank; flowering cherries; wisterias; a developing naturalistic extension with *Acer* glade, spring garden, quarry garden, wildflower meadow & South African garden; plant sales centre; tearoom with light lunches.

Owned by Fortescue Garden Trust
Number of gardeners 5
Size 4ha (10 acres)

From the horticultural point of view, Exeter has the most interesting university campus in England: the gardens are educational, attractive and important. At the centre are the gardens around Reed Hall, laid out by Veitch in the 1860s at the then phenomenal cost of £70,000. This explains the framework of splendid mature trees and shrubs which give such character to the whole site – especially conifers, rhododendrons, magnolias and hardy palm trees. Modern plantings have kept pace: there is a particularly fine collection of Australasian plants including acacias, callistemons and eucalyptus. Other tender plants that grow outside include *Albizia julibrissin*, cacti like *Opuntia humifusa* and the beautiful parrot-bill plant (*Clianthus puniceus*) from New Zealand. The gardeners also practise with great artistry the Victorian art of bedding out.

 tender plants; heathers; summer bedding; conifers; rhododendrons.

Owned by The University of Exeter
Number of gardeners 25
Size 100ha (250 acres)
NCCPG National Collections *Azara*

GIDLEIGH PARK HOTEL
Chagford TQ13 8HH

Tel: 01647 432367 **Fax:** 01647 432574
www.gidleigh.co.uk
Location 20 miles west of Exeter. Approach from Chagford: do NOT go to Gidleigh.
Opening hours Guests of the hotel & restaurant only. They reopen, after refurbishment, June 2006.
Admission fee Free to hotel & restaurant clients.
🅿 ⓦⒸ ⬙
Gidleigh has 45 acres of established woodland on the edge of Dartmoor. Many of the rhododendrons and conifers were planted in the 19th century and are wonderfully mature. Around the Tudorised house – now a top hotel – is a 1920s garden. Below is a fine 1930s water garden. The garden contains nothing very rare or special, but the position is stupendous and the sense of space, even

grandeur, is enhanced by immaculate maintenance. The hotel and restaurant have received innumerable awards over many years. Finding it needs careful map-reading: in Chagford Square turn right at Lloyds Bank and, after 150 yards, take the first fork to the right and follow the lane for two miles to its end. The excellent website includes a virtual tour of the garden.

woodland garden; delicious food in hotel.

Owned by Andrew Brownsword
Number of gardeners 4
Size 18ha (45 acres)

GLEBE COTTAGE PLANTS
Pixie Lane, Warkleigh, Umberleigh
EX37 9DH

Tel: 01769 540554
Location 4 miles south-west of South Molton.
Opening hours 10 am - 1 pm & 2 pm - 5 pm; Wednesday - Friday. And for NGS.
Admission fee £2.
🅿 ⓦⒸ ✿
Carol Klein has a sharp eye for worthwhile new introductions, yet does not forget the reliable old classics: her talents have brought her television popularity and many gold medals at Chelsea. Her nursery has an exceptional list of perennials, including lots of newly discovered species and promising cultivars. The garden – always good – is now developing fast.
Owned by Carol Klein

GNOME RESERVE & WILD FLOWER GARDEN
West Putford, Bradworthy EX22 7XE

Tel: 01409 241435
www.gnomereserve.co.uk
Location Between Bideford & Holsworthy, signed from A39, A386 & A388.
Opening hours 10 am - 6 pm; daily; 21 March to 31 October.

Admission fee Adults £2.75; OAPs £2.50; Children £2.25.

P ⇦ WC ⅙ ♣ ⬭

There are four reasons to visit this remarkable conservation centre which has been featured on television more than 60 times: first, the two-acre gnome reserve in a beech wood with a stream; second, the two-acre pixies' wildflower meadow, with 250 labelled species; third, the kiln where pottery gnomes and pixies are born; fourth, the museum of rare early gnomes. A large slice of gardening history is displayed in this garden and its museum, while the wildflower meadow is one of the best in the country.

 wildflower meadow; large shop selling gnomes; home-made food.

Owned by The Atkin Family
Number of gardeners 3
Size 1.6ha (4 acres)

GREENWAY
Greenway Road, Galmpton, Churston Ferrers TQ5 0ES

Tel: 01803 842382 **Fax:** 01803 661900
www.nationaltrust.org.uk
Location 6 miles east of Brixham, on the Dart estuary.
Opening hours 10.30 am – 5 pm; Wednesday – Saturday; 1 March to 7 October.
Admission fee £5, but £4.25 for visitors arriving on foot, bike or public transport.

WC ⅙ ♣ ⬭

Greenway is one of the National Trust's newest acquisitions, with a wonderful collection of sub-tropical exotica: among the best specimens are mimosas, myrtles, mahonias and puyas. The collection of camellias (over 200 different cultivars, most of them in the sensational camellia walk) is exceptional, and there are more than 50 different *Eucalyptus* species. All visitors intending to arrive by car must telephone 01803 842382 to book in advance a parking space at this property (the morning of the day in question is usually all right). Visitors arriving without having booked a parking space will not be admitted. There are no parking spaces on the narrow country lanes leading to the property.

camellias; sub-tropical plants; eucalyptus; National Trust shop; café.

Owned by The National Trust
Number of gardeners 3
Size 13ha (33 acres)

HIGHER KNOWLE
Lustleigh, Newton Abbot TQ13 9SP

Tel: 01647 277275
Location 3 miles north-west of Bovey Tracey. Turn off A382 towards Lustleigh; then first left, first right, & ½ mile on left.
Opening hours 11 am – 6 pm; Sundays & Bank Holiday Mondays; 19 March to 29 May.
Admission fee Adults £2.50; Children free.

P ⇦ WC

Higher Knowle was built by a pupil of Lutyens on a wooded slope on the south-eastern edge of Dartmoor: a stream flows down towards the Bovey valley – the views are stupendous. The first plantings date from the late 1950s – mature azaleas and magnolias around the house. The present owners bought the property in 1966 and have since planted up the lower woodland area with camellias, modern magnolias and rhododendrons. Bluebells, primroses and huge boulders of natural granite add to its charm, especially in spring.

Owned by Mr & Mrs David Quicke
Number of gardeners owners only
Size 1.2ha (3 acres)

HILL HOUSE
Landscove, Ashburton, Newton Abbot TQ13 7LY

Tel: 01803 762273 **Fax:** 01803 762716
www.hillhousenursery.co.uk
Location Off A384, follow signs for Landscove.

Opening hours 11 am – 5 pm; daily (including Bank Holidays); all year. Closed 15 December to 9 January. **Admission fee** Free.

P WC ❦ 🌰 ✕ ◘

This Victorian Old Vicarage was made famous by Edward Hyams's *An Englishman's Garden* but for many years now it has been the centre of a distinguished plantsman's nursery. Family-owned and family-run, the three-acre nursery has an excellent range of unusual or 'hard-to-find' plants – a list of over 3,000 in all, most of them available at any one time. In the glasshouses are handsome large specimens, particularly of fuchsias and passion flowers. Most of the stock is raised in the nursery. Raymond Hubbard breeds plants: this is where *Nemesia* 'Bluebird' originated. He is also the breeder of *Dianthus* 'Old Mother Hubbard', *Crocosmia* 'Krakatoa', *Plectranthus argentatus* 'Hill House' and *P. ciliatus* 'Sasha'.

🌿 mature conifers; daffodils; cyclamen and snowdrops; herbaceous borders; pond garden; conservatory; garden shop; tea-room (home-made cakes) March to September.

Owned by Raymond & Matthew Hubbard
Number of gardeners 2 part-time
Size 1.2ha (3 acres)

HOLBROOK GARDEN
Sampford Peverell, Tiverton EX16 7EN

Tel: 01884 821164
www.holbrookgarden.com
Location 1 mile north-east of Sampford Peverell, left-hand side on road to Holcombe.
Opening hours 9 am – 5 pm; Thursday – Saturday; March to October. Plus 10 am – 4 pm for NGS on 4 to 6 & 15 to 17 April; 1, 28 & 29 May; 26 to 28 September.
Admission fee Adults £2; Children free. RHS members free.

P WC ♿ ❦

This is the garden attached to Sampford Shrubs, an excellent plantsman's nursery just off the M5, which spills over into the garden itself. It was started in the early 1980s and has a good structure of garden-worthy rhododendrons and ornamental trees – many of them unusual, including a 6m *Pittosporum tenuifolium*. Daffodils and fritillaries have naturalised and there are interesting herbaceous underplantings everywhere. Part of the garden has been converted to a new-style jungle garden with bananas and foliage plants. Other parts are microhabitats, including a 'stone' garden and a damp summer meadow. There is lots to learn and admire here. There will be three RHS Special Events at Holbrook Garden in 2006; details from 020 7821 3408.

Owned by Martin Hughes-Jones & Susan Proud
Size 0.8ha (2 acres)

KILLERTON
Broadclyst, Exeter EX5 3LE

Tel: 01392 881345 **Fax:** 01392 883112
www.nationaltrust.org.uk
Location West side of B3181, Exeter to Cullompton road.
Opening hours 10.30 am – dusk; daily; all year.
Admission fee Adults £5.30; Children £2.65. Reduced rates in winter.

P WC ♿ ❦ 🌰 ◘

Killerton is an historic giant among gardens. Its long connections with Veitch's Nursery have bequeathed it a great tree collection. These include innumerable record-breaking specimens, many from collectors' seed, though one's sense of awe may be a little spoilt by droning traffic on the M5.

🌿 snowdrops; rock garden; rhododendrons & azaleas; daffodils; fine collection of trees; bluebells; tallest *Ostrya carpinifolia* (22m) in the British Isles (and eight further record trees); magnolias; drifts of *Crocus tommasinianus*; National Trust shop; small well-run plant centre; waitress-service restaurant and self-service tea-room.

Owned by The National Trust
Number of gardeners 5
Size 8.7ha (22 acres)
English Heritage Grade II*

KNIGHTSHAYES GARDEN
Tiverton EX16 7RG

Tel: 01884 254665 **Fax:** 01884 243050
www.nationaltrust.org.uk
Location Off A396 Tiverton to Bampton road.
Opening hours 11 am – 4 pm; Saturday – Monday; 4
to 20 March. 11 am – 5 pm; daily; 25 March to 31
October.
Admission fee Adults £5.50; Children £2.80.

P WC ♿ ❦ ▰ ☕

Knightshayes is a garden in a wood – one of
the best of its kind in the world. Much of the
original canopy is here – notably some very
fine oaks – but it is now supplemented by
magnolias, birches, nothofagus and sorbus.
The garden unveils as a series of walks and
glades, with beautiful rhododendrons,
camellias and rare shrubs underplanted by
hellebores, erythroniums, foxgloves,
cyclamen and bluebells. Closer to the house
are the stately formal gardens, enclosed by
immaculately clipped yew hedges. Here
alpine treasures and small bulbs grow in
raised beds. The old bowling lawn is filled by
a vast circular pool and a single weeping pear,
Pyrus salicifolia 'Pendula', which is pruned to
thin out its canopy of branches. The walled
garden, near the stables, is being restored and
run organically. In the surrounding park is a
very fine collection of trees, including several
record-breakers. The Douglas firs are
particularly impressive.

woodland garden; topiary; good
herbaceous borders; hellebores;
cyclamen; bulbs; peat beds; centenary planting of
100 trees along visitors' entrance; tallest *Quercus
cerris* (40m) in the British Isles; National Trust shop
& plant centre; licensed restaurant.

Owned by The National Trust
Number of gardeners 6
Size 20ha (50 acres)
English Heritage Grade II*

LUKESLAND
Harford, Ivybridge PL21 0JF

Tel: 01752 691749 **Fax:** 01752 698751
www.lukesland.co.uk
Location 1½ miles north of Ivybridge on the
Harford road.
Opening hours 2 pm – 6 pm; Wednesdays, Sundays
& Bank Holiday Mondays; 26 March to 11 June & 15
October to 12 November. And by appointment.
Admission fee Adults £3.50; Children free.

P ⟲ WC ♿ ❦ ☕

Lukesland is a woodland garden in a stream-
fed valley on the southern edge of Dartmoor:
it offers the perfect conditions for growing
rhododendrons, azaleas and many other
flowering shrubs. The house and the earliest
plantings date from the 1880s, but most of
what we see now has been planted by the
Howells since 1975. The family's policy is to
try to regenerate poor or over-mature areas,
so that the quality and display of plants are
improved: during the 1990s, for example,
they planted a good selection of late-
flowering rhododendrons at the north end of
the pinetum. Here, too, in 1992, they built a
striking reverse suspension bridge, designed
by the Scottish architect Sir James Dunbar-
Nasmith. The many paths and bridges
crossing the stream open up different views as
you progress through the garden. The fine
examples of rhododendron species include
the large-leafed *R. sinogrande, R.
macabeanum, R. falconeri* and *R. arizelum*.
The Exbury hybrids include 'Cornish Cross',
'Hawk Crest' and 'Jalisco'. Youngish camellias
are already making an impact, while other
good shrubs include *Drimys lanceolata,
Michelia doltsopa,* hoherias and eucryphias.
There are some very fine specimen trees:
Ginkgo biloba at 18m, *Davidia involucrata* var.
vilmoriniana planted in 1936 and now a broad
17m specimen, and a magnificent *Magnolia
campbellii* planted at the same time and now
19m high – its exceptionally wide girth
makes it a champion tree.

small pinetum; rhododendrons & azaleas;
stream, ponds & waterfalls; tea-room.

MARWOOD HILL GARDENS
Marwood, Barnstaple EX31 4EB

Tel & Fax: 01271 342528
www.marwoodhillgarden.co.uk
Location Signed from A361 Barnstaple to Braunton road.
Opening hours 9.30 am – 5 pm; daily; all year, except Christmas Day.
Admission fee Adults £4; Children free.

Marwood Hill is a remarkable plantsman's garden, conceived on a grand scale and fast maturing, though it is still expanding along the long sheltered valley which gives such vigorous growth to its plants. There is no better place in the South-West to learn about plants of every kind, especially as all the plants are clearly labelled. It is moreover a garden of year-round interest. Late in the year, *Galanthus reginae-olgae* flowers with the last of the *Cyclamen hederifolium*: these are followed in midwinter by many other snowdrops and *Cyclamen coum*. There is a wonderful collection of camellias at this season, too – some in the open, and others (huge bushes of Reticulata hybrids) under glass. Magnolias are numerous, including many of the Jury hybrids from New Zealand, the dark form of M. *campbellii* called 'Betty Jessel', M. *sprengeri* var. *diva*, M. *dawsoniana*, M. x *wieseneri* and the home-grown 'Marwood Spring'. Many are underplanted with drifts of narcissi. Come the spring, and the pergola draped with 12 different wisterias starts to flower (the colour is extended by interplanted clematis and climbing roses) and the walled garden begins to make an impact with ceanothus, *Clianthus puniceus* and the poppy bush (*Dendromecon rigida*). In early summer the bog garden comes into its own, starting with drifts of candelabra primulas and continuing with astilbes from the National Collection: in fact the bog garden is full of colour right through until autumn. Hydrangeas are another success story: a very large number of cultivars is planted throughout the garden. As the soil is acid, the 'mopheads' come out in many shades of blue, alongside the cultivars of *Hydrangea paniculata* (Dr Smart considered 'Pink Diamond' one of the best) and *Hydrangea quercifolia* whose oak-shaped leaves change to brilliant colours in the autumn. Leaves and bark are important elements of the garden: Dr Smart planted the birches close to the eucalyptus so that the contrasts of bark can be enjoyed together – he planted large numbers of both *Betula* and *Eucalyptus* species. He also had a high regard for the seldom-seen *Amomyrtus lechleriana* in the walled garden. And there is a fine collection of rhododendrons, including large plants of R. *macabeanum*, R. *sinograde*, R. *eximium*, R. *arizelum*, R. *arboreum* and R. 'Sir Charles Lemon'. There are additions and improvements every year: 2004 saw the start of a three-year project to plant up the hilltop with four acres of prairie garden – grasses, perennials and flower meadows among the eucalyptus.

a supreme example of a plantsman's collection of plants; roses (mainly old-fashioned & climbers); rhododendrons & azaleas; plants under glass; daffodils; good herbaceous plants; fine collection of trees; alpine plants; birches; *Eucalyptus*; camellias; hebes; teas, March to October.

Owned by Dr J.A. Snowdon
Number of gardeners 4
Size 8ha (20 acres)
NCCPG National Collections *Astilbe*; *Iris ensata*; *Tulbaghia*

Owned by Mr & Mrs J. Howell
Number of gardeners family, plus part-time help
Size 9.6ha (24 acres)

MOTHECOMBE HOUSE
Holbeton, Plymouth PL8 1LA

Tel: 01752 830444 **Fax:** 01752 830500
Location 10 miles south-east of Plymouth; signed from A379.
Opening hours 2 pm – 5 pm; 29 & 30 April; 21 May; 11 June.
Admission fee Adults £3; Children free.

Mothecombe is a beautiful, unspoilt estate which surrounds the Erme estuary. The walled garden has fruit, vegetables and flower borders. In the orchard are spring bulbs, flowering shrubs, streams and a bog garden, as well as a large pond. The camellia walk leads through a mass of bluebells and down to the sandy shore.

nursery plant sales; teas.

Owned by Mr & Mrs A. Mildmay-White
Number of gardeners 2
Size 6ha (15 acres)

NICKY'S ROCK GARDEN NURSERY
Broadhayes, Stockland, Honiton EX14 9EH

Tel: 01404 881213
Location 6 miles east of Honiton, off midpoint of north-south road between A30 & A35.
Opening hours 9 am – dusk; daily. Please telephone first.
Admission fee Free.

This nursery is one of few in the South-West which specialise in alpines. The owners are keen plantsmen and almost everything can be seen growing in their show garden, which is small and not always tidy. However, it is always worth rooting round the sales beds,

where there are treasures to find at very moderate prices. The owners enjoy looking at the garden with visitors and talking about the plants.

rockeries; troughs; scree; raised beds.

Owned by Bob & Diana Dark
Number of gardeners owners
Size 0.2ha (½ acre)

THE OLD GLEBE
Eggesford, Chulmleigh EX18 7QU

Tel & Fax: 01769 580632
Location South (& uphill) of Eggesford station for ⅔ mile; right into bridleway.
Opening hours 2 pm – 6 pm; 20, 21, 28 & 29 May for NGS. All customers by appointment.
Admission fee Adults £2 & Children £1 on NGS days.

This is a great rhododendron collection, well-known to the *cognoscenti*. Nigel Wright grows over 6,000 plants and 800 different cultivars, and his nursery sells over 200 of them. It is one of the best lists in the UK. The house is an old rectory, with fine lawns, mature trees, walled herbaceous borders, a bog garden and a small lake.

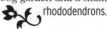

rhododendrons.

Owned by Mr & Mrs Nigel Wright
Number of gardeners 3 part-time
Size 2.8ha (7 acres)

ORCHID PARADISE
Burnham Nurseries, Forches Cross, Newton Abbot TQ12 6PZ

Tel: 01626 352233 **Fax:** 01626 362167
www.orchids.uk.com
Location Follow brown tourist signs from A382 between Newton Abbot & Bovey Tracey.
Opening hours 10 am – 4 pm; daily, except Christmas & New Year.
Admission fee Adults £2; Children free.

P WC & 🌱 🌰 ☕

The Rittershausens are famous for their orchids – their books, their expertise, their exhibits and the range of what they grow and sell. The display houses are open all year – a place of pilgrimage for beginners and experts alike, and a feast for the eyes whatever the weather outside.

 orchids for sale; tea, coffee & light refreshments.

Owned by Sara Rittershausen

OVERBECK'S MUSEUM & GARDEN
Sharpitor, Salcombe TQ8 8LW

Tel: 01548 842893 **Fax:** 01548 845020
www.nationaltrust.org.uk
Location 2 miles south of Salcombe.
Opening hours 10 am - 6 pm (or dusk, if earlier); daily; all year.
Admission fee Adults £5; Children £2.50.

P WC 🌱 🌰 ☕

Overbeck's has a small, intensely planted, almost jungly garden, perched above the Salcombe estuary. The formal terraces (rather 1930s) are stuffed with interesting tender plants: *Musa basjoo*, phormiums, agapanthus, self-sown *Echium pininana* and every kind of South African daisy, all held together in a framework of hundreds of *Trachycarpus* palms.

 sub-tropical plants; bluebells; palms; mimosas; cyclamen; *Magnolia campbellii*; National Trust shop; tea-room.

Owned by The National Trust
Number of gardeners 2
Size 2.4ha (6 acres)
English Heritage Grade II

PAIGNTON ZOO & BOTANICAL GARDENS
Totnes Road, Paignton TQ4 7EU

Tel: 01803 697500 **Fax:** 01803 523457
www.paigntonzoo.org.uk

Location On A385 Totnes Road, 1 mile from Paignton.
Opening hours 10 am - 6 pm (or dusk, if earlier); daily; all year. Closed 25 December.
Admission fee Adults £10; OAPs £8.25; Children £6.70.

P WC & 🌰 ☕

Once a private garden devoted to blue-flowered and blue-leaved plants, this is now an inspiring combination of zoo, botanic collection, public park and holiday entertainment. Themed plant collections are one of its more recent features: among them are economic plants, medical plants, palm species and a Mediterranean climate garden. There are tropical, temperate and desert-plant glasshouses.

 mature trees & shrubs; unusual exotics; glasshouses with tropical plants; shops; large self-service restaurant.

Owned by Whitley Wildlife Conservation Trust
Number of gardeners 6
Size 30ha (75 acres)
NCCPG National Collections *Buddleja*

PLANT WORLD BOTANIC GARDENS
St Marychurch Road, Newton Abbot TQ12 4SE

Tel: 01803 872939 **Fax:** 01803 875018
www.plantworld-devon.co.uk
Location Follow brown tourist signs from Penn Inn roundabout at Newton Abbot, at end of A380 dual carriageway from Exeter.
Opening hours 9.30 am - 5 pm; daily; April to September.
Admission fee Adults £3; Children free.

P WC & 🌱 ☕

This plantsman's nursery sells a selection of alpines, perennials and shrubs. There is an illustrated seed list with fresh material from the gardens and some interesting collected species. The National Collection of *Primula* extends only to the Cortusoides section of the genus, but the nursery used to collect the Capitatae and Farinosae, too, and it still grows many from those sections. The nursery also has a strong line in new strains of aquilegias and hardy geraniums. The mature four-acre gardens are planted out as special habitat zones representing the five continents. They burgeon with rare trees and shrubs: worth a long journey to visit in their own right.

 many good plants; innovative design; new café.

Owned by Ray Brown
Number of gardeners 3
Size 1.6ha (4 acres)
NCCPG National Collections *Primula* (Cortusoides section)

PLEASANT VIEW NURSERY & GARDEN

Two Mile Oak, Denbury, Newton Abbot TQ12 6DG

Tel: 01803 813388
Location Off A381 at Two Mile Oak pub towards Denbury, then ¾ mile on the left.
Opening hours Garden: 2 pm – 5 pm; 31 May, 11 & 25 June, 19 July & 9 August. Nursery: 10 am – 5 pm; Wednesday – Friday; mid-March to end of September. And by prior appointment. Groups welcome.
Admission fee Adults £2.50.

🅿 🆆🅒 ♿ 🌱

This garden is a remarkable achievement: the collection of trees and shrubs is exceptionally comprehensive – enough to be called an arboretum – and it has all been achieved from open pasture since 1988. Ceanothus and abelias flourish despite being some way inland from the South Coast. The nursery has lots of interesting shrubs, both for garden planting and for conservatories, with a special emphasis upon salvias. Pleasant View is the only place to offer some of the rarer species of every kind from all over the world.

Owned by Mr & Mrs B.D. Yeo
Size 1.6ha (4 acres)

POWDERHAM CASTLE

Exeter EX6 8JQ

Tel: 01626 890243 **Fax:** 01626 890729
Email: castle@powderham.co.uk
www.powderham.co.uk
Location Off A379 Dawlish to Exeter road at Kenton.
Opening hours 10 am – 5.30 pm; Sunday – Friday; 9 April to 29 October.
Admission fee Adults £4.90; Children £3.10. (2005 prices.)

🅿 ⬇ 🆆🅒 ♿ 🐛 ⬜

Powderham is not a major garden, though it has some good trees – notably the cork oak (*Quercus suber*) and its Devon hybrid *Q.* x *hispanica* 'Lucombeana'. Nevertheless the 18th-century landscaped park is serenely English, the woodland garden is stupendous in March and there is a cheerful modern rose garden all along the front of the house. The greenhouses in the Victorian walled garden are now back in commission after recent restoration.

🪴 roses (mainly modern); good trees in park; plant centre; gift shop; licensed restaurant.

Owned by Earl & Countess of Devon
Number of gardeners 3
Size 22ha (55 acres), including grounds
English Heritage Grade II

ROWDEN GARDENS

Brentor, Tavistock PL19 0NG

Tel & Fax: 01822 810275
www.rowdengardens.com
Location 1 mile west of North Brentor.
Opening hours For NGS (see Yellow Book) and by prior appointment at any season.
Admission fee £2 for charity.

🅿 🆆🅒 ♿ 🌱

Rowden Gardens is a nursery with a show garden attached. Its speciality is aquatic plants, and the remarkable thing about the garden is that it is planted around ten rectangular tanks, each resembling a canal,

RHS GARDEN ROSEMOOR
Great Torrington EX38 8PH

Tel: 01805 624067 **Fax:** 01805 624717
www.rhs.org.uk/rosemoor
Location 1 mile south of Great Torrington on A3124 (formerly B3220).
Opening hours 10 am - 6 pm (5 pm October to March); daily; all year, except 25 December.
Admission fee Adults £5.50; Children £1.50; Groups (10+) £4.50. RHS members (plus one guest) free.

The Royal Horticultural Society's garden at Rosemoor has proved a great success. When Lady Anne Palmer gave it to the Society in 1988, few people imagined that it would develop into such a major tourist attraction. The setting certainly helped – the Torridge valley is unusually wooded and sheltered – and Lady Anne's original garden was full of plants, but the achievement is largely due to the Society's good management and its original garden masterplan. Rosemoor is now an all-year garden, with a great variety of designs, styles, plants and plantings in both its formal 'rooms' and in the more natural parts. It is therefore a good place for ideas and inspiration at every season. The Winter Garden is designed to show what can be done to fill a garden with colour and interest during the colder months. The alpine display house provides colour and interest all the year round. Two major features for the summer and autumn months are the Queen Mother's Rose Garden, for modern roses, and its companion Shrub Rose Garden containing over 200 cultivars. The two colour-themed formal gardens provide strong contrasts: the Spiral Garden has cool, soft, pastel colours while the Square Garden contains 'hot' plantings. The cottage and herb gardens are more informal, but separated by the *potager* with its decorative vegetable planting. Leaf form and colour dominate in the foliage garden while the model gardens demonstrate three contrasting design solutions for the average domestic plot. Other attractions include the stream and bog garden; the lake; large areas of parkland; and the arboretum. An enormous number of events, shows, workshops, lectures, demonstrations and gardens walks take place at Rosemoor all through the year; for details see the Society's website.

woodland garden; roses (ancient & modern); plantsman's collection of plants; stream and bog garden; foliage garden; colour-themed gardens; fruit and vegetable gardens; herb garden; cottage garden; tallest *Eucalyptus glaucescens* (21m) in the British Isles (and seven further record trees); good range of book & gifts; plant centre; library; licensed restaurant; tea-room.

Owned by The Royal Horticultural Society
Number of gardeners 22, plus 40 volunteers
Size 26ha (65 acres)
NCCPG National Collections *Ilex, Cornus*

30m long. More than 3,000 different plants grow in the garden, which provides the propagating material for the nursery. As well as the four National Collections, there is a good choice of water lilies and *Iris ensata* cultivars, many of them raised by the nursery. Its list of non-aquatic herbaceous plants now totals nearly 2,000 cultivars, with a particularly strong hand of grasses, ligularias, rheums and rodgersias. But Rowden is also *the* place for marsh marigolds, celandines and water irises. From its National Collections it grows and offers for sale more species and cultivars than anyone else in Britain. The nursery prides itself on being an introducer of new plants.

Owned by John Carter
Number of gardeners 2
Size 0.4ha (1 acre)
NCCPG National Collections *Caltha; Iris (fulva, pseudacorus, versicolor, virginica & laevigata* cvs.); *Polygonum* (i.e. *Fagopyrum, Fallopia & Persicaria*); *Ranunculus ficaria*

SALTRAM
Plympton, Plymouth PL7 3UH

Tel: 01752 333500 **Fax:** 01752 336474
www.nationaltrust.org.uk
Location 2 miles west of Plympton.
Opening hours 11 am - 4.30 pm (4 pm from November to February); Saturday - Thursday & Good Friday; all year. Closed 22 December to 1 January 2007.
Admission fee Adults £4; Children £2.

Twenty acres of beautiful parkland, whose huge and ancient trees are underplanted with camellias and rhododendrons. Best in spring when the daffodils flower in hosts. rhododendrons & azaleas; camellias; parkland; handsome orangery; lime avenue; 'melancholy' walk; tallest *Acer palmatum* 'Osakazuki' (13m) in the British Isles; National Trust shop; restaurant.

Owned by The National Trust
Number of gardeners 3

Size 8ha (20 acres)
English Heritage Grade II*

SHERWOOD
Newton St Cyres, Exeter EX5 5BT

Tel: 01392 851216 **Fax:** 01392 851870
Location 2 miles south-west of Newton St Cyres, at end of a signed road.
Opening hours 2 pm - 5 pm; Sundays; all year.
Admission fee Adults £2.50.

This is an important rhododendron and magnolia garden with much more than the collection of Knap Hill azaleas to see and enjoy. The magnolias are good, and there are handsome collections of buddlejas, berberis, cotoneasters, hydrangeas and maples which take the garden through, with late-summer flowering and fine autumn colour, to the end of the year. And the planting continues: a new area of epimediums and similar small woodlanders is developing fast.

 rhododendrons; magnolias; good collection of ornamental shrubs.

Owned by Sir John & Lady Quicke
Number of gardeners 1½
Size 5.6ha (14 acres)
NCCPG National Collections *Berberis, Magnolia, Rhododendron* (Knap Hill azaleas)

TAPELEY PARK
Instow EX39 4NT

Tel: 01271 342558 & 860897 **Fax:** 01271 342371
www.tapeleypark.com
Location Off A39 between Barnstaple & Bideford.
Opening hours 10 am - 5 pm; daily, except Saturdays; 26 March to 31 October.
Admission fee Adults £4; OAPs £3.50; Children £2.50. RHS members free (only at some times).

Tapeley is a substantial house (early Georgian, plus Palladian additions) with fine views along Devon's north coast. Its garden's reputation rests upon three broad, impressive, Italianate terraces, dating from the early 20th century. The lowest has a handsome summerhouse at one end which recalls the garden's Edwardian heyday. The beds are planted with such tender plants as mimosas, giant echiums, *Sophora tetraptera* and *Myrtus communis* subsp. *tarentina*. One has fuchsia hedges. Nearby is an ilex tunnel that could have sprung from the Boboli gardens in Florence. An enticing staircase lined with tall cordylines and trachycarpus palms leads up to a shell house (in need of restoration), an ice house and the working kitchen garden with a long curvilinear range of glasshouses. Here, too, is a vast patch of *Iris unguicularis*. Rhododendrons, vast conifers and wild ramsons fill the woodland garden. Elsewhere are a lake surrounded by extremely ancient *Thuya plicata* and a new organic permaculture garden. Every corner of Tapeley has masses of horticultural interest – and charm.

woodland garden; plants under glass; fruit; gift shop; licensed lunches & cream teas.

Owned by NDCI Ltd.
Number of gardeners 2
Size 20ha (50 acres)
English Heritage Grade II*

THORNHAYES NURSERY LTD
Dulford, Cullompton EX15 2DF

Tel: 01884 266746 **Fax:** 01884 266739
www.thornhayes-nursery.co.uk
Location 10 mins from M5, Jct 28.
Opening hours 8 am – 4.30 pm; Monday – Friday.
Admission fee Free.

This nursery (retail and wholesale) was founded in 1991 with the aim of growing a wider range of ornamental and fruit trees than was generally available in the West Country. Now it offers one of the largest selection in the UK. Highlights include *Fitzroya cupressoides*, *Betula* 'Conyngham'

and good collections of sorbus, pyrus and crataegus: dendrophiles should take a closer look. Hard-to-get West Country apples for cider, cooking and eating are another speciality: these include 'Chorister Boy', 'Peter Lock' and 'Royal Somerset' – a total of 250 cultivars. There will be two RHS Special Events at Thornhayes Nursery in 2006; details from 020 7821 3408.

rare ornamental trees; West Country apples.

Owned by K.D. & P.M. Croucher
Size 13ha (33 acres)

UGBROOKE PARK
Chudleigh TQ13 0AD

Tel: 01626 852179 **Fax:** 01626 853322
www.ugbrooke.co.uk
Location Signed off A380.
Opening hours 1 pm – 5.30 pm; Tuesday – Thursday, Sundays & Bank Holiday Mondays; 9 July to 7 September. And by appointment for groups at other times.
Admission fee Adults £3; Children £2.

Ugbrooke's main claim to fame is the beautiful landscaped park laid out by Capability Brown in about 1770 and utterly unspoilt since then. His ponds and lakes still make for one of the best walks in Devon. In the park are mature specimens of Spanish chestnut, Turkey oak, holm oak and that West Country speciality *Quercus* x *hispanica* 'Lucombeana'. However, the gardens have been taken in hand in recent years, and now offer much to enjoy, including a rose garden, a maze, a small fernery, a lavender-and-box parterre, a hydrangea walk and a Spanish garden.

landscaped park; fine trees; attractive new gardens; tea-room.

Owned by Clifford Estate Company
Number of gardeners 3
Size 2 ha (5 acres), plus 40-ha (100-acre) park
English Heritage Grade II*

DORSET

Both Dorset's Grade I gardens – Abbotsbury and Athelhampton – have plenty of horticultural interest to offer their visitors as well as their historic importance. Abbotsbury has an especially good collection of old trees, including several UK record-holders. Minterne and Forde, too, are good for specimen trees, while one of the tallest in the British Isles of the dawn redwood (*Metasequoia glyptostroboides*) is a twin-stemmed specimen more than 25m high in Bournemouth's Central Park. Most of Dorset's leading nurseries are close to the coast – the chalk hinterland can be cold in winter – and there is a cluster of eminent nurseries on the sandy soils in the south-east of the county. The National Gardens Scheme is very well supported and lists well over 100 gardens – a remarkable number for such a small county. The NCCPG has a very active group in the county, but there are comparatively few National Collections – among them *Hoheria*, *Ceanothus* and *Penstemon* – all benefiting from the mild climate along the Dorset coast. Kingston Maurward is a RHS Partner College: the estate was first made famous by Sir Thomas Hanbury, who gave Wisley to the Royal Horticultural Society.

ABBOTSBURY SUB-TROPICAL GARDENS
Abbotsbury, Weymouth DT3 4LA

Tel: 01305 871387 **Fax:** 01305 871902
www.abbotsbury-tourism.co.uk/gardens.html
Location On B3157 coast road, in village.
Opening hours 10 am – 6 pm (dusk in winter); daily; all year. Closed over Christmas & New Year.
Admission fee Adults £7.50; OAPs £7; Children £4.50. RHS members free from October to February.

🅿 ⤵ 🚻 ♿ 🌸 🐾 ⟷

Abbotsbury is a woodland garden of splendid trees and shrubs of great rarity which has enjoyed a spectacular renaissance in recent years. Palms, eucalyptus, pittosporum and camellias all grow lushly in the sheltered valley and romantic walled garden. Among the trees are many exceptionally large specimens of species that are normally too tender to grow even in southern England – including *Buxus balearica*, *Ilex fargesii*, *Photinia nussia*, *Picconia excelsa*, and *Pittosporum crassifolium*. Spring colour gives way to a sub-tropical summer display – cannas, bananas, tree ferns, kniphofias, dahlias and bright bedding. There has been a lot of good planting in recent years, including many new species introduced by such collectors as Roy Lancaster. An excellent nursery makes for added value. There will be two RHS Special Events at Abbotsbury in 2006; details from 020 7821 3408.

🌿 fine collection of trees; magnolias; candelabra primulas; free-standing loquat *Eriobotrya japonica*; excellent collection of rare trees and shrubs; camellias; rhododendrons & azaleas; bluebells; sub-tropical rarities; tallest English oak *Quercus robur* (40m) in the British Isles; five other record trees; shop; plant centre; restaurant.

Owned by Ilchester Estates
Number of gardeners 5
Size 8ha (20 acres)
NCCPG National Collections *Hoheria*
English Heritage Grade I

ATHELHAMPTON
Dorchester DT2 7LG

Tel: 01305 848363 **Fax:** 01305 848135
www.athelhampton.co.uk
Location 5 miles east of Dorchester, off A35 at
Northbrook-Puddletown junction.
Opening hours 10.30 am – 5 pm; Sunday –
Thursday; March to October. 10.30 – dusk;
Sundays; November to February.
Admission fee House & Garden: £8.

Inigo Thomas designed these gardens
about 100 years ago as the perfect
complement for the perfect manor house.
Sharply cut pyramids of yew, a long canal
with water lilies, and rambling roses in
early summer are some of the main
features, alongside tulips, magnolias and
clematis. The overall effect is most
satisfying and harmonious.
gazebos; beautiful walls and hedges;
topiary; winner of HHA/Christie's
Garden of the Year Award in 1997; two
Metasequoia glyptostroboides from the original
seed; shop; restaurant; refreshments.

Owned by Patrick Cooke
Number of gardeners 3
Size 4ha (10 acres)
English Heritage Grade I

BENNETTS WATER LILY FARM
Water Gardens, Putton Lane, Chickerell,
Weymouth DT3 4AF

Tel: 01305 785150
www.waterlily.co.uk
Location 2 miles west of Weymouth, on B3157
Bridport road.
Opening hours 10 am – 5 pm; daily, except
Mondays & Saturdays, but open on Bank
Holidays; April to September.
Admission fee Adults £5.95; OAPs £5.50;
Children £3.50.

Bennetts Water Lily Farm is the leading

nursery in the South-West for aquatic
plants, especially waterlilies. The peak
flowering season is from early June to late
August, which coincides with the tourist
season. The gardens have been developed
as a visitor attraction: thousands of water
lilies and a 'Monet' bridge.
water lilies; tropical house; museum;
tea-room.

Owned by J.L. & A.J. Bennett
Number of gardeners 4
Size 2.4ha (6 acres)
NCCPG National Collections *Nymphaea*

CHETTLE HOUSE
Chettle, Blandford Forum DT11 8DB

Tel & Fax: 01258 830858
Location 6 miles north of Blandford; 1 mile west
of A354.
Opening hours 11 am – 5 pm; first Sunday of
each month; Easter to September. Groups by
appointment.
Admission fee Adults £3.50; Children free.

Chettle House is stunning – built by
Thomas Archer in the 1710s and actually
improved in the 1840s: it is full of
beautiful architectural detail. The gardens
are old and formal in structure, but have
been re-planted in the English style since
about 1970. A croquet lawn fringed by
herbaceous plantings fills the foreground
to the park, while the borders in the main
garden surround a sunken lawn. The
plantings are effective, and include a
variegated liriodendron, a stauntonia
growing over an old yew, a holboellia, a
small rose garden, a fine display of *Campsis*
in late summer, some 60 clematis cultivars
and 23 cultivars of lonicera. A walnut tree
planted in 1957 is already nearly 60ft
(18m) high. This garden is the original
home of the very pretty (and popular)
Campanula persicifolia 'Chettle Charm'
which is white with a blue edge. But the
really inspirational thing about the garden

is that it is all maintained by the husband-and-wife owners who inherited the estate in 1967 and have devoted themselves to restoring both house and garden.

 fine borders; tea-room.

Owned by Peter & Fiona Bourke
Number of gardeners owners only
Size 1.6ha (4 acres)

CHIFFCHAFFS
Chaffeymoor, Bourton, Gillingham
SP8 5BY

Tel: 01747 840841
Location At Wincanton end of Bourton, off A303.
Opening hours 2 pm - 5 pm; Wednesdays & Thursdays; March to October. Plus 19 March; 2, 16 & 30 April; 14 & 28 May; 11 & 25 June; 9 & 23 July; 27 August; and 10 & 24 September.
Admission fee Adults £2.50; Children 50p. RHS members free.

A pretty cottage, with an excellent small nursery attached, and just off the A303. Started in 1978, the garden has a flowing design, exploits a great variety of habitats and burgeons with good plants. Spring bulbs, herbaceous borders, shrub roses, lilies and clematis are among its key features. A bluebell-lined path leads to the woodland garden, which boasts a splendid collection of rhododendrons, drifts of daffodils and candelabra primulas, and yet more carpets of bluebells. It was originally a dank and scrubby alder copse – on a spring line – but the Potts have cleared it, drained it and planted ornamental trees and shrubs, with autumn colour in mind as much as spring flowers. Here are about a dozen cultivars of *Liquidambar styraciflua* and groups of *Disanthus cercidifolius*, as well as magnolias, meconopsis, maples and gunneras. The nursery is open at the same times as the garden. There will be two RHS Special Events at Chiffchaffs in 2006; details from 020 7821 3408.

woodland garden; plantsman's collection of plants, designed for all seasons; spring bulbs; dwarf rhododendrons; excellent nursery attached; refreshments for groups (15+), by appointment.

Owned by Mr & Mrs K.R. Potts
Number of gardeners part-time help
Size 1.4ha (3½ acres), including woodland

COMPTON ACRES GARDENS
Canford Cliffs Road, Poole BH13 7ES

Tel: 01202 700778 **Fax:** 01202 707537
www.comptonacres.co.uk
Location Well signed locally; follow brown tourist signs.
Opening hours 9 am - 6 pm (or sunset, if earlier); daily; all year. Closed 25 December.
Admission fee Adults £5.95; OAPs £5.45; Children £3.95. RHS members free.

Very touristy, very Bournemouth and very 1920s, Compton Acres offers ten totally unconnected but highly entertaining gardens, all in different styles but joined by tarmac paths. They include the Egyptian Court garden, the Spanish water garden, the Roman gardens and the Canadian woodland walk. Best are the Italian garden and the stupendous Japanese garden. The gardens are undergoing extensive renovation and replanting, and the views across Poole Harbour have been opened out again. The atmosphere is still fairly commercial, but the standards of maintenance are among the highest in any garden: no visitor could fail to be cheered up by the bravura of it all.

conifers; rock plants; modern roses; woodland walks; sub-tropical plantings; several shops; plant centre; tea-room & light lunches.

Owned by Red Sky Leisure Ltd
Number of gardeners 5
Size 4ha (10 acres)
English Heritage Grade II*

CRANBORNE MANOR
Cranborne, Wimborne BH21 5PP

Tel: 01725 517248 **Fax:** 01725 517862
www.cranborne.co.uk
Location 10 miles north of Wimborne on B3078.
Opening hours 9 am – 5 pm; Wednesdays; March to September.
Admission fee Adults £4; Concessions £3.50; Children 50p. RHS members free.

P WC ♿ ❀ ⚘ ♨

Much of the garden at Cranborne is modern, laid out and planted by Lord Salisbury's mother in the 1960s and 1970s. The Jacobean-style features are designed to complement the old house, which dates principally from the early 1600s, and to remind us that the first gardener was John Tradescant the Elder. You enter the garden through a large (and excellent) garden centre, passing through a small walled kitchen garden where apple trees are trained as 5ft espaliers. Espaliered apples appear almost as a *Leitmotif* in many other places in the garden. Everywhere are neat yew hedges and a little topiary. There are no horticultural rarities, but bulbs and polyanthus in spring and a cyclamen bank in autumn, and everywhere a sense of spaciousness, order and age. The classic view is of the narrow cottage garden walk, backed by more apple trees, leading towards the pretty flint church. Cranborne also has some fine old trees, notably beeches, limes and a vast low-branching ilex close to the house. You exit along an attractive double border, with windows cut into the yew hedge on one side, and finally through a herb garden.

🌿 topiary; roses (mainly old-fashioned); good herbaceous borders; Jacobean mount; new lavender garden (22 cultivars); garden centre; tea-room.

Owned by The Marquess of Salisbury
Number of gardeners 2, plus seasonal help
Size 3.2ha (8 acres)
English Heritage Grade II*

DEAN'S COURT
Wimborne BH21 1EE

Tel: 01202 882456
Location 2 mins walk from central Wimborne.
Opening hours For NGS.
Admission fee Adults £3; OAPs £2; Children £1. (Prices subject to review.)

P WC ❀ ♨

There are some very fine old trees in the lawns and wild gardens around Dean's Court, and a long serpentine wall. Behind the house is a small formal herb garden: everything is maintained organically.

🌿 monastery fishpond; good trees; all organic herb garden; old roses; cream teas.

Owned by Sir Michael & Lady Hanham
Number of gardeners 4
Size 5.2ha (13 acres)

EDMONDSHAM HOUSE
Edmondsham, Wimborne BH21 5RE

Tel: 01725 517207
Location Off B3081 between Cranborne & Verwood.
Opening hours 2 pm – 5 pm; Wednesdays & Sundays; April to October.
Admission fee Adults £2; Children 50p.

P WC ♿ ❀

The walled garden (one of the walls is of cob construction) is maintained organically, with beautiful herbaceous borders – go at midsummer to see the many hardy geraniums, or in August for the vast patches of white crinums. It is intensively cultivated and brims with interesting vegetables and fruit houses. There are fine trees around the main lawns and masses of spring bulbs.

🌿 herbaceous borders; fine kitchen garden; herbs; old roses, old grass cockpit; spring bulbs.

Owned by Mrs Julia E. Smith
Number of gardeners 1, plus 3 part-time
Size 2.4ha (6 acres), plus 0.4-ha (1-acre) walled garden

FORDE ABBEY
Chard TA20 4LU

Tel: 01460 221290
www.fordeabbey.co.uk
Location 4 miles south-east of Chard.
Opening hours 10 am – 4.30 pm; daily; all year.
Admission fee Adults £5.60; OAPs £5.10; Children free. RHS members free from October to February.

▣ ⬗ ⓦ ♿ ✿ ⬛ ⬭

The gardens of Forde Abbey surround the 12th-century Cistercian Monastery, a rambling private home since 1650, part Jacobean and part Gothic. They extend over 30 informal acres, with plants of interest and beauty throughout the year, set off by ancient and mellowed stone walls. Trees survive from 1700, although much has been planted in recent years: rhododendrons, azaleas, acers, magnolias, irises, meconopsis and candelabra primulas. But there are also mature Victorian conifers (*Sequoia sempervirens* and *Calocedrus decurrens*), lakes, ponds, streams, cascades, bogs and such oddities as a beech house and the highest powered fountain in England.

🌿 good herbaceous borders; fine collection of trees; rock garden planted by Jack Drake; Ionic temple (Ham-stone); 17th-century vistas; bog garden; working kitchen garden; HHA/Christie's Garden of the Year in 1993; tallest *Cornus controversa* (16m) in UK; gift shop; plant centre; cafeteria.

Owned by The Trustees of the G.D. Roper settlement
Size 12ha (30 acres)
English Heritage Grade II*

C.W. GROVES & SON LTD
Nursery & Garden Centre, West Bay Road, Bridport DT6 4BA

Tel: 01308 422654 **Fax:** 01308 420888
Email: garden@grovesnurseries.co.uk
www.grovesnurseries.co.uk

Location South of town centre, by river, next to the Crown roundabout on A35 Bridport bypass.
Opening hours 8.30 am – 5 pm (6 pm in summer); Monday – Saturday. 10.30 am – 4.30 pm; Sundays.

▣ ⬗ ⓦ ♿ ✿ ⬭

This modern, up-to-date garden centre (rose beds, Koi carp etc.) also has a traditional nursery attached. Founded in 1866 by the present owner's great-great-grandfather, it specialises in Sweet Victorian Hardy & Parma Violets. These are available from the garden centre as well as by mail order and include a large number of rarities – best seen when they flower in February and March.

🌿 old-fashioned violas; café with home cooking.

Owned by Clive & Diana Groves
NCCPG National Collections *Viola odorata* cvs.

IVY COTTAGE
Aller Lane, Ansty, Dorchester DT2 7PX

Tel & Fax: 01258 880053
Location Midway between Blandford & Dorchester.
Opening hours 10 am – 5 pm; Thursdays; May to September. Groups welcome by appointment at other times. Picnickers welcome.
Admission fee Adults £3; Children free.

▣ ⓦ ✿

This cottage garden has been made (and immaculately maintained) by the present owners since the mid-1960s and is crammed with interesting things, particularly moisture-loving plants. Springs and streams, combined with greensand soil, multiply the possibilities – drifts of marsh marigolds, astilbes and candelabra primulas. Many are chosen with wildlife in mind, especially birds, butterflies and bees. The new garage-roof garden is an interesting addition; it can be seen from steps nearby. The kitchen garden is good, too.

❧ plantsman's collection of plants; good herbaceous borders; small kitchen garden.

Owned by Anne & Alan Stevens
Number of gardeners owners only
Size 0.7ha (1¾ acres)

KINGSTON LACY
Wimborne Minster BH21 4EA

Tel: 01202 883402 **Fax:** 01202 882402
www.nationaltrust.org.uk
Location 1½ miles from Wimborne on B3082 to Blandford.
Opening hours 10.30 am - 6 pm; daily; 18 March to 29 October. 10.30 am - 4 pm; Friday - Sunday; 3 November to 17 December. 10.30 am - 4 pm; Saturdays & Sundays; 3 February to 11 March 2007.
Admission fee Adults £4.50; Children £2.30.

P WC ♿ ❁ ✿ ☕

The magnificent home of the Bankes family sits among 250 acres of parkland, filled in all directions as far as the eye can see with single specimen trees of great spread – beech, oak and chestnut. Nearer the house are a wonderfully gloomy cherry laurel walk, a newly restored Edwardian Japanese garden, a camellia walk, a lime avenue, and a cedar avenue planted piecemeal over the centuries to commemorate visits by everyone from the Duke of Wellington to the Kaiser. Next to the house is a pretty formal garden, first laid out in 1899 and still planted with the original scheme of pink begonias and purple heliotrope in summer. Nearby is a fern garden with 25 cultivars under a canopy of hollies, aucubas, bay and yew: gravel paths run between irregularly shaped raised beds planted with male ferns and hart's tongues. There is little of floral interest apart from snowdrops and daffodils in spring and some pretty roses near the stables restaurant – notably 'Bonica', 'Cardinal Hume' and 'Anna Zinkeisen' –

in summer. There are also many handsome trees, including a cut-leaved beech and several Lebanon cedars. The garden ornaments are, however, exceptional: they include an Egyptian obelisk (Ptolemy VII) and some first-class 19th-century marbles from Italy.

❧ snowdrops; mature conifers; Victorian fernery; Dutch parterre; huge cedars of Lebanon planted by visiting royalty; shop; licensed restaurant.

Owned by The National Trust
Number of gardeners 4, plus 1 part-time
Size 12ha (30 acres)
NCCPG National Collections *Anemone nemorosa; Convallaria*
English Heritage Grade II

KINGSTON MAURWARD GARDENS
Kingston Maurward College, Dorchester DT2 8PY

Tel: 01305 215003 **Fax:** 01305 250001
www.kmc.ac.uk/gardens
Location 1 mile east of Dorchester from A35: signed.
Opening hours 10 am - 5.30 pm (or dusk, if earlier); daily; 5 January to 21 December.
Admission fee Adults £5; Children £3; Family £15.50. RHS members free.

P WC ♿ ❁ ☕

Kingston Maurward belonged to the Hanbury family who owned La Mortola on the Riviera, and laid out the formal garden here in the Arts & Crafts style (with an Italianate overlay) in the 1920s. The parkland is older – a rolling 18th-century landscape. Much of the present planting is modern. The 'Grecian' temple was restored in 2000, and the hardy salvias in the National Collection have just been planted in a new parterre. The old kitchen garden is a splendid modern teaching garden with innumerable demonstrations of what can be grown in Dorset. Highly instructive.

cyclamen; autumn crocuses; fine borders; daffodils; topiary; parkland; cakes & drinks.

Owned by Kingston Maurward College
Number of gardeners 6
Size 14ha (35 acres)
NCCPG National Collections *Penstemon; Salvia*
English Heritage Grade II*

KNOLL GARDENS
Stapehill Road, Wimborne BH21 7ND

Tel: 01202 873931 **Fax:** 01202 870842
www.knollgardens.co.uk
Location Signed from B3073 at Hampreston.
Opening hours 10 am – 5 pm (or dusk, if earlier); Wednesday – Sunday; all year, except closed from 18 December to 31 January 2007.
Admission fee Adults £4.25; OAPs £3.75; Children £2.75. RHS members free (only at some times).

This garden was once an intimate and enclosed collection of tender exotics, many of them Australian trees and shrubs which now form the framework for extensive newer plantings. It was here, too, that the first owner, John May, bred the hybrid *Phygelius* x *rectus* 'African Queen'. The modern plantings have come together well and provide much to admire: this is a garden to interest the plantsman as much as the less horticulturally minded. The many different areas, winding pathways, and constantly changing views give an impression of a much larger area than its four acres. The owners continue to develop the garden and its plant collections, particularly of hardy perennials and grasses – in which the adjoining nursery specialises. There is a fine open area of lawn at the bottom which gives onto the gravel garden. The garden is maintained to a high standard. There will be two RHS Special Events at Knoll Gardens in 2006; details from 020 7821 3408.

rock garden; mature conifers; good herbaceous borders; *Eucalyptus*; gravel garden; ornamental grasses; self-service refreshments.

Owned by John & Janet Flude & Neil Lucas
Number of gardeners 2
Size 1.6ha (4 acres)
NCCPG National Collections *Ceanothus* (deciduous); *Pennisetum; Phygelius*

MAPPERTON GARDENS
Beaminster DT8 3NR

Tel: 01308 862645 **Fax:** 01308 863348
www.mapperton.com
Location 2 miles south-east of Beaminster.
Opening hours 11 am – 5 pm; daily, except Saturdays; March to October.
Admission fee Adults £4; Children £2 (under 5s, free). RHS members free.

Mapperton has spectacular hanging gardens that you see laid out in their entirety from the lawn beside the house. First comes an enchanting steep formal valley garden, running down from a pinnacled orangery to a handsome pool surrounded by Italianate terracing and gardens of clipped yew. Below are a 17th-century summerhouse, two canals and finally a long dell garden, with an excellent collection of spring-flowering trees and shrubs, some of them rare and many with good autumn colour.

terraced design; topiary; fine collection of trees; small gift shop; licensed café.

Owned by The Earl & Countess of Sandwich
Number of gardeners 3
Size 5.6ha (14 acres)
English Heritage Grade II*

MINTERNE
Minterne Magna, Dorchester DT 7AU

Tel: 01300 341370 **Fax:** 01300 341747
www.minterne.co.uk
Location On A352 Dorchester to Sherborne road,
2 miles north of Cerne Abbas.
Opening hours 10 am – 6 pm; daily; March to
October.
Admission fee Adults £4; Children free.

P 🐕 WC

A woodland garden, best in spring, and well
integrated into the park around the
handsome Edwardian house. The valley was
landscaped in the 18th century with a series
of small lakes and cascades. The oldest
rhododendrons came from Hooker's
collection, but the remarkable Lord Digby
(grandfather of the present owner)
supported Farrer, Forrest, Rock and
Kingdon Ward, which makes Minterne one
of the best Himalayan collections. The
circular walk down a greensand valley to
the woodland stream and back again is
ravishing: magnolias and Japanese cherries
are underplanted with camellias and
azaleas, while candelabra primulas and
astilbes line the pools at the bottom. The
fine collection of trees includes exceptional
specimens of *Corylus avellana* 'Heterophylla'
and *Cercidiphyllum japonicum*, while the
many handkerchief trees (*Davidia
involucrata*) are sensational in late May.
🌿 cherries; cyclamen; *Lathraea
clandestina*; rhododendrons & azaleas;
fine woodland walks; tallest *Chamaecyparis
pisifera* 'Filifera' (25m) in the UK.

Owned by The Hon. & Mrs Henry Digby
Number of gardeners 2
Size 11.5ha (29 acres)
English Heritage Grade II

SNAPE COTTAGE
Chaffeymoor, Bourton SP8 5BZ

Tel & Fax: 01747 840330 (evening)
www.snapestakes.com
Location At west end of Bourton, ¼ mile up
Chaffeymoor Hill.
Opening hours 10.30 am – 5 pm; last two
Sundays of each month; February to August. Plus
Thursdays from May to August.
Admission fee Adults £2.50; Children free.

P 🗓

This atmospheric cottage garden is
crammed with thousands of plants and
organically managed to attract wildlife. It
has masses to interest all visitors, and is
especially inspirational to those who
garden with plants in a small space. Plant
specialities include hellebores, narcissi,
pulmonarias, auriculas, geraniums,
dianthus, irises and asters, but perhaps the
most impressive collection is of snowdrops
(*Galanthus* species and cultivars) – over
250 different ones. There is a special
emphasis on plant history and the
conservation of 'old' cultivars of every sort.
🌿 lots of plants for plantsmen; home-
made teas.

Owned by Mr & Mrs I.S. Whinfield
Number of gardeners 1½
Size 0.2ha (½ acre)

STAPEHILL ABBEY
276 Wimborne Road West, Stapehill,
Wimborne BH21 2EB

Tel: 01202 861686 **Fax:** 01202 894589
Location Signed from A31.
Opening hours 10 am – 5 pm; daily; Easter to
September. 10 am – 4 pm; Wednesday – Sunday;
February to Easter & October to December.
Admission fee Adults £7.50; OAPs £7; Children
£4.50.

P WC ♿ 🌸 ☕ 🗓

A modern leisure development with
vintage tractors to admire and lots of
plants to sell – rather expensive if you are

only interested in seeing a garden. The
design is rather unco-ordinated but the
individual gardens are richly planted and
there are some handsome features: a small
rose garden, a laburnum pergola, a water
garden, a small tropical house and an
extensive rock garden (more noteworthy
for its size than for its plantings), a cottage
garden, good herbaceous borders, a sunken
garden and a Japanese garden.

 gift shop & many craft shops; licensed
coffee shop.

Owned by Stapehill Enterprises Ltd
Number of gardeners 4
Size 2ha (5 acres)

TREHANE CAMELLIA NURSERY
Stapehill Road, Hampreston, Wimborne
BH21 7ND

Tel & Fax: 01202 873490
www.trehane.com
Location Between Ferndown & Wimborne, off
A31. Next to Knoll Gardens.
Opening hours 8.30 am - 4.30 pm; Monday -
Friday; all year. 10 am - 4 pm; Saturdays &
Sundays; February to May. And by appointment.
Admission fee Free.

🅿 🚾 ♿ 🌱

This is a wholesale and retail camellia
nursery in a woodland setting. They have
a wide choice of *Camellia* cultivars, plus a
good range of magnolias, pieris,
rhododendrons, azaleas and blueberries
(plus 'pick-your-own' blueberries in
August!).

camellias; blueberries.

Owned by The Trehane family
Number of gardeners 3
Size 4ha (10 acres)

STICKY WICKET
Buckland Newton, Dorchester DT2 7BY

Tel & Fax: 01300 345476
www.stickywicketgarden.co.uk
Location 11 miles from Dorchester & Sherborne.
Opening hours 10.30 am – 8 pm; Thursdays & Fridays; June to September. For NGS: 2 pm – 8 pm on 18 June & 20 August. And by appointment at other times.
Admission fee Adults £3.50; Children £1.50.

Sticky Wicket is a highly original garden and worth revisiting frequently. Pam Lewis, like her late husband Peter who did so much to build up this garden, is both a designer and a conservationist. Her devotion to ecology guides her garden-making: she understands the need to attract birds, insects and other wildlife. Yet it is also one of the most photographed and admired of modern gardens, because of the subtlety and integrity of Pam Lewis's colour combinations. She and her husband began the garden in 1987 but the plantings are constantly reworked, so that you find new compositions and combinations every year. Berrying trees and shrubs and those with interesting winter stems are supplemented by plants chosen for their scent, decoration and usefulness to wildlife. The planting is increasingly naturalistic and draws upon a choice of native British plants. There are four principal wildlife gardens: the Frog and Bird gardens where ponds, bird baths, nesting boxes and feeders are thickly incorporated into the design, to attract wildlife close to the house where they can be seen; the beautiful Round Garden, whose colours move from pastel tints to richer hues and back again, but where the plants are chosen for the nectar and pollen they offer to insects; the White Garden, where ornamental grasses and flowers in loosely planted borders echo the grassy effect of the meadows beyond; and the half-acre wildflower meadow, started in 1997, sown with seed of local provenance and managed as a traditional hay meadow, at its most glamorous in June and July. Throughout the garden, information boards explain how Pam Lewis preaches and practises 'gardening in tune with Nature'. This is expanded in Pam Lewis's excellent books *Making Wildflower Meadows* [Frances Lincoln, 2003] and *Sticky Wicket: Gardening in Tune with Nature* [Frances Lincoln, 2005].

wide collection of interesting plants; strong ecological interest; many ornamental grasses; good colour associations; tea, coffee & home-made cakes.

Owned by Pam Lewis
Size 1ha (2½ acres)

DURHAM

Durham is too often – and wrongly – considered a horticultural wasteland, though it is true that in the 1980s the Royal Horticultural Society had fewer members in Durham than any other English county – less than 100. Things have come a long way since then. English Heritage has drawn attention to the importance of historic landscapes like Raby Castle and the Bowes Museum, and there are now six National Collections in the county. Horn's Garden Centre at Shotton Colliery has the National Collection of coleus (*Solenostemon* cvs.) and a large collection of *Streptocarpus* and pelargoniums, too. East Durham & Houghall College is a RHS Partner College.

BARNINGHAM PARK
Barningham, Richmond DL11 7DW

Tel: 01833 621202 **Fax:** 01833 621298
Location 10 miles north-west of Scotch Corner off A66.
Opening hours Parties only, by appointment.
Admission fee By arrangement.

P ✈ WC �而

This late 18th-century landscape includes terraces, an old bowling green and a skating pond. Humphry Repton may have had a hand in it. Keen horticultural Milbanks got to work in the 1920s. They designed the splendid rock garden and diverted a stream to form cascades and pools through it. Unknown and perhaps underrated, if Barningham were in the Home Counties everyone would rave about it.

🌿 hillside rock garden with stream; good herbaceous borders; terraced gardens; rhododendrons; woodland walks.

Owned by Sir Anthony Milbank Bt.
Number of gardeners 1
Size 1.6ha (4 acres), plus 24ha (60 acres) of woodland

THE BOWES MUSEUM GARDEN & PARK
Barnard Castle DL12 8NP

Tel: 01833 690606 **Fax:** 01833 637163
www.bowesmuseum.org.uk
Location In Barnard Castle town.
Opening hours Dawn – dusk; daily; all year.
Admission fee Free.

P ✈ WC 🚻 🍂 🇩

Twenty-one acres of Victorian splendour, now maintained by the trustees as a public amenity. The formal gardens around the fountain are good – a vast oval parterre re-made in the French style in 1982 – and mature trees pepper the park. Almost all were planted in the 1870s: some of the conifers are particularly fine. A tree trail highlights their splendour and diversity.

🌿 fine collection of trees; parterre; large monkey puzzle; gift shop; museum; café.

Owned by Trustees of the Bowes Museum
Number of gardeners 1
Size 8.3ha (21 acres)
English Heritage Grade II

CROOK HALL

Frankland Lane, Sidegate, Durham
DH1 5SZ

Tel: 0191 384 8028 **Fax:** 0191 386 4521
www.crookhallgardens.co.uk
Location Close to city centre.
Opening hours 1 pm - 5 pm; 14 to 17 April.
Then daily, except Mondays & Tuesdays;
28 May to 10 September. Plus Sundays & Bank
Holidays in May & 30 October (3 pm to dusk).
Admission fee Adults £4.50; Concessions £4.
[WC] ❁ ⬦

Crook Hall is a real gem of a cottage
garden – very peaceful and beautiful.
Ignore the trendy circular maze of
cotoneaster near the entrance and
make straight for the garden proper –
a series of many, small, enclosed gardens
with narrow paths. None of the plants
are rare, but the new owners have begun
to make additions. Old shrubs and hedges
give structure: new underplantings
supplement established colonies of
campanulas and Spanish bluebells.
Colour is important: the Cathedral
Garden takes its inspiration from stained
glass windows. The Silver Wedding
Garden is a contrast of greys, greens
and whites.
❧ tea-room; café.

Owned by Keith & Maggie Bell
Number of gardeners 2
Size 1.6ha (4 acres)

EAST DURHAM & HOUGHALL COMMUNITY COLLEGE

Durham DH1 3SG

Tel: 0191 375 4700 **Fax:** 0191 386 0419
Location Follow A177 from A1 to Durham.
Opening hours 1.30 pm - 4.30 pm; daily; all
year.
Admission fee Free.
[WC] ♿ ❁ ♣ ⬦

Houghall is a well-run teaching garden,
originally attached to Durham's
horticultural college. There is much to see
here: a fine arboretum (more than 600
different trees), an interesting young
pinetum, good displays of perennial plants
and shrubs (one of the best in northern
England), and a wildflower meadow for
summer interest. Many trials are
conducted here, for example on the
hardiness of fuchsias: the garden staff say
that 'if it grows at Houghall it will grow
anywhere'.

❧ roses (mainly modern); rock garden;
heathers; hardy fuchsias; seasonal
bedding; young pinetum & arboretum; shop;
good plant centre; refreshments available.

Owned by East Durham & Houghall Community
College
Number of gardeners 11
NCCPG National Collections *Sorbus*

EGGLESTON HALL GARDENS

Eggleston, Barnard Castle DL12 0AG

Tel: 01833 650115 **Fax:** 01833 650971
www.egglestonhall.co.uk/gardens.html
Location Off B6278, south of Eggleston village.
Opening hours 10 am - 5 pm; daily; all year.
Closed Christmas & New Year period.
Admission fee Adults £1; Children free.
[P] ⬦ [WC] ♿ ❁ ⬦

Eggleston Hall Gardens are attached to a
popular nursery with a lot to interest keen
plantsmen – the home of *Celmisia
spectabilis* 'Eggleston Silver'. The gardens
are informal but strongly designed to show
off good garden plants: *Syringa emodi*
'Aureovariegata', epimediums, abutilons,
variegated blackberries and much else
besides. Good at all seasons, too.
❧ refreshments.

Owned by Gordon Long & Malcolm Hockham
Size 1.8ha (4½ acres)

RABY CASTLE
Staindrop, Darlington DL2 3AH

Tel: 01833 660202 **Fax:** 01833 660169
www.rabycastle.com
Location On A688, 1 mile north of Staindrop.
Opening hours 11 am – 5.30 pm; daily, except
Saturdays; May to September. Plus Bank Holiday
weekends from Easter Saturday to August Bank
Holiday Monday.
Admission fee Adults £4; Concessions £3.50;
Children £2.50. RHS members free, except during
special events.

🅿 [wc] ♿ 🌿 🪴 ✗ 🗇

The 18th-century walled gardens at Raby
Castle are set within a 80-ha (200-acre)
deer park in the heart of Teesdale.
Designers such as Thomas White and
James Paine have worked on these
magnificent gardens, which incorporate
herbaceous borders, shrub borders, yew
hedges, a conservatory, formal rose gardens
and informal heather and conifer gardens.
The gardens were considerably altered
during the 20th century but many of the
original features remain, notably the two
fine 200-year-old yew hedges and the
ornamental pond that dominates the
central garden.

🌿 deer park; walled garden; fine yew
hedges; gift shop; cafeteria.

Owned by Lord Barnard
Number of gardeners 3½
Size 2ha (5 acres)
English Heritage Grade II*

UNIVERSITY OF DURHAM BOTANIC GARDEN
Hollingside Lane, Durham DH1 3TN

Tel: 0191 374 5524 **Fax:** 0191 374 7478
www.dur.ac.uk/botanic.garden/
Location In south of City of Durham.
Opening hours 10 am – 5 pm; daily; March to
October. 11 am – 4 pm; daily; November to
February. Closed for 2 weeks over Christmas &
New Year.
Admission fee Adults £2; Concessions £1.50;
Children £1.

🅿 [wc] ♿ 🌿 🗇

There is much to enjoy and masses of
interesting plants to see at the University
of Durham Botanic Garden. The cactus
house and tropical house each have good
collections. The Alpine garden has great
potential, and includes a 'dry' garden and
an area for South African plants. Elsewhere
are some surprisingly tender plants like
phormiums and a hedge of griselinia in the
collection of Antipodean plants. The
'North American arboretum' (very
attractive) was planted in 1980 to copy
natural associations. Gunneras flourish in
the pond garden alongside *Primula
pulverulenta*. A woodland garden dates from
1988, a wetland garden from 1989, and
1992 saw the opening of the 'Prince
Bishop's Garden' with statues transferred
from the Gateshead Garden Festival.
Unfortunately, the garden suffers from
under-funding: with a little more input, it
could become a major tourist attraction.

🌿 good collection of plants; tea, coffee,
cold drinks & snacks.

Owned by The University of Durham
Number of gardeners 3, plus volunteers

ESSEX

Considering its proximity to London, where fortunes have for centuries been made, Essex has few famous historic gardens: Audley End is the pre-eminent exception, and as important horticulturally as historically. It is the county's only Grade I garden. Few of the county's other historic gardens are open to the public. Essex's most famous gardener was Miss Ellen Willmott of Warley Place, Great Warley, but her house was demolished shortly after her death in 1934 and the garden (what remains of it) is now a nature reserve: arrangements to visit it may be made through Essex Wildlife Trust. It has one of Essex's few record trees, an *Umbellularia californica* 20m high. Low rainfall and hot summers define Essex gardening: Beth Chatto has made a study of dry gardening at her nursery near Elmstead Market. Other nurseries of exceptional interest to keen plantsmen are Glen Chantry and Langthorns Plantery. The National Gardens Scheme has a fair number of gardens opening for the Yellow Book, most of them medium-sized and good for seeing plants. There are 12 National Collections in the county. Writtle College near Chelmsford is a RHS Partner College, with lectures and workshops on a wide range of hands-on topics throughout the year. The garden at Hyde Hall has proved an interesting acquisition for the Royal Horticultural Society and is much improved by the Society's input – new design features and many new plants.

AUDLEY END
Saffron Walden CB11 4JF

Tel: 01799 522842/520052 **Fax:** 01799 522131
www.english-heritage.org.uk
Location On B1383, 1 mile west of Saffron Walden.
Opening hours 10 am – 6 pm; Wednesday – Sunday & Bank Holidays; April to 1 October. 10 am – 5 pm; weekends only; March and 7 to 29 October.
Admission fee Gardens: Adults £4.80; OAPs £3.60; Children £2.40; Family £12.

P ⊸ WC & ✿ ❀ ✕ ☕

Capability Brown landscaped the park in 1763 but work on rejuvenating the garden at Audley End started some years ago with the parterre garden behind the house towards the Temple of Concord. This dates from the 1830s and has 170 geometric flower beds crisply cut from the turf and planted with original varieties of perennials, bedding plants and annuals for spring and summer.

Nearby are the Elysian garden, designed in the 1780s by Placido Columbani, and the Victorian pond garden in the 'picturesque' style, whose walls and pergola are clad with climbing shrubs and roses. Work continues: the kitchen garden is now run as a joint venture with HDRA as a working organic garden. It looks much as it would have done in late Victorian times with vegetables, fruit, herbs and flowers to supply the household. The cultivation is, of course, entirely organic. The vinehouse is one of the earliest and largest in the country, with vines over 200 years old.

🌿 bedding out; parterre; magnificent plane trees; organic kitchen garden; ancient trees; shop; restaurant & picnic site.

Owned by English Heritage
Number of gardeners 9
Size 40ha (100 acres), including parkland
English Heritage Grade I

BETH CHATTO GARDENS
Elmstead Market, Colchester CO7 7DB

Tel: 01206 822007 **Fax:** 01206 825933
www.bethchatto.co.uk
Location 7 miles east of Colchester.
Opening hours 9 am – 5 pm; Monday – Saturday;
March to October; 9 am – 4 pm; Monday – Friday;
November to February.
Admission fee Adults £4.50; Children free. RHS
members free from January to March.

P WC & * D

This beautiful and instructive garden was begun in 1960 and uses a very wide range of plants, mostly species, chosen for their foliage and form as much as for their flowers. Beth Chatto's planting is based largely on ecological principles, following her late husband Andrew Chatto's lifetime research into the natural associations of garden plants. The original site was wasteland, unfit for farming and unfit for the planting of many conventional plants, especially cultivars. It had – and still has – three very different ecologies: areas of hungry sand and gravel, a clay-based spring-fed hollow, and elsewhere dry shade beneath ancient oaks. Beth Chatto has developed three contrasting types of planting, based on the principle of finding the right plant for the right place, and thus turning problem areas into advantages. Around the modest house, where the soil is thin and dry, Beth Chatto used plants mostly from the Mediterranean: cistus, broom, salvias, euphorbias, potentillas, verbascums, and the tree-like *Genista aetnensis* have come together on the warm sandy slopes. A short walk leads down to a water garden of remarkable luxuriance, made by damming the spring-fed ditch to create a series of ponds in the valley. The lush plantings are quite untypical of Essex, where rainfall averages 50cm a year. Here are gunneras, astilbes, lysichitons, hostas, phormiums, water irises and the ostrich fern *Matteuccia struthiopteris*. They have a continuous background, not too intrusive, of conifers, specimen trees and shrubs – but the emphasis throughout the garden is on the herbaceous plants for which the adjoining nursery is famous. A copse has been developed as a woodland garden and a canopy of young oaks underplanted with shade-lovers. Here, and in the long shady border above the water garden, are rich plantings of bulbs, woodlanders and groundcover – aconites, cyclamen, erythroniums and dicentras. The gravel garden was made in 1992 on the site of the old car park, where drought-resistant sun-lovers have been planted in a fluid sequence of island beds. Before planting, this ¾ acre of yellow sand and gravel was 'improved' with the addition of home-made compost, to give the plants a good start. Since then, however, the area has not been irrigated in any way, despite periods of drought, since it is a horticultural experiment to see which plants will survive and maybe inspire visitors who have hosepipe bans. But garden-making is only one of Beth Chatto's gifts: her writings and nursery have made her famous. And the standard of maintenance is impeccable.

colour contrasts; gravel garden; luxuriant water gardens; woodland garden; big nursery adjacent to the garden; tea-room (seasonal).

Owned by Beth Chatto
Number of gardeners 4, plus seasonal help
Size 2ha (5 acres)

COUNTY PARK NURSERY
384 Wingletye Lane, Hornchurch
RM11 3BU

Tel: 01708 445205
Location 2½ miles from M25, Jct 29. Off
Wingletye Lane, in Essex Gardens, Hornchurch.
Opening hours 10 am - 5 pm; daily, except
Wednesdays; March to October. Open in winter by
appointment only. Please telephone before visiting.
Admission fee Free.

This small nursery specialises in
Antipodean plants, many of them grown
from native seed and not available from
any other nursery in the UK. There is no
show garden to speak of, but every tiny
corner seems covered in pots of unusual
plants – some for display and others for
sale. There are hebes and parahebes, as
well as New Zealand *Clematis* species,
Coprosma and other shrubs like
leptospermums. They also have a long list
of podocarpus cultivars, selected for their
spreading habit and unusual leaf colours.
Very interesting.

plants from New Zealand & Australia.

Owned by Graham Hutchins
Size 0.2ha (½ acre)
NCCPG National Collections *Coprosma*

EASTON LODGE
Warwick House, Great Dunmow CM6 2BB

Tel & Fax: 01371 876979
www.eastonlodge.co.uk
Location Signed from A120 at Great Dunmow.
Opening hours 12 noon - dusk; daily; February to
early March (ring for exact dates) for snowdrops.
12 noon - 6 pm; Friday – Sunday & Bank Holiday
Mondays; Easter to October.
Admission fee Adults £3.80; OAPs £3.50;
Children £1.50.

The garden was laid out by Harold Peto in
1902 for the Countess of Warwick

(Edward VII's 'darling Daisy'), fell into
serious neglect, and has been wonderfully
restored since 1993. Much remains to be
done, as the owner is the first to admit,
but the lime grove has now been cleared
and the Peto shrubbery was rejuvenated in
2001. Work has begun on re-paving the
Italian garden. There is an exhibition of
how the house was built and the gardens
made. The roses are very beautiful in
high summer.

cream teas in courtyard & tea-room.

Owned by Brian Creasey
Number of gardeners 2
Size 9.2ha (23 acres)
English Heritage Grade II

THE GIBBERD GARDEN
Marsh Lane, Gilden Way, Harlow
CM17 0NA

Tel: 01279 442112
www.thegibberdgarden.co.uk
Location Leave Harlow on B183. Marsh Lane is on
left: follow brown tourist signs.
Opening hours 2 pm - 6 pm; Wednesdays,
Saturdays, Sundays & Bank Holidays; April to
September.
Admission fee Adults £4; Concessions £2.50;
Children free.

This was the private garden of Sir
Frederick Gibberd, the master planner of
Harlow New Town. It was designed as a
series of distinct rooms, and filled with
sculpture, pots and architectural salvage.
One of the most important architectural
gardens of the 20th century, it is being
restored with aid from the Heritage Lottery
Fund. The moated castle has been dredged
and repaired; the top lawns and beds have
been replanted; and much of the
restoration work featured in the BBC series
Hidden Gardens in December 2002. There
is an active Friends organisation: details
from Gordon Whittle on 01279 434840.

GLEN CHANTRY

Ishams Chase, Wickham Bishops, Witham CM8 3LG

Tel & Fax: 01621 891342
www.glenchantry.demon.co.uk
Location Turn off B1019, just south of A12 towards Benton Hall golf course & Wickham Bishops: immediately left after bridge & up track ½ mile.
Opening hours 10 am – 4 pm; Fridays & Saturdays; 7 April to 2 September. And for NGS.
Admission fee Adults £3; Children 50p. RHS members free.

P WC & 🌱 🍂 ▱

This remarkable garden has been made from a bare hillside since 1976: the owners have an excellent eye for good plants and for how to use them. You enter past a very pretty new *potager* and through the immaculately tidy nursery, itself a plantsman's treasure-house for herbaceous plants. Then you step down into the garden, filled with endless microhabitats, some exploiting the opportunities offered by dry, stony acid soil, and others defying it. Scree beds, peat beds, raised beds and an artificial stream are part of the story, but so is a winding pattern of ebbing and flowing island beds. Along the centre of these beds are trees and shrubs which screen the two faces from each other and make it possible to plant both sides of a path with the same colour. The owners also practise 'vertical planting', which means that season after season different displays are possible from the same patch: in one small area, for example, the spring-flowering fritillaries, erythroniums and corydalis are covered in summer by hostas, grasses and rushes. A new bed planted with a wide selection of grasses, interplanted with late-flowering perennials, is maturing well. Glen Chantry is a model of what devoted plantsmanship can achieve: educational, functional and beautiful all at once. There is one formal garden near the house, white and green in summer with 'Katharina Zeimet' and 'Iceberg' roses, campanulas, lilies, eryngiums, alliums and geraniums, but the rest of the garden is fluid, however disciplined may be the controlling hand. In fact, very little seeding around is allowed – perhaps a few plants of Martyn Rix's form of *Eryngium giganteum* 'Silver Ghost' – because the planting is intended to slow you down and stop you on your way, to admire individual plants. Besides, the standards of maintenance are immaculate. There will be two RHS Special Events at Glen Chantry in 2006; details from 020 7821 3408.

🌿 alpines; herbaceous plants; bulbs; special habitats; masses of fascinating plants for plantsmen; fine specialist nursery attached; light refreshments.

Owned by Sue & Wol Staines
Number of gardeners owners only
Size 1ha (2½ acres)

good modern design; wild garden; lime avenue; 'Roman Temple' vistas; shop; light refreshments.

Owned by Gibberd Garden Trust
Number of gardeners 2 part-time, plus volunteers
Size 2.8ha (7 acres)

GREEN ISLAND
Park Road, Ardleigh, Colchester CO7 7SP

Tel & Fax: 01206 230455
www.greenislandgardens.co.uk
Location Off B1029 from Ardleigh to Bromley; look out for brown tourist signs.
Opening hours 1 pm – 5 pm; Wednesdays, Thursdays & Sundays; March to October. And 11 November for NGS.
Admission fee Adults £3; Children £1. Groups and guided tours by appointment.

This is an old garden, redesigned by a professional designer in 1997 on a large scale, for all-year interest. It has a water garden, a pond, a bamboo dell, a Japanese garden, woodland gardens, a 'seaside' garden, and much else besides. But the main attractions are the fluid design, which leads you along quite naturally, and the spacious island beds, planted with a large number of herbaceous plants and shrubs. Seldom does a designer's garden display so much plantsmanship.

modern design; good plants; new woodland garden (2005); nursery; teas on Sundays.

Owned by Fiona Edmond
Number of gardeners 1 part-time
Size 8ha (20 acres)

LANGTHORNS PLANTERY
Little Canfield, Dunmow CM6 1TD

Tel & Fax: 01371 872611
www.langthorns.com
Location Between Takeley & Great Dunmow, signed off A120.
Opening hours 10 am – 5 pm; daily. Closed Christmas to New Year.
Admission fee Free.

Langthorns Plantery is a go-ahead modern nursery with an eye for good plants. Though best known for their wide range of hardy herbaceous plants, the owners apply their discriminating taste to all their stock – alpines, shrubs, trees and climbers, especially clematis. The garden is worth a visit in its own right but is not always open, so check before you visit.
Owned by The Cannon family
Size 1.2ha (3 acres)

OLIVERS
Olivers Lane, Colchester CO2 0HJ

Tel: 01206 330575 **Fax:** 01206 330366
Location 3 miles south-west of Colchester between B1022 & B1026.
Opening hours 2 pm – 6 pm; 27 & 30 April; 1, 4, 11 & 18 May. And by appointment.
Admission fee Adults £3; Children free.

Quite a modern garden, started in 1968 around three small lakes, with an eye-catching walk to one side leading down to a statue of Bacchus. Good plants and planting everywhere, from the parterres by the house to the woodland where roses and rhododendrons flourish. The main borders underwent a highly successful major re-design in 1998 and are looking very good now. This is the garden of enthusiastic and energetic owners: an inspiration.

roses (ancient & modern); bluebells; rhododendrons; fine borders; teas on 30 April & 1 May.

RHS GARDEN HYDE HALL

Buckhatch Lane, Rettendon, Chelmsford CM3 8ET

Tel: 01245 400256 **Fax:** 01245 402100
www.rhs.org.uk/gardens/hydehall
Location South-east of Chelmsford, signed from
A130. Exit for Rettendon turnpike, north through
Rettendon village and follow brown tourist signs.
Opening hours 10 am – 6 pm (5 pm or dusk from
October to March); daily; all year. Closed 25
December.
Admission fee Adults £5; Children (6-16) £1; Pre-
booked groups (10+) £3.50. RHS members (plus
one guest) free.

P WC &. 🌱 🦋 ☕ ⊄

You can see Hyde Hall long before you
reach the RHS garden. The approach is
so full of dramatic promise that it comes as
a surprise to learn that 50 years ago the
house had only six trees and no garden.
Dick and Helen Robinson started to
convert the 9.7ha (24 acres) of farmland
into a garden in 1955 and gifted it to the
RHS in 1993. Helen's first decision was to
buy some 60 young trees at an auction sale
in Wickford Market. She quickly became
an enthusiastic plantsman. The sheltered
woodland garden she made on the northern
side is a triumph of cultivation and helped
to create many microclimates: *Eriobotrya
japonica*, *Eucalyptus urnigera* and *Pittosporum
tenuifolium* are grown in the open, *Buddleja
officinalis* and *Crinodendron patagua* against a
wall of the yard and *Acca sellowiana* against
the house. The garden that the RHS
inherited had much to commend it: masses
of naturalised spring bulbs, a rich collection
of roses, the national collection of
viburnums and a striking collection of crab
apples (*Malus*). But it needed a lot of
infrastructure to turn it into a garden that
could welcome more than 100,000 visitors
a year. The challenge was to convert an

extensive private paradise into a garden
designed and maintained on a scale that
people could relate to at home. This
involved improvements like re-working the
long herbaceous border so that it had
shelter hedges of yew and tongues of yew to
divide the plantings into smaller bays. But
complete novelties were also needed. Hyde
Hall is in one of the driest areas of the
British Isles, with an average annual rainfall
of just 600mm (24in). The RHS designed
and planted the extensive Dry Garden to
demonstrate how a garden can be created
without the need for artificial irrigation. It
has over 4,000 plants representing 730
different species and cultivars from around
the world; many carry the RHS Award of
Garden Merit (AGM). Further new
gardens are now under way. A 1.5-ha (4-
acre) perennial wildflower meadow has
developed well since it was first sown in
2001. The Millennium Avenue in the
Malus Field (300m long and 20m wide) has
been planted with *Fraxinus excelsior*
'Westhof's Glorie' for short-term effect and
Quercus frainetto 'Hungarian Crown' for 100
years hence. Woodlands have been planted
in other parts of the estate – 25,000 trees so
far – and, over the next few years, Hyde
Hall will grow to 24ha (60 acres) or more.

🌿 good herbaceous borders; spring bulbs;
ponds; heathers; dry garden of
drought-tolerant plants; visitor centre; shop;
garden library; plant centre; licensed restaurant
serving hot & cold lunches, afternoon teas

Owned by The Royal Horticultural Society
Number of gardeners 14, plus students
Size 9.6ha (24 acres)
NCCPG National Collections *Viburnum*

Owned by Mr & Mrs David Edwards
Number of gardeners 2 part-time
Size 2.2ha (6 acres), plus woodland.

R & R SAGGERS
Waterloo House, High Street, Newport
CB11 3PG

Tel: 01799 540858 **Fax:** 01799 542900
Location On B1383 in centre of village.
Opening hours 10 am – 5 pm; Tuesday – Sunday
& Bank Holidays; all year. Closed on Sundays
from January to March.
Admission fee Free.

P ⏦ WC ♿ ❦ ●

This garden-nursery has a wide and ever-
changing stock of herbaceous plants, as
well as shrubs, climbers, old-fashioned
roses and trees. Many are grown from
seed. The owners offer a plant-finding
service. The garden is beautifully
maintained and runs down to a stream.
❧ unusual plants for sale.

Owned by Roger & Roslyn Saggers
Number of gardeners 4 part-time

SALING HALL
Great Saling, Braintree CM7 5DT

Location 2 miles north of B1256 (old A120),
between Great Dunmow & Braintree, at Blake
End.
Opening hours 2 pm – 5 pm; Wednesdays; May,
June & July. Groups by appointment on
weekdays; please apply in writing.
Admission fee Adults £3 (for NGS); Children
free.

P WC ♿

A thinking man's garden, Saling also
provokes thought in its visitors. The
plantsmanship is impressive, particularly
the choice and placing of trees and
shrubs, some of them extremely rare. Few
modern gardens are conceived on such a
scale, or mix classical and Japanese
elements so smoothly. The moods, and the
lessons, are endless. Hugh Johnson is *The
Garden's* Tradescant; his monthly column
is a rare source of wisdom.

❧ 17th-century walled garden with fruit
trees & borders; oriental touches; fine
standing stone; Temple of Pisces, moat & water
gardens.

Owned by Mr & Mrs Hugh Johnson
Number of gardeners 2
Size 5ha (12½ acres)
English Heritage Grade II

GLOUCESTERSHIRE

Gloucestershire is rich in nurseries and large important gardens. Six of its nine Grade I historic gardens (a remarkable number for one county) are regularly open to the public – Batsford Park, Frampton Court, Hidcote Manor, Sezincote, Stanway House and Westonbirt Arboretum – while a seventh, Stancombe Park, is open by appointment. Almost all the county's Grade II* gardens also welcome visitors, including Abbotswood, Berkeley Castle, Kiftsgate Court, Miserden Park, Painswick House, Rodmarton Manor, Sudeley Castle and Westbury Court. Most have important collections of plants as well as attractive design features. Indeed, almost all Gloucestershire's leading historic gardens have been highly graded precisely because of their horticultural attractions. Rich clay soils account for some of the popularity of gardening in Gloucestershire, though the inland, upland parts of the county can be very cold in winter. It is good to note that Rosemary Verey's garden at Barnsley House, now under new ownership, is once again open to visitors and hosting several RHS events in 2006. Among garden centres and nurseries, the Batsford Garden Centre has a very good general range and makes a speciality of ferns, while Hunt's Court is excellent for roses of every kind. A very large number of gardens – some 140 – open for the National Gardens Scheme though, slightly confusingly, the southern part of the county, which used to belong to Avon, is still separately organised: both continue to be very successful in persuading garden-owners to open their gardens and visitors to visit them. Permission to visit HRH The Prince of Wales's garden at Highgrove House near Tetbury may be given to garden clubs and similar organisations. In addition to the world-famous Westonbirt Arboretum, there are important collections of trees at Highnam Court, Batsford Park and Tortworth Court. The NCCPG is active in Gloucestershire and accounts for a large number of National Collections.

ABBOTSWOOD
Stow-on-the-Wold, Cheltenham
GL54 1LE

Tel: 01451 830173
Location 1 mile west of Stow-on-the-Wold.
Opening hours 1.30 pm – 6 pm; 9 April, 7 May, 4 June, 2 July, 6 August & 10 September.
Admission fee Adults £3; Children free.

🅿 ♿ 🚻 ♿ 🌺 ✕ ⛱

Abbotswood is one of the most interesting gardens in the Cotswolds – very Lutyens, very photogenic – with handsome formal gardens in front of the house. A stream meanders through a magnificent rock garden set with alpine meadows, bogs and moraines, past dwarf azaleas, primulas, lysichitons, heaths and heathers until it disappears. There is also a small, densely planted arboretum, with some unusual cultivars dating from about 100 years ago, fascinating to browse around: it is being cleared and replanted. The two-acre kitchen garden is worth the long walk on the occasions when it, too, is open: it has a fruit house, indoor roses and some interesting new plantings. Indeed there are plans for new developments throughout Abbotswood.

🌿 interesting topiary; fine collection of trees, including conifers; magnolias; heather garden; good borders; (roses ancient & modern); good for plants; teas.

Owned by Dikler Farming Co
Number of gardeners 4
Size 8ha (20 acres)
English Heritage Grade II*

BARNSLEY HOUSE GARDEN
Barnsley, Cirencester GL7 5EE

Tel: 01285 740000 **Fax:** 01285 740900
www.barnsleyhouse.com
Location On B4425 in Barnsley village.
Opening hours 11 am - 5 pm; 13 April, 13 May, 1 & 22 June, 27 July & 7 September.
Admission fee Adults £5.

P WC &

Rosemary Verey's famous garden was started in 1952 and more-or-less finished 25 years later. The bones were a pretty house (1697), an 18th-century wall ending in an original Gothic summerhouse and ha-ha, and some fine 19th-century trees. Her architect husband David helped with the design, and together they commissioned sculptures by Simon Verity for important focal points. The result was compact, neat, thickly planted, fairly labour-intensive – and very influential. Mrs Verey reflected the aspirations of many garden-owners in the difficult post-war years, so that when people had more money to spend again in the 1970s and 1980s, Barnsley was available to teach and inspire. The scale is surprisingly intimate – one of the garden's strengths – and the small decorative *potager* spawned many imitations. Barnsley is interesting at all seasons, particularly in early spring when it seems to have much more colour than other people's gardens, and again at midsummer rose time and when the salvias and asters flower in autumn. But it is probably at its best – and certainly at its most photographed – in late spring when the little laburnum walk and the purple alliums underneath are in flower together. The house is now an exclusive country house hotel. There will be five RHS

Special Events at Barnsley House in 2006; details from 020 7821 3408.

good borders; old roses; ornamental *potager*.

Owned by Tim Haigh & Rupert Pendered
Number of gardeners 6
Size 2.2ha (5½ acres)

BATSFORD ARBORETUM
Moreton-in-Marsh GL56 9QB

Tel: 01386 701441 **Fax:** 01386 701829
Location Off A44 between Moreton-in-Marsh & Bourton-on-the-Hill.
Opening hours 10 am - 5 pm; daily; 1 February to 15 November. Plus 10 am - 4 pm at weekends in winter.
Admission fee Adults £6; OAPs £5; Children £2. RHS members free except in October.

P WC &

Batsford has an openness which makes its hillside a joy to wander through, passing from one dendrological marvel to the next. Begun in the 1880s, the arboretum also has several oriental curiosities brought from Japan by Lord Redesdale – a large bronze Buddha and an oriental rest-house for instance. But the arboretum is mainly the work of the late Lord Dulverton, who added a large number of new plantings between 1956 and 1992. These include nearly 100 different magnolia cultivars, a comprehensive collection of Japanese cherries, some very beautiful conifers and excellent collections of such genera as Acer, Betula and Sorbus. Some are already record-breakers: all are in the prime of their life, well-grown and vigorous. The underplantings of spring bulbs are worth seeing, but visit Batsford at any season and you will find much to admire and enjoy.

Scottish native plants; oriental gardens; shop; garden centre; light meals & refreshments.

Owned by The Batsford Foundation
Number of gardeners 2
Size 22ha (55 acres)

BERKELEY CASTLE
Berkeley GL13 9BQ

Tel: 01453 810332
www.berkeley-castle.com
Location Off A38.
Opening hours 11 am – 4 pm; Tuesday – Friday; April to September. Plus 2 pm – 5 pm; Sundays; April to October. Gardens open at weekends only with combined Castle ticket.
Admission fee Garden only: Adults £4; Children £2. Garden & Castle: Adults £7.50; Concessions £6; Children £4.50.

🅿 🆆🅲 🌿 🐜 ⤾

The grim battlements of Berkeley Castle are host to an extensive collection of tender plants. On three terraces are *Cestrum*, *Cistus* and *Rosa banksiae* among hundreds of plant varieties introduced by the owner's grandmother, a sister of Ellen Willmott. An Elizabethan-style bowling green and a water lily pond fit well into the overall scheme.

🌿 roses (mainly old-fashioned); plantsman's collection of plants; mature conifers; good herbaceous borders; shop at Castle Farm; light lunches & afternoon tea.

Owned by R.J.G. Berkeley
Number of gardeners 2
Size 2ha (5 acres)
English Heritage Grade II*

BOURTON HOUSE
Bourton-on-the-Hill, Moreton-in-Marsh GL56 9AE

Tel: 01386 700754 **Fax:** 01386 701081
www.bourtonhouse.com
Location On A44, 1½ miles west of Moreton-in-Marsh.
Opening hours 10 am – 5 pm; Wednesday – Friday; 24 May to 31 August. Plus 28 & 29 May and 27 & 28 August, and Thursdays & Fridays in September & October.
Admission fee Adults £5; Children free.

🅿 🆆🅲 ♿ 🌿 ⤾

First laid out by Lanning Roper in the 1960s, but consistently improved by the present owners, the gardens at Bourton House are both fashionable and a delight. They include a knot garden, a small *potager*, a raised pond, the topiary walk, trellis work, a croquet lawn, and borders bulging with good colour schemes – purple-leaved prunus with yellow roses, for instance. The standard of maintenance is exemplary.

🌿 topiary; good colour plantings, especially of herbaceous plants; lots of unusual and little-known plants; light lunches and home-made teas.

Owned by Mr & Mrs Richard Paice
Number of gardeners 2, plus 2 part-time
Size 1.2ha (3 acres), plus 2.8-ha (7-acre) arboretum
English Heritage Grade II

DYRHAM PARK
Dyrham, Chippenham SN14 8ER

Tel: 0117 937 2501 **Fax:** 0117 937 1353
www.nationaltrust.org.uk
Location On A46, 8 miles north of Bath.
Opening hours 11 am – 5 pm; Friday – Tuesday; 24 March to 29 October.
Admission fee Garden only: Adults £3.50; Children £1.80.

🅿 🆆🅲 ♿ 🐜 ⤾

Dyrham is fascinating for garden historians, who can study the Kip plan and trace the lines of the 17th-century formal garden which Charles Harcourt Masters turned into classic English parkland. It is not a Mecca for the dedicated plantsman, but the impressive orangery is full of period plants. The BBC drama *Servants* was filmed here in 2003.

🌿 good herbaceous borders; deer park; handsome orangery; shop; tea-room.

Owned by The National Trust
Number of gardeners 3
Size 3.2ha (8 acres), plus park
English Heritage Grade II*

EASTLEACH HOUSE
Eastleach Martin, Cirencester GL7 3NW

Tel & Fax: 01367 850416
www.eastleachhouse.com
Location On edge of village, opposite church gates.
Opening hours 2 pm – 5 pm; Fridays; June & July. And by appointment for groups. For NGS on 1 May (teas in village hall).
Admission fee Adults £5; Children free.
[WC]

Eastleach House is at the top of a steep slope, and the garden has been laid out to provide enclosure and protection, while not interfering with the magnificent views. Each area is treated differently, but the garden is brought together by bold plantings, including an avenue of limes, and by inspired plantsmanship. There is colour at every season: in May from the iris borders, in June from rambling roses, in high summer from spectacular herbaceous borders, and in autumn from the small arboretum.

good design; rich plantings; wildflower meadow; good hedging & topiary; knot garden; herb garden.

Owned by Mrs David Richards
Number of gardeners 3 part-time
Size 5.6ha (14 acres)

ERNEST WILSON MEMORIAL GARDEN
High Street, Chipping Campden GL55 6AF

Tel: 01386 841298
Location North end of main street.
Opening hours 9 am - dusk; daily, except Christmas day; all year.
Admission fee Collection box for donations.
&

A collection of plants all introduced by Ernest H. Wilson, the greatest of European plant hunters in China: Chipping Campden was his birthplace. *Acer griseum*, *Clematis montana* var. *rubens* and the pocket-handkerchief tree (*Davidia involucrata*) are among his best-known introductions: all are represented here.

herbaceous borders; trees & shrubs.

Owned by Chipping Campden Town Council
Number of gardeners 1
Size 0.1ha (¼ acre)

FRAMPTON COURT
Frampton-on-Severn GL2 7EU

Tel: 01452 740267/740698 **Fax:** 01452 740698
www.framptoncourtestate.uk.com
Location Signed to Frampton-on-Severn from M5, Jct 13 (3 miles).
Opening hours By appointment all year.
Admission fee House & Garden: £5; Garden: £3. (2005 prices.)
[P] [WC]

A beautiful and mysterious garden, little changed since 1750. The Dutch water garden – a long rectangular pool – reflects the orangery of Strawberry Hill Gothic design. Nearby Frampton Manor, also owned by the Cliffords, may also be visited; it has a pretty walled garden with shrub roses.

gothic orangery; teas for pre-booked groups.

Owned by P.R.H. Clifford
Number of gardeners 1
Size 1.2ha (3 acres)
English Heritage Grade I

GOLDNEY HALL
Lower Clifton Hill, Clifton, Bristol BS8 1BH

Tel: 0117 903 4873 **Fax:** 0117 903 4877
www.goldneyhall.com
Location Top of Constitution Hill: entrance on Lower Clifton Hill.
Opening hours 2 pm – 6 pm; 7 May. Plus 21 May, 25 June & 6 August (see website for times).

Admission fee Adults £3; Concessions £1.50. (2005 prices.)

[wc] ⊅

A Bristol merchant's extravagance, nearly 300 years ago. Ten acres in the middle of the city, with an elegant orangery, a Gothic folly tower and the gorgeous Goldney Grotto, which sparkles with crystalline rocks among the shells and follies.

🌿 plants under glass; good herbaceous borders; holm oak hedge; many varieties of fruit; the *Chronicles of Narnia* were filmed in the grotto; cream teas in the orangery.

Owned by The University of Bristol
Number of gardeners 2
Size 4ha (10 acres)
English Heritage Grade II*

HIGHFIELD NURSERIES
School Lane, Whitminster, Gloucester GL2 7PL

Tel: 01452 740266 **Fax:** 01452 740750
www.highfield-nurseries.co.uk
Location Off A38, ½ mile from M5, Jct 13.
Opening hours 9 am – 4 pm; Monday – Friday. Closed Saturdays & Sundays; all year. The adjoining garden centre is open 9 am – 6 pm daily (5.30 pm in winter) and 10.30 am – 4.30 pm on Sundays.
Admission fee Free.

[P] [wc] 🌼 ⊅

Highfield is a large nursery, specialising in fruit trees and bushes: it offers a good choice of the best and most reliable cultivars. It also has a good list of roses, ornamental trees, shrubs and herbaceous plants – something for everyone, in fact.

🌿 restaurant at garden centre.

Owned by Joan Greenway

HIGHNAM COURT
Highnam, Gloucester GL2 8DP

Tel: 01452 308251
Location Entrance on A40 roundabout.
Opening hours 11 am – 5 pm; first Sunday of the month; April to September.
Admission fee Adults £4; Children free.

[P] ⇻ [wc] ♿ ⊅

Little remains of the original Highnam, laid out when the house was built in 1658. The garden was, however, very famous 100 years ago for the features designed or commissioned by Thomas Gambier-Parry in the middle of the 19th century: the terraces, the broad walk, the arboretum and, above all, the winter garden where natural stone is supplemented by Pulhamite – the largest and earliest surviving example of the artificial stone from which the rock garden at Wisley is also made. The estate was neglected for nearly 100 years, but the present owner started in 1994 first to restore it and then to add new features. The results are very impressive, and worth a long visit. They include a new, one-acre rose garden between the ha-ha and the lake, a vast new lake with a Giverny-inspired bridge and plantings, a knot garden, 60,000 bulbs and innumerable new island beds.

🌿 Pulhamite rock garden; fine conifers; tallest *Quercus acutissima* and *Fraxinus excelsior* 'Jaspidea' in the British isles; historic garden in restoration; tea & cakes.

Owned by Roger Head
Number of gardeners 2
Size 12ha (30 acres)
English Heritage Grade II*

HIDCOTE MANOR GARDEN
Hidcote Bartrim, Chipping Campden GL55 6LR

Tel: 01386 438333 **Fax:** 01386 438817
www.nationaltrust.org.uk
Location Signed from B4632, Stratford to
Broadway road.
Opening hours 10.30 am - 6 pm (5 pm from 2
October); Saturday - Wednesday & Good Friday;
25 March to 29 October. Last admissions one
hour before closing.
Admission fee Adults £7; Children £3.50.

One of England's great gardens,
Hidcote is an Arts & Crafts
masterpiece created by the American
plantsman and plant-collector Major
Lawrence Johnston. It was designed as a
series of outdoor rooms, each with a
different character and separated by walls
and hedges of many different species.
Hidcote therefore has a firm architectural
structure – many of Lawrence Johnston's
ideas came from France and Italy –
combined with a great love of plants. The
planting is exuberant but always considers
the contrasts and harmonies which can be
obtained by planting different things
together. Some of the rooms are very
small, like Mrs Winthrop's garden – no
more than a courtyard with a potted
cordyline at the centre – and others, like
the long walk and the great lawn, give a
great sense of space – though in fact the
garden is no more than ten acres in size.
Among the most famous features are: the
mixed borders richly planted with old
roses and companion plants; the red
borders, which were among the first 'hot'
borders in the country when planted in
1913; the sunken 'bathing pool' garden
where a huge circular swimming pool fills
a hedged compartment; and the woodland
area or wilderness, sometimes known as
Westonbirt, where Johnston planted long
vistas which run from end to end, but
which disappear and reappear as you
follow the paths back and forth. The
National Trust is working on a programme
of renewal and regeneration and it is fair
to say that Hidcote is now looking better
than it did ten years ago.

woodland garden; topiary; roses
(ancient & modern); rock garden;
plantsman's collection of plants; good
herbaceous borders; tallest pink acacia *Robinia*
x *ambigua* 'Decaisneana' (19m.) in the British
Isles; National Trust shop & plant centre;
licensed restaurant; teas.

Owned by The National Trust
Number of gardeners 7
Size 4.2ha (10.5 acres)
English Heritage Grade I

HODGES BARN
Shipton Moyne, Tetbury GL8 8PR

Tel: 01666 880202 **Fax:** 01666 880373
Location 3 miles south of Tetbury on
Malmesbury Road from Shipton Moyne.
Opening hours For NGS: 2 pm - 6 pm; 9 & 10
April; 21 & 22 May; 3, 4 & 7 July. Groups welcome
by appointment.
Admission fee Adults £5; Children free.
P ◁» WC &

This is a large garden – six acres
surrounding a converted 15th-century
columbarium – all intensively planted. The
terraces, courtyards and gardens are divided
into rooms (surrounded either by walls or
by tapestry, laurel or yew hedges) to give
year-round colour. Old-fashioned rose beds
are underplanted with tulips for spring and
with alliums and campanulas for summer.
There is a formal herbaceous border, a
water garden and a swimming pool area
with large planted pots. Shrub roses and
climbers are another Hornby passion and
are to be found winding up walls and trees.
The plantings reflect a desire to create an
informal feeling within a formal
framework. The woodland garden is almost
an arboretum of ornamental trees
(especially birches, maples, whitebeams
and many different magnolias),
underplanted with spring bulbs. In summer
the grass is left long in the wood and
wildflowers are encouraged to naturalise.
Hodges Barn is a garden of great energy
and diversity.

woodland garden; topiary; roses
(mainly old-fashioned & climbers);
plantsman's collection of plants; good
herbaceous borders; daffodils; bluebells;
cyclamen.

Owned by Mrs Charles Hornby
Number of gardeners 2 part-time
Size 2.4ha (6 acres)

HUNTS COURT
North Nibley, Dursley GL11 6DZ

Tel: 01453 547440 **Fax:** 01453 549944
Location Turn across front of Black Horse pub &
bear left for ¼ mile.
Opening hours 9 am - 12.30 pm & 1.45 pm - 5 pm;
Tuesday - Saturday (& Bank Holiday Mondays in
spring); all year, except August and Christmas to
New Year. For NGS: 2 pm - 6 pm; 11, 18 & 25 June
and 3 & 10 September.
Admission fee Adults £3; Children & Royal
National Rose Society members free.
P WC & ¥ ● ☞

The garden at Hunts Court has been
planted since 1976 by something of a
horticultural rarity – a plant-loving farmer,
and his wife. Keith and Margaret Marshall
say they have 'the collector's touch of
madness': the result is a garden which is
charming, peaceful and educational. Their
first love was old-fashioned roses, and they
moved their garden fence out into the
surrounding fields as the collection of
gallicas, damasks and hybrid perpetuals
began to grow: it is now the best in the
west of England, and still expanding. The
450 cultivars include climbers, species and a
few modern shrub roses. Many are
underplanted by the Marshalls' next great
passion – hardy geraniums and penstemons,
each of which is represented by over 100
cultivars. The fence has been moved out
several times now to accommodate a large
collection of ornamental trees and shrubs,
underplanted in turn by more unusual
herbaceous plants. These are the stock
plants for the thriving nursery they now run
in their old stockyard. It is surrounded by a
fine plantsman's garden with something for
all seasons, including good autumn colour
and winter-flowering shrubs. But the
Marshalls have just moved the fence again
to plant a mini-arboretum.

roses of every kind, especially 19th-
century cultivars; many other plants of
interest to the plantsman; first-rate nursery
attached; refreshments on NGS days.

Owned by T.K. & M.M. Marshall
Number of gardeners 1
Size 1ha (2½ acres)

KIFTSGATE COURT
Chipping Campden GL55 6LN

Tel & Fax: 01386 438777
www.kiftsgate.co.uk
Location 3 miles from Chipping Campden
opposite Hidcote Manor.
Opening hours 12 noon - 6 pm; Saturday -
Wednesday; May to July. 2 pm - 6 pm; Sundays,
Mondays & Wednesdays; April, August &
September.
Admission fee Adults £5.50; Children £1.50.

🅿 🚾 💐 ☕

Famous for its roses, especially the
eponymous *Rosa filipes*, Kiftsgate is all
about plants and the use of colour. The
best example is the yellow border, where
gold and orange are set off by occasional
blues and purples. After some dull years,
everything about Kiftsgate has revived
again: new thinking, new plantings and
new enthusiasm have more than restored
its excellence. The latest addition (2000) is
in marked contrast to the rest of the
garden: the tennis court has been
transformed into a contemporary water
garden, full of movement and sound, by
Simon Allison. Structure and form
predominate here over Kiftsgate's
traditional themes of colour and texture.
And the garden as a whole is remarkable
for its tender plants – abutilons, echiums,
azaras and wonderful tree peonies in May.
🌿 roses (mainly old-fashioned); colour
plantings; good borders; many
interesting plants; tea-room in the house.

Owned by Mr & Mrs J. Chambers
Number of gardeners 2
Size 1.6ha (4 acres)
English Heritage Grade II*

LYDNEY PARK GARDENS
Lydney Park GL15 6BU

Tel: 01594 842844 **Fax:** 01594 842027
Location Off A48 between Lydney & Aylburton.
Opening hours 11 am - 6 pm; Sundays, Wednesdays
& Bank Holidays; 26 March to 4 June. Plus daily; 1 to
7 May & 29 May to 4 June.
Admission fee Adults £4, but £3 on Wednesdays;
Children 50p.

🅿 ♿ 🚾 💐 🛍 ☕

There are fine formal gardens around the
house, but Lydney is famous for its
rhododendrons: a remarkable collection
planted over the last 50 years is the backbone
to the extensive woodland garden. And not
just rhododendrons, but azaleas and
camellias, too – all are carefully planted to
create distinct effects from March to June.
The numbers are still growing, and include
plants grown from collected seed and hybrids
from distinguished breeders, many as yet
unnamed, while others have yet to flower.
Lydney is now recognised as one of the best
rhododendron gardens in England.
🌿 rhododendrons & azaleas; woodland
garden; mature conifers; deer park;
daffodils; some souvenirs for sale; light teas.

Owned by Viscount Bledisloe
Number of gardeners 2, plus part-time help in
season
Size 3.2ha (8 acres) of woodland garden

MILL DENE GARDENS
School Lane, Blockley, Moreton-in-Marsh
GL56 9HU

Tel: 01386 700457 **Fax:** 01386 700526
www.milldenegarden.co.uk
Location First road on left as you come into
Blockley from Bourton-on-the-Hill. Follow brown
tourist signs.
Opening hours 10 am - 5.30 pm; Tuesday - Friday;
April to October. Plus occasional weekends for
charity. And by appointment.
Admission fee Adults £4.50; OAPs £4; Children £1.
RHS members free in April and October.

P WC ※ ⬭

This Cotswold water mill garden has been
designed and planted by the owner in an
English country garden style. Steep terraces
rise from the mill pond, stream and grotto.
Paths wander through the rose walk,
flanked by standard 'Sander's White
Rambler' roses and lavender, to the cricket
lawn. At the top of the garden, the *potager*
and the 'fantasy fruit garden' (all greys and
blues) have the church as a backdrop and
views of the hills. There will be an RHS
Special Event at Mill Dene in 2006; details
from 020 7821 3408.

 new walk with roses chosen for scent
(2005); refreshments.

Owned by Mr & Mrs B.S. Dare
Number of gardeners 1
Size 1ha (2½ acres)

MISERDEN PARK
Miserden, Stroud GL6 7JA

Tel: 01285 821303 **Fax:** 01285 821530
Location Signed from A417, or turn off B4070
between Stroud & Birdlip.
Opening hours 10 am – 5 pm; Tuesday – Thursday;
April to September. For NGS: 9 April & 25 June.
Admission fee Adults £4; Children free.

P WC ⅏ ※ ● ✕

The Cotswold house at Miserden
(Jacobean, with a Lutyens addition) has
wide views across the Golden Valley, while
the spacious, peaceful gardens lie to the
side. Most were laid out in the 1920s using
a 17th-century structure – a charming rose
garden, a long yew walk and expansive
herbaceous borders. Recent additions
include a rill and summerhouse, a parterre
of lavender and hebes, a shrub border and a
border of silvers and greys. Near the
entrance is an interesting nursery with a
stock of good herbaceous plants.

topiary; good trees; good herbaceous
borders; martagon lilies; roses; domed
yew walk; cyclamen; excellent garden nursery by
entrance (closed Mondays).

Owned by Major M.T.N.H. Wills
Number of gardeners 2
Size 5ha (12½ acres)
English Heritage Grade II*

OWLPEN MANOR
Uley, Dursley GL11 5BZ

Tel: 01453 860261 **Fax:** 01453 860819
www.owlpen.com
Location Off B4066 near Uley.
Opening hours 2 pm – 5 pm; Tuesdays, Thursdays &
Sundays; May to September.
Admission fee Adults £3.25; Children £1.25.

P WC ※ ● ⬭

Owlpen is a dreamy Cotswold manor house
whose loveliness depends upon its site. It
has a small formal garden which was
terraced in the 16th century, altered c.1720
and restored in the Old English style by
Norman Jewson in 1926. Jewson planted
the box parterres and topiary yews; the
present owners have added the roses and
herbs since 1980. The aim is to suggest an
earlier garden 're-ordered conservatively' in
about 1700. Owlpen is perhaps not worth a
special journey by keen plantsmen, but the
restaurant, the setting and the house all add
up to a good place for an outing.

topiary; roses (mainly old-fashioned);
standard gooseberries; guidebooks &
postcards for sale; licensed restaurant (noon – 5pm).

Owned by Nicholas & Karin Mander
Number of gardeners 1
Size 0.8ha (2 acres)
English Heritage Grade II

PAINSWICK ROCOCO GARDEN
Gloucester Road, Painswick GL6 6TH

Tel: 01452 813204 **Fax:** 01452 814888
www.rococogarden.co.uk
Location Outside Painswick on B4073.
Opening hours 11 am – 5 pm; daily; 10 January to
31 October.

Admission fee Adults £5; OAPs £4; Children £2.50.

P ⊲ WC 🌿 🍎 ⬚

Years of restoration work have saved the unique rococo garden at Painswick from back-to-nature woodland. A white Venetian Gothic exedra, a Doric seat, the plunge pool, an octagonal pigeon house, a Gothic gazebo called the Eagle House, a bowling green, the fish pond and a Gothic alcove have all been reconstructed in their original positions thanks to the efforts of Lord Dickinson and the Painswick Rococo Garden Trust. Recent additions include the Exedra Garden (18th-century herbaceous plantings in an informal structure, best in early summer) and the kitchen garden (best in late summer). A remarkable garden and a brilliant theatrical achievement.

🌿 woodland garden; snowdrop wood; new plant nursery; maze; gift shop; licensed restaurant, coffee, teas & light snacks.

Owned by Painswick Rococo Garden Trust
Number of gardeners 4
Size 2.4ha (6 acres)
English Heritage Grade II*

RODMARTON MANOR
Rodmarton, Cirencester GL7 6PF

Tel: 01285 841253 **Fax:** 01285 841298
www.rodmarton-manor.co.uk
Location Off A433 between Cirencester & Tetbury.
Opening hours 2 pm - 5 pm; Wednesdays, Saturdays & Bank Holiday Mondays; 17 April, then 1 May to 30 September. Plus 12, 16 & 19 February for snowdrops (open at 1.30 pm).
Admission fee Adults £4; Children £1.

P WC &

A splendid Arts & Crafts garden, with a strong design and exuberant planting. Simon Biddulph says there are 18 different areas within the garden, from the trough garden for alpine plants to the famous double herbaceous borders, now in the middle of a complete redesign, which lead to a Cotswold summerhouse. Highly

original – contemporary, but made without any contact with Hidcote.

🌿 interesting plants; old-fashioned roses; topiary; much renovation and replanting; snowdrops.

Owned by Simon Biddulph
Size 3.2ha (8 acres)
English Heritage Grade II*

SEZINCOTE
Moreton-in-Marsh GL56 9AW

Tel: 01386 700444
Location On A44 to Evesham, 1½ miles out of Moreton-in-Marsh.
Opening hours 2 pm - 6 pm (or dusk, if earlier); Thursdays, Fridays & Bank Holiday Mondays; January to November. Closed in August.
Admission fee Adults £4.50; Children free.

P WC

The house at Sezincote was the model for the Brighton Pavilion, and seems inseparable from the cruciform Moghul garden that sets off its Indian façade so well: yet this brilliant formal garden was designed as recently as 1965. On the other side are sumptuous borders planted by Graham Stuart Thomas and a luscious water garden of candelabra primulas and astilbes around the Temple to Surya, the Snake Bridge and Brahmin bulls. Humphry Repton had a hand in the original landscape, but the modern gardens are even more satisfying than the classical, 18th-century parkland setting.

🌿 good, bold plantings in the water garden; tallest maidenhair tree *Ginkgo biloba* (26m) in the British Isles and five other record trees. These include the blue-leaved noble fir *Abies procera* Glauca Group, the weeping hornbeam *Carpinus betulus* 'Pendula' and the yellow-leaved beech *Fagus sylvatica* 'Zlatia'.

Owned by Mr & Mrs D. Peake
Number of gardeners 3
Size 4ha (10 acres)
English Heritage Grade I

SNOWSHILL MANOR
Snowshill, Broadway WR12 7JU

Tel: 01386 852410 **Fax:** 01386 842822
www.nationaltrust.org.uk
Location In Snowshill village.
Opening hours 11 am – 5.30 pm; Wednesday –
Sunday & Bank Holiday Mondays; 18 March to 31
October.
Admission fee Gardens only: Adults £4; Children £2;
Family £10.

P WC 👜 ☕

Baillie Scott designed the garden at
Snowshill as 'an extension of the house, a
series of garden rooms'. It has often been
praised for its changes of levels and collection
of curious artefacts – an armillary sphere and
a gilt figure of St George and the Dragon, for
instance. Snowshill is as eccentric as its
owner, Charles Wade, and the spooky bric-a-
brac which fills his house, but many visitors
find it 'charming' or 'interesting'. Snowshill
was the National Trust's first organically run
garden.

🌿 unusual design; good borders; National
Trust shop; restaurant.

Owned by The National Trust
Number of gardeners 2
Size 0.8ha (2 acres)
English Heritage Grade II

SPECIAL PLANTS
Hill Farm Barn, Greenways Lane, Cold
Ashton, Chippenham SN14 8LA

Tel: 01225 891686
www.specialplants.net
Location Near Bath, just south of junction of A46 &
A420. Not in Cold Ashton.
Opening hours Nursery: 10 am – 5 pm; daily; March
to September. And by appointment. Garden: 11 am –
5 pm for NGS on Wednesdays in July & August.
Admission fee Adults £2.50.

P WC 🌼 ☕

The collection of hardy plants at this
connoisseur's nursery is excellent, but it is
for her tender perennials that Derry

Watkins's nursery is best known. Diascias,
salvias, pelargoniums and streptocarpus are
among her top lines, together with
conservatory climbers and shrubs. There
are also one-day courses at the nursery in
autumn. In 1996, Derry Watkins and her
architect husband bought a derelict barn
with three acres of steeply sloping fields.
Around the barn he designed bold shapes
in gravel, water and grass, terraced with dry
stone walls. Then she planted it up with
drifts of colour using many unusual plants
(not a rose or a clematis in sight, alas).
There is a 'black and white' border, a
sizzling hot red-and-orange bed and a
cooler lemon-and-lime slope, as well as a
gravel garden, grass garden, bog garden,
ponds, vegetable garden and now an
orchard and a woodland walk, all set off by
wonderful views down the valley.

🌿 unusual plants; home-made teas.

Owned by Derry Watkins
Number of gardeners 1
Size 0.3ha (¾ acre)

STANCOMBE PARK
Dursley GL11 6AU

Tel: 01453 542815
Location Off B4060 between Dursley & Wotton-
under-Edge.
Opening hours Groups by appointment.
Admission fee Adults £3; Children (under 10) £1.

P WC 🌼 ☕

Stancombe has everything: a handsome
house above a wooded valley, a flower
garden of wondrous prettiness, and a
Gothic horror of an historic folly garden at
the valley bottom. Start at the top. Peter
Coats, Lanning Roper and Nadia Jennett
all worked on the rose gardens and mixed
borders by the house: there is more to learn
about good modern design and planting
here than any other garden in
Gloucestershire. Then wander down the
valley where the path narrows and the

incline steepens to a ferny tunnel, and start the circuit of the follies, best described as an open-air ghost-train journey without the ghosts. Highly recommended.

fine collection of trees; excellent borders; fine spring bulbs; lots of roses; some interesting and unusual plants; refreshments by arrangement.

Owned by Mrs Basil Barlow
Number of gardeners 1
Size 6ha (15 acres)
English Heritage Grade I

STANWAY HOUSE
Stanway, Cheltenham GL54 5PQ

Tel: 01386 584528 **Fax:** 01386 584688
www.stanwayfountain.co.uk
Location On B4077.
Opening hours 2 pm - 5 pm; Tuesdays & Thursdays; June to August. Plus Saturdays in July & August. And groups by appointment. For NGS: 26 March & 21 May.
Admission fee Adults £4; OAPs £3; Children £1.

The important water gardens at Stanway are undergoing restoration: the 300ft gravity-fed fountain is the tallest in Britain. A pyramidal folly dominates the hillside behind the house. Repairs have begun on the 170m cascade which runs down to a long still tank known as the Canal. On the way up to the top are some interesting trees and shrubs. If you have not been to Stanway for a few years, you will be amazed by the changes; worth another visit.

woodland garden; mature conifers.

Owned by Lord Neidpath
Number of gardeners 1½
Size 8ha (20 acres)
English Heritage Grade I

STOWELL PARK
Northleach GL54 3LE

Tel: 01285 720308 **Fax:** 01285 720360
Location A429 between Cirencester & Northleach.
Opening hours 2 pm - 5 pm; 21 May (plus plant sale & country garden fête). 2 pm - 5 pm; 18 June for Royal British Legion.
Admission fee Adults £4. No concessions. Children free.

The most important feature at Stowell is its peach house, 180ft long, which has been in constant use since the early 19th century. Nowhere in England does such a glasshouse produce fruit in the manner perfected by our Victorian ancestors. Stowell also has an historic landscape in a magnificent position, with terraced gardens in front of the house looking down over the Coln valley and landscaped woodlands dating from the 18th century. The pleached lime avenue at the entrance to the house was planted in 1983 and is now fully established. In the superb traditional walled gardens are substantial herbaceous borders and some notable plantings of old-fashioned roses.

fine kitchen garden and glasshouses; roses; good herbaceous borders; plants for sale on 21 May only; excellent teas.

Owned by Lord & Lady Vestey
Number of gardeners 4
Size 3.2ha (8 acres)
English Heritage Grade II

SUDELEY CASTLE & GARDENS
Winchcombe GL54 5JD

Tel: 01242 602308 **Fax:** 01242 602959
www.sudeleycastle.co.uk
Location 8 miles north-east of Cheltenham on B4632.
Opening hours Not yet known as we went to press. Usually 10.30 am - 5.30 pm; daily; March to October.

Admission fee Adults £7.20; OAPs £6.20; Children £4.20. (2005 prices.)

P WC & ✿ ❀ ⟁

This large commercially run garden has features by many top garden designers: Jane Fearnley-Whittingstall did the roses and Charles Chesshire replanted the 'secret garden' (originally designed by Rosemary Verey) in the Mediterranean style. New plantings continue. The whole garden is organically managed. There are fine old trees, magnificent Victorian topiary (mounds of green and gold yew) and a raised walk around the pleasure gardens that may be Elizabethan in origin. Popular and successful.

topiary; roses (ancient & modern); herbs; mature conifers; good herbaceous borders; ruins of banqueting hall, now a pretty garden; wildflower meadow; gift shop; plant centre; coffee shop.

Owned by Lady Ashcombe
Number of gardeners 4
Size 5.6ha (14 acres)
English Heritage Grade II*

UNIVERSITY OF BRISTOL BOTANIC GARDEN
The Holmes, Stoke Park Road, Stoke Bishop, Bristol BS9 1JQ

Tel: 0117 331 4912 **Fax:** 0117 331 4909
www.bris.ac.uk/depts/BotanicGardens
Location North of city centre, off Stoke Hill; 200 yards on right.
Opening hours Not yet known as we went to press, but probably opening in April 2006.
Admission fee Free.
WC

Bristol Botanic Garden is on the move. The new site at Stoke Hill is expected to open in April 2006. The design has been worked out by Land Use Consultants and sets out to be both 'meandering' and 'organic', with a blend of informal and formal plantings that will be both educational and aesthetically pleasing. The botanic collections are in the process of being reorganised into four core collections: evolution; the five Mediterranean floras; useful plants; and rare and threatened plants of south-west England. Most of the plants for the new garden will come from the old Botanic Garden at Bracken Hill. These include the collections of *Aeonium* (the most comprehensive in the UK), *Pelargonium* species and Central American *Salvia* species. Please telephone or consult the website for details.

Owned by The University of Bristol
Number of gardeners 6½
Size 1.8ha (4½ acres)

WESTBURY COURT
Westbury-on-Severn GL14 1PD

Tel: 01452 760461 **Fax:** 01452 760461
www.nationaltrust.org.uk
Location 9 miles south-west of Gloucester on A48.
Opening hours 10 am – 5 pm; Wednesday – Sunday & Bank Holiday Mondays; 8 March to 29 October. Daily in July & August.
Admission fee Adults £4; Children £2.
P WC &

Westbury was restored in the 1970s to become the best example of a medium-sized 17th-century Dutch garden in England. An elegant pavilion, tall and slender, looks down along a long tank of water. On the walls are old apple, pear and plum cultivars. Parterres (now planted in the 17th-century style), fine modern topiary and a T-shaped tank with a statue of Neptune in the middle make up the rest of the garden. All the plants were known to cultivation before 1720. The garden is going through a period of consolidation; visitors should expect changes.

topiary; herbs; biggest holm oak *Quercus ilex* in the British Isles.

Owned by The National Trust
Number of gardeners 1
Size 1.6ha (4 acres)
English Heritage Grade II*

WILLOW LODGE
Gloucester Road (A40), Longhope,
Gloucester GL17 0RA

Tel & Fax: 01452 831211
www.willowgardens.fsnet.co.uk
Location On A40, 10 miles from Gloucester & 6 miles from Ross-on-Wye: ½ mile west of Dursley Cross.
Opening hours 1 pm - 5 pm; 16, 17 & 30 April; 1, 14, 15, 28 & 29 May; 2, 3, 16 & 17 July; 6, 7, 13 & 14 August. Groups and private visits by appointment.
Admission fee Adults £2.50; Children free.

P WC & 🌱 ▷

This garden has been entirely made by the owners, enthusiastic plantsmen, since they moved here in 1987. At first they developed just an acre around the house: it remains a good garden of mixed herbaceous and shrubby plantings, with some particularly fine shade-lovers – trilliums, erythroniums and dodecatheons. Then they started to plant the adjoining field as an arboretum, underplanted with native daffodils, snowdrops and ground orchids, *Dactylorhiza* species. Among the many interesting plants here are *Sinocalycanthus chinensis* and several *Lespedeza* species; some have been collected on their travels in China and North America. The stream that runs from end to end of the garden has been used to create a bog garden (lots of different primulas) and a pond, alongside a large alpine bed. There is much to enjoy and learn throughout the garden.

🌿 a good young arboretum; bog garden; maples; teas.

Owned by Mr & Mrs J.H. Wood
Number of gardeners 3
Size 1.6ha (4 acres)

WESTONBIRT THE NATIONAL ARBORETUM
Westonbirt, Tetbury GL8 8QS

Tel: 01666 880220 **Fax:** 01666 880559
www.forestry.gov.uk/westonbirt
Location 3 miles south-west of Tetbury on A433.
Opening hours 10 am - 8 pm (or dusk, if earlier); daily; all year. Visitor centre: 10 am - 5 pm; daily; March to December.
Admission fee Adults £6.50-£7.50 according to season; Children £1. RHS Members free.

P ⟨symbols⟩ WC ⟨symbols⟩

Westonbirt is the finest and largest arboretum in the British Isles: it contains one of the most important collections of trees and shrubs in the world. There are 18,000 of them, representing 3,700 species and cultivars, planted from 1829 to the present day, and covering some 600 acres of beautifully landscaped grounds. The maple glade is famous, and so are the bluebells in the part known as Silk Wood. Magnificent spring displays of rhododendrons, azaleas and magnolias, wildflowers in summer and architectural winter beauty are matched by the spectacular autumn colouring for which Westonbirt is justifiably famous. Westonbirt is also one of the best gardens in England for a winter walk but, with 17 miles of paths, you can find quiet areas even in the third week of October when the maples are at their most colourful.

over 1,000 species of record-breaking trees, including 24 maples (*Acer* species) and 16 *Sorbus*; other champion trees include the red horse-chestnut *Aesculus* x *carnea* at 27m; the upright birch *Betula pendula* 'Fastigiata' at 29m; the handkerchief tree *Davidia involucrata* at 24m; the home-sprung *Pinus* 'Holfordiana' at 36m; and the large-leaved deciduous oak *Quercus macranthera* at 31m; gift shop; plant centre; restaurant; cafeteria.

Owned by Forestry Commission
Number of gardeners 8
Size 240ha (600 acres)
NCCPG National Collections *Acer* (Japanese cvs.); *Salix*
English Heritage Grade I

HAMPSHIRE

For such a prosperous county, Hampshire has comparatively few historic gardens of the highest importance: only Hackwood Park (not open to the public) and Highclere Park (right in the north) are listed as Grade I. But Hampshire compensates with a wealth of 20th-century plantsman's gardens and nurseries. Indeed, the Sir Harold Hillier Gardens at Ampfield – the world's greatest collection of temperate trees and shrubs – was founded as recently as 1953 and grew out of the commercial activities of Hillier's Nursery. When modern gardens like Brandy Mount, Exbury, Longstock, Spinners and Meon Orchard are taken into account, and some of the small specialist nurseries like Blackthorn and Langley Boxwood, Hampshire emerges as one of the best places in Europe for plants and gardens, plantsmen and gardeners. Unfortunately, however, the great plantsman's garden at Longthatch will not be opening again in 2006. The National Gardens Scheme is extremely well represented in the county, with a very large number of gardens opening for charity. There are many good gardens that do not open often enough for us to list in this guide: Pylewell Park, Rotherfield Park and Conholt Park among them. And deep in the New Forest, at Rhinefield, is the best late-Victorian pinetum in southern England. The Hampshire Group of the NCCPG is strong – always a good measure of the interest in gardening with plants – with 43 National Collections. And the Hampshire Gardens Trust, founded more than 20 years ago by the energy and foresight of Gilly Drummond, has been the model for every county-based gardens trust since then. Sparsholt College, between Winchester and Stockbridge, is a RHS Partner College.

53 LADYWOOD
Eastleigh SO50 4RW

Tel: 023 8061 5389
Location M3, Jct 12; along A335, right at first roundabout (Woodside Ave); 2nd right into Bosville. Ladywood is 5th on right.
Opening hours 2 pm – 5 pm; Tuesdays; 4 April to 29 August. Plus 3 April & 8 May. Also 11 am – 5.30 pm on 2 April, 7 May & 23 July and 7 pm – 9 pm on 24 July to see border phloxes in evening light.
Admission fee Adults £2.50; Children £1.

Mrs Ward's garden is a model of how to design a very small garden to look much bigger than it really is, and then to fill it with interesting plants and attractive colour combinations. Screens and trellis-work divide up the space, and the compartments are so ornamented with decorative details that you have to stop and go round it very slowly, in case you might miss something. Contrasts of textures are another feature – brick, stone, concrete, gravel pebbles are mixed up to maximise variety – and so are flowering plants in pots. Leaves are as important as flowers; most of the shrubs are evergreen, and chosen for their foliage. The range of herbaceous and woodland plants is truly amazing, and they are all extremely well grown. A garden to admire and learn from.

plants from the garden for sale; refreshments on Sundays.

Owned by Mrs Sue Ward
Number of gardeners owner only
Size 14m x 14m

ABBEY COTTAGE
Rectory Lane, Itchen Abbas, Winchester
SO21 1BN

Tel & Fax: 01962 779575
Location On B3047, 1 mile east of the Trout Inn
at Itchen Abbas.
Opening hours 2 pm – 5 pm; 5 & 6 April. 12 noon
– 5 pm; 30 April, 1 May & 27 and 28 August. 10.30
am – 5 pm 14 & 15 June and 9 & 10 August. And
by appointment.
Admission fee Adults £2.50; Children free.

Abbey Cottage would be a fine garden by
any standards – it has a firm design,
beautiful flint and brick walls, good lines,
interesting plants, good colour schemes
and immaculate standards of tidiness – but
what makes it especially interesting is that
Colonel Daniell is a recent convert to
organic gardening. He says that 'organic
gardening was the element missing from
my gardening... now the garden feels
complete'. The garden is maintained as
much for the pleasure of his many friends
and visitors as for his own pleasure.
organic garden; good structure;
excellent maintenance; teas & plants
at weekend openings.

Owned by Col. Patrick Daniell CBE
Number of gardeners 1 part-time
Size 0.6ha (1½ acres)

APPLE COURT
Hordle Lane, Hordle, Lymington
SO41 0HU

Tel: 01590 642130 **Fax:** 01590 694220
www.applecourt.com
Location South of New Forest, just north of
A337 at Downton crossroads.
Opening hours 10 am – 5 pm; Friday - Sunday;
March to October.
Admission fee Adults £2.50; Children free.

The display gardens attached to this
specialist nursery (hostas, hemerocallis
and grasses) are firmly designed and would
be worth a visit even without plants. The
white garden is especially original: at its
heart is an oval-shaped lawn, surrounded
by pleached hornbeams. The white
plantings lie *outside* this oval of limes.
Elsewhere are about 300 cultivars of
Hosta, many of them – like the daylilies –
bred in the USA and offered for sale by
Apple Court but by no other UK nursery.
There are 400 *Hemerocallis* cultivars, too,
including spider and other unusual forms.
tea & coffee.

Owned by Charles & Angela Meads
Number of gardeners 2
Size 0.6ha (1½ acres)

BLACKTHORN NURSERY
Kilmeston, Alresford SO24 0NL

Tel: 01962 771796 **Fax:** 01962 771071
Location 1 mile south of Cheriton, off A272.
Opening hours 9 am – 5 pm; 13, 14, 27 & 28
January; 10, 11, 24 & 25 February; 10, 11, 24 & 25
March; 8, 9, 22 & 23 September.

Blackthorn's plants tend to be spring
beauties: the nursery's three specialities
are hellebores, epimediums and daphnes,
all of which they breed, as well as
introducing new species. Their most
striking hellebores are semi-doubles called
'Party Dress' hybrids. The list of
epimediums is the best in England – over
40 different names: their rarities include a
large number of collected species like *E.
fargesii* Og. 93057 and *E. franchetii*
'Brimstone Butterfly' Og. 87001. The
daphnes are no less remarkable: over 50
different names, including such little-
known hybrids as *D.* x *thauma* and no
fewer than seven cultivars of *D.* x
hendersonii. Their general list of alpines
and herbaceous plants is equally exciting:
they have a covetable and ever-changing
selection of good plants. For dedicated

plantsmen, a visit to Blackthorn on an open day in February or March is one of the social highlights of early spring: every fellow-plantsman in the country seems to be there, too. But, a warning – the Whites are planning to retire, or semi-retire.
Owned by R. & S. White
Size 0.1-ha (¼-acre) woodland walk

BRAMDEAN HOUSE
Bramdean, Alresford SO24 0JU

Tel: 01962 771214 **Fax:** 01962 771095
Location On A272, between Winchester & Petersfield.
Opening hours 2 pm – 5 pm; 19 February, 19 March, 16 April, 11 June, 9 July, 13 August, 10 September & by appointment. Plus 18 February 2007.
Admission fee Adults £4.50; Children free. For NGS: Adults £3.50.

P WC ✿ ▷

The gardens at Bramdean are much admired, and rightly so. Against a backdrop of mature trees, two wide mirror-image borders lead away from the back of the house. They are full of unusual shrubs, plants, bulbs and climbers. At the end of the central axis, steps lead to a one-acre walled kitchen garden whose central beds are planted with a range of herbaceous plants, roses, perennials and bulbs. The vista runs yet further, through an orchard underplanted with massed daffodils to an apple house some 300 yards from the house. The views in both directions are stunning.
climbing roses; herbaceous plants; peonies; ornamental shrubs; bulbs of every sort; climbing roses; clematis; sweet peas; vegetables; fruit; tender nerines; refreshments.

Owned by Mr & Mrs H. Wakefield
Number of gardeners 2
Size 2.6ha (6½ acres)
English Heritage Grade II

EXBURY GARDENS
Exbury, Southampton SO45 1AZ

Tel: 023 8089 1203 **Fax:** 023 8089 9940
www.exbury.co.uk
Location 3 miles south of Beaulieu.
Opening hours 10 am – 5.30 pm (or dusk, if earlier); daily; 1 March to 5 November.
Admission fee Adults £5; OAPs £4.50; Children £1. But in high season (20 March to 4 June) Adults £7.50; OAPs £6.50 (£7 on Saturdays & Sundays); Children £1.50. RHS members free in March.

P ⬧ WC ♿ ✿ ▦ ▷

Rhododendrons, rhododendrons, rhododendrons: over one million of them in 200 acres of natural woodland. More than 40 have won awards from the Royal Horticultural Society. But there are magnolias, camellias and rare trees, too, many grown from the original seed introduced by famous plant collectors. A place of wonder in May, but beautiful at every time of the year. The collection of nerines which Lionel de Rothschild bred between the wars was dispersed after his death but reassembled and developed by Sir Peter Smithers in Switzerland. A few years ago he returned them to Exbury where they may be seen once again in October. A new garden has been created in the style of Piet Oudolf and James Van Sweden – huge swathes of herbaceous perennials and grasses within a strong woodland structure. There will be two RHS Special Events at Exbury in 2006; details from 020 7821 3408.
good herbaceous borders; candelabra primulas; rare trees; rose garden; water garden; daffodils; massive two-acre rock garden; *Nerine* hybrids; hydrangea walk; plant centre; gift shop; hot & cold lunches; new tea-room.

Owned by Edmund de Rothschild
Number of gardeners 9
Size 80ha (200 acres)
English Heritage Grade II*

BRANDY MOUNT HOUSE
East Street, Alresford SO24 9EG

Tel: 01962 732189
www.brandymount.co.uk
Location Left into East Street from Broad Street, 50 yards, first right.
Opening hours 11 am – 4 pm; 1, 4 & 5 February. 2 pm – 5 pm; 5 March. And by appointment.
Admission fee Adults £2; Children free.

Brandy Mount is the garden of plantsmen – but plantsmen who are also distinguished cultivators and exhibitors of alpine plants. The first surprise is to find quite such a large and secluded garden so near the centre of a busy town. Then you discover that, although the underlying soil is chalky, a great variety of the rarer shade-loving plants thrive in the rich soil under the trees – as well as the snowdrops, for which the garden is famous among galanthophiles. The herbaceous borders in the sunnier parts support the many species of geranium, peonies, daphnes and spring-flowering bulbs which are happy in the warm, free-draining soil. The planting of all these areas is informal, with wide sweeps of lawn between the borders. The vegetable area has been reorganised as a formal *potager* with traditional box hedges and small beds to allow the owners to grow a greater variety of salad crops and more unusual vegetables, interspersed with flowering plants. Alpines have always been a speciality: they flourish around the terrace in front of the house, where there are over 30 kinds of smaller daphnes. Many alpines are also grown in troughs and sinks, which are organised as a group and replanted as small crevice gardens. These support many rare and tricky species which are also grown in frames and in the Alpine House. There is a fine collection of European primulas and saxifrages and an ever-increasing one of dwarf narcissi. This garden is fascinating, immaculately maintained, and forever changing, as the collection of rare plants grows ever larger. Strongly recommended.

plantsman's garden; woodland and herbaceous plants on a chalk soil; terrace and troughs for alpines; snowdrops; daphnes; peony species; European primulas; Alpine House; extensive plant sales area full of good plants; teas on 5 March.

Owned by Caryl & Michael Baron
Number of gardeners part-time (very)
Size 0.5ha (1¼ acres)
NCCPG National Collections *Daphne; Galanthus*

FURZEY GARDENS
Minstead, Lyndhurst SO43 7GL

Tel: 023 8081 2464 **Fax:** 023 8081 2297
www.furzey-gardens.org
Location Off A31 or A337 to Minstead.
Opening hours 10 am – 5 pm (dusk in winter);
daily, except 25 & 26 December.
Admission fee March – October: Adults £3.80;
OAPs £3; Children £1.50. (Prices under review.)
Reductions in winter. RHS members free from
March to October.

Furzey demonstrates how woodland
garden effects can be created in quite
small areas. Parts are a maze of narrow
curving paths running between hedges of
Kurume azaleas, unforgettable in April
and May, but the late-summer flowering of
eucryphias runs them close and the
autumn colours of nyssas, parrotias and
enkianthus are worth a visit in October.
rhododendrons & azaleas; mature
conifers; camellias; bluebells;
naturalised dieramas; heathers; spring bulbs;
small shop; refreshments.

Owned by Furzey Gardens Charitable Trust
Number of gardeners 2 horticultural
instructors with teams of students with learning
difficulties
Size 3.2ha (8 acres)

GILBERT WHITE'S HOUSE
High Street, Selborne, Alton GU34 3JH

Tel: 01420 511275 **Fax:** 01420 511040
www.gilbertwhiteshouse.org.uk
Location In centre of Selborne, on B3006.
Opening hours 11 am – 5 pm; daily; 1 January to
24 December.
Admission fee Adults £5; OAPs £4.50; Children
£3.

The house was bought some years ago,
and the museum founded to
commemorate the life and work of Gilbert
White, author of *The Natural History &*
Antiquities of Selborne. The garden
provides a very good example of how a
person of modest means might construct a
scaled-down landscaped park in the mid-
18th century. The flower borders display
plants and features described by White.
The 'wild' garden, orchard and vegetable
garden, with a 'wine pipe' and a herb
garden, complete the idyll.
plants associated with Gilbert White;
gift shop; tea parlour.

Owned by Oates Memorial Trust
Number of gardeners 2, plus volunteers
Size 12ha (30 acres)

HAMBLEDON HOUSE
Hambledon, Waterlooville PO7 4RU

Tel: 023 9263 2380
Location In village centre, 8 miles south-west
of Petersfield.
Opening hours 2 pm – 5.30 pm. For NGS: 9 April,
14 & 15 May, 16 & 17 June, 28 August & 17
September. And for groups by appointment.
Admission fee Adults £3; Children free.

Hambledon House sits in a frost pocket
on thin chalky soil, but Mrs Hart Dyke
has created a garden which is thick with
colour all through the year. She is a great
plantswoman, but it is the placing of
plants that interests her most. Brick and
flint walls, and hedges of yew and box
divide the garden into smaller areas.
Colour, shape and form determine where
plants look best: highlights include
clematis, salvias, lavender, hardy
geraniums, grasses and a great choice of
herbaceous plants.
plants for plantsmen; good colour
combinations; plants from garden for
sale; home-made teas.

Owned by Captain & Mrs David Hart Dyke
Number of gardeners owners only
Size 1ha (2½ acres)

HARDY'S COTTAGE GARDEN PLANTS
Priory Lane, Freefolk, Whitchurch
RG28 7NT

Tel: 01256 896533 **Fax:** 01256 896572
www.hardys-plants.co.uk
Location Off B3400 Whitchurch to Overton road:
1½ mile on left, up Priory Lane, past Watership
Down pub.
Opening hours 10 am – 5 pm; daily; March to
October. Evening visits by appointment.

P ◁ WC ¥

This family-run nursery offers over 1,200
different cottage garden perennials. Its
attractive exhibits have been a great
feature of RHS shows in recent years –
including Chelsea and Hampton Court. It
is one of the best nurseries in southern
England for a really wide choice of good
plants.
Owned by Rosy & Rob Hardy

HEATHLANDS
47 Locks Road, Locks Heath, Southampton
SO31 6NS

Tel: 01489 573598 **Fax:** 01489 557884
Location 2 miles from M27, Jct 9. Locks Road is
main north-south road through middle of Locks
Heath.
Opening hours 2 pm – 5.30 pm; 5 March, 2 April,
7 May & 27 August.
Admission fee Adults £2.50; Children free.

◁ & ¥

Since building his house in 1967, Dr
Burwell has filled his acre of stony soil with
a wonderful choice of immaculately grown
plants of every type. It is the embodiment
of careful plantsmanship, a garden to go
round slowly – looking, studying and
thinking. Your first sight is an 80m line of
Paulownia tomentosa grown from seed in
about 1970, flowering (in May) all along
the road and thought to be the longest line
in England. Next comes *Garrya elliptica*
trained as a small tree. Round the side of
the house is a tall yew hedge, topped by a
brooding topiary peacock. The design is a
mixture of formal and informal, with a
large number of different habitats. Under a
canopy of light oak woodland thrives a
shady fernery with orchids and
Rhododendron sinogrande. *Iris confusa*
flourishes against a wall of the house.
Cyclamen and bulbs are everywhere. The
climate is mild – the sea is only a mile or
so away – so there are hedges of griselinia,
a plant of *Pittosporum* 'Garnettii' 5m high,
and *Cleyera japonica* growing in the open.
The vegetable garden has a new cutting
garden, and an area for standing pots. In a
narrow alley between tall hedges of yew
and rhododendron is the National
Collection of Japanese Anemones. Dr
Burwell will tell you that, though first
described in 1695, they were not
introduced (from mainland Asia) until the
1840s by Robert Fortune. The collection
has about 40 cultivars, including a seedling
which will shortly be introduced as
'Heathlands Ruby'.

⚘ many different habitats; a very wide
range of plants of every kind; some
good combinations of colour & form.

Owned by Dr John Burwell
Number of gardeners owner only
Size 0.4ha (1 acre)
NCCPG National Collections *Anemone*
(Japanese anemones)

HIGHCLERE CASTLE
Highclere, Newbury RG20 9RN

Tel: 01635 253210 **Fax:** 01635 255315
www.highclerecastle.co.uk
Location South of Newbury off A34.
Opening hours 11 am – 4 pm; Monday – Friday;
June to August. Plus 16, 17 & 30 April; 1, 28 & 29
May; 27 & 28 August.
Admission fee Gardens only: free.

P WC & ¥ ⚘ ▷

A major historic garden – when Capability
Brown landscaped it in the 1770s he left
intact the avenues and follies of the early

18th century, but the park is dominated now by hundreds of huge cedars. Jim Russell advised on the planting in the walled garden. The 'Secret Garden' is not among his best, but the espaliered medlars and quince trees are good.

 rhododendrons & azaleas; herbaceous borders; good collection of cedars; long avenues; gift shop; self-service restaurant.

Owned by The Earl of Carnarvon
Number of gardeners 2
Size 2,400ha (6,000 acres) of parkland
English Heritage Grade I

HINTON AMPNER HOUSE
Bramdean, Alresford SO24 0LA

Tel: 01962 771305 **Fax:** 01962 793101
www.nationaltrust.org.uk
Location On A272, 1 mile west of Bramdean.
Opening hours 11 am – 5 pm; Saturday – Wednesday; 18 March to 11 October.
Admission fee Adults £5.50; Children £2.75.

The gardens at Hinton Ampner were laid out by the scholarly Ralph Dutton in the middle of the 20th century with great regard to line, landscape and historical propriety. Statues, buildings, axes and views have been placed with exquisite judgement to lead you subtly along the exact route that Dutton intended. He was also careful to choose plants which would do well on chalk and then planted lots of them – using always the best forms: among them are buddlejas, lilacs, philadelphus, cotoneasters, weigelas and shrub roses. It is now one of England's best mid-20th-century gardens, maintained to a high specification.

topiary; daffodils; yew trees; good plants; teas & home-made cakes.

Owned by The National Trust
Number of gardeners 3
Size 5ha (12½ acres)
English Heritage Grade II

HOUGHTON LODGE
Stockbridge SO20 6LQ

Tel: 01264 810502 **Fax:** 01264 810063
www.houghtonlodge.co.uk
Location Off A30 at Stockbridge. Well signed.
Opening hours 2 pm – 5 pm; daily, except Wednesdays; all year. And by appointment. Closed , Christmas & New Year.
Admission fee Garden & Hydroponicum: £5. Groups at special rates. Children free.

A lovely Gothic *cottage ornée* on a ledge above the River Test, with long spacious views down the river and across the water-meadows. Part of the BBC's *David Copperfield* was shot here. In the traditional walled garden are espaliered fruit trees, herbs, a glasshouse filled with tropical orchids and a topiary known as the snorting dragon. The owner has been restoring the 18th-century shrubbery: this means clearing seedling trees to open up the view across the river and replanting with trees and shrubs which were grown there 200 years ago. Houghton also boasts the leading hydroponic greenhouse in England, where plants are grown in nutrient-rich solutions instead of soil – salad vegetables and herbs, as well as bougainvilleas and bananas. The garden makes a great effort to be educational and entertaining.

plants under glass; daffodils; cyclamen; topiary snorting dragon; refreshments; windfall apples (free!).

Owned by Martin Busk
Number of gardeners 3 part-time
Size 7.2ha (18 acres)
English Heritage Grade II*

LANGLEY BOXWOOD NURSERY
Langley Lane, Rake, Liss GU33 7JN

Tel: 01730 894467 **Fax:** 01730 894703
www.boxwood.co.uk

THE SIR HAROLD HILLIER GARDENS

Jermyns Lane, Ampfield, Romsey SO51 0QA

Tel: 01794 368787 **Fax:** 01794 368027
www.hilliergardens.org.uk
Location Signed from A3090 & A3057.
Opening hours 10 am - 6 pm (dusk, if earlier);
daily, except 25 & 26 December.
Admission fee Adults £7.50; Concessions £6;
Children (under 16) free.

This is quite the most important modern arboretum in the UK. The gardens have the greatest collection of wild and cultivated woody plants in the world: over 12,000 taxa in 180 acres, totalling 42,000 plants. The arboretum was established in 1953 by the late Sir Harold Hillier: Hillier's Nursery aimed at the time to offer for sale every cultivar of every tree or shrub that was hardy in the British Isles. Sir Harold himself was an active importer and collector of new species from all over the world, at a time (of relative economic depression) when few British horticulturists had the impetus to look outside the United Kingdom for plants of any kind. Every part of the arboretum is an education and a pleasure, whatever the season or weather. It has so many unique features that the visitor needs all day to see more than a fraction of its riches: the collection of poplar trees called the Populetum; more than 100 pines (*Pinus* species), including the 'big cone' pine *P. coulteri* whose cones may weigh as much as two kilos; a maple valley; the largest winter garden of its kind in Europe and a Gurkha memorial garden. But it is the sheer number of trees and shrubs here that makes the most lasting impression: every time you visit, and wherever you walk, you see interesting plants that you have never seen before. The labelling is exemplary and a helpful guide is available. Hillier's Nursery shares a car park with the arboretum. Details of seasonal special events, workshops, evening talks, guided tours and children's activities can be obtained on request.

a plantsman's collection of trees and shrubs; mature conifers; good mixed borders; 51 record trees, including 11 *Sorbus*; plant centre; gift shop; restaurant.

Owned by Hampshire County Council
Number of gardeners 14, plus volunteers
Size 72ha (180 acres)
NCCPG National Collections *Carpinus; Cornus; Corylus; Cotoneaster; Hamamelis; Ligustrum; Lithocarpus; Photinia; Pinus* (excl. dwarf cvs.); *Quercus;* 'Hillier' plants

Location 5 miles north of Petersfield. Ring for map or directions (B2070).
Opening hours 8 am – 4.30; Monday – Friday. 10 am – 4 pm; Saturdays.
Admission fee Free

P wc &

These specialist growers of box have a comprehensive range of box plants for hedging, edging and topiary. There are over 50 cultivars of *Buxus* in their delightful catalogue, and some yew *Taxus* also. Both are available in a wide variety of topiary shapes, from simple balls to complex crowns and animals, and (given sufficient notice) they will create individual designs. Rare free-form specimens are also offered.

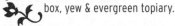 box, yew & evergreen topiary.

Owned by Russell Coates
Number of gardeners 7
Size 2ha (5 acres)
NCCPG National Collections *Buxus*

LITTLE COURT
Crawley, Winchester SO21 2PU

Tel: 01962 776365 **Fax:** 01962 776842
Location On main street through Crawley village, 300 yards from church/pond.
Opening hours 2 pm – 5.30 pm; 12, 19 to 21 February; 12 & 14 March; 9, 10 & 30 April; 21 & 23 May; 22 & 23 June (for eremurus display). Plus 11 & 18 to 20 February 2007. Extra evening opening 6 pm – 8.30 pm on 23 June. Groups by appointment until October.
Admission fee Adults £3; Children free. Evening opening £5.

P ⬚

Little Court fits a lot into its 1½ acres: the design allows for several distinct areas which are linked by spacious vistas and judiciously placed seats to emphasise the many views and axes. A sunken lawn, flint walls, orchards, fine trees, a copse (with a large tree-house), a grass labyrinth, and a 'proper' old-fashioned

kitchen garden are some of the features. The plantings are colour-themed, but some plants (like cyclamen and *Crocus tommasinianus*) have naturalised, too. The range of herbaceous plants is fairly impressive, especially hellebores, clematis and hardy geraniums. There is much to be learned and enjoyed here.

 plantsman's plants; herbaceous perennials; teas on Sundays.

Owned by Professor & Mrs A.R. Elkington
Number of gardeners 1 part-time
Size 0.6ha (1½ acres)

LONGMEAD HOUSE
Longparish, Andover SP11 6PZ

Tel: 01264 720386
Location 1½ miles from junction of A303 & B3048.
Opening hours 2 pm – 6 pm; 28 & 29 May. And by appointment for groups.
Admission fee Adults £4 for this special weekend opening jointly with another garden in Longparish.

P ⬚ wc &

Longmead House is an organic showcase: Wendy Ellicock is on the council of the Henry Doubleday Research Association. She and her husband started the garden when they returned from overseas in 1987. The wildflower meadow was one of their first endeavours, begun by planting plugs into areas cleared of turf: now it provides colour from February to November. The kitchen garden has 25 deep beds, much enriched by compost. There are also wildlife areas, a woodland walk, a fish pond and wildlife pond, as well as herbaceous and shrub borders, a polytunnel and greenhouse.

wildflower meadow; kitchen garden; all organically maintained.

Owned by Wendy & John Ellicock
Number of gardeners 1
Size 1ha (2½ acres)

MACPENNYS NURSERIES
154 Burley Road, Bransgore, Christchurch
BH23 8DB

Tel: 01425 672348
www.macpennys.co.uk
Location On the Burley road, on north-west edge of Bransgore.
Opening hours 9 am – 5 pm; Monday – Saturday.
10 am – 5 pm; Sundays. Closed at Christmas & New Year.
Admission fee Donation to NGS.

P ◁ WC ✿

This long-established nursery ('old-fashioned' in the best sense) has a reliable general range across the plant spectrum, plus a few rarities. It is particularly good for conifers, rhododendrons and shrubs. The large woodland garden next to the nursery is open for the National Gardens Scheme and full of interesting plants. Many have grown to a considerable size. The garden is perhaps at its best in late spring, when the rhododendrons and azaleas overlap with the last camellias.
Owned by Mr & Mrs T.M. Lowndes
Size 1.6ha (4 acres)

THE MANOR HOUSE
Upton Grey, Basingstoke RG25 2RD

Tel: 01256 862827 **Fax:** 01256 861035
www.gertrudejekyllgarden.co.uk
Location In Upton Grey village above & beside church.
Opening hours By appointment only: 9 am – 4 pm; Monday – Friday; April to July.
Admission fee £5, to include a copy of the guidebook & complete plant list. Groups of 20+ receive a personal guided tour and tea/coffee at £5 each.

P WC ⅙ ✿ ☕

Ros Wallinger has restored this Jekyll garden since 1984 using the original planting plans (now at Berkeley University, California, though copies are on display at Upton Grey). She has gone to great pains to recreate it exactly in all its Edwardian loveliness. In the Wild Garden, grass paths meander through wildflowers, rambling roses, shrubs and walnut trees to a water lily pond. In the Formal Garden the rich herbaceous borders drift from cool blues, white and pinks at either end to hot reds, oranges and yellows in the middle. There is no better place to study Gertrude Jekyll's plantings, but what makes it so special is that it is a 'young' garden again. And the restoration continues. Read more about it in Ros Wallinger's *Gertrude Jekyll's Lost Garden* (Garden Art Press, 2000).

roses (mainly old-fashioned & climbers); good herbaceous borders; refreshments for groups.

Owned by Mrs John Wallinger
Number of gardeners 1, plus very keen owners
Size 2ha (5 acres)
English Heritage Grade II

MEON ORCHARD
Kingsmead, Wickham, Fareham
PO17 5AU

Tel & Fax: 01329 833253
Location A32 north from Wickham for 1½ miles; turn left at Roebuck; ½ mile on left. Well signed on open days.
Opening hours 2 pm – 6 pm; 4 June & 30 July. Plus 2 pm – 6 pm on 3 September for NCCPG and specialist nursery plant sale. Groups welcome by appointment.
Admission fee Adults £2.50.

◁ WC ⅙ ✿ ☕

This stylish garden is a plantaholic paradise. The emphasis is upon difficult and tender plants which look their best in late summer. An extraordinary number of plants survive the winter outside with a little protection: bananas, hedychiums, *Impatiens tinctoria* and *Dahlia imperialis*, for example. The Smiths bought the property in 1986 and designed the garden as a series of interlinking paths and glades which radiate out and give the whole layout the impression of being much larger than it

LONGSTOCK WATER GARDENS
Longstock, Stockbridge SO20 6EH

Tel: 01264 810894/01264 810904
Fax: 01264 810924
www.longstockpark.co.uk
Location 1½ miles north-east of Longstock village.
Opening hours 2 pm – 5 pm; first & third Sundays in the month; April to September.
Admission fee Adults £4; Children 50p.

P WC & ✿

Longstock has quite the most extraordinary and beautiful water garden in England, a little Venice where dozens of islands and all-but-islands are linked by an apparently endless number of small bridges and intensely planted with water-loving plants: drifts of astilbes, primulas, kingcups, hemerocallis, musks, water irises and lilies. The ground is so soft that the islands seem to float, and a remarkable accumulation of peat has allowed such calcifuge plants as *Meconopsis betonicifolia* to flourish in this chalky valley. But the garden as a whole has an exceptional variety of habitats: parts are very dry. A seam of acid soil supports a collection of *Rhododendron orbiculare* and *R. williamsianum* cultivars and their hybrids like 'Temple Belle'. Around the perimeter are swamp cypresses and liquidambars: further away are oaks and Scots pines. On the other side of the road lies the splendid arboretum, open at the same time and with a vast collection of well-spaced specimen trees now approaching the prime of their life. Both the water gardens and the arboretum are open only rarely, so that they can be maintained principally for the benefit of partners of John Lewis, but up at the top, along a wooded drive, is an excellent nursery which is open daily throughout the year. It specialises in rare trees and shrubs, but also has a constantly changing stock of other interesting plants. Nearby is a beautiful, long pergola of fruit, rambling roses and clematis, and the National Collection of *Buddleja*. Every part of the Longstock estate – water gardens, arboretum, nursery and walled garden – are models of their kind, beautifully maintained and in top condition. There will be two RHS Special Events at Longstock in 2006; details from 020 7821 3408.

plantsman's collection of plants; good herbaceous borders; arboretum.

Owned by John Lewis Partnership
Number of gardeners 3 at water garden; 3 in arboretum
Size 4ha (10 acres) of water garden; 26ha (65 acres) in arboretum
NCCPG National Collections *Buddleja, Clematis viticella*

really is. It is not a quiet or refined garden, but exuberant and experimental, full of dramatic plants and contrasts. The 40 or so *Eucalyptus* species in their National Collection have grown quickly and give the garden an air of maturity. The speed has been extraordinary; a *Eucalyptus nitens*, planted a mere ten years ago is now a staggering 22m (70ft) tall. Cordylines, Italian cypresses and *Ligustrum japonicum* 'Rotundifolium' also recur throughout the garden and bind it together. In 2005, an overgrown bed of cypresses was cleared, allowing further planting of wild-sourced and hybrid *Podocarpus*, plus additions to their collection of *Araliaceae*, especially of *Pseudopanax*. These two collections were both awarded official National Collection status in 2005. A vast number of pots are planted out for the summer or grouped together. Some may be put in a strategic position for only a few weeks while their flowers associate well with another plant. The owners' plantsmanship is very broad and encompasses hardy plants and alpine plants, too: a laburnum hedge as you come down the drive, bulbs of every kind, a quincunx of Japanese anemones, a water garden, a pond, and hundreds of hardy trees and shrubs, too. This is a most imaginative and creative garden to visit for ideas about what to grow and how to display it.

southern hemisphere plants; tea/coffee & biscuits.

Owned by Dr D.J. & Mrs L.A. Smith
Number of gardeners owners, plus 3 hours' help a week
Size 0.6ha (1½ acres)
NCCPG National Collections *Eucalyptus, Podocarpaceae, Araliaceae*

MOTTISFONT ABBEY
Mottisfont, Romsey SO51 0LP

Tel: 01794 340757 **Fax:** 01794 341492
www.nationaltrust.org.uk
Location 4½ miles north-west of Romsey.
Opening hours 11 am – 4 pm; Saturdays & Sundays; 4 February to 26 February. 11 am – 5 pm; Saturday – Wednesday & Good Friday; 27 February to 31 May & 4 September to 29 October. 11 am – 8.30 pm; daily; 3 to 30 June for roses. 11 am – 6 pm; Saturday – Thursday; 1 July to 3 September.
Admission fee Adults £7; Children £3.50.

The park and gardens near the house are stately: Russell Page, Geoffrey Jellicoe and Norah Lindsay all worked here. A broad chalk spring surges out in the grounds and runs down to feed the River Test. One of the London planes *Platanus* x *hispanica* near the river has two huge trunks fused together, though nobody can work out whether the two stems are on the same roots. But it is the old rose collection in the walled garden which has made Mottisfont's name. It is Graham Stuart Thomas's best-known work, a collection of all the roses he has discovered, assembled, preserved and made popular through his writings. Mottisfont is surely the loveliest rose garden in Britain.

roses (mainly old-fashioned & climbers); good herbaceous borders; guided walks and 'rose clinics' in season; tallest *Platanus* x *hispanica* (42m) in the British Isles; good shop selling books; licensed restaurant.

Owned by The National Trust
Number of gardeners 4
Size 11.1ha (28 acres)
NCCPG National Collections *Platanus, Rosa*
English Heritage Grade II

SIR GEORGE STAUNTON COUNTRY PARK
Middle Park Way, Havant PO9 5HB

Tel: 023 9245 3405 **Fax:** 023 9249 8156
www.hants.gov.uk/countryside/staunton
Location North of Havant on B2149.
Opening hours Glasshouses: 10 am - 5 pm (4 pm in winter); daily; all year. Park: dawn - dusk; daily, all year, except 25 & 26 December.
Admission fee Adults £5; Concessions £4.10; Children £3.60. Parkland free.

🅿 ♿ ⚹ ✳ ✕ ⛿

The historic heart of this landscape garden is a Regency walled garden, pleasure grounds and *ferme ornée*, but the local authority has also restored and developed the Victorian glasshouses as an educational resource. Here you can see useful plants like tea, coffee, pineapple, coconut palms, papyrus and rice plants, as well as such ornamentals as passion flowers, sarracenias, *Nepenthes* and strelitzias. Recent additions include a Golden Jubilee maze and puzzle garden.

Chinese bridge; good trees; shell house; lakes; Regency farm; Victorian glasshouses; tea-room; light lunches & refreshments.

Owned by Hampshire County Council
English Heritage Grade II*

SPINNERS
Boldre, Lymington SO41 5QE

Tel: 01590 673347
Location Signed off A337 between Brockenhurst & Lymington.
Opening hours 10 am - 5 pm; Tuesday - Saturday; 1 April to 14 September. Nursery & part of garden open all year.
Admission fee £2.50 from 1 April to 14 September; free at other times. RHS members free at all times.

🅿 ♿ ✳

Only two acres, but what a garden! Spinners is a plantsman's paradise, where the enthusiast can spend many happy hours browsing at any time of the year. The habitat plantings and plant associations are particularly interesting to study. Much of the garden is light woodland, so it has good collections of hydrangeas, lilies, hostas, rodgersias and ferns. Peter Chappell's nursery sells an extraordinary range of good plants: you always come away with a bootful of novelties. The trilliums are, of course, one of the nursery's specialities: they include such rarities as *T. chloropetalum*. The list of magnolias is perhaps even more impressive: over 80 cultivars, including a great range of *M. acuminata* hybrids, Gresham hybrids and the new *M. stellata* x *liliiflora* hybrids, as well as such introductions as M. x *loebneri* 'Pirouette' and M. x *loebneri* 'Donna'. Roy Lancaster will give an RHS lecture and garden tour on 25 June 2006; details from 020 7821 3408.

woodland garden; an important plantsman's garden; fine collection of trees; rhododendrons; magnolias; woodland plants; rarities and novelties; new peat beds & bog garden; biggest *Eucalyptus perriniana* in the British Isles.

Owned by Peter Chappell
Number of gardeners several part-time helpers
Size 1ha (2½ acres)

STRATFIELD SAYE HOUSE
Stratfield Saye, Basingstoke RG7 2BZ

Tel: 01256 882882 **Fax:** 01256 881466
www.stratfield-saye.co.uk
Location 1 mile west of A33 between Reading & Basingstoke.
Opening hours 11.30 am - 5 pm (last admissions 3.30 pm); daily; 13 to 18 April & 6 to 31 July. Plus groups by prior arrangement.
Admission fee Garden only: £3 (weekdays); £3.50 (weekends).

🅿 ♿ ✳ 🌺 ⛿

Not a famous garden, but there are some fine incidents: a huge kitchen garden, a large and cheerful rose garden, rhododendrons in the park, and magnificent trees, including wellingtonias, named after the Iron Duke.

❧ tallest Hungarian oak *Quercus frainetto* (33m) in the British Isles; gift shop; light refreshments.

Owned by The Duke of Wellington
Number of gardeners 2
English Heritage Grade II

TUDOR HOUSE GARDEN
Bugle Street, Southampton SO14 2AD

Tel: 023 8063 5904 **Fax:** 023 8033 9601
Location Bugle Street runs parallel to the High Street in the old town.
Opening hours By arrangement for groups.
Admission fee Free.

[WC] [♿]

The house and garden are both closed for urgent repair to the house, but due to reopen in 2007. Pre-booked groups can, however, still be accommodated. Sylvia Landsberg's unique reconstruction of a Tudor garden has a knot garden, a fountain, a secret garden and contemporary plantings of herbs and flowering plants all crammed into a tiny area.

❧ Tudor-style knot garden; herbs.

Owned by Southampton City Council
Number of gardeners 1
Size 30m x 30m (100ft x 100ft)

THE VYNE
Sherborne St John, Basingstoke RG24 9HL

Tel: 01256 883858 **Fax:** 01256 881720
www.nationaltrust.org.uk
Location 4 miles north of Basingstoke.
Opening hours 11 am - 5 pm; Saturdays & Sundays; 4 February to 19 March. 11 am - 5 pm; Saturday - Wednesday & Good Friday; 23 March to 30 October.
Admission fee Adults £4.50; Children £2.25.

[P] [WC] [♿] [▷]

This historic garden has many fine features, including a 17th-century summerhouse which is said to be the earliest domed garden building in England. The horticultural interest lies in its fine old trees, an avenue of red-twigged limes, walnuts, and a venerable tree known as the 'Hundred Guinea Oak' because that was the price which a passing timber-merchant offered for it nearly 200 years ago. In the 1960s, Graham Stuart Thomas added herbaceous borders and old shrub roses.

❧ herbaceous borders; annuals; good trees; wild garden; restaurant.

Owned by The National Trust
Number of gardeners 2½
Size 5ha (12½ acres)
English Heritage Grade II

WATER MEADOW NURSERY AND HERB FARM
Cheriton, Alresford SO24 0QB

Tel: 01962 771895 **Fax:** 01962 771985
www.plantaholic.co.uk
Location Just off A272, on B3046 to Alresford.
Opening hours 10 am - 5 pm; Wednesday - Saturday; March to July. And by appointment between August and November.
Admission fee Garden: £2.50; Nursery: free.

[P] [♿] [✿]

This nursery offers a good list of water lilies – *Nymphaea* cultivars, of which they have 70 – and oriental poppies, which indicates that it is equally good for plants for wet situations and dry banks. Many of the hardy plants and herbs in the general list are unusual. The display garden is beautifully laid out – the nursery offers a design and landscaping service – especially when the National Collection of more than 100 cultivars of *Papaver orientale* is in flower. The owners run several 'Poppy Days' in May and June with walks and talks about the collection. Photographers welcome.

Owned by Roy & Sandy Worth
Number of gardeners 2 part-time
Size 1ha (2½ acres)
NCCPG National Collections *Papaver orientale*

WHITE WINDOWS
Longparish, Andover SP11 6PB

Tel & Fax: 01264 720222
Location In village centre, opposite village school.
Opening hours 2 pm - 6 pm; by appointment
from April to September on Wednesdays.
Admission fee Adults £2.50; Children free.
WC

White Windows is one of the best small
modern plantsman's gardens on chalk,
remarkable for the way Jane Sterndale-
Bennett, past Chairman of the Hardy Plant
Society, arranges her material. Layer upon
layer, White Windows bulges with good
plants, well grown and controlled, so that
the balance is kept between sun and shade.
Leaves and stems are as important as
flowers, especially in the combinations and
contrasts of colour – gold and yellow, blue
and silver, and crimsons, pinks and purples.
Much use is made of evergreens and
variegated plants. White Windows is a
garden which is always changing, not just
through the seasons (which it does very
well), but because Jane Sterndale-Bennett is
forever reworking its arrangements,
renewing its plants and readjusting the
balances. Perhaps the most luxuriant chalk
garden in Hampshire.

a plantsman's garden; good herbaceous
borders; euphorbias; pulmonarias;
hardy geraniums; sedums.

Owned by Mrs J. Sterndale-Bennett
Number of gardeners owner only
Size 0.3ha (¾ acre)
NCCPG National Collections *Helleborus* (part)

WEST GREEN HOUSE
Hartley Wintney, Basingstoke RG27 8JB

Tel & Fax: 01252 844611
www.westgreenhouse.co.uk
Location In West Green village; follow brown tourist signs.
Opening hours 11 am - 4.30 pm; Wednesday - Sunday & Bank Holiday Mondays; 25 March to 1 October.
Admission fee Adults £5; Children £2.50.

P WC & ❀ ◆ ✕ D

West Green house is 1720s, brick-and-ashlar, with classical busts along its garden façade. It looks onto a plain lawn, whose sides are hedged in hornbeam, running gently up to a woodland. Marylyn Abbott took a 99-year tenancy of West Green from the National Trust in 1993. The previous tenant was Lord McAlpine, who employed Quinlan Terry to create a modern Elysium which was pretty enough, but nothing like as good as the garden that Marylyn Abbott has now made. His garden was already going back when McAlpine left in 1990, so Abbott found the seats, statues and other structures buried in four or five years of undergrowth. Taming the inherited jungle was only a beginning: what the garden needed was vision, knowledge, taste, energy, expertise and imagination. Marylyn Abbott had all those qualities. She learned her gardening in New South Wales, where her garden at Mittagong is the most visited in Australia. She found the quality of the light in England so different from Australia that she made a special study of its effects upon colour in the garden. Her book *Gardening with Light and Colour* is a modern classic. It is in the mellow, 18th-century walled kitchen garden that Marylyn Abbott's sense of design and colour finds its fullest expression. Here, within neat clipped box hedges, the borders overflow with plants in stunning colour combinations that change from year to year and throughout the seasons. Elegant trellis-work fruit cages and attractive terracotta pots draw you up to the *potager* where fruit and vegetables are grown in a decorative way – always ornamental but never chi-chi. A grand water-staircase (inherited from McAlpine but much improved by Abbott) provides a focus point beyond. West Green has many other features which are original and inspirational. By the house is a charming small topiary garden – anyone could copy it – where waterlilies flourish in small water tanks sunk in the ground. It runs up to a handsome aviary inhabited by unusual breeds of bantams and chickens. Beyond, are a dramatic new Persian water garden in a woodland glade, a newly restored lake, more follies and fancies, new walks and massive plantings – 10,000 lilies, for example, snowdrops, daffodils and fritillaries. Lavishness is a hallmark of the Abbott style – 40,000 tulip bulbs are planted every year – but she also emphasises the importance of drama, colour, innovation and humour in the garden. The lessons for the visitor are endless: you cannot fail to be inspired, cheered, amused and delighted by this extraordinary garden.

exuberant plantings; colour combinations; woodland garden; parterre; great sense of style; new nursery; restaurant.

Owned by Marylyn Abbott
Number of gardeners 3
Size 3.2ha (8 acres)

HEREFORDSHIRE

There is, of course, no such county as Herefordshire – not any more. It was dissolved in 1974, when the old county was linked to its neighbour as 'Hereford & Worcester'. This was never a popular union, and Herefordshire people were always quick to point out that they retained their own identity and Lord Lieutenant. Herefordshire is now a District Council but, so distinct does it consider itself, that we list it as a county again. It is a pity that so few of its historic gardens are open to the public. Hergest Croft has by far the most important collection of trees, with a large number of 'record-breakers' among them: Eastnor Castle also has some magnificent conifers, the largest of their kind in England. Unfortunately, however, the important modern garden at Bryan's Ground will not be opening again in 2006. There are comparatively few top-class modern gardens – Arrow Cottage is a memorable exception (as is Sir Roy Strong's private garden at Much Birch) – and the county does not do conspicuously well for the National Gardens Scheme. Likewise, it has comparatively few National Collections and National Collection holders and no RHS Partner Colleges. But good nurseries exist – Kenchester Water Gardens is one of the best – and the extensive fruit orchards testify to the county's suitability for horticulture. The NCCPG group has worked with the Marcher Apple Network to identify old trees, propagate them and establish new orchards to preserve them.

ABBEY DORE COURT GARDEN
Abbey Dore, Hereford HR2 0AD

Tel: & Fax: 01981 240419
www.abbeydorecourt.co.uk
Location 3 miles west of A465, midway between Hereford & Abergavenny.
Opening hours 11 am – 5.30 pm; Tuesdays, Thursdays, Saturdays and Sundays & Bank Holidays; 1 April to 1 October.
Admission fee Adults £3.50; Children 50p.
🅿 ⬚ ♿ ❀ ⬤ ☕

This is a splendid plant-lover's garden on a difficult site, with fine borders leading down to the ferny river walk and a meadow planted with interesting trees. Mrs Ward says her 'rambling garden' has 'stopped getting any bigger', but the truth is that the garden grows, changes and improves with every visit and she has just taken in another acre of field – bamboos, trees, shrubs and more perennials than ever: very exciting.

good herbaceous borders; handsome wellingtonias; ferns; hellebores; good nursery; restaurant.

Owned by Mrs Charis Ward
Number of gardeners 1
Size 2.4ha (6 acres)

ARROW COTTAGE
Ledgemoor, Weobley HR4 8RN

Tel: 01344 622181
www.arrowcottagegarden.co.uk
Location 1 mile from Weobley: off Wormsley Road, signed Ledgemoor & second right, first house on left.
Opening hours 11 am (1 pm on Saturdays) – 4 pm; Wednesdays & Friday – Sunday; May to August.
Admission fee Adults £3.75; Children £1.
🅿 ⬚ ♿ ❀

Arrow Cottage has reverted to its original name, following its acquisition last year by

Mr and Mrs Martin. It was made in the 1990s by Lance Hattatt, a garden stylist who specialised in contemporary design, with a penchant for the surrealist. There are 24 garden rooms of immense variety, but all exhibit a large measure of plantsmanship as well as good lines. All are maintained to the highest standard. The keen plantsman will find *Iris confusa* 'Martyn Rix' flourishing outside, and pots of *Agapanthus africanus* along the rill in summer. The Martins' problem is how to stamp their own ideas on the garden without losing its unique charm and character. A gravel garden is planned for 2006.

good herbaceous borders; stream; wildflower orchard; 50m, yew-enclosed rill; good plants throughout; old roses.

Owned by David & Janet Martin
Size 0.8ha (2 acres)

THE BANNUT
Bringsty, Bromyard WR6 5TA

Tel: & Fax: 01885 482206
www.bannut.co.uk
Location On A44, 2½ miles east of Bromyard.
Opening hours 12.30 pm - 5 pm; Wednesdays, Saturdays, Sundays & Bank Holidays; Easter to September.
Admission fee Adults £3; Children £1.50.

Unlike many plantsman's gardens, the plants at The Bannut have been used to great decorative effect. The best example is the knot garden made from the contrasting leaf colours of different heathers, though the Everetts are fond of all heathers and grow a large number (over 10,000) in the summer heather garden. They are, however, interested in all types of plants and how to display them in the garden. The beds and borders are planted for colour harmonies and contrasts, mainly of herbaceous plants near the house, but with more shrubs

towards the little copse where cowslips flower in spring. Near the house are a formal yellow-and-white garden and an 'arbour garden' in silver, pink and blue. An old paddock is now planted with rhododendrons, azaleas, camellias and pieris, plus hydrangeas for late-summer interest. Recent additions include a laburnum and clematis walk and a 'secret' garden, with water features and a willow house. The standard of maintenance throughout is excellent.

over 300 different heathers; colour-themed plantings; island beds of shrubs and herbaceous plants; knot garden; cowslips; light lunches; teas.

Owned by Maurice & Daphne Everett
Number of gardeners owners, plus part-time help
Size 1ha (2½ acres)

BERRINGTON HALL
Leominster HR6 0DW

Tel: 01568 615721 **Fax:** 01568 613263
www.nationaltrust.org.uk
Location On A49, 3 miles north of Leominster.
Opening hours 12 noon - 5 pm; Saturday - Wednesday & Good Friday; 20 March to 1 November. Plus weekends only from 4 March to 19 March and 4 November to 17 December.
Admission fee £3.70.

This majestic park is classic Capability Brown. The National Trust has laid out a one-mile parkland walk which takes in the best vantage points and shows you how the landscape would have looked when young. The pleasure gardens around the house are Victorian – laurel walks and an avenue of golden yews. In the old walled garden, the Hereford & Marches Historic Apple Collection is supplemented by old pear varieties, quinces and medlars.

classic parkland; apples & pears; National Trust shop; licensed restaurant for lunch & teas.

Owned by The National Trust
Number of gardeners 2
Size 4.6ha (11½ acres)
English Heritage Grade II*

EASTNOR CASTLE
Eastnor, Ledbury HR8 1RL

Tel: 01531 633160 **Fax:** 01531 631776
www.eastnorcastle.com
Location 2 miles east of Ledbury on A438
Tewkesbury road.
Opening hours 11 am – 5 pm; 13 to 17 April, then
on Sundays & Bank Holiday Mondays to 1 October.
Also daily except Saturdays from 17 July to 31
August.
Admission fee Adults £3; OAPs £2; Children £1.

🅿 ⇦ 🚾 ♿ 🎖 🍂 ⇗

Eastnor is all about trees. The arboretum
planted by Lord Somers from 1852 to 1883
is now mature, and full of champion
specimens. Many are rare, including a tall
American beech (*Fagus grandifolia*) and an
enormous red hickory (*Carya ovalis*). It is,
however, the conifers which dominate the
setting for the neo-Norman castle, largely
because they were planted so thickly and in
such great numbers. Miles Hadfield wrote
that Eastnor was 'embowered by vast
conifers – plantations which spill out into
the surrounding hills and fields'. Quite
apart from the many hundreds of cedars,
the record-breaking specimens include the
Shensi fir (*Abies chensiensis*), the purple-
coned fir (*Picea purpurea*) from south-east
China, and *Pinus hartwegii* from Mexico.
The rest of the garden is less interesting,
but tree-lovers will find Eastnor a real treat.
🌿 mature conifers; fine collection of
trees; spring bulbs; tallest deodar
Cedrus deodara (38m) in the British Isles, plus 11
more record trees; souvenirs and gift shop;
lunches & teas.

Owned by James Hervey-Bathurst
Number of gardeners 2
Size 16ha (40 acres)
English Heritage Grade II*

HERGEST CROFT GARDENS
Kington HR5 3EG

Tel: 01544 230160 **Fax:** 01544 232031
www.hergest.co.uk
Location Signed from A44.
Opening hours 12.30 pm - 5.30 pm (12 noon –
6 pm in May & June); daily; 1 April to 29 October.
Admission fee Adults £5; Children free. RHS
members free (only at some times).

🅿 ⇦ 🚾 ♿ 🎖 🍂 ⇗

Hergest Croft is an extremely important
woodland garden and arboretum around a
whopping Edwardian house. It has over
4,000 rare trees and shrubs, but there
seems no end to the garden's marvels:
huge conifers, magnificent birches, scores
of interesting oaks, many acres of
billowing rhododendrons – Hergest Croft
is one of the best rhododendron gardens
in Britain. But it is also worth visiting for
its double herbaceous borders, alpine
collections, roses, autumn gentians and
kitchen garden, all on a scale that most of
us have forgotten.
🌿 fine collection of trees;
rhododendrons; tallest *Cercidiphyllum
japonicum* (25m) in the British Isles, among
some 50 record trees; gift shop; home-made
teas.

Owned by W.L. Banks
Number of gardeners 7
Size 22ha (56 acres)
NCCPG National Collections *Acer, Betula,
Zelkova*
English Heritage Grade II*

HOW CAPLE COURT
How Caple, Hereford HR1 4SX

Tel: 01989 740626 **Fax:** 01989 740611
www.howcaplecourt.com
Location Signed on B4224 & A449 junction.
Opening hours 10 am - 5 pm; daily; 13 March to
15 October.
Admission fee Adults £3; Children free.

Spectacular formal gardens laid out about 100 years ago (some Italianate, others more Arts & Crafts), and now undergoing restoration. Pergolas, loggias, dramatic terraces and *giardini segreti* with stunning views across a lushly wooded valley. How Caple is a garden of national importance, but little known even locally.

 mature conifers; Italian terraces surrounded by restored pergolas; old roses; topiary; woodland gardens; stable shop; tea-room.

Owned by Mr & Mrs Roger Lee
Number of gardeners 1
Size 4.4ha (11 acres)

IVY CROFT
Ivington Green, Leominster HR6 0JA

Tel: 01568 720344
www.ivycroft.freeserve.co.uk
Location Halfway between Ivington & Coldharbour, on north side of road.
Opening hours 9 am - 4 pm; Wednesdays & Thursdays; March to September. For NGS: 2 pm - 5 pm; 30 April, 28 May, 2 July, 27 August & 24 September. Plus 9 am - 4 pm on 1, 8, 15 & 22 February 2007.
Admission fee Adults £2.50; Children free.

Ivy Croft is a plantsman's garden, with a strong line in willows, snowdrops and cyclamen – and therefore especially good in late winter. But there is colour and interest at every season, and the nursery is always worth a visit.

nursery.

Owned by Sue & Roger Norman
Number of gardeners owners, plus 2 part-time
Size 0.8ha (2 acres)

KENCHESTER WATER GARDENS
Church Road, Lyde, Hereford HR1 3AB

Tel: 01432 270981 **Fax:** 01432 342243
Location On A49, 1 mile north of Hereford.
Opening hours 9 am - 6 pm (5.30 pm from October to March); daily; all year. 10.30 am - 4.30 pm on Sundays. Closed Christmas Day.
Admission fee Free.

The gardens and the nursery at Kenchester are equally important for anyone interested in water plants. The range of plants grown and offered for sale is excellent, and includes nearly 210 cultivars of *Nymphaea*, of which they have a National Collection. The gardens have pools and ponds over a large area – well worth a longish visit. This is a dynamic nursery which is getting bigger and better all the time.

water plants and water gardens; light lunches & teas.

Owned by Mr & Mrs M.R. Edwards
Number of gardeners 2
Size 2.4ha (6 acres)
NCCPG National Collections *Nymphaea*

KINGSTONE COTTAGE PLANTS
Weston under Penyard, Ross-on-Wye HR9 7PH

Tel: 01989 565267
Location Off A40, north of Weston under Penyard, on road to Rudhall.
Opening hours 10 am - 5 pm; Sunday - Friday; 1 May to 8 July. And by appointment.
Admission fee Adults £2 for NGS.

The main feature of this garden is its National Collection of old *Dianthus* cultivars, some 140, which flower in early summer. This is the place to see such rarities as *D*. 'Fenbow Nutmeg Clove' and *D*. 'Cranborne Seedling'. Mr and Mrs

Hughes also sell plants which they have propagated from their collection – the best way to promote a wider interest in old cultivars and guarantee their future survival. But there is much more to see as well as the pinks, including a sunken terrace garden, a large pond and a grotto.

🌿 ponds; grotto; summerhouse; pinks.

Owned by Michael & Sophie Hughes
Number of gardeners 2
Size 0.8ha (2 acres)
NCCPG National Collections *Dianthus*

LAKESIDE
Gaines Road, Whitbourne, Worcester WR6 5RD

Tel: 01886 821119
Location 9 miles west of Worcester off A44 at County boundary sign.
Opening hours Parties of 10+ by appointment only between April & July.
Admission fee Adults £3; Children free.

P 🚻 🌿

These six acres were dramatically planted by Chris Philip, who founded The *RHS Plant Finder*. Tender plants flourish against the old fruit orchard walls. Daffodils bred by Michael Jefferson-Brown run down to the lake, where clean-limbed alders stretch gothically heavenwards. Throughout the garden are good plants, used well: Lakeside is an inspiration to new gardeners, and a place from which all can learn.

🌿 woodland garden; small maturing pinetum; unusual plants; good herbaceous borders; ferns; hollies; heathers; lake; bog garden; teas.

Owned by Denys Gueroult
Number of gardeners 1 part-time
Size 2.4ha (6 acres)

THE PICTON GARDEN
Old Court Nurseries, Walwyn Road, Colwall, Malvern WR13 6QE

Tel: 01684 540416
www.autumnasters.co.uk
Location 3 miles west of Great Malvern; 5 miles east of Ledbury on B4218.
Opening hours 11 am – 5 pm; Wednesday – Sunday; August. And daily from 1 September to 22 October. Thereafter by prior appointment only.
Admission fee Adults £3 for NGS.

P 🚻 🌿

The Picton Garden at Old Court Nurseries holds the National Collection of Michaelmas daisies (*Aster*). This is also the nurseries' speciality: the extensive collection is fully described in Paul Picton's excellent book *Gardener's Guide to Growing Asters* (1999). When the Michaelmas daisies are in flower, the banks of colour, graded for height, recall the grandest of Edwardian gardens and the Picton Garden becomes one of the great showpieces of English horticulture. The new 'Jubilee Border' of *Aster nova-belgii* cultivars was planted in 2002 and is now in its prime. This year (2006), Old Court Nurseries celebrates its centenary; new plantings of Michaelmas daisies, backed by trees and shrubs, are planned as part of the celebration. There are also many other interesting perennials and cottagey plants here, some arranged in 'prairie-style' plantings.

🌿 magnificent collection of asters; herbaceous plants.

Owned by Paul & Meriel Picton
Number of gardeners 2
Size 0.6ha (1½ acres)
NCCPG National Collections *Aster* (autumn-flowering)

QUEEN'S WOOD ARBORETUM & COUNTRY PARK
Dinmore Hill, Leominster HR6 0PY

Tel: 01568 798320 **Fax:** 01568 798329
Location Midway between Leominster & Hereford on A49.
Opening hours 9 am – dusk; daily; all year.
Admission fee Free.

P ⚓ WC ♿ ❀ ✿ ☕

A vigorous young arboretum, first planted in 1953 with public amenity in mind. Wonderful for walking, whatever the season, and well run in a friendly, efficient manner so that visitors get the most from it. The rangers say that spring and autumn are the best time for colour, but there are lots of early purple orchids and spotted orchids in summer, too.

a fine collection of trees, including mature conifers; bluebells; wood anemones; gift shop; light meals from 9 am to 5 pm.

Owned by Hereford Council
Number of gardeners 4
Size 24ha (60 acres)

RUSHFIELDS OF LEDBURY
Ross Road, Ledbury HR8 2LP

Tel: 01531 632004 **Fax:** 01531 633454
www.rushfields.co.uk
Location ½ mile south-west of Ledbury off A449, behind Leadon House Hotel.
Opening hours 10 am – 5 pm (3 pm from November to February); Monday – Saturday; & by appointment.
Admission fee Free.

P ♿ ❀

Rushfields specialise in 'choice garden plants', most of them herbaceous. They are particularly good for hostas. Other specialities include geraniums, grasses, penstemons and monardas, but the nursery is a good place to see and buy a wide range of well-chosen herbaceous plants. More plants may be seen in a large undercover area. Rushfields are consistent medal winners at RHS shows.

 hostas.

Owned by Miss J. Nicholls

WHITFIELD
Wormbridge HR2 9BA

Tel: 01981 570727 **Fax:** 01981 570641
Location 8 miles south-west of Hereford on A465.
Opening hours For NGS: 2 pm – 6 pm; 21 May. And parties by appointment.
Admission fee Adults £3.

P ⚓ WC ♿ ☕

Whitfield has magnificent trees, most of them planted by the Clives over the last 200 years. *Zelkova serrata*, a weeping oak, and a ginkgo planted as early as 1778 are some of the highlights, but there is nothing to beat the grove of 20 or so *Sequoia sempervirens* now pushing 150ft (46m) in height.

topiary; mature conifers; fine collection of trees; huge grove of redwoods; tallest dwarf alder *Alnus nitida* and durmast oak *Quercus petraea* in the British Isles.

Owned by Mr & Mrs Edward Clive
Number of gardeners 1 full-time, 2 part-time
Size 5.2ha (13 acres)
English Heritage Grade II

HERTFORDSHIRE

Hertfordshire has two great historic gardens (Hatfield House and St Paul's Walden Bury) that are open to the public, and a couple of lesser ones (Ashridge and Knebworth), but few of the others admit visitors. Nor does Hertfordshire have as many good modern gardens as its proximity to London might suggest. However, the Royal National Rose Society's new display garden around its old offices near St Albans will open for the first time this year. The only garden with really good herbaceous plantings in Hertfordshire is Benington Lordship. There is a sprinkling of fine trees at such gardens as Bayfordbury (sometimes open

for the National Gardens Scheme) and Aldenham – both relics of keen gardening owners in the past – but no old-established arboretum or pinetum of special merit. The National Gardens Scheme can muster only about two-thirds of the number of gardens that open for charity in such a county as Northamptonshire and there are only eight National Collections in the county. But Hertfordshire has some good nurseries and a large number of excellent garden centres. Nevertheless, it remains difficult to explain why a county so close to London should not be endowed with horticultural wealth on anything like the scale of Surrey or Kent.

AYLETT NURSERIES LTD
North Orbital Road, London Colney, St Albans AL2 1DH

Tel: 01727 822255 **Fax:** 01727 823024
www.aylettnurseries.co.uk
Location On A414, on left-hand side when driving towards Hatfield.
Opening hours 8.30 am – 5.30 pm; Monday – Saturdays. 10.30 am – 4.30 pm; Sundays.
Admission fee Free.

This huge (and very successful) general garden centre has a prime trading position with a vast range of plants and every imaginable sundry. It also offers a design service and delivery. But Ayletts also has a speciality – its award-winning dahlias which have been a feature of RHS shows for many years and won 36 consecutive gold medals. The growing fields are a mile from the nursery and well worth a visit in late summer or early autumn. All the different classes of dahlia hybrids are represented in both quantity and quality.

There will be special dahlia weekends on 16-17 and 23-24 September 2006.
gift shop; coffee shop.

Owned by The Aylett family
Size 2.8ha (7 acres)

BENINGTON LORDSHIP
Benington, Stevenage SG2 7BS

Tel: 01438 869668 **Fax:** 01438 869622
www.beningtonlordship.co.uk
Location Off A602 Stevenage to Hertford, in Benington village, next to church.
Opening hours 12 noon – 4 pm; daily; 4 to 26 February for snowdrops. Spring & Summer Bank Holiday weekends: 2 pm – 5 pm; Sundays; 12 noon – 5 pm; Bank Holiday Mondays. Herbaceous Border week: 2 pm – 5 pm; daily; 26 June to 2 July. And on request, all year (please telephone).
Admission fee Adults £3.50; Children free. Sundays in February £4.50. RHS members free in February & Herbaceous Border week.

HATFIELD HOUSE
Hatfield AL9 5NQ

Tel: 01707 287010 **Fax:** 01707 287033
www.hatfield-house.co.uk
Location Off A1(M), Jct 4.
Opening hours 11 am - 5.30 pm; daily; 15 April to end of September. East Garden open only on Thursdays (closed in August).
Admission fee Park & garden: Adults £4.50, but £7 on Thursdays. RHS members free, except on Thursdays and major event days.

P WC & ✿ ☕ ☞

The gardens at Hatfield are mainly late 19th- and 20th-century. An 1890s parterre called the East Gardens is the outstanding feature: in 1977 The Dowager Marchioness of Salisbury enclosed it on either side with avenues of evergreen oaks – now grown as a high hedge-on-stilts – and replanted the formal beds. Two years later she started on the Knot Garden, an historical re-creation in front of the Old Palace. The designs are extracted from traditional English patterns in such herbaries as Parkinson's. Four central beds surround a small pool: the corners of the beds are marked by pyramids of box. Three are knots; the fourth is a gravel maze, to remind us that Hatfield already had a maze when Queen Elizabeth I visited it. The Elizabethan fruit garden is represented by pomegranates which are put out in the summer, another link to the earliest gardens at Hatfield. The planting is true to the period, too: every plant is one that would have been introduced to England before 1620. They include clove carnations, ancient roses and a collection of historical tulips given by the *Hortus Bulborum* in Holland. The Dowager's intention was to make the gardens as they might have been, and bring them back into sympathy with the great unchanging house. 'It is my dream, she wrote, 'that one day they will become again a place of fancies and conceits, where not only pleasure and peace can be found but a measure of surprise and mystery.' The gardens are now run by her daughter-in-law, the present Marchioness.

good herbaceous borders; knot gardens and good topiary; physic garden; organic kitchen garden (whole garden organically managed); souvenirs and gift shop; licensed restaurant, coffee shop, snacks & hot lunches.

Owned by The Marquess of Salisbury
Number of gardeners 6
Size 16.8ha (42 acres)
English Heritage Grade I

P WC & ▽

Benington Lordship is a Georgian house with an Edwardian add-on, a mock Norman gateway and the ruins of a real Norman castle in the grounds. The extensive gardens have been revived and replanted in recent years without destroying the older features: a Pulhamite folly, an Edwardian rock garden (now a grass dell with bulbs and small specimen trees) and a sense of spacious parkland. The late winter, the drifts of snowdrops and, a little later, of *Scilla bithynica* are quite spectacular. But the highlight of a visit today is the stupendous double herbaceous border that Mrs Bott has planted in gentle pastel shades: the best we know. There will be an RHS Special Event at Benington Lordship in 2006; details from 020 7821 3408.

🌿 roses (ancient & modern); rock garden; very good herbaceous borders; heather garden; cowslip bank; water features (& kingfishers); kitchen garden; refreshments.

Owned by R.R.A. Bott
Number of gardeners 1
Size 2.8ha (7 acres)
English Heritage Grade II

THE GARDENS OF THE ROSE
Chiswell Green, St Albans AL2 3NR

Tel: 01727 850461 **Fax:** 01727 850360
www.rnrs.org.uk
Location 1 mile from junction of M1 & M25; 2 miles south of St Albans.
Opening hours Not yet decided, but probably for about 8 weeks in June, July & early August.
Admission fee Not yet known as we went to press. RNRS members free.
P WC &

The gardens of the Royal National Rose Society have risen from the ashes of its well-publicised financial troubles. The Society is remaking the gardens on the old site, with a stunning design by

Michael Balston, and companion plantings by Tony Lord. The idea is to show, on a large scale, just how good roses can look in a garden setting. Although the construction of the first phase (6 acres) is complete, the roses and plantings went in only last winter, so everything is very much in its infancy – and there may be gaps in the planting, too. Elsewhere on-site are the international rose trials.

🌿 roses of every kind; Adrian Fisher maze.

Owned by The Royal National Rose Society
Number of gardeners 2
Size 10.7ha (27 acres)
NCCPG National Collections *Rosa* (species & cultivars)

HILL HOUSE GARDEN
Stanstead Abbots, Ware SG12 8BX

Tel: 01920 870013
Location Next to Parish Church in Capell Lane.
Opening hours Groups by appointment.
Admission fee Adults £4; Children 50p.
P WC & 🌷 ▽

Outstanding plantings in the old kitchen garden include colour borders, weeping pears, and vegetables, all as neat as imaginable. Pretty woodland garden and lush growth around the pond.

🌿 woodland garden; 20ft high original Victorian conservatory; good herbaceous borders; rose species; home-made teas.

Owned by Mr & Mrs Jonathan Pilkington
Number of gardeners 1, plus some extra help
Size 3.2ha (8 acres)

HOPLEYS PLANTS
High Street, Much Hadham SG10 6BU

Tel: 01279 842509 **Fax:** 01279 843784
www.hopleys.co.uk
Location 50 yards north of The Bull pub.
Opening hours 9 am (2 pm on Sundays) - 5 pm;
daily, except Tuesdays. Closed in January,
February, November & December.
Admission fee Donation. Coaches £1.50 per
person.

P WC ♿ ✿ ☕

Hopleys has a fine four-acre garden with
some excellent plants (notable conifers
and an ash tree said to be the fourth
largest in the UK), but the nursery is its
principal draw. It offers an extensive
choice of hardy shrubs and perennials,
with many half-hardy plants, too – being
particularly strong on diascias,
osteospermums, penstemons and salvias.
Since its foundation in 1968, the nursery
has been responsible for numerous
introductions: the most famous are
Lavatera 'Barnsley' and *Potentilla fruticosa*
'Red Ace'. The tradition continues with
its new *Abelia* x *grandiflora* 'Hopleys'. The
website is excellent – very comprehensive
and informative. There will be three RHS
Special Events at Hopleys Plants in 2006;
details from 020 7821 3408.

 self-service refreshments.

Owned by Aubrey Barker
Number of gardeners ½
Size 1.6ha (4 acres)

KNEBWORTH HOUSE
Knebworth, Stevenage SG3 6PY

Tel: 01438 812661 **Fax:** 01438 811908
www.knebworthhouse.com
Location Off A1(M), Jct 7.
Opening hours 11 am - 5.30 pm; daily; I to 17
April, 27 May to 4 June, 1 July to 5 September.
Plus weekends & Bank Holidays from 25 March
to 24 September.
Admission fee Adults, Concessions & Children
all £7 (excluding house).

P WC ♿ ✿ ☕

Most of the garden was laid out by
Lutyens, who married a daughter of the
house. It has been well restored in recent
years, with Jekyll plantings where
appropriate. These include some inventive
and harmonious colour-themed gardens
and a herb garden made from Jekyll's
original plans. In the park are fine
Victorian conifers and handsome avenues
of lime and horse-chestnut.

rose garden with herbaceous borders;
sunken lawn; gold garden; wilderness;
maze; ponds; herb garden; licensed tea-room.

Owned by The Hon. Henry Lytton Cobbold
Number of gardeners 4
Size 10ha (25 acres)
English Heritage Grade II*

ST PAUL'S WALDEN BURY
Whitwell, Hitchin SG4 8BP

Tel: 01438 871218 **Fax:** 01438 871229
Location B651 5 miles south of Hitchin.
Opening hours 2 pm - 7 pm; 9 & 23 April, 14
May, 4 June. And by arrangement at other times
for groups.
Admission fee Adults £3.50; Children 50p;
Groups £6 per person.

P ◁ WC ♿ ✿ ✕ ☕

St Paul's Walden Bury garden is highly
important as a unique example of the
French 18th-century style – hedged *allées*
forming a *patte d'oie* lead into the
woodland towards temples, statues and

pools. The present owner and his father (the Queen Mother's brother and a past President of the Royal Horticultural Society) added rhododendrons, camellias, maples and magnolias (plus much more besides) into parts of the woodland. Other areas are dedicated to shrub roses and mixed herbaceous borders: there are many small-scale gardens within the overall design. It is therefore a garden that appeals to historians, plantsmen and artists alike.

woodland garden; formal French landscape; rhododendrons; teas & home-made cakes (not 9 April).

Owned by Sir Simon Bowes Lyon
Size 24ha (60 acres)
English Heritage Grade I

THE VAN HAGE GARDEN COMPANY
Great Amwell, Ware SG12 9RP

Tel: 01920 870811 **Fax:** 01920 871861
www.vanhage.co.uk
Location On A1170.
Opening hours 9 am – 6 pm; Monday – Saturday. 10.30 am – 4.30 pm; Sundays. Opens at 9.30 am on Mondays.

P WC & ✿

This long-established and award-winning contemporary garden centre is particularly strong on house plants, specimen plants, hardy plants and bedding. The displays are excellent. Van Hage are also seed merchants: they sell their own flower and vegetable seed, including the record-breaking carrot 'Flak'. They have two other garden centres, one at Chenies near Rickmansworth and the other at Bragbury End on the south-east edge of Stevenage.
Owned by R.H. Van Hage

ISLE OF WIGHT

The Isle of Wight ('the Island' to its residents) may be small and deficient in wealth-creating industries, but it has two exceptional gardens: the 19th-century royal palace of Osborne which overlooks the Solent on the northern shores of the island, and the modern botanic garden at Ventnor on the sunny southern side. The two gardens have an unusual link: the head gardener at Osborne is married to the head gardener at Ventnor. The Isle of Wight also has some fine plantsman's gardens (most notably John Harrison's at North Court), an active Historic Gardens Trust and NCCPG group, several National Collections and some good nurseries. In addition to those listed below, there is a magnificent choice of daylilies available from A la Carte Daylilies (Little Hermitage, St Catherine's Down, Ventnor PO38 2PU – by appointment only), including many of the new American hybrids: the nursery has two National Collections of *Hemerocallis*, large-flowered cultivars that have received awards since 1960, and miniature and small-flowered cultivars. Another National Collection is held by Springbank Nurseries (Winford Road, Newchurch, Sandown PO36 0JX), whose nerines have won several awards at RHS.shows in recent years and extend to over 600 cultivars.

BARTON MANOR
Whippingham, East Cowes PO32 6LB

Tel: 01983 280676 **Fax:** 01983 293923
Location Next to Osborne House on East Cowes Road (A3021).
Opening hours By appointment.
Admission fee Adults £3; Children £1. For charity.
P **WC** **&**

Laid out by Prince Albert, Barton was for many years part of the Osborne estate. He planted some of the best trees, including the cork plantation near the house. The collection of kniphofias is the main modern attraction for garden-visitors: many are available by mail order.

woodland garden; roses (mainly modern); good herbaceous borders; rhododendrons.

Owned by Robert Stigwood
Size 10.3ha (26 acres)
NCCPG National Collections *Kniphofia*

DEACON'S NURSERY
Moor View, Godshill PO38 3HW

Tel: 01983 840750/522243 **Fax:** 01983 523575
www.deaconsnurseryfruits.co.uk
Location Moor View is next to school, down School Crescent.
Opening hours 8 am – 4 pm; Monday – Friday; all year. Boots advisable in winter.
P **❀**

Deacon's was established in 1966 and is celebrating its 40th birthday this year. It is one of the leading fruit tree nurseries in England, with trees and soft fruit of every size and variety, including 'family' trees. The very comprehensive list has over 600 different cultivars, including 300 apples: many are not listed elsewhere – such as regional specialities 'Devonshire Crimson Queen' and 'Welsh Russet'. They are particularly proud of the 20 tree fruits which originated in the Isle of Wight. All rootstocks are of virus-free origin. They mail anywhere in the UK, and abroad.

Owned by Brian & Grahame Deacon
Number of gardeners 5, plus owners
Size 6.7ha (17 acres)

MOTTISTONE MANOR
Mottistone, Newport PO30 4ED

Tel: 01983 741302
www.nationaltrust.org.uk
Location On B3399 west of Brighstone.
Opening hours 11 am – 5.30 pm; Sunday –
Thursday; 26 March to 29 October.
Admission fee Adults £3.40; Children £1.55;
Family £7.75.

P ◁ wc ♿ ☕

Mottistone has a cleverly designed modern
garden on a difficult site – steep and
narrow. Much has been terraced and
enclosed to allow a rose garden and good
herbaceous borders. Most of the rest is
given to a wide variety of fruit trees, trained
to make avenues and underplanted with
vegetables or spring bulbs. It is a model for
this type of planting, and made long before
the current fashion for ornamental *potagers*.
roses (mainly modern); fruit; mature
conifers; good herbaceous borders;
bluebells; irises; teas.

Owned by The National Trust
Number of gardeners 2
Size 2.4ha (6 acres)

NORTH COURT
Shorwell PO30 3JG

Tel: 01983 740415 **Fax:** 01983 821257
www.northcourt.info
Location 4 miles south-west of Newport, off
B3323.
Opening hours For NGS & by appointment.
Admission fee Adults £2.50 (in 2005).

P ◁ wc ♿ ☘ ☕

The Harrison family which owns the
substantial 17th-century North Court
inherited fine grounds with some
magnificent trees and a clear stream at the
bottom. John Harrison has extensively
replanted it with a plantsman's enthusiasm
and a special interest in tender exotica. It is
now the best private garden on 'the Island'.
woodland garden; sub-tropical plants;
roses (ancient & modern); plantsman's
collection of plants; fruit; good herbaceous
borders; large plane trees; B & B for garden-
lovers; refreshments; lunches for groups.

Owned by Mr & Mrs John Harrison
Number of gardeners 2 part-time
Size 6ha (15 acres)

NUNWELL HOUSE
Brading, Ryde PO36 0JQ

Tel: 01983 407240
Location Signed off A3055, 1 mile to west of
Brading.
Opening hours 1 pm – 5 pm; 28 & 29 May and 18
June; then Monday – Wednesday from 3 July to 6
September.
Admission fee Gardens only: £2.50.

P wc

The garden at Nunwell, with its peaceful
views across the Solent, dates back to about
1600. The walled garden was built about
100 years later and still has its original
paths, flanked by excellent double
herbaceous borders. Vernon Russell-Smith
planted a small arboretum about 30 years
ago. The present owners have added some
highly attractive garden ornaments and
have restored the fabric and the plantings
after some years of neglect. The mass of
'Frensham' roses and the long stone steps
lined with lavender are two of the more
striking features. Work continues.
roses (old-fashioned and modern);
plantsman's collection of plants; herbs;
fine collection of trees; statuary; 50m border of
'Frensham' roses.

Owned by Colonel & Mrs J.A. Aylmer
Number of gardeners owners, plus ½
Size 2.4ha (6 acres)
English Heritage Grade II

OSBORNE HOUSE
East Cowes PO32 6JY

Tel: 01983 200022 **Fax:** 01983 281380
www.english-heritage.org.uk
Location Follow brown tourist signs.
Opening hours 10 am – 5 pm (4 pm in October); daily; 24 March to 31 October.
Admission fee Garden only: Adults £5.50; Concessions £4.10; Children £2.80; Family £13.80.

P WC & ✿ ❀ ▭

Prince Albert laid out the stupendous Italianate terraces between the elegant Italianate palace and the parkland below. Starting in 1847, he embellished the terraces with balustrades, urns, steps, statues and fountains, all based on designs he had seen in northern and central Italy. The seasonal displays of massed bedding are still impressive, especially as they reach their peak in April to May and August to October: they employ Victorian period plants and designs. In the park are many fine trees, including stately cedars, cork oaks and holm oaks. The walled kitchen garden has been restored to use: English Heritage has repaired the wall and the old glasshouses, reinstated the original paths, started to train fruit trees against the walls (including 'Lane's Prince Albert' apples), and filled the beds with annual and perennial flowers for cutting. Heritage vegetables and fruit are grown organically at the royal children's gardens surrounding the Swiss Cottage.

✿ Italianate terraces; working walled garden - cut flowers & fruit; Victorian pleasure gardens; English Heritage shop; restaurant; tea-room.

Owned by English Heritage
Number of gardeners 9, plus seasonal extras
Size 20ha (50 acres)
English Heritage Grade II*

VENTNOR BOTANIC GARDEN
Undercliff Drive, Ventnor PO38 1UL

Tel: 01983 855397 **Fax:** 01983 856756
www.botanic.co.uk
Location 1½ miles west of Ventnor on A3055.
Opening hours Dawn – dusk; daily; all year. Show-house & plant sales open daily 10 am – 5 pm (but weekend only in winter, and closing at 4 pm). Visitor Centre open 10 am – 6 pm (4 pm in winter and closed on Mondays & Fridays November to March).
Admission fee Garden: free. Small charge to visit Show-house. car-parking charges.

⬦ WC & ✿ ❀ ✕ ▭

Ventnor Botanic Garden is devoted to exotic plants. It is not strictly a *botanic* garden, but it has a remarkable collection. Many of the plants – perhaps most – are from the southern hemisphere but flourish in the unique microclimate of the 'Undercliff': widdringtonias from Zimbabwe and Tasmanian olearias, for instance, as well as astelias, *Sophora microphylla* and *Griselinia lucida* from New Zealand. *Geranium maderense* has naturalised on the sunny slopes and so has an amazing colony of 4m *Echium pininana*. Elsewhere are such Mediterranean natives as acanthus, cistus and *Coronilla valentina*, and a remarkable area called the Palm Garden, where stately foliage plants like yuccas, cordylines, phormiums and beschornerias are underplanted with watsonias, cannas and kniphofias. The nursery sells some very interesting and often tender plants which are surplus to the garden's own requirements.

✿ sub-tropical plants; plantsman's collection of plants; good herbaceous borders; palms; olives; bananas; medicinal herbs from all over the world; largest collection of New Zealand plants in the UK; new nursery specialising in rare plants from the garden; licensed cafeteria with snacks, tea/coffee, lunches.

Owned by Isle of Wight Council
Number of gardeners 8
Size 8.7ha (22 acres)

KENT

Kent is thick with good gardens and nurseries: the Garden of England has the oldest market gardens in the country. These were developed in the 16th century to supply fresh fruit and vegetables to the fast-growing population of London: the men of Kent filled their barges up with the capital's night soil on the return journey and applied this bounty to their orchards. Kent has long been a rich county, not only because of its soil and climate, but also because many Londoners have traditionally spent the fortunes they made in the City on the acquisition of houses and gardens there. The number of arboreta and record-sized trees in Kent testifies to its long tradition of ornamental gardening. Not only does it have an exceptional number of important historic gardens, but all six of those which are rated Grade I by English Heritage are open regularly to the public – Godington, Hever, Knole, Penshurst, Scotney and Sissinghurst. Many of the other graded gardens are also open throughout the summer – among them are Chartwell, Emmetts, Goodnestone, Leeds Castle, Mount Ephraim, Port Lympne and Walmer Castle. Kent's historic gardens are supplemented by fine modern ones with important horticultural collections: the national pinetum at Bedgebury, for example, and the extensive fruit collections at Brogdale. The gardens at Yalding and Broadview are important examples respectively of organic gardening, and a teaching garden. The National Gardens Scheme thrives in Kent. Gardens and gardening flourish in every town and village: a great number of good garden centres and nurseries exist to satisfy the demand for plants. The nurseries include some of the leading specialists in their field: Brenda Hyatt, for example, has won many awards over the years for her auriculas, while Downderry Nursery (another regular at RHS shows in season) has National Collections of lavender and rosemary.

BEDGEBURY NATIONAL PINETUM

Park Lane, Goudhurst, Cranbrook
TN17 2SL

Tel: 01580 211044 **Fax:** 01580 212423
www.bedgeburypinetum.org.uk
Location 1 mile east of A21 at Flimwell on B2079.
Opening hours 10 am – 6 pm (4 pm in winter); daily; all year. Last admissions one hour before closing.
Admission fee Adults £4; OAPs £3.50; Children £2. RHS members free.

🅿 ⬦ 🚾 ♿ ☀ 🌑 ☂

Bedgebury Pinetum is the national conifer collection: the International Dendrological Research Institute considers it the best conifer collection in the world. It was founded as a joint venture between the Forestry Commission and the Royal Botanic Gardens at Kew: the first plants for the pinetum were raised at Kew in 1921 and planted out at Bedgebury four years later. The collection boasts some 330 different species and more than 2,000 cultivars growing in landscaped woodland around a series of lakes and streams. But Bedgebury is not just for conifer-lovers. The woodland garden is also well known for its deciduous trees: it has fine collections of oaks and maples, azaleas and rhododendrons. A new Japanese glade was added in 1996. Bedgebury is also good for its autumn colour and one of the best places we know for a winter walk. The extensive new plantings are promising.

mature conifers; rhododendrons; fungi; new Japanese maple glade; 18 record tree species, including two broadleaves; shop & visitor centre; tea-room (closed Mondays).

Owned by Forestry Commission
Number of gardeners 6
Size 130ha (320 acres)
NCCPG National Collections *Chamaecyparis lawsoniana* cvs.; *Juniperus, Taxus, Thuja,* x *Cupressocyparis*
English Heritage Grade II*

BEECH COURT GARDENS
Canterbury Road, Challock, Ashford TN25 4DJ

Tel: 01233 740735 **Fax:** 01233 740842
www.beechcourtgardens.co.uk
Location On A252 1 mile west of Challock (left-hand side).
Opening hours 10.30 am - 5.30 pm; Monday - Thursday; 18 March to 29 October. Plus 21 May & 6 August for NGS. And 12 noon - 6 pm on Saturdays & Sundays in October.
Admission fee Adults £4; OAPs £3.50; Wheelchair-bound £2; Children £1; Groups of 12+ £3 each.

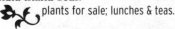

Beech Court is a fine woodland garden, very enjoyable to visit and explore at every season. It was mainly laid out in 1947, though parts have some much older trees and the property dates back to medieval times. There is lots to discover along its paths and glades – hydrangeas, azaleas, maples, magnolias, shrub roses, viburnums, climbing roses and magnificent rhododendrons. Nearer the house are expansive lawns (rather bumpy – visitors must be careful), pools, and well-planted, fluid island beds.

plants for sale; lunches & teas.

Owned by Mr & Mrs Vyvyan Harmsworth
Number of gardeners 3 part-time
Size 4ha (10 acres)

BELMONT PARK
Belmont, Throwley, Faversham ME13 0HH

Tel: 01795 890202 **Fax:** 01795 840042
www.belmont-house.org
Location Signed from A251 at Badlesmere.
Opening hours 10 am - 6 pm; Saturday - Thursday; April to September. For NGS: 2 July.
Admission fee Garden: Adults £2.75; Children £1.

Quiet parkland and the relics of a 200-year-old arboretum surround this handsome Samuel Wyatt house. The pleasure gardens include an ancient rock garden and a walled garden with herbaceous borders and a 7 m tree of *Ilex aquifolium* 'Ferox Argentea'. The Coronation Avenue was planted in 1937: a dead-straight, 274m (300-yard) pathway, lined with immaculately clipped yew hedges and leading to a Gothic flint folly. The old kitchen garden was prettily remade for the millennium by Arabella Lennox-Boyd. Pergolas hung with apples, pears, roses and vines lead to the central pool and flower garden. Further afield are metal arbours dressed with golden hop. The standard of maintenance everywhere is extremely high.

rock garden; shell grotto; rhododendrons; pinetum; teas.

Owned by The Harris (Belmont) Charity
Number of gardeners 3
Size 16ha (40 acres)
English Heritage Grade II

BROADVIEW GARDENS
Hadlow College, Hadlow, Tonbridge TN11 0AL

Tel: 01732 853211 **Fax:** 01732 853207
www.hadlow.ac.uk
Location Signed from A26, 3 miles north-east of Tonbridge.
Opening hours 10 am - 5 pm (4 pm on Sundays); daily; all year.
Admission fee Adults £2; Children free. RHS members free in September & October.

These new gardens attached to Hadlow College include a series of model designs and plantings which are intended to help students to learn the skills of garden design and horticulture. They are, of course, extremely interesting and inspiring for ordinary visitors: they include a sub-tropical garden, a low-maintenance garden, long herbaceous borders, an oriental garden and a cottage garden. The college also has a good garden centre.

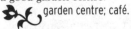 garden centre; café.

Owned by Hadlow College
Size 3.2ha (8 acres)
NCCPG National Collections *Anemone* (Japanese); *Helleborus*

BROGDALE
Brogdale Road, Faversham ME13 8XZ

Tel: 01795 535286 **Fax:** 01795 531710
www.brogdale.org
Location 1 mile south-west of Faversham.
Opening hours 10 am - 5 pm; daily; 26 March to 29 October. 9.30 am - 4.30 pm; daily; winter. Closed over Christmas period.
Admission fee Adults £5; OAPs £4.50; Children £3. RHS members free from Easter to November, except at special events.

Brogdale describes itself as 'a living museum' and claims to have the largest collection of fruit cultivars in the world: more than 2,300 apples, 550 pears and 350 plums. There are demonstrations, exhibitions, workshops and events throughout the year. Fruit from the collections is sold, and scion wood supplied.

hardy fruit of every kind - the biggest collection in Europe; excellent shop with rare fruit varieties for sale in season; light lunches & teas.

Owned by Brogdale Horticultural Trust
Size 64ha (160 acres)

NCCPG National Collections *Corylus* (cobnuts & filberts); *Malus* (apples, ornamental cvs. & cider apples); *Prunus* (cherries); *Prunus* (plums); *Pyrus*; *Ribes grossularia* (gooseberries); *Ribes nigrum* (blackcurrants); *Ribes sativum* (currants other than blackcurrants); *Vitis vinifera* (grapes)

CHARTWELL
Westerham TN16 1PS

Tel: 01732 868381 **Fax:** 01732 868193
www.nationaltrust.org.uk/chartwell
Location A25 to Westerham, then signed from B2026.
Opening hours 11 am - 5 pm; Wednesday - Sunday & Bank Holiday Mondays (plus Tuesdays in July & August); 25 March to 29 October.
Admission fee House & Gardens: Adults £10; Children £5.

Sir Winston Churchill lived here from 1924 on and laid out the spacious and extensive gardens in a slightly old-fashioned style. One of the rose gardens has the cultivar 'Winston Churchill' but every part has a deep sense of history and all is maintained to a very high standard. The Trust has started to restore the garden to a closer representation of the way it was in Churchill's time; the kitchen garden has just been reinstated.

roses (mainly modern); National Trust shop; restaurant.

Owned by The National Trust
Number of gardeners 5
Size 33ha (82 acres)
English Heritage Grade II*

COPTON ASH GARDENS
105 Ashford Road, Faversham ME13 8XW

Tel: 01795 535919
Location On A251, opposite M2 eastbound exit.
Opening hours 2 pm - 6 pm; Tuesday - Sundays. And by appointment.
Admission fee Free to nursery visitors.

This is a first-rate plantsman's garden, attached to a nursery specialising in real rarities. Started in 1978, the garden now has over 3,000 different plants growing in 1½ acres – the fruit of Tim Ingram's constant quest for new things to try out. His interests are omnivorous, with unusual plants from every corner of the globe and endless different microhabitats within the garden. Recent developments include extensive plantings of small bulbs like snowdrops, cyclamen and crocuses (species only – no hybrids) and the best woodland perennials, especially hellebores, erythroniums and trilliums. Seldom have so many good plants been grown in such a small area. Visitors are especially welcome early in spring when the garden starts to wake up, but there is much of interest at every season. It is a garden to explore slowly. The nursery is excellent, offering the best of these rarities, and with a catalogue that is based on Tim Ingram's own observations, not the recycled nursery-speak of others. A paradise for plantsmen.

important collection of dry-land plants of every kind.

Owned by Tim & Gillian Ingram
Number of gardeners 1½
Size 0.6ha (1½ acres)

DODDINGTON PLACE GARDENS
Sittingbourne ME9 0BB

Tel: 01795 886101
www.doddington-place-gardens.co.uk
Location Follow brown tourist signs from A2.
Opening hours 2 pm - 5 pm; Sundays & Bank Holiday Mondays; 16 April to 15 June. For NGS: 11 June, 6 & 20 August and 17 September.
Admission fee Adults £4; Children 75p. (2005 prices.)

P ⬧ WC & 🌿 ✕

The house and garden both date back to the 1870s: Markham Nesfield had a hand in the original formal gardens. The handsome *Sequoiadendron giganteum* and billowing yew hedges are also 19th-century, but this is a garden to which every generation has added something. From the Edwardian era dates the rock garden of local stone: cyclamen have naturalised all through it. The woodland garden was developed in the 1960s on a small outcrop of greensand: rhododendrons, camellias, styrax, eucryphias and maples flourish here as nowhere nearby. More recent are a paved rose garden (*very* pretty), an avenue of *Sorbus aucuparia* 'Beissneri' planted for its winter bark, and excellent colour borders (red and white). And the present owners are restoring the Edwardian rock garden and adding new architectural features and plantings with great verve.

woodland gardens (4 acres); magnificent lumpy yew hedges; fine old wellingtonias; rhododendrons & azaleas.

Owned by Mr & Mrs R. Oldfield
Number of gardeners 2, plus 1 part-time
Size 4ha (10 acres)
English Heritage Grade II

DOWNDERRY NURSERY
Pillar Box Lane, Hadlow, Tonbridge TN11 9SW

Tel: 01732 810081 **Fax:** 01732 811398
www.downderry-nursery.co.uk
Location Follow brown tourist signs off A26 north-east of Hadlow.
Opening hours 10 am - 5 pm; daily, except Mondays; May to October.
Admission fee Free. Tours (including distillation demonstration) available at £5 per adult.

P ⬧ WC & 🌿 🗂

This nursery in an old walled garden has the widest imaginable list of lavender and rosemary cultivars. Almost all the species are here, including the most unusual ones, and a wide number of hybrids and selections, some of them bred or chosen by the owner Dr Charlesworth himself. His exhibits at the major RHS summer shows have been a source of inspiration to many gardeners, and hurried them to visit his nursery, where his display garden has come together very well. Customers speak well of the quality of his plants. He has now started to distil lavender oils and sell the products. There will be a special 'Lavender Weekend' on 24 & 25 June 2006, when an admission price of £2 will include free tours and light refreshments.

lavender & rosemary; light refreshments.

Owned by Dr Simon J. Charlesworth
Size 0.4ha (1 acre) & 1ha (2½ acre) field of lavender
NCCPG National Collections *Lavandula*, *Rosmarinus*

EAST NORTHDOWN FARM NURSERY
Margate CT9 3TS

Tel: 01843 862060 **Fax:** 01843 860206
www.botanyplants.co.uk
Location On east fringes of town, along George Hill Road (B2052) between Cliftonville & Kingsgate.
Opening hours 10 am – 5 pm; daily; all year, except Christmas week.
Admission fee Free.

East Northdown Farm Nursery specialises in plants that will tolerate chalk soil, low rainfall and drying sea winds. There are many Mediterranean species, but the emphasis is always upon their toughness in cultivation. The farmhouse garden is worth a visit in its own right – many rare plants grown in a charming and traditional setting.

snacks & drinks.

Owned by William & Louise Friend
Number of gardeners owners only
Size 0.8ha (2 acres)

EDENBRIDGE HOUSE
Main Road, Edenbridge TN8 6SJ

Tel: 01732 862122 **Fax:** 01732 867385
Location On B2026, 1½ miles north of Edenbridge, near Marlpit Hill.
Opening hours 2 pm – 6 pm; 16 April, 7 May, 18 June, 9 July & 17 September. 1 pm – 5 pm 17 May & 13 September. 6 pm – 9 pm; 14 June. Plus 2 pm – 5 pm; Tuesdays & Thursdays; April to September. And groups by appointment.
Admission fee Adults £3; Children 25p.

This 1930s garden has been renewed and replanted by the present owner as a series of garden rooms to offer something of interest at every season. The spacious terraces are home to a rich mix of tender plants, many of them put out in pots for the summer months. A stream with bog plants along its edges runs down to a small pool. In the kitchen garden is a fine greenhouse and small collection of ornamental trees, as well as apples and an appetising vegetable garden.

plantsman's garden; roses; herbaceous plants; orchard; gravel garden; teas (not on Tuesdays or Thursdays).

Owned by Mrs M.T. Lloyd
Size 2ha (5 acres)

EMMETTS GARDEN
Ide Hill, Sevenoaks TN14 6AY

Tel: 01732 750367 **Fax:** 01732 750490
www.nationaltrust.org.uk
Location Between Sundridge & Ide Hill off B2042.
Opening hours 11 am – 5 pm (last admissions 4.15 pm); Tuesday – Sunday; 25 March to 31 May. Wednesday – Sunday; 1 June to 2 July. Wednesdays, Saturdays & Sundays; 5 July to 29 October.
Admission fee Adults £5; Children £1.

A short, stiff walk (or buggy ride) up from the car park brings you to this windswept hilltop garden, laid out in Edwardian times and maintained on a slim budget. The formal Italianate rose garden is pretty in July, but better still is the informal woodland garden laid out with unusual trees and shrubs in the William Robinson style. The bluebells are good; so is the autumn colour.

🌿 rock garden; bluebells; Italianate rose garden; rare trees and shrubs; autumn colour; azaleas; tea-room.

Owned by The National Trust
Number of gardeners 2
Size 7ha (17½ acres)
English Heritage Grade II

GARDEN ORGANIC YALDING
Yalding, Maidstone ME18 6EX

Tel & Fax: 01622 814650
www.gardenorganic.org.uk
Location On B2162, ½ mile south of village.
Opening hours 10 am - 5 pm; Wednesday - Sunday, plus all Bank Holidays; April to October.
Admission fee Adults £4; Concessions £3.50; Children £1. RHS members free, except for some special events, when £1.

P WC 👤 🌿 🐛 ☕

This is the new name for Yalding Organic Gardens, though it still has a series of 14 historically themed gardens run organically by Garden Organic (the new name for HDRA). They include an apothecary's garden in the 13th-century style, a late-19th-century artisan's garden and a post-war allotment: all very stylish and educational. Others show the influence of William Cobbett and Gertrude Jekyll through the centuries. There is a central hop-pole pergola – a good example of how design features should come out of their surrounding landscape. A recent addition is tall wooden henge. The garden sets out to inspire, to educate and to give pleasure – and succeeds.

🌿 gardens through the ages - modern reconstructions; shop; café.

Owned by Henry Doubleday Research Association
Number of gardeners 4
Size 2ha (5 acres)

GODINTON PARK
Ashford TN23 3BP

Tel: 01233 620773 **Fax:** 01233 647351
www.godinton-house-gardens.co.uk
Location A20 to Charing, then follow brown tourist signs.
Opening hours 2 pm - 5.30 pm; Thursday - Monday; 25 March to 29 October. Tours by arrangement. House open from 7 April to 8 October.
Admission fee Gardens only: Adults £3; Children free. Honesty box.

P WC 👤 🌿 ☕

Godinton is the prettiest house in Kent, a Jacobean mansion reworked in the 1920s by Sir Reginald Blomfield who advised on the spacious gardens for over 20 years. The charming Italian garden is his: statues, loggia, summerhouse, Persian rill, marble colonnade and Italian cypresses. The magnificent yew hedge dates from his first plantings in the 1900s: Dutch gables have been cut along its top to match the architecture of the house. Elsewhere are a sunken pool fringed with elegant weeping willows, a recently redesigned rose garden, herbaceous borders, sweeping lawns, a stupendous 18th-century park and a topiary garden with a statue of Pan at the centre. The wild garden is a carpet of daffodils and fritillaries in spring. In the kitchen garden are rows of fruit, vegetables and cut-flowers, and a border with rare cultivars planted by members of the Delphinium Society. Every part has recently been restored and is very well maintained, to an unusually high standard.

🌿 topiary; formal Italianate garden; redesigned rose garden; teas.

Owned by The Godinton House Preservation Trust
Number of gardeners 4
Size 5ha (12½ acres)
English Heritage Grade I

GOODNESTONE PARK
Wingham, Canterbury CT3 1PL

Tel & Fax: 01304 840107
www.goodnestoneparkgardens.co.uk
Location Follow brown tourist signs from B2046.
Opening hours 11 am – 5 pm; Wednesday – Friday
& Bank Holidays; 29 March to 30 September. Plus
12 noon – 5 pm on Sundays from 19 February.
Admission fee Adults £4; OAPs £3.50; Children
(under 12) £1; Wheelchair-bound £1; Group (20+)
£3.50; Guided Groups £5.50. RHS members free in
April, May & September.

P WC ♿ ☀ ▯

Goodnestone is a handsome Palladian
building. Jane Austen's brother married a
daughter of the house: she will have known
the fine chestnut avenue dating from about
1800 and the 18th-century parkland beyond.
Later came the formal 19th-century terraces
around the house, a 1920s woodland garden
(best in spring when the rhododendrons and
camellias are in flower) and the sloping
cricket ground below the house. Very recent
are a gravel garden on the edge of the wood,
and a formal parterre on one of the terraces.
The walled garden is quite exceptional.
Actually there are three walled gardens, one
after another, each of about one acre and
enclosed by beautiful, worn old bricks. A
long, broad, grass walk runs right down the
middle and connects them to one another,
with the flint tower of the parish church as a
focal point beyond. Drifts of shrub roses,
peonies, penstemons, clematis and
herbaceous plants fill the borders, stuffed
with interesting plants and arranged to create
pretty colour plantings. Here, above all, you
see the passionate plantsmanship which has
imbued the present owner since she first
started to garden here nearly 50 years ago.

woodland garden; topiary; snowdrops;
roses (mainly old-fashioned); good
herbaceous borders; teas; light lunches.

Owned by Lady FitzWalter
Number of gardeners 2 full-time, 2 part-time
Size 5.6ha (14 acres)
English Heritage Grade II*

GREAT COMP
St Mary's Platt, Borough Green, Sevenoaks
TN15 8QS

Tel: 01732 886154
www.greatcomp.co.uk
Location 2 miles east of Borough Green: take B2016
off A20.
Opening hours 11 am – 5.30 pm; daily; April to
October.
Admission fee Adults £4; Children £1.

P WC ♿ ☀ ✿ ▯

Great Comp is a monument to the energy
and enthusiasm of Eric Cameron who has
built up the garden over the last 40 years.
The plant content is of considerable
horticultural interest and includes some 30
magnolia cultivars and a good range of
rhododendrons, conifers, heathers and
herbaceous plants: over 3,000 different plants
in all. But the most interesting thing about
the garden is the way in which large areas
have been planted for minimum
maintenance. There is much to learn and
admire here. Dysons Nurseries, best known
for their salvias, are also based within the
grounds.

woodland garden; plantsman's collection
of plants; good herbaceous borders;
ground cover; dwarf conifers; salvias; gifts, plants
and souvenirs; refreshments.

Owned by Great Comp Charitable Trust
Number of gardeners 3
Size 2.8ha (7 acres)

GROOMBRIDGE PLACE GARDENS
Groombridge, Tunbridge Wells TN3 9QG

Tel: 01892 861444 **Fax:** 01892 863996
www.groombridge.co.uk
Location On B2110, 4 miles south-west of Tunbridge
Wells.
Opening hours 10 am – 5.30 pm; daily; 1 April to 4
November.
Admission fee Adults £8.50; OAPs £7.20; Children
£7.

P WC & ☘ ◼ ▯

Groombridge has lots to offer: a drunken garden where the yews lean at tipsy angles, an oriental garden, a white rose garden, a 'draughtsman's garden', a secret garden and a chessboard garden. Ivan Hicks has been at work in the 'Enchanted Forest', where the gardens are said to be 'interactive'. Best of all are the brilliant colour plantings, among the best we know. But the entry price is high, and some may question whether the garden offers good value.

 good colour plantings; gift shop; light lunches & teas.

Owned by Groombridge Asset Management Ltd
Number of gardeners 2 full-time, plus several part-timers
Size 0.6ha (1½ acres), plus 80ha (200 acres) of park & woods

HEVER CASTLE
Edenbridge TN8 7NG

Tel: 01732 865224 **Fax:** 01732 866796
www.hevercastle.co.uk
Location 3 miles south-east of Edenbridge, signed from M25, Jct 5 & 6.
Opening hours 11 am – 5 pm (4 pm in winter); daily; March to November.
Admission fee Adults £7.80; OAPs £6.70; Children £5.

P ◁ WC & ☘ ◼ ▯

Hever is one of the most important Edwardian gardens in England. The pretty moated castle sits in a park of oaks and firs (underplanted with rhododendrons) with a yew maze and formal neo-Tudor garden to one side. The best part is a spectacular five-acre Italian garden where a long pergola (cool dripping fountains all along) leads past a series of exquisite Italian gardens, stuffed with outstanding sculptures, urns, sarcophagi and other loot brought by William Waldorf Astor from Rome in 1903; it finally bursts onto a theatrical terrace, known as the Piazza, and a 35-acre lake, hand-dug by 800 workmen in less than two years.

woodland garden; topiary; 3,000 roses (old-fashioned and modern, with some climbers, too); rhododendrons & azaleas; snowdrops; crocuses; daffodils; bluebells; tulips; dahlias; autumn colour; Christie's/HHA Garden of the Year in 1995; plant centre; shop; two restaurants.

Owned by Broadland Properties Ltd
Number of gardeners 10
Size 16ha (40 acres)
English Heritage Grade I

HOLE PARK
Rolvenden, Cranbrook TN17 4JB

Tel: 01580 241386 **Fax:** 01580 241882
www.holepark.com
Location Off B2086 between Rolvenden & Cranbrook.
Opening hours 2 pm – 6 pm; Sundays & Bank Holiday Mondays; 2 April to 2 July, 8, 15 & 22 October. Plus Wednesdays & Thursdays from April to October. Also days for NGS & other charities (see website). Guided tours & groups by appointment at other times.
Admission fee Adults £4; Children 50p.

P WC & ◼ ▯

This great garden is far too little known. The drive runs under an avenue of horse-chestnuts through classical parkland with wonderful views. The pleasure garden is Edwardian in origin, but has been revived and replanted by the present owner. Solid hedges and clipped specimens of yew are everywhere: backing the excellent herbaceous borders, around the water lily pond and framing a croquet lawn with standard wisterias. The flowery woodlands have palm trees in the dell, surrounded by purple rhododendrons and orange azaleas. Daffodils abound from March onwards and the millions of bluebells in the woodland walk never cease to astonish in early May. Autumn colours are especially good, too.

good design and good plants; new millennium water garden; bluebells; plant stall on Sundays; teas on Sundays & Bank Holidays.

Owned by Mr & Mrs Edward Barham
Number of gardeners 2
Size 6ha (15 acres)

IDEN CROFT HERBS
Frittenden Road, Staplehurst TN12 0DH

Tel: 01580 891432 **Fax:** 01580 892416
www.herbs-uk.com
Location Signed from A229, south of Staplehurst.
Opening hours 9 am (11 am on Sundays & Bank Holidays) - 5 pm; daily; March to September. 9 am - 4 pm; Monday - Friday; October to February.
Admission fee Adults £4, Concessions £3; Children free.

This substantial nursery has been developed over the last 30 years and planted as a series of demonstration gardens. These incorporate a 16th-century walled garden, originally attached to Staplehurst Manor. Other gardens include a cottage garden near the café, and a 'sensory garden' which shows how herbs may be arranged and appreciated for their scent, colour, shape, form and texture. The intention is to provide design and planting ideas for all visitors, whatever the size of their garden. Insects and birds are encouraged and the catalogue which the nursery produces lists plants under both their Latin and common English names.

herbs.

Owned by Philip Haynes
Number of gardeners 2
Size 0.6ha (1½ acres)
NCCPG National Collections *Mentha, Origanum, Nepeta*

IGHTHAM MOTE
Ivy Hatch, Sevenoaks TN15 0NT

Tel: 01732 810378 **Fax:** 01732 811029
www.nationaltrust.org.uk
Location Signed from A25 in Ightham village.
Opening hours 10 am - 5.30 pm; daily, except

Tuesdays & Saturdays; 12 March to 29 October.
Admission fee Adults £8.50; Children £4.

Ightham Mote is a moated medieval manor in a wooded Kentish valley, with cottage-garden borders of pinks, old roses and lilies. These were remade about 100 years ago in a dreamily English style and give colour throughout the season. Fine lawns, natural springs, orchards and a kitchen or cut-flower garden are some of the other features. In the woodland parts are fine specimen trees, thick rhododendrons and a substantial collection of hydrangeas and philadelphus.

woodland garden; National Trust shop; restaurant.

Owned by The National Trust
Number of gardeners 3
Size 5.6ha (14 acres)
English Heritage Grade II

LADHAM HOUSE
Ladham Road, Goudhurst TN17 1DB

Tel: 01580 212511
Location Left at Chequers Inn on Cranbrook Road, then 2nd right into Ladham Road.
Opening hours 2 pm - 5 pm; 7 May. And by appointment (afternoons only).
Admission fee Adults £3.50; Children (under 12) 50p.

Ladham was laid out by a botanist Master of the Rolls in the mid-19th century, and has been enthusiastically restored and updated in recent years. There is a good mixture of new planting and old: the latter includes the deep red form of *Magnolia campbellii* which has been named 'Betty Jessel' and is now available commercially.

woodland garden; good herbaceous borders; fine collection of trees; magnolias; teas.

Owned by C.G. Johnson
Number of gardeners 2
Size 4ha (10 acres)

LEEDS CASTLE
Maidstone ME17 1PL

Tel: 01622 765400 **Fax:** 01622 735616
www.leeds-castle.com
Location M20, Jct 8.
Opening hours 10 am - 5 pm; April to October.
10 am - 3 pm; November to March. Closed on 25
December. Special pre-ticketed events on 10, 11, 24 &
25 June, 1 July, 2 & 3 September and 4 November
2006.
Admission fee Castle, park & gardens: Adults
£13.50; OAPs & Students £11; Children £8.

P WC 👤 ❀ ⊐

More a romantic castle than a garden, Leeds
is best seen across the lake (the 'Great
Water') which Russell Page created in the
1930s. Page also designed and planted the
Culpeper Garden, which takes its name
partly from Sir Thomas Colepeper, who
bought the castle in 1632, and partly from
Nicholas Culpeper, the 17th-century
herbalist. It could be said that the Culpeper
Garden does not show the 20th century's
greatest garden designer at his best. The
standard of maintenance is, however, very
high: informal plantings of old garden flowers
– roses, pinks, lavender, poppies and lupins.
Here, too, is the National Collection of
bergamot (*Monarda*) cultivars. The latest
development is the 'Lady Baillie Garden', a
series of sheltered terraces between the
Culpeper Garden and the lake. In this part of
the garden the planting is more
Mediterranean in character. The nearby
maze, planted in 1988, is fun to visit: it
resembles a topiary castle with towers and
bastions and, when you get to its centre, you
find the entrance to an underground grotto.
The 'wood garden' is planted with
rhododendrons and azaleas and underplanted
with daffodils and anemones and there are
further rhododendrons to the west of the
moat. Leeds is run by a high-profile
charitable trust which receives no
government funding or grant-aid, which may
help to explain the high entry charges. Are
they worth it for someone who is principally
interested in gardens and plants? The answer
– paradoxically – is yes, provided you also
visit the castle and some of the many other
attractions here. The owners say you need at
least three hours to experience and enjoy
them properly.

🌿 woodland garden; roses (mainly old-
fashioned); herbs; good herbaceous
borders; vineyard; plant centre; refreshments.

Owned by Leeds Castle Foundation
Number of gardeners 13
Size 5ha (12½ acres), plus 200ha (500 acres) of
parkland
NCCPG National Collections *Monarda*
English Heritage Grade II*

MADRONA NURSERY
Pluckley Road, Bethersden TN26 3DD

Tel: 01233 820100 **Fax:** 01233 820091
www.madrona.co.uk
Location Halfway between Bethersden village &
Pluckley railway station.
Opening hours 10 am - 5 pm; Saturday - Tuesday;
mid-March to end of October.

P WC 🌵 ⊐

This is a first-rate general nursery, with a
good choice of unusual cultivars across the
range. Trees and shrubs are perhaps its main
speciality – it is particularly strong on
arbutus, birches, *Aesculus* and unusual
conifers like *Podocarpus macrophyllus* and
several forms of *Sequoiadendron giganteum* –
but Madrona also offers a fine choice of
herbaceous perennials. All are well grown
and well displayed: a thoroughly satisfying
nursery to visit.

🌿 light refreshments.

MARLE PLACE GARDENS
Brenchley, Tonbridge TN12 7HS

Tel: 01892 722304 **Fax:** 01892 724099
www.marleplace.co.uk
Location Follow brown tourist signs from
Brenchley or Forstal Farm roundabout off A21.
Opening hours 10 am - 5 pm; Friday - Monday; 25

March to 3 October. And by appointment.
Admission fee Adults £4.50; Concessions £4.

P WC ♿ 🌺 🗗

The gardens around the Jacobean house are
mainly formal. They were imaginatively
designed and planted in the 1930s and
have been well preserved and improved by
the present owners since the early 1960s.
The sunken garden, laid out with scented
plants, is particularly charming. The
Edwardian kitchen garden has been
redesigned with exotic planters and the
Victorian greenhouse (recently restored)
holds a collection of over 200 orchids.
Recent additions include some unusual
sculptures, a 'mosaic terrace', a nut plat
and a bog garden. The wilder parts are full
of natural flowers, especially alliums. And
all around are orchards of Kentish apples
and pears.

🌿 good herbaceous borders; some
unusual plants; Victorian gazebo;
Edwardian rock garden; tea, coffee & cake.

Owned by Mrs Lindel Williams
Number of gardeners 2
Size 6ha (15 acres)

MOUNT EPHRAIM
Hernhill, Faversham ME13 9TX

Tel: 01227 751496 **Fax:** 01227 750940
www.mountephraimgardens.co.uk
Location Follow brown tourist signs from A2 &
A299.
Opening hours 1 pm – 5 pm; Wednesdays,
Thursdays, Saturdays, Sundays & Bank Holidays;
Easter to 30 September. Opens at 11 am on Bank
Holiday weekends.
Admission fee Adults £4; Children £1.

P 🔄 WC ♿ 🐞 🗗

Mount Ephraim is a handsome Edwardian
garden, in a spacious position surrounded
by orchards of apples and pears. The very
substantial rock garden, with pools of
water and Japanese influences, was laid
out by Waterers in about 1910. The
formal garden has a series of terraces with

yew topiary in combinations of gold and
green. Beyond are a lake, a stream, good
conifers and rhododendron woods. The
park trees include a venerable, gnarled
Robinia pseudoacacia on the lawn in front
of the house. Behind the house is a
magnificent topiary garden, with
geometric shapes, animals, birds and
Great War regimental badges. Beyond is
the millennium rose garden, pretty with
old and David Austin roses. Everything
has been restored and brought to life
again in recent years, with some good new
plantings. The newest feature (opening in
2006) is the 'mizmaze', a maze composed
of exotic grasses interplanted with
colourful perennials, but designed to look
like the spokes of a wheel. The idea came
from a picture of a mediaeval labyrinth.

🌿 rock garden; topiary; new maze of
grasses & perennials (2005); small
shop; plants for sale; teas.

Owned by Mrs Lesley Dawes
Number of gardeners 2½
Size 4ha (10 acres)
English Heritage Grade II

OLD BUCKHURST
Markbeech, Edenbridge TN8 5PH

Tel: 01342 850825
Location East of village on right-hand side of
road to Chiddingstone Hoath.
Opening hours 11 am – 5.30 pm: 26, 29 & 30 April;
3, 7, 20, 21 & 28 May; 4, 7, 11 & 25 June; 2, 5, 15, 16,
22, 23 & 30 July; 2, 5, 6, 12 & 13 August; 2, 3, 6, 9 &
10 September.
Admission fee Adults £3; Children free.

P WC 🌺

There was nothing but lawns and paving
when the Gladstones started the garden at
Old Buckhurst in 1988. It has been
designed and planted as a series of
compartments, each with its own
character and colour scheme – colours
and textures hold the garden together.
Shrub roses, clematis and foliage plants

are special favourites, but the garden is thickly planted, and intended to have as much interest as possible at every season of the year. A garden to enjoy and learn from.

Owned by Mr & Mrs John Gladstone
Number of gardeners owners only
Size 0.4ha (1 acre)

PENSHURST PLACE
Penshurst, Tonbridge TN11 8DG

Tel: 01892 870307 **Fax:** 01892 879866
www.penshurstplace.com
Location Follow brown tourist signs from A21 Hildenborough exit.
Opening hours 10.30 am - 6 pm; daily; 25 March to 29 October. Plus weekends earlier in March.
Admission fee Gardens only: Adults £6; OAPs £5.50; Children £4.50. RHS members free in April, September & October.

This is an historic garden of great importance: it has substantial genuine Tudor remains. Nevertheless, much of what we see now was developed in the mid-19th century as a re-creation of the ideal Elizabethan garden, divided into small self-contained garden rooms, each with its own style and character. They have been well restored and developed in recent years. A vast Italianate parterre dominates the immediate pleasure garden: it is planted with *Rosa* 'Surrey' – another is planted as a Union Jack. There are borders by Lanning Roper and John Codrington, a 100m bed of peonies, and a garden for the blind, bought off the peg at the Chelsea Flower Show in 1994. One impressive statistic: the garden has over one mile of yew hedging.

roses (mainly modern & climbers); daffodils; good herbaceous borders; formal Italian garden; spring bulbs; tea-room.

Owned by Viscount De L'Isle
Number of gardeners 6
Size 4.4ha (11 acres)
English Heritage Grade I

PORT LYMPNE
Lympne, Hythe CT21 4PD

Tel: 01303 264647 **Fax:** 01303 264944
www.totallywild.net
Location Exit 11 on M20 & follow brown tourist signs.
Opening hours 10 am - 6 pm in summer; 10 am - 5 pm in winter; daily, except 25 December. Last admissions 90 minutes before closing.
Admission fee Adults £13.95; OAPs £11.95; Children £10.95.

Ignore the zoo: Port Lympne is a stylish and luxurious house, with a seriously important 20th-century garden. It was laid out by Philip Tilden for Sir Philip Sassoon in 1911 on the steepest of slopes above Romney Marshes and worked on by Russell Page in the 1950s. The modern approach is nothing if not dramatic – an absolutely straight 100m walk lined with hydrangeas which brings you suddenly to the top of the stupendous, long stone staircase known as the Trojan stairs. Around the front door is a forecourt with 16 statues acquired from the sale at Stowe, in Buckinghamshire, in 1921; castellations in the yew hedges give views to the south. The slopes are terraced into five levels and include a vineyard and 'figyard'. The chess board garden – oblong rather than square – has squares of grass contrasted with beds for bulbs and annual displays: it is matched by a 'striped' garden on the other side of the main terrace. Down one side are the Long Borders, planted as mixtures of shrubs and perennials, and leading to the magnolia walk, the bowling green, the rose terrace, the dahlia terrace and the herbaceous border. Standards of maintenance remain high: a good garden for grandparents who want to see something more than animals.

topiary; good herbaceous borders; bedding out; dahlias; shop; restaurant.

Owned by The John Aspinall Foundation
Number of gardeners 9
Size 6.2ha (15½ acres)

RIVERHILL HOUSE GARDENS
Sevenoaks TN15 0RR

Tel: 01732 452557
Location 2 miles south of Sevenoaks on A225.
Opening hours 11 am – 5 pm; Sundays & Bank Holiday weekends; 2 April to 18 June.
Admission fee Gardens only: Adults £3; Children 50p. House open by appointment to groups.

🅿 🚻 ☕ ♿

Riverhill is a handsome Queen Anne house with grand views over the Weald; the garden suffered badly in the Great Storm of 1987. In the middle of the 19th century it belonged to John Rogers the botanist, who planted many of the surviving conifers and specimen trees. The vast billowing rhododendrons include original introductions by Hooker and Fortune. Rogers's descendants made the rose walk.

🌿 rhododendrons & azaleas; mature conifers; bluebells; tallest *Magnolia* x *soulangeana* (13m) in the British Isles; small gift shop; home-made teas.

Owned by The Rogers Family
Number of gardeners 1
Size 3.2ha (8 acres)
English Heritage Grade II

ROCK FARM
Gibbs Hill, Nettlestead, Maidstone ME18 5HT

Tel & Fax: 01622 812244
Location 1 mile south of Wateringbury, turn right up Gibbs Hill.
Opening hours 11 am – 5 pm; 17 & 20 May; 14, 17, 21, 24 & 28 June; 1, 5 & 8 July. And private visits by appointment.
Admission fee Adults £4; Children free.

🅿 🚻 🌿

Rock Farm is a plantsman's garden, made over many years by a (now retired) nurserywoman on alkaline soil. There are natural springs and ponds, a bog garden, iris beds, interesting trees and shrubs, and a spectacular herbaceous border designed to be at its best in high summer. All is maintained to a very high standard.
Owned by Mrs S.E. Corfe
Number of gardeners owner only
Size 1ha (2½ acres)

ROSEWOOD DAYLILIES
70 Deansway Avenue, Sturry, Canterbury CT2 0NN

Tel: 01227 711071
Location Off to right of Herne Bay Road, the main road leading north out of Sturry.
Opening hours By appointment. Special open day for NCCPG on 22 July (2 pm – 5 pm).
Admission fee Free.

🅿 🌿

Here is a splendid place to see more than 900 different daylilies, especially those bred and introduced since 1970. These include many of the hundreds of modern American hybrids: the owner trials new cultivars and then offers the best for sale. The nursery's list grows every year: a lot of cultivars with an RHS Award of Garden Merit have recently been added, as have many new spider forms and other specialities. It also offers a range of companion plants: agapanthus (80 cvs.), crocosmias (30 cvs.), and hardy geraniums.

🌿 *Hemerocallis; Agapanthus.*

Owned by Chris Searle
NCCPG National Collections *Hemerocallis* cvs. post-1970

SCOTNEY CASTLE GARDEN

Lamberhurst, Tunbridge Wells TN3 8JN

Tel: 01892 891081 **Fax:** 01892 890110
www.nationaltrust.org.uk/scotneycastle
Location On A21, south of Lamberhurst.
Opening hours 11 am – 6 pm; Wednesday –
Sunday & Bank Holiday Mondays; 18 March to 30
October. Plus 5, 6, 12 & 13 March.
Admission fee Adults £5.20; Children £2.60.
Guided tours by arrangement (extra fee).

P WC & ♈ ♣

The house (not open to the public) was
designed by Salvin in the late 1830s: the
quarry where they extracted the stone for
building is now a sheltered woodland dell.
During the 19th century, many specimen
trees were added to the parkland – cypresses,
cedars and wellingtonias: those that
survived the gales of 1987 still give
structure to the gardens in their maturity.
But the slopes between the house and the
moated and ruined castle at the bottom are
covered with ornamental trees and shrubs
planted by Christopher Hussey in the 1950s
– among them are many rhododendrons,
azaleas, hydrangeas, kalmias and maples.
The ruined castle is the focus of the whole
picturesque composition and the way it has
been richly draped in wisteria, clematis,
honeysuckles and roses is both romantic and
photogenic. Among the ruins are a herb
garden and a cottage garden designed by
Lanning Roper in about 1970, surprisingly
appropriate and effective. The views of the
castle as you meander round the edge of the
moat are little short of miraculous.

🌿 woodland garden; plantsman's collection
of plants; rhododendrons; azaleas; water
lilies; wisteria; good autumn colour; plantings in
ruins of 14th-century castle; shop.

Owned by The National Trust
Number of gardeners 4
Size 8ha (20 acres)
English Heritage Grade I

SISSINGHURST CASTLE GARDEN

Sissinghurst, Cranbrook TN17 2AB

Tel: 01580 710700 **Fax:** 01580 710702
www.nationaltrust.org.uk/sissinghurst
Location 1 mile east of Sissinghurst village, ½ mile
off A262. Cross-country footpath from village.
Opening hours 11 am – 6.30 pm; Friday – Tuesday;
18 March to 29 October. Opens at 10 am on
Saturdays, Sundays and Bank Holidays.
Admission fee Adults £7.80; Children £3.50;
Family £20.

P WC & ♈ ♣ ♫

So important, influential and well-known is
Sissinghurst that it comes as a shock to
realise that Harold Nicolson and Vita
Sackville-West began to make the garden
there as recently as 1930. Vita's writings
made it famous right from the beginning so
that it is possible to trace the history of such
features as the white garden in her many
books still in print. Harold Nicolson was a
careful designer who understood the
importance of line and measure: he was very
much a classicist in taste. Vita Sackville-
West was a romantic, exuberant, poetic
plantswoman. It was the combination of
these two complementary talents that made
the garden a source of wonder and
inspiration. Sissinghurst is now part of every
English gardener's education, and one to
which it is important to return time and
again. The garden is always changing and
developing. It was the Nicolsons' intention
that the garden should continue to develop
after they gave it to the National Trust, and
this principle – that the garden must be kept
up to date with new plants – is inherent in
the way that it has been managed. The
design is unaltered and unalterable, and the
plantings continue to be governed by the
Gertrude Jekyll principles of which
Sissinghurst is a supremely beautiful
interpretation. But the plants are always
changing and Sissinghurst therefore remains
an influential plantsman's garden, too.

🌿 influential 20th-century garden; roses
(mainly old-fashioned); plantsman's

collection of plants; herbs; good herbaceous borders; National Trust gift shop; self-service restaurant; coffee shop.

Owned by The National Trust
Number of gardeners 8
Size 2.2ha (5½ acres)
English Heritage Grade I

SQUERRYES COURT
Westerham TN16 1SJ

Tel: 01959 562345 **Fax:** 01959 565949
www.squerryes.co.uk
Location ½ mile from A25, signed from Westerham.
Opening hours 12 noon - 5.30 pm; Wednesdays, Thursdays, Sundays & Bank Holiday Mondays; April to September.
Admission fee Garden only: Adults £4; OAPs £3.50; Children £2. (2005 prices.)

P ⚬ WC ⚭ ⚮ ✕ ⚯

The gardens have been excellently restored with advice from Tom Wright since 1987, guided by a Badeslade plan of the original garden made in 1719, before they were landscaped later in the century. The main feature is a formal garden behind the house, where box-edged beds are filled with santolina, lavender and sage, alongside the beautifully planted Edwardian borders. The outline of the old formal garden is still apparent in the terracing and paths, and new borders have been added for year-round interest. The modern design and planting are inevitably a compromise, but Squerryes is a place of great beauty and variety. Beyond the formal gardens is a woodland garden planted with rhododendrons and azaleas, and it is all surrounded by an 18th-century park.

parterres; topiary; roses (mainly old-fashioned); herbaceous borders; formal design; gazebo; dovecote; woodland walks; lake; small shop in house; teas & light refreshments.

Owned by J. & A. Warde
Number of gardeners 1, plus 2 part-time

Size 10ha (25 acres)
English Heritage Grade II

STARBOROUGH NURSERY
Starborough Road, Marsh Green, Edenbridge TN8 5RB

Tel: 01732 865614 **Fax:** 01732 862166
Location On B2028 Edenbridge to Lingfield road.
Opening hours 9.30 am - 4 pm; daily, except Wednesdays & Sundays. Closed in January, July & August.

P WC ⚘

Starborough has for long been an important nursery for its wide range of trees and shrubs and, since it took over G. Reuthe Ltd, in the 1990s, for its rhododendrons and azaleas too. Its list of liquidambars, cornus, camellias and magnolias is particularly good.
Owned by Mr & Mrs C.B. Tomlin

STONEACRE
Otham, Maidstone ME15 8RS

Tel: 01622 862871 **Fax:** 01622 862157
www.nationaltrust.org.uk
Location 1 mile south of A20; north end of Otham village.
Opening hours 2 pm - 6 pm (last admissions 5 pm); Wednesdays, Saturdays & Bank Holiday Mondays; 18 March to 11 October.
Admission fee Adults £3; Children £1.50; Groups £2.50.

P ⚭ ⚘

Stoneacre is an important and influential garden because the tenant until 2000 was Rosemary Alexander, Principal of the English Gardening School at the Chelsea Physic Garden. It was where she worked out her ideas and showed her students how the principles of design and planting look 'on the ground'. The present tenants came to gardening from the fashion world and have made considerable alterations to the plantings around the house. They have incorporated their passion for strong textures and dark subtle colouring – for example, by contrasting dainty grasses with large-leaved shrubs. The old *potager* has been transformed into an intimate green-and-white garden. The back courtyard has an unusual collection of plants and flowers grouped around the doors. It is still one of the most exciting new gardens in southern England, and in perfect harmony with the Tudorised house.

 spring bulbs; autumn colour; strong design.

Owned by The National Trust
Number of gardeners 2

TILE BARN NURSERY
Standen Street, Iden Green, Benenden TN17 4LB

Tel & Fax: 01580 240221
www.tilebarn-cyclamen.co.uk
Location 2 miles south of Benenden; turn left at crossroads in Iden Green.
Opening hours 9 am - 5 pm, Wednesday - Saturday.

This is a splendid garden-nursery devoted to one genus – *Cyclamen*. Cyclamen are everywhere: they have spread through the lawns and into the drive, as well as under the shelter trees, shrubs and hedges. In the glasshouses are rows and rows of every imaginable hardy species and cultivar of cyclamen of different ages, all pot-grown and all of flowering size – a wonderful sight from August to April. Visitors will also find pots of some other unusual bulbs species, particularly the smaller, daintier colchicums, crocuses, fritillarias, snowflakes and narcissi.
Owned by Peter & Liz Moore

WALMER CASTLE & GARDENS
Kingsdown Road, Walmer, Deal CT14 7LJ

Tel: 01304 364288 **Fax:** 01304 364826
Location Follow brown tourist signs.
Opening hours 10 am - 6 pm (4 pm on Saturdays in March); daily, but Wednesday - Sunday only in October; March to October. Closed when the Lord Warden is in residence, 7 to 9 July.
Admission fee Adults £6.20; Concessions £4.70; Children £3.10.

The gardens at Walmer Castle are well worth a visit, partly for their horticultural interest and partly for their many historical associations – William Pitt, the Duke of Wellington and Winston Churchill were all Wardens of the Cinque Ports. The castle looks onto the Broad Walk, 100m long, on either side of a wide path backed by massive mature yew hedges (3m tall and 2m wide), and lined with fine herbaceous borders. Beyond are a croquet lawn, magnificent 19th-century terraces, and Penelope Hobhouse's new Queen Elizabeth the Queen Mother's Garden. To the north of the Broad Walk is the Kitchen Garden – an enclosed orchard with espaliered fruit trees, a cutting garden and glasshouses. Further away are drifts of daffodils, a lawnful of specimen trees planted by famous visitors from the 19th century onwards, a wildflower meadow, a thickly wooded quarry and a holm oak avenue planted in 1866.

magnificent old yew hedges; new garden by Penelope Hobhouse; English Heritage shop; tea-room.

Owned by English Heritage
Number of gardeners 4
Size 3.2ha (8 acres)
English Heritage Grade II

WAYSTRODE MANOR
Spode Lane, Cowden TN8 7HW

Tel: 01342 850695
Location In village.
Opening hours 2 pm - 5.30 pm; 17 & 21 May, 11 & 21 June & 5 July.
Admission fee Adults £3; Children 50p.

P WC & 🌹 ☕

The garden at Waystrode Manor has been developed over the last 35 years. You approach it along an avenue of pink horse-chestnuts, but the garden has a good collection of plants and is laid out in the cottage style. Highlights include a bog garden, an old-fashioned rose garden, a white garden, irises, geraniums, ornamental trees and tender plants put out for the summer.

good borders; interesting plants; unusual trees; small shop; plant stall; teas & cakes.

Owned by Mrs Jill Wright
Number of gardeners 2
Size 3.2ha (8 acres)

LANCASHIRE, MERSEYSIDE & GREATER MANCHESTER

There are few historic gardens in this industrial corner of the North-West, but several public parks whose importance is both historical and contemporary: Sefton Park in Liverpool was designed by Edouard André, Birkenhead Park by Sir Joseph Paxton, and Heaton Park in Manchester by William Emes. The public gardens at the seaside resorts of Blackpool and Southport are famous for their summer displays. Few private gardens are open to the public, though the National Gardens Scheme has in several villages managed to persuade a cluster of gardens to open simultaneously and make up a good afternoon's visiting. Myerscough College near Preston is a

RHS Partner College, with lectures and workshops all through the year. It also has a National Collection of *Eryngium* and is hoping for provisional acceptance for its collection of *Aesculus* (horse-chestnut) species and cultivars, of which it holds around 60. There is a handful of other National Collections in the three counties, but this is not a corner of England with any established interest in plants apart, perhaps, from alpines: Reginald Kaye at Carnforth and Holden Clough near Clitheroe are both long-established nurseries specialising in plants for cold climates. The new garden of the Lennox-Boyds at Gresgarth is a rising star.

CROXTETH HALL & COUNTRY PARK

Croxteth Hall Lane, Liverpool L12 0HB

Tel: 0151 228 5311 **Fax:** 0151 228 2817
www.croxteth.co.uk
Location Muirhead Avenue East.
Opening hours 10.30 am - 5 pm; daily; Easter to September.
Admission fee Walled garden: Adults £1.40; OAPs & Children 80p. Grounds: free.

🅿 ⬅ 🚻 ♿ 🌿 ♣ ☕

Very much a public amenity, Croxteth Hall has a fine woodland trail along the River Alt, but the main interest for gardeners is the Victorian walled garden. This aims to show visitors what they can achieve at home. There are lines of trained fruit trees, growing either against the walls or free-standing, a large

vegetable garden (lots of varieties grown from the HDRA), an area for soft fruit, a herb garden, and a mushroom house – to remind people how mushrooms were once cultivated in grand gardens. These are interplanted with more ornamental features – a bedding display, a rose garden, some herbaceous borders and the collection of fuchsias. There are also working greenhouses and some beehives, which add to the garden's interest.

🌿 herbs; plants under glass; fruit; good herbaceous borders; current holder of Sandford Award; shop; cafeteria.

Owned by City of Liverpool
Number of gardeners 5
Size 1.5ha (3¾ acres) walled garden
NCCPG National Collections *Fuchsia* (hardy)
English Heritage Grade II

DUNHAM MASSEY
Altrincham WA14 4SJ

Tel: 0161 941 1025 **Fax:** 0161 929 7508
www.nationaltrust.org.uk
Location 3 miles south-west of Altrincham off
A56, well signed (Dunham Massey Hall & Park).
Opening hours 11 am – 5.30 pm (4.30 pm from 24
October); daily; 25 March to 29 October.
Admission fee Gardens only: Adults £4.50;
Children £2.25. Car park £4.

🅿 🆆🅲 ♿ ❀ ● ⊕

Dunham Massey's 250 acres include an
ancient deer park, a medieval moat made
into a lake in the 18th century, an
Elizabethan mount, an 18th-century
orangery, a pump house and some early
landscape avenues. All remain as features of
the grounds, but the National Trust has
decided to major on its even more
interesting Victorian relics – evergreen
shrubberies, a bark house, ferns and
colourful bedding-out schemes. Serpentine
paths lead between borders thickly planted
for texture and colour. The bog garden and
moss garden take advantage of the unusual
opportunities of the site. The woodlands
are planted with Professor Pratt's azaleas,
cardiocrinums, meconopsis, and more than
60 different hydrangeas. There are more
unusual trees in the extensive lawns. The
result is a potent cross-section of historical
and modern styles with a solid core of
Victorian excellence, while the standard of
maintenance is one of the highest in any
National Trust garden.

🌿 topiary; good herbaceous borders;
hydrangeas; skimmias; Edwardian
parterre; garden shop; large restaurant.

Owned by The National Trust
Number of gardeners 5
Size 10ha (25 acres) of garden & 90ha (222 acres)
of park
English Heritage Grade II*

FLETCHER MOSS
BOTANICAL GARDENS
Mill Gate Lane, Didsbury M20 8SD

Tel: 0161 434 1877
Location In East Didsbury, off A5145.
Opening hours 8 am (9 am at weekends & Bank
Holidays) – dusk; daily; all year.
Admission fee Free.

🅿 ⊲ 🆆🅲 ♿ ✕ ⊕

Fletcher Moss is a model municipal botanic
garden, beautifully maintained but open
free to the public. In the rock garden,
which is substantially constructed on three
levels with a pool at the bottom, is a rich
collection of alpine plants, small conifers,
maples and aquatics. The woodland areas
have excellent autumn colour, but are
almost as good in spring.

🌿 rock garden; mature conifers; bulbs;
heathers; rhododendrons; cafeteria.

Owned by Manchester City Council
Size 8.5ha (21 acres)

HOGHTON TOWER
Hoghton, Preston PR5 0SH

Tel: 01254 852986 **Fax:** 01254 852109
www.hoghtontower.co.uk
Location A675 midway between Preston &
Blackburn.
Opening hours 11 am – 4 pm; Monday – Thursday;
July to September. 1 pm – 5 pm; Sundays; July to
September. Also Bank Holiday Mondays from
Easter to August.
Admission fee Adults £3; Children (under 5) free.

🅿 🆆🅲 ● ⊕

A series of spacious courtyards and walled
gardens surround this fierce castellated
house which is approached up a long
avenue. Its garden is not among the
greatest, but the setting is impressive and
there are fine spring walks in the
rhododendron woods below.

🌿 good herbaceous borders;
rhododendrons & azaleas; gift shop;
tea-room.

GRESGARTH HALL
Caton, Lancaster LA2 9NB

Tel: 01524 771838 **Fax:** 01524 771281
www.arabellalennoxboyd.com/gresgarth
Location ½ mile south of Caton.
Opening hours 11 am - 5 pm; 9 April, 14 May, 11 &
25 June, 9 July, 13 August, 10 September & 8
October.
Admission fee Adults £5; Children free.

P WC & ❦ ♣ ☞

Mark and Arabella Lennox-Boyd
bought Gresgarth Hall near Lancaster
in 1978. Arabella is a distinguished garden
designer, with a wonderful eye for structure,
line and colour. The main formal gardens
lie to the side of the house – terraces
elegantly laid out with octagonal platforms,
angled staircases and neat box edgings.
Much of the planting here is white:
Clematis 'Duchess of Edinburgh' and C.
'Henryi' grow against the retaining wall.
Here and throughout the garden are
magnificent hellebores, all the best modern
cultivars from Ashwood Nurseries, Helen
Ballard, Elizabeth Strangman and Will
McLewin in Cheshire. The surrounding
borders are all in yellow and orange:
rudbeckias, *Euphorbia dulcis* 'Chameleon',
and annual sunflowers. The main
herbaceous border is in pastel shades, and
designed to flower from April to October –
ending with a splendid show of Michaelmas
daisies. But the herbaceous plantings are
constantly changing as Arabella
experiments and tests out new ideas and
new combinations. The terraces run down
to the lake, which the Lennox-Boyds re-
landscaped. The damp border on its far side
has glorious blue meconopsis, candelabra
primulas in vast drifts, gunneras for late-
summer effect and both species of
Lysichiton. A handsome bridge crosses the
river to a long woodland garden which
stretches along the valley bottom for about
400 metres. The principal underplanting is
of winter-flowering witch-hazels –
Hamamelis 'Pallida', *H.* 'Diane' and many
new cultivars: they now have more than 50
different cultivars. The hillside across the
river is laid out with an extensive collection
of young rhododendrons and azaleas. The
Lennox-Boyds have also planted a very
large number of magnolias (over 300
different cultivars), an avenue of filberts
and cobs along the outside of the walled
garden and a substantial group of the
different cultivars of lilac. Microhabitats
support some surprisingly tender plants.
Drimys lanceolata and *Olearia scillonensis*
both grow out in the open: so does the
sweet-scented *Daphne bholua*, which has
started to seed around – there are over 60
bushes now, some grown from Sir Peter
Smithers's garden in Switzerland and others
of their own raising. Among the rarest
plants are a fine *Emmenopterys henryi*,
micropropagated by Kew. More and more
plants are being added from seed collected
all over the world. But it is above all the
energy and the scale of the Lennox-Boyds'
endeavours which create the greatest
impression. They have successfully
combined good design, passionate
plantsmanship and a fine eye for decoration
in a uniquely romantic natural setting.
There can be no doubt that Gresgarth is
one of the greatest gardens of our times.

good design; colour plantings;
rhododendrons; plant sales; teas &
cakes.

Owned by The Hon. Sir Mark & Lady Lennox-Boyd
Size 5ha (12 acres)

Owned by Hoghton Tower Preservation Trust
English Heritage Grade II

HOLDEN CLOUGH NURSERY
Holden, Bolton by Bowland, Clitheroe
BB7 4PF

Tel: 01200 447615 **Fax:** 01200 447197
www.holdencloughnursery.co.uk
Location 8 miles north-east of Clitheroe, off A59.
Opening hours 9 am – 5 pm; Monday – Friday;
March to October. Plus Saturdays all year. Other
times by appointment.
Admission fee Free.

P & ❀

This long-established working nursery
(founded in 1927) has a large range of
interesting alpines, perennials, crocosmias
(including some new cultivars), dwarf
conifers, shrubs, ferns, grasses and foliage
plants. It is well known at shows, all over
the country. One of its best introductions is
the hardy and vigorous hybrid *Iris* 'Holden
Clough'. Others, now available once again,
are the rare and beautiful *Astilbe* 'Holden
Clough' and the double-flowered
Rhodohypoxis 'Holden Rose'. The display
garden is still expanding, with new
plantings and a new alpine bed for 2006.
Owned by Peter Foley
Size 0.8ha (2 acres)

LEIGHTON HALL
Carnforth LA5 9ST

Tel: 01524 734474 **Fax:** 01524 720357
www.leightonhall.co.uk
Location Signed from A6 junction with M6.
Opening hours 2 pm – 5 pm; Tuesday – Friday &
Bank Holiday Sundays & Mondays; May to
September. Plus all Sundays in August. Open at
12.30 am in August.
Admission fee Adults £5.50; OAPs £5.

P WC & ❀ ❀ ☕

The handsome semi-castellated house at
Leighton is set in lush parkland with the
Lakeland Fells as a backdrop: the Victorian
conservatory to the side of the house has
just been restored. The main garden
features are in the 19th-century walled
garden, whose formal paths contrast with
the exuberant informality of the planting.
Here are herbaceous borders, a herb
garden, fruit trees, a vegetable plot and
masses of climbing roses – as well as the
unusual gravel maze.

🌿 roses (mainly old-fashioned); herbs;
fruit; good herbaceous borders;
'caterpillar' path maze; Victorian conservatory;
gift shop; tea-room.

Owned by R.G. Reynolds
Number of gardeners 1½
Size 2ha (5 acres)

RUFFORD OLD HALL
Rufford, Ormskirk L40 1SG

Tel: 01704 821254 **Fax:** 01704 823823
www.nationaltrust.org.uk
Location 7 miles north of Ormskirk on A59.
Opening hours 11 am - 5.30 pm; Saturday –
Wednesday & Good Friday; 25 March to 29
October.
Admission fee Garden only: Adults £2.80;
Children £1.30.

P ⬦ WC & ❀ ☕

One of the National Trust's most successful
re-creations, the gardens are laid out in the
Victorian style around a remarkable 15th-
century timber-framed house. The garden
had little character when the National
Trust took over, but Graham Stuart
Thomas was charged with adding exotic
shrubs and plants to make it more
interesting to visitors. The results include
box and yew topiary, a mixed border of
roses and herbaceous plants, and an
explosion of crocuses, daffodils, bluebells
and rhododendrons in spring.

🌿 roses (mainly old-fashioned);
rhododendrons & azaleas; good
herbaceous borders; National Trust shop; lunches
& teas.

Owned by The National Trust
Number of gardeners 1
Size 5.6ha (14 acres)

SPEKE HALL
The Walk, Liverpool L24 1XD

Tel: 0151 427 7231 **Fax:** 0151 427 9860
www.nationaltrust.org.uk
Location 1 mile off A561, surrounded by Liverpool Airport.
Opening hours 11 am - 5.30 pm (dusk from mid-October to March); Wednesday - Sunday & Bank Holiday Mondays and Tuesdays between 18 July and 10 September. Grounds closed 1 January & 24-26 & 31 December.
Admission fee Grounds and Home farm only: Adults £3.50; Children £1.80.
P WC &. ᗡ

Speke is an oasis among the concrete deserts of Merseyside's suburbs. At its heart is a substantial half-timbered house, dating back to the 14th century and surrounded by a moat, now dry. The garden is mainly modern, a sympathetic restoration of the one which a rich Liverpool merchant made in the mid-19th century. On the south lawn, three Victorian island beds have recently been remade. The nearby rose garden was planted in 1984 with shrubs and floribundas. All around are rhododendrons, daffodils and bluebells in spring.

roses; spring bulbs; summer borders; stream garden; restaurant.

Owned by The National Trust
Number of gardeners 3
Size 7ha (17½ acres)
English Heritage Grade II

LEICESTERSHIRE

One of the reasons why there are so few historic gardens in Leicestershire (no Grade I gardens and only two Grade II*) is that much of the county was open and unenclosed until the latter half of the 18th century. Even today, it is not as rich in interesting gardens as its neighbours, Northamptonshire and Warwickshire. However, the National Gardens Scheme offers a respectable number of gardens to visit in its Yellow Book, and the first-rate gardens at Wartnaby and Long Close show just how much can be grown by an adventurous plantsman – so does the excellent University of Leicester Botanic Garden. Leicestershire has some good garden centres, and a handful of first-rate specialist nurseries. Brooksby Melton College is a RHS Partner College with a fine teaching garden and collection of plants. It also has two National Collections: *Liriope* and *Ophiopogon*. Contrary to local belief, there is no such county as Rutland: it was dissolved in 1974 and absorbed into Leicestershire until eventually it re-emerged as a unitary authority. We include its gardens here for convenience.

BARNSDALE GARDENS
The Avenue, Exton, Oakham LE15 8AH

Tel: 01572 813200 **Fax:** 01572 813346
www.barnsdalegardens.co.uk
Location The Avenue is on south-west edge of Exton.
Opening hours 9 am – 5 pm (7 pm from June to August); daily; March to October. 10 am – 4 pm; daily; November to February. Last admissions 2 hours before closure. Closed on 22 & 25 December.
Admission fee Adults £6; Concessions £5; Children £2; Family £15; Groups £4.50. RHS members free.

P WC & ✿ ● ✕ ⬩

Barnsdale was famous for 20 years as Geoff Hamilton's BBC *Gardeners' World* garden. Within it are 37 smaller individual gardens and garden features, laid out and maintained with the same intention – to encourage people to make the most of their opportunities as garden-owners. The gardens are of every kind. Some have descriptive names like the Tranquil Garden and the Town Paradise: others are more specific like the Plantsman's Garden, the Fruit Orchard, the Rose Garden, the Stream and Bog Garden. But for many visitors the most interesting are those which match their own particular circumstances and inspire them to become better gardeners – the Cottage Gardens, the Small Town Garden, the Ornamental Kitchen Garden and the Allotment Garden. All are maintained to the highest standard and continue to educate, delight and inspire. The attached specialist nursery sells over 1,800 different plants, many of them rare and unusual. Owned and run by Geoff Hamilton's son and daughter-in-law, its policy is to offer the widest possible choice of good plants to its customers. There will be seven RHS Special Events at Barnsdale Gardens in 2006; details from 020 7821 3408.

✿ gift shop; nursery; licensed coffee shop.

Owned by Sue & Nick Hamilton
Number of gardeners 6
Size 3.2ha (8 acres)

BELVOIR CASTLE
Belvoir, Grantham NG32 1PD

Tel: 01476 871002 **Fax:** 01476 871018
www.belvoircastle.com
Location 6 miles west of Grantham.
Opening hours 11 am – 5 pm; daily; 1 April to 30 September.
Admission fee Gardens: Adults £5. RHS members free (only at some times).

Belvoir has formal gardens along the Victorian terraces beneath the castle, and a Broad Walk overlooking the newly restored 19th-century rose garden. Some way off is a hedged enclosure with seven statues by Caius Cibber. The Spring Garden, a pretty woodland garden, has recently been restored to its early 19th-century form.
woodland garden; roses (mainly modern); tallest bird cherry *Prunus avium* (28m) and yew tree *Taxus baccata* (29m) in the British Isles; gift shop; refreshments: lunches and teas; picnic site.

Owned by The Duke of Rutland
Number of gardeners 4
English Heritage Grade II

GOSCOTE NURSERIES LTD
Syston Road, Cossington LE7 4UZ

Tel: 01509 812121 **Fax:** 01509 814231
www.goscote.co.uk
Location 5 miles north of Leicester, on B5328.
Opening hours 9 am – 5 pm; Monday – Saturday. 10 am – 5 pm; Sundays. Closes at 4.30 pm in winter and between Christmas & New Year.
Admission fee Free.

Goscote has a wide range of reasonably priced plants of all types – more than 1,500 different kinds are propagated on-site. They offer an extensive collection of trees and shrubs, including acers, azaleas, clematis, conifers and rhododendrons, many of them rare or unusual but suitable to the cold Midlands. Plants can also be seen in the show gardens, laid out as island beds and borders, with a rock garden, a water garden and a 20m pergola. The website is helpful and comprehensive.
 mature show gardens.

Owned by Frank James Toone
Size 0.3ha (¾ acre)

THE HERB NURSERY
Thistleton, Oakham LE15 7RE

Tel: 01572 767658 **Fax:** 01572 768021
www.herbnursery.co.uk
Location In middle of village.
Opening hours 9 am – 6 pm (or dusk, if earlier); daily; closed from Christmas to New Year. Open weekend: 17 & 18 June.
Admission fee Donation.

This family-run nursery lists nearly 500 herbs and wildflower plants, with a special emphasis upon lavender, mint and thyme. The range of scented-leaf pelargoniums is particularly good (80+ cultivars), and there is a extensive range of cottage garden plants. The demonstration beds and borders around the nursery are a bonus. Ask to see the new knot garden.
Owned by Peter & Christine Bench

KAYES GARDEN NURSERY
1700 Melton Road, Rearsby, Leicester LE7 4YR

Tel: 01664 424578
Location On A607, north-east of Leicester.
Opening hours 10 am – 5 pm (10 am – 12 noon on Sundays); Tuesday – Sunday; March to October. By appointment from November to February.
Admission fee Garden: £2; Nursery: free.

This popular nursery has an excellent,

mature display garden, densely planted with a wide range of interesting plants. It also opens for the National Gardens Scheme. The nursery's specialities are hardy herbaceous plants, grasses, aquatics and climbers. Hazel Kaye has a plantsman's eye for quality, and the list includes many of the best forms of a wide range of plants.

 eryngiums; tradescantias; teas.

Owned by Hazel Kaye
Number of gardeners 2
Size 0.6ha (1½ acres)
NCCPG National Collections *Tradescantia* Andersoniana Group

LONG CLOSE

Main Street, Woodhouse Eaves, Loughborough LE12 8RZ

Tel: 01509 890616 (daytime)
www.longclose.org.uk
Location 4 miles south of Loughborough.
Opening hours 9.30 am - 5.30 pm; Tuesday - Saturday & Bank Holiday Mondays; March to October, but closed in August. Groups also welcome at other times by appointment. For NGS: 2 pm - 5.30 pm on 2 April (plant fair), 2 pm - 6 pm on 28 May (plants for sale). Also 6 pm - 8.30 pm on 11 May (£5).
Admission fee Adults £3; Children 50p. Tickets from Pene Crafts Gift Shop, opposite (open 9.30 am - 1 pm and 2 pm - 5.30 pm). Groups & on Sundays pay at garden.

This is a plantsman's garden, made over many years and now magnificently mature. Some of the plants might be thought too tender for so far north, and it has been called 'a Cornish garden in Leicestershire'. The entrance courtyard has *Crinum* x *powellii* 'Album', *Sophora tetraptera* and *Clematis armandii*. As you go round the side of the house, suddenly a spacious series of terraced gardens opens out below you, lined by clouds of rhododendrons and venerable conifers. The terraced lawns lead to a fine woodland garden, underplanted with bulbs, magnolias, camellias and massed rhododendrons and azaleas. Elsewhere are good herbaceous plantings, a thicket of *Prunus tenella*, penstemons (quite a collection), a box-edged *potager*, a very handsome, bulging, pendulous ash *Fraxinus excelsior* 'Pendula', aged wisterias, *Azara microphylla* 6m tall, Italian cypresses *Cupressus sempervirens* Stricta Group, a stream and pond thickly planted with both species of *Lysichiton*, and *Lathraea clandestina* spreading upon the roots of an old poplar. Soaring above are huge English oaks, and arborescent hawthorns (*Crataegus monogyna*) as much as 20m high. The whole garden is run organically.

woodland garden; rhododendrons; azaleas; spring bulbs; lots of other interesting plants; plants for sale, especially penstemons; tea & coffee; refreshments for groups by arrangement; teas on Sundays.

Owned by John Oakland & Pene Johnson
Size 2ha (5 acres) plus 1.2-ha (3-acre) meadow

UNIVERSITY OF LEICESTER BOTANIC GARDEN

Beaumont Hall, Stoughton Drive, Oadby LE2 2NA

Tel: 0116 271 7725
www.le.ac.uk/biology/botanicgarden/
Location 3 miles south of Leicester on A6 London Road opposite racecourse: visitor entrance at The Knoll, Glebe Road.
Opening hours 10 am - 4 pm; Monday - Friday; all year. Plus Saturdays & Sundays from 18 March to 12 November. Closed 1 January, 25 & 26 December. Special Open Days: 11 am - 4 pm; 2 & 30 July & 3 September.
Admission fee Free, but charge for special events.

The University of Leicester Botanic Garden moved to its present site in 1947. It fills the grounds surrounding four houses, which were built early in the 20th century and are now used as student residences. The four (once separate) gardens have been merged into a single entity, the University Botanic Garden with some 16 acres. They now support a wide variety of plants from historic trees to an 1980s ecological meadow. A pretty Edwardian pergola draped with roses, a well-planted rock garden and a splendid display of hardy fuchsias from the National Collection all add to its interest. In 1997 the garden opened an out-station at Knighton, known as the Attenborough Arboretum. Though its plantings are still few and the trees very young, it is designed to display the native tree flora of England in an historical sequence of arrival dates – ending with beech (*Fagus sylvatica*) after the last Ice Age.

rock garden; rhododendrons & azaleas; plants under glass; mature conifers; cacti; succulents; heathers; fuchsias.

Owned by The University of Leicester
Number of gardeners 5
Size 6.4ha (16 acres)
NCCPG National Collections *Aubrieta; Chamaecyparis lawsoniana; Fuchsia; Skimmia*

WARREN HILLS COTTAGE
Warren Hills Road, Coalville LE67 4UY

Tel: 01530 812350
www.warrenhills.co.uk
Location On B587 near the schools on Copt Oak to Whitwick road.
Opening hours 12 noon – 5 pm; 7 May, 4 June, 16 July (plant fair) & 20 August. And by appointment; groups welcome. All for NGS.
Admission fee Adults £2; Children 50p.

This maturing garden is attached to a small nursery specialising in hardy plants, many of them unusual. The owner describes it as 'a plantaholic's garden', planted to provide year-round interest. The main feature is the collection of over 55 different astrantias, each growing in its own labelled bed. Other features include hellebores, bulbs and early perennials underscoring the rhododendrons. There have been extensive new plantings recently. A garden to watch.

astrantias; campanulas; penstemons; salvias; cream teas on open days.

Owned by Graham Waters
Number of gardeners 2 part-time
Size 0.8ha (2 acres)
NCCPG National Collections *Astrantia*

WARTNABY GARDENS
Wartnaby, Melton Mowbray LE14 3HY

Tel: 01664 822549 **Fax:** 01664 822231
www.wartnabygardenlabels.co.uk
Location 3 miles north of Melton Mowbray on A606. Left at A6 Kettley, then 1 mile.
Opening hours Not available as we went to press. 9.30 am – 12.30 pm; Tuesdays; April to July. And parties by appointment.
Admission fee Adults £2.50; Children free. (2005 prices.) RHS Members free.

Wartnaby is the garden of someone who loves roses and is prepared to make them one of the principal elements of her garden design: the result is one of the best modern examples of how to grow roses in mixed borders. Even in the so-called rose garden, the roses do not dominate: they are interplanted instead with other shrubs, like ceanothus, hebes and tree peonies, and underplanted with geraniums and bulbs. Foliage, shapes, colours and textures take over when the roses are not in flower. The long central path in the substantial kitchen garden is flanked by massed plantings of hybrid musks, including 'Felicia', 'Prosperity' and 'Pink Prosperity', underplanted with the grey-leaved *Stachys byzantina* and *Lychnis flos-*

jovis, and edged with lavender and box. Recent developments include spring plantings around the ponds and pools in the woodland and a new walk through the young arboretum. Wartnaby is a garden of enormous interest and charm.

🌿 roses (mainly old-fashioned) used in mixed borders; fruit; fine collection of trees; colour borders; many new features; refreshments.

Owned by Lady King
Size 2ha (5 acres)

WHATTON HOUSE
Long Whatton, Loughborough LE12 5BG

Tel & Fax: 01509 842268
www.whattongardens.co.uk
Location 3 miles from Jct 24, Kegworth A6 towards Hathern.
Opening hours 11 am – 4 pm; Sunday – Friday; March to September. Groups welcome by arrangement.
Admission fee Adults £2.50; Children free.

🅿 ♿ 🚾 ♿ 🌾 ☕

The garden at Whatton was started in 1880, and many of the older features date from about 1900, but there has been much replanting over the years, especially recently. A rose garden, a fine herbaceous border and some magnificent specimen trees are among the attractions. It is particularly interesting in spring when the bulbs and flowering shrubs are in full display.

🌿 roses (ancient & modern); good herbaceous borders; arboretum; climbing plants; bark temple; canyon garden; bulbs; teas on Sunday afternoons.

Owned by Lord Crawshaw
Number of gardeners 2
Size 6ha (15 acres)
English Heritage Grade II

LINCOLNSHIRE

Lincolnshire, with which we include what was for a while south Humberside, has long been known for its horticultural industry based on bulb-growing, and it still has a high number of producers, both wholesale and retail. The show garden at Springfields is one of the great attractions of Lincolnshire in spring. The county has its fair share of important historic gardens: Belton House and Grimsthorpe Castle are both open to the public, though the third Grade I garden at Brocklesby Park (Capability Brown, Humphry Repton and Reginald Blomfield all worked there) remains strictly private. The National Gardens Scheme has a fair number of gardens opening for charity and the county is blessed with several specialist nurseries of national importance. In addition to the alpine experts Pottertons Nursery near Caistor, there are two nurseries with significant National Collections – the fuchsia enthusiast Kathleen Muncaster on the north-west outskirts of Gainsborough and the auricula specialists Martin Nest Nurseries to the east of the same town. RHS members have free access to Normanby Hall Country Park, one of the most interesting restoration projects on the East Coast of England.

BAYTREE NURSERIES

High Road, Weston, Spalding PE12 6JU

Tel: 01406 370242 **Fax:** 01406 372829
www.baytree-gardencentre.com
Location 1½ miles east of Spalding, on A151.
Opening hours 9 am – 6 pm; summer. 9 am – 5 pm; winter. Closed for Easter Day, Christmas Day & Boxing Day.

Baytree won the Garden Centre of Excellence Award some years ago: in 2000 it also won the growers' Retailer of the Year Award. Its six hectares include a pets and aquatic department, a leisure complex devoted to selling garden furniture and an owl centre. But it also aims to carry the largest selection of bulbs available at retail level anywhere in the country and a very large stock of plants, many of them grown on-site. Roses are a speciality: Baytree lists over 300 cultivars including some which it has bred and introduced itself.

 self-service licensed restaurant.

Owned by Reinhard Biehler
Size 6.2ha (15½ acres)

BELTON HOUSE

Grantham NG32 2LS

Tel: 01476 566116 **Fax:** 01476 579071
www.nationaltrust.org.uk
Location 3 miles north-east of Grantham on A607.
Opening hours 11 am (10.30 am in August) – 5.30 pm; Wednesday – Sunday & Bank Holiday Mondays; 25 March to 29 October. Plus 12 noon – 4 pm; Friday – Sunday; 3 November to 17 December. Closed on 15 July.
Admission fee Adults £8; Children £4.50.

Grandeur and amenity go hand in hand at Belton. There are 1,000 acres of wooded deer park, a Wyattville orangery, a Dutch garden and an Italian garden with statues and parterres. But the adventure playground and other facilities make it popular with all ages.

woodland garden; topiary; snowdrops; daffodils; bluebells; good herbaceous borders; biggest sugar maple Acer saccharum in the British Isles; gift shop; lunches, teas, licensed restaurant.

Owned by The National Trust
Number of gardeners 4
Size 14ha (35 acres)
English Heritage Grade I

DODDINGTON HALL
Doddington, Lincoln LN6 4RU

Tel: 01522 694308 **Fax:** 01522 682584
www.doddingtonhall.com
Location Signed off A46 Lincoln bypass.
Opening hours 1 pm – 5 pm; Sundays & Bank
Holiday Mondays; 19 February to 30 September.
Plus Wednesdays from May to September.
Gardens open at 12 noon from May onwards.
Admission fee Garden only: Adults £3.80;
Children £1.90. RHS members free from February
to June.

🅿 🆆 ♿ ✂ ⬭

Doddington is a ravishing Elizabethan
house around which successive generations
have made a successful Tudor-style garden.
The owners keep it simple and formal at
the front, but in the walled garden (thickly
and richly planted) are Edwardian knots
and parterres, a modern herb garden and
pleached hornbeams. Wonderfully
harmonious and strongly recommended in
early summer. There will be three RHS
Special Events at Doddington Hall in
2006; details from 020 7821 3408.
good herbaceous borders; long
succession of spring bulbs; irises;
peonies; box-edged parterres; topiary; tea shop.

Owned by Antony Jarvis
Number of gardeners 1
Size 2.4ha (6 acres)
English Heritage Grade II*

EASTON WALLED GARDENS
Easton, Grantham NG33 5AP

Tel: 01476 530063 **Fax:** 01476 550116
www.eastonwalledgardens.co.uk
Location Between A1 & B6403, 2 miles north of
Colsterworth.
Opening hours 11 am – 3 pm; daily; 11 to 19
February for snowdrops. 11 am – 4 pm;
Wednesdays, Fridays, Sundays & Bank Holiday
Mondays; 2 April to 29 September. For NGS: 7
June.

Admission fee Adults £4; Children free. Coaches
by appointment only.

🅿 🆆 ♿ 🌱 🍂 ⬭

Easton has a spectacular display of
snowdrops in late winter, and the garden is
always open for a week or ten days when
they are at their peak. But there is even
more to see at other times of the year,
because the whole garden is undergoing a
substantial restoration and reinterpretation
by its young, enthusiastic owners. Easton
Hall, the house, was pulled down in 1948
and the garden abandoned. Now – starting
in 2002 – the avenues have been cleared,
stonework restored and new planting
schemes devised. Do not expect an instant
garden, but visit Easton now as it emerges
from 50 years of neglect, and then return
to measure the progress. Work continues –
new in 2006 is a David Austin rose garden,
a turf maze, an iris collection and some
sweet pea trials. There will be four RHS
Special Events at Easton Walled Gardens
in 2006; details from 020 7821 3408.

plants for sale; gift shop; tea-room.

Owned by Sir Fred & Lady Cholmeley
Number of gardeners 3
Size 4.8ha (12 acres)
English Heritage Grade II

GRIMSTHORPE CASTLE
Grimsthorpe, Bourne PE10 0LY

Tel: 01778 591205 **Fax:** 01778 591259
www.grimsthorpe.co.uk
Location On A151, 4 miles north-west of Bourne.
Opening hours 11 am – 6 pm; Thursdays, Sundays
& Bank Holiday Mondays; April to September. Plus
daily from June to August, except Fridays &
Saturdays.
Admission fee Adults £3.50; Concessions £3;
Children £2.

🅿 🆆 ♿ 🍂 ⬭

Much is happening at Grimsthorpe. Recent
researches have unearthed traces of the
Stephen Switzer garden design from about

1700 and shown that it was probably a local engineer called John Grundy who designed the lake in 1771, not Capability Brown. Yew hedges have been planted to enclose the Victorian Italian garden, which is stylishly maintained with summer bedding among the topiary, urns and sculptures. The most interesting horticultural feature is a formal vegetable garden, made in the 1960s before the craze for *potagers*, right below the Italian garden. The ornamental ponds, complete with fountains, have just (2005) been re-instated within the topiary squares, and further developments are planned for the near future.

topiary; roses (mainly modern); fine collection of trees; shop; tea-room (licensed).

Owned by Grimsthorpe & Drummond Castle Trust Ltd
Number of gardeners 4
Size 10.7ha (27 acres)
English Heritage Grade I

GUNBY HALL
Gunby, Spilsby PE23 5SS

Tel: 01909 486411 **Fax:** 01909 486377
www.nationaltrust.org.uk
Location 2½ miles north-west of Burgh-le-Marsh.
Opening hours 2 pm - 6 pm; Wednesdays (plus Thursdays for garden only); 29 March to 28 September.
Admission fee Adults £3.30; Children £1.70.

Rich herbaceous borders, an arched apple walk, shrub roses, herbs and traditional English vegetables are planted in the exquisite walled garden.

roses (mainly old-fashioned); herbs; fruit; good herbaceous borders.

Owned by The National Trust
Number of gardeners 2, plus volunteers
Size 2.8ha (7 acres)
English Heritage Grade II

HALL FARM & NURSERY
Harpswell, Gainsborough DN21 5UU

Tel: 01427 668412 **Fax:** 01427 667478
www.hall-farm.co.uk/nursery
Location On A361, 7 miles east of Gainsborough.
Opening hours 10 am - 5 pm (or dusk, if earlier); weekdays; all year. For NGS: 10 am - 5.30 pm on 3 September.
Admission fee Adults £3; Children 50p on NGS day; otherwise a charity donation is requested.

This garden is intensely planted and beautifully maintained as an adjunct to the nursery, and for the owners' pleasure. There are plants of every kind – trees, shrubs, bulbs and herbaceous plants – and over 100 different roses. The National Gardens Scheme day (always on the first Sunday in September) is a 'free seed collection' day.

roses (mainly old-fashioned) in a newly made rose garden; plantsman's collection of plants; good herbaceous borders; sunken garden; good nursery next door.

Owned by Pam & Mark Tatam
Size 0.6ha (1½ acres)

HIPPOPOTTERING NURSERY
Orchard House, Brackenhill Road, East Lound, Haxey, Doncaster DN9 2LR

Tel: 07979 764677
www.hippopottering.com
Location Off A161 at Haxey on Owston Ferry Road to East Lound.
Opening hours By appointment.
Admission fee Free.

Hippopottering Nursery – the name has its origins in a family joke – are specialists in Japanese maples. They offer everything from selected colourful seedlings and bonsai material to mature specimens. Cultivars are selected from their collection of over 120; they also sell rootstocks. Look out for them at Chelsea and other RHS shows.

 maples.

Owned by Margaret & Patricia Gibbons
Number of gardeners 2
Size 0.4ha (1 acre)

KATHLEEN MUNCASTER FUCHSIAS
18 Field Lane, Morton, Gainsborough DN21 3BY

Tel: 01427 612329
www.kathleenmuncasterfuchsias.co.uk
Location North-west of Gainsborough: Field Lane is off the minor road to Walkerith.
Opening hours 10 am – 5 pm; Thursday to Tuesday; February to mid-June. Phone first at other times.
Admission fee Free.

This is the nursery of a fuchsia specialist who began as an amateur and now has a National Collection of hardy cultivars and one of the largest nurseries in the country which specialises in the genus. The hardy fuchsias can be seen in the garden, together with the stock plants: almost all the glasshouses may also be visited. The list is impressive, though not all the cultivars in the collection are propagated regularly – ask if they have a cutting available. They will introduce six new fuchsias in 2006, including a stunning red, green and orange hybrid between *F. magdalenae* and *F. splendens* which they call 'Morton Splendide'.

 teas for pre-arranged groups.

Owned by Kathleen Muncaster
Size 0.25ha (2/3 acre)
NCCPG National Collections *Fuchsia* (hardy)

MARTIN NEST NURSERIES
Grange Cottage, Hemswell, Gainsborough DN21 5UP

Tel: 01427 668369 **Fax:** 01427 668080
Location 6 miles east of Gainsborough on A631.
Opening hours 10 am – 4 pm; daily; all year. By appointment only at weekends from November to January.

Martin Nest Nurseries are wholesalers and retailers with a good business-like range of tough pot-grown hardy alpine plants. Primulas and auriculas are their speciality: some of their cultivars are unique to them. Visitors may be shown the National Collection of *Primula auricula* cultivars on request. A new display garden will be open soon.
Owned by Joe Shardlow

NORMANBY HALL COUNTRY PARK
Normanby, Scunthorpe DN15 9HU

Tel: 01724 720588 **Fax:** 01724 721248
www.northlincs.gov.uk/normanby
Location 3 miles north of Scunthorpe.
Opening hours Walled garden: 10.30 am – 5 pm (4.30 pm in winter); daily; all year; closed 1 January, 25 & 26 December. Park: 9 am – dusk; daily; all year.
Admission fee Adults £4.20; Children £2.10. (2005 prices.) RHS members free.

The Victorian Walled Garden (actually built in 1817, before Queen Victoria was even born) has been restored and planted – with help from the National Lottery – as a living museum of 19th-century horticulture. Old varieties of fruit and vegetables are grown organically. The glasshouses have recently been rebuilt to house peaches and other fruit. Ferns and exotic ornamentals fill a display house. Recent developments include a bog garden along the base of the ha-ha (125m long), a Christmas garden of hollies, ivies, hellebores and ferns, and herbaceous borders in the Secret Garden and Sunken Garden. Now they are developing a Victorian woodland garden. Four RHS special events will take place during 2006; details from 020 7821 3408.

🌿 fruit & vegetables; herbaceous borders; woodland walks and parkland outside; deer park; shop; new nursery; refreshments.

Owned by North Lincolnshire Council (tenants)
Number of gardeners 4
Size 0.4ha (1 acre), plus 120ha (300 acres) of parkland.

POTTERTONS NURSERY
Moortown Road, Nettleton, Market Rasen LN7 6HX

Tel: 01472 851714 **Fax:** 01472 852580
www.pottertons.co.uk
Location 20 miles north-east of Lincoln, on B1205: leave A46 at Nettleton.
Opening hours 9 am - 4.30 pm; daily.
Admission fee Free.
🅿 ♿ 🚻 🌿

This alpine, bulb and rock plant specialist (formerly known as Potterton & Martin) has an interesting and extensive range of plants for sale, running from the easy to the unusual. All are propagated on-site, and most can be seen in the extensive display garden. The rock garden has a stream course, waterfalls and pools: elsewhere are raised beds, troughs, woodland and peat beds. The nursery holds many Chelsea gold medals, and has won the RHS Farrer Trophy (best alpine display) on several occasions. Satisfied customers praise not only the nursery's wide choice of plants, but also its cultivation skills and reasonable pricing policy. There will be an RHS Special Event at Pottertons Nursery in 2006; details from 020 7821 3408.

🌿 large rock garden.

Owned by Robert & Jackie Potterton
Number of gardeners 1 part-time
Size 2ha (5 acres)

SPRINGFIELDS FESTIVAL GARDENS
Camelgate, Spalding PE12 6ET

Tel: 01775 724843 **Fax:** 01775 711209
www.springfields.mistral.co.uk
Location 1 mile from Spalding, signed off A17 bypass.
Opening hours 10 am - 6 pm (8 pm on Thursdays & Saturdays); Monday - Saturday; 11 am - 5 pm on Sundays; all year, except 25 December.
Admission fee Free. Parking charge.
🅿 🚻 ♿ 🌱 🍽 📷

Springfields Festival Gardens, a registered charity, are the show gardens for the UK flower bulb industry. They were re-landscaped as part of a major out-of-town retail centre in 2003-2004. They include formal gardens, seasonal flower beds, celebrity gardens (Charlie Dimmock, Chris Beardshaw, Kim Wilde), a Japanese garden, woodland walks, natural wetlands and water features. But best of all are the spectacular displays of bulbs – daffodils, tulips, hyacinths and many others, all donated by the industry.

 millions of bulbs; shopping mall; restaurant & café.

Owned by Springfields Horticultural Society Ltd
Number of gardeners 5
Size 8ha (20 acres)

LONDON

London gardeners are much more fortunate than they would have you believe. They have a microclimate that enables them to grow plants that are tender anywhere except in the mildest corners of the South-West, and they enjoy a good choice of suitably stylish plants from garden centres and other outlets within the city itself. Some of the world's greatest gardens are within a short journey: among them are the Chelsea Physic Garden, Chiswick House, the Royal Botanic Gardens at Kew, Richmond Park and Syon Park. The Royal Parks Agency manages the inner-city green spaces like Hyde Park and Regent's Park with immense horticultural skill: almost all the parks contain acres of well-kept grass and trees of record size. London is, of course, the seat of the Royal Horticultural Society, whose Chelsea Flower Show is traditionally regarded as the start of the London summer season. The Hampton Court Palace Flower Show in July is, if possible, even more of a Londoners' show, while the regular London shows at the RHS's own halls in Westminster are attended by thousands of London gardeners keen to see plants and buy them. Nowhere has so many lectures and other educational garden events as London does. The RHS's Partner College at Capel Manor has a long programme of lectures, demonstrations and workshops throughout the year. Many of the specialist plant societies have their shows and administrative offices in London, too: if you want to see plants as diverse as orchids, carnations, vegetables, daffodils or camellias, London is the place to do so. The National Gardens Scheme thrives there; the Museum of Garden History is based there – just across the river from the Houses of Parliament; the Association of Gardens Trusts has its office in London and so does the Institute of Horticulture. The London Historic Parks & Gardens Trust is one of the country's most successful conservation societies. The greater part of the RHS's Lindley Library – Britain's largest collection of horticultural books and primary sources about gardening – is based in London and now housed in spacious purpose-built accommodation at 80 Vincent Square. Perhaps the only thing that a Londoner cannot do is to garden on a large scale. That apart, there is no better place to be a garden-lover.

BEALE ARBORETUM
West Lodge Park Hotel, Cockfosters Road, Hadley Wood EN4 0PY

Tel: 020 8216 3905 **Fax:** 020 8449 9916
www.bealeshotels.co.uk
Location A111 1 mile south of M25, Jct 24.
Opening hours 2 pm - 5 pm; Monday - Friday; April to October. For NGS: 15 May (2 pm - 5 pm) & 16 October (1 pm - 4 pm).
Admission fee £2.50.

P WC & D

The Beale Arboretum has been developed since 1963 by adding to the original plantings around the house. Young trees are planted among much older specimens – Victorian cedars and redwoods – with a view to the overall effect. A grassy glade runs down from the hotel terrace to a classical cupola at the bottom, inviting exploration. There are fine collections of oaks, hornbeams, liquidambars and nyssas, as well as buddlejas, elaeagnus and rhododendrons. The arboretum is maintained to a high standard, primarily as a facility for hotel guests. It is an excellent example of what can be achieved by an enthusiastic individual.

20-acre arboretum; mature conifers; fine collection of young trees; 200-year-old *Arbutus unedo*; refreshments in hotel.

Owned by Beales Hotels
Number of gardeners 2
Size 8ha (20 acres)
NCCPG National Collections *Carpinus betulus* cvs.; *Elaeagnus*

CANNIZARO PARK
West Side Common, Wimbledon
SW19 4UE

Tel: 020 8545 3657
www.cannizaropark.org.uk
Location West side of Wimbledon Common.
Opening hours 8 am – sunset, Monday – Friday; 9 am – sunset, Saturday, Sunday & Bank Holidays; all year.
Admission fee Free.

Cannizaro is well known among connoisseurs for its azaleas, planted about 40 years ago and a magnificent spectacle when in full flower. It is one of the best woodland gardens of its type in the country and especially beautiful when the underplantings of bulbs are in flower. There are some fine specimen trees, including birches, horse-chestnuts and the tall sassafras.

woodland garden; mature conifers; azaleas; magnolias; several *Sassafras albidum* 15m or more; some refreshments at summer weekends.

Owned by London Borough of Merton
Size 15.5ha (39 acres)
English Heritage Grade II*

CAPEL MANOR
Bullsmoor Lane, Enfield EN1 4RQ

Tel: 08456 122 122 **Fax:** 01992 717544
www.capel.ac.uk
Location A10 by M25, Jct 25.
Opening hours 10 am – 6 pm (or dusk, if earlier); daily; March to October. Weekdays only from November to February.
Admission fee Adults £5; OAPs £4; Children £2.

There are three main areas at this high-profile demonstration garden attached to a horticultural college 'where the City meets the Countryside'. First, there is the National Gardening Centre, where dozens of small model gardens are designed and planted to give people state-of-the-art ideas for their own gardens. Second, there are the trial grounds run by *Gardening Which?*, where this influential monthly magazine carries out all its trials and experiments, long-term and seasonal. Third, there is the series of themed gardens laid out for students to learn from: a walled garden, a herb garden, a knot garden, a disabled person's garden, a shade garden, an Italianate holly maze, a magnolia border, a pergola, a Japanese garden, alpine beds and some historical re-creations. Other themes include Mediterranean, modern, cottage, rustic, family and minimalist gardens. The latest additions are model gardens which include a 'Sunflower Street' taken from the Chelsea Flower Show, a 'Diana, Princess of Wales Garden' and a 'H.M. The Queen Mother Garden', featuring some of the favourite plants of the two royal ladies. Whatever your interests and whatever the time of year, Capel Manor is a garden which educates and delights. And it is brilliant for new ideas, especially for small gardens. There is a substantial programme of RHS workshops, lectures and garden walks at Capel Manor during 2006; details from 020 7821 3408.

vegetables & fruit; topiary; plantsman's collection of plants; herbs; plants under glass; daffodils; good herbaceous borders;

fine collection of trees; alpine plants; roses of every kind; small shop; restaurant.

Owned by Capel Manor Corporation
Number of gardeners 8
Size 12ha (30 acres)
NCCPG National Collections *Achillea*, *Sarcococca*

CHELSEA PHYSIC GARDEN
66 Royal Hospital Road SW3 4HS

Tel: 020 7352 5646 **Fax:** 020 7376 3910
www.chelseaphysicgarden.co.uk
Location Entrance in Royal Hospital Road, towards Chelsea Embankment end, on Swan Walk on public days.
Opening hours 12 noon – 5 pm, Wednesdays; 12 noon – 6 pm, Sundays; 2 April to 29 October. Plus 12 noon – 5 pm on 22 to 26 May (for Chelsea Flower Show), 20 & 22 June, and 18 July to 7 September.
Admission fee Adults £6.50; Children £3.50.
[wc] ⬧
This oasis of peace between Royal Hospital Road and the Chelsea Embankment started life in 1673 as a pharmacological collection, and has kept its original design – hence the word 'Physic' in its name. But it also has the oldest rock garden in Europe, the largest olive tree in Britain, extensive botanical order beds, a vast number of rare and interesting plants, including the long-flowering form of *Rosa chinensis* known as 'Crimson Bengal'. An historical walk emphasises the importance of the garden through the ages by drawing attention to the number of plants first introduced to Britain by the garden and its curators.
herbs; plants under glass; good herbaceous borders; 18th-century rock garden; large olive tree growing outside; light refreshments.

Owned by Chelsea Physic Garden Company
Number of gardeners 5
Size 1.6ha (4 acres)
English Heritage Grade I

CHISWICK HOUSE
Burlington Lane, Chiswick W4 2RP

Tel: 020 8742 1225
Location South-west London on A4 & A316.
Opening hours 8 am – dusk; daily; all year.
Admission fee Free.
[P] [wc] ⬧ ⬧
Laid out by Bridgeman and Kent for Lord Burlington, Chiswick is the best baroque garden in southern England, and the exquisite house is pure Palladian. The bachelor Duke of Devonshire added an Italian renaissance garden early in the 19th century, and a Camellia House with slate benches and huge bushes, mainly of old Japonica hybrids. But it is the lay-out and buildings which are so exceptional: the Ionic temple, the Inigo Jones gateway, the obelisk and the statues. Forget the dogs and the joggers – almost all free-entry gardens have a municipal heart – but explore the *pattes d'oie*, *allées* and ilex groves of the main garden on a hot July morning and you might be doing a Grand Tour of Italy 250 years ago.
plants under glass; camellias; parterres; summer bedding; luxuriant evergreens; refreshments.

Owned by London Borough of Hounslow
Number of gardeners 5
Size 16ha (40 acres)
English Heritage Grade I

CLIFTON NURSERIES
5A Clifton Villas, Little Venice W9 2PH

Tel: 020 7289 6851 **Fax:** 020 7286 4215
www.clifton.co.uk
Location In Little Venice, 100 yds from Warwick Avenue Tube Station.
Opening hours 8.30 am – 6 pm, Monday – Saturday; 10.30 am – 4.30 pm, Sundays; March to September. 8.30 am – 5.30 pm, Monday – Saturday; 10 am – 4 pm, Sundays; October to February.
[P] ❀

Clifton Nurseries were founded in 1854 and are now the capital's oldest garden centre. They have become one of the smartest and most stylish sources of good plants and designer sundries for Londoners. They concentrate on supplying town gardens with containers, statuary, climbers and shrubs in specimen sizes, indoor and conservatory plants. Topiary is one of their specialities: so are mature plants for instant gratification.
everything for London gardeners.

DOWN HOUSE
Luxted Road, Downe, Orpington BR6 7JT

Tel: 01689 859119 **Fax:** 01689 862755
www.english-heritage.org.uk
Location In Downe, on right side of Luxted Road.
Opening hours 10 am – 6 pm; Wednesday – Sunday & Bank Holiday Mondays; 1 February to 17 December. Closes at 5 pm from 7 July to 31 August and in October, and at 4 pm in February, March, November & December.
Admission fee Adults £6.90; Concessions £5.20; Children £3.50.

Charles Darwin's house and garden have been restored as they were in the great scientist's lifetime. It is a thoughtful, practical, middle-class garden with none of the extravagances of 'great' gardens. The borders, orchards and kitchen gardens are just as they were in the 1860s: there are orchids and carnivorous plants in the greenhouse and grassland fungi in the lawns. Visitors can also explore the 'sandwalk' where Darwin thought through his ideas as he paced along.
Charles Darwin's garden; gift shop; tea-room.

Owned by English Heritage
Number of gardeners 2, plus many volunteers
Size 1.6ha (4 acres)

ELTHAM PALACE
Court Yard, Eltham SE9 5QE

Tel: 020 8294 2548 **Fax:** 020 8294 2621
www.english-heritage.org.uk/elthampalace
Location Follow English Heritage signs off Court Road (A208).
Opening hours 10 am – 5 pm; Sunday – Wednesday; April to October & 10 am – 4 pm; Sundays; February, March, November & December.
Admission fee Adults £4.60; Concessions £3.50; Children £2.30.

The ramparts and moat of the old royal palace give structure to the modern garden. There are fine rose gardens, herbaceous borders, rock gardens and shade borders dating from the 1930s, but restored recently. Also from the pre-war period are several huge specimens of *Ligustrum lucidum*. Perhaps the best modern planting is the 110m South Moat border by Isabelle van Groeningen, which won the English Heritage Contemporary Gardens competition, though climate change has required some alterations in the original choice of plants.
historic royal palace; unusual 1930s garden; modern prairie-style garden; tea-room.

Owned by English Heritage
Number of gardeners 3, plus volunteers
Size 7.6ha (19 acres)
English Heritage Grade II*

FENTON HOUSE
Windmill Hill, Hampstead NW3 6RT

Tel: & Fax: 020 7435 3471
www.nationaltrust.org.uk
Location Entrances in Hampstead Grove near Hampstead tube station.
Opening hours 2 pm – 5 pm; Saturdays & Sundays; 4 to 26 March. Then 2 pm – 5 pm; Wednesday – Sunday & Bank Holiday Mondays; 29 March to 29 October. Opens at 11 am on

Saturdays, Sundays & Bank Holiday Mondays.
Admission fee Adults £2; Children £1.
wc &

Fenton House has a country garden in Hampstead, with neat, terraced gardens near the house, and a rather more informal design at the bottom. The 300-year-old apple orchard boasts 300 cultivars of English apples, and there is a working kitchen garden. It is not outstandingly flowerful, but the hedges are good, plants are firmly trained, and there is something to see throughout the year: definitely worth knowing, and very popular with visitors.

roses (mainly old-fashioned); herbs; good herbaceous borders; restored Edwardian garden.

Owned by The National Trust
Number of gardeners 1, plus several volunteers
Size 0.6ha (1½ acres)

FULHAM PALACE GARDEN CENTRE
Bishops Avenue, Fulham SW6 6EE

Tel: 020 7736 2640 **Fax:** 020 7371 8468
Email: enquiries@fulhamgardencentre.com
www.fulhamgardencentre.com
Location Corner of Fulham Palace Road & Bishops Avenue.
Opening hours 9.30 am - 5.30 pm, Monday - Thursday; 9.30 am - 6 pm, Friday - Saturday; 10 am - 5 pm, Sundays. Shuts earlier in winter months.
P ⬦ wc & 🌽

Fulham Palace Garden Centre has everything for the town gardener, including specimen-sized plants, topiary and a good range of containers. The general range includes herbs, vegetables, fruit trees, herbaceous plants, climbers, ferns, grasses, olives, figs and oranges. The nursery will deliver seven days a week in London and further afield. It is owned by Fairbridge, the charity which arranges training for inner-city youth. The Fairbridge Garden Society, based at the Fulham Palace Garden Centre, runs a lively programme of lectures, demonstrations, and garden visits at home and abroad. For details ring 020 7736 2640 or see the website.

excellent general garden centre.

HAM HOUSE
Ham, Richmond TW10 7RS

Tel: 020 8940 1950 **Fax:** 020 8439 8241
www.nationaltrust.org.uk
Location On River Thames, signed from A307.
Opening hours 11 am - 6 pm (or dusk, if earlier); Saturday - Wednesday; all year, except 1 January and 25 & 26 December.
Admission fee Adults £4; Children £2.
P wc & 🌽 ♣ ⬩

Ham is a modern re-creation of the original 17th-century garden. It is not a literal copy, but more of a free-handed re-interpretation. The best part is a grand series of hornbeam enclosures with white summerhouses and seats, known as the Wilderness. The borders are all planted, so far as possible, in the 17th-century style. There are plans to redevelop the kitchen garden in front of the orangery to contrast its 17th-century design and plantings with the better-known 19th-century ones that are commonly seen elsewhere. The garden buildings include a dairy, ice house and still-house.

formal gardens in 17th-century style; roses (mainly modern & climbers); herbs; fruit; parterres; holm oak avenue; National Trust shop; tea-room.

Owned by The National Trust
Number of gardeners 4
Size 8ha (20 acres)
English Heritage Grade II*

HAMPTON COURT PALACE
Hampton KT8 9AU

Tel: 0870 752 7777
www.hrp.org.uk
Location North side of Kingston Bridge over the Thames on A308 junction with A309.
Opening hours 10 am – 6 pm (4.30 pm from November to March); daily; all year.
Admission fee Formal Gardens: Adults £4; Concessions £3; Children £2.50. Maze: Adults £3.50; Concessions £3; Children £2.50. (Prices under review.)

William III was responsible for the main features at Hampton Court today. His Privy Garden has been reconstructed as it was in 1702 and remains the outstanding example of a successful historic restoration from the 1990s. Even the planting is accurate – roses, fritillaries and other flowering plants chosen and cultivated exactly as they would have been 300 years ago. Note how widely spaced they are in their slightly raised beds, an exact copy of horticultural practices of the time. Next to the vast Privy Garden is the Pond Garden, a sunken formal garden with magnificent displays of bedding – tulips in spring and tender perennials in summer. Nearby is the Great Vine – actually 'Black Hamburgh' – planted in 1768 on the advice of Capability Brown: it is the world's oldest known vine and produces, on average, 300 kilos of grapes every year. To one side of the Privy Garden lies the great formal East Garden. Its central feature is the Long Water which cuts right through the deer park: the Hampton Court Palace Flower Show (organised by the Royal Horticultural Society) takes place astride its banks on 4 to 9 July 2006 (tickets from 0870 906 3791). The garden at the palace end of the Long Water was laid out as a parterre by William III with 12 marble fountains: Queen Anne added the semi-circular canals in 1710. On the other side of the palace are the Wilderness gardens, extending over a considerable area, and a mass of naturalised daffodils in spring. Here too is the famous Hampton Court Maze, which covers about one third of an acre and has yew hedges totalling nearly half a mile. Other areas in the Wilderness also have considerable horticultural interest, including the rose garden, a herbaceous garden, and walls covered with climbing plants. Hampton Court is large and you need several hours to appreciate all the gardens, their different styles and what they offer. The website is excellent – educational and helpful.

topiary; roses (ancient & modern); herbs; fruit trees; good herbaceous borders; the famous maze; laburnum walk; knot gardens; the Great Vine; the Wilderness; shop; café; coffee shop.

Owned by Historic Royal Palaces
Number of gardeners 40
Size 24ha (60 acres) of formal gardens & 240ha (600 acres) of deer park
NCCPG National Collections *Heliotropium*
English Heritage Grade I

ISABELLA PLANTATION
Richmond Park, Richmond TW10 5HS

Tel: 020 8948 3209 **Fax:** 020 8332 2730
www.royalparks.gov.uk
Location Richmond Park.
Opening hours Dawn – dusk; daily; all year.
Admission fee Free.

P ⬆ WC ♿

The Isabella Plantation in Richmond Park is at last getting the recognition it deserves: these 42 acres of rhododendrons and azaleas under a mature deciduous canopy are one of the finest woodland gardens in the country. They are probably best visited in late April and May, when the azaleas are accompanied by lush streamside plantings of candelabra primulas, ferns and hostas. And it all gets better still: the new bog garden is a great addition.

🌿 woodland garden; rhododendrons & azaleas; camellias and magnolias; good ornamental trees; primulas.

Owned by The Royal Parks
Number of gardeners 5
Size 17.2ha (42 acres)
NCCPG National Collections *Rhododendron* (Kurume azaleas, the Wilson 50)
English Heritage Grade I

KENWOOD
Hampstead Lane NW3 7JR

Tel: 020 8348 1286
www.english-heritage.org.uk
Location North side of Hampstead Heath, off B519.
Opening hours 8 am - dusk (8.30 pm, if earlier); daily; all year.
Admission fee Free.

⬆ WC ♿ ⴵ

Parts of this superb 18th-century parkland around two glittering lakes have recently been restored to Repton's original designs. There are splendid plantings of rhododendrons, fine azaleas, a mature

Davidia involucrata and wonderful landscaped views to London and Westminster. Work continues.

🌿 woodland garden; good herbaceous borders; fine collection of trees; restaurant; café.

Owned by English Heritage (Iveagh Bequest)
Number of gardeners 5
Size 44ha (112 acres)
English Heritage Grade II*

MUSEUM OF GARDEN HISTORY
Lambeth Palace Road SE1 7LB

Tel: 020 7401 8865 **Fax:** 020 7401 8869
www.museumgardenhistory.org
Location Between Lambeth Bridge & Lambeth Palace.
Opening hours 10.30 am – 5 pm; daily; all year, except Christmas & New Year period. For NGS: 3 June, in conjunction with Lambeth Palace Gardens next door.
Admission fee £3 voluntary admission charge (£2.50 concessions).

WC ♿ 🌱 🍵 ✕ ⴵ

The garden is small, and complements the museum's fascinating collections and excellent exhibitions. Nevertheless, it is neatly designed and planted – with a fair degree of historical correctness – as a 17th-century knot garden, using plants associated with the Tradescant period. A garden for contemplation. But the events, exhibitions, lectures and courses are well worth knowing about: the museum is undergoing major redevelopment with the aim of becoming a first-class information resource about the history of gardening in Britain.

🌿 17th-century plants; good exhibitions; historic tool collection; books, cards and gifts; light refreshments.

Owned by Museum of Garden History
Number of gardeners 10 part-time volunteers

MYDDELTON HOUSE
Bulls Cross, Enfield EN2 9HG

Tel: 01992 702200 **Fax:** 01992 650714
www.leevalleypark.org.uk
Location Off A10 onto Bullsmoor Lane: right at Bulls
Cross. Or train to Turkey Street station.
Opening hours 10 am – 4.30 pm (3 pm from
October to March); weekdays, except Christmas
Holidays; all year. Plus 12 noon – 4 pm; Sundays &
Bank Holiday Mondays; Easter Sunday to 31 October.
For NGS: 12 noon – 4 pm on 30 April, 28 May, & 25
February 2007.
Admission fee Adults £2.40; Concessions £1.80.
(Subject to review.)

🅿 🚾 ♿ ❦

Holy ground for plantsmen with a sense of
history, E.A. Bowles's garden was abandoned
for 30 years: Lee Valley Regional Park
Authority has started to restore it. Thousands
of naturalised bulbs have survived: snowdrops,
crocus and narcissi in spring, and cyclamen,
colchicums and sternbergias in autumn. The
large wisteria planted in 1903 has also
survived, while the rose garden has been
replanted with varieties that Bowles grew.
The iris borders are spectacular in May but it
is true to say that, as with all plantsman's
gardens, there is much to see throughout the
year. A current project is to restore the
Lunatic Asylum, Bowles's collection of freak
plants like the double-flowered (but non-
berrying) blackberry *Rubus ulmifolius*
'Bellidiflorus'. The RHS thought so highly of
this part of the garden that, even in the cash-
strapped 1950s, it propagated the plants and
created its own Lunatic Asylum corner at
Wisley. And the Lee Valley Regional Park
Authority has just reacquired the kitchen
garden and has plans to restore it, too. The
E.A. Bowles of Myddelton House Society
which has an active programme of events:
details from Mr A. Pettitt, 2(A) Plough Hill,
Cuffley, Potters Bar, Hertfordshire EN6 4DR
or from *roger@holland900.freeserve.co.uk*.

🌿 snowdrops; roses (mainly old-fashioned &
climbers); plantsman's collection of
plants; daffodils; good herbaceous borders; fine
collection of trees.

Owned by Lee Valley Regional Park Authority
Number of gardeners 3
Size 2.4ha (6 acres)
NCCPG National Collections *Iris*
English Heritage Grade II

OSTERLEY PARK
Jersey Road, Isleworth TW7 4RB

Tel: 020 8232 5050 **Fax:** 020 8232 5080
www.nationaltrust.org.uk/osterley
Location 5 miles west of central London on A4.
Opening hours 9 am – 7.30 pm (or dusk, if earlier);
daily; all year. Closed 25 & 26 December.
Admission fee Park & Pleasure Grounds: free. Car
park £3.50.

🅿 ♻ 🚾 ♿ ❦ 🍴 🛈

Osterley has much of its 18th-century design
intact. Within the park are formal gardens,
meadows, lakes and garden buildings: the
Temple of Pan is especially fine. The Pleasure
Grounds served as a garden to the neo-
classical house, one of Robert Adam's best,
and have recently been restored. Adam also
built the semi-circular Garden House (1780)
at the centre of the design. The many fine
trees include cedars, oaks and an oriental
plane planted in 1755, while the American
garden has unusual conifers and
rhododendrons.

🌿 woodland garden; herbs; fruit; fine rare
oaks; autumn colour; tallest variegated
chestnut *Castanea sativa* 'Albomarginata' (16m) in
the British Isles; National Trust shop; tea-room.

Owned by The National Trust
Size 56ha (140 acres)
English Heritage Grade II*

THE PALM CENTRE
Ham Nursery, Ham Street, Ham,
Richmond TW10 7HA

Tel: 020 8255 6191 **Fax:** 020 8255 6192
www.thepalmcentre.co.uk
Location Near Ham House, on right-hand side of
Ham Street, opposite Riverside Drive.

Opening hours 9 am – 5 pm (or dusk, if earlier); daily; all year.
Admission fee Free.

P ⏏ WC ✿

The Palm Centre, close to Ham House, is a five-acre nursery with half an acre of glass. It specialises in hardy exotic plants, especially palms, bamboos, tree ferns, cycads, yuccas, cordylines, Mediterranean plants and grasses. It lists over 300 species. There are planted-out areas which display hardy palms and some impressive mature trees to admire. Customers are encouraged to browse.
Owned by Martin Gibbons
Size 2ha (5 acres)

QUEEN MARY'S GARDENS
Inner Circle, Regent's Park NW1 4NR

Tel: 020 7486 7905
Location In middle of Regent's Park.
Opening hours Dawn – dusk; daily; all year.
Admission fee Free.

P WC &. ✿

Queen Mary's Gardens are contained within Regent's Park's Inner Circle. Originally a display garden for the Royal Botanic Society (a 19th-century rival to the Royal Horticultural Society; Robert Marnock and William Robinson both worked there), the Japanese garden, the lake and the mound made from the excavations all date from the 1850s. The horticultural interest comes from the excellent herbaceous borders, tender bedding plants, displays of annuals and spring bulbs. Above all, Queen Mary's Gardens are known for their rose gardens, where large beds are planted each with just one cultivar – mainly modern hybrid teas and floribundas, though there are English roses and old-fashioned ones, too, often in mixed borders. At one end is a circular catenary of climbing and rambling roses around yet more beds of bright modern roses: a spectacular sight in early June – roses flower earlier in the London parks

than anywhere else in England, and are worth a visit at any time after about the middle of May.

🌿 massed displays of roses; fine herbaceous borders.

Owned by Royal Parks Agency

SYON PARK
Brentford TW8 8JF

Tel: 020 8560 0881/2 **Fax:** 020 8568 0936
www.syonpark.co.uk
Location Between Brentford & Isleworth, north bank of Thames.
Opening hours 10.30 am – 5.30 pm (4 pm or sunset, if earlier, from November to March); daily, except 25 & 26 December; all year.
Admission fee Adults £3.75; Concessions £2.50. RHS members free.

P WC &. ✿ 🌼 ✕ ▱

Syon is a wonderful mixture of 18th-century landscape, 19th-century horticultural seriousness, 20th-century plantsmanship and 21st-century theme park. The Great Conservatory was designed by Charles Fowler in the 1820s; the formal terraces followed in the 1830s. But one of the nicest details about Syon is the way the water meadows along the banks of the Thames are still grazed by cows: it creates a unique rural prospect so close to the heart of London. There are fine trees, too, the relic of a botanical collection dating back to the 1820s: some, including four species of oak, are record-breakers.

🌿 spectacular Great Conservatory; woodland garden; mature conifers; good herbaceous borders; fine collection of trees; cacti; ferns; tallest *Catalpa ovata* (22m) in the British Isles (and 14 further record trees); Wyevale Garden Centre on-site; shop; café.

Owned by The Duke of Northumberland
Number of gardeners 7
Size 16ha (40 acres)
English Heritage Grade I

ROYAL BOTANIC GARDENS, KEW
Kew, Richmond TW9 3AB

Tel: 020 8332 5655
www.kew.org
Location Kew Green (parking), tube to Kew Gardens tube Station, or train from Waterloo to Kew Bridge.
Opening hours 9.30 am - 6.30 pm (7.30 pm at weekends), but closes at 5.30 pm from mid-February to last Saturday in March and 6 pm from early September to end of October, & at 4.15 pm in November & December; daily; all year, except 24 & 25 December. Last admissions 30 minutes before closing.
Admission fee Adults £10; Concessions £7; Children free. (Subject to review.)

P WC & * * *

Kew Gardens are enormous – the guidebook advises people to allow a whole day for their visit – and have one of the largest collections of plants in the world. The emphasis is upon species rather than garden cultivars, but there is an immense amount for gardeners to see and admire and – of course – to learn from. There are seasonal features like the winter garden and historic areas like the Queen's garden behind Kew Palace which was designed in the 1960s as a reconstructed 17th-century garden. Nor should the famous pagoda and Japanese landscape gardens be forgotten. There are also many horticulturally themed gardens. The azalea garden divides azaleas into 12 distinct horticultural groups, e.g. the Ghent hybrids and the Knap Hill hybrids, and arranges them all systematically in historic order. The bamboo garden has over 120 cultivars arranged to maximise the contrast between their forms and leaf shapes. The berberis dell is a unique feature with a comprehensive collection of berberis and mahonia – the tallest is a 5m specimen of *Berberis lycoides*. Kew has one of the best bluebell woods in the London area, behind Queen Charlotte's cottage. The grass garden has over 550 species and is being added to continuously: although the scientific purpose is to display the diversity and importance of grasses, the garden is arranged ornamentally. The holly walk was laid out in 1874 by Sir Joseph Hooker: the original specimens are therefore over 130 years old and as high as 30m. The collection has over 600 hollies. The juniper collection is the largest in Europe. The lilac garden ('Go down to Kew in lilac time') was renovated in 1993 and has over 100 specimens in ten separate beds. The rhododendron dell (700 plants) includes some unique Kew hybrids as well as hardy species. The rose garden was created in 1923 and is very popular in high summer: it has roses of all types and an area which illustrates the history of roses in cultivation. There is also a rose pergola running through the order beds, which were originally designed as a living library of flowering plants systematically arranged for students of botany. The pinetum has an important collection of conifers and there are many record-breakers among the deciduous species at Kew, too. The rock garden was rebuilt in the 1980s to include more microhabitats. It has over 2,500 different plants roughly arranged in geographical areas, e.g. the mountains of Europe, the

Mediterranean and Patagonia. The glasshouses also contain a vast collection of plants. The Palm House was built in the 1840s to house tropical trees and shrubs – these include coconuts, bananas, bread-fruit, mangoes and paw-paws. The Princess of Wales Conservatory opened in 1987 and has ten distinct climatic zones ranging from arid to moist-tropical: here are such plants as ginger, pineapple and orchids. The Temperate House is set out geographically: among its most striking plants are proteas from South Africa. In the hot and humid water lily house are tropical *Nymphaea* and *Victoria cruziana*, as well as such economic plants as rice and lemon grass. The alpine house was opened in 1981 and its systems of refrigeration and ventilation enable Kew to grow plants which would not otherwise survive the damp, mild climate of England. Other glasshouses to visit include the Evolution House, which tells the story of plant evolution over the last 3,500 million years and the unique filmy fern house. There are twice-daily hour-long guided tours which leave from the Guides' Desk, just inside the Victoria Gate Visitors Centre, at 11 am and 2 pm (no extra fee payable). Kew has every imaginable facility for visits by schools, groups, tourists and students of botany. In summer it also has very good bedding-out schemes, but the garden is somewhat bedevilled by Canada geese, which foul the grass, and by aircraft noise.

woodland garden; sub-tropical plants; snowdrops; roses of every kind; rock garden; plantsman's collection of plants; herbs; plants under glass; fruit; mature conifers; good herbaceous borders; fine collection of trees; alpine plants; heather gardens; 138 record trees - more than any other garden in the British Isles - including 38 different oaks (*Quercus spp.*); gift & book shop; three restaurants; café.

Owned by Trustees of the Royal Botanic Gardens
Number of gardeners 150
Size 121ha (302 acres)
English Heritage Grade I

NORFOLK

Norfolk has a large number of important historic gardens. Only a few are open to the public, but they include Blickling, Felbrigg, Holkham, Sheringham and the royal gardens at Sandringham – an impressive list. The garden with the finest collection of trees is Ryston Hall, but it is not open to the public. The same is true of Talbot Manor, which was planted from about 1950 onwards by the late Maurice Mason with advice from Sir Harold Hillier. Nevertheless, the National Gardens Scheme does fairly well in Norfolk and the county also has a good number of first-rate nurseries: Peter Beales Roses, Norfolk Lavender, P.W. Plants, Reads Nursery at Hales Hall Gardens and the Romantic Garden Nursery are all of national importance. There are 13 National Collections in the county, including a collection of *Elaeagnus* which is spread among several members of the Norfolk Group of the NCCPG. The Royal Horticultural Society has good links with Norfolk: Easton College near Norwich is a RHS Partner College, while Sandringham and Mannington are RHS Free Access gardens. Many people consider that East Ruston Old Vicarage, free to RHS members in September and October, is the most important new garden to have been made in the UK during the last few years. And there is no doubt that both the Dell Garden and Foggy Bottom (now jointly known as Bressingham Gardens) at Bressingham continue to be immensely influential: the Bloom family at Bressingham was largely responsible for the enormous renewal of interest in herbaceous plants from about 1970 onwards. Unfortunately, however, the important modern rose garden at Elsing Hall was sold last year and will not be opening again in 2006.

AFRICAN VIOLET & GARDEN CENTRE
Station Road, Terrington St Clement, King's Lynn PE34 4PL

Tel: 01553 828374 **Fax:** 01553 828376
www.africanvioletcentre.ltd.uk
Location 3 miles west of King's Lynn, on A17.
Opening hours 9 am (10 am on Sundays) - 5 pm; daily; all year. Closed for New Year's Day, Christmas Day & Boxing Day.
Admission fee Free.

African violets; house plants; gift shop; café.

Owned by Paul Crake & Mark Leach

This nursery built its reputation on African violets, and its Chelsea exhibits have been memorable. It offers 140+ cultivars and one of the largest collections of *Saintpaulia* species in the UK. The display house always has a good showing.

BLICKLING HALL
Blickling, Norwich NR11 6NF

Tel: 01263 738030 **Fax:** 01263 738035
www.nationaltrust.org.uk
Location 1½ miles north-west of Aylsham on B1354.
Opening hours 10.15 am - 5.15 pm; Wednesday - Sunday & Bank Holiday Mondays; 29 March to 29 October. Plus Tuesdays in August. 11 am - 4 pm; Thursday - Sunday; 2 November to 23 December 2006, then 4 January to 24 March 2007.
Admission fee Adults £5; Children £2.50.

P WC & ❀ ● ☐

Blickling is the garden with everything: a Jacobean mansion, handsomely symmetrical; an early landscape layout (the Doric Temple was built in about 1735); a pretty orangery by Samuel Wyatt; a large mid-19th-century parterre, later simplified, with fine yew hedges and topiary; and 1930s herbaceous plantings by Norah Lindsay (her masterpiece). The spring bulbs are magnificent, and there are sheets of bluebells in the woods, but Blickling is a garden to visit at all seasons. woodland garden; rhododendrons & azaleas; good herbaceous borders at peak July/August; bluebells; shops; plant sales in season; restaurant.

Owned by The National Trust
Number of gardeners 5, plus volunteers
Size 20ha (50 acres)
English Heritage Grade II*

BRADENHAM HALL
Bradenham, Thetford IP25 7QR

Tel: 01362 687243/687279 **Fax:** 01362 687669
www.bradenhamhall.co.uk
Location West of East Dereham, north of Bradenham.
Opening hours 2 pm – 5.30 pm; second & fourth Sundays of month; April to September. Groups at other times by appointment. And for NGS.
Admission fee Adults £4; Children free.

P WC & ❀ ☐

This is an exceptional plant-lover's garden for all seasons, made over the last 40 years in a windy, open position at the top of what passes in Norfolk for a hill. The first thing you notice is that the house (early Georgian) and garden walls are covered with unusual shrubs, climbers and fruit. The flower gardens are formally designed and richly planted within beautiful yew hedges: formal rose gardens, a paved garden, and herbaceous and shrub borders. The arboretum has a remarkable collection of trees – more than 800 different species and forms, many of them rare or very rare. All are labelled. The walled kitchen gardens are traditionally managed, with vegetables, cut-flowers, mixed borders, and two glasshouses. In spring, the parkland and arboretum are filled with daffodils – massed plantings of more than 90 carefully chosen and graded cultivars. A delight and an education. roses (mainly old-fashioned); plantsman's collection of plants; daffodils; good herbaceous borders; fine collection of trees; tea-room.

Owned by Chris & Panda Allhusen
Number of gardeners 3
Size 8.3ha (21 acres)

CHANTICLEER
Dereham Road, Ovington, Watton, Thetford IP25 6SA

Tel: 01953 881194
Location On A1075, 2 miles from Watton on the Dereham road.
Opening hours 10 am – 4 pm; 10 & 11 June, 8 & 9 July, 5 & 6 August. And groups by appointment.
Admission fee Adults £2; OAPs £1.50; Children free.

P WC & ❀ ☐

Chanticleer is a former 1830s public house, converted to a private dwelling in the 1950s and since extended. The present owners have lived and gardened here for 25 years, originally in just under two acres, but then with three further acres for a small flock of Jacob sheep, Vietnamese pot-bellied pigs, goats, geese, chickens and ducks. The main garden includes a kitchen garden, greenhouses, orchard, herb garden and a large wildlife garden with a pond: all are managed organically. Great emphasis is placed on working with nature: the wildlife garden is frequented by birds, insects and small mammals, including breeding water voles. Most native shrubs and trees are represented, as are many wildflowers – including two species of

BRESSINGHAM GARDENS
Bressingham, Diss IP22 2AB

Tel: 01379 688585 **Fax:** 01379 688490
www.bressinghamgardens.com
Location On A1066, 3 miles west of Diss.
Opening hours 10.30 am – 4.30 pm; daily; April to October. Groups by appointment at other times.
Admission fee Not yet known as we went to press.

🅿 🚾 ♿ ❀ ✗ 🖰

Bressingham Gardens combines two major gardens made by the Bloom family which were until recently open at different times – Alan Bloom's Dell Garden, and Adrian Bloom's Foggy Bottom. There is no better place to learn about herbaceous plants – what they look like, how they grow and how to place them – than the Dell. This is a six-acre complex of about 50 island beds, which act as a trial-ground and conservation resource for the herbaceous and alpine plants (over 5,000 of them) for which Alan Bloom is famous. The new Summer Garden was designed by Adrian Bloom to provide a new and more dramatic entrance to the garden. It has a stunning display of *Crocosmia* and *Miscanthus* cultivars interplanted with other perennials. The Blooms are keen to emphasise that the Dell Garden is not a museum piece but a carefully tended collection of perennials, developing and growing all the time. The same is true of Foggy Bottom, which Adrian Bloom started planting in about 1975 as a garden for year-round seasonal colour and interest. Its centrepiece was his unique collection of conifers, collected from all over the world and tested for English conditions. They were, for many years, the dominant plants in the garden, and he used them to show off the innumerable contrasts of form, colour, texture and shape between different cultivars. Then he began to use them in other plant combinations – with ornamental grasses, perennials and shrubs – chosen to give a succession of colour, texture and other interest throughout the year. Renovation and renewal are ongoing – new beds are constantly developed and new plant associations created. The All-Seasons Bed is a recent example: its 'river of blood' is a meandering 30ft planting of *Imperata cylindrica* 'Rubra'. Another new feature is Adrian's Wood, two acres connecting the two gardens which is being planted with North American natives. The net result is that all parts of Bressingham Gardens continue to be an inspirational source of ideas for the smaller garden.

🌿 superb herbaceous borders; some alpine plants; beautiful plantings; island beds; plantsman's collection of plants; mature dwarf conifers; refreshments in adjoining plant centre.

Owned by Alan & Adrian Bloom
Number of gardeners 4
Size 4.8ha (15 acres)
NCCPG National Collections *Miscanthus*

orchid, which have colonised parts of the wildlife area. A small willow plantation supplies materials for hurdle-making. There are demonstrations of how to make compost (including the use of wormeries and liquid compost) during open weekends.

 organic garden of great interest; refreshments.

Owned by Mr & Mrs T. Rands
Number of gardeners owners only
Size 2ha (5 acres)

CORPUSTY MILL GARDEN
The Mill House, Corpusty, Norwich
NR11 6QB

Tel: 01263 587223
Location In middle of village on B1149.
Opening hours Groups by appointment.
Admission fee Adults £6.

Corpusty Mill has been made and developed by Roger Last and his late brother John since 1965. Water is used extensively (ponds, streams, a small lake and a river) and there are strong architectural elements, garden buildings or follies, including a vast flint wall with the heads of Roman emperors, a Gothic arch and window, a grotto (with four chambers), a ruined tower, a classical pavilion and stainless steel spire. The planting is knowledgeable, varied and controlled. Most visitors come away quite amazed by the beauty and ingenuity of what they have seen.

stylish design.

Owned by Roger Last
Number of gardeners owner only
Size 1.6ha (4 acres)

EAST LODE
Nursery Lane, Hockwold, Thetford
IP26 4ND

Tel: 01842 827096
Location Down Church Lane in Hockwold, left at iron seat, then first house on right.
Opening hours By arrangement. Special Hellebore and Spring Bulbs Open Day: 10 am – 4 pm on Saturday 18 March.
Admission fee Adults £2.

This half-acre cottage garden is absolutely full of interest – shrubs, roses, clematis, and many unusual plants – all put together in the cottage style. Mrs Mansey is a skilful plantswoman and fills it with colour throughout the year: many hellebores in spring, roses and clematis in summer, evergreens and silvers for autumn and winter, and tremendous underplantings of bulbs. There is a small pond, a greenhouse, some scree beds and a conservatory. It is also intended to be a haven for bees, birds and butterflies.

 plantsman's garden with many unusual plants; cottagey mix.

Owned by Mrs P. Mansey
Number of gardeners 1
Size 0.2ha (½ acre)

FAIRHAVEN WOODLAND & WATER GARDEN
School Road, South Walsham, Norwich
NR13 6DZ

Tel & Fax: 01603 270449
www.fairhavengarden.co.uk
Location Follow brown tourist signs off A47 on to B1140.
Opening hours 10 am – 5 pm; daily; all year, except 25 December. Closes 9 pm on Wednesdays & Thursdays from May to August.
Admission fee Adults £4; OAPs £3.50; Children £1.50. (Under review.) RHS members free from February to April & in October.

EAST RUSTON OLD VICARAGE
East Ruston, Norwich NR12 9HN

Tel: 01692 650432 **Fax:** 01692 651246
www.e-ruston-oldvicaragegardens.co.uk
Location Turn off A149 near Stalham or to B1159 signed Walcott, Bacton, Happisburgh. Left at T-junction. On right after 2 miles, next to East Ruston Church.
Opening hours 2 pm - 5.30 pm; Wednesdays, Fridays, Saturdays, Sundays & Bank Holidays; 26 March to 28 October.
Admission fee Adults £4.50; Children £1. RHS members free in September & October.

P WC & ♥ ⊡

This fine modern garden has been conceived on the grand scale. The owners, Graham Robeson and Alan Gray, combine the rare qualities of superb architectural design and exceptional plantsmanship. The house was built by a Surrey architect in 1913 in the Arts & Crafts style, which is uncommon in Norfolk. When the owners started to make their garden in 1988, it sat in an empty field. It was then that they planted the shelter belts, almost all tough evergreens. The garden has been designed as a series of 'rooms', getting larger the further you move from the house. There are fine views borrowed from the landscape of two local churches and a whimsical porthole view of Happisburgh lighthouse. The gardens and grounds include superb long borders abundantly and richly planted, a box parterre annually bedded out with unusual and original plant combinations, a gravelled forecourt with large groups of *Aeonium* 'Zwartkop' and various echeverias, a sunken garden containing many varieties including a large group of *Lobelia tupa*, and the newly relocated and much extended exotic garden with fabulously bold plantings of palms, bananas, shrubby salvias and many tender exotics which are propagated on the premises. Much thought has gone into the design and preparation of beds for plants. The Mediterranean garden, for example, faces south and has a lot of brickwork and paving to preserve the warmth which plants need to survive through the winter. The beds are heavily mulched with gravel, and the result is that many plants survive which are typical of the Mediterranean *maquis*, the Californian chaparral and Australasia – clouds of yellow Australian mimosa, a very dark blue rosemary from the Mediterranean and *Beschorneria yuccoides* from Mexico. Even more impressive is the newly planted desert wash, made from over 350 tons of flints of varying sizes and covering an acre. It is intended to imitate the Arizona desert where the only rainfall is one of tumultuous thunderstorms every year. The plantings include some great specimens of palm trees, *Trithrinax campestris* from Argentina and *Brahea armata*, the Mexican blue palm, plus dasylirions, agaves, aloes and other succulents, some of which were grown from seed imported by the owners. East Ruston also has a pretty no-nonsense vegetable garden, a cutting garden, woodland walks, wildflower meadows, a walled garden and a spectacular corn field, brimming with field poppies, cornflowers and corn marigold. There will be four RHS Special Events at East Ruston Old Vicarage in 2006; details from 020 7821 3408.

🌿 a young garden on a large scale; architectural plants, tea-room.

Owned by Graham Robeson & Alan Gray
Size 12.5ha (32 acres)

This is a vast woodland garden of naturalised rhododendrons under a canopy of ancient oaks – one pollarded specimen known as the King Oak is estimated to be 950 years old. In 1946, Lord Fairhaven laid two fairly narrow paths straight across a section of boggy land where sheets of candelabra primulas flourish in alder woodland. On the drier ground he planted masses of rhododendrons and azaleas among the naturalised R. ponticum. The garden is at its loveliest throughout May and June, when the rhododendrons and candelabras are reflected in the still waters of the dykes and private Broad. It is a bit short on follow-up later in the year, though there are effective plantings of hydrangeas, hostas, Osmunda regalis, ligularias and gunneras. The snowdrops, too, are good in February, and the lysichitons in March and April. The garden is managed organically. Many people are more interested in the wildlife and the Broad than the garden, so that even in high season the horticultural visitor may be almost alone in the woodland garden. There will be two RHS Special Events at Fairhaven in 2006; details from 020 7821 3408.

woodland garden; bluebells; snowdrops; rhododendrons; lilies; candelabra primulas; shop; excellent plant sales area; tea-room.

Owned by Fairhaven Garden Trust
Number of gardeners 2 full-time; 2 part-time
Size 52ha (130 acres)

FELBRIGG HALL
Felbrigg, Norwich NR11 8PR

Tel: 01263 837444 **Fax:** 01263 837032
www.nationaltrust.org.uk
Location Entrance off B1436, signed from A148 & A140.
Opening hours 11 am - 5 pm; Saturday - Wednesday; 25 March to 29 October. Daily from 20 July to 1 September.
Admission fee Adults £3.

There are fine trees in the park, but the best bit of Felbrigg is the walled kitchen garden, oriented on a large brick dovecote flanked by Victorian vineries. Fruit trees are trained against the walls (figs, pears, plums) and the garden laid to neatly grown vegetables with herbaceous borders, ribbon borders and a hot border enclosed by box-edged gravel paths.

fruit; good herbaceous borders; National Trust shop; restaurant & tea-room.

Owned by The National Trust
Number of gardeners 3, plus 1 trainee
Size 2.4ha (6 acres)
NCCPG National Collections Colchicum
English Heritage Grade II*

HALES HALL GARDENS & READS NURSERY
Hales Hall, Loddon NR14 6QW

Tel: 01508 548395 **Fax:** 01508 548040
www.readsnursery.co.uk
Location Off A146, 1 mile south of Loddon.
Opening hours 10 am - 5 pm (4 pm in winter); Monday - Saturday; all year. Plus 11 am - 4 pm on Sundays from April to October.
Admission fee Garden: £2; Nursery: free.

This important and long-established family nursery specialises in citrus fruit trees and conservatory plants. Its extensive list of Citrus cultivars is based upon the centuries-old collection made by Rivers of Sawbridgeworth. Rivers were famous fruit-breeders in the 19th century, and their citrus trees supplied the scions needed to start the California fruit industry. Reads acquired their stock when Rivers closed in 1983. They also grow and sell over 70 different grape cultivars, including many more English-raised vines than any other nursery: this is the place to find such Victorian delicacies as 'Lady Downe's Seedling' and 'Mrs Pince's Black Muscat'.

Their list of figs is equally extensive, and unparalleled among UK nurserymen: 'Goutte d'Or', 'Malcolm's Giant' and 'White Ischia' are among their specialities. But they also stock a large number of proper traditional conservatory plants – abutilons, bougainvilleas, brugmansias, gardenias, jasmines, passionflowers, sparmannias and hundreds more. In the adjoining two-acre garden are the moated remains of a medieval hall, planted with topiary, a 'potted' fruit orchard, a *potager*, a vegetable garden and a plantsman's collection of shrubs, herbaceous plants and bulbs.

🌿 conservatory plants; fruit; teas by arrangement for groups.

Owned by The Read Family
Number of gardeners 1
Size 0.8ha (2 acres)
NCCPG National Collections *Citrus*; *Ficus*; *Vitis vinifera* (grapes)

HOECROFT PLANTS
Severals Grange, Holt Road, Wood Norton, Dereham NR20 5BL

Tel & Fax: 01362 684206
www.hoecroft.co.uk
Location 2 miles north of Guist on B1110 (not in Wood Norton village).
Opening hours 10 am - 4 pm; Thursday - Sunday; April to October. For NGS: 13 August.
Admission fee Donation to NGS.

P ⬇ WC 🌱

Hoecroft is a small but well-known specialist nursery which began by concentrating upon variegated and coloured foliage plants. These range from the smallest alpines to large shrubs. Perhaps more prominent now is its list of ornamental grasses, rushes, sedges and bamboos: it offers over 250 different cultivars, which may be seen in the attached display gardens. These were started 15 years ago with the specific purpose of showing how to achieve year-round colour with foliage rather than flowers. They also incorporate grasses to give movement and a sense of lightness between the more solid shapes of the shrubs.

🌿 grasses; mixed borders.

Owned by Jane Lister
Size 0.4ha (1 acre)

HOLKHAM HALL
Holkham, Wells-next-the-Sea NR23 1AB

Tel: 01328 710227 **Fax:** 01328 711707
www.holkham.co.uk
Location Off A149, 2 miles west of Wells.
Opening hours 1 pm - 5 pm; daily, except Tuesdays & Wednesdays; June to September. Plus 12 noon - 5 pm; 15 to 17 April, 29 April to 1 May, 27 to 29 May, & 26 to 28 August. Park: 9 am; daily, except Christmas Day.
Admission fee Park: free.

P ⬇ WC & 🌱 🌲 ✕ 📷

Holkham is a big landscape garden, worked on by Kent, Brown and Repton. Formal terraces were added in the 1850s. Holkham Gardens are in the walled garden, laid by Samuel Wyatt in the 1780s. The glasshouses include a vinery and recently restored fig- and peach-houses. The website is excellent.

🌿 gift shop; garden centre; café.

Owned by The Earl of Leicester
Number of gardeners 4
English Heritage Grade I

HOUGHTON HALL
King's Lynn PE31 6UE

Tel: 01485 528569 **Fax:** 01485 528167
www.houghtonhall.com
Location Signed from A148 between King's Lynn & Cromer.
Opening hours 11 am - 5.30 pm; Wednesdays, Thursdays, Sundays & Bank Holidays; Easter Sunday to 28 September. For NGS: 7 July.
Admission fee Adults £4.50; Children £2. RHS members free in June.

P WC & ● ᗡ

Sir Robert Walpole made the park, now stocked with white fallow deer, but it is the new plantings which draw visitors to Houghton today. The huge old kitchen garden at Houghton has been transformed by the present Marquess in memory of his grandmother Sybil Sassoon, an enthusiastic gardener. The new layout is modern but formal, drawing on the best Italianate tradition of design and a family fondness for lavish planting. The herbaceous borders (130m long) are stupendous – so are the roses; both depend for their effect upon big designs and large-scale planting. The results are inspirational, and very impressive.

🌿 shop; tea-room.

Owned by The Marquess of Cholmondeley

HOVETON HALL
Wroxham, Norwich NR12 8RJ

Tel: 01603 782798 **Fax:** 01603 784564
www.hovetonhallgardens.co.uk
Location 9 miles north of Norwich: follow brown tourist signs from A1151.
Opening hours 10.30 am - 5 pm; Wednesdays, Fridays, Sundays & Bank Holiday Mondays; Easter to 16 September. Also open on Thursdays in May & June. For NGS: 17 June & 21 August.
Admission fee Adults £4; Wheelchair-bound & carers £2; Children £1.50. Free to RHS members on 8 June.

P WC & 🌱 ᗡ

The gardens are laid out around a series of streams, with beautiful waterside plantings, gunneras and candelabra primulas. Rhododendrons and azaleas fill the woodland gardens – at their peak in May. Daffodils are a spring feature, and the many-coloured hydrangeas are impressive later in the year. A moon-gate in the shape of a spider's web was added in 1936 to enclose the walled herbaceous garden. The walled kitchen garden is

divided into three: a knot garden, a circular herb garden (designed by Tessa Hobbs) and a vegetable garden. Old fruit trees line the walks, and the peonies are a sight in June.

🌿 rhododendrons & azaleas; daffodils; good herbaceous borders; water garden; light lunches & teas.

Owned by Mr & Mrs Andrew Buxton
Number of gardeners 3
Size 6ha (15 acres)

LYNFORD ARBORETUM
Munford, Thetford IP26 5HW

Tel: 01842 810271
Location Turn right off A1065 just north of Munford.
Opening hours Dawn - dusk; daily; all year.
Admission fee Free.

P

The Lynford Arboretum was started in 1947 by students at the Forester Training School who at that time occupied nearby Lynford Hall. They planted about 100 species of conifers and broadleaves, some in forestry plots but mostly as individual specimens within the parkland and policies surrounding the house. The soil is thin and sandy, but some of those original plantings are already handsome specimens, including a *Nothofagus obliqua* and a *Pinus banksiana* each 20m tall. Rather simply maintained by the Forestry Commission, the arboretum has considerable potential for development. Lynford Hall is now a hotel: the extensive formal garden (rather gone back) was laid out by William Burn in the 1860s and was famous for its bedding until 1914. Beyond is a curving lake. Rather surprisingly, the Forestry Commission does not permit dogs in the arboretum.

🌿 trees, deciduous & evergreen.

Owned by Forestry Commission

MANNINGTON GARDENS
Mannington Hall, Norwich NR11 7BB

Tel: 01263 584175 **Fax:** 01263 761214
www.manningtongardens.co.uk
Location Signed from B1149 at Saxthorpe.
Opening hours 12 noon – 5 pm; Sundays; May to
September. 11 am – 5 pm; Wednesday – Friday; June
to August.
Admission fee Adults £4; Concessions £3; Children
free. RHS members free.

🅿 🚾 ♿ 🌟 🍎 🏳

The gardens at Mannington embrace a
moated house, the ruins of Mannington
Church, two lakes, a scented garden, an
arboretum of native trees, a new 'sensory
garden', genuine wildflower meadows and
handsome herbaceous borders. But the best
part is the Heritage Rose Garden, made in
association with Peter Beales, where
thousands of old-fashioned roses are planted
to illustrate the history of roses in
cultivation. The developments are
represented by beds which display roses
according to their periods, from the 15th
century up to today. There will be three
RHS Special Events at Mannington in
2006; details from 020 7821 3408.
🌿 roses (mainly old-fashioned & climbers);
natural surroundings; colour borders;
lakes; wildflowers; roses for sale; light
refreshments, teas.

Owned by Lord Walpole
Number of gardeners 2 full-time, 3 part-time
Size 8ha (20 acres)
English Heritage Grade II

OXBURGH HALL
Oxborough, King's Lynn PE33 9PS

Tel: 01366 328258 **Fax:** 01366 328066
www.nationaltrust.org.uk
Location 7 miles south-west of Swaffham on Stoke
Ferry Road.
Opening hours 11 am – 4 pm; Saturdays & Sundays;
7 January to 19 March & 4 November to 17
December. 11 am – 5.30 pm (4.30 pm after 30

September); Saturday – Wednesday; 25 March to 29
October. Daily in August.
Admission fee Adults £3.25; Children £1.65.

🅿 🚾 ♿ 🌟 🍎 🏳

The baroque 19th-century parterre has been
replanted by the National Trust with such
herbs as rue and cineraria making permanent
companions for annuals and bedding plants.
Good fruit trees in the walled garden,
especially medlars and quinces. A good
garden – and getting better all the time.
🌿 roses (mainly modern); good herbaceous
borders; French-style parterre; trained
fruit trees; woodland walks; vegetable garden; gift
shop; licensed restaurant.

Owned by The National Trust
Number of gardeners 2, plus volunteers
Size 6.2ha (15½ acres)
English Heritage Grade II

P.W. PLANTS
Sunnyside, Heath Road, Kenninghall
NR16 2DS

Tel & Fax: 01953 888212
www.hardybamboo.com
Location South-west of Norwich, between
Kenninghall & North Lopham.
Opening hours 9 am – 5 pm; Fridays; all year. Plus
the last Saturday of the month from October to
March and every Saturday from April to September.
Admission fee Free.

🅿 🚾 ♿ 🌟

This enterprising nursery offers a wide range
of plants chosen for their general garden-
worthiness, interesting foliage and shape. It is
perhaps best known for its bamboos, which
have won the nursery many medals at RHS
shows, but P.W. Plants also stock grasses,
shrubs, perennials and climbers. Most can be
seen growing in the display gardens.
 bamboos.

Owned by Paul Whittaker
Number of gardeners 1
Size 0.6ha (1½ acres)

PETER BEALES ROSES
London Road, Attleborough NR17 1AY

Tel: 01953 454707 **Fax:** 01953 456845
www.classicroses.co.uk
Location 2 miles south of Attleborough: leave A11 at Breckland Lodge. Follow brown tourist signs.
Opening hours 9 am – 5 pm (4.30 pm from October to March, and 4 pm in January); Monday – Saturday. 10 am – 4 pm; Sundays & Bank Holidays.
Admission fee Free.

There is a small display garden attached to this well-known rose nursery and latest reports say that it is well maintained. A good range of older and classic roses is offered for sale, both at the nursery and from its mail-order catalogue and website, which list over 1,300 species and cultivars, many not available elsewhere in the United Kingdom.

roses (mainly old-fashioned); garden sundries & gift shop; licensed bistro.

Owned by Peter Beales
Number of gardeners 2
Size 1ha (2½ acres)
NCCPG National Collections *Rosa* (species)

PLANTATION GARDEN
4 Earlham Road, Norwich NR2 3DB

Tel: 01603 455223/621868 **Fax:** 01603 631166
www.plantationgarden.co.uk
Location Between The Beeches Hotel and Roman Catholic Cathedral.
Opening hours 9 am – 6 pm (or dusk, if earlier); daily; all year.
Admission fee Adults £2; Children free. Honesty box when unattended.

The Plantation Garden was made in an abandoned chalk quarry by Henry Trevor, a successful Norwich businessman, between 1856 until his death in 1897. In the ensuing years the garden passed through various hands until, in 1980, it was totally overgrown, abandoned and forgotten. In that year it was rediscovered and the Plantation Garden Preservation Trust formed to save and restore the garden. The area, nearly three acres in all, contains many features including woodland walkways, flower beds, lawns, a Gothic fountain, an Italianate terrace, a 'Mediaeval' terrace wall, a rustic bridge and a reconstruction of the original thatched summerhouse. There are many unique aspects to this very idiosyncratic garden making it a haven of peace and tranquillity – a refuge from the hurly-burly of modern life and a glimpse into a bygone age. Sir Roy Strong is patron of the Trust and points out that the garden is 'something of a rarity, for in most cases it is usually only the grandest of gardens which survive from earlier periods'. The original house, designed by Edward Boardman for Henry Trevor, is now part of The Beeches Hotel.

historic Victorian suburban garden undergoing restoration; crocosmias; tea & cakes (on Sunday afternoons, May to September).

Owned by The Plantation Garden Preservation Trust
Number of gardeners 1 part-time, plus volunteers
Size 1.2ha (3 acres) approx.
English Heritage Grade II

RAVENINGHAM HALL GARDENS
Raveningham, Norwich NR14 6NS

Tel: 01508 548152 **Fax:** 01508 548958
www.raveningham.com
Location Signed off A146 at Hales.
Opening hours 1 pm – 4 pm on weekdays & 2 pm – 5 pm on Bank Holiday Sundays & Mondays. 12 to 17 February; 19 February; 15, 16 & 30 April; 1 May; 28 May to 2 June; 4 to 9 June; 11 & 12 June; 27 & 28 August.
Admission fee Adults £4; OAPs £3; Children free.

The house at Raveningham is partly Georgian and partly 20th-century: the 14th-century church of St Andrew near the house is an integral part of the landscape. Both are set in a splendid 18th-century park and enhanced by 19th-century tree plantings. Despite all this history, the main attraction now is the modern plantings. These were largely the work of Priscilla, Lady Bacon, who collected rare plants and arranged them beautifully in areas like the long herbaceous border. She was also a keen dendrologist and planted the young arboretum. In the working walled garden (very pretty) is a recently restored Victorian glasshouse. Outside the walled garden are an orchard and herb garden. A new lake has been made in the park, and there are contemporary sculptures by the present owner's wife throughout.

roses (mainly modern); good herbaceous borders; fine collection of trees; splendid 18th-century walled garden and Victorian glasshouses.

Owned by Sir Nicholas Bacon Bt.
Number of gardeners 3
Size 2ha (5 acres)
English Heritage Grade II

THE ROMANTIC GARDEN NURSERY
Swannington, Norwich NR9 5NW

Tel: 01603 261488 **Fax:** 01603 864231
www.romantic-garden-nursery.co.uk
Location 7 miles north-west of Norwich.
Opening hours 10 am – 5 pm; Wednesdays, Fridays, Saturdays & Bank Holidays.
Admission fee Free.

The Romantic Garden Nursery sells topiary: ornamental standards, bobbles and pyramids in *Cupressus* and *Ilex*, as well as box in animal and other shapes. It is a specialist nursery holding one of the largest selections of topiary and ornamental standards in the country. It offers topiary packages, too – these include a layout together with the necessary plants – and a range of wire frames for growing and shaping your own topiary. Also available are large specimens of conservatory plants and a 'plant hire' service, borrowing topiary and specimen plants for special occasions.
Owned by John Powles

SANDRINGHAM HOUSE
Sandringham, King's Lynn PE35 6EN

Tel: 01553 612908 **Fax:** 01485 541571
www.sandringhamestate.co.uk
Location Signed from A148.
Opening hours 10.30 am – 5 pm (4 pm in October); daily; 15 April to 20 July & 29 July to 29 October.
Admission fee Adults £5.50; OAPs £4.50; Children £3.50. RHS members free.

The best of the royal gardens, with much of interest at all seasons. The woodland and lakes are rich with ornamental plantings. The splendid herbaceous borders were designed by Eric Savill and the North Garden by Geoffrey Jellicoe, but it is the scale of it all that most impresses, and the grandeur, too. There will be two RHS Special Events at Sandringham in 2006; details from 020 7821 3408.

good herbaceous borders; rhododendrons; azaleas; maples; hydrangeas; gift shop; plant centre; restaurant & tea-rooms.

Owned by H.M. The Queen
Number of gardeners 8
Size 24ha (60 acres)
English Heritage Grade II*

SHERINGHAM PARK
Sheringham NR26 8TB

Tel: 01263 820550 **Fax:** 01263 820556
www.nationaltrust.org.uk
Location Junction of A148 & B1157.
Opening hours Dawn - dusk; daily; all year.
Admission fee Cars £3.20 (National Trust
members free)

P 🐕 WC ♿ ☕

This is one of the best Repton landscapes
to have survived the last 200 years, but it
was also fleshed out with a great 19th- and
20th-century collection of rhododendrons.
The owners also subscribed to E.H. Wilson's
expeditions and bought a great variety of
choice trees and shrubs from the Surrey
nurseries between the wars. The elegant
classical temple was built in 1975 to a
design by Repton. Recent clearing and
replanting have opened up the
rhododendron woods very successfully.
       woodland garden; mature conifers;
       rhododendrons; refreshments.

Owned by The National Trust
Number of gardeners 3
Size 20ha (50 acres)
English Heritage Grade II*

STOW HALL
Stow Bardolph, King's Lynn PE34 3HU

Tel: 01366 383194
Location 2 miles north of Downham Market, off
A10.
Opening hours 2 pm - 5 pm; 23 April. 5 pm -
9 pm; 23 June (plus flower arrangement
demonstration). And by appointment.
Admission fee Adults £3; Children free.

P 🐕 WC ♿ 🌱 🌺 ☕

Although the Hares have lived here for
450 years, the gardens at Stow Hall are
largely modern. Little remains of earlier
gardens except for their outline and the
magnificent, mature trees. These include
London plane trees, cedars of Lebanon
and vast beeches. The outbuildings, stables

and walled gardens are covered in climbing
roses and tender plants like *Azara microphylla*.
There is a working kitchen garden, and a
young collection of old apple cultivars. Old-
fashioned roses are everywhere.
       roses; kitchen garden; plant stall; home-
       made teas.

Owned by Lady Rose Hare
Number of gardeners 1½
Size 8ha (20 acres)

THORNCROFT CLEMATIS NURSERY
The Lings, Reymerston, Norwich
NR9 4QG

Tel: 01953 850407 **Fax:** 01953 851788
www.thorncroft.co.uk
Location Between Dereham & Wymondham on
B1135.
Opening hours 10 am - 4 pm; Tuesday - Saturday
& Bank Holiday Mondays; all year.
Admission fee Free.

P WC ♿ 🌾

This family-run specialist nursery began as a
hobby and has now developed into a
substantial business. In the display garden
attached to the nursery, the owners have set
out some of the many ways that clematis
may be grown – in borders and island beds,
over shrub roses, through ornamental trees
and in containers. There is also a formal
sunken garden with clipped box hedges and
classical obelisks (covered by yet more
clematis, and roses). The nursery does not
stock all clematis cultivars, but prefers to
list those it regards as best, selected for such
qualities as their length of flowering, colour,
form, quantity of bloom, strength of growth
and so on. These amount to some 300+
cultivars, including many new
introductions from around the world.
Owned by Ruth & Jonathan Gooch

NORTHAMPTONSHIRE

Despite its industrial importance and its proximity to London, Northamptonshire is still a county of large estates. Three of the four Grade I historic gardens are open to the public (Althorp, Boughton House and Castle Ashby), while the fourth (Drayton) is occasionally open to groups from organisations like the Garden History Society. Althorp and Boughton House also have good arboreta, each with a few champion trees. The National Gardens Scheme does well in Northamptonshire: it is particularly successful in persuading groups of gardens, as many as eight or nine in a village, to open together on the same day. It is therefore something of a paradox that there appear to be comparatively few nurseries in the county and only two National Collections. On the other hand, its RHS Free Access garden – Cottesbrooke – is a modern classic, an historic landscape with a really good horticultural garden inserted into it.

ALTHORP
Northampton NN7 4HQ

Tel: 01604 770107 **Fax:** 01604 770042
www.althorp.com
Location Signed from M1, Jct 16.
Opening hours 11 am – 5 pm; daily; July to September (provisional dates). Closed 31 August. All visits must be pre-booked on website: www.althorp.com
Admission fee Adults £10.50; OAPs £9.50; Children £5.50. (2005 prices.) Pre-booked only.

🅿 📶 ♿ 🌰 ☕

Althorp is interesting more for its ex-royal associations than as a great garden. However, it is said to be undergoing some improvement under the direction of Dan Pearson. The 19th-century formal gardens are impressive and the traditional parkland deeply pastoral. In the arboretum are some fine mature trees, including a record-breaking Santa Lucia fir (*Abies bracteata*) over 30m high.

🌿 mature conifers; formal gardens; biggest *Abies bracteata* (38m) in the British Isles; gift shop; café.

Owned by Earl Spencer
English Heritage Grade I

BOUGHTON HOUSE
Kettering NN14 1BJ

Tel: 01536 515731 **Fax:** 01536 417255
www.boughtonhouse.org.uk
Location A43, 3 miles north of Kettering, signed through Geddington.
Opening hours 1 pm – 5 pm; Saturday – Thursday; 1 May to 1 September. Daily in August.
Admission fee Adults £1.50; OAPs & Children £1.

🅿 🚗 📶 ♿ 🌱 🌰 ☕

Boughton has a seriously important landscaped park (350 acres/ 140ha) dating from the early 18th century. The layout is intact, and some of the plantings too – one of the lime avenues was planted in 1715. The original landscaping features have been purposefully restored over the last 20 years or so: rides, avenues, *allées*, lakes, canals and prospects – the restoration plan is ongoing. There is little of horticultural interest, but the sense of history is strongly felt.

🌿 roses (mainly modern); good herbaceous borders; good website; current holder of Sandford Award; shop; plant centre in walled kitchen garden; tea-rooms (weekends only; daily in August).

Owned by The Duke & Duchess of Buccleuch & The Living Landscape Trust
Number of gardeners 5
Size 8ha (20 acres) garden; 150-ha (350-acre) park
English Heritage Grade I

CANONS ASHBY HOUSE
Daventry NN11 3SD

Tel: 01327 861900 **Fax:** 01327 861909
www.nationaltrust.org.uk
Location Signed from A5 & A422.
Opening hours 11 am - 5.30 pm (4.30 pm in October & November); Saturday - Wednesday; 25 March to 5 November. 11 am - 4 pm; Saturdays & Sundays; 11 November to 13 December.
Admission fee Garden only: Adults £2.20.

Canons Ashby is a rare survivor among gardens. The Drydens, who owned it, never really took to the landscape movement. The early 18th-century layout is intact and has been carefully restored by the National Trust. The terraces below the house (*very* pretty) are planted with clipped Portugal laurel (*Prunus lusitanica*) and period fruit trees. A place to contemplate old Tory values.

 topiary; fruit; good herbaceous borders; light lunches & teas.

Owned by The National Trust
Number of gardeners 2
Size 1.4ha (3½ acres)
English Heritage Grade II*

CASTLE ASHBY GARDENS
Castle Ashby, Northampton NN7 1LQ

Tel: 01604 696696 **Fax:** 01604 696516
www.castleashby.co.uk
Location Off A428 between Northampton & Bedford.
Opening hours 10 am - 5.30 pm (or dusk, if earlier); daily; all year. Closes at 4.30 pm from October to March.
Admission fee Adults £2.80; OAPs & Children £1.90. (Under review.)

Much thought and money has recently been spent on restoring the gardens at Castle Ashby. The Italian formal gardens were among the first to be renewed, and the arboretum has been restocked. There are stylish terraces, an orangery and greenhouses built by Sir Matthew Digby Wyatt in the 1860s, but perhaps the best thing about Castle Ashby is the park – 200 acres of it, designed by Capability Brown.

topiary; fine collection of trees; gift shops; plant centre; tea-rooms.

Owned by The Marquess of Northampton
Number of gardeners 5
Size 8ha (20 acres)
English Heritage Grade I

COTON MANOR
Guilsborough NN6 8RQ

Tel: 01604 740219 **Fax:** 01604 740838
www.cotonmanor.co.uk
Location Signed from A5199 (formerly A50) & A428.
Opening hours 12 noon - 5.30 pm; Tuesday - Saturday & Bank Holiday weekends; April to September. Plus Sundays in April & May.
Admission fee Adults £4.50; OAPs £4; Children £2.

The Pasley-Tylers have lived at Coton since the 1920s, and every generation has left its mark upon the garden. Among the best features are a rose garden, a herb garden, a woodland garden, colour plantings (including a wonderful crimson and pink border), a Mediterranean bank, a five-acre bluebell wood, an apple orchard with 80 English cultivars, and a wildflower meadow. Water is everywhere: pools, streams and ponds support hostas, primulas and the black-and-yellow flowers of *Kirengeshoma palmata*. There are surprises, too: one might suppose that the sweet-scented *Trachelospermum asiaticum* and long-flowering *Fremontodendron californicum* were too tender for Northamptonshire, but they both grow against the walls of the house. Recent plantings include a bog garden and an extension to the woodland garden. The whole garden comes together nicely because the plants are chosen for their overall contribution as well as their intrinsic merits. The standard of maintenance is excellent, while the presence of a few ornamental birds adds quite another dimension to a visit.

roses (mainly old cultivars); good herbaceous borders; bluebells; waterfowl; lots of pots; good garden nursery; home produce & gifts; light lunches & teas.

Owned by Ian Pasley-Tyler
Number of gardeners 3
Size 4ha (10 acres)

COTTESBROOKE HALL
Northampton NN6 8PF

Tel: 01604 505808 **Fax:** 01604 505619
www.cottesbrookehall.co.uk/frameset
Location 10 miles north of Northampton.
Opening hours 2 pm – 5.30 pm; Thursdays; May to September. Plus Wednesdays in May & June, 1 & 29 May & 28 August. For NGS: 6 August (2 pm – 5 pm).
Admission fee Garden only: Adults £5; Concessions £4; Children £2.50. RHS members free.

Cottesbrooke is the garden with everything: a two-mile drive, majestic parkland, a classical bridge, a fabulously pretty house, an 18th-century park, lakes, waterfalls, bluebell woods, rhododendrons, acres of daffodils, 27 cultivars of naturalised snowdrops, half-a-dozen garden rooms, Scheemakers's statues from Stowe, an armillary garden, pergolas, *allées*, 300-year-old cedars, new developments every year, immaculate maintenance, plants a-plenty, and the signatures of Geoffrey Jellicoe and Sylvia Crowe among the designers who have helped to develop it.

roses (mainly old-fashioned); good herbaceous borders; exceptionally harmonious design; thoughtful plantings; water gardens; wild gardens; HHA/Christie's Garden of the Year in 2000; tea-room.

Owned by Mr & Mrs A.R. Macdonald-Buchanan
Number of gardeners 6
English Heritage Grade II

HOLDENBY HOUSE GARDENS
Holdenby, Northampton NN6 8DJ

Tel: 01604 770074 **Fax:** 01604 770962
www.holdenby.com
Location 6 miles north-west of Northampton, off A5199 or A428.
Opening hours 1 pm – 5 pm; Sundays & Bank Holiday Mondays; April to September.
Admission fee Adults £4.50; OAPs £4; Children £3. Different tariffs for special events.

The outlines of the garden at Holdenby are Elizabethan: a bowling alley, some parterres and terraces which were built in 1580 to impress Queen Elizabeth on one of her progresses through England. They explain why Holdenby is so highly regarded as an historical garden. What we see now is modern and pretty. The Elizabethan-style garden was planted by Rosemary Verey, using only those plants which were available in 1580. Rupert Golby planted the 'fragrant border' and there is a charming 'silver border' made to display the owners' ever-growing collection of silver- and grey-leaved plants.

roses (mainly old-fashioned); herbs; good herbaceous borders; Elizabethan-style garden; fragrant and silver borders; kitchen garden; current holder of Sandford Award; souvenirs and crafts for sale; tea room in original Victorian kitchen.

Owned by Mr & Mrs James Lowther
Number of gardeners 2
Size 6ha (15 acres)
English Heritage Grade II*

KELMARSH HALL
Northampton NN6 9LU

Tel: 01604 686543 **Fax:** 01604 686437
www.kelmarsh.com
Location On A508 at crossroads in Kelmarsh.
Opening hours 2 pm – 5.30 pm; Tuesday –
Thursday & Sundays; 16 April to 28 September.
For NGS: 23 April.
Admission fee Adults £3.50; Concessions £3;
Children £2.

🅿 ⬆ 🅆🅲 ♿ ❦ ⛾

Kelmarsh is a handsome Palladian house: it
looks out over a formal terrace, designed by
Geoffrey Jellicoe in 1936, to formalised
parkland. The view extends across a
meadow lined with horse-chestnuts to a
lake before wilder, open semi-parkland
carries the eye to the horizon. Most of the
horticultural interest is off to the side,
around the outside of a triangular walled
garden. First come lumpy box hedges,
pleached limes and a pretty sunken garden,
designed as a quincunx and planted with
white and scented flowers. Further on,
Tropaeolum speciosum clambers through the
hedges which flank a sequence of narrow,
intimate beds, designed by Nancy
Lancaster with help from Norah Lindsay.
Some of the yew hedges have been
breached by cutting the yew trees back to
the trunks and letting them grow into
curious hump-backed shapes – a very
effective and unique feature of the garden.
At the furthest extremity, the narrow path
bursts out into a fan-shaped old-fashioned
rose garden, recently remade, with a
splendid view of the parish church across
parkland. On the way back (outside the
walled garden again) is the long border,
another Lancaster-Lindsay collaboration,
which is currently being restored and
replanted. This is a fine garden, which will
be interesting to watch as it develops in
years to come. A Heritage Lottery grant
has funded the restoration of the vinery
and back sheds, which means that the
walled garden with its cut-flower borders is
now fully accessible.

❧ spring bulbs; old hedges; lots of recent
restoration; teas.

Owned by The Kelmarsh Trust
Number of gardeners 3½
Size 5.6ha (14 acres)

OLD RECTORY
Sudborough NN14 3BX

Tel: 01832 733247 **Fax:** 01832 733832
www.oldrectorygardens.co.uk
Location A14, Exit 12. In village centre, by church,
off A6116.
Opening hours By appointment.
Admission fee Adults £4; Children free.

🅆🅲 ♿ ❦ ⛾

This immaculately maintained modern
garden has been made around a handsome
Georgian rectory with a bit of advice from
Rosemary Verey and Rupert Golby. In front
of the house, on the edge of the lawn, is a
handsome and ancient *Robinia
pseudoacacia*: everything else is fairly recent
and extremely well grown. The garden is
thickly and thoughtfully planted so that
every season is rich in interest. Few of the
plants are rare, but all are well chosen –
some for their flowers, some for their
foliage and others because they look good
in mixed groups. Roses are much in
evidence throughout the garden and in a
dedicated rose garden. The best feature is
an extensive and very pretty *potager*, which
has an infinite number of beds edged and
fairly narrow brick paths between them.
Clematis and roses cover the framework of
a tunnel: they are joined, in season, by
ornamental gourds which are encouraged
to grow up the same structure. The fruit
trees are trained in many different ways
and good use is made of flowers in pots to
ensure that the *potager* has colour at all
seasons.

❧ roses (ancient & modern); herbs; fruit;
good herbaceous borders; handsome
new *potager*; tea, coffee & biscuits.

Owned by Mr & Mrs A.P. Huntington
Number of gardeners 2
Size 1.2ha (3 acres)

ROCKINGHAM CASTLE
Market Harborough LE16 8TH

Tel: 01586 770240 **Fax:** 01586 771692
www.rockinghamcastle.com
Location 2 miles north of Corby on A6003.
Opening hours 12 noon – 5 pm; Sundays & Bank
Holiday Mondays; 16 April to September. Plus
Tuesdays from June to September.
Admission fee £4.50.

🅿 ⏴ 🆆🅲 ⅃ 🐜 🗗

Rockingham has centuries of garden
history in its layout: the park was
landscaped in the 18th century but goes
back to the 13th century as a deer park.
The formal circular rose garden on the site
of the old keep was added in the 19th
century: it is surrounded by a billowing yew
hedge 400 years old, known as the
'Elephant Hedge'. The wild garden in a
ravine was replanted 20 years ago as a
mini-arboretum: all the modern plantings
are very effective.

🌿 roses (mainly old-fashioned); good
herbaceous borders; fine collection of
trees; gift shop; tea-room.

Owned by James Saunders Watson
Number of gardeners 3
Size 5ha (12½ acres)
English Heritage Grade II*

SULGRAVE MANOR
Sulgrave, Banbury OX17 2SD

Tel: 01295 760205 **Fax:** 01295 76805
www.sulgravemanor.org.uk
Location 7 miles from Banbury.
Opening hours 12 noon – 5.30 pm; 1 April to 31
October. Closed Mondays & Fridays except Bank
Holidays. Groups at other times by appointment.
Admission fee Adults £5.75; Children £2.50. But
Adults £6.50; Children £3.25 for special events.

🅿 🆆🅲 ⅃ 🌱 🗗

There are two reasons for visiting Sulgrave.
The first is that it belonged to George
Washington's family or, at least, to his
ancestors. This places the Great American
firmly among the English minor gentry.
The second is that, after the estate was
underwritten by the Colonial Dames in
1924, Sir Reginald Blomfield was called in
to design a period garden. In his day,
Blomfield was one of England's foremost
architect-designers, and the garden he
made for Sulgrave is formally laid out in a
simple, 17th-century style, to complement
the old house. The plantings are suitably
olde worlde. The Herb Society moved its
headquarters to Sulgrave in 2001 and has
planted a herb garden which is full of
interest but rather spoils the spirit of the
place.

🌿 herbs; tea-room.

Owned by Sulgrave Manor Board
Number of gardeners 2
Size 2ha (5 acres)
English Heritage Grade II

NORTHUMBERLAND AND TYNE & WEAR

Northumberland and Tyne & Wear are two sides of the same historical phenomenon: men made their fortunes in Newcastle or Sunderland, both now in Tyne & Wear, and then moved out to build houses and plant gardens in Northumberland. Belsay, Cragside and Lindisfarne all owe their gardens to this social pattern. Belsay is a Grade I garden: the only other one in Northumberland is Alnwick, where the Duchess of Northumberland has nearly finished building a spectacular new garden. The greatest 19th-century garden in Northumberland is Cragside, which now has a collection of champion conifers. There are record-breakers, too, at Alnwick, and a very good arboretum at Howick, where many new plantings have also been made in recent years. The National Gardens Scheme does not have a large portfolio of gardens in Northumberland and Tyne & Wear, but there are several first-rate nurseries in the two counties, including Halls of Heddon, Herterton House and Hexham Herbs. The real interests of ordinary gardeners in Northumberland and Tyne & Wear are quite different: alpines and leeks. Both the Alpine Garden Society and the Scottish Rock Garden Club are well supported here, while the National Pot Leek Society could be described as a uniquely Geordie success story.

THE ALNWICK GARDEN
Denwick Lane, Alnwick NE66 1YU

Tel: 01665 511350 **Fax:** 01665 511351
www.alnwickgarden.com
Location Signed in Alnwick & from A1.
Opening hours 10 am - 7 pm (4 pm in winter); daily; all year. Closed Christmas Day.
Admission fee Adults £6; Concessions £5.75; Children free.

🅿 🚾 ♿ ♣ ♿

The Alnwick Garden has become a major tourist attraction in a very short time – and deservedly so, because it is wonderful to visit. First open to the public in 2001, it is a continuing project, with new features appearing all the time. The Duchess of Northumberland is the driving force behind it, and the gifted Jacques Wirtz is its designer. The main feature is already impressive – a grand neo-baroque water cascade flanked by hornbeam arcades in the Belgian style and ending in fountains. At the top, you enter the Ornamental Garden, a place of box-lined paths, pleached apples, tender climbers (tea roses and ceanothus against the walls) and the best continental-style of planting outside Belgium. Here, too, are rare roses from Lens in Belgium, like 'Frisson Frais' and 'Lieve Louise', seldom seen in England. Whole beds are dedicated to a single genus, like hellebores, irises, Japanese anemones and delphiniums, so that there is always something to see, whatever the season. Down the hill again (the cascade flows down a north-facing slope and is difficult to photograph well – photographers, please note) is an excellent, thickly planted David Austin rose garden, with pergolas, climbers, shrub roses and a few mixed plantings – very beautiful. In fact the whole garden is probably best when all the roses are out in high summer. Work continues. The poison garden, serpent garden and bamboo labyrinth all opened last year (2005). The garden will be more-or-less complete this year (2006) when the new visitor centre and pavilion open. The standard of maintenance is exemplary. The lack of a decent horticultural guidebook is regrettable, but this should not detract from the enormous pleasure of a visit to this enormous, sumptuous, inspirational and fascinating garden.

 grand cascade; roses; shop; restaurant.

Owned by The Alnwick Garden Trust
Number of gardeners 8
Size 16ha (40 acres) including 4.8ha (12 acres) of walled garden

BEDE'S WORLD HERB GARDEN
Bede's World, Church Bank, Jarrow NE32 3DY

Tel: 0191 489 2106 **Fax:** 0191 428 2361
www.bedesworld.co.uk
Location Signed from A185 & A19.
Opening hours 10 am – 5 .30 pm; daily; all year. Opens 12 noon on Sundays. Closes 4.30 pm from November to March. Closed Good Friday and Christmas to New Year.
Admission fee Herb Garden only: free.
🅿 🚾 ♿ 🌱 🐌 📷

Bede's World is an educational experience: one of its main parts is an 'Anglo-Saxon farm' with a vegetable garden where early cultivars of vegetables are grown. But there is also a herb garden, based on a plan of the 9th-century original at St Gall in Switzerland, where culinary, aromatic and medicinal herbs are grown. It is a small part of an ambitious enterprise which seeks to impart a feeling for the Anglo-Saxon world.

herbs; shop for herbal products; lunches & light refreshments.

Owned by Bede's World

BELSAY HALL
Belsay, Newcastle-upon-Tyne NE20 0DX

Tel: 01661 881636 **Fax:** 01661 881043
www.english-heritage.org.uk
Location At Belsay on A696 Ponteland to Jedburgh road.
Opening hours 10 am – 6 pm (4 pm in October); daily; April to October. 10 am – 4 pm; Thursday – Monday; November to March. Closed 1 January & 24 to 26 December.
Admission fee Adults £5.30; Concessions £4; Children £2.70. (2005 prices.)
🅿 🍴 🚾 ♿ 🌱 🐌 📷

The wildly Picturesque gardens at Belsay were created by Sir Charles Monck in the 19th century around his new Greek Revival house. The outstanding feature is 11 acres (4.4ha) of disused quarry with a sequence of gloomy chasms, corridors and pinnacles, which house all manner of exotic and rare plants. Rhododendron species flower here from November to August, climbers scramble 10m up the quarry faces, spring bulbs carpet the meadow and modern underplantings like lilies flower from May to September. The ravines create a microclimate which allows such plants as *Trachycarpus* palms and eucryphias to flourish in a cold upland site: Belsay is of great interest to plantsmen. The house is very austere – inspired by ancient Athens – but underpinned by fine formal terraces where the gardeners arrange magnificent displays of bedding. Down the valley are splendid woods planted with two acres of hardy hybrid rhododendrons – not open to the public, but a magnificent sight from the terraces. Elsewhere are fine weed-free lawns (one is for croquet), intensive modern herbaceous plantings, a magnolia terrace, a recently restored rose border, tall heathers, brooding conifers (some of the earliest Douglas firs in England) and the stately ruins of Belsay Castle. The standard of maintenance is superb.

snowdrops; rhododendrons & azaleas (species & hardy hybrids); formal terraces; winter garden; unique quarry garden;

BIDE-A-WEE COTTAGE
Stanton, Netherwitton, Morpeth NE65 8PR

Tel & Fax: 01670 772238
www.bideawee.co.uk
Location 7 miles north-west of Morpeth.
Opening hours 1.30 pm – 5 pm; Wednesdays &
Saturdays; 22 April to 26 August. Parties by
arrangement at other times.
Admission fee £2.50. RHS members free.
P ❦ ♣

The situation of the garden at Bide-a-
Wee Cottage is extraordinary: most
of the garden is hidden in a disused
quarry on the edge of a 160m (500ft)
ridge. The unusual site means that there
are enormous variations within its two
acres – variations of aspect, topography,
soil-type and moisture. Over the last 20
years, Mark Robson has seized on this
natural diversity to plant a remarkably
wide spectrum of plants. In the wet,
shaded quarry bottom, by the ponds, are
swathes of primulas, rodgersias, ostrich
ferns, sensitive ferns and gunneras. Away
from the water, on the north-facing
slopes of the quarry and in the shade of
trees, are meconopsis, rhododendrons
and gentians. Quite a different type of
plant grows on the south-facing slopes:
abutilons, agapanthus and eryngiums, for
example. Throughout the garden, the
natural rock walls are contrasted with
hedges and complemented by evergreens
– conifers, rhododendrons and grasses.
Then more ephemeral perennials and
wildflowers are woven into the design, as
are the more unusual plants that are the
hallmark of a plantsman. Robson
describes his garden as 'bold perennial
plantings linked with a network of
winding paths and steps, all associated
with dramatic changes of level'. These
are designed to create views across the
garden or down onto lower levels, as well
as into the countryside beyond. To the
east, above the quarry, drifts of late-
flowering perennials (including lythrum,
eupatorium and helianthus) melt into
the half-acre wildflower meadow that is
also home to the beehives. Then the
garden opens out and blends into the
rough landscape of Northumberland –
tough grassland grazed by sheep.
❧ rock garden; plantsman's collection
of plants; excellent nursery selling
plants from garden.

Owned by Mark Robson
Size 0.8ha (2 acres)
NCCPG National Collections *Centaurea*

gift shop; refreshments in summer.

Owned by Managed by English Heritage on behalf of the Belsay Trust
Number of gardeners 4, plus 1 trainee
Size 16ha (40 acres)
NCCPG National Collections *Iris spuria*
English Heritage Grade I

BIRKHEADS COTTAGE GARDEN NURSERY
Birkheads Lane, Causey Arch, Sunniside, Newcastle-upon-Tyne NE16 5EL

Tel: 07778 447920 **Fax:** 01207 232262
www.birkheadsnursery.co.uk
Location Follow brown tourist signs on A6076 between Sunniside & Stanley.
Opening hours 10 am – 5 pm; daily, except Mondays; March to October. And by appointment at other times and seasons. Guided walks at 2 pm on the first Tuesday of the month (booking essential – £3.50). Groups by appointment.
Admission fee Garden: £2. Nursery: free.

This nursery offers a varied and informed selection of alpines, perennials and shrubs, all of which can be seen growing in the adjoining gardens; the owner is a garden designer with a passion for plants. The gardens include an avenue of soft blue, pink and silver perennials, the Bowes railway heritage garden, over half a mile of colour-themed borders, a mini-arboretum underplanted with spring bulbs, the roundel slate garden with old roses and scented shrubs, a wildflower mead, an oriental-style meditation garden with pond, the spring garden planted with a woodland theme for all-year interest, a wildlife pond, the beachcombers' garden, a gravel and rock garden.

a plantsman's garden attached to a plantsman's nursery; small coffee shop.

Owned by Christine Liddle
Number of gardeners 3
Size 1.2ha (3 acres)

CHESTERS WALLED GARDEN
Chollerford, Hexham NE46 4BQ

Tel: 01434 681483
www.chesterswalledgarden.co.uk
Location 6 miles north of Hexham, off B6318 near Chollerford.
Opening hours 10 am – 5 pm; daily; 21 March to October. Telephone for winter opening times.
Admission fee Adults £2.50; Children (under 10) free.

This energetic and successful garden-nursery is strategically placed near the fort at Chesters. The original name of the nursery was 'Hexham Herbs'. Now the garden is a tourist attraction in its own right, and the nursery better than ever. The herb collection is remarkable (over 900 cultivars) and the design within a two-acre brick-walled garden is charming. Dye plants, a Mediterranean garden, two ponds, an astilbe bed and a knot garden are just some of the features. Much of the structure comes from box hedges, but wildflowers have been allowed to seed alongside the more exotic plants, which gives an air of naturalness. In addition to their National Collections of *Origanum* and *Thymus*, the nursery has a very good collection of mint cultivars. The garden has over 3,000 different plant cultivars growing in it, and the owner aims to propagate and sell them all in rotation, which means that if they do not have something just at the moment, you should be able to buy it from them in the future.

thyme bank; roses (mainly old-fashioned); herbs; 'Roman' garden; grass garden; wildlife ponds; nursery attached; gift & produce shop.

Owned by Mrs S. White
Size 0.8ha (2 acres)
NCCPG National Collections *Origanum, Thymus*

CRAGSIDE
Rothbury, Morpeth NE65 7PX

Tel: 01669 620333 **Fax:** 01669 620066
www.nationaltrust.org.uk
Location 15 miles north-west of Morpeth, off
A697 & B6341.
Opening hours Gardens: 10.30 am – 7 pm (last
admissions 5 pm); Tuesday – Sunday & Bank
Holiday Mondays; 1 April to 29 October. 11 am –
4 pm; Wednesday – Sunday; 1 November to 17
December.
Admission fee Adults £5.70; Children £2.60.

P WC ♿ ❀ 🌰 ☕

There are three gardens at Cragside: all
were made by the armaments millionaire
Lord Armstrong when he started to build
the house in 1863. First comes the
Italianate formal garden with splendid
carpet bedding, ferneries and a fruit house
with rotating pots. Then there is the
large, semi-natural rock garden by the
house. But most impressive of all are the
rhododendron woods – hundreds and
hundreds of acres of 19th-century hybrids,
plus trusty *R. ponticum* and *R. luteum*. The
estate drives take you for six miles all the
way round, past granite boulders,
moorland, heather and conifers – but the
rhododendrons dominate the journey,
breathtaking in early June.

fruit; mature conifers; massive rock
garden; tallest *Abies nordmanniana*
(50m), *Cupressus nootkatensis* (33m) and *Picea
glauca* (28m) in the British Isles; National Trust
shop; refreshments.

Owned by The National Trust
Number of gardeners 4
English Heritage Grade II*

THE GARDEN STATION
Langley-on-Tyne, Hexham NE47 5LA

Tel: 01434 684391
www.thegardenstation.co.uk
Location A686 Alston road off A69 for 2½
miles, then follow yellow signs on left.

Opening hours 10 am – 5 pm; daily, except
Mondays; May to August.
Admission fee Free. Donation welcome.

P ♿ ❀ 🌰 ☕

A small centre for gardening and art
courses, The Garden Station is a very
attractive restored Victorian railway
station in a sheltered, tranquil woodland
garden. Following along the old track
under stone arched bridges, the garden
extends into a walk planted with
foxgloves, *Meconopsis*, hostas, ferns and
primulas. There will be two RHS Special
Events at The Garden Station in 2006;
details from 020 7821 3408.

plants for sale; light refreshments.

Owned by Jane Torday
Number of gardeners 2 part-time

HALLS OF HEDDON
West Heddon Nurseries, Heddon on the
Wall, Newcastle-upon-Tyne NE15 0JS

Tel: 01661 852445 **Fax:** 01661 852398
www.hallsofheddon.co.uk
Location 1 mile north-west of Heddon, off
B6318.
Opening hours 9 am – 5 pm, Monday –
Saturday; 10 am – 5 pm, Sundays.
Admission fee Free.

P WC ❀

Halls produced their first dahlia and
chrysanthemum catalogue in 1931: now
they offer cultivars for many purposes,
including showing, cutting, garden
display, greenhouse cultivation and
growing in pots and containers. Their
extensive list includes many cultivars
which are unique to them. Their
magnificent show fields are open from
September until the plants are cut down
by the frosts: they have over 10,000 plants
on display. The garden centre carries a
good general range.
Number of gardeners 4
Size 0.4ha (1 acre)

HERTERTON HOUSE GARDENS & NURSERY
Hartington, Cambo NE61 4BN

Tel: 01670 774278
Location 2 miles north of Cambo (B6342).
Opening hours 1.30 pm - 5.30 pm; daily except Tuesdays & Thursdays; April to September. For NGS: on 15 June, 13 July & 3 August.
Admission fee Adults £2.80; Children £1.

P WC ❧ ❧

This excellent plantsman's garden is firmly designed and meticulously planted. The formal garden (very simple, very full) relies on contrasts of colour, texture and shape of clipped evergreens – a model of how to impart a sense of size and space to a very small space. There is topiary throughout the garden; it also provides shelter for tender plants like 'Gloire de Dijon' roses. The knot garden is famous, and much photographed, full of herbs and pharmacological plants. The main garden is best seen from the staircase at the back of the house; it has a very firm structure, furnished with evergreen shrubs clipped into endless inventive forms to give interest all through the year. More impressive still are the cottagey herbaceous plantings, all weaving through each other in beautifully co-ordinated colours. In the gazebo at the top are photographs showing how the garden has developed, expanded, grown up and intensified over the years: a most inspirational display. A modern masterpiece.

❧ plantsman's collection of plants; small formal garden; physic garden; nursery garden; first-class nursery attached.

Owned by Mr & Mrs Frank Lawley
Number of gardeners 2
Size 0.4ha (1 acre)

HOWICK HALL
Alnwick NE66 3LB

Tel: 01665 577285
www.howickgarden.org.uk
Location Off B1399 between Longhoughton & Craster.
Opening hours 1 pm - 6 pm; daily; Easter to October.
Admission fee Adults £4; OAPs £3; Children free.

P WC ♿ ⚐

Howick is a very good garden, full of interesting plants. It is also rather un-Northumbrian, because its closeness to the sea makes possible the cultivation of such tender plants as tree-fuchsias, carpenterias, olearias and ceanothus. The handsome Palladian house has well-planted formal terraces below – you cannot miss the 70m ribbon of agapanthus in high summer – and there is a rock garden to one side. The woodland garden has acid soil, and was planted in the 1930s with a fine collection of rhododendrons and camellias together with shrubs like linderas and underplantings of lilies, hellebores and candelabra primulas. Elsewhere are fine parkland, a large bog garden, lots of new plantings (groves of cercidiphyllums) from collected seed, daffodils, colchicums and curiosities like an oak tree and a beech tree all intermingled because they were planted in the 19th century in the same hole. The present Lord Howick is an avid plant-collector: new this year (2006) is an arboretum planted with some 11,000 trees and shrubs (1,700 taxa) all grown from wild-collected seed.

❧ roses (mainly old-fashioned); rhododendrons & azaleas; plantsman's collection of plants; mature conifers; spring bulbs; eucryphias; much new planting; champion *Magnolia wilsonii*; tea-room.

Owned by Howick Trustees Ltd
Number of gardeners 5
English Heritage Grade II

KIRKLEY HALL GARDENS
Ponteland NE20 0AQ

Tel: 01670 841200 **Fax:** 01661 860047
Location Signed in Ponteland.
Opening hours 10 am - 5 pm; weekdays; all year.
And by appointment at weekends. Closes at 3
pm from October to March.
Admission fee Free.

P WC & ✿ ✿

The Victorian, walled garden at Kirkley
Hall is one of the best in the north of
England in which to learn how to garden.
The emphasis is on plants – their
selection, cultivation and enjoyment –
though cutbacks mean that standards of
maintenance are somewhat relaxed.
Further demonstration gardens have been
laid out between the walled garden and
the house, with some interesting trees and
shrubs along the way.

woodland garden; plantsman's
collection of plants; plants under
glass; fruit; mature conifers; good herbaceous
borders; plant centre.

Owned by Northumberland College at Kirkley
Hall
Number of gardeners 3
Size 4ha (10 acres)
NCCPG National Collections *Fagus*

LONGFRAMLINGTON GARDENS
Swarland Road, Longframlington,
Morpeth NE65 8BE

Tel & Fax: 01665 570382
www.longframlingtongardens.co.uk
Location ³⁄₄ mile east of Longframlington along
B6345.
Opening hours 8.30 am - 5 pm (or dusk, if
earlier); daily; all year. Closed Christmas to New
Year. Evenings by appointment.
Admission fee Adults £3. Nursery free.

P ◁ WC & ✿ ▢

This young garden was started in 1998 in a
cold, open, windy, greenfield position and
has a chirpy, modern design where low-
maintenance is important. It is worth
visiting to see how many plants have
survived recent winters in this
unpromising site – including cistus, hebes
and *Olearia macrodonta*. The main problem
at this stage is to acquire sufficient shelter
to allow ornamentals to grow and establish
well. The nursery is said to offer over
2,500 different plants, all of them suitable
for the Northumbrian climate.

young nursery; new garden; coffee
shop.

Owned by Hazel Huddleston
Size 5ha (12½ acres)

SEATON DELAVAL HALL
Seaton Sluice, Whitley Bay NE26 4QR

Tel: 0191 237 1493
Location ½ mile from coast between Whitley
Bay & Blyth.
Opening hours 2 pm - 6 pm; Wednesdays &
Sundays; June to September. Plus Bank Holidays
in May & August.
Admission fee Adults £4; OAPs £3.50; Children
£1. (2005 prices.)

P WC

The garden is modern: one of Jim Russell's
earliest works, it dates from 1948 and is
stylish, expansive, and easy to maintain.
Parterres and topiary of yew and box are
used to enclose old-fashioned roses,
handsome ornaments and a fountain: a fair
match for the sumptuous house –
Vanbrugh's masterpiece. The horticultural
interest comes from a fine weeping ash (it
dates back to before 1750), good plantings
of rhododendrons and azaleas, and a
laburnum walk.

rhododendrons & azaleas; laburnum
tunnel; ice house; roses.

Owned by Lord Hastings
Number of gardeners 2
Size 0.8ha (2 acres)
English Heritage Grade II*

ST LUKE'S COTTAGE
North Road, Wooley, Hexham NE46 1TN

Tel: 01434 673445
Location 3 miles south of Hexham (A69); 3 miles east of A68.
Opening hours By appointment.
Admission fee Donation to Multiple Sclerosis Society.

P WC ❧

Alan Furness is a long-standing stalwart of the Alpine Garden Society, that most august of specialist horticultural societies. His garden in a cool valley in southern Northumberland illustrates the enormous opportunities for growing alpine plants which such a situation offers. Within his garden is a wide range of specially constructed habitats to suit an equally wide range of plants: a large limestone scree, and one for acid-loving plants; several high humus beds and meadow beds; a tufa rock bed; a crevice bed, a raised bed and several damp areas; and four alpine houses. Celmisias (species and garden hybrids), primulas, saxifrages, gentians and pulsatillas are especially well represented, but the whole garden is both a revelation and an inspiration.

❧ alpine plants; screes; many different microhabitats.

Owned by Alan Furness
Size 0.3ha (¾ acre)
NCCPG National Collections *Celmisia*

WALLINGTON
Cambo, Morpeth NE61 4AR

Tel: 01670 773600 **Fax:** 01670 774420
www.nationaltrust.org.uk
Location 6 miles north-west of Belsay (A696).
Opening hours 10 am - 7 pm; daily; all year. Closes at 6 pm in October & 4 pm between November and March. Grounds open daily in daylight hours.
Admission fee Adults £5.20; Children £2.60.

P ⬧ WC ♿ ❧ ✿ ◗

There are three reasons to visit Wallington. First, because Capability Brown was born in nearby Kirkharle. Second, to gawp at the ancient tree-like specimen of *Fuchsia* 'Rose of Castile' in the conservatory. Third, to admire the modern mixed borders (*very* Graham Stuart Thomas) in the long, irregular, walled garden, in a sheltered valley far from the house. Worth the journey for any of them, but prepare for a longish walk to the walled garden.

❧ woodland garden; roses (mainly old-fashioned & climbers); rhododendrons & azaleas; plants under glass; daffodils; good herbaceous borders; tallest *Sorbus discolor* (7m) in the British Isles; shop; restaurant.

Owned by The National Trust
Number of gardeners 5
NCCPG National Collections *Sambucus*
English Heritage Grade II*

NOTTINGHAMSHIRE

For a county of such historic importance, Nottinghamshire has comparatively few historic gardens. Clumber Park has lost the house that was once at its centre, and Newstead Abbey has long lost its most famous owner, Lord Byron. Nevertheless, there are some interesting 19th-century gardens in Nottinghamshire, including the curious little arboretum at Papplewick Pumping Station. One of the best civic parks in England is the Nottingham Arboretum, 8ha (20 acres) in extent, which opened in 1852: the architect Sir Joseph Paxton and the nurseryman Samuel Curtis both advised the founders. Nowadays there are few nurseries of national importance in the county. Nevertheless, the *RHS Plant Finder* had its origins in the list of nurseries prepared by the Nottingham Group of the Hardy Plant Society in the 1970s and early 1980s. The county also has some nine National Collections. The National Gardens Scheme lists a fair number of gardens of all sizes that open in Nottinghamshire for charity: the RHS Free Access garden at Felley Priory is one of exceptional interest and beauty, and a good example of what can be achieved on an unpromising site in only a few years. One further sight should not be missed – the incredible hulk of the Major Oak, also known as Robin Hood's Oak, in Sherwood Forest.

CLUMBER PARK
Worksop S80 3AZ

Tel: 01909 476592/544917 **Fax:** 01909 500721
www.nationaltrust.org.uk
Location Off A614 Nottingham Road, 4 miles south of Worksop.
Opening hours Park: dawn - dusk; daily; all year, but closed on 8 July, 19 August & 25 December. Walled garden: 10 am - 5.30 pm; Monday - Friday; 10 am - 6 pm; Saturdays, Sundays & Bank Holidays; 1 April to 1 October.
Admission fee Walled garden: Adults £2. Cars £4.30; Pedestrians, Cyclists & coaches free.

🅿 ⬙ ♿ ⚲ ☕ ⬗

Clumber has over 3,800 acres of thickly wooded parkland with a Gothic chapel, classical bridge, temples, an avenue of cedars, a heroic double avenue of limes and masses of rhododendrons. There are good conservatories and a garden tools exhibition in the old walled garden. The main glasshouse range, at 150m, is the longest owned by the National Trust. But the scale of everything at Clumber is enormous: very impressive.

🌿 woodland garden; autumn colour; vineries; old rhubarb cultivars; superb trees; tallest *Ilex aquifolium* 'Laurifolia' (20m) in the British Isles; National Trust shop; restaurant.

Owned by The National Trust
Number of gardeners 4, plus seasonal help
Size 13ha (32 acres) of gardens in 1,500ha (3,800 acres) of park
English Heritage Grade I

HODSOCK PRIORY
Blyth, Worksop S81 0TY

Tel: 01909 591204 **Fax:** 01909 591578
www.snowdrops.co.uk
Location Signed off B6045 between Blyth & Worksop.
Opening hours 10 am - 4 pm; daily; 28 January to 5 March.
Admission fee Adults £4; Children £1.

FELLEY PRIORY
Underwood NG16 5FJ

Tel: 01773 810230 **Fax:** 01773 580440
Location ½ mile west of M1, Jct 27, on A608.
Opening hours 9 am - 12.30 pm; Tuesdays,
Wednesdays & Fridays; all year. Plus 9 am -
4 pm; second & fourth Wednesday of every
month; March to October. And 11 am - 4 pm;
every third Sunday of month; March to October.
For NGS: 11 am - 4 pm; 9 April. NCCPG plants
fairs: 12 noon - 4 pm; 4 June & 1 October.
Parties welcome, by appointment.
Admission fee Adults £3; OAPs £2.50; Children
& RHS members free.

P WC & 🌱 🌺 ⬧

Parts of the house at Felley Priory – a
wonderful brick and dark red sandstone
building – date back to 1150. One link with
the 16th century is a venerable pear tree
which grows against the house: the Royal
Horticultural Society has identified it as
'Jargonelle', an ancient cultivar well known
before 1600. Major and Mrs Chaworth-
Musters started work on the garden in 1976
and were, from the start, adventurous
gardeners, willing to try plants which might
be considered doubtfully hardy at 180m
(600ft) so far inland. The results are
astonishing. Against the garden walls are
Buddleja colvilei, nandinas, eucryphias,
several hebes and *Drimys winteri*: elsewhere
in the garden are *Podocarpus salignus* and
Correa backhouseana. Felley Priory is an
excellent garden for plants, with a very
large number of interesting ones in flower
at every season – enough to start a nursery
where everything is propagated from the
garden. Shrubs are a major interest, and

Felley has good collections of magnolias,
cornus, hydrangeas, *Paeonia suffruticosa* and
viburnums. Bulbs are planted in great
numbers: as well as snowdrops and
cyclamen there are massive displays of
daffodils in spring. The handsome yew
hedges are little more than 20 years old, yet
they fill the garden with their bulk: some
have been turned into objects of topiary,
with curvy tops and bobbles and birds. In
the rose garden is a good display of well-
grown old-fashioned roses: there are about
90 different cultivars, some imported
directly from French nurseries. The rarities
include a pink-and-white form of *Rosa
multiflora* which was collected in Korea by
Jamie Compton. The mediaeval garden
harks back to the original priory which was
lost at the time of the Reformation: it is
planted with plants that were known in the
15th century – among them are lilies, roses,
violas, columbines, irises, tulips and
Phillyrea latifolia. Everything at Felley is
charming, stylish well trained and well
grown. New plants arrive constantly from
all the best nurseries: the garden gets better
all the time.

old-fashioned rose gardens; good
herbaceous borders; knot gardens,
two pergolas and thousands of daffodils; new
pleached hedge of *Crataegus tanacetifolia*;
unusual trees and shrubs; nursery attached;
refreshments.

Owned by The Hon. Mrs Chaworth-Musters
Size 1ha (2½ acres)

⊞ ⬚ ✦ ⬡

The gardens at Hodsock are unique in February when visitors can see a remarkable winter feature – snowdrops. There are thousands and thousands of them. They have also been planting ferns and lots of winter-flowering plants: *Cyclamen coum*, sarcococcas, daphnes and loniceras.

✿ aconites; hellebores; hepaticas; winter-flowering plants of all kinds; large *Catalpa* (Indian bean tree); tea-room.

Owned by Sir Andrew & Lady Buchanan
Number of gardeners 1 full-time, 3 part-time
Size 2ha (5 acres) plus woodland

HOLME PIERREPONT HALL
Holme Pierrepont, Nottingham NG12 2LD

Tel & Fax: 0115 933 2371
www.holmepierreponthall.com
Location 3 miles east of Trent Bridge.
Opening hours 2 pm – 5 pm; Monday – Wednesday; 1 February to 23 March. And 9 April for *Tulipa sylvestris*, and for NGS. Groups by appointment at other times.
Admission fee House & gardens: £4.50; Gardens: £2.

⊞ ⬚ ✦

The house at Holme Pierrepont is both beautiful and historic. The main attraction of the garden is a large courtyard garden, designed in 1875, whose box parterre is filled with modern plantings. But there are fine recent additions, too, including splendid herbaceous borders and interesting fruit trees. The rare English tulip *Tulipa sylvestris* grows wild in a remote part of the fields. The main openings, in late winter and early spring, are planned for when the snowdrops and winter-flowering plants are at their peak. The April opening is when the rare wild English tulip *Tulipa sylvestris* is at its peak in the

meadows; Holme Pierrepont is thought to have the largest colony in the country.

✿ roses (mainly old-fashioned); formal gardens; good topiary; teas in the long gallery.

Owned by Mr & Mrs Robin Brackenbury
Number of gardeners 2½ part-time
Size 1ha (2½ acres)
English Heritage Grade II

MILL HILL PLANTS
Mill Hill House, Elston Lane, East Stoke, Newark NG23 5QJ

Tel: 01636 525460
www.come.to/mill.hill.plants&garden
Location 5 miles south-west of Newark. Leave A46 at East Stoke, for Elston; ½ mile down, on right.
Opening hours 11 am – 5 pm; 29 May & by appointment; April to October.
Admission fee Garden: £2.

⊞ ⬚ ✦

The garden is generously planted for year-round interest with hardy and half-hardy perennials, annuals and shrubs. Wildlife is encouraged. The nursery has now closed down, but the garden gets better and better.
Owned by Mr & Mrs R.J. Gregory
Size 0.2ha (½ acre)
NCCPG National Collections *Berberis*

NATURESCAPE
Lapwing Meadows, Coach Gap Lane, Langar NG13 9HP

Tel: 01949 860592 **Fax:** 01949 869047
www.naturescape.co.uk
Location Signed off A46 & A52.
Opening hours 11 am – 5.30 pm; daily; April to September.
Admission fee Free.

⊞ ⬚ ✦ ⬡

Naturescape is a significant nursery, specialising in British wild plants. These include wildflowers, bulbs, native shrubs and trees, pond and marsh species and cottage garden favourites: many are available both as plants and as seeds. The principle behind the nursery is the realisation that many garden-owners want to attract wildlife to their gardens, and that growing native plant species is the best way to do so. The visitor centre opened in 1990 and is set in a wildlife garden showing different habitats. Meadows, hedges, ponds, woodland edges and wetlands are supplemented by cottage gardens and such features as a bee garden.

wildflowers; native plants; tea-room.

Owned by Mr & Mrs B. Scarborough
Number of gardeners 2½
Size 18ha (45 acres)

NEWSTEAD ABBEY
Newstead Abbey Park, Ravenshead NG15 8NA

Tel: 01623 455900 **Fax:** 01623 455904
www.newsteadabbey.org.uk
Location 4 miles south of Mansfield on A60; 12 miles north of Nottingham.
Opening hours 9 am – dusk; daily; all year, except the last Friday in November & Christmas Day.
Admission fee Adults £3; Concessions £2.50; Children £1.50; Family £8.50.

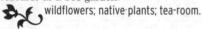

Chiefly of interest for being the debt-ridden estate which Lord Byron the poet inherited and had to sell, Newstead has a good modern garden. Features include a Spanish garden, a tropical garden, an iris garden, a rose garden, a heather garden, a fern garden, ponds and lakes. Best are the Japanese garden and the substantial rockery. The Council has restored and extensively replanted it as a public amenity: lots of cheerful roses and summer bedding.

rock garden; herbs; Japanese garden; water features; shop; café.

Owned by Nottingham City Council
Number of gardeners 5
Size 120ha (300 acres) of parkland
English Heritage Grade I

SALLEY GARDENS
Simkins Farm, Adbolton Lane, West Bridgford NG2 5AS

Tel: 0115 923 3878 or 07811 7039
www.thesalleygardens.co.uk
Location Just off A52 from Nottingham to Grantham.
Opening hours 9 am – 5 pm; Sundays; April to September. And by appointment.
Admission fee Free.

Salley Gardens is a nursery which concentrates upon plants that are especially beneficial to mankind: all are organically grown. They include dye and beverage plants, and culinary and aromatic herbs and spices. The main emphasis, however, is on plants with medicinal properties. Three major herbal traditions are represented: North American, European, and Traditional Chinese Medicine. Plants used in homoeopathy, ayurveda, and conventional medicine are also listed. 2003 saw an expanded section of culinary herbs, including some 30 different types of basil.

herbal and medicinal plants.

Owned by Richard Lewin
Size 0.2ha (½ acre)

OXFORDSHIRE

Oxfordshire is one of the best counties for keen gardeners. The natives may grumble about the cold, wet, heavy, clay soils of the Thames Valley, but they have some of the finest English gardens, ancient and modern, to show what those soils can do for them. There are no fewer than nine Grade I historic gardens in the county, and all are open to the public. Both the Oxford Botanic Garden and its country offshoot the Harcourt Arboretum at Nuneham Courtenay have seriously important plant collections, laid out to attract the ordinary garden-owner. It is in these two collections, too, that many of the county's record-breaking trees grow. Several 20th-century gardens were also laid out on a grand scale, including Sutton Courtenay, Buscot, Garsington, Waterperry and Pusey – the latter, alas, no longer open to the public. The county also has a host of good small gardens: it has long been a matter of pride that Oxfordshire should have more gardens open for the National Gardens Scheme and raise more money for its charities than any other English county. Nevertheless, it has only a handful of National Collections and comparatively few first-rate nurseries – Mattocks Roses, now part of the Notcutt chain, is perhaps the best known. It is as if Oxford were relying for its horticultural reputation more upon its past achievements than its present – rather like its university, some would say. Nevertheless, it was at Oxford University that the Garden History Society was born, thanks to the energy and acumen of Mavis Batey. And the many college gardens that open to the public are another of the city's gifts to garden-lovers: Robin Lane-Fox looks after the Fellows' garden at New College.

BLENHEIM PALACE
Woodstock, Oxford OX20 1PX

Tel: 01993 811091 **Fax:** 01993 813570
www.blenheimpalace.com
Location 8 miles north of Oxford.
Opening hours 10.30 am - 5.30 pm (or dusk, if earlier; last admissions 4.45 pm); daily; 11 February to 29 October. And daily, except Mondays & Tuesdays, from 1 November to 10 December. Park open daily all year.
Admission fee Park, gardens & maze: Adults £9; OAPs £7; Children £2.50. RHS members free 11 February to 13 April, 18 April to 26 May and 11 September to 10 December.

Blenheim is the grandest of grand gardens. Vanbrugh, Bridgeman, Hawksmoor and Wise worked here: the grand bridge, the triumphal arch and the column of victory all date from the 1720s. The huge park (800ha/2,000 acre) was landscaped by Capability Brown. Achille Duchêne designed the formal gardens in the 1920s: the Water Terraces centre on a Bernini fountain and took five years to build. The Italian garden focuses on the neo-classical mermaid fountain and is decked with orange trees in summer. There is a pretty Victorian rose garden and, in the old walled garden ('The Pleasure Gardens'), a maze and a lavender garden. The 'Secret' Garden, made by the 10th Duke in the Japanese style, has been restored as a garden for all seasons with original trees, plants and water features. The arboretum has some interesting trees, including four fine upright incense cedars (*Calocedrus decurrens*). In 1908, Winston Churchill proposed to his wife Clementine in the

Temple of Diana. There will be three RHS Special Events at Blenheim in 2006; details from 020 7821 3408.

🌿 formal gardens; new maze; current holder of Sandford Award; good shops; one restaurant & two self-service cafés.

Owned by The Duke of Marlborough
Number of gardeners 12
Size 40ha (100 acres)
English Heritage Grade I

BROOK COTTAGE
Well Lane, Alkerton, Banbury OX15 6NL

Tel: 01295 670303/670590 **Fax:** 01295 730362
Location 6 miles north-west of Banbury, ½ mile off A422.
Opening hours 9 am - 6 pm; Monday - Friday; Easter Monday to 31 October. Group, evening & weekend visits by appointment.
Admission fee Adults £4; OAPs £3; Children free.

P ♿ WC 🌿 🌰 ☕

Brook Cottage is *not* a dinky little cottage garden: it is a first-rate plantsman's garden, made by the present owner and her husband since 1964, on four acres of sloping pasture. The good plants are moreover displayed with a fine sense of colour and form. Parts of the garden are winding and cottagey, parts more spacious and open. Beautiful flowering trees in spring are followed by opulent old roses in summer and rich autumn colour. A recent addition is a border of blue and white agapanthus interspersed with kniphofias in shades of lemon and lime. The yellow border is backed by a hedge of copper beech, while the white border is brought to life by a dark hedge of yew. The diversity of planting is supplemented by tender perennials displayed in numerous ornamental containers. All the wooden furniture has been designed and hand-made to complement the character of the different areas. There is much to study and enjoy here.

🌿 plantsman's collection of plants; roses (over 200, mainly species & shrubs); good herbaceous borders (colour co-ordinated); 50 different clematis; gravel & water gardens; plants for sale; DIY tea & coffee; refreshments for groups by arrangement.

Owned by Mrs D.M. Hodges
Number of gardeners 1, plus some part-time help
Size 1.6ha (4 acres)

BROUGHTON CASTLE
Banbury OX15 5EB

Tel: 01295 722547 **Fax:** 01295 276070
www.broughtoncastle.demon.co.uk
Location 2½ miles west of Banbury on B4035.
Opening hours 2 pm - 5 pm; Wednesdays & Sundays; 1 May to 14 September. Plus Thursdays in July & August, Bank Holiday Sundays & Mondays (including Easter). For NGS: 30 July.
Admission fee Castle & gardens: Adults £6; OAPs & Students £5; Children £2.50.

P WC ♿ 🌿 🌰 ☕

The garden at Broughton Castle dates back to the 19th century: the neat formal garden with roses and lavender (best seen from the house) was designed by Lady Algernon Gordon-Lennox in the 1890s. The modern garden was established in 1970 with advice from Lanning Roper. It has two pretty colour-themed mixed borders – blue-yellow-and-white and pink-and-silver – both at their best towards the end of June when the roses are in full flower. The plants play second fiddle to the stupendous setting – the castle, the moat and the spacious parkland beyond.

🌿 roses (mainly old-fashioned & climbers); good herbaceous borders; shop; tea-room.

Owned by Lord Saye
Number of gardeners 1
Size 0.8ha (2 acres)
English Heritage Grade II*

BUSCOT PARK
Faringdon SN7 8BU

Tel: 01367 240786 **Fax:** 01367 241794
www.buscotpark.com
Location On A417 west of Faringdon.
Opening hours Garden only: 2 pm - 6 pm;
Monday - Friday; 3 April to 29 September. Plus
Saturdays & Sundays on second & fourth
weekends from Easter to September. And 29 &
30 April.
Admission fee Adults £5; Children £2.

[WC] ❀ ▱

There are three fairly distinct gardens at
Buscot. You enter through the newest
– a series of colour plantings and
horticultural features created by Lord
Faringdon over the last 20 years. Here is
the 'Parents' Walk', a lush double
herbaceous border designed by Peter Coats
in 1986: he uses a lot of yellow foliage and
contrasts it with purple, to create a sense of
lightness and brightness even on the
dullest of days. Next to it is the old kitchen
garden which was turned into a 'Four
Seasons' garden in the early 1980s: the four
quadrants planted by Tim Rees in the early
1990s have recently been further
developed and revised to represent each of
the four seasons. It also has prettily trained
fruit trees, vegetables used as climbing
plants and gooseberries grown as standards.
You climb out of the walled garden, up a
steep staircase lined with yews, and walk
past the front of the house on your way to
the second of the gardens: a perfect *patte
d'oie*, focused on the Theatre Arch. The
temptation is to explore all three avenues
of the *patte d'oie* at once, but they are
linked by cross-paths which run between

further gardens cut out of the woodland:
these include a circular sunken garden
furnished in summer with orange and
lemon trees in pots, and a pretty white-
and-green garden which is known as the
'Swinging Garden' because of the swinging
seats which surround it. But the third and
best-known garden at Buscot is Harold
Peto's water garden, which dates from the
1900s and stretches down over hundreds of
yards in a series of steps and then along a
long, narrow, straight canal punctuated
towards the end by a chunky Italianate
bridge until it bursts out into the view of
the lake at the bottom. The canal – little
more than a rill really – is framed first by
Irish yews and then by clipped box hedges.
It has an amazing dynamism and strength
of design which makes it an entirely self-
contained garden. The only downside to a
visit is that the lake is actually the furthest
point of the garden, and there is then no
other way out except to retrace your steps
across the park and through the modern
gardens. But Peter Coats's borders look
even better as you approach them again
from outside the walled gardens. And a
word of warning: Buscot is a big garden, so
allow lots of time for your visit.

topiary; roses (mainly old-fashioned);
fruit; good herbaceous borders;
tallest *Pinus nigra* var. *cebennensis* (32m) in
the British Isles; light refreshments.

Owned by The National Trust (administered by
Lord Faringdon)
English Heritage Grade II*

GARSINGTON MANOR
Garsington, Oxford OX44 9DH

Tel: 01865 361234 **Fax:** 01865 361566
Location East of B480 Oxford to Watlington road.
Opening hours For NGS: 2 pm - 5 pm.
Admission fee Adults £3; Children free.

P ◁ WC & ▱

The gardens at Garsington were laid out in the 1920s in the Italian style by Lady Ottoline Morrell and her husband. The parterre has 24 square beds with Irish yews at the corners; the Italian garden has a large ornamental pool enclosed by yew hedges and set about with statues; beyond, is a wild garden, with lime tree avenues, shrubs, a stream and pond. They make an incomparable setting for the summer opera season.

Italianate gardens; modern plantings; teas.

Owned by Mrs L.V. Ingrams
Number of gardeners 3
Size 1.6ha (4 acres)
English Heritage Grade II*

GREENWAYS
40 Osler Road, Headington, Oxford OX3 9BJ

Tel: 01865 767680 (after dark) **Fax:** 01865 767922
Location Osler Road is in Headington, off A420 London Road, within the ring road.
Opening hours 2 pm - 6 pm; 21 May, 16 July & 13 August. And by appointment.
Admission fee Adults £2.50; Children free.

This garden is totally different and – incredibly – now 30 years old. The Cootes have emphasised the Provençal look of the house by planting a rich Mediterranean garden – glittering evergreens, terracotta pots, old oil jars, gravel, parterres, mosaic water garden – with an exuberance of tender plants including olives, brugmansias, yuccas, oleanders, palms, bougainvillea, agaves, lantana, and echiums. It is quite the most stylish small garden in England, and intensively maintained to the highest standard.

beautiful modern Italianate garden; sub-tropical plants; plantsman's collection of plants; good herbaceous borders; painted obelisks; long view to monumental classical vase.

Owned by Mr & Mrs N.H.N. Coote
Number of gardeners owners only
Size 0.3ha (¾ acre)

HARCOURT ARBORETUM
Nuneham Courtenay OX44 9PQ

Tel: 01865 343501 **Fax:** 01865 341828
www.botanic-garden.ox.ac.uk
Location On A4074, just south of village of Nuneham Courtenay.
Opening hours 10 am - 5 pm; daily; April to November. 10 am - 4.30 pm; Monday - Friday; December to March. Closed over the Christmas period.
Admission fee Free. £2 for car park.

P WC &

Though it belongs to the University of Oxford Botanic Garden, Harcourt Arboretum is best regarded as a stand-alone woodland garden with a distinct history and character. It has been developed since 1950 around a nucleus of magnificent American conifers planted about 1840 in a corner of the Nuneham Courtenay estate. The new plantings include 'plants from high places' (geographically arranged), conservation areas, an extensive glade of ornamental maples, and fine modern features like collections of *Nothofagus*, magnolias and camellias. The labelling is fairly good and there are useful information boards in front of specimens of particular interest. It is perhaps best visited in May, when the mature oak woodland which surrounds the conifers is filled with vast oceans of bluebells.

🌿 woodland garden; rhododendrons & azaleas; mature conifers; camellias; fine collection of trees; bluebells.

Owned by The University of Oxford
Number of gardeners 3½
Size 32ha (80 acres)

KELMSCOTT MANOR
Kelmscott, Lechlade GL7 3HJ

Tel: 01367 252486 **Fax:** 01367 253754
www.kelmscottmanor.co.uk
Location Signed from B4449 & A4095.
Opening hours 11 am – 5 pm (gates open
10.30 am); Wednesdays; April to September. Plus
2 pm – 5 pm (gates open 1.15 pm) on Thursdays
from May to September. Plus the third Saturday
of the month from April to September & the first
Saturday of the month in July & August.
Admission fee Adults £8.50; Students £4.25.
Gardens only: Adults £2; Children free.
🚾 ♿ ❀ ☕

Kelmscott Manor was the summer home of
William Morris, an unspoilt Tudor
farmhouse on the banks of the Thames.
The surrounding countryside, river and
garden were inspirational to Morris's
designs and writings. Work on restoring
the garden started in 1996 and the result is
something that Morris would recognise –
all typical of the 1890s, with rustic
fencing, herbaceous borders edged by box,
and an orchard and pergola. The planting
reflects the rich botanical content of his
designs – wild tulips (*T. sylvestris*) and
fritillaries (*F. meleagris*) grow thickly under
the original mulberry tree. Elsewhere are
crocuses, aconites and snowdrops, followed
by roses, hollyhocks, cottage annuals,
poppies, pinks and China asters. Morris's
original topiary dragon 'Fafnir' is currently
being restored and the standard rose
bushes flanking the garden path featured
in his most famous book *News from
Nowhere*.

🌿 gift shop; licensed restaurant for coffee, lunches & teas.

Owned by The Society of Antiquaries of London
Number of gardeners 1 part-time
Size 1.3ha (3¼ acres)
English Heritage Grade II

LIME CLOSE
35 Henley's Lane, Drayton, Abingdon
OX14 4HU

Tel: 07831 861463
Location Off main road through Drayton.
Opening hours 2 pm – 5.30 pm; 16 April & 4 June.
And groups by prior appointment.
Admission fee Adults £3; Children free.
⬦ ♿ ❀ ☕

This modern garden has been much
praised, and deservedly, for its wide range
of plants and the way in which they are
grouped. As well as rare trees, shrubs,
alpines, perennials and bulbs, it can boast a
recently planted shade border, a pond, a
pergola, some unusual topiary, an
ornamental kitchen garden, a herb garden
designed by Rosemary Verey and a
wonderful selection of raised beds and
troughs planted by the owner's aunt Miss
C. Christie-Miller. A new cottage garden
has just been made with beds planted in
different tones of single colours and a
bearded iris collection.

🌿 good mixed borders; unusual plants; cream teas.

Owned by M-C. de Laubarède
Size 1.2ha (3 acres)

LE MANOIR AUX QUAT'SAISONS
Church Road, Great Milton, Oxford
OX44 7PD

Tel: 01844 278881 **Fax:** 01844 278847
www.manoir.com
Location Signed in village.
Opening hours All year; patrons only.
Admission fee Free to patrons.
🅿 🚾 ♿ ❀ ☕

Raymond Blanc insists that the gardens at Le Manoir aux Quat'Saisons are 'very much a part of the Le Manoir experience and are as important as the cuisine'. Features include a Japanese water garden and a 17th-century pond, but the soul of the garden is a two-acre kitchen garden. It is organically run, and registered with the Soil Association. The herb garden grows about 120 different herbs, alongside some 90 different vegetables. There will be several RHS Special Events at Le Manoir aux Quat'Saisons in 2006; details from the restaurant directly on 01844 278881.

 2-star Michelin restaurant.

Owned by Raymond Blanc
Number of gardeners 6
Size 11ha (27 acres)

MATTOCKS ROSES
Nuneham Courtenay, Oxford OX44 9PY

Tel: 01865 343454 **Fax:** 01865 343267
Email: oxford@notcutts.co.uk
www.mattocks.co.uk
Location On B4015, Golden Balls Roundabout (A4074).
Opening hours 9 am – 6 pm; Monday – Saturday. 10.30 am – 4.30 pm; Sundays.
Admission fee Free.

This is one of the oldest nurseries in England, founded in 1875 and now part of the Notcutts Group. Mattocks have been particularly successful in promoting their 'County' series of groundcover roses, though most of them were actually raised in Germany and Denmark. They offer a large choice of all kinds of roses, and on-line ordering, too. One of their specialities, bred by John Mattock and introduced in 1973, is the yellow repeat-flowering climber 'Dreaming Spires'. The new rose garden, opened in 2001, is now in its prime: it contains many of the roses in the list.
Owned by Notcutts Garden Centres

OXFORD BOTANIC GARDEN
Rose Lane, Oxford OX1 4AZ

Tel: 01865 286690 **Fax:** 01865 286693
www.botanic-garden.ox.ac.uk
Location East end of High Street next to river, opposite Magdalen College tower.
Opening hours 9 am – 5 pm (4.30 pm from November to February; 6 pm from May to August); daily; all year, except Good Friday & Christmas Day. Glasshouses: 10 am – 4 pm. Late night openings to 8 pm on Thursdays from June to August.
Admission fee Adults £2.70; OAPs £2; Children free. Donation box from November to February.

This is the oldest botanic garden in England, first laid out in 1621: the handsome gateways were added a few years later. It has kept its original rectangular design and many of the statues and garden ornaments. It also has a calm that is far from the bustle outside and has proved a refuge for generations of undergraduates. There are good and representative collections of almost every type of plant, including a grass garden, carnivorous plants, a water garden, fernery, orangery and several conservatories. Everything is well labelled, of course, and designed not only as an aesthetically pleasing living collection of plants for the university botanists but, much more generally, as an educational resource. In recent years the area outside the walled garden has been developed as a garden to inspire gardeners: here are a new water garden, rock garden, herbaceous border and autumn border. The palm house was redesigned in 2000 so that visiting schoolchildren could enjoy 'the ultimate rainforest experience'. The garden is very good on education, and its website is brilliant.

roses (mainly old-fashioned); rock garden; herbs; plants under glass; systematic beds; *Sorbus domestica*; *Victoria amazonica*.

Owned by The University of Oxford
Number of gardeners 9
Size 1.8ha (4½ acres)
NCCPG National Collections *Euphorbia*
English Heritage Grade I

ROUSHAM HOUSE
Steeple Aston, Bicester OX6 3QX

Tel: & Fax: 01869 347110
www.rousham.org
Location A4260 then off B4030.
Opening hours 10 am - 4.30 pm; daily; all year.
Admission fee Adults £4. No Children under 15.
P WC &

Rousham is the most perfect surviving example of William Kent's landscaping: *Kentissimo*, according to Horace Walpole. The main axis brings you to Scheemakers's statue of a lion devouring a horse, high above the infant River Cherwell. Follow the correct circuit: the serpentine landscape lies away to the side. Here are Venus's Vale, the Cold Bath and Townsend's Building, from which a lime walk will lead you to the Praeneste. Rousham is an Arcadian experience. The pretty herbaceous border in the walled garden and the modern rose garden by the dovecote seem almost an irrelevance.

early 18th-century landscape; important sculptures & garden buildings.

Owned by C. Cottrell-Dormer
Number of gardeners 4
Size 10ha (25 acres)
English Heritage Grade I

STANSFIELD
49 High Street, Stanford-in-the-Vale SN7 8NQ

Tel: 01367 710340
Location Off A417 opposite Vale garage.
Opening hours 10 am - 4 pm; first Tuesday of the month; April to September. And by appointment, including evenings. Garden clubs especially welcome.
Admission fee Adults £2; Children free.

Stansfield is a modern plantsman's garden, and a fascinating model of what an enthusiastic collector and cultivator of plants can achieve in a few years. Over 2,000 different plants grow in just over one acre. The special features include troughs, screes, open borders and endless microhabitats.

plantsman's collection of plants; good herbaceous borders; Mediterranean garden.

Owned by Mr & Mrs D. Keeble
Number of gardeners owners only

STONOR
Henley-on-Thames RG9 6HF

Tel: 01491 638587 **Fax:** 01491 639348
www.stonor.com
Location On B480, 5 miles north of Henley-on-Thames.
Opening hours 1 pm - 5.30 pm; Sundays & Bank Holiday Mondays; 2 April to 24 September; Wednesdays 5 July to 30 August. (Closed 18 June)
Admission fee £3.50.
P WC & 🌸 ☕

Stonor fills a hillside: classical parkland (with a deer park, too), the Elizabethan house, lawns, terraces, a 17th-century walled garden, and finally the wood with wonderful views at the top. Nothing appears to have changed for 200 years: the effect is miraculous.

roses (mainly old-fashioned); rock garden; daffodils; souvenir shop; tea room.

Owned by Lord Camoys
Number of gardeners 1
English Heritage Grade I

WATERPERRY GARDENS
Waterperry, Wheatley, Oxford OX33 1JZ

Tel: 01844 339226 **Fax:** 01844 339883
www.waterperrygardens.co.uk
Location M40, Jct 8 or 8a. Well signed locally.
Opening hours 9 am – 5 pm; daily; all year,
except 13 to 16 July and Christmas/New Year
period.
Admission fee April to October: Adults £4.25;
OAPs £3.75; Children £3. November to March: all
£3. RHS members free in September.
P ⏃ WC ♿ ♣ ⫐

The gardens at Waterperry are extensive,
well-maintained and full of interesting
plants. Much has been redesigned and
replanted in recent years, with some fine
formal features and pleasing plant
combinations. The Virgin's Walk is a good
place to study shade-loving plants, but the
main feature of this area is a long classical
herbaceous border brilliantly colourful from
late May until October. The Mary Rose
Garden, enclosed by yew hedges, illustrates
both modern and older roses, and the
formal garden is particularly neatly
designed and colourful, with a small knot
garden, herbaceous border and wisteria
tunnel. Nearby are some interesting ways
of training apples and roses, but the main
part of the garden is the extensive shrub
borders, alpine beds and flower borders.
Waterperry offers much to enjoy and learn
from at every season.

🌿 roses; rock garden; good herbaceous
borders; apple orchards; irises; home
produce, stoneware, books; excellent plant
centre; tea shop; wine licence.

Owned by School of Economic Science
Number of gardeners 3½
Size 2.8ha (7 acres)
NCCPG National Collections Saxifraga

WESTWELL MANOR
Burford OX18 4JT

Location 2 miles from A40, west of Burford
roundabout.
Opening hours 2 pm – 6.30 pm; 11 June. And by
prior appointment for serious horticultural
groups of 20+.
Admission fee Adults £3; Children 50p.
WC 🌸

Westwell is a large and peaceful Cotswold
garden with several distinct 'rooms'. The
features include rills, a water garden,
herbaceous borders, an orchard, a lavender
meadow, lots of hazel and willow fencing, a
vegetable garden, a moonlight garden, a
clematis wall and a small rice paddy.

🌿 topiary; roses (mainly old-fashioned);
good herbaceous borders; water garden.

Owned by Mr & Mrs T.H. Gibson
Number of gardeners 2
Size 2.8ha (7 acres)

SHROPSHIRE

Shropshire has the reputation of being a remote and quasi-feudal county. It is certainly true that very few of its historic gardens are ever open to the public. Hawkstone is the most notable exception, but this – the county's only Grade I garden – is now in multiple occupation: nevertheless, its principal parts are still highly visitable and also have the best collection of trees, mainly conifers, in Shropshire. Among 20th-century gardens, Hodnet Hall is of national importance, and a sizeable achievement by modern standards. Unfortunately, however, the owners have decided that, from 2006 onwards, they can no longer open it to visitors on a regular basis. Three further recent gardens are also outstanding, each in its own way – Burford House, the David Austin rose gardens and Wollerton Old Hall. There are 24 National Collections in Shropshire; and the National Gardens Scheme is well supported, mainly by gardens that are large or medium-sized.

ATTINGHAM PARK
Shrewsbury SY4 4TP

Tel: 01743 708123 **Fax:** 01743 708155
www.nationaltrust.org.uk
Location 5 miles south-east of Shrewsbury on B4380.
Opening hours 10 am - 8 pm (5 pm from November to February); Friday - Tuesday; 1 March to 29 October. Weekends only at other times.
Admission fee Adults £3.30; Children £1.65.
🅿 ⬩ 🚾 ♿ ⬥ ⬩
No garden to speak of, but the classical late 18th-century parkland round the vast Georgian house is a joy to walk around.
rhododendrons & azaleas; daffodils; newly restored orangery; National Trust shop; light lunches & teas.

Owned by The National Trust
Number of gardeners 1
Size 20ha (50 acres)
English Heritage Grade II*

BENTHALL HALL
Broseley TF12 5RX

Tel & Fax: 01952 882159
www.nationaltrust.org.uk

Location 1 mile north-west of Broseley (B4375).
Opening hours 2 pm - 5.30 pm; Tuesdays, Wednesdays & Bank Holiday Sundays & Mondays; 16 April to 27 September. Plus all Sundays from July to September.
Admission fee Adults £2.75; Children £1.35.
🅿 🚾 ♿ 🌾
The smallish garden has been well restored with a Graham Stuart Thomas rose garden. Home of the 19th-century botanist George Maw, his Mediterranean collection is still the backbone of the garden – crocuses naturalised everywhere.
roses (mainly old-fashioned); herbs; good herbaceous borders; spring bulbs.

Owned by The National Trust
Number of gardeners 1
Size 1.2ha (3 acres)

BURFORD HOUSE GARDENS
Tenbury Wells WR15 8HQ

Tel: 01584 810777 **Fax:** 01584 810673
www.burford.co.uk
Location A456 between Tenbury Wells & Ludlow.
Opening hours 9 am - 6 pm (gardens close at dusk, if earlier); daily; all year. Closed 25 & 26 December.

Admission fee Adults £3.95; Children £1; Groups (20+) £3. RHS members free.

P WC ♿ ✿ ✕ ☐

This glamorous seven-acre garden, made to complement a stylish Georgian house, is now beautiful and mature. The fluid design is enhanced by interesting plants, imaginatively used and comprehensively labelled. There are good roses and herbaceous borders, the original *Wisteria* 'Burford' on the back of the house, and a magnificent series of water gardens, but Burford means *Clematis* – over 500 cultivars – cleverly trained, grown and displayed among shrubs and in the new Clematis Maze near the coach house. Charles Chesshire has renewed and reordered much of the planting, and the results are excellent. There are new developments on the other side of the river, too: bulbs and wildflower plantings in particular.

❧ clematis; roses (mainly old-fashioned & climbers); plantsman's collection of plants; mature conifers; good herbaceous borders; *Rosa* 'Treasure Trove'; new wildflower garden; new collection of bamboos; café; morning coffee, lunches & teas.

Owned by Burford Garden Company
Number of gardeners 4
Size 2.8ha (7 acres)
NCCPG National Collections *Clematis*

DAVID AUSTIN ROSES
Bowling Green Lane, Albrighton,
Wolverhampton WV7 3HB

Tel: 01902 376376 **Fax:** 01902 372142
www.davidaustinroses.com
Location Signed in Albrighton.
Opening hours 9 am - 5 pm; daily; all year, except Christmas to New Year. For NGS: last Sunday in June.
Admission fee Free.

P ⬆ WC ♿ ● ☐

David Austin has developed an entirely new strain of 'English' roses which combine the shape and scent of old-fashioned roses with the colours, health and floriferousness of modern types. The display gardens adjoining

his nursery are impressive: five different sections, each extensive and thickly planted with old-fashioned roses and his own hybrids – over 700 different cultivars of English Roses, old roses, shrub roses, climbers, ramblers and species, as well as some modern hybrid teas and floribundas. In late June and early July it is a place of magic beauty. The garden is maintained to an extremely high standard: all the roses look happy and healthy, and flower profusely. Sculptures by David Austin's wife add a further dimension to a visit. Groups are sometimes allowed to see the breeding houses and trial grounds. There will be four RHS Special Events at David Austin Roses during 2006; details from 020 7821 3408.

❧ roses of every kind, especially 'English' roses; important rose nursery & plant centre; tea-room & light refreshments.

Owned by David Austin
Number of gardeners 1
Size 0.8ha (2 acres)
NCCPG National Collections *Rosa* (David Austin 'English Rose' cultivars)

THE DOWER HOUSE
Morville Hall, Morville, Bridgnorth
WV16 5NB

Tel & Fax: 01746 714407
www.stmem.com/dower-house-garden/
Location At junction of A458 & B4368, 3 miles from Bridgnorth.
Opening hours 2 pm - 6 pm; Wednesdays, Sundays & Bank Holiday Mondays; 1 April to 30 September. Groups by appointment at other times.
Admission fee Adults £3; Children 50p.

P ⬆ ♿ ✿ ● ☐

Dr Swift is a distinguished garden-writer with a special gift for putting our gardening practices in an historical context. Her own garden is both beautiful and instructive. The aim is to tell the story of English gardening in a series of gardens which represent the styles and aspirations of different historical periods. The oldest feature, in spirit, is a turf maze, followed by a medieval cloister garden. Then come the Elizabethan-style knot garden, a 17th-century 'plat', a William-and-Mary canal garden and so on, up to a stupendous Victorian rose border. Dr Swift is also a dedicated conservationist, not just of historical style, but also of old garden cultivars of everything from roses to apples and vegetables. The Dower House is therefore of great interest both to modern plantsmen and to lovers of things ancient.

plants from garden for sale; home-made teas.

Owned by Dr Katherine Swift, as tenant of the National Trust
Number of gardeners owner, plus part-time help
Size 0.6ha (1½ acres)

DUDMASTON
Quatt, Bridgnorth WV15 6QN

Tel: 01746 780866 **Fax:** 01746 780744
www.nationaltrust.org.uk
Location 4 miles south-east of Bridgnorth on A442.
Opening hours 12 noon – 6 pm; Sunday – Wednesday; 2 April to 27 September.
Admission fee Adults £4; Children £2.

Dudmaston has a fine collection of trees and shrubs, put together by several generations of keen plantsmen in the 19th and 20th centuries. Rhododendrons form the background: there are many magnolias, cherries, kalmias, maples and roses, underplanted with daffodils and primroses, which makes this a particularly fine garden in spring. But there is also a natural rock garden made of the local red sandstone. Elsewhere are a bog garden and a good herbaceous border, recently replanted.

rhododendrons & azaleas; fine trees; sculptures; shop; plant sales; tea-room.

Owned by The National Trust
Number of gardeners 2
Size 3.2ha (8 acres)
English Heritage Grade II

HALL FARM NURSERY
Vicarage Lane, Kinnerley, Oswestry
SY10 8DH

Tel & Fax: 01691 682135
www.hallfarmnursery.co.uk
Location 2 miles from A5, between Shrewsbury & Oswestry.
Opening hours 10 am – 5 pm; Tuesday – Saturday; 1 March to 7 October.
Admission fee Free.

Hall Farm Nursery carries a good range of fashionable herbaceous perennials, including a great number of ornamental grasses, echinaceas, bog plants, asters and heleniums. All its plants are grown and propagated on-site: requests for cultural advice are therefore welcome. The display borders around the nursery are attractive and well maintained. Four RHS Special Events will take place at Hall Farm Nursery during 2006; details from 020 7821 3408.

herbaceous plants; ornamental grasses.

Owned by Christine & Nick Foulkes Jones

HAWKSTONE HISTORIC PARK & FOLLIES
Weston under Redcastle, Shrewsbury
SY4 5UY

Tel: 01939 200611 **Fax:** 01939 200311
Location Off A49 between Shrewsbury & Whitchurch.
Opening hours 10 am – 4 pm; daily; 21 March to 10 April & 25 May to 11 September. Wednesday – Sunday; 13 April to 22 May & 14 September to 30 October.
Admission fee Adults £5.75; OAPs £4.75; Children £3.75.

Sir Rowland Hill began landscaping Hawkstone in the 1750s, but most of what remains was initiated by his elder son Sir Richard and completed by his grandson, another Sir Rowland Hill, best known for inventing the postage stamp. It is a fine example of the 'sublime' movement, which sought to create contrasts of emotion in the natural landscape. Hawkstone has deep ravines and gloomy chasms, accompanied by dizzying pinnacles, soaring sandstone rocks, and ornamental follies which fill the whole estate, once more than 700 acres in extent. It is the contrasts which make this landscape unique: the mosses, ferns, and dampness of its dark gullies turn suddenly into dramatic cliffs, tunnels, crags and bridges, while the peaks of the precipitous outcrops offer views across 13 counties. But allow lots of time for your visit – the owner recommends at least three hours. remarkable series of landscaped follies; some good trees.

Owned by M.C. Boler
Size 40ha (100 acres)
English Heritage Grade I

HILLVIEW HARDY PLANTS
Worfield, Bridgnorth WV15 5NT

Tel & Fax: 01746 716454
www.hillviewhardyplants.com
Location Between Worfield & Albrighton, off B4176.
Opening hours 9 am – 5 pm; Monday – Saturday; March to mid-October. And by appointment.
Admission fee Free.

This is a good nursery for hardy herbaceous perennials. Its range of primulas and auriculas, aquilegias and South African plants is especially noteworthy. Guided tours of the nursery and well-planted display garden can be arranged for groups. Seven RHS Special Events will take place at Hillview Hardy Plants during 2006; details from 020 7821 3408.
refreshments by arrangement.

Owned by John & Ingrid Millington
Number of gardeners 3½
Size 0.4ha (1 acre)
NCCPG National Collections Acanthus

HODNET HALL GARDENS
Hodnet, Market Drayton TF9 3NN

Tel: 01630 685786 **Fax:** 01630 685853
Location Near junction of A53 & A442.
Opening hours For NGS: 10 May. And by appointment for groups of 20+.

In the 1950s, *The RHS Journal* (forerunner of *The Garden*) described Hodnet as a 'small modern garden'. Now it has more than 60 acres of woodland garden around a chain of ornamental pools. The woodlands are planted with exotic trees like magnolias, maples and davidias against a background of native oaks, sycamores, limes and beech trees. Underneath are rhododendrons, azaleas, camellias, prunus and berberis, themselves underplanted when they flower in spring with a wide variety of herbaceous plants, especially hostas, primulas, daffodils and bluebells. The spacious mixed borders near the house are particularly interesting in July, when they are complemented by the beds of old-fashioned roses and modern floribundas. But Hodnet is a garden for everyone and every season – good in late summer, too, when the hydrangeas and astilbes flower. Allow lots of time for a thorough visit to one of the greatest 20th-century gardens.
woodland garden; roses (mainly old-fashioned); good herbaceous borders; camellias; primulas; rhododendrons; HHA/Christie's Garden of the Year in 1985.

Owned by A.E.H. Heber-Percy
Number of gardeners 4
Size 24+ha (60+ acres)
English Heritage Grade II

JESSAMINE COTTAGE
Kenley, Shrewsbury SY5 6NS

Tel: 01694 771279
www.stmem.com/jessamine-cottage
Location Signed from B4371 & A458.
Opening hours 2 pm – 6 pm; Wednesday – Sunday &

Bank Holiday Mondays; 28 April to 3 September.
Admission fee Adults £3; Children 50p.

P WC 🌿 🍴 📷

This is a new garden, made from an open
paddock since 1999: the owners seek to
combine good plants, fluid design, and all-
season interest. Features include a parterre, a
wildflower meadow, a stream and pond,
island beds (mainly herbaceous), a rose walk
and young shrub borders. Worth visiting now,
and returning to see how it grows up.

🌿 good plants; fluid design; plants for sale;
home-made teas.

Owned by Leon & Pamela Wheeler
Number of gardeners 2
Size 1.2ha (3 acres)

LINGEN NURSERY AND GARDENS
Lingen, Bucknell SY7 0DY

Tel & Fax: 01544 267720
www.lingennursery.co.uk
Location Follow brown tourist signs from A4113 &
A4362, north-east of Presteigne.
Opening hours 10 am – 5 pm; Thursday – Monday;
Easter to September. Nursery opens from February
to October.
Admission fee Garden: £2.50. Nursery: free.

P ⬅ WC ♿ 🌿 📷

Since it was started in 1979, Lingen has
become one of the best-known specialist
nurseries for unusual alpine and herbaceous
plants. In addition to their two National
Collections, the owners have put together
notable collections of auriculas and
penstemons (both alpine and herbaceous)
and have a number of interesting aquilegias
and irises, too. But it is true to say that you
will not visit Lingen without seeing a plant
that you have never seen before. The gardens
are worth a visit in their own right: one acre
is intensively planted with a rock garden and
cottage garden, supplemented by an alpine
house and raised beds. Two further acres are
under development to create a bog garden,
further herbaceous borders, a scree and a rock

outcrop. There will be three RHS Special
Events at Lingen Nursery in 2006; details
from 020 7821 3408.

🌿 auriculas; penstemons; tea-room.

Owned by Kim & Maggie Davis
Size 1.2-ha (3-acre) garden; 0.4-ha (1-acre) nursery
NCCPG National Collections *Iris sibirica*,
Campanula

LOWER HALL
Worfield, Bridgnorth WV15 5LH

Tel: 01746 716607 **Fax:** 01746 716325
Location In centre of village of Worfield.
Opening hours By appointment. Groups welcome.
Admission fee Adults £3.50; Children free.

⬅ WC

Lanning Roper helped to get this splendid
garden going in the 1960s. It bestrides the
River Worfe and every part has a distinct
character. There are lush streamside plantings
(some replanted in 2002-2003), infinite
colour schemes, and a woodland area at the
bottom. These contrast with formal designs,
straight brick paths, a pergola and more
colour themes in the old walled garden. It is
one of the best gardens to be made since
World War II, still evolving and neatly kept.

🌿 roses (all sorts); plantsman's collection of
plants; good herbaceous borders.

Owned by C.F. Dumbell
Number of gardeners 1
Size 1.7ha (4¼ acres)

PREEN MANOR
Church Preen, Church Stretton SY6 7LQ

Tel & Fax: 01694 771207
Location Signed from B4371 Much Wenlock/Church
Stretton.
Opening hours 2 pm – 6 pm; 30 April, 1 & 27 June,
14 & 28 July, 1 October (4.30 pm Harvest
Thanksgiving). And parties by appointment in June
& July.

Admission fee Adults £3.50; Children 50p.

P wc ✺ ◗

Preen has a stylish new garden with some original ideas to complement the historic old site. These include a chess garden, a collection of plants in handsome old pots, a pebble garden, a fern garden and that symbol of the 1990s – a gravel garden. Down in the woodland garden are rhododendrons and candelabra primulas. And it gets better every year.

 woodland garden; fruit; fern garden; home-made teas.

Owned by Mrs Philip Trevor-Jones
Number of gardeners 2½
Size 2.4ha (6 acres), plus woodland

SWALLOW HAYES
Rectory Road, Albrighton, Wolverhampton WV7 3EP

Tel: 01902 372624 **Fax:** 01902 373151
Location M54, Jct 3, then A41 towards Wolverhampton & first right after garden centre.
Opening hours 2 pm – 5 pm; 21 & 28 May. And by appointment.
Admission fee Adults £3; Children 10p. £3.50 per head for groups, to include tea & biscuits.

P ⇨ wc ⏃ ✺ ◗

Swallow Hayes is a plantswoman's garden (3,000 plants) entirely made since 1968 and a model of its kind, where groundcover helps to minimise labour and maximise enjoyment. The garden started life as a stock-ground and trial-ground for the owner's wholesale nursery. Mrs Edwards has more than 100 different cultivars of *Geranium* in a garden which is packed with different microhabitats, each of them themed and exploited as fully as possible. There is much to see and enjoy at every season. The garden is open every January for about a week to view the National Collection of winter-flowering witch-hazels *Hamamelis* of which there are over 50 cultivars. Please telephone for January 2007 dates.

rock garden; herbs; fruit; mature conifers; good herbaceous borders; ferns; geraniums; trees & shrubs; teas on open days.

Owned by Mrs P. Edwards
Number of gardeners owner, plus some very part-time help
Size 0.8ha (2 acres)
NCCPG National Collections *Hamamelis; Lupinus* (Russell strains)

WOLLERTON OLD HALL
Wollerton, Market Drayton TF9 3NA

Tel: 01630 685760 **Fax:** 01630 685583
www.wollertonoldhallgarden.com
Location Follow brown tourist signs from A53/A442 or A53/A41 junctions.
Opening hours 12 noon – 5 pm; Fridays, Sundays & Bank Holidays; Good Friday to end of September.
Admission fee Adults £4; Children £1. RHS members free in April, May & September.

P wc ⏃ ✺ ✂ ◗

Started in 1984, this outstanding garden creation seeks to combine horticultural excellence with unrestrained planting of perennials, careful colour design with strong contrasts, and intimacy with bold design structure. As the site is centuries old, the dominant theme is of linear formality but this gradually gives way to total informality where the garden meets the Shropshire countryside.

plantsman's collection of plants; good herbaceous borders; deciduous euonymus; salvias; clematis; shrub roses; crocosmias; lunches & teas.

Owned by Lesley Jenkins
Number of gardeners 2½
Size 1.2ha (3 acres)

SOMERSET

Like its neighbour Devon, Somerset is rich in both gardens and nurseries: it is a county where gardeners are well served. Four of its five Grade I historic gardens – Dunster, East Lambrook, Hestercombe and Montacute – are regularly open to the public. Somerset also has an exceptional number of good small and medium-sized gardens, often made by the present owners – as witness the large number (in quite a small county) that open in aid of the National Gardens Scheme. Somerset is famous for its mild climate – warm and wet – and the rich soils that are put to cider and dairying: they also induce good growth in gardens. It has long been recognised that along the coast – at Porlock and Cannington, for example – plants flourish that would not survive in any but the mildest parts of Devon and Cornwall. Unfortunately, however, two of Somerset's most admired modern gardens, Hadspen House and

Cannington Gardens, have each decided to take a year 'off' and will not be opening in 2006. Nevertheless, the county has no arboreta of note and few trees that are thought to be among the tallest or largest of their kind. Somerset has many nurseries and among them are several of national or international importance: Avon Bulbs and Broadleigh Gardens for bulbs, Kelways for peonies, Mallet Court for rare trees, P.M.A. Plants for Japanese maples. Somerset also has a large number (over 20) of National Collections, which is always a good indicator of the general level of interest in gardening. And it has long been well served by the county horticultural college at Cannington, which is one of the leading centres in all England for the teaching of amenity horticulture. Cannington's own sub-tropical gardens are closed for restoration in 2006, but the college hopes to open again in 2007-2008 at the latest.

THE AMERICAN MUSEUM
Claverton Manor, Bath BA2 7BD

Tel: 01225 460503 **Fax:** 01225 469160
www.americanmuseum.org
Location Off A36 south of Bath.
Opening hours 12 noon - 6 pm; daily, except Mondays; 19 March to 30 October.
Admission fee Adults £4; Children £2.50.
Private tours by prior arrangement.
P ♿ WC ⚘ ☕ 🛈

The 15 enchanting acres of garden at Claverton Manor were created by two artistic Americans, Dallas Pratt and John Judkyn, from about 1960 onwards. They bought the handsome classical house, built in 1820, to hold their collection of early American domestic art and artefacts:

the American Museum is now the largest of its kind outside the USA and well worth a visit. The house has a stunning situation with wide views across to the west-facing slopes of the Avon valley, yet sheltered and screened from all but the prettiest eye-catchers on the other side. Tea is served on the terrace in front of the house, next to the little Colonial herb garden ('Colonial' = pre-1778). Sloping lawns lead to the Mount Vernon garden, a box-edged re-creation of George Washington's own original. The first enclosure has beds of old roses: the main section is a herbaceous garden. Despite a little historical latitude with the choice of 18th-century plants, it is all very neat and instructive, and prettily enclosed by white

picket fencing. Also of horticultural interest is a young arboretum which opened in 1985 on the slopes below and recently expanded. This celebration of hardy American trees and shrubs adds up to a fine, well-labelled collection, and includes (among many other rarities) *Alnus rhombifolia*, *Salix mackenziana* and *Philadelphus insignis*. The new part is planted with trees discovered on the first expedition across America – the Lewis and Clark Trail. Also worth discovering are the new (2006) woodland and parkland walks, a ferny dell at the bottom of the arboretum and a collection of American apple cultivars, with such names as 'Smokehouse' and 'Sheep's Nose'. The American Museum is a well-endowed foundation and its gardens are very well maintained, which adds enormously to the pleasure of a visit, though rabbits and deer are a problem.
topiary; roses (mainly old-fashioned); herbs; fruit; good herbaceous borders; fine collection of trees; book shop, herb shop and country store; light lunches at weekends; tea, coffee and American cookies.

Owned by Trustees of the American Museum in Britain
Number of gardeners 4
Size 6ha (15 acres)
English Heritage Grade II

AMMERDOWN PARK
Kilmersdon, Radstock, Bath BA3 5SH

Tel: 01761 432227 **Fax:** 01761 433094
Location West of Terry Hill crossroads: A362/A366.
Opening hours 11 am - 5 pm; 17 April, 1 & 29 May, 28 August.
Admission fee Adults £3; OAPs £2 ; Children free.

Ammerdown's layout is Lutyens at his most ingenious. The lie of the land precludes right angles, but long straight views cover up the irregularities. It has some nice plants, particularly trees, but the design is everything and there are good spring bulbs. A restoration plan has recently got under way.
major Lutyens garden; good design; refreshments in May & August.

Owned by The Hon. Andrew Jolliffe
Number of gardeners 3
Size 6ha (15 acres)
English Heritage Grade II*

AVON BULBS
Burnt House Farm, Mid-Lambrook, South Petherton TA13 5HE

Tel & Fax: 01460 242177
www.avonbulbs.co.uk
Location Turn south, down 'no through road', halfway between West Lambrook & East Lambrook.
Opening hours 9 am - 4.30 pm; Thursday - Saturday; mid-February to end of March & mid-September to end of October.
Admission fee Free.

Avon Bulbs offers an impressive variety of bulbs (and close relatives) of all sizes, types and seasons – mainly by mail order. The nursery is well run and the plants are beautifully grown. It is well worth a visit early in the year to see the wide range of its stock, including much which is not listed in the catalogue. The opening hours are limited because of the seasonal nature of the business and the nursery's show commitments. It is a good idea to check with them before visiting. There will be an RHS Special Event at Avon Bulbs in 2006; details from 020 7821 3408.
hardy bulbs of every kind.

Owned by Chris Ireland-Jones
Number of gardeners 4
Size 1.2ha (3 acres)

BARRINGTON COURT
Barrington, Ilminster TA19 0NQ

Tel: 01460 241938 **Fax:** 01460 243133
www.nationaltrust.org.uk
Location In Barrington village.
Opening hours 11 am - 4.30 pm (5.30 pm from
April to September); Thursday - Tuesday; 2 March
to 31 October.
Admission fee Adults £7; Children £3.

🅿 ⓦ ♿ ❀ ☕ ⬥

There is still an Edwardian opulence about
Barrington. Massive plantings of irises, lilies
and rich dark dahlias. And good design
detail, too: the patterns of the brick paving
are a study in themselves.
🌿 roses (mainly old-fashioned); fruit; fine
collection of trees; shop; tea-room;
licensed restaurant.

Owned by The National Trust
Number of gardeners 3, plus 2 trainees & 1
seasonal gardener
Size 4ha (10 acres)
English Heritage Grade II*

BATH BOTANIC GARDENS
Royal Victoria Park, Bath BA1 2NQ

Tel: 01225 448433 **Fax:** 01225 480072
Location West of city centre by Upper Bristol
Road.
Opening hours 9 am - dusk; daily; all year, except
Christmas Day.
Admission fee Free.

🅿 ⬥ ⓦ ♿ ❀

Bath Botanic Gardens were founded in
1887, extended in 1926 and again in 1987.
It has nine acres of trees, shrubs, borders,
limestone-loving plants and scented walks.
It has never been attached to a university or
institute, so it is more of a horticultural
collection than a botanic garden, and public
amenity is its main function. The central
feature is a rocky pool designed in the
Japanese style, surrounded by venerable not-
so-dwarf maples. Standards are high,
maintenance is good, and the seasonal

highlights of bulbs, bedding and herbaceous
plants are among the best. The excellent
guidebook is a model of visitor-friendliness.
🌿 rock garden; autumn colour; fine
bedding displays; good *Scilla* collection;
tallest tree of heaven *Ailanthus altissima* (31m)
and tallest hornbeam *Carpinus betulus* (27m) in
England (and 11 other record trees).

Owned by Bath & North East Somerset Council
Number of gardeners 4
Size 3.8ha (9½ acres)
English Heritage Grade II

BLACKMORE & LANGDON
Stanton Nurseries, Pensford, Bristol
BS39 4JL

Tel: 01275 332300 **Fax:** 01275 331207
www.blackmore-langdon.com
Location 8 miles south of Bristol on B3130,
between A37 Wells road & A38.
Opening hours 9 am - 5 pm; Monday - Friday; all
year. 10 am - 4 pm; Saturdays & Sundays; April to
September.

🅿 ⓦ ♿ ❀

This family business was started in 1901 and
is still run by the founder's grandsons.
Blackmore & Langdon has a long tradition
of breeding and growing showy border
plants – huge begonias and tall delphiniums,
in particular. The nursery's immaculately
grown flowers have been a feature of RHS
flowers shows – and especially the Chelsea
Flower Show – for many years. What is not
so well known is that the nursery also
produces phlox, aquilegias and polyanthus.
All its plants are grown on-site. The
begonias and delphiniums fill a 0.4ha (1-
acre) glasshouse; there are also delphiniums
in flower in the field from the end of May
until September. There will be an annual
plant sale (combined with a Chelsea
preview) from 12 to 14 May.
🌿 delphiniums; begonias.

Owned by The Langdon family

BROADLEIGH GARDENS
Bishops Hull, Taunton TA4 1AE

Tel: 01823 286231 **Fax:** 01823 232464
www.broadleighbulbs.co.uk
Location At Barr, ¾ mile north-west of Bishops Hull.
Opening hours 9 am – 4 pm; Monday – Friday. Viewing & collection of pre-booked orders.
Admission fee £1 charity donation.

P WC & ❦

This nursery, with strong RHS connections, is best known for its small bulbs, though it now grows almost as many foliage and woodland perennials. Look out for the agapanthus, crocosmias, snowdrops, the many miniature narcissus and species tulips, and Broadleigh's own Pacific Coast hybrid irises. The three-acre display garden is planted for year-round effect, and includes formal and informal areas.

❧ spring bulbs (especially miniature narcissus); agapanthus.

Owned by Christine Skelmersdale
Number of gardeners 4
Size 2ha (5 acres)
NCCPG National Collections Narcissus (miniature)

CLEEVE NURSERY
Cleeve, Bristol BS49 4PW

Tel: 01934 832134 **Fax:** 01934 876498
www.cleevenursery.co.uk
Location On A370 between Bristol & Weston-super-Mare.
Opening hours 9 am – 6 pm (5 pm in winter); Monday – Saturday; all year. Plus 10 am – 5 pm on Sundays & Bank Holidays. Closed 25 December to 1 January.
Admission fee Free.

P WC & ❦ ☕

This is a well-regarded garden centre with a wide range of plants of all sorts for sale. There will be an RHS Special Event here during 2006; details from 020 7821 3408.

❧ garden centre; coffee shop.

Owned by Alan & Felicity Down

COTHAY MANOR
Greenham, Wellington TA21 0JR

Tel: 01823 672283 **Fax:** 01823 672345
Location Off A38, 1½ miles from Greenham.
Opening hours 2 pm – 6 pm; Wednesdays, Thursdays, Sundays & Bank Holiday Mondays; Easter to September. Groups (21+) by appointment throughout the season.
Admission fee Adults £4.50; Children £2. Special rates for pre-booked groups.

P WC & ❦ ☕

Cothay is an exciting old/new garden on either side of the River Tone. The seven acres of formal gardens designed in the 1920s by Reggie Cooper (a friend of Lawrence Johnston, and Harold Nicolson & Vita Sackville-West, too) have now been completely replanted, room by room, colour by colour, since the Robbs came here in 1993. Cothay makes a model study of how a garden can be rejuvenated. It is now in the prime of life, brimming with vigour. The avenue of mop-headed acacias (*Robinia pseudoacacia* 'Umbraculifera'), nearly 100m long, looks stunning underplanted with nepeta and a thousand white tulips. New for 2004 were a mount, planted with wildflowers and bulbs, and a lake – work continues.

❧ stylish 1920s design; good plants; cream teas.

Owned by Mr & Mrs Alastair Robb
Number of gardeners 1½
Size 2.8ha (7 acres); plus 2ha (5 acres) of new trees
English Heritage Grade II*

CROWE HALL
Widcombe Hill, Bath BA2 6AR

Tel: 01225 310322
Location Off A36 up Widcombe Hill.
Opening hours 2 pm - 6 pm; 9 April, 14 May, 11 June & by appointment.
Admission fee Adults £3; Children £1.

🅿️ ⟡ 🆆🅲 ♿ 🚻

Crowe Hall is a most extraordinary and exciting garden. It looks straight out at the Capability Brown landscape at Prior Park, and 'borrows' it. Mown grass paths have been cut through the meadows above the house to create an ever-changing view of the park and Palladian bridge. Below the house is an Italianate terrace, which leads to a ferny rock garden (real rocky outcrops here) and down into a semi-woodland garden. Recent developments include a 'Sauce' garden, in memory of Lady Barratt (a former owner), a 'Hercules' garden and the 'Teazle' garden with a cascade, pool and pergola in memory of a much-loved dog.

🌿 roses (mainly old-fashioned); fine greenhouse & grotto; teas.

Owned by John Barratt
Number of gardeners 2
Size 4.4ha (11 acres)
English Heritage Grade II

DUNSTER CASTLE
Dunster, Minehead TA24 6SL

Tel: 01643 821314 **Fax:** 01643 823000
www.nationaltrust.org.uk
Location 3 miles south-east of Minehead on A39.
Opening hours 11 am - 4 pm; daily; January to 17 March & 30 October to 31 December. 10 am - 5 pm; daily; 18 March to 29 October. Closed 25 & 26 December.
Admission fee Adults £4.10; Children £2.

🅿️ 🆆🅲 ♿ 🌳 🚻

Dunster is a Victorian woodland (with older features) on a steep slope, terraced in places and planted with tender exotica – mimosa, *Beschorneria* and a collection of citrus plants in an unheated conservatory.

🌿 *Arbutus* grove; woodland garden; sub-tropical plants; National Trust shop; tea-room at Dunster Mill.

Owned by The National Trust
Number of gardeners 4
Size 6.7ha (17 acres)
NCCPG National Collections *Arbutus*
English Heritage Grade I

EAST LAMBROOK MANOR
East Lambrook, South Petherton TA13 5HL

Tel: 01460 240328 **Fax:** 01460 242344
Email: garden@eastlambrook.com
www.eastlambrook.com
Location Signed from A303 at South Petherton.
Opening hours 10 am - 5 pm; daily; all year. Plus special openings for NGS.
Admission fee Adults £3.95; OAPs £3.50; Children free.

🅿️ 🆆🅲 🌸 🚻

East Lambrook is the archetypal cottage garden, made by Margery Fish, the popular gardening writer, and charmingly restored in recent years. Margery Fish was an important influence in British gardening in the 1950s and 1960s. She learnt about gardening not from books but from her own observations, so that she developed her own unselfconscious style of gardening. As a journalist, she knew how to communicate, and her books about the garden she made at East Lambrook have been very influential. The new owners are continuing the work of restoration begun in the 1980s, and have updated the plantings while respecting the original spirit. They have returned Margery Fish's nursery to its original site, made a special bed for hardy geraniums and restored the malthouse. They also run RHS courses for gardeners all through the year.

Margery Fish's garden; plantsman's collection of plants; good herbaceous borders; 150 different snowdrops; hellebores; euphorbias; geraniums; cottage garden plants; lunches & teas from Easter to end of September.

Owned by Marianne & Robert Williams
Number of gardeners 1½
Size 0.8ha (2 acres)
English Heritage Grade I

ELWORTHY COTTAGE PLANTS
Elworthy Cottage, Elworthy, Lydeard St Lawrence, Taunton TA4 3PX

Tel: 01984 656427
www.elworthy-cottage.co.uk
Location 10 miles north-west of Taunton, on B3188 in Elworthy village centre.
Opening hours 10 am - 4.30 pm; Thursday – Saturday; mid-March to end of May. Then Thursdays only from June to mid-October. And by appointment.
Admission fee £2.

Elworthy offers a pleasant selection of perennials and cottage garden plants, including quite a number which are uncommon or hard-to-find, as well as old favourites. The nursery is strong on geraniums (over 200), clematis (c.100), pulmonarias (over 50), as well as geums, violas, crocosmias and grasses. Some of the plants the nursery offers are not available from any other source. It has also introduced a number of new plants, including *Geranium* x *oxonianum* 'Elworthy Misty' and G. 'Elworthy Eyecatcher'. Most of the plants can be seen growing in the garden, which is neatly laid out with island beds and themed colours for year-round interest but also to blend into the surrounding countryside (Exmoor National Park) and to encourage wildlife. Other features include a gravel area for shade-tolerant plants, a decorative vegetable garden, an autumn bed of hot colours, hedges of native species, wildflower areas and a living willow screen.

raised beds; troughs; wildflowers.

Owned by Mike & Jenny Spiller
Number of gardeners owners only
Size 0.4ha (1 acre)

GAULDEN MANOR
Tolland, Lydeard St Lawrence TA4 3PN

Tel: 01984 667213
Location 1 mile east of Tolland church, off B3224.
Opening hours 2 pm - 5 pm; Thursdays, Sundays & Bank Holidays; June to August. And groups by appointment at other times.
Admission fee £3.25.

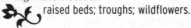

Gaulden is a modern garden, well designed and well planted. It has a series of small garden rooms, each devoted to a different theme (roses, herbs etc.) which makes it seem much larger than it really is and a pleasure to explore. The stream garden – very pretty – is below the monks' pond, its sides planted with candelabra primulas, ferns and gunneras.

woodland garden; roses (ancient & modern); herbs; good herbaceous borders; scent gardens; secret garden.

Owned by James Starkie
Number of gardeners 2
Size 0.8ha (2 acres)

GREENCOMBE GARDENS
Porlock TA24 8NU

Tel: 01643 862363
www.greencombe.org.uk
Location ½ mile west of Porlock on left of road to Porlock Weir.
Opening hours 2 pm - 6 pm; Saturday – Wednesday; April to July & again in autumn.

Admission fee Adults £5; Children (under 16) £1.

🅿 🚻 ♿ 🌱

Greencombe is an organic showpiece of international renown. The garden stretches across a sheltered hillside which looks up to the tree-covered slopes of Exmoor, behind and down across ancient fields to Porlock Bay and an uninterrupted view of the sea. It is a woodland garden, long and narrow, with a rich underplanting of ornamental plants beneath an outstanding canopy of oaks, hollies, conifers and sweet chestnuts. Camellias, rhododendrons, azaleas, maples, lilies, roses, clematis, and hydrangeas all flower in turn among many ferns and the garden's four National Collections: *Erythronium*, which are small mountain-lilies; *Vaccinium*, which the curator Joan Loraine calls 'whortleberries worldwide'; *Gaultheria*, which she refers to as 'whortleberries for bears'; and *Polystichum*, the 'thumbs-up' fern. The garden is completely organic, with compost heaps and leaf mould pits on show, and a riot of birds, butterflies and lesser insects. But, above all, like all good plantsman's gardens, Greencombe is full of rare plants and has lots to interest the visitor at every time of the year.

🌿 woodland garden; plantsman's collection of plants; good herbaceous borders; organically run.

Owned by Greencombe Garden Trust
Number of gardeners 2 part-time
Size 1.4ha (3½ acres)
NCCPG National Collections *Erythronium; Gaultheria; Polystichum; Vaccinium*

HADSPEN GARDEN
Castle Cary BA7 7NG

Tel & Fax: 01749 813707
www.hadspengarden.co.uk
Location 2 miles east of Castle Cary on A371. New access off A359.
Opening hours 10 am - 5 pm; Thursday -

Sunday & Bank Holiday Mondays; March to September.
Admission fee Adults £4; Children 50p.

🅿 🚻 ♿ 🌱 🌰 🍴

Part garden, part nursery specialising in colour plantings and unusual plants. Little remains of Penelope Hobhouse's first garden: the Popes have remade it in the modern idiom, using a wide range of rare plants to create decorative effects. Most visitors speak highly of it. The Popes' book on using colour in the garden has now been reprinted as *Planting with Colour*. It is published by Conran Octopus and based on their work at Hadspen.

🌿 roses (mainly old-fashioned); plantsman's collection of plants; good herbaceous borders; Eric Smith's *Hosta* collection; tulips; excellent nursery; colour gardening; nursery; light lunches & teas.

Owned by N. & S. Pope
Number of gardeners 2½
Size 2ha (5 acres)
NCCPG National Collections *Rodgersia*

HESTERCOMBE GARDENS
Cheddon Fitzpaine, Taunton TA2 8LG

Tel: 01823 413923 **Fax:** 01823 413747
www.hestercombegardens.com
Location 4 miles north of Taunton.
Opening hours 10 am - 5 pm; daily; all year. Closed 25 December.
Admission fee Adults £6.60; OAPs £6; Children £1.50.

🅿 ♿ 🚻 🌱 🌰 🍴

Ignore the house – a Victorian mansion now used as Council offices – and look at the famously restored garden. Lutyens hallmarks are everywhere: iris-choked rills, pergolas, seats, relieved staircases and pools where reflections twinkle on recessed apses. Gertrude Jekyll's planting is bold and simple, which adds to the vigour. The combination of Lutyens design and Jekyll plants is extremely photogenic: Hestercombe is a highly rewarding garden to learn about symmetry, balance and proportion. The secret landscape garden which Coplestone Warre Bampfylde laid out in the late 18th century reopened in 1997: 40 acres of lakes, temples, combes and woodlands which have not been seen for over 100 years. The Heritage Lottery Fund has made a grant of £3.7m to be paid between 2003 and 2008 which will confirm Hestercombe as Somerset's most visited garden.

good herbaceous borders; classical landscaping; Lutyens design & Jekyll planting; gift shop; plant sales (March to October); café.

Owned by Hestercombe Gardens Trust
Number of gardeners 8
Size 20ha (50 acres)
English Heritage Grade I

KELWAYS LTD
Barrymore Farm, Langport TA10 9EZ

Tel: 01458 250521 **Fax:** 01458 253351
www.kelways.co.uk
Location On B3153, just east of Langport.
Opening hours 9 am – 5 pm; Monday – Saturday. 10 am – 4 pm; Sundays; all year.

Long famous for its peonies (500+ herbaceous and 35 tree peonies), Kelways also has a large range of irises (700+), and an expanding range of perennials, shrubs and bedding plants. An orchid house displays and sells English-grown orchids. The peony fields will be open at their peak – usually the first two weeks of June, but please telephone before travelling to check the dates.

peonies; irises; orchids.

Owned by C. Johnson
NCCPG National Collections *Paeonia lactiflora*

LOWER SEVERALLS GARDENS & NURSERY
Crewkerne TA18 7NX

Tel: 01460 73234 **Fax:** 01460 76105
www.lowerseveralls.co.uk
Location 1½ miles north-east of Crewkerne. Signed from A30 & A352.
Opening hours 10 am – 5 pm; Tuesdays, Wednesdays, Fridays and Saturdays & all Bank Holiday Mondays; 1 March to 30 September. Plus some Sundays for NGS.
Admission fee Adults £3.

Both the garden and nursery started in 1985. At first, the nursery specialised in herbs, of which it still has a wide range. However, there are also good selections of hardy geraniums, salvias and lots more besides. The garden is set in front of an 18th-century Ham-stone farmhouse: it has fine herbaceous borders, island beds, a living 'dogwood basket' and an area for bog plants known as 'the Wadi'. There will be two RHS Special Events at Lower Severalls in 2006; details from 020 7821 3408.

herbaceous borders; island beds; herbs; self-service tea; lunches & teas for groups by arrangement.

Owned by Mary Pring
Number of gardeners 2
Size 1.2ha (3 acres)

LYTES CARY MANOR
Charlton Mackrell, Somerton TA11 7HU

Tel & Fax: 01458 224471
www.nationaltrust.org.uk
Location Near A303 junction with A372 & A37.
Opening hours 11 am – 5 pm; Wednesdays, Friday – Sunday & Bank Holiday Mondays; 22 March to 29 October.
Admission fee Adults £3.50; Children £1.50.

Lytes Cary has a neo-Elizabethan garden to go with the prettiest of manor houses: yew hedges, hornbeam walks, alleys and lawns, medlars, quinces and a simple Elizabethan flower border.

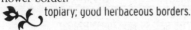 topiary; good herbaceous borders.

Owned by The National Trust
Number of gardeners 1, plus seasonal help & volunteers
Size 2.4ha (6 acres)
English Heritage Grade II

MALLET COURT NURSERY
Curry Mallet, Taunton TA3 6SY

Tel & Fax: 01823 481493
www.malletcourt.co.uk
Location In centre of Curry Mallet.
Opening hours 10 am - 4 pm; Mondays - Fridays. Plus special open days in April and October. Weekends by appointment.
Admission fee Free.

P ⬩ WC ♿ ❋

This is a wonderful specialist tree nursery with an excellent list of unusual trees. Its displays at RHS flower shows, including Chelsea and Hampton Court, have been a delight and a revelation over many years now. Many of the species it sells are offered by no other nursery anywhere in the world. It is particularly good for *Quercus* and *Acer*, and strong on species from China and Korea, but the nursery's list is full of species of every imaginable genus of rare tree. Every dendrophile in Britain knows of it and buys from it: the array of plants to be seen at the nursery is itself an education. Two RHS Special Events will take place at Mallet Court during 2006; details from 020 7821 3408.
Owned by J.G.S. Harris & Mrs P.M.E. Mallet-Harris

MEADOWS NURSERY
5 Rectory Cottages, Selwood Street, Mells, Frome BA11 3PN

Tel: 01373 812268
Location In centre of village.
Opening hours 10 am - 6 pm; Wednesday - Sunday; February to October.
Admission fee Free.

P ❋ ⬧

Meadows Nursery has a pretty, cottage-style garden, well maintained and boosted by putting out some spectacular succulents and other glasshouse plants in summer. The nursery specialises in perennials and has a particularly good line in kniphofias. Both make very good use of a confined space.

 good nursery.

Owned by Sue Lees & Eddie Wheatley
Number of gardeners owners
Size 0.2ha (½ acre)

MILL COTTAGE PLANTS
Henley Mill, Wookey BA5 1AW

Tel & Fax: 01749 676966
www.millcottageplants.co.uk
Location 2 miles from Wells, off A371. Left into Henley Lane, then 50 yards on left.
Opening hours Nursery: 10 am - 5.30 pm; Wednesdays; March to September. Garden also open by appointment.
Admission fee Garden: £1.50; Nursery: free.

P ❋

The nursery grows a selection of unusual perennials, including a wide range of geraniums, hellebores, oriental poppies, dieramas, ferns and grasses. It also has a good line in rare hydrangea cultivars. The garden is well worth seeing, though it is best to ask if you can see it in advance of your visit. It includes a sunny formal garden, a shaded 'folly' garden, a kitchen garden, 'hot red' borders, and a late summer bed (mainly grasses and perennials). Groups are especially welcome.

 beautiful waterside setting; hardy perennials.

Owned by Peter & Sally Gregson
Number of gardeners 2½
Size 1ha (2½ acres)

MILTON LODGE
Old Bristol Road, Wells BA5 3AQ

Tel: 01749 672168
Location Old Bristol Road off A39.
Opening hours 2 pm - 5 pm; Tuesdays, Wednesdays, Sundays & Bank Holidays; Easter to 31 October.
Admission fee Adults £3; Children (under 14) free. Groups by arrangement.

This impressive Edwardian garden is terraced down a hillside against a backdrop of Wells Cathedral. Most of the plantings are modern, and look good against the walls and bulky yew hedges. In a combe, across the main road, is an eight-acre 19th-century arboretum. Both parts are full of interesting plants, excellently maintained and constantly improving, with considerable new planting in recent years.

roses (mainly modern); good herbaceous borders; fine collection of trees; tallest *Populus alba* (20m) in the British Isles; teas on Sundays (May to August).

Owned by D.C. Tudway Quilter
Size 1.6ha (4 acres)
English Heritage Grade II

MONTACUTE HOUSE
Montacute, Yeovil TA15 6XP

Tel: 01935 823289 **Fax:** 01935 826921
www.nationaltrust.org.uk
Location In Montacute village, 4 miles west of Yeovil.
Opening hours 11 am - 6 pm (or dusk, if earlier); daily, except Tuesdays; 22 March to 29 October. 11 am - 4 pm; Wednesday - Sunday; 1 November to 17 March 2007.
Admission fee Adults £4.50; Children £2.

The sunken gardens at Montacute are a perfect foil for the amazing Elizabethan mansion, and are beautifully maintained. They cannot be beaten for the sense of English renaissance grandeur they impart. The National Trust has recently had the courage to replant the borders not as they were originally planned by Vita Sackville-West, nor as subsequently laid out by Graham Stuart Thomas in pretty pastel shades, but using the brilliant colours devised by Phyllis Reiss of nearby Tintinhull in the 1950s. The vivid colours of 'Frensham' roses, purple berberis and late-summer dahlias are the ideal complement to the Ham-stone house.

good herbaceous borders; exquisite gazebos; shop; light lunches & teas; licensed restaurant.

Owned by The National Trust
Number of gardeners 4
Size 5ha (12½ acres), plus 10.2ha (26 acres) of parkland
English Heritage Grade I

P.M.A. PLANT SPECIALITIES
Junker's Nursery Ltd, Lower Mead, West Hatch, Taunton TA3 5RN

Tel: 01823 480774 **Fax:** 01823 481046
www.junker.co.uk
Location West Hatch is 4 miles south of Taunton.

Opening hours By appointment only.
Admission fee Free.

P 🌿

P.M.A. has some interesting container-grown trees and shrubs. It is particularly strong on Japanese and snakebark acers, daphnes, magnolias and the ornamental tree *Cornus* (flowering dogwoods). Some plants are available in larger sizes for instant impact. The display borders are particularly instructive – new areas are planted and developed every year – and visitors also have free access to the stock plants. The new *Betula* glades are shaping up well. Look out for the many epimediums and hellebores in the woodland plantings.

Owned by Nick & Karan Junker
Number of gardeners owners only
Size 1.2ha (3 acres)

PRIOR PARK LANDSCAPE GARDEN
Ralph Allen Drive, Bath BA2 5BD

Tel: 01225 833422
www.nationaltrust.org.uk
Location 1½ miles south of Bath city centre. No on-site or nearby parking.
Opening hours 11 am - 5.30 pm (or dusk, if earlier); Wednesday - Monday; 2 February to 30 November. 11 am - dusk; Friday - Sunday; 1 December to 28 January 2007.
Admission fee Adults £4.50; Children £2.50.

WC &

The classical landscape at Prior Park was laid out between 1734 and 1764 by a property developer called Ralph Allen, who was a friend of Pope and Burlington. Pope advised extensively on the original layout and buildings before Capability Brown gave them a make-over in the early 1760s. The park is no more than 28 acres, stretching from the extremely handsome Palladian house (not National Trust) at the top of the steep valley to the exquisite Palladian bridge right at the bottom, which is the focus of the entire landscape

and reflected in three lakes. It is reached by a rugged and sometimes slippery path through the woods on either side, quite unfitted for wheelchairs and buggies and only suitable for the sure-footed and confident. Now the National Trust has started on its final programme of restoration, by reviving the Wilderness, its Gothic temple, serpentine lake and cascade. There is nothing of horticultural interest, but some fine trees – mainly beech, with some yew, sycamore and seedling ashes – underplanted with ferns and laurels. Nevertheless, it is hard to imagine a more elegant landscape than this one, which uses the busy and fashionable city of Bath as its background. Photographers may wish to visit it early in the afternoon, when the sun shines on the Palladian bridge. There is one snag, however; the Trust can offer no on-site parking, except for disabled visitors. Buses (Nos. 2 & 4) run from the Grand Parade every 15 minutes on weekdays and every 20 minutes from Dorchester Street on Sundays: further details on the National Trust's website.

❧ Palladian bridge; handsome parkland.

Owned by The National Trust
Number of gardeners 3, plus volunteers
Size 11.1ha (28 acres)
English Heritage Grade I

SHERBORNE GARDEN
Pear Tree House, Litton BA3 4PP

Tel: 01761 241220
Location On B3114, ½ mile west of Litton village, 7 miles north of Wells.
Opening hours 11 am - 5 pm; Sundays & Mondays; June to October. For NGS: 11 to 15 February for snowdrops, and 4 June.
Admission fee Adults £3; Children free. Groups welcome by appointment.

P 🌿 WC & ✕ ▷

This plantsman's garden started in a

modest enough way in 1964 but now extends to more than six acres. It is very thickly planted, yet it also seems to sit very well in the countryside. The owners are particularly interested in trees and plant them in groups for comparison: hence the 'prickly wood' (of hollies), the pinetum and an acer glade, as well as some 40 different oaks. But there are also good herbaceous plantings and bulbs, a fine collection of *Rosa* species, hemerocallis (250) and ferns (200), which makes it an excellent garden to dawdle in and learn from.

🌿 woodland garden; roses (ancient & modern, plus many species); plantsman's collection of plants; small pinetum; collection of hollies (180 varieties) and hardy ferns (250 varieties); 29 different water lilies; tea/coffee.

Owned by Mr & Mrs John Southwell
Number of gardeners owners, with part-time help
Size 2.4ha (6 acres)

TINTINHULL HOUSE
Tintinhull, Yeovil BA22 8PZ

Tel: 01935 823289 **Fax:** 01935 826357
www.nationaltrust.org.uk
Location In Tintinhull village, 5 miles north-west of Yeovil.
Opening hours 11 am – 5 pm; Wednesday – Sunday & Bank Holiday Mondays; 22 March to 29 October.
Admission fee Adults £5; Children £2.50; Family £12.50.

🅿 🚾 ♿ ☕

This small garden – less than two acres – is the most famous example of a Jekyll-style garden on a small scale. It combines great design with a wide range of plants and the most skilful use of colour combinations in planting them. The garden looks larger than it really is because it has been divided into a sequence of small rooms of different size,

all of them hedged or walled. Perhaps the most famous part is the largest, around a formal rectangular pool in front of a pillared summerhouse. The borders on either side are in complete contrast to each other: one is made in the bright bold colours of scarlet, yellow, orange and white, while the other is dominated by pastel pinks, mauves, blues and pale yellows. Yet they are also mirror images of each other because each uses grey-leaved plants and striking leaf shapes as well as colour. No garden employs such a wide palette of plants so rigorously as elements of design. There has been much cutting back, clearing, renewal and replanting recently.

🌿 topiary; roses (mainly old-fashioned); good herbaceous borders; colour borders; kitchen garden; light refreshments.

Owned by The National Trust
Number of gardeners 1
Size 0.8ha (2 acres)
English Heritage Grade II

TYNTESFIELD
Wraxall BS48 1NT

Tel: 01275 461900
Location On B3128 at Wraxall.
Opening hours 10 am – 5.30 pm; Mondays, Wednesdays, Saturdays & Sundays; 18 March to 30 October.
Admission fee Adults £4.50; Children £2.30; Family £11.30.

🅿 🚾 ♿ ☕

The National Trust has already worked wonders to restore the gardens and parkland at Tyntesfield. It was laid out in the 1860s and 1870s in a mixture of the Gothic and Italianate styles. The formal garden is Italianate, with eight cruciform beds set into a grass terrace and enclosed by gravel paths. Beyond is a choice of three paths leading to the arboretum known as Paradise. One has hollies cut as mushrooms, another Irish yews and the third an avenue of Portugal laurel. Paradise itself is a Victorian collection of oaks, cedars, hollies and conifers. The walled garden, remodelled in 1889 in the Georgian style, has a cut-flower garden, an orangery (built for Queen Victoria's Diamond Jubilee), and a series of glasshouses, bothies and sheds all in good working order.

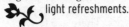 light refreshments.

Owned by The National Trust
Number of gardeners 4
Size 8ha (20 acres)

WAYFORD MANOR
Crewkerne TA18 8QG

Tel: 01460 73253 **Fax:** 01460 76365
Location 3 miles south-west of Crewkerne off A30 or B3165.
Opening hours For NGS: 9 & 30 April; 1 & 21 May; 11 June. And parties by appointment.

Admission fee Adults £3; Children 50p.

Wayford is one of the best gardens designed by Harold Peto: terraces and courtyards, pools and arbours, balustrades and staircases, Tuscan and Byzantine. Down in the wild garden is an extensive collection of mature acers and magnolias, as well as many rhododendrons, dogwoods, candelabra primulas, bog plants and daffodils. The whole garden is being restored by the enthusiastic and knowledgeable owners: they recently reinstated the pergola with stone Tuscan columns as Peto originally designed it.

good herbaceous borders; rhododendrons; spring bulbs; maples; tallest *Photinia davidiana* (13m) in the British Isles; plants for sale; teas.

Owned by Mr & Mrs R.L. Goffe
Number of gardeners 1
Size 1.6ha (4 acres)
English Heritage Grade II

STAFFORDSHIRE

Staffordshire has three historic gardens to which English Heritage has accorded Grade I status: Alton Towers, Biddulph Grange and Shugborough. All are open to the public. The county is not, however, a magnet for garden-visitors with horticultural interests. The Dorothy Clive Garden is the only really first-rate garden in Staffordshire to have come out of the 20th century. There are only three National Collections and the National Garden Scheme has comparatively little success within the county. Why this should be remains a puzzle: the county is fairly wealthy, its soils are fertile, and its climate is not too subject to extremes.

Staffordshire's Historic Gardens Trust is, however, very active and its historic gardens are well visited – Shugborough, Weston and Trentham have all enjoyed long traditions of popular participation in their public events. There are few arboreta of note and practically no record-sized trees anywhere in the county. Even the Royal Horticultural Society seems unable to stir up enthusiasm for gardening: Staffordshire is one of the few counties where it has no partners, except for the Dorothy Clive Garden. But Ashwood Nurseries, on the borders of the West Midlands, is a place of international standing.

ALTON TOWERS
Alton, Stoke-on-Trent ST10 4DB

Tel: 0870 5204060 **Fax:** 01538 704092
www.altontowers.com
Location Signed for miles around.
Opening hours 9.30 am - 5/6/7 pm, depending on season; daily; 1 April to 29 October.
Admission fee Tickets vary in cost according to season but are always fairly expensive (typically £29.50 for an adult), but Alton offers much more than gardens to visit.

P WC & X D

Alton has 300 acres of dotty and exuberant display, best seen from the sky-ride. The gardens are by and large detached from the razzmatazz of the theme park. There are splendid Victorian conifers and gaudy bedding, magnificently done. The highlights include a Swiss Cottage, a Roman bridge, a Chinese pagoda, a flag tower, and a corkscrew fountain. It is seriously important to garden historians and

excellent entertainment still – but not for contemplative souls. Best in term time.

woodland garden; roses (mainly modern); rock garden; mature conifers; good herbaceous borders; many restaurants.

Owned by Tussauds Group
Number of gardeners 10
Size 120ha (300 acres)
English Heritage Grade I

ASHWOOD NURSERIES LTD
Ashwood Lower Lane, Kingswinford DY6 0AE

Tel: 01384 401996 **Fax:** 01308 401108
www.ashwood-nurseries.co.uk
Location 2 miles west of Kingswinford, near A449.
Opening hours 9 am - 6 pm, Monday - Saturday; 9.30 am - 6 pm, Sundays; all year, except 25 & 26 December.

Admission fee Free.

P WC ⚹ 🌱 🍵 ⟁

Ashwood is a rising star among nurseries.
The owner and his associates have the
happy knack of anticipating trends in
horticultural fashion: then they put a lot of
thought into developing new plants and,
thus, new markets. They began in the
1970s with lewisias, crossing and selecting
them until they could offer a remarkable
range of colours. In 1996 they were
awarded a gold medal for their lewisias at
the Chelsea Flower Show, their first ever
exhibit at the Royal Horticultural Society's
most prestigious show. Next they began to
breed hellebores – strains of H. *orientalis* in
particular. The Ashwood hybrids are
remarkable for their purity of colour, vigour
and form – but, above all, for the new
developments that they have brought to
the genus: doubles, anemone-centred and
upright forms. Now they are turning their
attention to hybrids of H. *niger*. More
recent, but no less promising, has been
their involvement with hardy cyclamen,
auriculas, hepaticas and salvias. Hepaticas
are extremely fashionable in Japan, where
rare cultivars may cost the equivalent of
several hundred pounds, and there is clearly
money to be made from developing this
genus yet further. Above all, Ashwood
means quality: the exhibits the nursery
brings to RHS flower shows are beautifully
grown. The hydrangeas they brought last
year (2005) to the Chelsea Flower Show
were a real eye-opener. A visit to their
nursery is strongly recommended. There
will be five RHS Special Events at
Ashwood Nurseries in 2006; details from
020 7821 3408.

🌿 hellebores; cyclamen; lewisias;
hepaticas; auriculas; gift shop; tea-
room.

Owned by John Massey
Size 2ha (5 acres)
NCCPG National Collections *Lewisia*

BIDDULPH GRANGE GARDENS
Biddulph, Stoke-on-Trent ST8 7SD

Tel: 01782 517999 **Fax:** 01782 510624
www.nationaltrust.org.uk
Location ½ mile north of Biddulph, 3½ miles south-
east of Congleton.
Opening hours 11.30 am – 5.30 pm; Wednesday –
Sunday & Bank Holiday Mondays; 25 March to 29
October. 11 am – 3 pm; Saturdays & Sundays; 4
November to 17 December.
Admission fee Adults £5.30; Children £2.60, but
less from 4 November to 17 December.

WC 🌱 🍵 ⟁

The garden at Biddulph was made in the
middle of the 19th century by James
Bateman – an important amateur garden
designer, plantsman and writer. His wife
Maria and their friend Edward Cooke also
had a hand in it. Their garden has several
microclimates, compartments, follies and
whimsies: it is, in fact, the earliest example of
a garden being divided into a series of smaller
rooms, each designed and planted to a
different theme. Some are so original and
inventive that they still strike us as frankly
rather wacky – the Dragon Parterre, for
example, which is dominated by a golden
cow (or, possibly, buffalo), or the stumpery
where carefully excavated and inverted tree
stumps and roots form a framework for
trailing ivies and other plants. One of the
more eccentric novelties is the 'upside-down
tree' replanted with its roots in the air
between the Rhododendron Ground and the
Lime Avenue. Others are the Egyptian
courtyard with its own pyramid, a bowling
green and quoits ground, the Chinese garden
(surprisingly large and beautiful, with a joss
house, temple and section of the Great Wall)
and the ferny Scottish glen. Elsewhere are
areas devoted to collections of plants – a
wellingtonia avenue, a pinetum and the
dahlia walk. The estate suffered years of
neglect when the house was used as a
hospital but the National Trust has restored
the garden energetically and many of the
quirkier features are as good as ever again.

The trees survived best: some of the conifers are very large handsome specimens in the prime of middle age now.

🌿 Victorian garden with many different styles & rooms; excellent plants & plantings; mature conifers; mosaic parterre; gift shop; tea-room.

Owned by The National Trust
Number of gardeners 4, plus 1 student
Size 6ha (15 acres)
English Heritage Grade I

DOROTHY CLIVE GARDEN
Willoughbridge, Market Drayton TF9 4EU

Tel: 01630 647237 **Fax:** 01630 647902
www.dorothyclivegarden.co.uk
Location A51, midway between Nantwich & Stone.
Opening hours 10 am - 5.30 pm; daily; mid-March to October.
Admission fee Adults £4.20; OAPs & Groups (20+) £3.60; Children £1 (under 11s free). RHS members free in July & August.

P ⬧ WC ♿ ☕

Meticulously maintained and still expanding, this garden was begun in 1940 but seems ageless. It was made on an unpromising site, a cold, windy hilltop, but advice on plants and planting came from Frank Knight, then director of Wisley. The layout is informal, yet full of incidents, each with a distinct character. They include a superb woodland garden, an alpine scree, a gravel garden, a fine collection of trees and spectacular flower borders. The Dorothy Clive Garden is best perhaps in May, when the woodland quarry is brilliant with rhododendrons, but the great range and variety of plants ensure that there is always much to see whatever the season.

🌿 woodland garden; mature conifers; camellias; good herbaceous borders; heather; cyclamen; tea-room with beverages & home-baked food.

Owned by Willoughbridge Garden Trust
Number of gardeners 3
Size 5ha (12 acres)

MOSELEY OLD HALL
Moseley Old Hall Lane, Fordhouses WV10 7HY

Tel: 01902 782808
www.nationaltrust.org.uk
Location South of M54 between A449 & A460.
Opening hours 12 noon - 5 pm (11 am to 5 pm on Bank Holiday Mondays); Wednesdays, Saturdays, Sundays, Bank Holiday Mondays & the following Tuesdays; 18 March to 29 October. 1 pm - 4 pm; Sundays; 6 November to 18 December.
Admission fee Adults £5.

P ⬧ WC ♿ ☀ ☕ ☕

This is a modern reconstruction of a 17th-century, walled, town garden: neat box parterres, a nut walk and an arched pergola hung with clematis and vines. The plantings are all of the period, including the fruit trees: quietly inspirational.

🌿 topiary; snowdrops; herbs; current holder of Sandford Award; gift shop; tea-room.

Owned by The National Trust
Number of gardeners 1 part-time
Size 0.4ha (1 acre)

OULTON HOUSE
Oulton, Stone ST15 8UR

Tel: 01785 813556 **Fax:** 01785 816141
Location From Stone take Oulton Road & turn left after Oulton sign. 3rd driveway on right. Steep, winding drive; house at top of hill.
Opening hours By appointment, February to end of July.
Admission fee Adults £3; Children 75p.

P WC ☀ ☕ ☕

This three-acre garden has been made by Mrs Fairbairn over many years, essentially for private enjoyment not for public display. It is full of good plants – roses, rhododendrons, geraniums and clematis – arranged in colour groupings. The snowdrops and hellebores are especially good early in the year, followed by more spring bulbs and a field of daffodils, but the high point comes with the herbaceous borders and roses in June and July.

snowdrops; roses (mainly old-fashioned); rock garden; plants under glass; good herbaceous borders; hellebores; spring bulbs; plants for sale sometimes; teas.

Owned by Mr & Mrs W.A. Fairbairn
Number of gardeners owners, plus part-time help
Size 1.4ha (3½ acres)

SHUGBOROUGH HALL
Milford, Stafford ST17 0XB

Tel: 01889 881388 **Fax:** 01889 881323
www.shugborough.org.uk
Location On A513 from Stafford to Lichfield. Signed from M6, Jct 13.
Opening hours 11 am – 5 pm (last admissions 4.30 pm); daily; 17 March to 27 October.
Admission fee House & Garden: Adults £10; Concessions £7; Children £6; Family £15.

This classical and neo-classical landscape has Chinese additions; a handsome William Andrews Nesfield terrace dominated by dumplings of clipped golden yew; and a walled garden, due to open this year (2006). It is managed by Staffordshire County Council, and is very popular with the locals.

woodland garden; good herbaceous borders; formal terraces with rhododendrons; current holder of Sandford Award; National Trust shop; licensed restaurant; tea-rooms.

Owned by The National Trust
Number of gardeners 4
Size 8.7ha (22 acres)
English Heritage Grade I

TRENTHAM GARDENS
Stone Road, Stoke-on-Trent ST4 8AX

Tel: 01782 646646 **Fax:** 01782 644536
www.trenthamleisure.co.uk
Location Signed from M6.
Opening hours 10 am – 6 pm (4 pm in winter; last admissions one hour before closing); daily; all year. Closed 25 December.

Admission fee Not yet known as we went to press.

The Trentham estate has been substantially redeveloped and this includes restoring the important Victorian formal gardens, park, lakes and woods. Most of the gardens are now open and the rest are expected to be visitable again during the course of this year (2006). Tom Stuart-Smith and Piet Oudolf are the main designers: the results so far are very promising.

important Italianate formal gardens; summer bedding; shops; tea-room.

Owned by Trentham Leisure Ltd
English Heritage Grade II*

WESTON PARK
Weston-under-Lizard, Shifnal TF11 8LE

Tel: 01952 852100 **Fax:** 01952 850430
www.weston-park.com
Location Off A5 to Telford.
Opening hours 11 am – 6.30 pm (last admissions 5 pm); 15 to 23, 29 & 30 April; 1, 6, 7, 13, 14, 20, 21 & 27 to 31 May; 1 to 4, 10, 11, 17, 18, 24 & 25 June; daily in July & August, except 29 July & 17 to 23 August; 1 to 3 September.
Admission fee Adults £4; OAPs £3.50; Children £3.

Weston has a fine 18th-century landscape (Capability Brown worked there) and a 19th-century Italianate parterre, a temple of Diana, a grotto called Pendrill's Cave, and a handsome orangery by James Paine. It is not of major horticultural interest, but the rose walk and rhododendrons are worth seeing. It is perhaps best for its fine collection of trees, some of them record-breakers, and the collection of *Nothofagus* planted by the late Lord Bradford.

fine collection of trees; landscaped park; rhododendrons; gift shop; restaurant.

Owned by The Weston Park Foundation
Number of gardeners 3
English Heritage Grade II*

SUFFOLK

Suffolk has comparatively few historic gardens of national importance but, such as they are, they are of great interest to the garden-lover. Both Helmingham and Shrubland are rated as Grade I gardens, while Euston, Ickworth and Somerleyton are all Grade II*. There is a particularly fine collection of trees at East Bergholt Place, which has a good nursery attached. Suffolk is a rich county but was, until recently, rather cut off from London and its markets, which may help in part to explain why it has so many good nurseries. Notcutts is one of the largest quality nurseries in the country, with a long and distinguished history of plant introductions and exhibits at RHS flower shows. Unfortunately, however, they have decided to remake their display garden in 2006 and move their National Collection of *Hibiscus syriacus* cultivars, which means that they will not be opening again until 2007 or 2008 – the nursery and garden centres are, of course, unaffected. The leading seedsmen Thompson & Morgan have been at Ipswich for over 100 years: their trial grounds may also be visited in season. But it is the sheer number of good small modern nurseries which is so surprising: we list Goldbrook, Park Green and Rougham Hall among others – but Gardiner's Hall Plants at Braiseworth (over 3,000 different plants) and North Green Snowdrops (sent 'in the green') are also worth knowing. Suffolk has many good modern gardens like Wyken Hall and others that we do not list, including the Blakenham Woodland Garden at Little Blakenham (made by the late Lord Blakenham, Treasurer of the RHS). The National Gardens Scheme does well in the county and there is an active Historic Gardens Trust, too. The NCCPG is represented by about a dozen National Collections, including some horticulturally important genera like lilacs (*Syringa*), delphiniums and fuchsias. Otley College near Ipswich is a RHS Partner College, with lectures, workshops and garden walks throughout the year: further details from 020 7821 3408.

EAST BERGHOLT PLACE
East Bergholt CO7 6UP

Tel: & Fax: 01206 299224
Location 2 miles east of A12, on B1070, east-north-east of East Bergholt.
Opening hours 10 am - 5 pm; daily; March to October.
Admission fee Adults £3; Children free. RHS members free from March to June.

P [WC] & ✿ ◆

East Bergholt has a wonderful woodland garden (best in spring) planted by Charles Eley, the present owner's great-grandfather, at the start of the 20th century. It is the home of *Malus x purpurea* 'Eleyi' and has been called a 'Cornish Garden in Suffolk'. Of greatest interest is a collection of trees known as the 'Swale', around a gentle valley with a small brook running down the middle. Many of the older trees and shrubs were grown from original collections by George Forrest: others represent modern plantings and replantings. The collection is well labelled and well maintained – a fine place to see a wide range of trees and shrubs. Good specimens include a very handsome variegated cherry-laurel *Prunus laurocerasus* 'Castlewellan' 5m high, a magnificent *Quercus castaneifolia* and a fine three-stemmed *Davidia involucrata* var. *vilmoriniana*. Some are record-breakers, including a *Lithocarpus densiflorus* 12m tall.

The valley is sheltered by hedges of holly and yew and a mature collection of hardy rhododendrons. And it is good for insects and wildlife, too. Restoration and replanting continue. There will be three RHS Special Events at East Bergholt Place in 2006; details from 020 7821 3408.

topiary; rhododendrons & azaleas; camellias; fine collection of trees; specialist plant centre in walled garden.

Owned by Mr & Mrs Rupert Eley
Number of gardeners 2
Size 6ha (15 acres)

EUSTON HALL
Euston, Thetford IP24 2QP

Tel: 01842 766366 **Fax:** 01842 766764
www.eustonhall.co.uk
Location On A1088 3 miles south of Thetford & 12 miles north of Bury St Edmunds.
Opening hours 2.30 pm – 5 pm; Thursdays; 15 June to 14 September, plus 25 June, 16 July & 3 September. NCCPG plant sale on 28 May.
Admission fee £3.

The classical 18th-century landscaping at Euston is very beautiful. William Kent made the serpentine lake, though it was later modified by Capability Brown. Kent also built the elegant banqueting house. There are avenues of beech and lime, and clumps, spinneys and belts of mature trees. The formal terraces by the house lead to herbaceous borders and rose gardens. It all adds up to a most satisfying composition where horticulture plays second fiddle to landscaping.

roses (mainly old-fashioned); William Kent temple and summerhouse; new 'Monet' bridge on lake; river walk & water mill; craft shop; home-made teas.

Owned by The Duke of Grafton
Number of gardeners 2
Size 28ha (70 acres)
English Heritage Grade II*

GOLDBROOK PLANTS
Hoxne, Eye IP21 5AN

Tel & Fax: 01379 668770
Location On south-east edge of Hoxne.
Opening hours 10 am – 5 pm; Thursday – Sunday; April to September. Saturdays & Sundays only; October to March. Other days by appointment. Closed January & around Chelsea & Hampton Court Shows.

Goldbrook's exhibits at Chelsea and other RHS flower shows have won them much praise – and an impressive run of gold medals. Their collection of hostas is quite exceptional – over 1,000 cultivars, of which a great many are available from no other nursery. The same is true of their hemerocallis. Look out for their American introductions, too – many of the hemerocallis bear the prefix 'Siloam' (e.g. H. 'Siloam Fairy Tale') – while the hostas they have raised themselves are often prefixed by 'Goldbrook'.

hostas; hemerocallis.

Owned by Sandra Bond

HARVEYS GARDEN PLANTS
Great Green, Thurston, Bury St Edmunds IP31 3SJ

Tel & Fax: 01359 233363
www.harveysgardenplants.co.uk
Location In middle of Great Green, on road between Thurston & Norton.
Opening hours 9.30 am – 4.30 pm; Tuesday – Saturday; 10 January to 23 December.
Admission fee Free.

Harveys Garden Plants is a family-run nursery in Suffolk growing an extensive range of hardy herbaceous plants. They specialise in unusual perennials, especially those not commonly found in garden centres. Their specialities include hellebores, heleniums and shade-loving woodland plants. They have now started to develop their own strain of more vertical-facing hellebores which are called Bradfield hybrids. The nursery moved to a new site in 2004, and will be developing new display borders, a woodland area and visitor centre this year (2006). There will be six RHS Special Events at Harveys Garden Plants in 2006; details from 020 7821 3408.

Korean chrysanthemums; excellent specialist nursery.

Owned by Roger & Teresa Harvey
Size 4ha (10 acres)

HAUGHLEY PARK
Stowmarket IP14 3JY

Tel: 01359 240701 **Fax:** 01359 243001
www.haughleyparkbarn.co.uk
Location Signed from A14.
Opening hours 2 pm - 5.30 pm; Tuesdays; May to September, plus 30 April & 7 May for bluebells.
Admission fee Adults £3; Children free.

Haughley has a Jacobean mansion with well-kept modern flower gardens and fine trees (especially a magnolia, probably *Magnolia denudata*, 8m high and 11m across). In the walled garden are vegetables, trained fruit trees, a rose arbour and other ornamental features. But the acres of lily-of-the-valley and bluebells in the woodland garden are worth the journey no matter how far. There is a choice of three woodland walks, from 1½ to 2½ miles long: the camellias are good in May and the rhododendrons in June. In the West Woods, the owners have been carrying out an interesting experiment since the great gale of 1987. This arises from the different way in which each part was subsequently managed. Some areas were undamaged and remain 'natural'; one area of damaged woodland has been left in place to recover naturally; one area had the stumps left in place to shoot as coppice timber; and

several areas were cleared and replanted between 1992 and 1996.

woodland garden; rhododendrons & azaleas; good herbaceous borders; bluebells; lily-of-the-valley; 1,000-year-old oak with 9.15m girth.

Owned by Robert Williams
Number of gardeners 3
Size 3.2ha (8 acres), plus 105ha (265 acres) of park & woods.

ICKWORTH
Horringer, Bury St Edmunds IP29 5QE

Tel: 01284 735270 **Fax:** 01284 735175
www.nationaltrust.org.uk/ickworth
Location 3 miles south-west of Bury St Edmunds.
Opening hours 10 am - 5 pm; Friday - Tuesday; 20 March to 1 October. 11 am - 4 pm; Friday - Tuesday; 2 October to 18 March 2007. Open daily during half-term holidays, Easter holidays and summer holidays (24 July to 3 September). Closed 25 December.
Admission fee Adults £3.40; Children 90p.

Ickworth is an extraordinary garden for an extraordinary house: both were influenced by Italy. The main borders follow the curves of the house. There is also an Italian garden with Mediterranean plants and long vistas in the park. Capability Brown had a hand in it. Please note that parts may be closed off from time to time for essential work.

autumn colour; Italian garden; Victorian 'stumpery'; display of lemon trees in orangery; tallest *Quercus pubescens* (29m) in the British Isles; National Trust shop; large self-service restaurant.

Owned by The National Trust
Number of gardeners 5, plus a trainee
Size 28ha (70 acres)
NCCPG National Collections *Buxus*
English Heritage Grade II*

HELMINGHAM HALL
Stowmarket IP14 6EF

Tel: 01473 890799 **Fax:** 01473 890776
www.helmingham.com
Location 9 miles north of Ipswich on B1077.
Opening hours 2 pm – 6 pm; Wednesdays &
Sundays; 7 May to 17 September.
Admission fee Adults £4.50; Concessions £4;
Children £2.50.

A visit to Helmingham is a step back into history, to a time of ancient certainties, order and peace. The Tollemaches have lived here since 1487. The house is a moated manor, half-timbered when built in 1480, but given a cladding of bricks and tiles in the 18th century. It is set in the most spacious 400-acre deer park, loosely studded with vast centennial oaks grown to their full spread. Helmingham's formal garden lies beyond the moat to the south of the house. It is surrounded by 60 hybrid musks, lightly pruned and allowed to billow out, to fill the beds. The entire garden, about 100m long, is edged with 'Hidcote' lavender, underplanted with variegated London pride, and complemented by *Campanula lactiflora*, alstroemerias, foxgloves and peonies. This is gardening on a large scale, and makes its impact through simplicity and repetition: it is immensely grand. Beyond the formal garden is the walled garden proper, built of brick in 1745. On either side of the central grassy path runs a broad and stately double herbaceous border perhaps 120m long. Climbing roses are tied to straining wires all along its back: they include 'Guinée', 'Long John Silver', and *Rosa multiflora* var. *cathayensis*. The roses are underplanted with herbaceous plantings chosen to blend with the soft colours of the roses: pinks, blues, mauves,

whites and the palest of creamy-yellows. Not until the main rose-flowering has finished in mid-August do yellows, bronzes, oranges and reds come to the fore. A spring border runs the whole way along one of the outer walls of the walled garden and is planted mainly with irises, tulips and peonies, backed by more climbing roses, vines, clematis, chaenomeles, ceanothus and myrtle from Queen Victoria's wedding posy. Nearer the house is a new series of knot gardens planted in 1982, which look as if they have been here for hundreds of years. The knots include the Tollemaches' heraldic device, a fret or interlacing pattern of bands, which has been made to interweave by pruning the strips of box at different levels. It leads to another rose garden: albas and species roses, centifolias and mosses, a large choice of gallicas and so on, underplanted with spring bulbs, white foxgloves, *Campanula persicifolia*, *Alchemilla mollis*, purple violas and geraniums. One reason why the garden is so successful is that the roses and their companion plantings all fall within a narrow colour range. But everything here is carefully thought through and controlled: you see this firmness, too, in the immaculately edged lawns and weedless borders. Everywhere at Helmingham order prevails over anarchy.

roses (mainly old-fashioned); good herbaceous borders; deer park; moat; fine walled garden; good parterres and knots; shop; tea-room.

Owned by Lord Tollemache
Number of gardeners 3 full-time, 1 part-time
Size 4ha (10 acres)
English Heritage Grade I

PARK GREEN NURSERIES
Wetheringsett, Stowmarket IP14 5QH

Tel: 01728 860139 **Fax:** 01728 861277
www.parkgreen.co.uk
Location 6 miles north-east of Stowmarket.
Opening hours 10 am - 4 pm; Monday - Saturday;
1 March to 30 September.
Admission fee Free.

P WC

This excellent nursery specialises in
ornamental grasses and other hardy
perennial plants, but its most important
line is hostas. It stocks over 200 different
cultivars and introduces new ones every
year. Recent home-raised releases include
Hosta 'Delia', *H.* 'Fran Godfrey', *H.* 'Sarah
Kennedy', *H.* 'Gay Search' and *H.* 'Royal
Golden Jubilee'. A very large number can
be seen in the demonstration beds. Park
Green Nurseries will host two RHS Special
Events in 2006, on 18 May and 29 June;
details from 020 7821 3408.

light refreshments.

Owned by Richard & Mary Ford

ROUGHAM HALL NURSERIES
A14 Rougham, Bury St Edmunds IP30 9LZ

Tel: 0800 970 7516 **Fax:** 01359 271149
www.roughamhallnurseries.co.uk
Location Off west-bound carriageway of A14.
Opening hours 10 am - 4 pm; daily; all year,
except Christmas to New Year.

P

Rougham Hall Nurseries – always very
popular when they come to RHS flower
shows – are breeders, introducers and
growers of an extensive and interesting
range of perennials. Their selection of
asters is particularly good, as is their list of
delphiniums, of which they have a
National Collection. Their other National
Collection is of gooseberries: they have by
far the most extensive list anywhere in the

world. The whole history of this most
highly prized of dessert fruits is contained
within the hundreds of cultivars which
they list. The range is always increasing,
too: it is worthwhile enquiring if they do
not appear to have one that you are
looking for. They will be hosting two RHS
Special Events during 2006; details from
020 7821 3408.

Owned by K. Harbutt
NCCPG National Collections *Delphinium, Ribes
grossularia* (gooseberries)

SHRUBLAND PARK GARDENS
Coddenham, Ipswich IP6 9QQ

Tel: 01473 830221 **Fax:** 01473 832202
www.shrublandpark.co.uk
Location Between Claydon & Barham: come by
A14 or A140.
Opening hours 2 pm - 5 pm; Sundays & Bank
Holiday Mondays; 16 April to 31 August. Plus
Wednesdays in July & August.
Admission fee Adults £3; OAPs & Children £2.
(Subject to review.)

P WC

This grand Victorian garden was designed
by Charles Barry and has been famous ever
since for the spectacular Italianate staircase
which connects the terrace around the
house with the formal gardens below.
William Robinson later helped with the
planting, both around the formal garden
and in the park and woodland gardens
beyond. Much restoration and recovery has
been completed in recent years: Shrubland
is getting better and better.

spectacular garden architecture;
woodland garden; roses (mainly
modern); good herbaceous borders; box maze;
Swiss châlet.

Owned by Lord de Saumarez
Number of gardeners 5
Size 16ha (40 acres)
English Heritage Grade I

SOMERLEYTON HALL
Somerleyton, Lowestoft NR32 5QQ

Tel: 01502 730224 **Fax:** 01502 732143
www.somerleyton.co.uk
Location 4 miles north-west of Lowestoft on
B1074.
Opening hours In 2005: 10 am – 5 pm; Thursdays,
Sundays & Bank Holidays, plus Tuesdays &
Wednesdays in July & August; 2 April to 29
October.
Admission fee Adults £4.50; OAPs £3.50;
Children £2.50.

P WC & 🌿 🍂 ⬠

Somerleyton is a splendid place to visit:
there is much for the garden- and plant-
lover to see and enjoy. In front of the
house (palatial, Victorian) is an extremely
grand formal garden. William Andrews
Nesfield laid out the terraces and the yew
maze, which was planted in 1846: it is not
too difficult to get to the centre, which is
less than 400m from the entrance. The
gardens are full of topiary and good
statuary, including a great equatorial
sundial, encircled by signs of the Zodiac.
Near the house are quantities of roses,
herbaceous borders and seasonal bedding.
Further afield are large plantings of
rhododendrons and azaleas. Though none
is actually a record-breaker, Somerleyton
has some very fine specimen trees,
including a giant redwood (*Sequoiadendron
giganteum*), *Eucalyptus gunnii*, Monterey
pine (*Pinus radiata*), Atlas cedar (*Cedrus
atlantica*) and a particularly good
maidenhair tree (*Ginkgo biloba*). There has
been much replanting since the hurricane
of 1987 and the new plantings are already
making quite an impact. The walled garden
was once the kitchen garden but is now
planted with flowers: on the walls are many
different climbers including roses, clematis,
figs, climbing hydrangeas and such wall-
shrubs as *Hoheria sexstylosa*. The
glasshouses and peach-cases were designed
by Sir Joseph Paxton, architect of the
Crystal Palace, with his characteristic
ridge-and-furrow roofs. They are now
planted with tender ornamentals like
Meyer's lemon, abutilons, *Cassia* (*Senna*)
corymbosa and the sweetly-scented *Dregea
sinensis*. An old boiler house has a
collection of old garden equipment in it.
Other good features include an elegant,
long, metal pergola with lots of different
wisterias and a young avenue of lime trees
along the driveway, planted in 1981. The
whole estate is well kept and well run for
visitors' enjoyment.

🌿 roses (mainly modern); plants under
glass; maze; new bamboo bed; fine
statues; magnificent trees; pergola; formal
garden; walled garden; new pond (2004);
souvenir gift shop; tea-room for light lunches &
teas.

Owned by The Hon. Hugh Crossley
Number of gardeners 4½
Size 5ha (12½ acres)
English Heritage Grade II*

WHITE HALL PLANTS
Southolt Road, Worlingworth IP13 7HW

Tel: 01728 628490 **Fax:** 01728 628160
Location Follow brown tourist signs on A1120
from Earl Soham.
Opening hours 10 am – 5 pm; Thursday – Sunday;
Easter to October.
Admission fee Free.

P 🔄 WC & 🌿 🍂

There are stock beds and sale displays for
over 2,000 different plants in this excellent
nursery. There are good numbers of
heucheras, ligularias, dicentras, grasses,
salvias, penstemons, lilies, hellebores,
foxgloves, cardamines and epimediums –
and much else besides.

🌿 excellent plantsman's nursery.

Owned by Charles Walker
Number of gardeners 3
Size 1.2ha (3 acres)

WYKEN HALL
Stanton, Bury St Edmunds IP31 2DW

Tel: 01359 250287 **Fax:** 01359 253420
Location 9 miles north-east from Bury St Edmunds; follow brown tourist signs from A143 at Ixworth to Wyken Vineyards.
Opening hours 2 pm – 6 pm; Sunday – Friday; 1 April to 1 October. For NGS: 13 May.
Admission fee Adults £3; OAPs £2.50; Children free.

P ⟲ WC ♿ ❦ ● ⌂

The garden at Wyken is ingeniously designed: a series of old-style gardens to complement the Elizabethan house. These include a knot garden, a herb garden, a traditional English kitchen garden, wildflower meadows, a nuttery and a copper beech maze. All are in scale with the house and the farmland around. Stylish and well maintained, this is one of the best modern private gardens in the country. The restaurant features in the *Good Food Guide*. The 'Giant Stride' (a sort of revolving maypole) was added to commemorate the millennium.

woodland garden; roses (ancient & modern); plantsman's collection of plants; herbs; fruit; good shrubs; good herbaceous borders; award-winning seven-acre vineyard; country store shop; lunches & teas at excellent Vineyard Restaurant.

Owned by Sir Kenneth & Lady Carlisle
Number of gardeners 2
Size 1.6ha (4 acres)

SURREY

A Martian could be excused for thinking that Surrey was the centre of the horticultural universe. It is the county with everything that gardeners could ever want. Its six Grade I gardens include two very important landscapes – Claremont and Painshill – and two highly influential 20th-century gardens – Munstead Wood and the Savill Garden. Because of its closeness to London, it has become a very rich county during the last 100 years, which means that people have the time and money to garden on a large scale. The National Gardens Scheme does extremely well in Surrey, with a large number of medium-sized gardens opening for charity, as well as a handful of intensely cultivated smaller gardens. It is the county where the National Gardens Scheme has its headquarters. Surrey has many of the country's best-known nurseries – the light soils being poor for agriculture but excellent for growing plants: the floral mile along the A30 is a famous landmark, where some of the trees and shrubs in the old Waterer nurseries have grown to exceptional size. There are good trees, too – and many record-breakers – at Winkworth Arboretum, the Savill Garden and the RHS Garden Wisley. Surrey still has a large number of first-class nurseries. Those that we do not have space to list but which are well worth visiting include Secretts near Godalming and Lincluden at Bisley. The Surrey Gardens Trust and the Surrey Group of the NCCPG are both very active in the county: the NCCPG has its base at Wisley. There are some 33 National Collections in Surrey, including seven at Wisley and nine at the Savill Garden. And of course the Royal Horticultural Society's own flagship garden at Wisley dominates every aspect of gardens and gardening in the county: as many as 20 per cent of the Society's members live in Surrey.

CADENZA
Butterfly Walk, Warlingham CR6 9JA

Tel: 01883 623565
Location M25, Jct 6; A22 northbound for 4 miles; fourth exit at large roundabout; uphill & turn right.
Opening hours By appointment only, at most times.
Admission fee Free.

🅿 🚾 ♿ ✿

This is the private garden of keen plantsmen. Their special interest is small bulbs, and they have one of England's most interesting collections of hardy cyclamen and *Fritillaria* species. Frames and greenhouses extend the range of what is grown. An education and an inspiration.

cyclamen; fritillaries; bulbs.

Owned by Mr & Mrs Ronald Frank
Number of gardeners part-time help
Size 0.3ha (¾ acre)

CLANDON PARK
West Clandon, Guildford GU4 7RQ

Tel: 01483 222482 **Fax:** 01483 223479
www.nationaltrust.org.uk/clandonpark
Location Off A247 at West Clandon.
Opening hours 11 am – 5 pm; Tuesdays – Thursdays & Sundays; 26 March to 29 October.
Admission fee House & Garden: Adult £6.50; Children £3.20. No garden-only prices.

🅿 🚾 ♿ 🍴 ☕

Capability Brown's magnificent mature beeches are now underplanted with sombre Victorian shrubberies and slabs of comfrey, bergenias and *Geranium macrorrhizum* – the apotheosis of National Trust groundcover. There is a modern pastiche of a Dutch garden at the east end of the grounds but the daffodils in spring are breathtaking. A recent addition are two dicksonias, fresh from the New Zealand garden at Chelsea in 2004. Unfortunately, the National Trust no longer sells garden-only tickets, and £6.50 is expensive for what the garden offers.

parterres; grotto; Dutch garden; Maori meeting-house; Clandon Park Garden Centre is nearby; restaurant; shop.

Owned by The National Trust
Number of gardeners 1
Size 3.8ha (9½ acres)
English Heritage Grade II

CLAREMONT LANDSCAPE GARDEN
Portsmouth Road, Esher KT10 9JG

Tel: 01372 467806 **Fax:** 01372 476420
www.nationaltrust.org.uk/claremont
Location On southern edge of town (A307).
Opening hours 10 am – 6 pm (but dusk from November to March & 6 pm or sunset if earlier on Saturdays, Sundays & Bank Holiday Mondays from April to October); daily, all year, but closed on Mondays from November to March. Closed on 25 December and major events days in July.
Admission fee Adults £5; Children £2.50.
🅿 🚾 ♿ 🍴 ☕

This vast historic landscape – now much reduced – was worked over by Vanbrugh, Bridgeman, Kent and Capability Brown and has been energetically restored in recent years. The elegant green theatre is best seen flanked by spreading cedars from across the dark lake. Very popular locally, it is apt to get crowded at summer weekends.

laurel lawns; tallest service tree *Sorbus domestica* (23m) in the British Isles, and two further record trees; shop; tea-room.

Owned by The National Trust
Number of gardeners 3, plus volunteers
Size 19.6ha (49 acres)
English Heritage Grade I

HANNAH PESCHAR SCULPTURE GARDEN
Black and White Cottage, Standon Lane, Ockley RH5 5QR

Tel: 01306 627269 **Fax:** 01306 627662
www.hannahpescharsculpture.com
Location Turn off A29 down Cathill Lane, left at T-junction, over bridge & entrance is 400 yards on right.
Opening hours 11 am – 6 pm, Fridays & Saturdays; 2 pm – 5 pm, Sundays & Bank Holidays; May to October. And by appointment.
Admission fee Adults £9; Concessions £7; Children £6.
🅿 🚾 ♿

The lush water garden and woodlands surrounding a black-and-white cottage are the setting for this remarkable and ever-changing collection, mainly of contemporary British sculpture. The water-garden has been revamped by Anthony Paul with lots of architectural plants. There are pools and a stream, and surprisingly few flowers but lots of contrasts of light and shade. The background is more important for sculpture than any transient colour. An earlier owner was the distinguished horticulturist Dick Trotter, Mr Bowles's 'nephew Dick' and sometime Treasurer of the RHS.

sculptures; water; glass.

Owned by Hannah Peschar
Number of gardeners 2 part-time
Size 4ha (10 acres)

HATCHLANDS PARK
East Clandon, Guildford GU4 7RT

Tel: 01483 222482 **Fax:** 01483 223176
www.nationaltrust.org.uk/hatchlands
Location Off A246 Guildford to Leatherhead.
Opening hours House: 2 pm - 5.30 pm; Tuesday -
Thursday, Sundays & Bank Holiday Mondays; April to
October. Also Fridays in August. Park walks in
Repton Park: 11 am - 6 pm; daily; April to October.
Admission fee Park walks: Adults £3; Children £1.50.

Apart from the Jekyll garden (roses, lupins,
box and columbines) Hatchlands is an 18th-
century landscape with parkland. Four
marked ways include a magnificent bluebell
wood. The garden buildings are charming
and the National Trust has made some
progress with restoration and replanting.
woodland garden; National Trust shop;
restaurant.

Owned by The National Trust
Number of gardeners 2
Size 180ha (450 acres) of parkland

HERONS BONSAI LTD
Wire Mill Lane, Newchapel, Lingfield
RH7 6HJ

Tel: 01342 832657
www.herons.co.uk
Location Turn left off A22, ¼ mile south of junction
with B2028.
Opening hours 9.30 am - 5.30 pm; Monday -
Saturday. 10.30 am - 4.30 pm; Sundays. Closes at
dusk in winter months.
Admission fee £1 donation to charity. Nursery free.

This bonsai nursery has a string of gold
medals behind it from Chelsea Flower Shows.
As well as trees for indoors and outdoors,
there are ornaments, pots, tools and
accessories (retail and wholesale). The Chans
are recognised experts and donated the
bonsai collection and Japanese garden at
RHS Garden Wisley. They run bonsai classes
and offer Japanese garden design. The whole
nursery is landscaped in the Japanese style,
with several examples of different types of
Japanese gardens.
Owned by Peter & Dawn Chan
Number of gardeners 3
Size 3ha (7½ acres)

HYDON NURSERIES
Clock Barn Lane, Hydon Heath, Godalming
GU8 4AZ

Tel: 01483 860252 **Fax:** 01483 419937
Location 2 miles east of A3, Milford exit. Near
Cheshire Home.
Opening hours 8.30 am - 5 pm (4 pm in winter);
Monday - Friday. Plus Saturdays 9.30 am -
12.45 pm (5 pm from 1 March to 15 June and from
late September to October). Sundays by
appointment. Closed for lunch 12.45 pm - 2 pm.
Conducted tours for small groups by prior
appointment.
Admission fee Free. Parties by arrangement.

These rhododendron and azalea specialists
have an extensive range of all classes,
including some tender species and their own
hybrids (*Rhododendron yakushimanum* and
others). They have a comprehensive stock of
evergreen azaleas, including 36 of the Wilson
Kurume azaleas. They also sell companion
trees and shrubs, especially camellias
(another speciality – 100+ cultivars). The
nursery extends over 25 acres: among the
many fine trees are five large trees of the dark
pink form of *Magnolia campbellii* and fine
mature specimens of *Nothofagus dombeyi* and
N. antarctica, as well as the two record-
breakers. Visitors are particularly welcome to
see the magnolias in early spring; the gardens
are at their best between mid-March and
June and there is an annual sale of plants
during March.
rhododendrons & azaleas; tallest
Eucalyptus pauciflora subsp. *niphophila*
and *Sorbus* 'Joseph Rock' in the British Isles.

Number of gardeners 5
Size 10ha (25 acres)

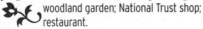

LOSELEY PARK
Guildford GU3 1HS

Tel: 01483 304440 **Fax:** 01483 302036
www.loseley-park.com
Location Off B3000 at Compton, south of
Guildford.
Opening hours 11 am – 5 pm; Tuesday – Sunday; 1
May to 30 September. Plus Bank Holiday Mondays
in May & August.
Admission fee Garden & grounds only: Adults £4;
Children £2; Concessions £3.50. RHS members free
in May & September.
P WC ♿ ☀ ✿ ✕ ☕

The walled garden attached to this fine
Elizabethan house has recently been re-made
and replanted in the Jekyll style, with 1,000
old-fashioned roses framed by long, low, box
hedges. Other good features include a herb
garden, a fruit and flower garden, a fountain
garden (planted in cream, white and silver),
a cut-flower garden and an organic vegetable
garden. A new wildflower meadow will open
this year (2006). There will be seven RHS
Special Events at Loseley Park in 2006;
details from 020 7821 3408.

roses (mainly old-fashioned); herbs; fruit;
lakeside walk; gift shop; courtyard tea-
room; restaurant.

Owned by Michael More-Molyneux
Number of gardeners 3
Size 1ha (2½ acres)

MILLAIS NURSERIES
Crosswater Farm, Crosswater Lane, Churt,
Farnham GU10 2JN

Tel: 01252 792698 **Fax:** 01252 792526
www.rhododendrons.co.uk
Location Off Jumps Road, ½ mile north of Churt
village.
Opening hours Nursery: 10 am – 1 pm & 2 pm –
5 pm; Monday – Friday. Also Saturdays in spring &
autumn. And daily in May. Garden: mid-April to
early June.
Admission fee Garden: £2.50; Nursery: free.
P WC ☀ ☕

This important and dynamic rhododendron
and azalea nursery has an extensive range of
species and hybrids, including some new
Himalayan species, late-flowering cultivars
chosen to avoid the frost, large-leaved
species for sheltered gardens, scented
deciduous azaleas, *R. yakushimanum* hybrids
for the smaller garden, dwarf cultivars for the
rock garden and Maddenia series
rhododendrons for the conservatory. The
six-acre garden (ponds, stream and
companion plantings) has an extensive
collection of new magnolias and acers.
There is also a trials garden where hundreds
of new cultivars from around the world are
labelled and tested.

rhododendrons; sorbus; tea & coffee.

Owned by The Millais family
Size 2.4ha (6 acres)

MUNSTEAD WOOD
Heath Lane, Busbridge, Godalming
GU7 1UN

Tel: 01483 417867 **Fax:** 01483 425041
Location 1 mile south of Godalming on B2130: turn
along Heath Lane. Parking in field 300 yards along
on left.
Opening hours 2 pm – 6 pm; 23 April, 28 May & 25
June.
Admission fee Adults £3; OAPs £1.50; Children free.
◁ WC ♿ ☀ ☕

Munstead Wood is important for being
Gertrude Jekyll's own garden. Here she
worked out the principles she expounded in
her best-known books *Wood and Garden*
(1899) and *Colour in the Flower Garden*
(1908). Her garden has now been split into
several smaller holdings each in separate
ownership, but the main parts are still
attached to the house which Lutyens
designed in 1896. The wood garden is fairly
intact: the views up and down its main path
to and from the lawn in front of the house
seem just as they were a hundred years ago:
birches underplanted mainly with

rhododendrons and azaleas. Closer to the house is a block of borders full of good plantings – herbaceous plants, in particular. The nut walk and its nearby borders have recently been replanted: the Clarks have spent many years restoring the garden – and the results are admirable.

🌿 woodland garden; roses (mainly old-fashioned); sunken rock garden; good herbaceous borders; rhododendrons & azaleas; spring garden; cream teas.

Owned by Sir Robert & Lady Clark
Number of gardeners 2
Size 4ha (10 acres)
English Heritage Grade I

PAINSHILL PARK
Portsmouth Road, Cobham KT11 1JE

Tel: 01932 868113 **Fax:** 01932 868001
www.painshill.co.uk
Location Signed from M25, Jct 10 & A3.
Opening hours 10.30 am - 6 pm (last admissions 4.30 pm); daily; March to October. 11 am - 4 pm (last admissions 3 pm); daily; November to February. Closed 25 & 26 December.
Admission fee Adults £6; Concessions £5.25; Children (under 16) £3.50.

🅿 🚾 ♿ 🌺 🛏

Charles Hamilton was the plantsman, painter and designer who created Painshill between 1738 and 1773, when he finally went bankrupt. His lasting achievement was to transform a barren heathland into ornamental pleasure grounds and parkland of dramatic beauty. A 14-acre lake is at the centre of the design: it offers a focus for the garden's most famous features, the white Gothic temple and the grotto, which is approached across a 'Chinese' bridge. Hamilton sought to provoke the greatest variety of moods: other features included a ruined abbey, a Turkish tent and the newly restored hermitage. Hamilton was a pioneer of the naturalistic landscape style, and very influential, but never a rich man: he leased Painshill from the Crown and had little to

spend, which makes his achievement all the more remarkable. He was also a great plantsman, importing many new species from North America for his shrubberies. After 1948 the garden fell into dereliction. Over the past 20 years it has been meticulously restored (for which it won a Europa Nostra award) and the Painshill Park Trust has made enormous progress in raising the substantial funds needed. The Heritage Lottery Fund is a major supporter and grant-aided the new Visitor and Education Centre.

🌿 'American' garden; grotto; Turkish tent; tallest *Juniperus virginiana* (26m) in the British Isles; gift shop; visitor centre; licensed tea-room.

Owned by Painshill Park Trust
Number of gardeners 4
Size 63ha (158 acres)
English Heritage Grade I

POLESDEN LACEY
Great Bookham, Dorking RH5 6BD

Tel: 01372 452048 **Fax:** 01372 452023
www.nationaltrust.org.uk/polesdenlacey
Location Off A246 between Leatherhead & Guildford.
Opening hours 11 am - 5 pm (4 pm from November to February); daily; all year.
Admission fee Adults £6; Children £3; Family £15.

🅿 🚾 ♿ 🌿 🌺 🛏

Polesden Lacey is best for the long terraced walk, laid out by Sheridan, and the return through an Edwardian-style rose garden whose pergolas drip with rambling roses. The park is good and there are fine views and walks around the estate.

🌿 snowdrops; roses of every kind; good herbaceous borders; lavender garden; large National Trust shop; self-service tea-room.

Owned by The National Trust
Number of gardeners 6, plus 1 trainee
Size 12ha (30 acres), plus landscaped park
English Heritage Grade II*

RAMSTER
Chiddingfold GU8 4SN

Tel: 01428 654167 **Fax:** 01428 658345
www.ramstergardens.co.uk
Location 1½ miles south of Chiddingfold on A283.
Opening hours 10 am – 5 pm; daily; 8 April to 25
June. 10 am – 4 pm; 28 & 29 October and 4 & 5
November for autumn colour. Parties by
appointment at other times.
Admission fee Adults £4; Children free.

P ◁ WC & ☀ ↻

Ramster was first laid out in 1890, with
help from a local nursery, Gauntletts of
Chiddingfold, who were known for their
interest in flowering shrubs and especially
for Japanese plants and planting. From this
original influence date the ornamental
stone lanterns, the large plantings of
bamboos, and the avenue of *Acer palmatum*
var. *dissectum* seedlings, now over 100 years
old. In 1922 the property was bought by
Miranda Gunn's grandparents Sir Henry
and Lady Norman. Lady Norman was a
keen gardener, the sister of the 2nd Lord
Aberconway, who was President of the
RHS. She had been brought up at
Bodnant, where she imbibed the family's
great love of rhododendrons: many of the
plants at Ramster came from Bodnant, and
some of the rhododendrons and azaleas are
her own hybrids. Ramster is an important
garden for rhododendrons and, in the part
known as Ant Wood, the Gunns have
been building up a comprehensive
collection of the old Hardy Hybrids – over
200 plants. But the garden is full of other
projects and developments: the bog garden
has come together very quickly since it was
planted in 1998, and there is a new
Millennium Garden. The garden is
maintained in such a way as to allow
meadow grasses, wildflowers and orchids to
flourish and flower later in the year, but
Ramster is essentially a garden for spring
and early summer.

🌿 mature woodland garden with
rhododendrons, magnolias, camellias,
azaleas; bluebells; largest *Euonymus europaeus*

(6m) in the British Isles; home-made teas in May
& at weekends.

Owned by Mr & Mrs Paul Gunn
Number of gardeners 1
Size 10ha (25 acres)

TITSEY PLACE
Oxted RH8 0SD

Tel: 01273 407056 **Fax:** 01273 478995
www.titsey.com
Location Off B269 north of Limpsfield.
Opening hours 1 pm – 5 pm; Wednesdays,
Sundays & Bank Holiday Mondays; 10 May to 27
September. Plus 17 April & 1 May.
Admission fee Adults £2.50; Children £1.

P WC

The historic garden at Titsey has been well
restored with advice from Elizabeth Banks
since it first opened to the public in 1993.
The layout is gardenesque and most of the
plantings date from the middle of the 19th
century. The large triple-trunked horse-
chestnut (*Aesculus hippocastanum*) on the
upper terrace dates from that time. The
formal gardens are planted with roses
(replanted in 2002) and herbaceous plants,
while the old walled kitchen garden has
been planted as an example of how fruit,
vegetables and flowers were grown in
Victorian times.

🌿 fine parkland.

Owned by The Trustees of the Titsey Foundation
Number of gardeners 5
Size 5ha (12½ acres)

VALE END
Albury, Guildford GU5 9BE

Tel & Fax: 01483 202296
www.ngs.org.uk
Location 500 yards west of Albury on A248.
Opening hours 10 am – 5 pm; 11 & 12 June. 6 pm –
8.30 pm; 8 June (music by members of Guildford

Philharmonic Orchestra) & 6 July. Groups by arrangement.
Admission fee Adults £2.50; Children free; 11 & 12 June. Adults £4; Children free; 8 June & 6 July.

⊞ ⟿ 🚻 ❋ ⌶

Vale End is a traditional plantsman's garden, one of the best on Bagshot sand, where a love of plants has not been allowed to obscure either the design or the landscape beyond. It is walled around, and made on many levels, on a site that faces south-west: the owners have taken the opportunity to grow sun-loving and Mediterranean plants. Daphne Foulsham is a Vice-President (and a very successful ex-Chairman) of the National Gardens Scheme.

plantsman's collection of plants; good herbaceous borders; roses (mainly old-fashioned); vegetables; fruit; herbs; refreshments.

Owned by Mr & Mrs John Foulsham
Size 0.4ha (1 acre)

VALLEY GARDENS
Wick Road, Englefield Green, Windsor TW20 0UU

Tel: 01753 847518 **Fax:** 01753 847536
www.theroyallandscape.co.uk
Location At Englefield Green, 5 miles from Windsor, off A30: follow signs for Savill Garden.
Opening hours 8 am - 7 pm (3.30 pm in winter); daily; all year.
Admission fee Cars £4 (£5.50 in April & May); occupants free.

⊞ ⟿ 🚻 ⌶

This is a woodland garden on a royal scale. The Valley Gardens have over 200 acres of plantings across a site of great natural beauty which falls in vast sweeps to the open expanse of Virginia Water. As in the Savill Garden, huge trees of oak, beech, sweet chestnut and Scots pine provide a magnificent framework and have been used with great sensitivity. The whole composition conveys the feeling of a flowering forest from some far-off corner of Asia. From March and April until the end of June, a succession of camellias, rhododendrons and azaleas provide an unbelievable kaleidoscope of colour, most notably in the Punch Bowl where a natural combe is filled with terrace upon terrace of brightly coloured Japanese Kurume azaleas. Giant magnolias garland themselves overhead with thousands of chalice-shaped blooms. A huge array of supporting trees, shrubs and perennials jostles for attention. Enormous groups of hydrangeas provide late-summer colour, from the white foaming flowers of *H. paniculata* to the blues and pale pinks of the lacecaps and mopheads. In autumn the hillsides light up in a spectacle unrivalled this side of the Appalachian Mountains. In the nearby heather garden an old gravel pit has been transformed into a horticultural wonder to rival the Punch Bowl: ostensibly dominated by heathers and dwarf conifers (there is a National Collection here), the garden contains unrivalled collections of exotic and native birches, whitebeams and rowans, wild roses, cotoneasters and cistus. Recent plantings have made extensive use of ornamental grasses to provide relief amongst the stolid conifers. On the next hillside is to be found the National Collection of *Rhododendron* species, brought here in the 1950s from the famous garden of Tower Court near Ascot. A sweeping valley also contains a pinetum of some note, carpeted by countless thousands of dwarf narcissi in March and April. All in all, a garden of the blue-stocking variety.

outstanding collection of trees; hydrangeas; heathers; primulas; magnolias; rhododendrons & azaleas; refreshments at the Savill Garden.

Owned by Crown Estate
Number of gardeners 16
Size 87ha (220 acres)
NCCPG National Collections *Ilex, Magnolia, Mahonia, Pernettya, Rhododendron* (species & Glenn Dale azaleas); ferns; dwarf & slow-growing conifers

RHS GARDEN WISLEY
Woking GU23 6QB

Tel: 01483 224234 **Fax:** 01483 211750
www.rhs.org.uk/gardens/wisley
Location M25, Jct 10. Follow brown tourist signs.
Opening hours 10 am (but 9 am at weekends) - 6 pm; daily; all year, except Christmas Day. Closes at 4.30 pm from November to February. Last admissions one hour before closing.
Admission fee Adults £7.50; Children £2. Discounts for groups - telephone 01483 212307 or 212308. RHS members (plus one guest) free.

Wisley is the most important horticultural demonstration garden in Europe – perhaps in the world. It has many incidents of great intrinsic value – the vast Pulhamite rock garden which fills an entire hillside, for example – but its true worth lies in its comprehensiveness: everything that a gardener could possibly want to see and learn from is here within its 240 acres. The only problem is its very size: Wisley is not a garden you could ever hope to get round properly in just a day, let alone a few hours. It is somewhere to explore over many visits at different times of the year, until the layout and the principal features become familiar and you learn where you should go to see what is good and instructive at the time of your visit.

In 2004, the Royal Horticultural Society celebrated the bicentenary of its foundation. 2003 marked the centenary of the Royal Horticultural Society at Wisley. It was in 1903 that Sir Thomas Hanbury bought the Wisley estate and gave it to the Society for 'the encouragement and improvement of the science and practice of horticulture in all its branches.' When the Society moved its experimental garden from Chiswick, Wisley was in a remote part of Surrey with no public transport to serve it. The move would not have been possible without the invention of the motor car: 6,000 Fellows (as members were then called) visited it during its first 12 months. Now more than 700,000 visitors come to the garden every year. Wisley was unashamedly a trials garden where the Society practised the perfect cultivation of every type of plant that could be grown in the British Isles from alpines to hothouse orchids, whether in the open ground or in artificial conditions. This was backed up – then, as now – by an important system of trials which grew, tested, examined and made awards to flowers, fruit and vegetables. Those trials remain one of the garden's most important activities. Wisley was, above all, conceived as a scientific garden: to this day, the main building which dominates the formal garden near the entrance is known as the Laboratory and contains scientific and administrative offices.

Sir Simon Hornby, President of the RHS until 2001, describes Wisley as 'a garden to delight, instruct and inspire.' His assertion is true at every time of the year. For many visitors the pulling power of Wisley is greatest in the short, dark days of winter. That is the time when such plants as cyclamen and narcissi fill the alpine pan house: there is always colour and interest here because suitable pots are brought from the growing-frames and plunged into its sandy benches specifically to maintain the display through every week of the year. In the landscaped alpine house, too, there is much of interest even in deep midwinter. The main glasshouses certainly come into their own in winter. The display range has three sections – cool, warm and hot. Each is landscaped and supports a large number of plants growing in the soil that are suitable for greenhouses and conservatories at home. Sometimes the seasonal display is augmented by pots brought from the growing areas behind and placed on the benches: 'Charm' and 'Cascade' chrysanthemums in November, for example. There are many other houses open to visitors: the orchid collections and the cacti house are among the most popular.

Wisley really begins to come into its own in spring. The alpine meadow is the best of its kind anywhere in Britain: from about the middle of March onwards, for at least four weeks, it is completely carpeted with hoop-petticoat narcissi (forms of *N. bulbocodium*). In September, the same meadows are thick with autumn-flowering crocuses. Beyond them is the Pulhamite rock garden, constructed in 1911-1912, which is probably the finest in Britain. It does not provide the variety of habitats which more modern rock gardens offer, but it is a majestic and beautiful construction. It covers the whole hillside from the 'monocot border' (full of such plants as agapanthus, daylilies, amaryllis, nerines and kniphofias – best in late summer) at the top to the stream at the bottom of the valley, whose margins are thick with such plants as *Lobelia cardinalis* and

lysichitons. Beyond is an area of light woodland where magnolias and tall rhododendrons give shelter to such woodlanders as meconopsis, hellebores and snowdrops and huge patches of candelabra primulas.

By late spring, one of the best areas is Battleston Hill, the highest point in the gardens, where winding paths take you through a beautifully laid out woodland garden underplanted with rhododendrons, azaleas, magnolias and camellias. Crocuses in late winter, lilies in high summer and colchicums in autumn extend the season so that this is always an area of colour and interest. Here, and throughout the garden, are many unusual rare and interesting plants which add so much to the horticultural quality of Wisley. Also on Battleston Hill is a 'Mediterranean' garden where an extensive collection of plants with a reputation for tenderness shows what can be grown successfully on light, well-drained soil when trees provide shelter and frost rolls away downhill.

Wisley has a fine collection of roses, from rare species to the massed ranks of modern roses which fill the beds around the Bowes-Lyon Pavilion and in behind the mixed borders. Wisley is, in short, one of the best places in Britain to see roses of every sort, including some which are rare elsewhere in English gardens open to the public. The mixed borders also come into their own from midsummer onwards: there are two of them, and they face each other on either side of the broad, grass ride which leads up to Battleston Hill. These borders are 130m long, backed by beech hedges and have a light framework of shrubs as a background for deep plantings of all the traditional perennials of the English herbaceous border. In contrast to the mixed borders are the new Piet Oudolf borders. Planted in 2001, the borders were designed by the Dutch plantsman Piet Oudolf, who has used the modern style of perennial planting. The borders, 147m long and 11m wide, are planted with over 16,000 perennials and grasses. The RHS says that the plants are chosen for their movement and colour and planted in diagonal 'rivers' across the borders, which gives a feeling of walking in a meadow.

Wisley has many other areas dedicated to the cultivation and display of particular plants. The pinetum is one example – an under-visited area of stately conifers, some of them record-breakers and all of them interesting at every season. The heather garden in Howard's Field is another dedicated garden, a National Collection with probably the best collection of heathers in England. The fruit fields, too, are a part of the garden that far too few venture into: over 1,400 cultivars of top, bush and soft fruit are grown here, including more than 670 apple cultivars. The Society has been associated with the cultivation of fruit ever since its foundation in 1804, and displays of Wisley fruit have long been a feature of RHS London shows.

Wisley has its formal gardens, too. These centre upon the long rectangular canal in front of the Laboratory and the walled gardens beyond. Designed by Geoffrey Jellicoe and Lanning Roper, the canal is a formal setting for water lilies while the walled enclosures have spectacular summer and winter bedding displays. Rare and tender climbers cover their walls. Formal in a different sense are the model gardens which seem to grow and develop every year. The first were model fruit gardens, which showed people how to grow a great variety of fruit (and grow it well) in a small area. Nearby are model vegetable gardens, now supplemented by many ornamental model gardens, which serve the same function – to show visitors what may be achieved in their own gardens. Each is full of design ideas on a realisable scale, reflecting changing styles and new techniques. Up by the Orchard Café, eight small gardens are under construction, aimed at young professionals who may be moving into new starter homes but whose interest in gardening is tempered by limited spare time at weekends. These gardens – the first two opened in 2005 – offer a dramatic choice of design, materials, features and planting styles. New for the millennium was the renovation of the Walled Garden (west) to create a plantsman's corner filled with a mixture of hardy and tender plants.

For many people, one of the most fascinating areas is the main Trials Field – over the brow of Battleston Hill and down towards the furthest boundary with the A3. This is where the Royal Horticultural Society runs most of its trials (more than 50 every year, some short- and some long-term) on a very wide selection of annuals, perennials, shrubs, bulbs, fruit and vegetables. The permanent trials are conducted (among others) with border carnations, chrysanthemums, daffodils, dahlias, daylilies, delphiniums, garden pinks, irises and sweet peas. These trials continue from year to year with periodic replanting, at which time additions and removals are made. They are of exceptional interest to visitors, and often of remarkable beauty, too. There can be few horticultural experiences more exciting than to walk through the massed ranks of thickly planted delphiniums or sweet peas that tower over you in July or August.

Wisley is always changing. The new Family Garden opened in 2005 and shows how a garden can adapt to the expectations of family members with different needs and ages. It illustrates, for example, how a play area for children may be changed into an open-air room as children move towards adolescence. The biggest project at the moment is the Bicentenary Glasshouse, costing £7.7m and the subject of an ongoing appeal. It incorporates a learning-centre where a classroom, 'Growing Lab' and teaching garden will give hands-on experience of growing plants to visitors from primary school-age upwards. The Bicentenary Glasshouse is near the Piet Oudolf borders and, at 3,000 sq. metres, is more than twice the size of the current display glasshouses. The 12m-high glasshouse will display plants from all five continents and visitors will be able to

see them from a viewing platform. It incorporates several water features (waterfalls, rock cliffs, scree and still ponds) and is divided into three main planting zones – desert, tropical and temperate climates. It is scheduled to open in spring 2007.

woodland garden; snowdrops; roses (ancient & modern); rock garden; plantsman's collection of plants; plants under glass; fruit; mature conifers; good herbaceous borders; fine collection of trees; heather garden; herb garden; horticultural trials; vegetable gardens; tallest *Ostrya virginiana* (15.5m) in the British Isles, and 25 further record trees; marvellous book and gift shop; plant centre; restaurant & café.

Owned by The Royal Horticultural Society
Number of gardeners 79
Size 96ha (240 acres)
NCCPG National Collections *Calluna vulgaris*; *Crocus*; *Daboecia*; *Epimedium*; *Erica*; *Galanthus*; *Rheum* (culinary)
English Heritage Grade II*

VANN
Hambledon, Godalming GU8 4EF

Tel & Fax: 01428 683413
www.caroe.com
Location 2 miles from Chiddingfold. Signs from
A283 at Hambledon on NGS days.
Opening hours 10 am – 6 pm; daily; 26 March to 2
April, 16 to 21 April, 7 to 14 May. And by
appointment. Opens at 2 pm on 16 & 17 April.
Admission fee Adults £4; Children free. Pre-
booked groups welcome.

P WC ⬥ ❀ ☕

This high-profile Jekyll garden has been
well restored and meticulously maintained
by the present Caroes, the third generation
to live here. Start with the old cottage
garden at the front of the house and move
round the house to the Arts & Crafts
pergola straight to the lake. This is the
heart of the garden, from which several
distinct gardens lead from one to the next
and melt into the Surrey woods: among
them, a yew walk (1909), island beds,
mixed borders, the Jekyll water garden
(1911) and a woodland garden under vast
oaks leading to a hazel coppice. The
plantings are dense and thoughtful.

🌿 woodland garden; good herbaceous
borders; bluebells; fritillaries; wood
anemones; teas on 17 April.

Owned by Mrs Martin Caroe
Number of gardeners ½
Size 2ha (5 acres)
English Heritage Grade II

THE VERNON GERANIUM NURSERY
Cuddington Way, Cheam, Sutton
SM2 7JB

Tel: 020 8393 7616 **Fax:** 020 8786 7437
www.geraniumsuk.com
Location South-west of Cheam.
Opening hours 9.30 am – 5.30 pm; Monday –
Saturday. 10 am – 4 pm; Sundays. March to June.

P WC ⬥ ❀

As it names indicates, this is a specialist
pelargonium nursery. The number of
pelargonium cultivars here speaks for itself
– over 1,100 doubles and semi-doubles,
Deacons, stellars, rosebuds, finger-
flowered, fancy-leaved, speckled, uniques,
dwarfs, miniatures, angels and regals – the
list seems endless. Guided tours are given
daily at 11 am and 2.30 pm between 17
and 25 June.

🌿 pelargoniums.

WINKWORTH ARBORETUM
Hascombe Road, Godalming GU8 4AD

Tel: 01483 208477 **Fax:** 01483 208252
www.nationaltrust.org.uk/winkwortharboretum
Location 2 miles south-east of Godalming, off
B2130.
Opening hours Dawn – dusk; all year. Groups
must pre-book in writing.
Admission fee Adults £4.50; Children £2.

P 🍴 WC ⬥ ❀ ☕

Winkworth is a true arboretum in the sense
that it has a large collection of full-sized
trees – as many taxa as possible – planted
liberally over a large area. Many of the
plantings are now in their prime. The red
oaks (*Quercus coccinea*), tupelos *Nyssa
sylvatica* and sweet gums *Liquidambar
styraciflua* are quite spectacular in autumn.

🌿 woodland garden; fine collection of
trees; bluebells; wood anemones;
autumn colour; tallest *Acer davidii* (19m) in the
British Isles, and five further record trees; shop;
tea-room.

Owned by The National Trust
Number of gardeners 3
Size 49ha (123 acres)
NCCPG National Collections *Sorbus* (Aria &
Micromeles groups)

SAVILL GARDEN
Wick Lane, Englefield Green, Windsor TW20 0UU

Tel: 01753 847518 **Fax:** 01753 847536
www.savillgarden.co.uk
Location Off Wick Lane at Englefield Green, 3 miles west of Egham off A30 & 5 miles from Windsor.
Opening hours 10 am – 6 pm (4 pm from November to February); daily, except 25 & 26 December.
Admission fee Adults £5.50; OAPs £4.95; Children £2.75 from March to October. Less in other months.

This is quite simply the finest woodland garden in England, developed since 1932 on an undulating site framed by magnificent deciduous trees. There are, in fact, several gardens here, some formal and some informal, but all are seamlessly linked together. The woodlands contain unrivalled spring plantings with masses of camellias, rhododendrons, azaleas, maples and flowering dogwoods underplanted with subtle drifts of bulbs, ferns and herbaceous plants. Recent refurbishment of the bog garden has allowed the development of stunning associations of meconopsis, primulas, astilbes, hostas and wild narcissi. The primulas have just been replanted, and come in monospecific masses, from the earliest *P. rosea* and *P. denticulata* through to *P. florindae* in July and August. In high summer, the rose garden and tremendous set-piece double herbaceous borders are worth a long trip to see. The nearby gravel garden is one of England's oldest and largest: parts of it have recently been replanted with a fine display of drought-tolerant plants – many of them rare – and plants which benefit from the mulching effect of the gravel. Extensive and intelligent use is made of a wide range of summer perennials in the borders and in containers. The new Golden Jubilee Garden has a formal structure, informal planting, and exquisite pastel shades. By late summer the woods are filled with hydrangeas, whose cool blues and whites are stunningly effective. Then the deciduous broad-leaved trees begin their autumn spectacle. From November to March the newly created winter beds display flowers, stems and berries in effective colour groupings. But there are many reasons to visit the Savill Garden at other times of the year – the drifts of *Narcissus bulbocodium* (second only in their splendour to the alpine meadow at Wisley) in March, for example, and the floods of lysichitons in April. The collections of maples, camellias, rhododendrons and azaleas are also exemplary. The raised beds, the cool greenhouse and the monocot border are each full of interest in due season. The guidebook, the plant centre and the website are all alike excellent. A spectacular new visitor centre is due to open in April 2006.

roses (mainly modern); camellias; fine collection of trees; mahonias; magnificent late-summer borders; tallest silver birch *Betula pendula* (30m) in the British Isles (& 13 other record trees); gift and plant shop; licensed restaurant.

Owned by Crown Estate
Number of gardeners 12
Size 14ha (35 acres)
NCCPG National Collections *Ilex, Magnolia, Mahonia, Pernettya, Rhododendron* (species & Glenn Dale azaleas); ferns; dwarf & slow-growing conifers
English Heritage Grade I

SUSSEX, EAST

The two historic gardens in East Sussex that English Heritage has rated Grade I could not be more different – Great Dixter and Sheffield Park. Yet they have one thing in common which is typical of East Sussex gardens generally – they are gardens whose historic features have been overlaid with plants. Few of the other historic gardens in the county are open to the public, but plant-lovers are almost spoiled for choice. Every corner of East Sussex seems to brim with good modern gardens – those like Pashley Manor and Merriments have been widely recognised for their beauty and invention – and good collections of trees, including those at Sheffield Park and Stanmer Park, near Brighton. The National Gardens Scheme does well in East Sussex, especially in the area around Crowborough where there are many medium-sized gardens to see. Nurseries, too, are good and fairly plentiful: some of the best are attached to gardens, like Great Dixter, or have a fine display garden attached to them, like Merriments. There are comparatively few National Collections: one of the most interesting is the collection of lilacs (*Syringa* cvs.) kept by the City of Brighton & Hove Parks Department.

BATEMAN'S
Burwash, Etchingham TN19 7DS

Tel: 01435 882302 **Fax:** 01435 882811
www.nationaltrust.org.uk/batemans
Location Signed at west end of village.
Opening hours 11 am – 5 pm; Saturday – Wednesday; 18 March to 29 October.
Admission fee Adults £6.20; Children £3.10.

🅿 🚻 ♿ ♣ ⏟

These ten acres on the banks of the River Dudwell were Rudyard Kipling's home from 1902 until his death in 1936. The garden is fun for children, because there is a working flour mill, but not spectacular for the knowledgeable gardener, except for the *Campsis grandiflora* on the house and the herbaceous borders designed by Graham Stuart Thomas.

🌱 roses (mainly old-fashioned); herbs; good herbaceous borders; Kipling pear arch; National Trust shop; tea-room.

Owned by The National Trust
Number of gardeners 2
Size 4ha (10 acres)
English Heritage Grade II

BATES GREEN FARM
Tye Hill Road, Arlington, Polegate BN26 6SH

Tel: 01323 485152 **Fax:** 01323 485151
Location 3 miles south-west of Hailsham.
Opening hours For NGS: 11 am – 5 pm; 9 April, 18 June & 17 September. And by appointment.
Admission fee Adults £3; Children free.

🅿 🚻 ♿ 🌼 ⏟

Made by the present owners since the mid-1970s, the garden at Bates Green Farm has several different areas. These include: a shady garden with narcissus, geraniums and cyclamen; a vegetable garden with raised beds; a monocot border; mixed borders planted for year-round colour associations.

🌱 woodland garden; good herbaceous borders; colour borders; bluebells; rockery; pond; light lunches & teas on NGS days.

Owned by Mr & Mrs J.R. McCutchan
Number of gardeners 1 part-time
Size 0.8ha (2 acres)

BRICKWALL HOUSE & GARDENS
Frewen College, Northiam TN31 6NL

Tel: 01797 253388 **Fax:** 01797 252567
Location Off B2088.
Opening hours By appointment for groups and on some afternoons in school holidays. For NGS: 2 pm - 5 pm on 20 August.
Admission fee £5.

This is an important historic garden, with 17th-century features which were reworked in the 19th century, a chess garden where green and yellow yew shapes are grown in squares of black or white chips, and attractive mixed plantings of perennials and annuals. The bluebells in the arboretum are magnificent.

topiary; herbs; good herbaceous borders; fine collection of trees; bluebells; extensively redesigned since 1980; teas by arrangement.

Owned by Frewen Educational Trust
English Heritage Grade II*

CLINTON LODGE
Fletching, Uckfield TN22 3ST

Tel: 01825 722952 **Fax:** 01825 723967
Location In main village street.
Opening hours For NGS: 2 pm - 5.30 pm; 7, 9, 16 & 18 June, 14 July & 4 August. And by appointment on weekdays.
Admission fee NGS days: Adults £4; Children £2.

Clinton Lodge is a rising star among new gardens, designed round a handsome 17th-century house. There are formal gardens of different periods, starting with a 'medieval' *potager* and an Elizabethan-style herb garden with camomile paths and turf seats. The most successful parts are the pre-Raphaelite walk of lilies and pale roses, the Victorian-style herbaceous borders in soft pastel shades and a very cheerful garden of old roses. A canal garden and an *allée* of fastigiate

hornbeams were added in 2001, and a knot garden and 'shade glade' in 2003.

 roses (mainly old-fashioned); herbs; good herbaceous borders; yew hedges; lime walks; *potager*; knot gardens; teas.

Owned by Sir Hugh & Lady Collum
Number of gardeners 2
Size 2.4ha (6 acres)

MARCHANTS HARDY PLANTS
2 Marchants Cottages, Ripe Road, Laughton BN8 6AJ

Tel & Fax: 01323 811737
Location ½ mile east of Laughton; take right turn signed to Ripe.
Opening hours Mid-March to end of October.
Admission fee Adults £2.

This acclaimed young garden is especially good from June onwards, and peaks early in autumn. It is attached to a nursery with an excellent selection of herbaceous plants and grasses. Their many introductions include *Sedum* 'Purple Emperor'.

herbaceous plants; grasses; good nursery.

Owned by Graham Gough & Lucy Goffin
Number of gardeners 1
Size 0.4ha (1 acre)

MERRIMENTS GARDENS
Hawkhurst Road, Hurst Green TN19 7RA

Tel: 01580 860666 **Fax:** 01580 860324
www.merriments.co.uk
Location On A229.
Opening hours 10 am (10.30 am on Sundays) - 5.30 pm; daily; 16 April to mid-October.
Admission fee Adults £4; Children £2.

The gardens at this nursery are young – started in 1991 on a bare clay field – but the tail is already wagging the dog. Four

GREAT DIXTER
Dixter Road, Northiam TN31 6PH

Tel: 01797 252878 **Fax:** 01797 252879
www.greatdixter.co.uk
Location Off A28 at Northiam Post Office.
Opening hours 2 pm - 5 pm; Tuesday - Sunday
& Bank Holiday Mondays; 1 April to 29 October.
Open at 11 am on the Sundays & Mondays of
Bank Holiday weekends.
Admission fee Adults £6; Children £2.

Christopher Lloyd's father Nathaniel bought Great Dixter in 1910: Lutyens did a conversion job on the house and laid out part of the gardens. Most of the brickwork, yew hedges, steps, walls, doorways and Arts & Crafts details date back to the original design – contemporary with Hidcote and earlier than Sissinghurst. The topiary was Nathaniel Lloyd's contribution – he wrote a book about it. But the main reason for the garden's pre-eminent reputation is the decades of horticultural skill which Christopher Lloyd himself put into its planting. He was a knowledgeable plantsman who once taught horticulture at Wye College and had a remarkable eye for combining plants in harmonious groupings throughout the year. His books – especially the compilation of articles from *Country Life* published as *The Well-Tempered Garden* – have been popular and influential, so the Lloyd style of planting and maintaining a garden is probably more widely copied now than any other. The heart of the garden is the Long Border, about 65m long and 4½m deep, which has become a showcase and trial ground for his experiments. It is a series of compositions loosely strung together with a wide variety of weaving colours, heights and textures but unified as much by good foliage as by flowers. Every section of it teaches you something new that could be made to work in your own garden. One of Lloyd's strengths was his fondness for change – his desire to refine and improve his garden all the time. He was one of the first garden-owners to use lots of annuals and tender perennials to extend the summer season right through into autumn. He shocked the country's rosarians by replacing his parents' collection of old-fashioned roses with a late-summer explosion of dahlias, cannas and exotic foliage. And nobody has practised the gentle, patient art of long-term meadow gardening so successfully as Christopher Lloyd: indeed, he has written so eloquently and prolifically about the principles and practices of meadow gardening that, even if he had never penned a word on any other aspect of ornamental horticulture, he would be established as a great apostle of this charming and relaxed art form which he sometimes refers to as 'tapestry gardening'. Visiting Great Dixter should be a compulsory part of every gardener's ongoing education.

topiary; sub-tropical plants; plantsman's collection of plants; good herbaceous borders; meadow garden; colour schemes; gift shop.

Owned by The Lloyd Trustees
Number of gardeners 5
Size 2ha (5 acres)
English Heritage Grade I

remarkable acres of imaginative design and striking planting are kept meticulously tidy. The planting has been chosen so that each area blends seamlessly into the next and creates a satisfying and harmonious whole. The deep sweeping borders are designed and planted to combine colour, form and texture in endlessly imaginative planting schemes. The features include foliage borders, two ponds, a border for spring, several borders designed to peak in summer and autumn, a blue garden – and dozens more. Recent developments include a dry area which has been transformed into a Mediterranean-inspired scree garden and a waterlogged area which has been turned into a bog garden and planted with moisture-loving plants. The formal gardens have been redeveloped, and wheelchair access is now good. The nursery is excellent.

plantsman's collection of plants; good herbaceous borders; brilliant modern design; tropical border; first-rate nursery attached; garden café.

Owned by David & Peggy Weeks
Number of gardeners 3
Size 1.6ha (4 acres)

MICHELHAM PRIORY
Upper Dicker, Hailsham BN27 3QS

Tel: 01323 844224 **Fax:** 01323 844030
www.sussexpast.co.uk
Location Signed from A22 & A27.
Opening hours 10.30 am - 4.30 pm; Tuesday – Sunday; March & October. 10.30 am - 5 pm; Tuesday – Sunday; April to July & September; 10.30 am - 5.30 pm; daily; August.
Admission fee Adults £5.60; OAPs £4.70; Disabled £2.80; Children £2.90.

The old Augustinian priory has an Elizabethan barn, a blacksmith's shop, a rope museum, a working water mill and England's largest medieval water-filled moat. Within the garden are several distinct areas, including a physic garden and cloister garden, with medieval plantings (faithful, if a little dull), some very good borders, a bog garden, a kitchen garden and several wildflower areas. It all makes for an enjoyable visit, highly educational for children and interesting for parents, too.

herbs; mature conifers; good herbaceous borders; sculpture trail; dovecote gift shop; licensed restaurant & tea-room.

Owned by The Sussex Archaeological Society (Sussex Past)
Number of gardeners 2, plus volunteers
Size 2.8ha (7 acres)

MOORLANDS
Friars Gate, Crowborough TN6 1XF

Tel: 01892 652474
Location 2 miles north of Crowborough, off B2188 & along St John's Road, on right.
Opening hours 11 am - 5 pm; Wednesdays; 1 April to 1 October. For NGS: 2 pm - 6 pm on 25 June.
Admission fee Adults £3; Children free.

The garden at Moorlands was begun by Dr Smith's parents in 1929: Dr Smith took over in 1974, made a lake and ponds, and planted a lot of woodland and bog-loving plants. The garden now combines mature trees with modern herbaceous plantings. By the house, on a sloping site, is a long herbaceous border. This leads to the main stream, red with iron ore but clean enough for trout and protected enough for kingfishers. It is spring-fed, full of waterfalls, and planted with grasses and bamboos. Moorlands is a plantsman's garden of fine trees, rhododendrons and collectors' shrubs, underplanted with bog plants as well as wildflowers such as native daffodils (*Narcissus pseudonarcissus*) and orchids.

good plants for plantsmen; Japanese anemones; teas on NGS open day.

Owned by Dr & Mrs Steven Smith
Number of gardeners 3 part-time
Size 1.6ha (4 acres)

PARADISE PARK
Avis Road, Newhaven BN9 0DH

Tel: 01273 512123 **Fax:** 01273 616000
www.paradisepark.co.uk
Location Signed from A26 & A259.
Opening hours 9 am - 6 pm; daily; all year,
except 25 & 26 December.
Admission fee Adults £6.99; Children £4.99.
(Subject to review.)

P WC &

Part of a leisure complex attached to a
garden centre, the most interesting
features are a tropical house and a cactus
house, each landscaped with handsome
plant collections chosen for display. There
are some imaginative garden designs –
Caribbean, seaside, desert and oriental, for
example. It is a haven in winter, and the
outside gardens are a pleasure to explore in
summer, full of contrasting designs and
splendid water features. They contain a
Sussex History trail – beautiful models of
important historic buildings in the county,
each in a different setting. Other
attractions include a hemerocallis
collection, a fuchsia border and an alpine
rock garden.
plants under glass; hydroponic
demonstration area; *Streptocarpus*
collection; plant centre; large coffee shop.

Owned by Jonathan Tate
Number of gardeners 3
Size 1ha (2½ acres) of garden and 0.1ha (¼ acre)
under glass

PASHLEY MANOR GARDENS
Ticehurst TN5 7HE

Tel: 01580 200888 **Fax:** 01580 200102
www.pashleymanorgardens.com
Location On B2099 between A21 & Ticehurst
village.
Opening hours 11 am - 5 pm; Tuesday -
Thursday, Saturdays & Bank Holiday Mondays; 4
April to 30 September.

Admission fee Adults £6; Children £5.50.

P WC &

Pashley Manor is a new/old garden, made
or remade in the Victorian style over the
last ten years or so with advice from the
brilliant Anthony du Gard Pasley. The
original structure came from fine old trees,
fountains, springs and large ponds or small
lakes. The modern plantings have added
gentle shapes, spacious expanses,
harmonious colours and solid plantings.
There is a sumptuous series of new
enclosed gardens where colour gardening is
practised to brilliant effect. And it gets
better every year.
roses (mainly old-fashioned &
climbers); mature conifers; Victorian
shrubberies; hydrangeas; irises; HHA/Christie's
Garden of the Year in 1999; lunches & teas.

Owned by James & Angela Sellick
Number of gardeners 5
Size 5ha (12½ acres)

SHEFFIELD PARK GARDEN
Uckfield TN22 3QX

Tel: 01825 790231 **Fax:** 01825 791264
www.nationaltrust.org.uk/sheffieldpark
Location Between East Grinstead & Lewes on
A275.
Opening hours 10.30 am - 6 pm; Tuesday -
Sunday & Bank Holidays; 14 February to 23
December. Open daily from 1 May to 4 June and
from 2 to 30 October. Closes at 4 pm from 1
November to 25 February 2007.
Admission fee Adults £6.20; Children £3.10. RHS
members free.

P WC &

Sheffield Park is a beautiful 120-acre
garden around five lakes. These were laid
out in the 18th century by Capability
Brown and Humphry Repton. The result is
landscaping on the grandest of scales,
though the lakes now reflect the 20th-
century plantings of exotics. Carpeted
with daffodils and bluebells in spring, its
rhododendrons, azaleas and stream garden

are spectacular in early summer. In autumn, the garden is ablaze with wonderful leaf colours, and long beds of gentians. But the collection of rare trees and shrubs makes it a fascinating visit at any time of year and the National Trust is in the middle of a major restoration project which will involve planting 9,000 trees and shrubs between 2003 and 2008. There will be two RHS Special Events at Sheffield Park in 2006; details from 020 7821 3408.

mature conifers; fine collection of trees; bluebells; daffodils; kalmias; autumn crocuses; rhododendrons; tallest *Nyssa sylvatica* (21m) in the British Isles, plus two other record trees; National Trust shop.

Owned by The National Trust
Number of gardeners 6
Size 48ha (120 acres)
NCCPG National Collections *Rhododendron* (Ghent azaleas)
English Heritage Grade I

STANDEN
West Hoathly, East Grinstead RH19 4NE

Tel: 01342 323029 **Fax:** 01342 316424
www.nationaltrust.org.uk/standen
Location 2 miles south of East Grinstead, signed from B2110.
Opening hours 11 am – 6 pm; Wednesday – Sunday & Bank Holidays; 25 March to 29 October. 11 am – 3 pm; Saturday – Sunday; 18 November to 17 December.
Admission fee Adults £4; Children £2.

This early Edwardian garden has a compartmentalised structure (very Arts & Crafts) but also enjoys magnificent views across the Medway valley. It is currently undergoing restoration, and the kitchen garden and bamboo garden will reopen in 2006. A series of enclosed gardens around the house gives way to woodland slopes and an old quarry furnished with ferns and azaleas.

roses (mainly rugosas & old-fashioned); rock garden; mature conifers; good herbaceous borders; rhododendrons; azaleas; woodland shrubs; National Trust shop; restaurant.

Owned by The National Trust
Number of gardeners 2½
Size 5ha (12½ acres)

SUSSEX, WEST

West Sussex is even better endowed with fine gardens and interesting nurseries than East Sussex. All five Grade I gardens are open to the public – Goodwood, Leonardslee, Parham, Petworth House and Stansted Park – though only Leonardslee and Parham are of great horticultural interest. However, there is also a glut of Grade II* gardens open to the public, and all of them chiefly of importance for their plant collections – Borde Hill, Cowdray, Gravetye, Highdown, Nymans, High Beeches, Wakehurst and West Dean. These are matched by a great number of good medium-sized gardens that open for the National Gardens Scheme and a large number of good nurseries and garden centres. Architectural Plants, Rotherview Nursery and Ingwersens are all nurseries of national or international status and often seen at RHS flower shows. The NCCPG has a good number of National Collections in the county. Borde Hill and Nymans offer free access to RHS members, though Borde Hill extends this privilege only in the quiet months. The old county horticultural college at Brinsbury, now part of Chichester College, is a RHS Partner College with a series of public lectures, demonstrations and workshops throughout the year: details from 020 7821 3408.

ARCHITECTURAL PLANTS
Cooks Farm, Nuthurst, Horsham
RH13 6LH

Tel: 01403 891772 **Fax:** 01403 891056
www.architecturalplants.com
Location 3 miles south of Horsham, behind the Black Horse pub in Nuthurst.
Opening hours 9 am – 5 pm; Monday – Saturday; all year.
Admission fee Free.

P ◁⟩ WC ᕦ ❦

Somewhat out of the ordinary, Architectural Plants specialises in exotic-looking, evergreen foliage plants, often with architectural or sculptural shapes. 'Architectural' means that the plants themselves have strong, sometimes spectacular, shapes which bring a distinctive year-round presence to a garden. Examples include eucalyptus, bamboos, hardy palms, hardy bananas and evergreen magnolias. Larger specimens are available for immediate impact. The display area around the nursery is stylishly laid out and a pleasure to visit in its own right. The nursery also has a branch at Lidsey Road, Woodgate, near Chichester (open 10 am – 4 pm, Sunday to Friday): it has phillyreas, arbutus and many rare trees, plus seaside exotics, but no display garden.

❧ architectural plants; large specimens.

Owned by Angus White
Size 1.2ha (3 acres)

BORDE HILL GARDEN
Balcombe Road, Haywards Heath
RH16 1XP

Tel: 01444 450326 **Fax:** 01444 440427
www.bordehill.co.uk
Location 1½ miles north of Haywards Heath.

Opening hours 10 am - 6 pm (or dusk, if earlier); daily; all year.
Admission fee Adults £6; OAPs £5 (£6 in May & June); Children £3.50. RHS members free (only at some times).

P ⬦ WC ⚲ ✹ ● ⟱

This important woodland garden has been significantly developed and improved in recent years. It was originally planted in the early 1900s with exotic trees and shrubs, notably a large collection of rhododendron species grown from such introducers as Forrest and Kingdon Ward. Some of those trees are record-breakers, including *Sorbus hupehensis*, a splendid *Magnolia hypoleuca* and the rare Chinese tulip tree (*Liriodendron chinense*) now 19m tall. The garden has recently been substantially redeveloped for the recreation market and is all the better for the new capital. The gardens surrounding the house are divided into 'rooms'. These include the Garden of Allah with a new wildlife pool; a ring of Knap Hill azaleas backed by rhododendrons from Farrer and Cox's expedition to Burma and China in 1919; the newly restored Victorian greenhouses, one of which is a peach house and another devoted to South African plants (including nerines); a small Mediterranean garden designed by Robin Williams; a rose garden planted with 500 David Austin roses; the Italian garden and two dells with *Trachycarpus* palms. There will be three RHS Special Events at Borde Hill in 2006; details from 020 7821 3408.

🌿 woodland garden; plantsman's collection of plants; fine collection of trees; rhododendrons; azaleas; magnolias; plants from original seed; 80 champion trees, one of the largest collections in the British Isles; gift shop; tea-room & restaurant.

Owned by Borde Hill Garden Ltd
Number of gardeners 5
Size 6.7ha (17 acres) of formal gardens, plus 8ha (20 acres) of woodland and 150 acres of parkland
English Heritage Grade II*

CHAMPS HILL
Coldwaltham, Pulborough RH20 1LY

Tel: 01789 831868 **Fax:** 01789 831536
Location West of Coldwaltham, on road to Fittleworth (Waltham Park Road).
Opening hours 2 pm - 5 pm; 25 & 26 March, 21 May and 12 & 13 August. Plus special openings for an Art Exhibition on 12 May (6 pm - 9 pm; £7) and 13 & 14 May (11 am - 4 pm; £6).
Admission fee Adults £4; Children free.

P WC ⚲ ✹ ⟱

This garden has been developed around three disused sand quarries since 1960. The woodlands are full of beautiful rhododendrons and azaleas, but the most striking feature is the collection of heathers – over 300 cultivars – interplanted with dwarf conifers. The garden also has some interesting sculptures, and stupendous views.

🌿 heathers; rhododendrons & azaleas; teas.

Owned by Mr & Mrs David Bowerman
Number of gardeners 2
Size 10.7ha (27 acres), including woodland

COWDRAY PARK
Midhurst GU29 0AY

Tel: 01730 812461 **Fax:** 01730 812122
Location South of A272, 1 mile east of Midhurst.
Opening hours For NGS: 2 pm - 5 pm on 14 May. And possibly in the autumn, too.
Admission fee Adults £3; Children £1.

P WC ⟱

Cowdray is seldom open, but worth a long journey to see the ornate house and its contemporary (100-year-old) collection of trees, particularly conifers – don't miss the avenue of wellingtonias up at the top. Some are now record-breakers, and the sweeps of rhododendrons and azaleas, especially the hardy hybrids down 'the dell', are on the grand scale, too. There are also two lakes, waterfalls, wildflower areas and a lot of new plantings.

300-year-old Lebanon cedar; wellingtonia avenue; rhododendrons; grapes & fruit in the glasshouses; valley garden; tallest *Abies concolor* f. *violacea* (28m) and *Chamaecyparis pisifera* (29m) in the UK; refreshments.

Owned by Viscount & Viscountess Cowdray
Size 10ha (25 acres)
English Heritage Grade II*

DENMANS GARDEN
Fontwell, Arundel BN18 0SU

Tel: 01243 542808 **Fax:** 01243 544064
www.denmans-garden.co.uk
Location Off A29 or A27, near Fontwell racecourse.
Opening hours 9 am – 5 pm (dusk in winter); daily; all year. Closed 1 January, 24 & 25 December.
Admission fee Adults £3.95; OAPs £3.45; Children (4-16) £2.25. RHS members free November to February.

🅿 ♿ ✿ 🌱 🐚 ☕

This modern garden is a showpiece for John Brookes's ideas and commitment to easy care. He uses foliage, gravel mulches, contrasts of form, coloured stems, winter bark and plants as elements of design. The garden's design is so fluid that you feel carried along by its momentum and, of course, it is a brilliant source of ideas for your own garden.

excellent modern design; gravel and grass; roses (mainly old-fashioned); herbs; good herbaceous borders; spring bulbs; shop; plant centre; lunches & teas.

Owned by John Brookes & Michael Neve
Size 1.6ha (4 acres)

GRAVETYE MANOR HOTEL
East Grinstead RH19 4LJ

Tel: 01342 810567 **Fax:** 01342 810080
www.gravetyemanor.co.uk

Location 4 miles south-west of East Grinstead.
Opening hours Hotel & restaurant guests only; all year. The perimeter path is open to the public free of charge from 10 am to 5 pm on Tuesdays & Fridays.

🅿 ♿ ✕

Gravetye was William Robinson's own garden, very influential about 100 years ago, and scrupulously maintained as it was in its prime. It was here that Robinson put into practice the natural style of gardening which he promoted so vigorously in his magazines and books. Robinson's own original woodland garden has many of the trees he planted – fine davidias and nyssas, for example. And the meadows below the house are planted with naturalised bulbs in the style that Robinson made popular through his writings. Gravetye is still a garden to learn from: there is much to admire and copy.

William Robinson's woodland garden; topiary; roses (mainly old-fashioned); plantsman's collection of plants; good herbaceous borders; fine collection of trees; alpine meadow; gazebo.

Owned by Mark Raffan & Andrew Russell
Number of gardeners 4
Size 12ha (30 acres)
English Heritage Grade II*

HIGH BEECHES
Handcross RH17 6HQ

Tel: 01444 400589 **Fax:** 01444 401543
www.highbeeches.com
Location South of B2110, 1 mile east of M23 at Handcross.
Opening hours 1 pm – 5 pm; daily, except Wednesdays; 17 March to 31 October.
Admission fee Adults £5.50. Reductions for groups of 30+. Coaches by appointment.

🅿 ♿ ✿ 🌱 ☕

One of the best (and most magical) of the famous Sussex woodland gardens, High Beeches was originally laid out by Colonel Giles Loder, a cousin of the Loders of

Wakehurst. In 1966 it was acquired by Anne and Edward Boscawen, who have devoted many years to its maintenance and improvement. Now it is managed by a non-profit-making charitable trust. The original woodland has been thinned and underplanted with exotics, many of them rare. Some are trees like nyssas, magnolias, *Tetracentron sinense* and davidias; others are shrubs – there is a 'Loderi Walk' planted with *Rhododendron* x *loderi* cultivars. A valley of ponds and woodland glades is beautifully planted with splendid rhododendrons, azaleas and camellias for spring, and swathes of native bluebells. The garden has wonderful autumn colours, too, and a policy of letting good plants naturalise – cowslips, wild orchids, willow gentians and *Primula helodoxa*. The clock in the Clock Tower (now the restaurant) was installed to commemorate Colonel Loder's Derby winner, Spion Cop.

woodland garden; plantsman's collection of plants; mature conifers; fine collection of trees; rhododendrons; five-acre natural wildflower meadow; tallest *Stewartia monodelpha* (11m) in the British Isles; restaurant open from noon; pretty tea garden.

Owned by High Beeches Gardens Conservation Trust
Number of gardeners 2
Size 10ha (25 acres)
NCCPG National Collections *Stewartia*
English Heritage Grade II*

HIGHDOWN
Littlehampton Road, Goring-by-Sea
BN12 6PE

Tel: 01903 239999 ext 1112 **Fax:** 01903 821384
Location Signed from A259.
Opening hours 10 am - 6 pm (4.30 pm in February, March, October & November, & 4 pm in January & December); daily (but not weekends from October to March); all year.
Admission fee Free. Donations welcome.
🅿 🚾 ♿

This is the most famous garden to be made on chalk, and one of the best. It was actually laid out in a disused chalk quarry and on the surrounding, south-facing downland. Its maker, Sir Frederick Stern, was determined to try anything that might grow in these unusual conditions. Eighty years on, the results are some handsome trees, vigorous roses, and long-forgotten peony hybrids. The gardens are designed on a large grid and planted mainly as mixed borders. Mediterranean plants do especially well: hellebores, tulips, daffodils and anemones have naturalised over large areas. Stern was a fine plantsman and scholar, and wrote the classic book *A Chalk Garden* as a memoir of his gardening experiences. He was also a distinguished plant breeder: Highdown has given us two very fine roses in *Rosa* 'Highdownensis' and 'Wedding Day'. The garden is now well maintained by Worthing Borough Council and a pleasure to visit at any season, but perhaps especially in spring.

woodland garden; roses (mainly old-fashioned); rock garden; plantsman's collection of plants; mature conifers; good herbaceous borders; fine collection of trees; tallest specimen of *Carpinus turczaninowii* in the UK, a handsome tree; refreshments (March to September).

Owned by Worthing Borough Council
Number of gardeners 4
Size 4ha (10 acres)
NCCPG National Collections plants introduced by Sir Frederick Stern
English Heritage Grade II*

HOLLY GATE CACTUS NURSERY
Billingshurst Road, Ashington RH20 3BB

Tel: 01903 892930
www.hollygatecactus.co.uk
Location ½ mile from Ashington, on B2133 to Billingshurst.
Opening hours 9 am - 5 pm; daily. Closed 25 -

27 December.
Admission fee Adults £2.50; OAPs & Children £2.
🅿 [wc] ✿

Holly Gate specialises in cacti and
succulents. It carries over 50,000 plants of
all types in stock and sells them both retail
and wholesale. Many are also planted in
the cactus garden, which has some fine
specimens and a wide range of taxa –
fascinating for the *cognoscenti* and an eye-
opener for the uninitiated, whatever the
weather.

🐛 cacti; succulents.

Owned by J.M. Hewitt
Number of gardeners 2
Size 930 sq.m. (10,000 sq.ft.)

W.E.TH. INGWERSEN LTD
Birch Farm Nursery, Gravetye, East
Grinstead RH19 4LE

Tel: 01342 810236
www.ingwersen.co.uk
Location 4 miles south-west of East Grinstead
off B2110.
Opening hours 9 am – 1 pm & 1.30 pm – 4 pm;
daily, except Sundays & Bank Holidays; March to
September. Weekdays only from October to
February. Closed for 2 weeks at Christmas.
Admission fee Free.
🅿 ⬆ [wc] ♿ ✿

This was the first alpine nursery in the
south of England: when it started in
March 1927, Walter Ingwersen was a
tenant of William Robinson at nearby
Gravetye Manor. The company's exhibits
at RHS flower shows have been a source of
much praise. It still has one of the best
collections in the country of traditional
alpines, especially European primulas,
sempervivums and autumn-flowering
gentians, but it is also a good place to find
less common rock plants, the smaller
perennials, dwarf shrubs and conifers.
There are many raised beds and troughs to
see at the nursery (which is in a most

beautiful setting): one can spend a long
and very happy time here looking at
alpines and browsing through possible
purchases. And the Bluebell Line runs
right past the nursery.

🐛 rock plants; troughs; lots of small
plants for interested plantsmen.

Owned by Paul Ingwersen
Number of gardeners 4
Size 0.4ha (1 acre)

NYMANS
Handcross, Haywards Heath RH17 6EB

Tel: 01444 400321 **Fax:** 01444 400253
www.nationaltrust.org.uk/nymans
Location Handcross, off the main road on B2114.
Opening hours 11 am – 6 pm; Wednesday –
Sunday & Bank Holiday Mondays; 15 February to
29 October. 11 am – 4 pm; Saturdays & Sundays; 4
November to 11 February 2007.
Admission fee Adults £7; Children £3.50.
Reductions in winter. RHS members free.
🅿 [wc] ♿ ✿ 🌲 🗗

The garden at Nymans was made in the
early years of the 20th century by Leonard
Messel, and his head gardener James
Comber. Although it is now owned by the
National Trust, there is still a substantial
input from latter-day members of the
Messel family. Nymans is a stupendous
plantsman's garden with a wonderful
collection of plants of every type which
have been marshalled with a fair degree of
artistry and made to fit within a strong
overall design. It is one of the best gardens
of the Sussex Weald, and one which
retains much of the distinctive style
dictated by its historic collection of shrubs
and trees. There are opulent yellow-and-
blue herbaceous borders in the walled
garden, a pioneering collection of old
roses, a stupendous wisteria pergola and
vast collections of magnolias and
camellias. Further afield, the woodland
and wild garden have a great collection of
rare trees and shrubs. Nymans suffered

LEONARDSLEE LAKES & GARDENS
Lower Beeding, Horsham RH13 6PP

Tel: 01403 891212 **Fax:** 01403 891305
www.leonardslee.com
Location 4 miles south-west of Handcross at junction of B2110 & A281.
Opening hours 9.30 am – 6 pm; daily; April to October.
Admission fee Adults £6 (but, in May, £8 on weekdays and £9 at weekends); Children £4 at all times.

🅿 🚾 🌾 🍂 📷

Leonardslee is a plantsman's garden on an enormous scale. It was begun in 1801 and enlarged from 1889 by Sir Edmund Loder – and still belongs to his descendants. It is important historically as one of the earliest examples of a collection of rare plants in a designed setting – a series of woodland valleys with panoramic views on the edge of the Wealden Forest. The gardens are beautiful when they first open in April with magnificent magnolias and camellias. Autumn colour is another feature: from the middle of September onwards maples, azaleas, liquidambars, carryas and nyssas produce one of the finest arrays of autumn colour in England. But Leonardslee is famous above all for its rhododendrons and azaleas which line the many miles of paths up and down the hillsides and around the seven lakes. Sheets of bluebells accompany their main flowering in May, while the banks of the lakes and streams are densely planted with candelabra primulas, lysichitons and gunneras. There are many other fascinating features: magnificent conifers; large plantings of modern *Rhododendron yakushimanum* hybrids; several original plants of *Rhododendron* x *loderi* hybrids; a large area naturalised by *Scilla liliohyacinthus*; rare shrubs like *Ilex dipyrena*; a European cork oak (*Quercus suber*) and the Amur cork oak (*Phellodendron amurense*); a magnificent Pulhamite rock garden about 100 years old, which has a very striking clump of the hardy Chusan palm (*Trachycarpus fortunei* and a fine form of *T. fortunei* var. *surculosa*) and a bright mixture of evergreen azaleas; and a truly beautiful valley on the other side of the main lake which is filled from top to bottom with a flood of sweet-scented yellow azaleas (*Rhododendron luteum*). The garden is very large – allow lots of time – and the labelling sparse.

🌿 rock garden; plantsman's collection of plants; mature conifers; new millennium plantings (100 oak species; 100 maple species; many flowering *Cornus*); bonsai; tallest fossil tree *Metasequoia glyptostroboides* (28m) and *Magnolia campbellii* (27m) in the British Isles, and five further champion trees; gift shop; licensed restaurant/café.

Owned by The Loder family
Number of gardeners 7
Size 100ha (250 acres)
English Heritage Grade I

very severely from the great storm of 1987, but has since made a brilliant recovery and many would say now that the garden looks better than ever.

🌿 woodland garden; topiary; roses (mainly old-fashioned); plantsman's collection of plants; good herbaceous borders; fine collection of trees; eight different record-breaking trees; shop; plant centre open daily (11 am – 6 pm); licensed restaurant.

Owned by The National Trust
Number of gardeners 7
Size 12ha (30 acres)
English Heritage Grade II*

PARHAM
Storrington, Pulborough RH20 4HS

Tel: 01903 742021 **Fax:** 01903 746557
www.parhaminsussex.co.uk
Location On A283 midway between Pulborough & Storrington.
Opening hours 12 noon – 6 pm; Wednesdays, Thursdays, Sundays & Bank Holiday Mondays; Easter to September. Plus Saturday 8 July (Garden Weekend), and Tuesdays & Fridays in August.
Admission fee Gardens only: Adults £5; OAPs & Disabled £4.50; Children £1.50.

🅿 🍽 [wc] ♿ ❀ ● ✂ ♥

Parham is an ethereal English garden for the loveliest of Elizabethan manor houses. In the deer park are a landscaped lake and a cricket ground. The fun for garden-lovers is in the old walled garden: four acres of lush borders, colour plantings in yellow, blue and mauve, old and new fruit trees, and all maintained to the highest standard. The aim is to achieve 'Edwardian opulence...without being too purist'. There are striking colour combinations, too, within the vegetable garden, while extensive cutting borders supply material for the arrangements of cut-flowers for which the house is famous. The voluminous conservatory has a splendid display of fuchsias and old-fashioned pelargonium cultivars.

🌿 roses (mainly old-fashioned); trained fruit; good herbaceous borders; organic kitchen garden; HHA/Christie's Garden of the Year in 1990; shop; light lunches & teas.

Owned by Parham Park Trust
Number of gardeners 4½, plus volunteers
Size 4.4ha (11 acres)
English Heritage Grade I

PETWORTH HOUSE
Petworth GU28 0AE

Tel: 01798 342207 **Fax:** 01798 342963
www.nationaltrust.org.uk/petworth
Location At Petworth, well signed.
Opening hours Garden: 11 am – 6 pm; Saturday – Wednesday & Good Friday; 18 March to 29 October. Park: 8 am – dusk; daily; all year (but may close at 12 noon on concert days).
Admission fee Garden ('Pleasure Grounds'): Adults £3; Children £1.50. Park: free.

🅿 [wc] ♿ ● ♥

One of the best Capability Brown landscapes in England sweeps right up to the windows of Petworth House. The National Trust has added acres of bright azaleas to the woodland garden. Both park and garden have enjoyed a renaissance since the damage caused by the great storm of 1987. The Pleasure Ground is one of the most historically interesting parts of Petworth: the layout dates back to Elizabethan times. Winding pathways lead through shrubberies, punctuated by unexpected vistas and areas for quiet contemplation.

🌿 Capability Brown landscape; woodland garden; good herbaceous borders; deer park; one million daffodils; shop; restaurant.

Owned by The National Trust
Number of gardeners 4
Size 12ha (30 acres) of Pleasure Grounds; 280-ha (700-acre) park.
English Heritage Grade I

WAKEHURST PLACE
Ardingly, Haywards Heath RH17 6TN

Tel: 01444 894066 **Fax:** 01444 894069
www.kew.org
Location On B2028 between Turners Hill &
Ardingly.
Opening hours 10 am - 6 pm (4.30 pm in winter);
daily, except 24 & 25 December; all year. Last
admissions 30 minutes before closing.
Admission fee Adults £8; OAPs £7; Children free.
(Subject to review.) Free to National Trust
members.

🅿 ♿ ⛲ 🌿 🍂 ✕ 🏷

Wakehurst Place, now managed by the
Royal Botanic Gardens at Kew as a
country outlier, has a long horticultural
history. Most of the planting, however,
began after Gerald Loder bought the estate
in 1903 and began to introduce exotic
trees and shrubs – a development which
continued throughout the mid-20th
century under the next owner Sir Henry
Price. The planting suffered badly in the
great storm of 1987 but the survivors
include many rare trees including the King
William pine (*Athrotaxis selaginoides*).
Among the record-breaking trees which
survived the gales are *Cornus nuttallii* and
Torreya nucifera, both 17m high, *Carya
tomentosa* at 27m, and two cultivars of
Chamaecyparis lawsoniana – 'President
Roosevelt' at 15m and 'Winston
Churchill', slightly shorter, at 13m. A
recent addition has been the 'iris dell',
planted with authentic Japanese cultivars
of water iris (*Iris ensata*), against a brilliant
background of Kurume azaleas –
Wakehurst has significant connections
with Japan. The water garden is
surrounded by sheets of blue meconopsis
and the giant Himalayan *Cardiocrinum
giganteum*. Wakehurst also has its botanic
collections, including a monocot border –
wonderful ginger plants (*Hedychium*) in
autumn – and specimen beds with
especially comprehensive collections of
hypericums, hydrangeas and agapanthus.
Many parts of the woodland garden are
underplanted with rhododendrons, which
are at their best in April and May.
Wakehurst has also benefited from major
funding by the Millennium Commission,
which has enabled it to develop the
world's largest seed bank: it aims to collect
and conserve some ten per cent of the
world's flora – 24,000 species – by the year
2010.

🌿 ornamental woodland garden; roses
(mainly old-fashioned & climbers);
rhododendrons & azaleas; plantsman's collection
of plants; daffodils; camellias; fine collection of
trees; alpine plants; bluebells; Asian heath
garden; pinetum; cardiocrinums; good autumn
colour; *Iris ensata* dell; water garden; tallest
Ostrya japonica (15m) in the British Isles, plus 25
further tree records; gift shop; plant sales
(March to October); light refreshments &
restaurant.

Owned by RBG Kew, on lease from the National
Trust
Number of gardeners 40
Size 127ha (316 acres)
NCCPG National Collections *Betula; Hypericum;
Nothofagus; Skimmia*
English Heritage Grade II*

WEST DEAN GARDENS
West Dean, Chichester PO18 0QZ

Tel: 01243 818210 **Fax:** 01243 811342
www.westdean.org.uk
Location 6 miles north of Chichester on A286.
Opening hours 11 am (10.30 am from May to
September) - 5 pm; daily; March to October. 11
am - 4.30 pm; Wednesday - Sunday; November to
February. Closed 24 December to 3 January.
Admission fee Adults £6; OAPs £5.50; Children
£2.50. Reductions in winter. RHS members free
from October to March, except on show days.

🅿 ♿ 🌿 🍂 🏷

Laid out in the 1890s and 1900s, West
Dean has now been extensively restored.
Harold Peto's 100m pergola has been
replanted with roses. Much of the damage
to the 20ha (49 acre) St Roche's arboretum

caused by the 1987 storm has been made good. The great range of glasshouses in the walled garden has been repaired and the garden itself planted as a working kitchen garden which is now the crowning glory of West Dean. A huge variety of plants – from peaches to peppers, cucumbers to coleus, aubergines to orchids – grows in the 16 glasshouses and frames. Out of doors are orderly rows of cabbage, carrots, lettuce and beetroot, alongside herbaceous borders in rich reds, oranges and yellows. No space is wasted: the kitchen garden has over one mile of walls covered in trained fruit trees – over 200 different apples, pears and plums. No private garden has so many beautifully grown fruit and vegetables. Beyond the walled garden (2½ acres in size) are 35 acres of ornamental gardens, the St Roche's arboretum and 240 acres of landscaped park – all linked by a 2¼-mile walk. Herbaceous borders and annual bedding schemes have been reinstated, rustic summerhouses rebuilt and the arboretum taken in hand. The redevelopment of the spring garden, including the 1820s rustic thatched summerhouse with its moss- and heather-lined interior and its floor of knapped flints and horses' molars is now complete. In the wild garden are new (2005) woodland and herbaceous plantings (lots of grasses), a pond and wetland area.

roses (mainly old-fashioned & climbers); plants under glass; museum of old lawn mowers; long pergola with roses & clematis; tallest *Cupressus goveniana* (22m) and *Ailanthus vilmoriniana* (26m) in the UK; amazing kitchen garden; good shop; licensed restaurant.

Owned by The Edward James Foundation
Number of gardeners 10
Size 36ha (90 acres) in all
NCCPG National Collections *Aesculus*, *Liriodendron*
English Heritage Grade II*

WARWICKSHIRE

Warwickshire has for centuries been a prosperous county: it has the rich clay soils, the country estates and the gardens to prove it. Many of its historic gardens are open to the public throughout the season, including such top attractions as Arbury Hall, Charlecote Park, Farnborough Hall, Packwood House, Upton House and Warwick Castle. The National Gardens Scheme is very successful in persuading the owners of modern gardens to open them to the public, especially by grouping several together within a village. Warwickshire has many first-rate garden centres and a few top-class specialist nurseries, too – notably Fibrex Nurseries, who specialise in pelargoniums, ivies, hardy ferns and hellebores. Fibrex also have two of the county's National Collections. The Henry Doubleday Research Association, the organic gardening organisation, has its headquarters at Ryton near Coventry. Its garden, now known as Garden Organic Ryton, offers free access to RHS members throughout the year.

ARBURY HALL
Nuneaton CV10 7PT

Tel: 024 7638 2804 **Fax:** 024 7664 1147
Location 3 miles south-west of Nuneaton off B4102.
Opening hours 2 pm – 6 pm; Bank Holiday Sundays & Mondays (8 days in total); Easter Sunday to August.
Admission fee Adults £5; Children £3.50.

P ⟳ WC ㋡ ✿ ☕

Arbury is more important historically than horticulturally: Sanderson Miller was involved in some 18th-century improvements and there is a wonderfully landscaped sequence of canals and lakes. During the 19th century, many good trees were planted, now in the full-grown beauty of their maturity: purple beeches and a golden sycamore, for example. Then there are bluebell woods, pollarded limes, a large rose garden, a walled garden and a huge wisteria. Nothing is outstanding in itself, but the ensemble is an oasis of peace on the edge of industrial Daventry and worth the journey from far away.

woodland garden; roses (mainly modern); rhododendrons & azaleas; daffodils; bluebells; gift & crafts shop; tea-room.

Owned by Viscount Daventry
Number of gardeners 4
English Heritage Grade II*

BADDESLEY CLINTON
Baddesley Clinton Village, Knowle, Solihull B93 0DQ

Tel: 01564 783294 **Fax:** 01564 782706
www.nationaltrust.org.uk
Location 1 mile west of A4141.
Opening hours 12 noon – 5.30 pm; Wednesday – Sunday; 1 March to 10 December. Also open on Bank Holiday Mondays. Closes at 5 pm in March, April, October & 1 to 5 November; closes at 4.30 pm from 8 November to 10 December.
Admission fee Adults £3.40; Children £1.70.

P WC ㋡ ✿ ✿ ☕

The walled garden at Baddesley Clinton has fine mixed plantings, including a good collection of shrub roses, herbaceous plants, herbs and annuals. One of the Victorian lean-to glasshouses has recently been restored. In front of the house (an ancient manor house) is a formal courtyard garden. Further away are woodland walks, a lake, stew ponds and wildflower meadows.

 formal courtyard garden; walled garden; shop; plant sales; restaurant.

Owned by The National Trust
Number of gardeners 2
Size 4.4ha (11 acres)
English Heritage Grade II

CHARLECOTE PARK
Wellesbourne, Warwick CV35 9ER

Tel: 01789 470277 **Fax:** 01789 470544
www.nationaltrust.org.uk
Location Signed from A429.
Opening hours 10.30 am – 6 pm; Friday – Tuesday; 4 March to 29 October. Plus Wednesdays in July & August. 11 am – 4 pm; Saturdays & Sundays 4 November to 17 December.
Admission fee Adults £3; Children £1.50.

Fine cedars and a Capability Brown park are Charlecote's main claims to fame, but the young William Shakespeare is reputed to have poached deer from the park, so the National Trust has planted a border with plants mentioned in his works. Recent additions include a parterre, a large herbaceous border, a sensory garden and 'green court' garden designed by the tenant, Sir Edmund Fairfax-Lucy.

topiary; parterre; mature conifers; deer park; orangery; National Trust shop; restaurant.

Owned by The National Trust
Number of gardeners 2
Size 1.6ha (4 acres)
English Heritage Grade II*

COUGHTON COURT
Alcester B49 5JA

Tel: 01789 400777 **Fax:** 01789 765544
www.coughtoncourt.co.uk
Location 2 miles north of Alcester on A435.
Opening hours 11 am – 5.30 pm; Wednesday – Sunday; April to September. Plus Tuesdays in July & August. Plus May & August Bank Holidays, and Saturdays & Sundays in October.
Admission fee Adults £5.90; Children £2.95. RHS members free. Parking £1 per car.

The garden at Coughton has all been made since 1992, designed by Christina Williams, Mrs Throckmorton's daughter. The Throckmortons have lived at Coughton for 300 years. An Elizabethan-style knot garden fills the courtyard, and extensive new plantings beyond lead the eye out to the distant landscape. The walled garden has a rose labyrinth, a new vegetable garden, fine herbaceous borders and a bog garden, as well as an orchard planted with local varieties of fruit. The family is building up a collection of daffodil cultivars bred by their American namesake Dr Tom Throckmorton.

interesting historic gardens (new) around the house (old); pretty plants and plantings; gift shop & plant centre; restaurant/café.

Owned by Mrs Clare Throckmorton & the National Trust
Number of gardeners 5
Size 10ha (25 acres)

FARNBOROUGH HALL
Banbury OX17 1DU

Tel: 01295 690002
www.nationaltrust.org.uk
Location Off A423, 6 miles north of Banbury.
Opening hours 2 pm – 5.30 pm; Wednesdays & Saturdays; April to September and 1 & 2 May. Terrace walk also open on Wednesdays & Saturdays, by prior appointment.

Admission fee Garden & Terrace walk £2.10.

P ◁ wc ⅃

Farnborough Hall is Sanderson Millar's masterpiece – a broad grass walk leads gently uphill for ¼ mile to an obelisk erected in 1751. On the way are an Ionic temple and the Oval Pavilion, both hemmed in by vegetation now. Below the house lies a pretty series of landscaped lakes. There is no garden, as such, but a sense of space and peace: only the distant roar of the M40 takes the edge off the sense of awe. The National Trust suggests taking the woodland walk back – pretty with wild flowers in spring.

 historic landscape.

Owned by The National Trust
Number of gardeners 1 full-time, 1 part-time
Size 4.8ha (12 acres)
English Heritage Grade I

FIBREX NURSERIES LTD
Honeybourne Road, Pebworth, Stratford-upon-Avon CV37 8XP

Tel: 01789 720788 **Fax:** 01789 721162
www.fibrex.co.uk
Location South-east edge of village, on road to Honeybourne.
Opening hours 9 am – 4 pm; Monday – Friday; all year. Plus weekends (10.30 am – 4 pm) from March to July. Closed for last two weeks of December & first week of January. Also closed on Easter Sunday and August Bank Holiday Monday.
Admission fee Free.

P wc 🌱

Fibrex is a family nursery, built up over more than 40 years and a regular prize-winner at RHS flower shows. It has four specialities – pelargoniums, ivies, hardy ferns and hellebores – and holds National Collections of two of them. The National Collection of pelargoniums has over 2,000 different species and cultivars and claims to be the largest in the world. The National Collection of ivies (*Hedera*) has

over 300 different species and cultivars. The ferns are planted out in the show garden in a natural manner using mature plants: the ivies can be seen growing both outside and in a covered exhibition area. There will be an RHS Special Event at Fibrex Nurseries in 2006; details from 020 7821 3408.

pelargoniums; ivies; hardy ferns; hellebores.

NCCPG National Collections *Hedera*, *Pelargonium*

GARDEN ORGANIC RYTON
Ryton, Coventry CV8 3LG

Tel: 024 7630 3517 **Fax:** 024 7663 9229
www.gardenorganic.org.uk
Location 5 miles south-east of Coventry off A45.
Opening hours 9 am – 5 pm; daily; all year, except Christmas week.
Admission fee Adults £5; Concessions £4.50; Children £2.50. RHS members free (except for some special events, when £1.50).

P wc ⅃ 🌱 🌰 ✕ 🏷

This is the new name for Ryton Organic gardens, though it remains the UK's centre of excellence for organic gardening. It is very well laid out and landscaped, with 30 different small gardens, all highly instructive. The gardens include herb gardens, rose gardens, fruit and vegetable displays plus wildlife and conservation areas. A new development is the area called the Vegetable Kingdom, which tells the history of British vegetables. The website is good.

organic gardens; considerable educational interest; shop with gardening products, books, food, wine & gifts; organic whole-food restaurant.

Owned by Henry Doubleday Research Association
Number of gardeners 7
Size 4ha (10 acres)

THE HILLER GARDEN

Dunnington Heath Farm, Dunnington,
Alcester B49 5PD

Tel: 01789 491342 **Fax:** 01789 490439
Location On B4088 near Ragley Hall, 2 miles
south of Alcester.
Opening hours 10 am – 5 pm (4 pm in winter);
daily; all year. Nursery open from March to
November.
Admission fee Free.

This is an unusually fine display garden,
with colour and interest all the year
round. The rose garden has roses from
mediaeval times through to the latest
David Austin English roses. The nursery
specialises in old roses and perennial
plants, of which it has a wide range.

gift shop; garden centre; farm shop;
restaurant.

Owned by Richard Beach
Number of gardeners 1½
Size 0.8ha (2 acres)

THE MILL GARDEN

55 Mill Street, Warwick CV34 4HB

Tel: 01926 492877
Location Off A425, beside the old castle gate,
at the bottom of Mill Street. Use St Nicholas car
park.
Opening hours 9 am – 6 pm; daily; April to
October.
Admission fee Adults £1; Children free.

No garden has such an idyllic setting, on
the banks of the Avon at the foot of
Warwick Castle: the views in all
directions are superb. The garden is
planted in the cottage style and seems
much larger than its half acre: it burgeons
with plants, and the use of annuals to
supplement the varied permanent
planting enables it to have colour and
form, contrasts and harmonies, at every
season. This garden was made by Arthur

Measures over a long period: it remains
open in his memory.

plantsman's collection of plants; water
plants; magnificent riverside position.

Owned by D.G. & J. Measures
Number of gardeners owners & part-time help
Size 0.2ha (½ acre)

PACKWOOD HOUSE

Packwood Lane, Lapworth, Solihull
B94 6AT

Tel: 01564 783294 **Fax:** 01564 782706
www.nationaltrust.org.uk
Location 2 miles east of Hockley Heath: signed
from A3400.
Opening hours 11 am – 5.30 pm; Wednesday –
Sunday & Bank Holiday Mondays; 1 March to 5
November. Closes at 4.30 pm in March, April,
October & November.
Admission fee Garden only: Adults £3.20;
Children £1.60.

Long famous for its topiary, Packwood also
has magnificent herbaceous borders which
make a visit in July or August particularly
rewarding.

shop; plants for sale.

Owned by The National Trust
Number of gardeners 3½
Size 2.8ha (7 acres)
English Heritage Grade I

RAGLEY HALL

Alcester B49 5NJ

Tel: 01789 762090 **Fax:** 01789 764791
www.ragleyhall.com
Location 2 miles south-west of Alcester, off
A435/A46
Opening hours 10 am – 6 pm; daily; April to
September. Closed Monday – Wednesday in
term-time.
Admission fee Adults £6; OAPs £5.50; Children

£4.50. (2005 prices.) RHS members free for some of the time.

🅿 🆆🅲 ♿ ⏏

Ragley Hall has a Capability Brown park, overlaid by a horticultural landscape started by Robert Marnock in the 1860s. Mature trees, including vast wellingtonias, are the background for modern gardens – roses, bulbs, azaleas, bog plants and mixed borders.

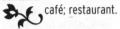 café; restaurant.

Owned by The Marquess of Hertford
English Heritage Grade II*

UPTON HOUSE & GARDENS
Banbury OX15 6HT

Tel: 01295 670266 **Fax:** 01295 671144
www.nationaltrust.org.uk
Location A422, 7 miles north-west of Banbury & 12 miles south-east of Stratford-upon-Avon.
Opening hours 12 noon (11 am on Saturdays, Sundays & Bank Holidays) – 5 pm; Saturday – Wednesday; 18 March to 1 November. 12 noon – 4 pm; Saturdays & Sundays only; 4 November to 17 December.
Admission fee Adults £4.20; Children £2.10

🅿 🆆🅲 ♿ 🌱 🌺 ⏏

Upton House is set off by a flat and spacious expanse of grass; only when you reach the far side of this immense lawn do the real gardens appear, tumbling down the terraced hillside to the pool at the bottom. The structure is early 1700s: the gardens are 1930s – Kitty Lloyd-Jones's masterpiece. It is dominated by a sloping kitchen garden, reached by flights of Italianate stairs. There are also small formal gardens, one with standard *Hibiscus syriacus* 'Bluebird' underplanted with eryngiums, and another planted with roses. One way back runs through good herbaceous borders – simply planted, but effective. The best area for interesting plants is the bog garden, once a mediaeval

fish pond, with fine cercidiphyllums, gunneras, magnolias and an *Acer carpinifolium* leaning low over another pool. Be prepared for quite a long walk from the car park – and be careful on the slopes in wet weather.

good herbaceous borders; bog garden; National Trust shop; licensed restaurant.

Owned by The National Trust
Number of gardeners 5, plus 2 students
Size 14ha (35 acres)
NCCPG National Collections *Aster*
English Heritage Grade II*

WARWICK CASTLE
Warwick CV34 4QU

Tel: 0870 442 2000 **Fax:** 0870 442 2394
www.warwick-castle.co.uk
Location In town centre.
Opening hours 10 am – 6 pm (5 pm from October to March); daily; all year, except 25 December.
Admission fee Peak season (22 July to 3 September): Adults £17.95; OAPs £12.95; Children £10.95. Slightly less out-of-season. Ticket price includes entry to Castle (no 'garden only' price).

🅿 🆆🅲 ♿ 🌺 ⏏

This classic 18th-century landscape looks good after some recent restoration, as do the late 19th-century formal garden (the 'Peacock' garden) and the recreated Victorian rose garden, both by Robert Marnock. But the price is expensive unless you take in the castle, too.

topiary; roses (mainly old-fashioned); rhododendrons & azaleas; mature conifers; Capability Brown landscape; handsome conservatory; shop; refreshments.

Owned by The Tussauds Group
Number of gardeners 9
Size 23ha (58 acres)
English Heritage Grade I

WEST MIDLANDS

As an administrative entity, West Midlands was a short-lived county, created in 1974 from parts of Warwickshire and Staffordshire, it is now entirely split up into unitary authorities. Its historic gardens are few, but they include what is left of the poet Shenstone's The Leasowes, together with the Birmingham Botanical Gardens and Castle Bromwich Hall. The latter are both highly visitable and highly visited – excellent gardens, deservedly popular still. Being such an urban county, West Midlands is short on old estates, landscaped parks and arboreta, but full of large villa-gardens like the one in Edgbaston that became the University of Birmingham Botanic Garden. This is the area, too, where the National Gardens Scheme does best. The biggest RHS event in the Midlands takes place at the NEC from 14 to 18 June 2006: *BBC Gardeners' World Live* is very different from such shows as Chelsea and Hampton Court, though the great draw is the enormously long floral marquee that the Royal Horticultural Society runs with great aplomb. The county, though small, also has a surprisingly large number of National Collections, including two, *Ceanothus* and *Rudbeckia*, held by Dudley Borough Council.

BIRMINGHAM BOTANICAL GARDENS & GLASSHOUSES
Westbourne Road, Edgbaston, Birmingham B15 3TR

Tel: 0121 454 1860 **Fax:** 0121 454 7835
www.birminghambotanicalgardens.org.uk
Location Follow brown tourist signs in Edgbaston.
Opening hours 9 am (10 am on Sundays) - 7 pm (5 pm or dusk from October to March); daily; all year, except Christmas Day.
Admission fee Adults £6.10 (£6.40 on summer Sundays); Concessions £3.60.

P WC & 🌺 🐛 ▽

Part botanic garden, part public park, wholly delightful, the Birmingham Botanical Gardens & Glasshouses can boast an historic layout (John Claudius Loudon), rare trees and shrubs, gardens for rhododendrons, roses, herbs and alpines, and four glasshouses (tropical, sub-tropical, Mediterranean and arid) as well as a good tea-room, brilliant standards of maintenance and a brass band playing on Sunday afternoons in summer. The plant highlights are innumerable, but include water hyacinths (the weed that is choking the Nile), rice plants, papyrus plants, coffee and sugar, bananas and pineapples, many cycads, insectivorous plants, 'living stones', *Paulownia tomentosa*, good herbaceous plants (phlox, euphorbias, geraniums, delphiniums) and the National Collection of bonsai housed in a secure courtyard.

🌿 roses (ancient & modern); rock garden; plantsman's collection of plants; plants under glass; fruit; mature conifers; good herbaceous borders; alpine yard; bonsai; three 'historic' gardens - Roman, Mediaeval & Tudor; gift shop; tea-room & light refreshments.

Owned by Birmingham Botanical & Horticultural Society
Number of gardeners 10, plus students
Size 6ha (15 acres)
NCCPG National Collections Bonsai
English Heritage Grade II*

CASTLE BROMWICH HALL GARDENS

Chester Road, Castle Bromwich B36 9BT

Tel & Fax: 0121 749 4100
www.cbhgt.colebridge.net
Location 5 miles from city centre, just off B4114.
Opening hours 1.30 pm - 4.30 pm; Wednesday - Friday. 1.30 pm - 5.30 pm; Saturdays, Sundays & Bank Holiday Mondays. 1 April to 1 October.
Admission fee Adults £3.50; Concessions £3; Children 50p.

P ⊸ WC ও ❀ ● ⊘

The gardens at Castle Bromwich Hall are garden archaeology at work – educational, instructive and highly enjoyable. They are being restored as they were in about 1700 by a privately funded trust. For many years they were neglected, lost beneath a tangled mass of vegetation. Work began in 1985 and has been very successful: the result is both beautiful, inspiring and educational. The gardens contain a large collection of unusual period plants, and a 19th-century holly maze. There is also a holly walk – a broad path lined with variegated hollies. At its end, the elegant Summer House looks across to an early orangery known as the Green House. Nearby is the formal vegetable garden, laid out to the design of Batty Langley's *New Principles of Gardening* (1728). Many historic vegetables and herbs are grown, along with unusual varieties like the black 'Congo' potato and white carrot. Fruit trees are formally trained – apples, pears, apricots, figs and cherries. The Upper and Lower Wildernesses have grown to maturity, with period underplanting. The North Garden has recently been restored to the design shown in Henry Beighton's Prospect of 1726, its parterre outlined with yew, mown grass and gravel.

❧ walled gardens; historic vegetables, fruit and herbs; holly maze; gift shop; coffee shop.

Owned by Castle Bromwich Hall Gardens Trust
Number of gardeners 3, plus volunteers
Size 4ha (10 acres)
English Heritage Grade II*

WIGHTWICK MANOR

Wightwick, Wolverhampton WV6 8EE

Tel: 01902 761400 **Fax:** 01902 764663
www.nationaltrust.org.uk
Location 3 miles west of Wolverhampton on A454.
Opening hours 11 am - 6 pm Wednesday - Saturday & Bank Holidays; 1 March to 24 December.
Admission fee Adults £3.30; Children free.

⊸ WC ও ● ⊘

Wightwick is a substantial Victorian garden, designed by Alfred Parsons and Thomas Mawson. The upper garden is held together by yew hedges, which separate it into a series of smaller gardens. These include fine herbaceous borders, shrub borders, and the famous Poets' Borders (currently undergoing a redesign) where all the plants were taken as cuttings from the gardens of literary men – Keats, Tennyson and Dickens among them. The Victorian peach house, topiary, rose arbour and avenues of Irish yews are also worth seeing.

❧ topiary; roses (mainly old-fashioned & climbers); rock garden; good herbaceous borders; current holder of Sandford Award; shop; tea-room.

Owned by The National Trust
Number of gardeners 3, plus 6 volunteers
Size 6.7ha (17 acres)

WINTERBOURNE BOTANIC GARDEN, UNIVERSITY OF BIRMINGHAM

58 Edgbaston Park Road, Edgbaston B15 2RT

Tel: 0121 414 5590 **Fax:** 0121 414 8128
www.botanic.bham.ac.uk
Location Off A38 Bristol Road, ½ mile.
Opening hours 11 am - 4 pm; Monday - Friday; all year from 3 April. Plus 2 pm - 5 pm on Sundays & Bank Holiday Mondays from May to September. Closed Easter & Christmas holidays.

Admission fee Adults £3.

[WC] ♿ ⚘ ☕

This was originally a private garden, belonging to one of Birmingham's great-and-good families: it was given to the university in 1944 but still has the 'feel' of a private garden – one with a fine collection of plants. The rhododendrons and naturalised bulbs are very pretty: even the roses, chosen to illustrate their history in cultivation, fit well into an ornamental garden. There are some geographic beds which put together plants that combine naturally in the wild, and an interesting sandstone rock garden. The garden went back a little during the 1980s and early 1990s, but is now being restored and redeveloped most effectively. It is a charming place to spend a couple of hours at almost any time of the year.

roses of every kind; a good collection of plants of every kind; shop; tea & coffee.

Owned by The University of Birmingham
Number of gardeners 4
Size 2.4ha (6 acres)
NCCPG National Collections *Anthemis*, *Rosa* (History of European roses); *Iris unguicularis* (provisional)

WILTSHIRE

Wiltshire is the county that people travel through on their way to somewhere else. For gardeners, this is a mistake. Unlike so many counties whose great Grade I historic gardens are often rather dull, Wiltshire's are all supremely beautiful – Bowood, Iford, Longleat, Stourhead and Wilton. All are open to the public, as are many of the other graded gardens. Wiltshire also has a number of very good plantsman's gardens – notably Broadleas and Home Covert near Devizes, and the Old Vicarage at nearby Edington. It has some fine arboreta: tree-enthusiasts should also try to see the record-breaking multi-stemmed specimen of *Zelkova carpinifolia* at Wardour Castle – 35m high when last officially measured in 1977. The National Gardens Scheme does well in the county, particularly among the owners of medium-sized and large gardens. Unfortunately, however, Barbara Austin's beautiful garden at Pound Hill was sold last year and will not be opening again in 2006. The Wiltshire Gardens Trust is active in conservation and also represents the NCCPG in the county: there is a sprinkling of National Collections among its members. Wiltshire does not, however, do so well for nurseries: perhaps only the Botanic Nursery at Atworth can be said to have a national profile. Geoffrey Jellicoe's masterpiece at Shute House, Donhead St Mary, has recently been open to groups by prior appointment. It is worth noting that, contrary to widespread belief, both Shute House and Larmer Tree Gardens are actually in Wiltshire, not in Dorset.

THE ABBEY HOUSE
Market Cross, Malmesbury SN16 9AS

Tel: 01666 822212 (information)
Fax: 01666 822782
www.abbeyhousegardens.co.uk
Location In town centre, behind abbey. Public car parks nearby.
Opening hours 11 am – 5.30 pm; daily; 21 March to 21 October.
Admission fee Adults £5.50; Concessions £5; Children £2.

wc &. ❀ ☕

This remarkable five-acre garden has all been made by the Pollards since 1995. They planted 2,000 different roses to celebrate the millennium, and 2,000 different herb cultivars. The roses are now (2006) underplanted with 100,000 tulips. Other features include an arcaded fruit walk, a knot garden, huge herbaceous borders, a striking laburnum tunnel, a new fuchsia gallery and a formal garden. But it is the design and planting which are so distinctive: bold, varied and inspirational. The woodland garden running down to the river is home to more than 40,000 spring bulbs and 60 different hellebore cultivars. At the bottom are fish ponds, a 6m waterfall, heather banks, 10,000 narcissi and a fernery. Alan Titchmarsh came here for *BBC Gardeners' World* in June 2002. His verdict: 'the Wow factor is here in abundance!'. But that was four years ago, and the development since then is amazing: the Wow factor is now here in *super*abundance!

❧ plantsman's collection of plants; herbaceous borders; roses of every kind; good design; colour contrasts; light refreshments.

Owned by Ian Pollard
Number of gardeners 1, plus enthusiastic owners
Size 2ha (5 acres)

AVEBURY MANOR GARDEN
Avebury, Marlborough SN8 1RF

Tel: 01672 539250 **Fax:** 01672 538038
www.nationaltrust.org.uk
Location In village, well signed.
Opening hours 11 am – 5 pm; daily, except
Wednesdays & Thursdays; 1 April to 31 October.
Open Bank Holiday Mondays.
Admission fee Adults £3; Children £1.50.

The National Trust is continuing the work
of restoration at this great Edwardian
garden and the 'garden rooms' are being
revived and replanted: the results are well
worth another visit.

topiary; roses (mainly old-fashioned);
good herbaceous borders; double
lavender walk; shop; National Trust restaurant in
village.

Owned by The National Trust
Number of gardeners 2
Size 2.4ha (6 acres)

BOLEHYDE MANOR
Allington, Chippenham SN14 6LW

Tel: 01249 652105 **Fax:** 01249 659296
Location 2 miles west of Chippenham.
Opening hours 2.30 pm – 6 pm; 18 June. And by
appointment.
Admission fee Adults £3; Children 50p.

This charming house is surrounded by
outbuildings and walls of old Cotswold
stone, which form the background to a
series of enclosed gardens. Each is very
prettily designed and planted in the modern
style – using plants for their contrasts and
combinations of flower, shape, colour and
form. The gardens seem to brim over with
flowers and an abundance of beauty. If only
it were open more often.

roses (mainly old-fashioned); pretty
potager, good herbaceous borders;
climbing roses; teas.

Owned by Earl & Countess Cairns
Number of gardeners 1
Size 1.2ha (3 acres)

THE BOTANIC NURSERY
Cottles Lane, Atworth, Melksham
SN12 8NU

Tel: 07850 328756 **Fax:** 01225 700953
www.thebotanicnursery.com
Location Next to grounds of Stonar School, just
outside Atworth on road to South Wraxall.
Opening hours 10 am – 5 pm; Tuesday –
Saturday; March to November. And by
appointment.
Admission fee Free.

The Botanic Nursery built its reputation
on growing lime-tolerant plants, but has
become better known as a plantsman's
nursery, where a long browse will winkle
out all sorts of rarities. It is best known at
RHS flower shows for its spectacular
displays of foxgloves (*Digitalis*) from its
National Collection, though it also has
very good collections of unusual shrubs,
eryngiums and dieramas. The one-acre
display garden (mainly trees and shrubs) is
well worth a visit, too. There will be
several events at The Botanic Nursery
during 2006; details from 020 7821 3408.

2,000 different plants, many rare, all
lime-tolerant.

Owned by Terence & Mary Baker
Number of gardeners 1
Size 0.8ha (2 acres)
NCCPG National Collections *Digitalis*

BOWOOD HOUSE & GARDENS
Calne SN11 0LZ

Tel: 01249 812102 **Fax:** 01249 821757
www.bowood.org
Location Off A4 in Derry Hill village between
Calne & Chippenham.

Opening hours 11 am - 6 pm; daily; April to October.
Admission fee Adults £7.50; OAPs £6.50; Children (under 15) £5; Children (2-4 yrs) £3.80. Separate charge of £4.80 for rhododendron walks, open from mid-April to early June (telephone for exact dates, which depend upon the flowering season).

🅿 🆆 ♿ ♣ ✕ ▷

Beautifully maintained and welcoming, Bowood has something from every period of English garden history. Capability Brown made the lake and planted many of the trees and lawns which give such a beautiful setting to the house. Charles Hamilton added the famous cascade below the lake in the picturesque style. There is an important 19th-century pinetum, laid out on pre-Linnaean principles – geographically – with oceans of grass to separate the continents. It is not just a collection of magnificent conifers, but contains many rare and beautiful deciduous trees, too, including the tallest specimen of the cut-leaved horse-chestnut (*Aesculus hippocastanum* 'Laciniata') in the British Isles. By the house are handsome Italianate formal gardens designed by Smirke and Kennedy in the 19th century and recently replanted by Lady Mary Keen. Up in the woods in a separate part of the estate, and entered directly from the A342, is a magnificent display of modern rhododendrons around the beautiful Robert Adam mausoleum. The ocean of bluebells which surrounds these rhododendron drives is one of the finest in the south of England. Be sure to miss the reclining nude above the formal gardens.

🌿 lake; 100-acre Capability Brown landscaped parkland; famous old arboretum; topiary; mature conifers; modern borders; rhododendrons, azaleas & bluebells (separate garden); tallest *Thuya occidentalis* 'Wareana' in the UK; gift shop; coffee shop; buffet lunches & afternoon teas in licensed restaurant.

Owned by The Marquis of Lansdowne
Number of gardeners 4
Size 80ha (200 acres) of grounds
English Heritage Grade I

BROADLEAS
Devizes SN10 5JQ

Tel: 01380 722035 **Fax:** 01380 722970
Location 1 mile south of Devizes.
Opening hours 2 pm - 6 pm; Wednesdays, Thursdays & Sundays; April to October.
Admission fee Adults £5; Children £1.50; Groups (10+) £4.50.

🅿 🍽 🆆 ♿ 🌱 ♣ ▷

Lady Anne Cowdray started to make this garden – now owned by a charitable trust – in 1947. Since then it has grown into a very fine plantsman's garden, with lots of different kinds of plants but an especially good collection of ornamental trees and shrubs. Broadleas has a rose garden, a grey border, a rock garden and a perennial garden, all near the Regency house. But the main attraction is the Dell, a greensand combe that stretches down to the valley below, its sides just stuffed with good things. At the top are two tall magnolias, M. *sargentiana* var. *robusta* and the very rare cultivar now known as 'Broadleas'. Pass between them, and past a very tall paulownia, and you come into a world of rare trees, a large yellow magnolia, sheets of unusual bulbs, trilliums, erythroniums and many others. And Broadleas has two characteristics common to all good plantsman's gardens: it is worth visiting at any time of the year and it gets better all the time. The nursery sells surplus plants propagated from the garden.

🌿 a plantsman's collection of plants; woodland garden; roses (ancient & modern); good herbaceous borders; fine ornamental trees; excellent small nursery for rare plants; teas for groups by arrangement.

Owned by Lady Anne Cowdray & Broadleas Gardens Charitable Trust
Number of gardeners 2½
Size 3.6ha (9 acres)
English Heritage Grade II

CONOCK MANOR
Devizes SN10 3QQ

Tel: 01380 840227
Location 5 miles south-east of Devizes off
A342.
Opening hours For NGS: 2 pm – 6 pm on 21 May.
And by appointment.
Admission fee Adults £2.50; Children free.
🅿 ♿ 🌾 🗗

Beautiful flat parkland surrounds this
covetable Georgian house. Behind the
copper-domed stables, an elegant shrub
walk meanders past *Sorbus*, maples and
magnolias. Some of the trees which have
been planted in recent years are already
making a good show. A recent addition is
a Persian garden – brickwork in stylised
script with water runnels and small
fountains.

cottages orneés; fine trees and mixed
borders; good *Sorbus* and *Eucalyptus*;
woodland walk; cream teas.

Owned by Mrs Bonar Sykes
Number of gardeners 1 part-time
Size 0.8ha (2 acres), plus parkland
English Heritage Grade II

CORSHAM COURT
Corsham SN13 0BZ

Tel & Fax: 01249 701610
www.corsham-court.co.uk
Location Signed from A4 Bath to Chippenham.
Opening hours 2 pm – 5 pm; Tuesday –
Thursday, plus Saturdays, Sundays & Bank
Holiday Mondays; 20 March to 30 September. 2
pm – 4.30 pm; Saturdays & Sundays; 1 January
to 19 March & October to December.
Admission fee Adults £2.50; OAPs £2; Children
£1.50. RHS members & wheelchair-users (plus
one helper) free.
🅿 ⬧ 🆆🅲 ♿

Corsham is a major 18th-century
landscape garden, one of the few where
both Capability Brown and Humphry
Repton worked. Then the flower garden

was developed in the middle of the 19th
century: box-edged borders and a pretty
fountain, all kept up with some good
modern planting. An 18-acre (7-ha)
arboretum was planted in the 1980s: there
are plans to landscape it and enlarge its
collections.

fine trees; designed by Capability
Brown and Humphry Repton; young
arboretum; magnolias; amazing oriental plane
Platanus orientalis whose sweeping limbs have
rooted over a huge area.

Owned by James Methuen-Campbell
Number of gardeners 4
English Heritage Grade II*

THE COURTS GARDEN
Holt, Bradford-on-Avon BA14 6RR

Tel: 01225 782340 **Fax:** 01225 782340
www.nationaltrust.org.uk
Location In middle of Holt village, 2½ miles
east of Bradford-on-Avon.
Opening hours 11 am – 5.30 pm; Thursday –
Tuesday; 25 March to 15 October.
Admission fee Adults £5; Children £2.50.
🅿 🆆🅲 ♿ 🌼

Holt Court (as it used to be called) is a
1920s masterpiece in the Hidcote style. It
has rich colour plantings in a series of
garden rooms and excellent plants,
beautifully used. The design is
asymmetrical, with both formal and
informal lines. The sunken garden has just
been restored.

plantsman's collection of plants; good
herbaceous borders; fine collection of
trees; tea-room.

Owned by The National Trust
Number of gardeners 2
Size 2.8ha (7 acres)
English Heritage Grade II

HEALE HOUSE GARDEN
Middle Woodford, Salisbury SP4 6NT

Tel: 01722 782504
Location Signed off the western Woodford valley road, & from A345 & A360.
Opening hours 10 am - 5 pm; daily; all year. Closed on Mondays, except Bank Holidays.
Admission fee Adults £4; OAPs £3.75; Children £1.50.

Many would agree that Heale is the prettiest garden in southern England. It sits at the bottom of a broad, chalk valley, with the River Avon and its leats flowing through. The house is Carolean, with substantial additions so sympathetically designed by Detmar Blow that it is difficult to know which parts belong to the original house. Harold Peto laid out the garden: you see his handiwork in the formal gardens which run up towards the south along an avenue of *Robinia pseudoacacia* 'Umbraculifera' (recent replacements for the original laburnums). There are formal pools, terraces, balustrades and Italianate garden architecture on the way. Alongside the river are more balustrading, old rambling roses and a lawn which is richly planted with hybrid musk roses and herbaceous plants. On an island in the river is a Japanese garden, laid out in 1901 and much altered by the sheer growth of the original Japanese maples: however, the scarlet lacquered bridge and the neat tea-house seem almost new. Perhaps the best part of the garden is the old kitchen garden, surrounded by cob walls and designed around 100-year-old box balls and tunnels of trained apples and pears. Here, over 30 years from the mid-1960s onwards, Lady Anne Rasch developed a wonderful series of mixed borders, exuberantly planted with roses, clematis and herbaceous plants which is one of the best examples of the genre in England. But the garden and its excellent nursery are open all through the year, and there is always something to see, including swarms of cyclamen in autumn, and woodlands full of snowdrops and aconites in winter.

roses (mainly old-fashioned); good herbaceous borders; Japanese garden; good plant associations; first HHA/Christie's Garden of the Year in 1984; plant centre; garden & gift shop; coffee shop, with teas & light lunches.

Owned by Mr & Mrs Guy Rasch
Number of gardeners 2, plus owners
Size 3.2ha (8 acres)
English Heritage Grade II*

HOME COVERT GARDEN & ARBORETUM
Roundway, Devizes SN10 2JA

Tel: 01380 723407
Location 1 mile north of Devizes in Roundway village.
Opening hours For NGS. And groups welcome at any time by appointment,
Admission fee Adults £3; Children free.

Home Covert is one of the most influential and largest plantsman's gardens in England. The knowledge and taste of the owners – together with their generosity towards visitors – have made it a cult garden among *cognoscenti* and learner-gardeners alike. The Phillips describe it as 'a botanical mad-house': it would be truer to call it a horticultural treasure-house. Every type of plant is grown but, above all, rare trees: *Cercis racemosa*, for example, and hundreds of plants – perhaps thousands – grown from seeds collected by such friends as Roy Lancaster, Martyn Rix and Maurice Foster. An older generation of plantsmen is also commemorated here – Maurice Mason, Norman Haddon and Margery Fish, for example. Home Covert is a large garden, informally laid out within natural oak woodland, and it needs a long time to see round. Down in the bog garden are collections of willows and alders, naturalised *Lathraea clandestina* and swathes of candelabra primulas. Near the house is an enormous lawn, completely free of weeds, with a view for miles down the Avon valley. Raised beds, a rock garden, shade borders, protected beds for tender plants, swarms of erythroniums, fat clumps of lilies, old-fashioned roses and wild species – there seems no end to the number and variety of what is grown here. woodland garden; plantsman's plants of every kind.

Owned by Mr & Mrs John Phillips
Number of gardeners owners only, plus part-time help
Size 13ha (33 acres)

IFORD MANOR
Bradford-on-Avon BA15 2BA

Tel: 01225 863146 **Fax:** 01225 852364
www.ifordmanor.co.uk
Location 7 miles south-east of Bath, signed from A36 & Bradford-on-Avon.
Opening hours 2 pm - 5 pm; Sundays & Easter Monday; April & October. Plus Tuesday – Thursday, Saturdays, Sundays & Bank Holiday Mondays from May to September.
Admission fee Adults £4.50; OAPs & Children (over 10) £4. Children under 10 free, but weekdays preferred for safety reasons.

Harold Peto's own Italianate garden on a steep wooded hillside is meticulously maintained and a delight to visit. Peto was a fashionable architect with a passion for classical Italian architecture and landscaping. When he returned from working in France and Italy, he bought Iford to house his collections of statues and architectural marbles. He planted phillyreas, Italian cypresses and other Mediterranean species and laid out the garden as a series of formal terraces on the steep hillside behind the house. The architectural highlights include a Romanesque cloister, an octagonal gazebo, and a gloriously colonnaded terrace. Every detail is wonderfully photogenic, especially when contrasted with wisterias, roses or well-chosen acanthus. The woodland garden is worth exploring (it hides a recently restored Japanese garden) and there is much of horticultural interest, too, at Iford, notably a meadow of naturalised martagon lilies.

Harold Peto's own garden; opulent Edwardian design; Italian cypresses and handsome *Phillyrea*; martagon lilies; cyclamen; roses; teas on Bank Holidays and weekends from May to August.

Owned by Mrs E. Cartwright-Hignett
Number of gardeners 2
Size 0.6ha (1½ acres), plus 5ha (12 acres) of woodland
English Heritage Grade I

LACKHAM COUNTRY PARK
Lacock, Chippenham SN15 2NY

Tel: 01249 466800 **Fax:** 01249 444474
Location 3 miles south of Chippenham on A350.
Opening hours 10 am - 5 pm; 18 & 19 March; 16 & 17 April; 4, 11 & 18 June; 23 July; 13, 27 & 28 August; 17 September; 8 October.
Admission fee Adults £2; Concessions £1.50; Children free. More for some events.

Lackham is among the best of the old county college gardens. Its response to the usual shortfall in funding has been to establish a Museum of Agriculture, which now also shelters the historic teaching garden. Its open days cater for every interest, from the 'lambing weekend' on 18 and 19 March to the NGS day on 23 July which is entitled 'woodwork in action'. The gardens are open during all these events and featured in the 13-part TV gardening programme *Gardeners To Be*. The heart of Lackham is its walled garden of flowers, ornamentals, herbs, fruit and vegetables, beautifully laid out to educate and delight. In one of the glasshouses is the champion plant of *Citrus medica* which grew the largest citron (over 10lbs) ever seen in Britain (according to the *Guinness Book of Records*). The grounds are good for an exploration, too, especially in bluebell time: there has been a lot of attractive companion planting for the National Collection of poplars.

plantsman's collection of plants; herbs; fruit & vegetables; plants under glass; daffodils; good herbaceous borders; fine collection of trees; alpine plants; bluebells; roses of every kind; sensory garden; laurel maze; woodland walk; souvenirs for sale; refreshments.

Owned by Wiltshire College Lackham
Number of gardeners 4, plus students
Size 8ha (20 acres)
NCCPG National Collections *Populus*

LACOCK ABBEY
Lacock, Chippenham SN15 2LG

Tel: 01249 730459 **Fax:** 01249 730501
www.nationaltrust.org.uk
Location 3 miles south of Chippenham, just east of A350.
Opening hours 11 am - 5.30 pm; daily; 25 February to 29 October. Closed on Good Friday.
Admission fee Adults £4.80; Children £2.40.

The National Trust has recently laid out a 'botanic garden' in the style of an earlier one planted by Lacock's most famous past owner, William Fox Talbot, the 'inventor' of photography. It was he who planted many of the mature trees in the park, including the London plane (*Platanus* x *hispanica*), swamp cypress (*Taxodium distichum*) and walnut (*Juglans nigra*). Part of the *Harry Potter* series was filmed at Lacock.

snowdrops; crocuses; parkland.

Owned by The National Trust
Number of gardeners 1, plus 1 part-time
Size 3.4ha (8½ acres)

LANDFORD TREES
Landford Lodge, Landford, Salisbury SP5 2EH

Tel: 01794 390808 **Fax:** 01794 390037
www.landfordtrees.co.uk
Location By junction of A36 & B3079.
Opening hours By appointment for groups at weekends. Visitors to nursery & tree collection at all times.
Admission fee Free.

This is an excellent tree nursery, with over 700 lines on sale. These include 40 different acers, 20 birches, 15 crataegus, 10 beech, 70 *Malus*, 40 *Prunus*, 50 *Sorbus* and 30 different pines. There will be a RHS Special Event at Landford Trees on 11 May 2006; details from 020 7821 3408.

well-known tree nursery.

Owned by Christopher Pilkington
Size 12ha (30 acres)

LARMER TREE GARDENS
Tollard Royal, Salisbury SP5 5PT

Tel: 01725 516228 **Fax:** 01725 516449
www.larmertreegardens.co.uk
Location Follow brown tourist signs from A354 or B3081.
Opening hours Not available as we went to press. In 2005: 11 am - 5 pm; Sunday - Thursday; April to September.
Admission fee Adults £3.75; OAPs £3; Children £2.50. (2005 prices.)

The Larmer Tree Gardens were laid out by General Augustus Pitt-Rivers as a public amenity. He put up a series of eccentric garden buildings around a spacious lawn of perhaps two acres: they include the Singing Theatre, the Indian Room, the Roman Temple and the Lower Indian Building in the Nepalese style, brought here in 1880 after the Colonial Exhibition in London. In the 1880s and 1890s, trainloads of East-enders were brought there by the philanthropic owner for a jolly cultural day in the country. His descendants have entirely restored the gardens since about 1990 and added some modern horticultural features. The best of these is a series of artificial pools in an artificial dell, surrounded by multi-coloured hydrangeas. All is set in light oak woodland with splendid thickets of cherry laurel. It is not a garden of the highest horticultural interest, though there are some venerable eucryphias, crinodendrons and stewartias. It is, however, spaciously laid out and very enjoyable to visit.

hydrangeas; woodland gardens; remarkable series of follies; tea-room on Sundays in season.

Owned by W. Gronow-Davies & Trustees
Number of gardeners 2
Size 4.4ha (11 acres)
English Heritage Grade II

LONGLEAT HOUSE
Warminster BA12 7NW

Tel: 01985 844400 **Fax:** 01985 844885
www.longleat.co.uk
Location Off A362 Warminster to Frome road.
Opening hours 10 am - 5.30 pm; daily; 1 April to 5 November.
Admission fee Grounds & gardens: Adults £3; OAPs & Children £2.

Longleat has a classic 18th-century landscape by Capability Brown, a home park of 900 acres best seen from Heaven's Gate and a grand Victorian garden reworked by Russell Page in the 1930s. Capability Brown's landscape has been carefully managed and replanted over many years, so that it keeps its intended form. The Victorian garden between the house and the elegant conservatory built by Wyatville in the 1820s is now a very beautiful rose garden. The plantings of ornamental trees and rhododendron

woodlands have been thickened and updated with many new introductions. In short, Lord Bath (like his father before him) has conserved the best of Longleat and reinvigorated the rest. Worth another visit.

woodland garden; topiary; rhododendrons & azaleas; fine collection of trees; orangery; rose garden planted as a 'love labyrinth'; sun maze & lunar labyrinth; shops; cafeterias & restaurants.

Owned by 7th Marquess of Bath
Number of gardeners 8
Size 8-ha (20-acre) garden; 200-ha (494-acre) park
English Heritage Grade I

THE MEAD NURSERY
Brokerswood, Westbury BA13 4EG

Tel: 01373 859990
www.themeadnursery.co.uk
Location Off A36 or A361, between Rudge & Brokerswood Country Park.
Opening hours 9 am - 5 pm, Wednesday - Saturday & Bank Holiday Mondays; 12 noon - 5 pm, Sundays, 1 February to 10 October. For NGS: 12 noon - 5 pm on 20 August.
Admission fee £2.50 (tea & cake included) on 20 August. Otherwise free.

The Mead Nursery specialises in alpine plants (including varieties suitable for trough plantings), pot-grown bulbs and herbaceous perennials. All plants are grown in peat-free compost. The display garden is excellent: raised alpine beds, a sink garden, a bog bed, a small wildlife pond, a Mediterranean raised bed, and herbaceous borders planted with colour combinations in mind.

perennials; alpines; bulbs; all plants grown on-site; pretty demonstration garden.

Owned by Stephen & Emma Lewis-Dale
Size 0.3ha (¾ acre)

OLD VICARAGE
Edington, Westbury BA13 4QF

Tel: 01380 830512
Location On B3098 in Edington village.
Opening hours 2 pm – 6 pm; 11 June. And by appointment.
Admission fee Adults £5; Children free.

John d'Arcy bought the Old Vicarage in 1982: it is now one of the best examples of a plantsman's garden in southern England. The site offers a surprising range of mini-habitats, and d'Arcy took advantage of their potential to grow the widest possible number of plants. The features now include a sunken garden, a shady pergola, an avenue of fastigiate hornbeams *Carpinus betulus* 'Fastigiata', a gravel garden where *Morina afghanica* and *Ptilostemon afer* seed around, hot walls, raised beds, peat beds and shady beds – all blended with the rest of the garden so that no feature dominates any part of it. D'Arcy's great skill is as a cultivator: the fact that there is so much colour and interest at every time of the year proves that good plantsmanship can produce effects to challenge the most carefully designed and planted of gardens. Trees are underplanted with shrubs, which are underscored in turn by herbaceous plants and bulbs, several different plants being placed together to give a succession of interest throughout the year. D'Arcy's special interests include mahonias, cyclamen, nerines and hollies. He is also well known as a plant collector. *Corydalis flexuosa* came from Sichuan in 1989; several new species of *Dierama* came from South Africa, together with such new species of *Geranium* as *G. harveyi* and *G. pulchrum*. All are still here, together with the living holotype of *Salvia darcyi*.
plantsman's plants – a collector's collection; herbaceous borders; alpine plants; shade plants; gravel garden; small arboretum.

Owned by John d'Arcy
Number of gardeners 1
Size 1ha (2½ acres)
NCCPG National Collections *Oenothera*

SHARCOTT MANOR
Pewsey SN9 5PA

Tel: 01672 563485
Location Off A345, one mile south-west of Pewsey.
Opening hours 11 am – 5 pm; first Wednesday of every month; April to October. Plus two Sundays for NGS. And by appointment.
Admission fee Adults £3; Children free. All for NGS.

This extensive modern garden has been quite transformed over the last 25 years into a densely planted plantsman's paradise. There is much to see as you move gently between the garden rooms near the house and out into the spacious lawns and woodland garden. There are harmonies and contrasts to please the most colour-conscious, while the dark shady lake at the bottom is a haven of romantic broodiness. New (in 2003) is an avenue of *Pyrus calleryana* 'Chanticleer'. Sharcott is an excellent garden which deserves to be better known.
plantsman's collection of plants; good herbaceous borders; woodland and stream gardens; good plant sales area, all propagated from garden; home-made teas.

Owned by Captain & Mrs David Armytage
Number of gardeners 2 part-time
Size 2.4ha (6 acres)

SHUTE HOUSE
Donhead St Mary, Shaftesbury SP7 9DG

Tel: 01935 814389 **Fax:** 01935 815535
Location In village, near church.
Opening hours By appointment, for groups of 20+. Must be 10 am – 12 noon or 2 pm – 4 pm.

Admission fee Adults £3.50.

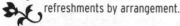

Geoffrey Jellicoe's favourite garden – and his masterpiece – is open to groups by special arrangement. The most famous feature is the stream garden, where water runs straight down the hillside, over copper steps and circular pools. But it is all a place of rare enchantment.

refreshments by arrangement.

Owned by Mr & Mrs John Lewis
Number of gardeners 1, plus 2 part-time
Size 2.8ha (7 acres)

STOURHEAD
Stourton BA12 6QD

Tel: 01747 841152 **Fax:** 01747 842006
www.nationaltrust.org.uk
Location 3 miles north-west of Mere, signed off A303/B3092.
Opening hours 9 am – 7 pm (or dusk, if earlier); daily; all year.
Admission fee Adults £6.20; Children £3.60.

Whatever the weather or season, Stourhead conveys a sense of majesty and harmony. Try it early on a May morning, when the air is sweet with azaleas. Or scuff the fallen leaves in late November. Think of it 200 years ago, without the rhododendrons or exotic trees, when all the beech trees were interplanted with spruces and the colours came all from shades of green. Ponder the 18th-century aesthetic, which esteemed tones and shades more highly than colours, and follow the iconographic tour inspired (they say) by Virgil. Spot the change from Classical to Gothic, from Pope to Walpole, and wonder at the National Trust's ability to maintain it so well with only six gardeners.

snowdrops; rhododendrons & azaleas; mature conifers; fine collection of trees; good autumn colour; tallest tulip tree *Liriodendron tulipifera* (37m) in the British Isles, and seven other record tree species; shop & plant centre; restaurant.

Owned by The National Trust
Number of gardeners 6, plus 2 students
Size 40ha (100 acres)
English Heritage Grade I

WESTDALE NURSERIES
Holt Road, Bradford on Avon BA15 1TS

Tel & Fax: 01225 863258
www.westdalenurseries.co.uk
Location 1 mile east of Bradford town centre; left-hand side.
Opening hours 9 am – 6 pm (10 am – 5 pm from October to March, and 10 am – 4 pm on Sundays); daily; all year, except Christmas.

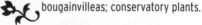

Westdale has made quite an impact at RHS flower shows in recent years with its wonderful displays of bougainvilleas. It lists over 200 different cultivars, which are available in different sizes. All can be seen growing in their extensive glasshouses outside Bradford-on-Avon. But their range of other conservatory plants is very wide, and they are enthusiastic plantsmen, willing to try any plant which may have value as an ornament to the conservatory or greenhouse. Well worth a visit.

bougainvilleas; conservatory plants.

Owned by C.W. & P.A. Clarke
Number of gardeners 3
Size 0.4ha (1 acre) of glass

WILTON HOUSE
Wilton, Salisbury SP2 0BJ

Tel: 01722 746720 **Fax:** 01722 744447
www.wiltonhouse.com
Location In village, 3 miles west of Salisbury by
A36.
Opening hours 10.30 am – 5.30 pm; daily; 9
April to 30 September.
Admission fee Adults £4.50; Children £3.50.

P WC 🚻 ✕ ☕

Wilton has a sublime 18th-century park
around its classical Inigo Jones house, which
is famous for its paintings. It is this
stupendous parkland setting above the River
Nadder which is the chief delight of visiting
the gardens at Wilton. There are
comparatively few horticultural excitements,
though the house has pleasant mixed borders
along one of its sides and a stylish modern
garden, rather formal, in the entrance court
designed by Lady Tollemache. On the edge
of the park are a pretty new garden of old-
fashioned roses and an oriental water garden:
opinions are divided as to the merits of the
new millennium water feature.

🌿 roses; handsome cedars; famous
Palladian bridge; magnificent golden-
leaved oak; self-service restaurant.

Owned by Earl of Pembroke/Wilton House Trust
Number of gardeners 4
Size 8.3ha (21 acres)
English Heritage Grade I

WORCESTERSHIRE

Worcestershire has been reconstituted not as a county (which it was until 1974) but as a District Council. But such is its feeling of distinct identity that we have treated it in this book as a legal county again: the same applies to Herefordshire, to which it was yoked for 25 years. Worcestershire has a lot going for it: a flourishing National Gardens Scheme, the site of the only dedicated horticultural college in England at Pershore (a RHS Partner College), the headquarters of the Alpine Garden Society, 11 National Collection holders, and two of the most popular gardening shows in the country – the Spring Gardening Show (12-14 May 2006) and the Autumn Garden & Country Show (23-24 September 2006), both at the Three Counties Showground at Malvern. Worcestershire also has some excellent specialist nurseries, including Cotswold Garden Flowers, Old Court Nurseries and Stone House Cottage Garden. Though few of its historic parks and gardens are open to the public, they include that great plantsman's garden Spetchley Park (substantially re-made by a great-nephew of Miss Ellen Willmott) and Witley Court (now undergoing extensive renovation by English Heritage).

ARLEY ARBORETUM
Arley, Bewdley DY12 1XG

Tel: 01299 861368 **Fax:** 01299 861330
www.arley-arboretum.org.uk
Location Follow brown tourist signs from A442.
Opening hours 11 am - 5 pm; Wednesday – Sunday & Bank Holiday Mondays; 15 March to 5 November.
Admission fee Adults £4; Children £1. RHS members free.

This beautiful arboretum opened to the public in 2002. It was first planted in the 1820s (very early for arboreta) and has been continuously expanded and replanted since. There are very fine Crimean pines *Pinus nigra* var. *caramanica*, one of which is the tallest in the United Kingdom. In all there are over 300 different taxa. Within the arboretum is a walled garden with a formal Italian garden and fine herbaceous borders – quite a contrast to the awesome trees outside.

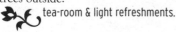 tea-room & light refreshments.

Owned by R.D. Turner Charitable Trust

Number of gardeners 4
Size 14ha (35 acres)

BODENHAM ARBORETUM
Wolverley, Kidderminster DY11 5SY

Tel: 01562 852444 **Fax:** 01562 852777
www.bodenham-arboretum.co.uk
Location B4189 or B4190 to Wolverley village and follow brown tourist signs.
Opening hours 11 am - 5 pm or dusk; Wednesday – Sunday & Bank Holiday Mondays; all year. Daily in October. Weekends only in January & February.
Admission fee Adults £5; Children £2.

Bodenham Arboretum has more than 2,700 different trees and shrubs in a total of 156 acres, containing eleven pools and four miles of footpaths. In May and early June, the rhododendrons, azaleas and laburnum tunnel are spectacular but, like all arboreta, there is much to enjoy in all seasons.

light refreshments & lunches.

Size 62ha (156 acres)

COTSWOLD GARDEN FLOWERS
Sands Lane, Badsey, Evesham WR11 5EZ

Tel: 01386 422829 **Fax:** 01386 49844
www.cgf.net
Location On south-east edge of village (last left turning off Sands Lane)
Opening hours 9 am – 5.30 pm; Monday – Friday. 10 am – 5.30 pm; Saturday – Sunday. Closed at weekends from mid-October to March. Other times by appointment.
Admission fee Free.

P ◁ WC ❀

Don't be put off by the bumpy driveway – the nursery is right at the end of Sands Lane. Cotswold Garden Flowers is a treasure-house of rare plants: over 8,000 different cultivars are grown in the display garden. Actually the garden is no more than the nursery's stock beds, but quite spectacular, because the owner has a knack for seeking out and introducing plants which are highly 'garden-worthy'. The catalogue is both amusing and informative, but it is nothing compared to the joy of visiting the nursery and having the opportunity to see so many well-grown, new and interesting plants.
Owned by Bob Brown
Size 0.4ha (1 acre)
NCCPG National Collections *Lysimachia*

EASTGROVE COTTAGE GARDEN
Sankyns Green, Shrawley, Little Witley, Worcester WR6 6LQ

Tel: 01299 896389
www.eastgrove.co.uk
Location On road between Great Witley (on A443) & Shrawley (on B4196).
Opening hours 2 pm – 5 pm; Thursday – Saturday & Bank Holiday Mondays in April & May; 13 April to 29 July & 7 September to 14 October.
Admission fee Adults £3.50 (£4 May – July); Children free; RHS members free.

P WC ♿ ❀

Eastgrove is a very attractive, 17th-century, half-timbered, black-and-white cottage in a beautiful country setting. It has an equally pretty cottage garden that has been entirely made by the Skinners since they bought the near-derelict property in 1970. The scale is small, but the quality and variety of the plantings are stunning. There is a developing collection of trees, a raised bed (known as the 'Great Wall of China') and, above all, thickly planted herbaceous plants. The design and planting of the borders is carefully thought through, with curving borders and several enclosed rooms. The 'secret garden' concentrates on mauves, pinks, silvers and crimsons. Although perhaps best in high summer, the garden is good enough to visit at any season, and beautifully maintained. Beyond the garden is a two-acre field planted with trees in 2004, complete with a ride and a grass labyrinth. The nursery propagates only plants from the garden and has a list of over 1,000 different varieties. Specialities include aquilegias, hardy chrysanthemums, dianthus, heleniums, irises, peonies, rosemary, salvias and violas.

🌿 cottage garden; rose arches; plantsman's plants; herbaceous borders; wall plantings; pots & containers; attached to a good small nursery.

Owned by Malcolm & Carol Skinner
Number of gardeners owners only
Size 0.6ha (1½ acres)

OVERBURY COURT
Tewkesbury GL20 7NP

Tel: 01386 725111 **Fax:** 01386 725678
Location 5 miles north-east of Tewkesbury.
Opening hours By appointment.
Admission fee Adults £2.50. Minimum charge for groups £15.

P ◁ ♿

A peaceful and expansive garden laid out around the large, handsome, Georgian house, with a view of the Parish church

worked in. Aubrey Waterfield, Geoffrey Jellicoe, Russell Page, Peter Coates and James Alexander Sinclair all worked on the design and planting. Their work is not always distinguishable, because the result is a garden of exceptional harmony.

 topiary; landscaped park; daffodils.

Owned by Mr & Mrs Bruce Bossom
Number of gardeners 2

PERSHORE COLLEGE
Pershore WR10 3JP

Tel: 01386 554609 **Fax:** 01386 556528
www.pershore.ac.uk
Location On B4084 (formerly A44).
Opening hours 10 am – 4.30 pm; daily; all year. AGS garden closed at weekends.
Admission fee Free.

Pershore College specialises in horticultural education. Within its grounds are a 15-ha (37-acre) fruit and vegetable production unit, an 8-ha (20-acre) nursery stock and specialist plant unit, and a plant centre. The garden centre sells a selection of college-grown trees and shrubs including plants from the National Collection of penstemons, alpines, herbaceous plants, climbers, roses, house plants and fruit trees and bushes in season. It is open daily from 9 am – 5 pm (10.30 pm – 4.30 pm on Sundays; 4 pm in winter). The college also has show gardens designed and maintained by the Hardy Plant Society and the Alpine Garden Society. Both are full of interesting plants and ideas for design and cultivation. The RHS Centre at Pershore was established in 1989 to offer a variety of courses, lectures and workshops on all aspects of horticulture for both members and non-members in the Central Region. There is a long list of RHS Special Events at Pershore in 2006.
Size 54ha (135 acres)
NCCPG National Collections *Penstemon, Philadelphus*

SPETCHLEY PARK
Worcester WR5 1RS

Tel: 01453 810303 **Fax:** 01453 511915
www.spetchleygardens.co.uk
Location 3 miles east of Worcester on A44.
Opening hours 11 am – 6 pm; Wednesday – Sunday & Bank Holiday Mondays; 21 March to 30 September. Plus 11 am – 4 pm at weekends in October. Last admissions one hour before closing.
Admission fee Adults £5; Children £2.

In a classic English landscaped park, three generations of Berkeleys have created one of the best plantsman's gardens in the Midlands. Ellen Willmott was the owner's great-aunt and many of the most exciting trees and shrubs date from her time – a gnarled specimen of the laciniate walnut (*Juglans nigra* 'Laciniata'), for example. In the Fountain Gardens, *Tulipa sprengeri* has seeded and naturalised over a large area. Other spring flowers include peonies, columbines and masses of bulbs. In summer, there are hundreds of different roses – old-fashioned roses, tea roses, David Austin roses, floribunda roses – every type of rose is here. Martagon lilies have naturalised in large quantities. The conservatory is crammed with unusual plants. The planting continues: everywhere in the garden are new designs, new plants and new combinations. A whole new garden has been planted to commemorate the millennium, with tunnels of *Cercis canadensis* 'Forest Pansy' and *Robinia hispida* 'Macrophylla'. Because of its scale and variety, this garden offers something to everyone, but most especially to the plantsman.

many good plants of every kind for plantsmen; roses (ancient & modern); rhododendrons & azaleas; daffodils; good herbaceous borders; fine trees; deer park; good new plantings in the kitchen garden; naturalised lilies; teas & refreshments.

Owned by R.J. Berkeley

Number of gardeners 4
Size 12ha (30 acres)
English Heritage Grade II*

STONE HOUSE COTTAGE GARDEN
Stone, Kidderminster DY10 4BG

Tel: 01562 69902
www.shcn.co.uk
Location In village, 2 miles from Kidderminster on A448.
Opening hours 10 am – 5 pm; Wednesday – Saturday; March to mid-September. And by appointment between mid-September & March.
Admission fee Adults £3; Children free. RHS members free.
🅿 ⏻ 🆆🅲 ♿ ❦ 🏛

This is the garden of a famous nursery, which it matches for the range of beautiful and unusual plants it offers. The owners are compulsive plantsmen and, as the garden is small, they have to move plants around or replace them altogether to make room for new arrivals. This means that the garden is constantly developing and improving – especially since much thought is given to the way each plant will associate with its neighbours. Around the walls is an eccentric collection of follies built as towers, which makes this garden quite unique.
 plantsman's plants; herbs; good herbaceous borders; alpine plants; unusual climbing plants; roses (mainly old-fashioned & climbers); excellent nursery attached.

Owned by James & Louisa Arbuthnott
Number of gardeners 1
Size 0.3ha (¾ acre)

THE WALLED GARDEN
6 Rose Terrace, Worcester WR5 1BU

Tel & Fax: 01905 354629
Location Off Fort Royal Hill (which is off A44); ½ mile from Cathedral.

Opening hours 1 pm – 5 pm; 15 April, 6 & 20 May, 10 & 24 June & 8 July.
Admission fee Adults £2; Children 50p.
🆆🅲 ❦

This all-organic private garden has an integrated mixture of flowers, fruits and herbs. The owners have reclaimed the walled garden, dating from Victorian times, and planted a series of areas for studying and demonstrating organic gardening techniques and the uses of herbs.
herb gardens.

Owned by William & Julia Scott
Number of gardeners owners only
Size 0.3ha (¼ acre)

WEBBS OF WYCHBOLD
Wychbold, Droitwich Spa WR9 0DG

Tel: 01527 860000 **Fax:** 01527 861284
www.webbsofwychbold.co.uk
Location 1 mile from M5, Jct 5: follow brown tourist signs.
Opening hours 9 am – 6 pm; Monday – Friday (8 pm from spring to Christmas). 9 am – 6 pm; Saturdays & Bank Holidays. 10.30 am – 4.30 pm; Sundays. Closed Easter Sunday, 25 & 26 December.
Admission fee Free.
🅿 🆆🅲 ♿ 🏛 ✕ ⎇

Webbs are a major garden centre, a regional heavyweight with several trade awards for excellence. They have an extremely large stock of plants of every kind, as well as a range of in-house retail opportunities of interest to gardeners and non-gardeners alike. They have a reputation as plant introducers, too: *Diascia fetcaniensis* 'Daydream' and *Dianthus* 'Tickled Pink' are two of their plant introductions. Their Riverside display gardens (over 2 acres of them) include a National Collection of *Potentilla fruticosa* cultivars, colour spectrum and white gardens, plantings for dry, sunny and damp, shady conditions, and displays of grasses and bamboos. The adjacent New Wave Gardens, designed in conjunction with Noel Kingsbury, mix perennial shrubs and grasses in a series of different naturalistic styles. They also contain trial beds of mixed annuals from Suttons, a bog garden and an extensive planting of perennial salvias which Webbs are assessing for winter hardiness.

model gardens; award-winning garden centre; gift shop; restaurant.

Size 10ha (25 acres)
NCCPG National Collections *Potentilla fruticosa* cvs.

WITLEY COURT
Great Witley WR6 7JT

Tel & Fax: 01299 896636
www.english-heritage.org.uk
Location 10 miles north-west of Worcester on A443.
Opening hours 10 am – 5 pm (6 pm from June to August); daily; March to October. 10 am – 4 pm; Thursday – Monday; November to February. Closed 1 January, 25 & 26 December.
Admission fee Adults £5.20; Concessions £3.90; Children £2.60.

The gardens at Witley Court have undergone extensive restoration and are increasingly in good condition. You enter through rhododendron woods, planted mainly with hardy hybrids under a canopy of American conifers. More interesting, though, is the spectacular ruined mansion and the immense formal gardens behind. They are one of William Andrews Nesfield's masterpieces, built on a monumental scale by the 1st Earl of Dudley: English Heritage has restored the gardens and the famous Perseus and Andromeda fountain. The sheer size of the roofless conservatory and the fountains is remarkable: a place to fantasise about life among the plutocrats 100 years ago. The fountains start running from about Easter onwards – usually at noon, 2 pm and 4 pm on weekdays, but hourly (on the hour) from 11 am to 4 pm at weekends.

Victorian formal garden; rhododendron woodlands; sculpture.

Owned by English Heritage
Number of gardeners 2
Size 16ha (40 acres)
English Heritage Grade II*

YORKSHIRE, EAST RIDING OF

Since the demise of much-disliked Humberside, the East Riding has been reconstituted as an administrative area. Many of Yorkshire's gardening institutions are organised on an all-Yorkshire basis: thus, for example, the Yorkshire Gardens Trust and the Yorkshire Group of the NCCPG are county-wide societies. Sledmere House is the outstanding historic garden in East Yorkshire, though Burton Constable is also well known for its Capability Brown landscape garden. There are comparatively few good modern gardens in East Yorkshire, apart from the charming water gardens at Burnby, where a National Collection of water lilies (*Nymphaea*) is displayed in a beautifully landscaped site. There are four further National Collections in East Yorkshire, including a collection of *Crataegus laevigata* and *C. monogyna* cultivars at the University of Hull's garden at Cottingham – a botanic garden that has lost the botany department that was once the reason for its existence. There is a sprinkling of gardens that open for the National Gardens Scheme in East Yorkshire, which has its own county organiser. There are few nurseries of national repute: one that is not listed below is Swanland Nurseries, which has a good collection of *Pelargonium* cultivars – over 800 of them. Burnby Hall and Burton Agnes offer free entry to RHS members – both very enjoyable gardens to visit – and the garden at Bishop Burton College is a stunner.

BISHOP BURTON BOTANIC GARDEN

Bishop Burton College, Beverley
HU17 8QG

Tel: 01964 553000 **Fax:** 01964 553101
Location In Bishop Burton: entrance to west of village green.
Opening hours 9 am – 5 pm; Monday – Friday; all year.
Admission fee Free.

🅿 🚻 ♿ 🌼 ♿

Bishop Burton is a college where horticulture is taught, so this is not so much a botanic garden as a demonstration garden to teach students about plants – and a very good one, too. There are areas for fruit, vegetables and herbs, fine herbaceous borders supplemented by annuals and bedding, hot-colour borders, a heather collection, dwarf conifers, trees, shrubs, ponds and show gardens, some of them designed by students. The glasshouses include a cactus house and tropical house. Outside, in the park, is a 19th-century landscape with good wellingtonias, cedars and a cucumber tree (*Magnolia acuminata*).

🌿 good collection of plants; fine trees in park; *Gardening Which?* Garden Trials; café open in term-time.

Owned by Bishop Burton College
Number of gardeners 4, plus students
Size 0.8-ha (2-acre) walled garden, plus park

BURNBY HALL GARDENS
Pocklington YO42 2QF

Tel: 01759 307125 **Fax:** 01377 288359
www.burnbyhallgardens.com
Location Off A1079, 13 miles east of York.
Opening hours 10 am – 6 pm; daily; 25 March to
1 October.
Admission fee Adults £3.50; OAPs £2.75;
Children £1.60. RHS members free from April to
June.

Burnby Hall is famed for its water lilies, planted by Amos Perry in the 1930s and now totalling over 100 different cultivars. They are grown in two long, landscaped lakes. But there is much more to Burnby: a large, walled Victorian garden, a rock garden, a woodland walk, heather beds, a 'secret garden', seasonal bedding and a good collection of conifers all contribute to its visitor-friendly air. Follow the tarmac path around the lakes: Burnby is a grand place for a promenade, especially when a brass band is playing on Sunday afternoons in summer.

water lilies; rock garden; mature conifers; plants for sale; café; gift shop.

Owned by Stewarts Trust
Number of gardeners 3
Size 3.2ha (8 acres)
NCCPG National Collections *Nymphaea*

BURTON AGNES HALL GARDENS
Burton Agnes, Driffield YO25 0ND

Tel: 01262 490324 **Fax:** 01262 490513
www.burton-agnes.com
Location On A166 Driffield to Bridlington road.
Opening hours 11 am – 5 pm; daily; April to
October.
Admission fee Adults £2.75; OAPs £2.50;
Children £1.30. RHS members free. House extra.

The old walled garden has been redesigned in a neo-Elizabethan style (to complement the nearby house) and cut up into numerous, thickly planted gardens with narrow paths and changes of level. As well as a *potager* and herb garden it has such unconventional features as life-size games boards for chess, draughts and snakes-and-ladders, a jungle garden and a maze with a riddle. Rather more conventional are the colour-schemed gardens and sumptuous plantings of shrub roses, clematis and herbaceous plants. There are also some enjoyable horticultural surprises, including cordylines and *Echium pininana* growing outside, and lots of furcraeas put out in pots for the summer.

good modern plantings; inventive design; café & ice-cream parlour.

Owned by Burton Agnes Hall Preservation Trust
Ltd
Number of gardeners 3½
NCCPG National Collections *Campanula*

BURTON CONSTABLE
Skirlaugh, Hull HU11 4LN

Tel: 01964 562400 **Fax:** 01964 563229
www.burtonconstable.com
Location Via Hull, A165 Bridlington road, then
B1238 to Sproatley – follow brown tourist signs.
Opening hours 12.30 pm – 5 pm (last admission
4 pm); Saturday – Thursday; Easter Saturday to
31 October.
Admission fee Grounds only: Adults £1.50;
Children 75p.

The main feature around the massive house is a Capability Brown landscape: his original plans are still shown. However, the foundation has recently received Heritage Lottery Funding for a major restoration of the gardens, including the four acres of 19th-century pleasure grounds, so this is a garden to watch in future.

woodland garden; fine 18th-century orangery; Victorian parterre; shop; light snacks.

Owned by Burton Constable Foundation
Number of gardeners 3
English Heritage Grade II

SLEDMERE HOUSE
Sledmere, Driffield YO25 3XG

Tel: 01377 236637 **Fax:** 01377 236500
www.sledmerehouse.com
Location Off A166 between York & Bridlington.
Opening hours 10 am – 5 pm; daily, except
Mondays, Tuesdays & Saturdays; Easter weekend,
then from 29 April to 17 September.
Admission fee Adults £3; Children £1.

P ◁» WC ₺ ❀ ♣ ☕

Sledmere has a classical Capability Brown
landscape: his original plans can be seen in
the museum. An Italianate formal garden
was added in 1911, with Greek and Roman
busts swathed in climbing roses. In recent
years, Sledmere has enjoyed extensive
replanting in the 18th-century walled
garden: a new rose and clematis arcade;
young roses and fruit trees on the walls; a
dedicated rose garden; and a
Mediterranean border. And it gets better
every year as the head gardener restores,
improves, takes more borders in hand and
adds more plants. There are fine purple
beeches in the park.

roses; Capability Brown landscape;
craft & gift shop; tea-terrace & licensed
cafeteria.

Owned by Sir Tatton Sykes
Number of gardeners 3
English Heritage Grade I

YORKSHIRE, NORTH

North Yorkshire corresponds with the old North Riding of Yorkshire: it is a county of large estates and small market towns. Among its historic gardens are some of the grandest landscapes in England: Castle Howard, Duncombe Park and Studley Royal are all Grade I gardens. North Yorkshire also has three very important modern gardens – Harlow Carr, Newby Hall and Thorp Perrow – each quite different in character but all horticultural heavyweights. Harlow Carr, for years the flagship of the Northern Horticultural Society, joined the RHS's growing fleet of top gardens in 2001 and has now embarked on substantial redevelopment and improvement at the RHS's hands.

The National Gardens Scheme does well in North Yorkshire and so does the NCCPG, which has over 20 National Collections in the county. The best nurseries are also in North Yorkshire, including R.V. Roger Ltd, which has a good line in exotic 'architectural' plants, and the *Pulmonaria* and rare plant specialist Stillingfleet Lodge Nurseries: Stillingfleet also has a good garden that RHS members can visit free. There are many others that offer free access to RHS members for all or part of their open season: Duncombe Park, Harewood House, Millgate House, Newby Hall, Parceval Hall, Ripley Castle and Thorp Perrow.

BENINGBROUGH HALL & GARDENS
Beningbrough, York YO30 1DD

Tel: 01904 470666 **Fax:** 01904 470002
www.nationaltrust.org.uk
Location 8 miles north-west of York off A19.
Opening hours 11 am – 5.30 pm; Saturday – Wednesday; 25 March to 31 October. Plus Good Friday, & Fridays from 7 July to 1 September. Plus 11 am – 3.30 pm; Saturdays & Sundays; 4 November to 17 December.
Admission fee Adults £5.30; Children £2.70.
🅿 📶 ♿ � 🛍 ☕

The National Trust calls Beningbrough 'York's Country House and Garden'. It is approached by an avenue of limes through stately parkland. Apart from a gloomy Victorian shrubbery, the gardens are modern and pretty. Two small formal gardens, one with reds and oranges and the other with pastel shades, lie on either side of the early Georgian house. A sumptuous mixed border, graded from hot colours to cool, runs right to the gate of the walled kitchen garden.

fruit; good herbaceous borders; American garden; good conservatory on house; traditional Victorian kitchen garden undergoing restoration; 'Lady Downe's Seedling' grape, raised at Beningbrough in 1835; vast Portuguese laurel *Prunus lusitanica*; National Trust gift shop; morning coffee, hot & cold lunches, afternoon teas.

Owned by The National Trust
Number of gardeners 4½, plus volunteers
Size 2.8ha (7 acres)
English Heritage Grade II

DUNCOMBE PARK
Helmsley YO62 5EB

Tel: 01439 770213 **Fax:** 01439 771114
www.duncombepark.com
Location Off A170; signed from Helmsley.
Opening hours 11 am – 5.30 pm (or dusk, if earlier); Sunday – Thursday; 30 April to 29 October.
Admission fee Adults £3.50; OAPs £3; Children £1.75. RHS members free.

CASTLE HOWARD
York YO6 7DA

Tel: 01653 648333 **Fax:** 01653 648529
www.castlehoward.co.uk
Location 15 miles north-east of York, off A64.
Opening hours 10 am - 6 pm (or dusk, if earlier); daily; all year.
Admission fee Adults £7; Concessions £6.50; Children £5.

P ◁ WC & ❀ ♣ ☕

Be prepared to spend all day at Castle Howard: it is essential visiting both for plantsmen and for anyone with a sense of history. At every time of the year, there are really good walks through woodlands and formal gardens, along the terraces and beside the water, and views of the buildings and sculptures in the landscape. The heroic megapark was first laid out by the 3rd Earl of Carlisle in 1700. Vanbrugh filled the five axes with landscapings and important buildings: the south lake, the terraces, the statues and the waterfalls down to the new river are all his. Vanbrugh's masterpiece, built in 1724-6, is the Temple of the Four Winds. The Mausoleum was designed by Hawksmoor in 1728. In front of the house are the remains of a vast 19th-century parterre, whose centrepoint is the Atlas fountain built by William Andrews Nesfield in the 1850s. Within a walled garden is a series of grand 1980s rose gardens (slightly Surrey) designed by Jim Russell, with every type of rose from ancient to modern. Of more interest to gardeners and plantsmen is Ray Wood, where a fine and historic collection of rhododendrons and other ericaceous plants (all meticulously labelled) is destined to develop as one of the greatest woodland gardens in Europe. The rhododendrons and other plants of 20th-century plant hunters are here in abundance – collections by Forrest, Rock, Kingdon Ward, Ludlow and Sheriff are all represented, as are more recent collections from Nepal, Bhutan, Japan, and China. Since 1999 the wood has been managed jointly by Castle Howard and the Royal Botanic Gardens at Kew: there is a small additional charge to visit it.

important buildings; impressive landscape; sculptures; woodland garden; roses (ancient & modern); good herbaceous borders; tallest elm *Ulmus glabra* (37m) in the British Isles; shops; plant centre; cafeteria.

Owned by Castle Howard Estates Ltd
Size 400ha (1,000 acres)
English Heritage Grade I

P WC & ※ 🐜 ☕

Christopher Hussey wrote that 'the grass terraces of Duncombe are unique, and perhaps the most spectacularly beautiful among English landscape conceptions of the 18th century'. They were probably completed between 1713 and 1730 to the designs of either Charles Bridgeman or Stephen Switzer, or both. A long, broad, grass terrace curves along the edge of a steep escarpment from an Ionic rotunda to the north. Woodland clothes the hillside: you see nothing until you reach the Doric temple at the southern end and look down to the ruins of Rievaulx Abbey. Hidden in more woodland is a small, classical conservatory fronting the ruins of a Victorian rose garden. Duncombe has little or nothing of horticultural interest, but it can scarcely be bettered for Palladian grandeur.

🌿 stately 18th-century landscape; gift shop; licensed tea-room.

Owned by Lord Feversham
Number of gardeners 1
Size 14ha (35 acres), within 160ha (400 acres) of parkland
English Heritage Grade I

FIR TREES PELARGONIUM NURSERY
Fir Trees Cottage, Stokesley TS9 5LD

Tel & Fax: 01642 713066
www.firtreespelargoniums.co.uk
Location South of Stokesley, by junction of A172 & B1365.
Opening hours 10 am - 4 pm; daily; all year. Closed at weekends between October & February.
Admission fee Free.

P WC & ※

This family-run nursery specialises in pelargoniums, and stocks more than 370 cultivars. Visitors are free to wander around the nursery, including its stock and show plant areas and propagation unit. Four RHS Special Events will take place at Fir Trees Pelargonium Nursery during 2006;

details from 020 7821 3408.
Owned by Helen Bainbridge
Number of gardeners 3
Size 0.4ha (1 acre) of glass

HELMSLEY WALLED GARDEN
Cleveland Way, Helmsley YO62 5AH

Tel & Fax: 01439 771427
www.helmsleywalledgarden.org.uk
Location Behind castle. Park in Cleveland Way long-stay car park.
Opening hours 10.30 am - 5 pm; daily; April to October.
Admission fee Adults £4; Concessions £3; Children free.

◁ WC & ※ 🐜 ☕

This was originally the walled kitchen garden of Duncombe Park; it is now run by a charitable trust devoted to horticultural therapy which received a £½m grant from the Heritage Lottery Fund, principally for the restoration of the glasshouses. Apart from its sheer size and splendour, the main features of horticultural interest in the walled garden are some 300 clematis cultivars, 52 different Yorkshire apples, 34 Victorian vines and a splendid Orchid House. The nursery has some interesting and unusual plants.

🌿 rare plant nursery; restaurant.

Owned by Helmsley Walled Garden Ltd
Number of gardeners 3, plus volunteers
Size 2ha (5 acres)
English Heritage Grade I

MIDDLETHORPE HALL & SPA
Bishopthorpe Road, York YO23 2GB

Tel: 01904 641241 **Fax:** 01904 620176
www.middlethorpe.com
Location 1½ miles south of city centre, by York racecourse.

Opening hours Residents & guests of the hotel, all year round.

🅿 🆆 ☕

Middlethorpe Hall is a William III country house close to the city, set in 8ha (20 acres) of its own gardens and parkland. After a period of neglect, the gardens have been carefully restored to their 18th-century splendour and include ha-has, a white garden, a walled garden, a small lake and some beautiful specimen trees. Three RHS Special Events will take place during 2006; details from 020 7821 3408.

 renowned hotel & restaurant.

Owned by Historic House Hotels Ltd
Number of gardeners 2
Size 8ha (20 acres)

MILLGATE HOUSE
Richmond DL10 4JN

Tel: 01748 823571 **Fax:** 01748 823571
www.millgatehouse.com
Location Bottom of Market Place; first house in Millgate on left.
Opening hours 10 am - 5 pm; daily; April to October. And by appointment on Sundays in February & March for snowdrops.
Admission fee Adults £2; Children free. RHS members free, except for charity days.

This is a walled garden in the middle of the town, and thus remarkably sheltered. Since starting work in the garden in 1980, the owners' aim has been to create structure, bulk, year-round interest and a sense of profusion. They have achieved this by redesigning the garden to suggest that it is much larger than it really is, and by planting only the best plants of every type. The most prominent are roses, clematis, hostas, snowdrops, hellebores, ferns and foliage shrubs. By 1995 the owners had won the National Garden Competition, against 3,200 other entries. The garden continues to improve: Professor David

Stevens calls it 'a sophisticated study in both the manipulation of spatial concepts and [in] planting design'. It is immensely stylish and closely planted, a model for all town gardens. Only one caveat – it is so dense that your trousers will get soaked by brushing against plants in wet weather!

Owned by Tim Culkin & Austin Lynch
Number of gardeners owners only
Size 0.15ha (⅓ of an acre)

MOUNT GRACE PRIORY
Osmotherley, Northallerton DL6 3JG

Tel: 01609 883494 **Fax:** 01609 883361
www.nationaltrust.org.uk
Location 12 miles north of Thirsk on A19.
Opening hours 10 am - 4 pm; daily; 1 April to 30 September. 10 am - 4 pm; Thursday - Monday; 1 October to 31 March 2007. Closed 1 January & 24 to 26 December.
Admission fee Adults £3.60; Concessions £2.70; Children £1.80.

🅿 🆆 ♿ 🌸 ☕

The herb garden, designed by Stephen Anderton in 1994, is of most interest to gardeners. It is a re-creation of a 15th-century monastic garden. Around the house, the 1920s flower borders are being restored: there are terraces, acers, rhododendrons and azaleas. It is not a garden in which to dally, but an interesting add-on to the whole experience of a visit to the property.

 herbs; shop; hot & cold drinks.

Owned by The National Trust (managed by English Heritage)
Number of gardeners 2
Size 5ha (12½ acres)

NEWBY HALL
Ripon HG4 5AE

Tel: 01423 322583 **Fax:** 01423 324452
www.newbyhall.co.uk
Location Off B6265, 2 miles from A1 between
Boroughbridge & Ripon.
Opening hours 11 am – 5.30 pm; Tuesday –
Sunday & Bank Holiday Mondays; April to
September. Plus Mondays in July & August.
Admission fee Adults £6.90; OAPs £5.90;
Children £5.20. RHS members free in April, May
& September.

P ⓦ ⅋ ❀ ✖ ☕

Newby is the garden with everything: firm
design, an endless variety of features, great
plantsmanship and immaculate
maintenance. Its axis is a bold, wide,
double border stretching gently down to
the River Ure. The National Collection
of *Cornus* now extends to 32 species and
53 cultivars, planted to give colour,
beauty and interest. Newby also has a
large number of other rare trees and
shrubs and a comprehensive collection of
shrubby salvias, many of them collected in
Central and southern America by the
owner's brother Dr James Compton.
Newby is second only to Hidcote as an
example of 20th-century gardening, but
very much grander: visit it at any season
and expect to spend all day there.

woodland garden; roses (mainly old-
fashioned & climbers); rock garden;
plantsman's collection of plants; daffodils; good
herbaceous borders; HHA/Christie's Garden of
the Year in 1986; tallest *Acer griseum* (15m) in
the UK; adventure garden for children; shop and
plant centre; licensed restaurant.

Owned by Richard Compton
Number of gardeners 7
Size 10ha (25 acres)
NCCPG National Collections *Cornus* (excluding
C. florida cvs.)
English Heritage Grade II*

PARCEVALL HALL GARDENS
Skyreholme, Skipton BD23 6DE

Tel & Fax: 01756 720311
www.parcevallhallgardens.co.uk
Location Off B6160 from Burnsall.
Opening hours 10 am – 6 pm; daily; April to
October; winter visits by appointment. For NGS:
23 April.
Admission fee Adults £4; Children 75p. RHS
members free from May to August.

P ⇦ ⓦ ❀ ☕

The gardens at Parcevall Hall have a
breathtaking architectural layout and views
of the Yorkshire dales. They were largely
designed and planted by Sir William
Milner in 1927 and benefit from a great
variety of soils (limestone and gritstone)
which means that rhododendrons and
camellias grow alongside limestone
outcrops. It is something of a plantsman's
garden, too: the naturalised daffodils in the
orchard include 'W.P. Milner' while the
Primula florindae given by Kingdon Ward
has now naturalised around the lily pond.
Within the grounds are 14 Stations of the
Cross.

woodland garden; climbing roses; rock
garden; rhododendrons & azaleas;
water features; candelabra primulas; tea-room.

Owned by Walsingham College (Yorkshire
Properties) Ltd
Number of gardeners 3
Size 6.4ha (16 acres)

RIPLEY CASTLE GARDENS
Ripley, Harrogate HG3 3AY

Tel: 01423 770152 **Fax:** 01423 771745
www.ripleycastle.co.uk
Location 3½ miles north of Harrogate, off A61.
Opening hours 9 am – 5 pm (or dusk, if earlier);
daily; all year.
Admission fee Adults £4; OAPs £3.50; Children
£2.50. RHS members free.

P ⓦ ⅋ ❀ ❀ ☕

RHS GARDEN HARLOW CARR

Crag Lane, Beckwithshaw, Harrogate HG3 1QB

Tel: 01423 565418 **Fax:** 01423 530663
www.rhs.org.uk/harlowcarr
Location Crag Lane is off Otley Road (B6162),
1½ miles from Harrogate centre.
Opening hours 9.30 am – 6 pm (4 pm from
November to February); daily; all year. Closed
25 December. Last admissions one hour before
closing.
Admission fee Adults £6; Children (6-16) £1.60;
Children (under 6) free. RHS members (plus one
guest) free.

🅿 🅦 ♿ 🌱 🌰 ✕ ▯

For more than 50 years, Harlow Carr has set itself the challenge of educating, inspiring and delighting northern gardeners. The garden was opened in 1950, by the Northern Horticultural Society, as a trial ground for assessing the suitability of various plants for growing in northern climates. The gardens are comprehensive and spectacular. One of the highlights is the famous Streamside Garden – possibly one of the longest in the country – a breathtaking sight from spring onwards. It peaks in June and July with the vivid colours of the famous Harlow Carr hybrid candelabra primulas, along with blue Himalayan poppies, astilbes and hostas. The woodland, arboretum and wildflower meadow are home to insects, birds, squirrels, stoats and roe deer, and, as such, form a pivotal role in encouraging biodiversity. The ornamental gardens include scented, foliage, herb, grasses and winter gardens, alpine display houses and herbaceous beds. The newly redesigned scented garden mixes contemporary planting with gently curving rustic willow screens. New features appear every year: look out for the new kitchen garden and fruit garden, the redesigned main borders, and the new mixed border which combines herbaceous plants with grasses and roses in a contemporary design. Another significant addition is the opening of the Gardens Through Time – seven new historical gardens created to commemorate the RHS bicentenary in 2004; they were the centrepiece of a BBC television series. Each garden represents a different phase in gardening history: c.1804, the 1850s, the end of the 19th century, a garden in the style of Gertrude Jekyll, a modern garden from the Festival of Britain (1951), a scene from the 1970s and finally a contemporary garden by Diarmuid Gavin. The Royal Horticultural Society also ensures that Harlow Carr is an important centre for horticultural learning, with a full programme of workshops and longer courses on all aspects of gardening and horticulture, plus year-round events for all the family.

🌿 fruit; vegetables; herbs; daffodils; fine collection of trees; heathers and alpines; good autumn colour; gift shop; large book shop; plant centre; café; tea-rooms.

Owned by The Royal Horticultural Society
Number of gardeners 17
Size 23ha (58 acres)
NCCPG National Collections *Dryopteris*;
Fuchsia section Quelusia; *Polypodium*; *Rheum*
(viewable on request)

Ripley has a garden with something for everyone: a 15th-century castle (restored); a 120-acre deer park; 1,000-year-old oaks; temples; a landscape designed by Capability Brown; a fine Regency conservatory; a Victorian formal garden; evergreen shrubberies (handsome yews); rare vegetables from Henry Doubleday Research Association in the traditional Victorian walled garden; colour at every season; over 2,000 hyacinths in 40 varieties; woodland walks; herbaceous borders; and hundreds of thousands of bulbs – daffodils in hosts.

hyacinths; sub-tropical plants; parkland; bluebells; gift shop with plants, fruit and vegetables; castle tea-room.

Owned by Sir Thomas Ingilby Bt.
Number of gardeners 4
NCCPG National Collections *Hyacinthus orientalis*
English Heritage Grade II

R.V. ROGER LTD
The Nurseries, Pickering YO18 7HG

Tel: 01751 472226 **Fax:** 01751 476749
www.rvroger.co.uk
Location 1 mile south of Pickering, on A169.
Opening hours 9 am – 5 pm, Monday – Saturday; 1 pm – 5 pm, Sundays; all year.

R.V. Roger was founded in 1913 and is still run by the family. It is best known for its excellent and extensive range of rare bulbs, conifers, perennials, roses, ornamental trees, hedging and shrubs. However, it also specialises in trained fruit trees – everything from espaliered apples to gooseberries grown as standards (it still lists 60 different apples and almost as many gooseberries). Excellence and variety remain the nursery's guiding principles.

trained fruit trees.

NCCPG National Collections *Erythronium*

SCAMPSTON HALL
Malton YO17 8NG

Tel: 01944 758224/759111 **Fax:** 01944 758700
www.scampston.co.uk
Location 4 miles east of Malton on north side of A64.
Opening hours 10 am – 5 pm; daily, except Mondays; 15 March to 15 October. Plus Bank Holiday Mondays.
Admission fee Adults £5; Concessions £4.50; Children £3. RHS members free in April, May, September & October.

Scampston is a Georgian house with a Capability Brown landscape, but the reason for visiting it is the new Piet Oudolf garden, planted in 1999 and open for the first time in 2004. It occupies the old kitchen garden and has been divided into sections, each with a distinct but complementary character. Most spectacular is the perennial flower meadow, planted with rich colours – red, yellow, orange and purple – in a characteristic modern mix of salvias, echinaceas, achilleas, monardas and grasses. But there are good herbaceous borders, avenues and hedges, too, and a grassy pyramid from which to survey the splendour.

modern plantings; shop; restaurant.

Owned by Sir Charles & Lady Legard
Number of gardeners 4
Size 1.8ha (4½ acres), plus parkland
English Heritage Grade II*

SLEIGHTHOLMEDALE LODGE
Fadmoor, Kirkbymoorside YO62 7JG

Tel: 01751 431942 **Fax:** 01751 430106
Location Signed from Fadmoor.
Opening hours For NGS: 27 May, 3 June, 15 & 16 July. And by written appointment at any time.
Admission fee Adults £2.50; Children 50p.

This family garden – Mrs James is the third generation to garden here – is a plantsman's paradise right on the edge of the moors. The walled garden was built on a south-facing slope, which makes it possible to grow a wide range of plants that might not otherwise survive. As well as magnificent meconopsis and hardy herbaceous plants it has Mexican and Mediterranean rarities (a cistus walk, for example) which are a triumph for good cultivation and manipulation of the microclimate. The herbaceous borders are held together by repeating certain plants throughout: foxgloves, campanulas and martagon lilies, for example. Outside the walled garden is an orchard underplanted with snowdrops and narcissi. Up at the top is a hollyhock walk. And there are roses of every sort – hundreds of them.

roses (ancient & modern); plantsman's collection of plants; good herbaceous borders; teas in July.

Owned by Mrs R. James
Number of gardeners 1, plus 2 very part-time
Size 1.2ha (3 acres)

STILLINGFLEET LODGE NURSERIES
Stillingfleet, York YO19 6HP

Tel & Fax: 01904 728506
www.stillingfleetlodgenurseries.co.uk
Location 6 miles south of York: turn opposite church.
Opening hours 1 pm - 4 pm; Wednesdays & Fridays; May to September. Plus Saturdays in May & June. For NGS: 7 May & 18 June (1.30 pm - 5 pm).
Admission fee Adults £3; Children 50p. RHS members free.

Stillingfleet is a series of small gardens surrounding a late-18th-century farmhouse. The emphasis is on a cottage garden style of planting, and every part is maintained organically. Foliage is used to add interest

and texture: the result is a sequence of sumptuous herbaceous borders – a living lesson in how to plant a garden. The collection of pulmonarias is fascinating: 13 species and over 150 cultivars flower over a long period. A wildflower walk leads to a pond planted for natural effect. The nursery has an excellent herbaceous list with a high proportion of unusual plants: the catalogue changes each year but is always good for geraniums and pulmonarias. Worth a long journey to visit. There will be three RHS Special Events at Stillingfleet Lodge Nurseries in 2006; details from 020 7821 3408.

herbaceous plants; wildflower walk.

Owned by Vanessa Cook
Number of gardeners owner, plus a little part-time help
Size 0.6ha (1½ acres)
NCCPG National Collections *Pulmonaria*

STUDLEY ROYAL
Fountains, Ripon HG4 3DY

Tel: 01765 608888 **Fax:** 01765 601002
www.nationaltrust.org.uk
Location 3 miles west of Ripon off B6265, via the Visitor Centre.
Opening hours 10 am - 4 pm (5 pm in summer); daily; all year, except Fridays from November to February. Closed 24 & 25 December.
Admission fee Adults £6.50; Children £3.50.

Studley Royal is inextricably linked to Fountains Abbey: nothing can beat the surprise view of the ruined Cistercian abbey from Anne Boleyn's Seat. The most spectacular water garden in England was laid out between 1716 and 1781 in the sheltered flat bottom of the River Skell. The Abbey is at one end, the deer park at the other. The combination of the formal canal, moon pools, grotto springs, rustic bridge, sculptures and the Temple of Piety against a dark background of trees is a supreme example of 18th-century landscaping at its most individual.

🐝 topiary; snowdrops; World Heritage site; 400-acre deer park; water garden; biggest *Prunus avium* (bird cherry) in the British Isles; National Trust visitor centre shop; tea-room.

Owned by The National Trust
Number of gardeners 9, plus volunteers
Size 60ha (150 acres)
English Heritage Grade I

SUTTON PARK
Sutton-on-the-Forest, York YO6 1DP

Tel: 01347 810249 **Fax:** 01347 811251
www.statelyhome.co.uk
Location 8 miles north of York on B1363.
Opening hours 11 am – 5 pm; daily; 3 April to 27 September.
Admission fee Adults £3.50; OAPs £2.50; Children £1.

📧 [WC] ♿ ✿ 🍂 ⼞

Capability Brown was here in the 18th century, but the joy of Sutton is the formal garden laid out on three broad terraces below the house. It was designed by Percy Cane in the 1960s and planted by the late Nancie Sheffield with exquisite taste. It was one of the first to throw off the austerity of the post-war years and insist upon floral profusion and segregated colour schemes, though it looks a little dated nowadays – rather a period piece. In the grounds are a Georgian ice-house, a woodland walk, some fine Victorian conifers, and a tulip tree *Liriodendron tulipifera* planted by Prince George, later Duke of Kent, on 7 October 1933.

🐝 influential formal gardens; plantsman's plants; good herbaceous borders; plants for sale occasionally; refreshments Wednesday - Sunday in summer.

Owned by Sir Reginald & Lady Sheffield
Number of gardeners 2½
Size 3.2ha (8 acres), plus parkland

THORP PERROW ARBORETUM & WOODLAND GARDEN
Bedale DL8 2PR

Tel & Fax: 01677 425323
www.thorpperrow.com
Location On the Bedale to Ripon road, 2 miles south of Bedale.
Opening hours Dawn - dusk; daily; all year.
Admission fee Adults £5.95; OAPs & Students £4.60; Children £3.10. RHS members free from Monday to Friday, excluding Bank Holidays & event days.

📧 ⤳ [WC] ♿ 🍂 🍂 ⼞

Thorp Perrow is the most important arboretum in the north of England, with more than 20 record-breaking trees among the thousands planted since Sir Leonard Ropner started work in 1931. There was already a pinetum on the estate, planted by Lady Augusta Milbank in the 1840s and 1850s. Ropner surrounded it with his new plantings – over 1,000 different taxa still survive, to which his son Sir John has added at least another 600. There are handsome avenues to walk along, often lined with a single genus or species – red oaks, rowans, cherries or cypresses, for example. Many are thickly lined with daffodils in spring, as are the glades and bays where you can study a particular collection like acers or hollies. The only downside to Thorp Perrow is that all the trees are identified only with a number, which you then have to look up in the catalogue of plantings. This minor irritation apart, Thorp Perrow is in every way an inspiring and enjoyable place to visit. There will be two RHS Special Events at Thorp Perrow in 2006; details from 020 7821 3408.

🐝 the best collection of trees in northern England; daffodils; bluebells; new Millennium Glade; information centre; plant centre; licensed tea-room.

Owned by Sir John Ropner Bt.
Size 34ha (85 acres)
NCCPG National Collections *Fraxinus, Juglans, Laburnum, Tilia*
English Heritage Grade II

VALLEY GARDENS
Valley Drive, Harrogate

Tel: 01423 500600 **Fax:** 01423 556720
www.harrogate.gov.uk
Location Signed from town centre.
Opening hours Dawn - dusk; daily; all year.
Admission fee Free.

The Valley Gardens at Harrogate are a
good example of plantsmanship in a public
garden, first laid out between 1880 and
1900. The gardens have alpine rarities in
spring, a romantic rhododendron dell, good
roses, a fine dahlia display in late summer
and good colour bedding.

 rock garden; herbaceous borders;
bedding; small cafeteria.

Owned by Harrogate Borough Council
Size 6.7ha (17 acres)
English Heritage Grade II

WYTHERSTONE GARDENS
Pockley YO62 7TE

Tel: 01439 770012 **Fax:** 01439 770468
www.wytherstonegardens.co.uk
Location In middle of village, on left side,
coming from A170.
Opening hours 1 pm - 5 pm; Wednesdays; 31 May
to 30 August. Plus 28 May, 11 & 25 June, 16 July &
13 August for charity. And by appointment at
other times.
Admission fee Adults £3; Children £1.

There is a lot to see – and tender plants
especially – in this remote garden, which
has received a boost in recent years by the
arrival of a plant-wise head gardener. In a
sheltered area near the entrance are
bananas, *Pinus montezumae*, trachycarpus,
cordylines and phormiums. Rhododendrons
thrive nearby in a specially made-up bed.
Fremontodendrons and (remarkably)
Eucalyptus gunnii have been trained against
the south-facing side of the house. Around
the house is a series of small, linked
gardens with mixed borders, often backed
by climbing roses, and good colour-
schemed plantings. A garden made of old
railway sleepers is terraced up with raised
beds full of interesting plants –
zauschnerias, succulents (put out for the
summer), agapanthus and *Lobelia tupa*.
Elsewhere are carpenterias, phlomis,
crinums, *Melianthus major* and *Salvia greggii*
and its hybrids, all apparently quite hardy
in the free-draining, limestone soil.
Buddleja colvilei is grown as a free-standing
shrub. Further away from the house, a
collection of trees around a pond promises
to develop into a domestic arboretum. The
nursery is excellent.

 tender plants; good colour
combinations; interesting nursery; teas
on charity Sundays.

Owned by Lady Clarissa Collin
Number of gardeners 2
Size 3.2ha (8 acres)

YORKSHIRE, SOUTH

The county of South Yorkshire was invented in 1974 and is, in effect, Greater Sheffield. Nevertheless, it has a couple of good historic gardens that are open to the public – Wentworth Castle and Brodsworth Hall. The Sheffield Botanical Gardens, too, are of great horticultural interest, having been planted and maintained over many years as a garden of ornamental plants of every kind. Both the Sheffield Botanical Gardens and the gardens at Wentworth Castle have benefited from lottery funding in recent years and are very visitor-friendly as a result. The National Gardens Scheme has very few gardens opening for it in the county and, though it is well provided with garden centres, South Yorkshire has no specialist nurseries of national importance. There are several NCCPG National Collections – including two at Sheffield Botanical Gardens and three at Wentworth Castle.

BRODSWORTH HALL & GARDENS

English Heritage, Brodsworth, Doncaster DN5 7XJ

Tel: 01302 722598 **Fax:** 01302 337165
Location 6 miles north-west of Doncaster.
Opening hours 10 am - 6 pm; Tuesday – Sunday & Bank Holiday Mondays; April to September. Then 11 am - 4 pm; weekends only.
Admission fee Garden only: Adults £4.80; OAPs £3.75; Children £2.40. Cheap rates in winter.

🅿 🚾 ♿ ♣ ⴲ

Brodsworth has proved a triumph for English Heritage – a splendid Victorian garden, unkempt for 50 years, but now spectacularly restored as first laid out in the 1860s. It offers Italianate terraces, statues and classical follies; a rose garden where the vigorous ramblers are trained on bizarre ironwork arcades and box-edged beds are filled with period roses; magnificent trees (especially cedars, pines and monkey puzzles); bright Victorian bedding in a huge formal garden; and lots of clipped evergreens – laurels, yews, aucubas and many more, even free-standing griselinias. Best of all, perhaps, are the hollies – hundreds and hundreds of them, planted to display their vast colour palette. The spring bulbs, too, are exceptional. Every part of the garden is well maintained and a joy to visit at any time of the year.

🌿 good specimen conifers; Victorian spring & summer bedding; large fern collection; significant clipped evergreen shrubberies; statuary; shop; licensed restaurant.

Owned by English Heritage
Number of gardeners 6
Size 5.2ha (13 acres)
English Heritage Grade II*

SHEFFIELD BOTANICAL GARDENS

Clarkehouse Road, Sheffield S10 2LN

Tel: 0114 268 6001 **Fax:** 0114 255 2375
www.sheffield.gov.uk
Location M1, Jct 33, follow A57 signs to Glossop, left at Royal Hallamshire Hospital, 500 yards on left.
Opening hours 7.30 am (10 am at weekends) - 7.45 pm (4 pm in winter); daily; all year. Closed 1 January, 25 & 26 December.
Admission fee Free.

◁ 🚾 ♿ 🌱 ♣ ⴲ

The Sheffield Botanical Gardens were founded in 1833 by public subscription and designed by Robert Marnock in the gardenesque style. A £6.69m Heritage

Lottery grant has repaired the gardens and their buildings. The glass pavilions are among the earliest curvilinear glasshouses ever built and now contain a temperate plant collection from around the world. There is much to interest the plantsman, too. The features include good camellias and magnolias; heathers; a rock garden; and good trees. The garden has splendid summer bedding, too, and lots of seats: an exemplary combination of botany and amenity.

rock garden; mature conifers; good herbaceous borders; historic conservatories; peat garden; heath garden; roses (mainly modern); new shop; restaurant; tea-room.

Owned by Sheffield Town Trust (managed by Sheffield City Council)
Number of gardeners 6, plus 2 part-time
Size 7.6ha (19 acres)
NCCPG National Collections *Diervilla*, *Weigela*
English Heritage Grade II

WENTWORTH CASTLE GARDENS
Lowe Lane, Stainborough, Barnsley
S75 3ET

Tel: 01226 776040 **Fax:** 01226 776041
www.wentworthcastle.org
Location Signed 'Northern College'. 2 miles south of Barnsley; 2 miles from M1.
Opening hours 12 noon – 5 pm; Saturdays, Sundays & Bank Holidays; April to October. Guided tours at 2 pm. Guided tours also at 2 pm on Tuesdays & Thursdays from April to October. Details from 01226 776040 or website.

Admission fee Adults £2.50; Concessions £2 (£2.50 on 28 & 29 May); Children £1. RHS members free, except 28 & 29 May.

Wentworth Castle has a major landscape garden, one of the earliest in England, which accounts for the amazing series of buildings in the grounds – among them are an Ionic rotunda, the Gothic folly of Stainborough Castle, an obelisk to Queen Anne and another to Lady Mary Wortley-Montagu to commemorate her introduction of smallpox inoculation to England. The garden was then overlaid with a seriously important collection of hardy hybrid rhododendrons at the end of the 19th century. It was in the same era that the handsome cast-iron conservatory was built: it was recently featured on BBC Two's *Restoration* series. The need to preserve the original landscape features has been the basis of an ambitious £15m restoration project. Go now to see this important landscape (South Yorkshire's only Grade I listed landscape) as it emerges from disrepair, and return to watch restoration progress. Stout footwear essential. There will be two RHS Special Events at Wentworth Castle in 2006; details from 020 7821 3408.

historic landscape; woodland garden; newly excavated 19th-century rock garden; educational collection of rhododendrons.

Owned by Wentworth Castle Trust
Number of gardeners 8
Size 16ha (40 acres)
NCCPG National Collections *Rhododendron* species; *Magnolia* species; *Camellia* x *williamsii*
English Heritage Grade I

YORKSHIRE, WEST

West Yorkshire corresponds to the old West Riding. It is a county of great contrasts, from the industrial and commercial cities of Bradford and Leeds to the wool towns of Huddersfield and Halifax, with a chunk of the Peak District in the south-west and some large agricultural estates in the north. The most important historic gardens are Bramham Park – a remarkable pre-landscape garden on a big scale – and the opulent Harewood House. But they are matched for sheer horticultural value by four gardens which all have an historic past but are now owned and managed by Leeds City Council as gardens for public recreation – Lotherton Hall, Temple Newsam, The Hollies, and the Canal Gardens & Tropical World in Roundhay Park. The NCCPG has no fewer than 11 National Collections in the care of the Leeds City Parks Department. There are rather few specialist nurseries of national standing in the county, though it is well served by garden centres.

8 DUNSTARN LANE
Adel, Leeds LS16 8EL

Tel: 0113 267 3938
Location Off Long causeway, Adel.
Opening hours By appointment.
Admission fee Adults £2; Children free.

[P] ⟁ & ❀ ☞

The Wainwrights have grown delphiniums here for more than half a century. It is probably the finest and most extensive collection of delphiniums in private hands, with nearly seventy cultivars. They are interplanted with their traditional border companions – roses (mainly modern), phlox, dahlias, Michaelmas daisies and many unusual perennials.

   roses; delphiniums; fine trees; tea & coffee.

Owned by Mrs Richard Wainwright
Number of gardeners ½
Size 1.2ha (3 acres)

BRAMHAM PARK
Wetherby LS23 6ND

Tel: 01937 846000 **Fax:** 01937 846007
www.bramhampark.co.uk
Location 5 miles south of Wetherby on A1.
Opening hours 11.30 am – 4.30 pm; daily; April to September. Closed for horse trials from 5 to 11 June, Leeds Festival from 14 August to 1 September & occasionally for other events. Ring before visiting.
Admission fee Gardens only: Adults £4; OAPs & Children £2.

[P] [WC] &

Bramham is a very important pre-landscape formal garden, laid out in the grand manner in the early 18th century. A long driveway winds through the woods, turns a corner, and suddenly reveals the magnificent Palladian house, framed by the most spacious of avenues. Behind the house are long, straight rides carved through dense woodland and edged with tall beech hedges, neatly cut. Focal points include loggias,

statues, temples, an obelisk and a sequence
of formal cascades running down to a
square, lake-sized pond. The parkland turf is
speckled with cowslips and orchids, while
wild onions run amok in the woods, but the
scale and complexity of the design have
nothing to match them anywhere in the
British Isles: Bramham is the finest French
garden in England – awesome, uplifting and
built to impress.

 very important pre-landscape park;
daffodils.

Owned by George Lane Fox
Number of gardeners 3
Size 27ha (68 acres)
English Heritage Grade I

GOLDEN ACRE PARK
Otley Road, Bramhope, Leeds LS16 5NZ

Tel: 0113 267 3729
www.leeds.gov.uk
Location 6 miles north-west of Leeds city centre on
A660 Otley Road.
Opening hours Dawn - dusk; daily; all year.
Admission fee Free.

Golden Acre is part historic park, part
botanic collection, part demonstration
garden and part test ground for Fleuroselect
and *Gardening Which?*. It began life in the
1930s as an amusement park, but the City
Council decided after the war to develop it as
a public garden with a strong botanical
interest. Perhaps the best of the five
impressive public gardens in Leeds, it is
certainly the most popular.

rock garden; large heather garden; new
'harmony' garden; herb garden; limestone
rock garden; sandstone rock garden; arboretum;
pinetum; display houses; rhododendrons & azaleas;
cherry orchard; gifts/souvenirs; restaurant.

Owned by Leeds City Council
Size 54ha (135 acres)
NCCPG National Collections *Primula auricula,
Syringa*

HAREWOOD HOUSE
Harewood, Leeds LS17 9LQ

Tel: 0113 218 1010 **Fax:** 0113 218 1002
www.harewood.org
Location Between Leeds & Harrogate on A61.
Opening hours Not yet known as we went to press:
probably 10 am - 6 pm; daily; April to October.
Admission fee 2005 prices: Grounds (weekdays):
Adults £8.25; OAPs £7.50; Children £5.50. Grounds
(weekends): Adults £10.25; OAPs £9.50; Children £7.
RHS members free in April & May, excluding
weekends & Bank Holidays.

Capability Brown was the first famous
landscaper to work at Harewood for the
super-rich Lascelles family: he was followed
by Humphry Repton, John Claudius Loudon
and Sir Charles Barry. The latter came in the
1840s, to build the stupendous Italianate
terrace whose grand parterre and ornate
fountains are the perfect link between the
house and the landscaped park. Bedding out
is practised here on a large scale – very
impressive – and ensures colour throughout
the year. The border below the parterre is
planted with bold foliage plants – yuccas,
phormiums, irises, artichokes, peonies,
eriobotryas, bananas, callistemons and
acanthus. Around the lake at the bottom are
hundreds of rhododendrons, and unusual
shrubs and bulbs, particularly daffodils. The
waterfall at the lake head feeds a picturesque
rock garden where primulas, astilbes, hostas
and gunneras grow rampantly in the damp.
The rose garden at the end of the lakeside
walk is an extra delight in early summer. The
large, traditional walled garden displays a
wide selection of vegetables and economic
crops from around the world: Harewood is a
registered Seed Library garden.

formal terraces; good bedding; woodland
garden; rhododendrons; current holder of
Sandford Award; two shops; licensed café .

Owned by Harewood House Trust Ltd
Number of gardeners 12
Size 56ha (140 acres)
English Heritage Grade I

THE HOLLIES PARK
Weetwood Lane, Leeds LS16 5NZ

Tel: 0113 278 2030 **Fax:** 0113 247 8277
www.leeds.gov.uk
Location 3 miles north of city off A660.
Opening hours Dawn – dusk; daily; all year.
Admission fee Free.

This public park is made in a plantsman's garden, and is well run by a hard-pressed and enthusiastic team. Visitors wishing to see the National Collections are advised to make a prior appointment.

 woodland garden; rhododendrons; eucryphias.

Owned by Leeds City Council
Size 37ha (93 acres)
NCCPG National Collections *Deutzia, Hemerocallis* (Coe hybrids); *Hosta* (large-leaved); *Philadelphus, Syringa*

LAND FARM GARDENS
Colden, Hebden Bridge, Halifax HX7 7PJ

Tel: 01422 842260
Location On right, 2 miles from Hebden Bridge on Colden Road.
Opening hours 10 am – 5 pm; Saturdays, Sundays & Bank Holiday Mondays; May to August.
Admission fee Adults £4. Guided parties £5 per head, including refreshments.

This is a pioneering plantsman's garden, high in the Pennines and facing north. The range of plants that can successfully be grown in such an unpromising situation is an eye-opener – lots of hardy rhododendrons, shrubs, trees, alpines, cardiocrinums and meconopsis. There is also a good collection of sculpture, with more pieces arriving all the time.

garden created by owners on greenfield site; good conifers and herbaceous borders; new woodland garden (2 acres); *Meconopsis, Tropaeolum*, art gallery.

Owned by John Williams
Number of gardeners 3 part-time
Size 1.6ha (4 acres)

LOTHERTON HALL
Aberford, Leeds LS25 3EB

Tel: 0113 281 3259 **Fax:** 0113 281 3068
www.leeds.gov.uk/lothertonhall
Location Off A1, ¾ mile east on B1217.
Opening hours 8 am – 8 pm (or dusk, if earlier); daily; all year.
Admission fee Garden free, but charges for parking (£3 in 2005).

This showpiece garden was laid out between 1885 and 1915 by a friend of Ellen Willmott. Given to the Council in 1968, it has been well restored in recent years. It offers gazebos, walks, yew hedging, rose gardens, and a lily pond recently replanted with period varieties. The rock garden known as the Dell is especially good. The formal garden is laid out with gravel paths and lots of bedding. Lotherton is a garden that is on the move again, with a woodland trail recently added for disabled users and a new (2005) orchard planted in partnership with the Northern Fruit Group. Lotherton is extremely popular – over ¾ million visitors a year.

Edwardian plantswoman's garden; roses (mainly modern); good trees; fine hedges; mature layout; shop; cafeteria.

Owned by Leeds City Council
Number of gardeners 2
Size 4ha (10 acres)
English Heritage Grade II

ROUNDHAY PARK & TROPICAL WORLD
Roundhay Park, Princes Avenue, Leeds LS8 2ER

Tel: 0113 266 1850 **Fax:** 0113 237 0077
www.leeds.gov.uk
Location 3 miles north-west of city centre, off

A6120 ringroad.
Opening hours Open at 10 am all year. Close at 4 pm in January & December; 5 pm in February & November; 6 pm in March & October; 7 pm in April & September; 8 pm from May to August.
Admission fee Tropical World: Adults £3; Children £2. Gardens: free.

Tropical World's glasshouses contain South American rainforest plants, bromeliads, hoyas, cacti and a butterfly house. It is said to have the largest collection of tropical plants outside Kew. It is in any event a wonderful retreat from a Yorkshire winter and a triumph of municipal horticultural excellence. Roundhay Park has a £6.1m project to preserve and enhance the gardens which has received support from the Heritage Lottery Fund. Tropical World is visited by over a million people every year. The gardens outside have fine herbaceous and mixed borders, and splendid formal bedding schemes, including a clock surrounded by carpet bedding and two further raised carpet beds. Nearby is a reinterpretation of Monet's garden at Giverny and another of the Alhambra Gardens in Granada, complete with fountains. Add in two lakes and extensive woodland walks in the park and you have a most enjoyable place to visit at any time of the year.

sub-tropical plants; roses (mainly modern); plants under glass; good carpet bedding; orchids; desert house; souvenirs; cafeteria by lakeside.

Owned by Leeds City Council
Number of gardeners 40
Size 240ha (600 acres)
English Heritage Grade II

TEMPLE NEWSAM PARK
Leeds LS15 0AD

Tel: 0113 264 5535
www.leeds.gov.uk/templenewsam
Location 3 miles south-east of city, off A63 Selby Road.

Opening hours Dawn – dusk; daily; all year.
Admission fee Free. Admission charge to house.

This prodigious house on a windy bluff, surrounded by 1,500 acres of parkland, has been a 'green lung' for Leeds since 1923. Somewhat dilapidated in the past, the garden is now improved by some recent plantings. These include a spring garden full of bulbs; the Italian garden with formal flower beds; box, yew and beech hedges; pleached laburnum walks; and a clipped hornbeam stilt hedge. A fine rhododendron and azalea walk runs down to the lakes. Nearby is a specimen tree area and a bog garden. Further on still, the old walled kitchen garden is planted with roses and wide herbaceous borders. The long conservatory has a fine display of flowering plants, ivies and cacti: its back wall (1788) still has the flues which were used to keep it warm with hot air.

spacious parkland; roses (ancient & modern); good herbaceous borders; rhododendrons; visitor centre & gift shop; tea-room open daily from 10.30 am.

Owned by Leeds City Council
NCCPG National Collections *Aster*, *Chrysanthemum* (Charms & Cascade); *Delphinium*, *Phlox paniculata*, *Solenostemon*
English Heritage Grade II

YORK GATE
Back Church Lane, Adel, Leeds
LS16 8DW

Tel: 0113 267 8240
www.perennial.org.uk/yorkgate.html
Location 2¼ miles south-east of Bramhope and ½ mile east of A660, behind Adel Church.
Opening hours 2 pm – 5 pm; Thursdays, Sundays & Bank Holiday Mondays; April to September. Plus 6.30 pm – 9 pm on 22 & 29 June & 6 July. And by appointment.
Admission fee Adults £3.50 (more for private visits); Children free. RHS members free in April, May & September.

This one-acre masterpiece – a modern icon – was made by the Spencer family between 1951 and 1994. It is of equal interest to the designer and the plantsman. Its marvels include shrub and herbaceous borders, an arbour, a miniature pinetum, a dell with a stream, a folly, a nut walk, a peony bed, water features, a fern border, the famous herb garden, a pretty summerhouse, an alley, a white and silver garden, a kitchen garden, and a pavement maze. This combination of tight design, invention, colour sense and sheer creative opportunism is now in the care of Perennial, formerly the Gardeners' Royal Benevolent Society. 'Sybil's Garden' reopened in 2005 with a new, contemporary design.

brilliant design; plantsman's collection of plants; famous herb garden; endless inventive details; plants for sale (usually); tea & biscuits, May to September (& BH weekends).

Owned by Perennial – Gardeners' Royal Benevolent Society
Number of gardeners 1, plus part-timers & volunteers
Size 0.4ha (1 acre)

SCOTLAND

Scottish gardens are very variable – this is a result of their soil and climate. All along the west coast, from Dumfries & Galloway up to Ullapool and beyond, are fine, sub-tropical woodland gardens, where one can enjoy acres of large-leaved rhododendrons and eucalyptus trees and all manner of curiosities like *Myosotidium hortensia*, which would not be hardy in any but the most favoured parts of England. There is no better place to go visiting gardens in May or June – provided the weather is kind. There are comparatively few good gardens in inland Scotland. Historically, the big estates were (and still are) in remote places where the land is unsuitable for agriculture and, in consequence, their gardens tend to be few and disappointing. In the Borders, for example, there are several estates along the valleys of Tweed and the Teviot whose gardens are open to the public: all have collections of 19th-century conifers underplanted with hardy hybrid rhododendrons or common *R. ponticum*, but little else in the way of horticultural interest. On the east coast, however, there are once again many worthy gardens, above all the superb botanic garden at Edinburgh, which (like all botanic gardens nowadays) is laid out to please visitors, and other good botanic gardens at Dundee, St Andrews and Aberdeen. There are interesting gardens, too, near Edinburgh (especially Malleny at Balerno) and on Deeside (Crathes, Kildrummy and Drum).

Trees flourish in much of Scotland – especially those North American conifers for which the cool, damp west coast provides perfect growing conditions: many of the tallest pines, firs and spruces in Britain are in Scotland. The largest collection of record-breaking trees is at the Royal Botanic Gardens in Edinburgh, which has 45.

We have listed the gardens to visit in Scotland under the old 1974 regions, rather than the historic counties or the plethora of more recent local councils. The regions divide the country into areas of acceptable size for the purpose of this book, though there is a preponderance of gardens in the old region of Strathclyde – as indeed there still is in Argyll & Bute. If readers can suggest a better way than the old regions to list gardens, we would be pleased to hear from them. Scotland's Gardens Scheme divides the country into areas which are even more confusing – 'Etterick & Lauderdale', for example, and 'Lochaber, Badenoch & Strathspey'. The 1974 regions do at least have the advantage of having been administrative areas until recently.

Scotland has many great historic gardens. The basis of the protection they enjoy is the Inventory of Gardens & Designed Landscapes in Scotland which was published in 1987. The Inventory listed 275 sites, which are graded in a more specific way than the gardens on the English register, for example, according to the value of their horticultural content or historic importance. Historic Scotland has recently begun to extend the Inventory.

Nobody has done more to acquire, save, restore and redevelop Scotland's great gardens than the National Trust for Scotland. Its portfolio of properties includes many of the best historic and horticultural gardens in the country: Branklyn, Brodick, Crathes, Culzean and Inverewe are gardens of international renown. It has now taken the splendid garden at Crarae into its care. The Royal

Botanic Garden in Edinburgh, too, has developed four of the finest gardens anywhere in the world – Dawyck, Logan, Benmore (Younger Botanic Garden) and its own incomparable garden in north Edinburgh.

Members of the Royal Horticultural Society have free access for at least some months of the year to a fine list of Scottish gardens from Dunrobin Castle in the north to Harmony Garden in the Borders. More may be added during the course of the year: see the Society's website (www.rhs.org.uk) for the latest news. Scotland also has its own Yellow Book called *The Gardens of Scotland*, available from Scotland's Gardens Scheme, 31 Castle Terrace, Edinburgh EH1 2EL. It lists some 350 gardens throughout Scotland and, like its English equivalent, is the essential starting point for choosing more gardens to visit than this book recommends.

Scotland is well served by garden centres, especially by such chains as Dobbies in the Lowlands, which now also has branches in northern England.

Scotland has some excellent specialist nurseries, too: Jack Drake is Britain's premier alpine nursery; nobody has bred more or better new rhododendrons than Peter Cox at Glendoick; and Cally in Dumfries & Galloway has a great reputation for rare plants. However, it is fair to say that there are fewer nurseries *per capita* in Scotland as a whole than in England.

Scotland also has its own rather basic horticultural structures: these include, for example, such societies as the Scottish Rock Garden Club, the Scottish Rhododendron Society, the Royal Caledonian Horticultural Society and the Scottish Orchid Society. All are excellent organisations and some, like the Scottish Rock Garden Club and the Scottish Rhododendron Society, are substantial societies with good programmes of events and publications of record. Scotland also has a number of horticultural training colleges, notably Threave and the Scottish Agricultural College at Auchincruive, both of them RHS Partner Colleges.

BORDERS

ABBOTSFORD
Melrose TD6 9BQ

Tel: 01896 752043 **Fax:** 01896 752916
www.scottsabbotsford.co.uk
Location On B6360, 2 miles west of Melrose.
Opening hours Not yet known as we went to
press. In 2005: 9.30 am -5 pm (but 2 pm - 5 pm
on Sundays in March, April, May & October); daily;
Easter to 31 October.
Admission fee Adults £4.75; Children £2.40.
(2005 prices.)

P WC & ♣ ☞

Sir Walter Scott laid out the gardens at
Abbotsford in the 1820s: he designed the
formal Court garden by the house and
planted the surrounding woodlands. The
walled garden centres on a handsome
orangery, with roses, fruit trees and
herbaceous borders planted for late-
summer effect.

fine walled garden; orangery; topiary;
herbaceous borders; gift shop; self-
service tea-room.

Owned by The Trustees of Dame Jean Maxwell-
Scott DCVO
Number of gardeners 2
Size 0.4ha (1 acre)

DAWYCK BOTANIC GARDEN
Stobo EH45 9JU

Tel: 01721 760254 **Fax:** 01721 760214
www.rbge.org.uk
Location 8 miles south-west of Peebles on B712.
Opening hours 10 am - 6 pm (4 pm in February &
November and 5 pm in March & October); daily;
February to November.
Admission fee Adults £3.50; Concessions £3;
Children £1.

P WC ♣ ♣ ☞

Dawyck is a woodland garden, run as a
regional garden of the Royal Botanic Garden
Edinburgh. It is very different from
Edinburgh's other outliers: its 60 acres are
high in the hills and north-facing, and the
climate is more continental than temperate.
The trees for which the garden is famous
were first planted in the 1830s: the owners
subscribed to the great plant-hunting
expeditions of the day, including those of
David Douglas. This explains the many fine
North American conifers in the garden. In
the early 20th century, the owners received
plants from the early Chinese collections of
E.H. Wilson. The gardens are also famous for
their rhododendrons, berberis and
cotoneasters and – of course – the Dawyck
beech, an upright, fastigiate form of the
common beech, first found in the policies in
the mid-19th century. Good for lichens and
fungi, too – over 1,750 different fungi grow
in Heron Wood.

Chinese conifers; Dawyck beech;
Douglas fir from original seed; *Torreya
californica*; tallest *Abies mariesii* (21m) in the
British Isles, and 12 further record trees; gift
shop; light refreshments.

Owned by Royal Botanic Garden Edinburgh
Size 24ha (60 acres)

EDROM NURSERIES
Coldingham, Eyemouth TD14 5TZ

Tel: 01890 771386 **Fax:** 01890 771387
www.edromnurseries.co.uk
Location A1107, 5 mins from A1.
Opening hours 9 am - 5.30 pm; daily; mid-March
to mid-October.
Admission fee Free.

P ♣ ♣

This nursery specialises in primulas,
arisaemas, fritillarias, trilliums, gentians

and meconopsis. The list of these genera is particularly comprehensive, and includes many forms that are not available elsewhere. *Rhodohypoxis* is another speciality, and the list of Japanese *Hepatica nobilis* cultivars is stunning. As with the other plants it lists, many are new to commerce or grown under collectors' numbers. The display gardens are varied and interesting, including woodland areas, raised beds and gravel-topped troughs.

Owned by T. Hunt & C. Davis
Number of gardeners 2
Size 0.2ha (½ acre)

FLOORS CASTLE
Kelso TD5 7SF

Tel: 01573 223333 **Fax:** 01573 226056
www.floorscastle.com
Location Signed in Kelso.
Opening hours 11 am - 5 pm; daily; 1 April to 29 October.
Admission fee Adults £3; OAPs £1.50. RHS members free.

🅿 ⋖⃗ 🆆🅲 ⛧ ✿ ☕

Floors Castle is impressively sited in its parkland. There are some good trees in the park, including a holm oak (*Quercus ilex*) and a Dawyck beech (*Fagus sylvatica* 'Fastigiata'), and a venerable holly on the spot where King James II of Scotland was blown up while besieging Roxburgh Castle in 1460. The horticultural interest is all in the old walled garden, which has been restored as a visitor attraction. Here are old vineries and fruit houses, a rose catenary, a very long border of pink crinums, and massive herbaceous borders, each designed with a different colour scheme and supplemented by dahlias and annuals so that it is full of colour even in late summer. There will be three RHS Special Events at Floors Castle in 2006; details from 020 7821 3408.

🌿 good borders; garden centre in walled garden; gift shop; licensed restaurant; coffee shop.

Owned by The Duke of Roxburghe
Number of gardeners 5

HARMONY GARDEN
St Mary's Road, Melrose TD6 9LJ

Tel: 01721 722502
www.nts.org.uk
Location In Melrose, opposite abbey.
Opening hours 10 am - 5 pm, Monday - Saturday; 1 pm - 5 pm, Sundays; Good Friday to 30 September.
Admission fee Adults £3; Concessions £2. RHS members free.

🆆🅲 ⛧

'Harmony' takes its name from the Jamaican pimento plantation where its original builder James Waugh made his fortune. It is a modest, quiet, walled garden, but very much more interesting to visit than some of the private gardens in the area. There are lawns, herbaceous and mixed borders, vegetable and fruit areas, lots of spring bulbs, a turning circle edged with Scotch roses and hedges of yew with the Scottish flame flower *Tropaeolum speciosum* growing through. The views of Melrose Abbey and the Eildon Hills are a bonus.

Owned by The National Trust for Scotland
Number of gardeners 1
Size 0.8ha (2 acres)

KAILZIE GARDENS
Kailzie, Peebles EH45 9HT

Tel & Fax: 01721 720007
Location On B7062, 2 miles east of Peebles.
Opening hours 11 am - 5.30 pm; daily; all year.
Admission fee Adults £3; Children £1 (but £2.50 & 75p respectively from mid-March to 1 June, and £2 & 50p from November to mid-March).

🅿 ⋖⃗ 🆆🅲 ⛧ 🌱 ✿ ☕

Kailzie has been revived over the last 20 years. The large walled garden has a mixture of flowers and produce: a laburnum alley, a rose garden and double herbaceous borders are some of the attractions. There are displays of gunneras, meconopsis, primulas and massed snowdrops.

 good conifers; snowdrops; daffodils; shop; restaurant & teas.

Owned by Lady Angela Buchan-Hepburn
Number of gardeners 3
Size 8ha (20 acres)

LILLIESLEAF NURSERY
Garden Cottage, Linthill, Lilliesleaf TD6 9HU

Tel & Fax: 01835 870415
Location On B6359 between Midlem & Lilliesleaf.
Opening hours 10 am - 5 pm, Monday - Saturday; 10 am - 4 pm, Sundays. November to March. Phone first.
Admission fee Free.

P ◁ WC & ✻

This nursery, in a pretty position on the bank of the River Ale, has a general plant range, with an emphasis on perennials and hard-to-find plants of every kind. It is particularly good for epimediums, and offers a number of hybrids listed by no other nursery. The demonstration garden is also worth seeing: attractive mixed borders in a walled garden.

Owned by Teyl de Bordes
Number of gardeners 2
Size 0.4ha (1 acre)
NCCPG National Collections *Epimedium*

MANDERSTON
Duns TD11 3PP

Tel: 01361 883450 **Fax:** 01361 882010
www.manderston.co.uk
Location On A6105, 2 miles east of Duns.
Opening hours 11.30 am - dusk; Sundays & Thursdays; mid-May to September. Parties at any time by appointment.
Admission fee Gardens only: free. Parties £3.50 per person.

P ◁ WC ☕

The house is Edwardian, built in classical neo-Georgian style, and was the location for Channel 4's *The Edwardian Country House*. Below it are four expansive terraces with rich planting around clipped yews and hollies and fountains on the upper terrace. Below is a small lake with an ornamental boathouse and an 18th-century Chinese-style bridge. On the other side of the lake are the woodland gardens with a large collection of unusual species of trees and shrubs: the extensive collection of rhododendrons and azaleas dates back 100 years. This woodland garden is criss-crossed with numerous paths so that visitors can see all parts of it. On the north side of the house, after crossing wide lawns set about with mature trees, visitors reach the formal garden and herbaceous borders, both at their best in summer.

woodland garden with rhododendrons & azaleas; mature conifers; good herbaceous borders; good bedding out on the formal terraces; tea-room.

Owned by Lord Palmer
Number of gardeners 2
Size 22ha (56 acres)

MELLERSTAIN
Gordon TD3 6LG

Tel: 01573 410225 **Fax:** 01573 410636
www.mellerstain.com
Location 1 mile west of A6089 Kelso to Edinburgh road.
Opening hours 11.30 pm - 5.30 pm; daily, except Tuesdays, Fridays & Saturdays; 14-17 April & 1 May to 30 September. Plus Sundays in October.
Admission fee £3.50.

P ◁ WC & ☕

The house has extensive views south to the Cheviots: it was built by the Adams (father and son) between 1725 and 1778. It is set off by Sir Reginald Blomfield's formal garden, balustraded and terraced, but now rather covered by lichen. The garden is planted with floribunda roses and catmint. Beneath it runs the landscaped park, also laid out by William and Robert Adam, sauntering down to a lake. The whole picture is uncompromisingly grand.

topiary; roses (mainly modern); Italian terraced garden by Sir Reginald Blomfield; licensed restaurant.

Owned by Mellerstain Trust
Number of gardeners 1, plus 1 seasonal assistant
Size 1.8ha (4½ acres)

MERTOUN GARDENS
St Boswells, Melrose TD6 0EA

Tel: 01835 823236 **Fax:** 01835 822474
Location B6404, 2 miles north-east of St Boswells.
Opening hours 2 pm - 6 pm; Friday - Monday; April to September.
Admission fee Adults £2.50; OAPs £1.50; Children 50p.

Mertoun is the home of the Duke & Duchess of Sutherland, on the banks of the Tweed, with rolling lawns, herbaceous borders and azaleas. Its gardens are best known for their immaculately maintained, traditional, three-acre kitchen garden in which is situated Old Mertoun House. Here is a great variety of fruit trees, vegetables, flowers and a range of heated greenhouses and cold frames. Nearby is a circular dovecot dated 1567 and thought to be the oldest in the region. Mertoun also has a young arboretum, established since 1975, with a good selection of conifers and hardwoods, most of which have grown away very well. For many years now, the Dukes have grown a strain of pea which is said to have come from one found by Lord Carnarvon in the tomb of Tutenkhamen.

vegetables; herbs; plants under glass; daffodils; good herbaceous borders.

Owned by Mertoun Gardens Trust
Number of gardeners 2½
Size 10.3ha (26 acres)

MONTEVIOT HOUSE GARDENS
Jedburgh TD8 6UQ

Tel: 01835 830380/830704 **Fax:** 01835 830288
Location Off A68 north of Jedburgh & B6400 to Nisbet.
Opening hours 12 noon - 5 pm; daily; April to October.
Admission fee Adults £2.50; Children free. (Under review.)

The gardens at Monteviot lie along a dramatic slope of the Teviot valley. The box-hedged herb garden and terrace along the front of the house have a breathtaking view of the river below. The sheltered terraced rose garden is Victorian: the river garden at the bottom was originally designed in the 1930s by Percy Cane. Italianate in inspiration, this sheltered garden slopes down between curved borders of herbaceous plants, shrubs, bulbs and roses, to a broad stone landing stage above the waters of the Teviot itself. In the nearby water garden, fed by a natural spring, three islands are linked by elegant curved wooden bridges. Here are bog plants and bamboos. The dramatic impact of the garden as a whole is heightened by the contrast between the formal and the informal and by the way that the planting leads seamlessly through the different parts. The trees in the arboretum are exceptional: recent clearing has displayed them in their glory. *Fagus sylvatica* 'Riversii' is 30m high.

fine collection of trees; water garden; Victorian rose garden; refreshments for pre-booked groups.

Number of gardeners 3

PRIORWOOD GARDEN
Melrose TD6 9PX

Tel: 01896 822493 **Fax:** 01896 823181
www.nts.org.uk
Location Next to Melrose Abbey.

Opening hours 10 am (1 pm on Sundays) - 5 pm; daily; 1 April to 24 December.
Admission fee Adults £3; Concessions £2. Honesty box.

Priorwood is best known for its shop, which was recently extended and improved. Everything in the garden is geared towards dried flowers. The plants are chosen because they are suitable for drying, but they are also very colourful. Courses on drying flowers are held here. In the orchard is a collection of historic apple cultivars, all organically grown.

dried flower shop and The National Trust for Scotland gift shop; plant sales.

Owned by The National Trust for Scotland
Number of gardeners 1

TRAQUAIR HOUSE
Innerleithen EH44 6PW

Tel: 01896 830323 **Fax:** 01896 830639
www.traquair.co.uk
Location Signed from Innerleithen.
Opening hours 12 noon (10.30 am from June to August) - 5 pm; daily; 25 March to 30 October. 11 am - 4 pm in October. 12 noon - 4 pm on weekends only in November.
Admission fee Grounds only: Adults £3.50; Children £2.

The main attraction is a large maze, planted in 1980, of beech and Leyland cypress. The house is a Catholic time-warp, said to be the oldest inhabited and most romantic house in Scotland. The Bear Gates in the park, once the main entrance to the estate, have been closed ever since Bonnie Prince Charlie passed through them for the last time in 1746.

gift shop; restaurant serving lunch & tea; Traquair ale.

Owned by Catherine Maxwell Stuart
Number of gardeners 1
Size 12ha (30 acres)

DUMFRIES & GALLOWAY

BROUGHTON HOUSE GARDENS
12 High Street, Kirkcudbright DG6 4JX

Tel & Fax: 01557 330437
Location Signed in centre of Kirkcudbright.
Opening hours 11 am - 4 pm; daily; February & March. 12 noon (10 am in July & August) - 5 pm; daily; April to October.
Admission fee Donations.

P WC &

E.A. Hornel the artist laid out the Japanese-style garden in the 1900s: it is the best-known part of the garden here and featured in many of his portraits. Most of the rest is a 'Scottish' garden with a fine position above the River Dee. The house contains many of Hornel's works and an extensive collection of Scottish books.
Owned by The National Trust for Scotland
Number of gardeners 1
Size 0.8ha (2 acres)

CALLY GARDENS
Gatehouse of Fleet, Castle Douglas DG7 2DJ

Tel: 01557 815029 (info line)
www.callygardens.co.uk
Location 12 miles west of Castle Douglas, on Gatehouse road off A75.
Opening hours 10 am - 5.30 pm; Saturdays & Sundays; 2 pm - 5.30 pm Tuesday - Friday. Easter Saturday to last Sunday in September.
Admission fee Adults £2.50; Children free.

P ◁ WC & ✿

Cally is a nursery for the horticultural *avant-garde*. It specialises in new and rare perennials, including some from wild-collected and botanic garden seed. Many are culled from a collection of over 3,000 plants, which makes it one of the most interesting in Scotland – the owner,

Michael Wickenden, has an excellent eye for quality. The walled garden has 30 large borders where all these novelties and rarities can be seen growing. It is particularly good in September but it is also spectacular in early June, when 1,000 *Meconopsis betonicifolia* and 1,000 M. x *sheldonii* come into flower. The list of what is for sale changes by as much as half each year.
Owned by Michael Wickenden
Number of gardeners 2, plus students
Size 1.2ha (3 acres)

CRAIGIEBURN CLASSIC PLANTS
By Moffat DG10 9LF

Tel: 01683 221250
Location 2½ miles east of Moffat, on A708. On left, beyond Craiglochan signs.
Opening hours 11 am - 6 pm; Thursday - Sunday; Easter to mid-October. Other times by prior arrangement.
Admission fee Adults £2.50; Children (under 12) free.

P ◁ WC ✿

Craigieburn continues to develop and improve every year. The Wheatcrofts have close links with Nepal, and Himalayan plants – including many found by Janet – flourish in the mild, damp climate. The long (75m) herbaceous borders are now fully planted but, as in all good gardens, the Wheatcrofts are always in the process of changing, moving and adding to the contents. Craigieburn is particularly good for *Meconopsis*, of which they used to have a National Collection, and *Primula*. The mild climate means that *Lobelia tupa* grows to 2.5m and *Impatiens tinctoria* flourishes voluptuously. 'Meconopsis Month' from 20 May to 20 June is perhaps the peak time to

CASTLE KENNEDY GARDEN

Stair Estates, Rephad, Stranraer DG9 8BX

Tel: 01776 702024 **Fax:** 01776 706248
www.castlekennedygardens.co.uk
Location 5 miles east of Stranraer on A75.
Opening hours 10 am – 5 pm; daily; April to
September.
Admission fee Adults £4; OAPs £3; Children £1.

🅿 ⬦ ♿ ⚘ 🐞 ⬦

Castle Kennedy is a ruined keep, destroyed in the first half of the 18th century when the bedding which was being aired for the return of the master, the 2nd Earl of Stair, caught fire. Its imposing bulk overlooks the walled garden, which is a riot of herbaceous colour in the summer, with gnarled old apple trees heavy with lichen in its midst, and some interesting tender shrubs, including bottle-brushes (*Callistemon* species) against its walls. The main horticultural interest lies outside, although the romantic planting continues. The 2nd Earl was a military man, and bequeathed to the garden its highly original structure of dashing rides, ridges and earthworks which represent battle encampments. They were made by the Royal Scots Greys and the Inniskilling Fusiliers when they should have been occupied suppressing religious dissent in the area. The extensive gardens now occupy an isthmus bounded by two lochs, with the ruined castle at one end, and its 19th-century replacement Lochinch Castle at the other – the place where *Buddleja* 'Lochinch' originated. There is a two-acre round pond, from which an ancient, slightly decrepit avenue of monkey puzzle trees leads off. These trees, *Araucaria araucana*, were grown from original seed sent from Chile: elsewhere are plants garnered by Stair forbears who subscribed to the collecting expeditions of Sir Joseph Hooker (*Rhododendron arboreum*, for example). The gardens generally are well stocked with rhododendrons, at their best in April and May. Later in the season, in an area known as the Dancing Green, a semi-circle of crimson *Embothrium coccineum* (June) is interplanted with flower-decked *Eucryphia* x *nymansensis* (August). There are more conventional flower borders in the area beside Lochinch Castle. In gardens as old as these, time has started to take its toll, but restoration and replanting is underway. The owners recommend visitors to follow one of four graded walks to get the most out of their visit. For the energetic, this is a marvellous place just to wander at will.

woodland garden; good herbaceous borders; rhododendrons; embothriums; eucryphias; monkey puzzle avenue; tallest *Pittosporum tenuifolium* (17m) in the British Isles, tallest *Rhododendron arboreum* (16m) and three other record-breaking trees; plant centre; tea-room.

Owned by Lochinch Heritage Estate
Size 30ha (75 acres)

visit, but there is always lots of interest to the plantsman. The nursery sells seeds and plants grown from the garden.

 meconopsis; woodland plants; Himalayan plants.

Owned by Janet & Andrew Wheatcroft
Number of gardeners 2
Size 3.2ha (8 acres)

ELIZABETH MACGREGOR
Ellenbank, Tongland Road, Kirkcudbright DG6 4UU

Tel & Fax: 01557 330620
Location On A711, 1 mile north of Kirkcudbright.
Opening hours 10 am - 5 pm; Mondays, Fridays & Saturdays; May to September.
Admission fee Free.

Violas – over 100 of them – are the speciality at this excellent nursery: some are not available from any other source. They are complemented by a lively selection of 500 other perennials for cottage gardens and mixed-border planting. The walled garden is worth a visit in its own right.

violas; perennials.

Owned by Elizabeth & Alasdair MacGregor
Size 0.2ha (½ acre), plus 0.6ha (1½ acres) of stock beds & trials

GALLOWAY HOUSE GARDENS
Garlieston, Newton Stewart DG8 8HF

Tel & Fax: 01988 600680
Location Off B7004 at Garlieston.
Opening hours 9 am - 5 pm; daily; March to October.
Admission fee £1.

Galloway House is where Neil McEacharn learnt to garden, before moving to Lake Maggiore to create the great gardens of Villa Taranto. A *Davidia involucrata* dates from his ownership, as do many of the tender trees and shrubs which he planted to take advantage of the mild maritime climate – eucryphias, for example. The fine conifers date back to the Earls of Galloway in the 19th century, while most of the *Rhododendron* species were planted after the war. The garden is still undergoing restoration, but is already a great pleasure to visit, especially in late spring.

snowdrops; rhododendrons & azaleas; daffodils; camellias; bluebells; camellia house; extensive new plantings.

Owned by Galloway House Gardens Trust
Number of gardeners 1
Size 26ha (65 acres)

LOGAN HOUSE
Port Logan, Stranraer DG9 9ND

Location 14 miles south of Stranraer, next to Logan Botanic Garden.
Opening hours 10 am - 5 pm; daily; March to September.
Admission fee Adults £2; Children free.

Logan Botanic Garden occupies the walled garden of Logan House. The rest of the Logan estate is still privately owned, and richly endowed with the rare plant collection built up by the McDouall family between 1870 and 1945. The real highlight is the collection of rhododendrons, including scores of self-seeded *R. augustinii*, *R. grande*, *R. macabeanum* and *R. sinogrande*, and the original *R.* 'Logan Damaris'. But the exotic trees are stunning at all seasons: embothriums, nothofagus, araucarias, metrosideros, clethras and several UK record-holders, including *Leptospermum lanigerum* and *Eucryphia cordifolia* (20m tall).

Owned by Mr & Mrs Andrew Roberts
Size 8ha (20 acres)

GLENWHAN GARDEN
Dunragit, by Stranraer DG9 8PH

Tel & Fax: 01581 400222
www.glenwhangardens.co.uk
Location 1 mile off A75 at Dunragit village. Follow brown tourist signs.
Opening hours 10 am – 5 pm; daily; April to October. And by appointment.
Admission fee Adults £4; OAPs £3; Children £1.50; Family £8.50. RHS members free after 1 August.

P ⌇ WC & ✿ ♣ ◻

Glenwhan is a plantsman's garden which has been created since 1979 by its present owners, starting from moorland, bog and scrub. Ambitious in scale, the heart of the garden is a pair of lochans or bog lakes. Above them rises a series of roped terraces, planted with heathers, azaleas, small conifers, golden elders, hardy fuchsias and massed Rugosa roses. A small folly stands at the peak. In prospect, the whole design is beautifully composed and tranquil. From the folly there are extensive views across the garden to Luce Bay and the Mull of Galloway beyond. Tessa Knott's first plantings (in 1980) were a sturdy shelter belt of small trees, including native Scots pines, English oaks and mountain ashes. Now maturing very well, there are occasional glimpses through these lichen-stained ancients to the gorse scrub and bog which surround the garden. The shelter belt is a transitional feature: it is a refinement of the more primitive vegetation beyond the perimeter fence, and it introduces planting themes which are then developed within the garden, in the form, for example, of collections of choicer *Sorbus* and *Quercus* species (including *Q.* x *bushii* and *Q. dentata*). Pools have been cut out of the blackest peat to make an attractive sequence of grassy water gardens, planted with primula and meconopsis cultivars. Glenwhan is very much a plantsman's garden, but Tessa Knott also uses plants to create effects, and she has capitalised upon the lie of the land to produce different habitats. The new plantings include large-leaved rhododendron species (*R. fictolacteum* for example), and some interesting southern hemisphere plants, including eucalyptus and olearias around the summerhouse, embothriums, eucryphias, callistemons and dicksonias. Another highlight is the dappled woodland walk with yet more new planting. Indeed many parts of this garden are 'work in progress' which will be worth returning to see again as they mature.

woodland garden; roses (mainly old-fashioned); plantsman's collection of plants; bluebells; cistus; camellias; primulas; bog plants; trees and shrubs; many new *Rhododendron* species from collected seed; shop; nursery with interesting plants; licensed garden restaurant.

Owned by Tessa & William Knott
Number of gardeners 2
Size 5ha (12½ acres)

LOGAN BOTANIC GARDEN
Port Logan, Stranraer DG9 9ND

Tel: 01776 860231 **Fax:** 01776 860333
www.rbge.org.uk
Location 14 miles south of Stranraer on B7065.
Opening hours 10 am - 6 pm (5 pm in March &
October); daily; March to October.
Admission fee Adults £3.50; Concessions £3;
Children £1; Family £8.

This extraordinarily exotic garden, started by the McDouall family in the 19th century, is now part of the Royal Botanic Garden Edinburgh. Logan's sheltered aspect and proximity to the warming waters of the Atlantic enable a wide range of tender and southern hemisphere plants to be grown out of doors. The bedding out of thousands of half-hardy perennials makes the garden a blaze of colour on bright sunny days. In the walled garden, overlooked by the slender remains of Castle Balzieland, there is a fine collection of established tree ferns (*Dicksonia antarctica*). They are underplanted with the smaller fern, *Blechnum chilense*, which creates an impression of lush fertility, as if the dicksonias have seeded themselves everywhere. The formal lily pond is partly framed by a diagonal avenue of cabbage palms (*Cordyline australis*) 10m high. Around the pond are waving wands of *Dierama pulcherrimum* and *Kniphofia*, and the air glints with dragonflies in summer. Among the trees which flower in the sheltered walls are a tall *Metrosideros umbellatus* and the flame tree *Embothrium coccineum*. Also flowering freely here, as it does in other gardens in south-west Scotland, is *Eucryphia* x *nymansensis*

'Nymansay'. Beyond the brilliance of the walled garden, and past an avenue of Chusan palms (*Trachycarpus fortunei*), lies Logan's woodland garden. Some of its pleasures are more hidden than others, but a spectacular specimen of *Magnolia campbellii* 'Charles Raffill' stands on the edge, in flower in April, and decked with swollen red pods by August. Look out in particular for plants from the southern hemisphere, including *Leptospermum lanigerum*, *Crinodendron hookerianum*, and the Chatham Island daisy bush *Olearia semidentata* (syn. *O*. 'Henry Travers'). Do not miss the gunneras bog either, where this giant rhubarb-like plant grows so tall and thick that you can lose yourself under its prickly, slightly sinister canopy. In the Discovery Centre there are reference books, computers and microscopes which the visitor can use, perhaps to learn more about the Maddenia section of the genus *Rhododendron*, in which the garden specialises. Visitors can borrow innovative free audio guides, which are keyed to numbers marked on labels throughout the gardens. It is slightly surreal to see your fellow visitors wandering around clasping these futuristic wands, but the guide is informative and chatty.

sub-tropical plants; good herbaceous borders; tree ferns; cardiocrinums; gunneras; cordylines; trachycarpus palms; tender perennials (diascias, fuchsias, salvias); eucalyptus; shop; café.

Owned by Royal Botanic Garden Edinburgh
Size 12ha (30 acres)

THREAVE GARDEN
Castle Douglas DG7 1RX

Tel: 01556 502575 **Fax:** 01556 502683
www.nts.org.uk
Location Off A75, 1 mile west of Castle Douglas.
Opening hours 9.30 am - sunset; daily; all year.
Walled garden & glasshouses close at 5 pm.
Admission fee Adults £6; Concessions £4.50. RHS
members free in April, May, September & October.

🄿 ⋙ 🆆🅲 ♿ 🌼 🐛 ✕ ☕

Threave is a teaching garden with a very
wide range of attractions – something to
interest every gardener, in fact. It has been
developed since 1960 with the needs of
students at the School of Horticulture,
garden-owners and tourists all in mind.
There are over 200 daffodil cultivars to
admire in spring; roses and colourful
herbaceous borders in summer; and good
autumn colour. A new Victorian-style
conservatory has recently been built in the
walled garden.

🌿 tallest *Alnus rubra* (23m) in the British
Isles, and two other record trees; shop;
plant centre; restaurant & snacks.

Owned by The National Trust for Scotland
Number of gardeners 2, plus 3 instructors
Size 26ha (65 acres)

WOODFALL GARDENS
Glasserton, Whithorn, Newton Stewart
DG8 8LY

Tel: 01988 500692 **Fax:** 01988 500080
www.woodfall-gardens.co.uk
Location By Glasserton Church, 2 miles south of
Whithorn.
Opening hours 2 pm - 5.30 pm; 14 May & 9 July
for SGS and 11 June for Marie Curie. 2 pm -
4.30 pm on 28 August for St Ninian Festival.
Other dates not yet fixed.
Admission fee For SGS: Adults £2.50;
Concessions £1.50; Children free.

🄿 ♿ 🌼 🐛

After the big house at Glasserton was
demolished in 1952, the large 18th-century
walled garden gradually declined into
disrepair. Successive owners have brought
it to life again as a private garden. A small
area is devoted to raising and selling box
and yew for topiary, parterres and knots.
The rest is a garden of great interest at all
seasons, with a parterre, a woodland area, a
grasses garden and a fern garden, as well as
colourful mixed borders and a productive
potager.

🌿 topiary plants; *Parthenocissus*; plant
sales area.

Owned by Lesley & David Roberts
Number of gardeners owners, plus 1 part-time
Size 1.2ha (3 acres)

FIFE

CAMBO GARDENS
Kingsbarns, St Andrews KY16 8QD

Tel: 01333 450054 **Fax:** 01333 450987
www.camboestate.com
Location On A917 between Kingsbarns & Crail.
Opening hours 10 am - dusk; daily; all year.
Guided tours by arrangement.
Admission fee Adults £3.50; Children free. RHS
members free.

Cambo's large, romantic, Victorian walled
garden is built around the Cambo Burn, a
most unusual feature which, with its
summerhouse, willows, elegant wrought-
iron bridges and waterfall, gives the
garden its unique character. The
atmosphere is informal, with naturalistic
plantings of herbaceous perennials, many
of them unusual. There are also masses of
spring bulbs, a lilac walk, rambler roses,
and fine herbaceous borders for summer
and autumn. An ornamental *potager* and
cutting garden add to the variety and a
traditional vegetable garden supplies fruit
and vegetables to the handsome Victorian
house. A woodland garden with masses of
colchicums in autumn is traversed by
walks that lead down to the sea,
spectacular in early spring when carpeted
with aconites, snowflakes and snowdrops.
A National Collection of snowdrops is in
the pipeline. There will be three RHS
Special Events at Cambo Gardens in
2006; details from 020 7821 3408.
roses (mainly old-fashioned);
daffodils; snowflakes; aconites;
colchicum meadows; autumn colour; plants for
sale.

Owned by Mr & Mrs T.P.N. Erskine
Number of gardeners 3
Size 1ha (2½ acres), plus 28ha (70 acres) of
woodland

FALKLAND PALACE
Falkland, Cupar KY15 7BU

Tel: 01337 857397 **Fax:** 01337 857980
www.nts.org.uk
Location On A912, 11 miles north of Kirkcaldy. 10
miles from M90, Jct 8.
Opening hours 10 am - 6 pm; daily; Sundays 1 pm
- 5.30 pm (last admissions one hour before
closing); March to October.
Admission fee Adults £5; Concessions £4.

The palace at Falkland is old: it dates from
the first half of the 16th century. Today's
flower garden was built in 1952 by Percy
Cane. The pastiche of a Scottish
renaissance garden has a herb garden in
the Jacobean style, an astrolabe walk and
formal parterres prettily planted in pastel
colours.
gift shop; plant centre.

Owned by The National Trust for Scotland
Number of gardeners 2
Size 4.4ha (11 acres)

HILL OF TARVIT
Cupar KY15 5PB

Tel & Fax: 01334 653127
www.nts.org.uk
Location Off A916, 2½ miles south of Cupar.
Opening hours 9.30 am - sunset; daily; all year.
Admission fee Adults £2; Concessions £1.
Honesty box. RHS members free.

Both house and garden at Hill of Tarvit
were designed by Lorimer. The formal
garden is not so well planted and
maintained as it used to be, but the Trust
has begun to restore and replant the borders
on the top terrace in an Edwardian style.

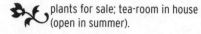 plants for sale; tea-room in house (open in summer).

Owned by The National Trust for Scotland
Number of gardeners 2
Size 8ha (20 acres)

KELLIE CASTLE
Pittenween KY10 2RF

Tel: 01333 720271 **Fax:** 01333 720736
www.nts.org.uk
Location On B9171, 3 miles north-west of Pittenween.
Opening hours 9.30 am - 5.30 pm; daily; all year.
Admission fee Adults £4. RHS members free.

Kellie Castle was Sir Robert Lorimer's own family house: it was he who initiated the reconstruction of the garden in its present form. The walled garden is no more than one acre in extent, but strong lines and thick planting create a sense of both space and enclosure. Much of the planting is a modern reinterpretation of Lorimer's original design: later family members have made alterations and additions. The organic walled garden contains a fine collection of old-fashioned roses, fruit trees and herbaceous plants: there are displays in the summerhouse about the history of the walled garden. The yew hedges are threaded with scarlet *Tropaeolum speciosum*.
extended collection of historic vegetables; gift shop; tea-room.

Owned by The National Trust for Scotland
Number of gardeners 2
Size 6.4ha (16 acres)

ST ANDREWS BOTANIC GARDEN
The Canongate, St Andrews KY16 8RT

Tel: 01334 476452 **Fax:** 01334 476452
www.st-andrews-botanic.org
Location A915, Largo Road, then entrance in The Canongate.
Opening hours 10 am - 7 pm (4 pm October to April); daily; all year.
Admission fee Adults £2; OAPs & Children £1. RHS members free.

The botanic garden at St Andrews is currently undergoing much improvement. The garden's main asset, the peat, rock and water complex (crag, scree, moraine, alpine meadow and bog) is being repaired and replanted. The succulent house, alpine house and tropical house are now well established and there is a house for Maddenia rhododendrons, too. A new Mediterranean Climate house is under development. The garden caters particularly well for children and is interesting to visit at every season.
woodland garden; rock garden; rhododendrons & azaleas; plants under glass; fine collection of trees; peat beds; ferns; heath garden; order beds; herbaceous borders; self-service tea/coffee.

Owned by St Andrews University, but managed by Fife Council
Number of gardeners 4
Size 7.2ha (18 acres)

GRAMPIAN

BLACKHILLS
by Elgin, Moray IV30 3QU

Tel: 01343 842223 **Fax:** 01343 842223
www.blackhills.co.uk
Location 1 mile south of Lhanbryde, near Elgin on the B9103.
Opening hours 12 noon - 6 pm; 14 & 21 May. And by appointment.
Admission fee Adults £2; Children free.

P 🐾 WC ♿ 🌾

Blackhills is a magnificent collection of rhododendrons in two steep-sided glacial valleys: these possess a microclimate which allows many plants to grow that are normally considered too tender for the north-east coast of Scotland. The rhododendrons were planted throughout the 20th century by successive generations of the Christie family, along with many other Himalayan and Chinese plants, in a woodland garden which is now fully mature. There are about 360 different rhododendron species growing at Blackhills, all of wild origin: most were collected in the Himalayas, some came from North America, Central Asia and Northern Europe. The garden now contains one of the finest and most extensive private collections of species rhododendrons in the world.

🌿 rhododendrons.

Owned by T.S. Christie
Number of gardeners 1
Size 20ha (50 acres)

BRODIE CASTLE
Brodie, Forres, Moray IV36 2TE

Tel: 01309 641371 **Fax:** 01309 641600
www.nts.org.uk
Location Signed from A96. 4½ miles west of Forres.

Opening hours Grounds: 9.30 am - sunset; daily; all year.
Admission fee £2. Honesty box.

P WC ♿ 🌾 🌰 🛍

Brodie Castle sits in a flat landscaped park with an ornamental woodland garden behind: here a young lime avenue leads to a polyhedral sundial and opens out attractive plantings of ornamental maples, liquidambars, sorbus, birches and rhododendrons. Brodie is, however, famous for its daffodils. Many were bred here at the turn of the 19th century and the Trust has tried assiduously to identify, propagate and distribute them more widely. They are a glorious sight when they bloom in the lawns around the baronial battlements.

🌿 daffodils; colchicums; NTS shop; tea-room in castle (closes at 4.30 pm).

Owned by The National Trust for Scotland
Number of gardeners 6, plus 2 part-time
Size 32ha (80 acres)
NCCPG National Collections *Narcissus*

CRATHES CASTLE
Banchory AB31 5QJ

Tel: 01330 844525 **Fax:** 01330 844797
www.nts.org.uk
Location On A93, 15 miles west of Aberdeen.
Opening hours 9 am - sunset; daily; all year.
Admission fee Adults £8; Concessions £6.

P 🐾 WC ♿ 🌾 🌰 ✗ 🛍

Crathes is famous for its walled garden, which started as a kitchen garden and was later developed as a flower garden, both before World War I and in the 1920s and 1930s. It is divided into eight distinct gardens, each with its own character. These include a white border, a yellow enclosure known as the Golden Garden, a misty-blue garden, and a dreamy high-summer border with pastel shades for long Highland evenings. The garden is intensively planted to give colour all the year round. Some of the topiary yew hedges date back to 1702.

current holder of Sandford Award; tallest *Zelkova* x *verschaffeltii* in the British Isles, and four further tree records; NTS shop; plant centre; restaurant/café open most of the year.

Owned by The National Trust for Scotland
Number of gardeners 5
Size 1.5ha (3¾ acres)
NCCPG National Collections *Dianthus* (Malmaison carnations)

CRUICKSHANK BOTANIC GARDEN
St Machar Drive, Aberdeen AB24 3UU

Tel: 01224 272704 **Fax:** 01224 272703
www.abdn.ac.uk/biologicalsci/pss/gardens
Location Follow signs for University of Aberdeen and/or Old Aberdeen. Entrance in The Chanonry.
Opening hours 9 am - 4.30 pm; Monday - Friday; all year. Plus 2 pm - 5 pm; Saturdays & Sundays; May to September.
Admission fee Free.

Cruickshank Botanic Garden was founded in 1898 for the teaching and study of botany at the University of Aberdeen. Its 12 acres still have an educational element but also serve as an amenity for the wider public. Its leading features include: a rock garden for alpine plants and bulbs, where wild orchids seed around; an arboretum, planted with natives, exotics and garden cultivars, many of them now semi-mature; collections of native plants, including all the endemic *Sorbus* species of the British Isles; and a rose garden which has been laid out to illustrate the history of the rose in cultivation. The garden is well maintained and – like all botanic gardens – worth visiting at any time of the year. It is also supported by an enthusiastic Friends organisation.

lots of plants; roses (mainly old-fashioned); rock garden; good

herbaceous borders; fine collection of trees; stone troughs; peat beds; Scottish upland plants; *Meconopsis* x *sheldonii*.

Owned by University of Aberdeen & Cruickshank Botanic Garden Trust
Number of gardeners 3
Size 4.4ha (11 acres)

DRUM CASTLE
Drumoak, Banchory AB31 3EY

Tel: 01330 811204 **Fax:** 01330 811962
www.drum-castle.org.uk
Location Off A93, 10 miles west of Aberdeen.
Opening hours Grounds: 9.30 am - sunset; daily; all year. Garden: 12.30 pm (10 am from June to August) - 5.30 pm; daily; April to September.
Admission fee Adults £3; Concessions £2.50.

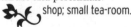

Modern gardens – begun in 1991 with the intention of providing an appropriate historic setting for the castle and a place where old Scottish roses could be grown. There is a knot garden planted with herbs in the style of the early 17th century and a formal garden with *allées* and topiary to represent the early 18th century. The Victorian-style garden has a decorative, rose-covered catenary and the sunken garden a collection of modern roses, shrubs and perennials.

shop; small tea-room.

Owned by The National Trust for Scotland
Number of gardeners 2
Size 8ha (20 acres)

DUTHIE PARK
Polmuir Road, Aberdeen AB11 7SL

Tel: 01224 522984
Location By river, in Ferryhill area of Aberdeen.
Opening hours 9.30 am - dusk; daily; all year. Closed 1 January & 25 December.
Admission fee Free.

Duthie Park is one of Scotland's top tourist attractions: 350,000 people visit it every year – and it is free. The park was laid out in 1883, but substantially improved when David Welch was director in the 1970s and 1980s. Its main attraction in summer is the Rose Mountain, a massed display of bright modern roses, themselves quite a feature of Aberdeen's roadside landscaping. But the jewel in the crown are the Winter Gardens, a series of linked glasshouses with beautiful and instructive plant displays. They include the Bromeliad House, Cacti & Succulents Hall, Victorian Corridor, Floral Hall, Corridor of Perfumes and Fern House.
Owned by Aberdeen City Council
Number of gardeners 9

KILDRUMMY CASTLE
Kildrummy, Alford AB33 8RA

Tel: 01975 571203/571277
www.kildrummy-castle-gardens.co.uk
Location On A97, off A944.
Opening hours 10 am - 5 pm; daily; April to October.
Admission fee Adults £2.50; Children free.

Kildrummy has a glen-garden, laid out about 100 years ago. The richly planted pools and ponds are complemented by a plantsman's collection on the hillside, and a large mature rock garden made from the natural sandstone. It is one of the most romantic gardens in Scotland.
roses (mainly old-fashioned); plantsman's collection of plants; fine collection of trees; autumn colour; heathers; tea & coffee.

Owned by Kildrummy Castle Garden Trust
Number of gardeners 2½
Size 8ha (20 acres)

LEITH HALL
Kennethmont, Huntly AB54 4NQ

Tel: 01464 831216 **Fax:** 01464 831594
www.nts.org.uk

Location On B9002, 1 mile west of Kennethmont.
Opening hours 9.30 am - sunset; daily; all year.
Admission fee Adults £3; Concessions £2. RHS members free.

From this garden's historic past come two ponds and an ice house, but richly planted borders are the pride of Leith Hall today: they are full of colour all through the summer. Also impressive is the rock garden, restored and replanted by that most successful of societies, the Scottish Rock Garden Club. Leith gets better and better.
sculptures in woodland walk; refreshments May to September, 12 noon to 5 pm.

Owned by The National Trust for Scotland
Number of gardeners 2
Size 2.4ha (6 acres)

PITMEDDEN
Ellon, Aberdeen AB41 7PD

Tel: 01651 842352 **Fax:** 01651 843188
www.nts.org.uk
Location 1 mile west of Pitmedden on A920.
Opening hours 10 am - 5.30 pm; daily; May to September.
Admission fee Adults £5; Concessions £4; Children £2.

The formal garden at Pitmedden was created in the 1950s by the National Trust for Scotland, using 17th-century Scottish designs. Three of the four parterres came from patterns associated with Holyroodhouse: the fourth is an heraldic design based on the coat-of-arms of Sir Alexander Seton, who first laid out a garden here in 1675. The result has three miles of box hedging and uses 40,000 bedding plants every summer.
plants for sale; tea-room.

Owned by The National Trust for Scotland
Number of gardeners 5
Size 6ha (15 acres)

HIGHLAND

ABRIACHAN GARDENS
Loch Ness Side, by Inverness IV3 8LA

Tel & Fax: 01463 861232
www.lochnessgarden.com
Location Just off A82.
Opening hours 9 am - 7 pm (5 pm in British Winter Time); daily; February to November.
Admission fee Adults £2; OAPs £1; Children 20p. RHS members free.

🅿 ⟁ 🌿 ▷

Abriachan is a fine plantsman's garden, cut from native scrub – hazel, birch and rowan – on a steep, south-east-facing slope above Loch Ness. The views across to the other side and down the Great Glen are spectacular. The garden is absolutely full of interesting plants of every kind and the owners have created endless different habitats to accommodate the widest possible variety. There are lots of new projects under way. The nursery is a treasure-house of good plants.

🌿 good modern garden; herbaceous plants; geraniums, helianthemums and Barnhaven primulas; hot drinks machine.

Owned by Mr & Mrs D. Davidson
Number of gardeners 2
Size 1.6ha (4 acres)

ARDFEARN NURSERY
Bunchrew, Inverness IV3 8RH

Tel: 01463 243250 **Fax:** 01463 711713
www.ardfearn-nursery.co.uk
Location On A862, 5 miles west of Inverness.
Opening hours 9 am - 5 pm; daily.

🅿 ♿ 🌿 ▣ ▷

Alpines, ericaceous plants and shrubs, and trees are produced at this intensive nursery in a lovely Highland farmstead. It is particularly good for plants from New Zealand and the Himalayas and, above all, for primulas. But the stock is always changing and expanding – especially of rare and unusual plants – which is what draws back both novices and the nursery's discriminating clientele year after year.

 gift shop; coffee facilities.

Owned by Alasdair Sutherland

ARDTORNISH GARDENS
Lochaline, Morvern by Oban PA34 5VZ

Tel: 01967 421288 **Fax:** 01967 421211
www.ardtornishgardens.co.uk
Location 2 miles north-east of Lochaline.
Opening hours 8 am - dusk; daily; all year
Admission fee £3.

🅿 ⟁ ⌨ 🌿

This is Faith Raven's other garden – see Docwra's Manor in Cambridgeshire – and a complete contrast: 28 acres of rocky hillside full of rhododendrons and acid-loving trees and shrubs. The oldest plantings date back to the 19th century but the real horticultural interest began in the 1930s when Mrs Raven's parents began to plant a great range of *Rhododendron* species. A large number of unnamed hybrid seedlings came from Sir John Stirling Maxwell of Pollock House, Glasgow, which fill the rhododendron glen with colour. Flowering continues into August with *R.* 'Polar Bear', when the flowers also start with *Eucryphia* x *nymansensis* 'Nymansay' and *Hoheria lyallii*. Mrs Raven has actively improved the garden with further plantings of eucryphias, embothriums and acers and much else. The spring bulbs and early rhododendrons are fine from March onwards. Peak time for rhododendrons is May/June, but the autumn colours are also spectacular – the leaves of acers, cercidiphyllums, enkianthus, prunus, and berries of sorbus, berberis and cotoneaster. plantsman's collection of plants; mature conifers; bluebells; kitchen garden; gunneras; rhododendrons; autumn colour.

Owned by Mrs John Raven
Number of gardeners 1
Size 11.1ha (28 acres)

ATTADALE GARDENS
Strathcarron, Wester Ross IV54 8YX

Tel: 01520 722217/722603 **Fax:** 01520 722546
www.attadale.com
Location On A890 between Strathcarron & South Strome.
Opening hours 10 am - 5.30 pm; Monday - Saturday; April to October. Coaches by prior arrangement only. For SGS: 2 pm - 5.30 pm on 3 June.
Admission fee Adults £3; Children £1; Disabled free.

The gardens at Attadale were started in the 1890s: many rhododendrons, azaleas and specimen trees date from that time. The recent expansion of planting began in the 1980s, with over 2,000 trees and shrubs, which are now underplanted with irises, candelabra primulas, gunneras and bamboos. The ponds and waterfalls are spanned by bridges and richly planted with marginals and water lilies. Handsome sculptures add quite a different dimension. In an old quarry, a geodesic dome houses an exotic fern collection. There is also a Japanese garden and a kitchen garden. The nursery specialises in bog plants – among them, primula, gunneras, darmera – as well as more than 80 different ferns. rhododendrons; meconopsis; primulas; bog plants; ferns; nursery; tea-room.

Owned by Mr & Mrs Ewen Macpherson
Number of gardeners 4½
Size 8ha (20 acres)

AUCHGOURISH GARDENS & ARBORETUM
Street of Kincardine, by Boat of Garten PH24 3BY

Tel: 01479 831464 **Fax:** 01479 831672
Location Follow brown tourist signs from Aviemore & Inverness.
Opening hours 10 am - 5 pm; daily; March to October. 11 am - 3 pm in winter.
Admission fee Adults £3.50; Children free.

Auchgourish is a new garden, begun in 2001 as a tourist attraction with botanic and horticultural interest. It is particularly interesting to learn what will survive in extreme conditions – short summers, frost in every month of the year and a soil so poor and sandy that it has neither slugs nor worms. Many East Asian plants do well, especially loniceras, malus and pyrus, and there is a slight Japanese overlay to the design. But the plants are the real interest. Most are grown from seed that is wild-collected or collected from parents of known wild origin: over 120 *Primula* species, over 80 *Sorbus*, 73 *Betula*, 67 *Iris*, 59 *Fritillaria* and even 24 *Lonicera*. And there are always surplus plants for sale which are unavailable elsewhere. Scottish native plants; oriental gardens; surplus plants for sale.

Owned by Iain Brodie of Falsyde
Number of gardeners 1
Size 4ha (10 acres)

CAWDOR CASTLE
Cawdor, Nairn IV12 5RD

Tel: 01667 404401 **Fax:** 01667 404674
www.cawdorcastle.com
Location Between Inverness & Nairn on B9090.
Opening hours 10 am - 5.30 pm; daily; 1 May to 8 October.
Admission fee £3.70. RHS members free to gardens in May, June, September & October.

Cawdor Castle could claim to be the most romantic castle in the Highlands – the 14th-century home of the Thanes of Cawdor. It has several gardens: the earliest dates from the 16th century. Best of all is an 18th-century flower garden with large herbaceous borders, a lavender-edged garden with shrub roses, whole borders of lilies and galtonias, spring-flowering trees and shrubs, and an arch of rambling roses. The 19th-century wild garden has a good collection of rhododendrons and spring bulbs as well as huge lime trees and fine Victorian conifers. Recent additions to the walled garden include a holly maze, a laburnum walk, several modern designs, and coloured planting schemes. The Auchindoune garden, originally planted in the 1920s with plants brought back by Lord Cawdor from his expedition to the Himalayas with Frank Kingdon Ward, is being restored with many of the species they collected in the Tsangpo Gorges: it is open on Tuesdays and Thursdays from May to July, and by appointment at other times.

woodland garden; roses (mainly old-fashioned); fruit; good herbaceous borders; good late-summer plantings; gift shop; licensed restaurant in castle.

Owned by The Dowager Countess Cawdor
Number of gardeners 4
Size 1.4ha (3½ acres)

COILTIE GARDEN
Divach, Drumnadrochit IV63 6XW

Tel: 01456 450219
Location Take the small uphill road off A82 at Drumnadrochit to Divach for about 2 miles. Garden 150m beyond Divach Lodge.
Opening hours 12 noon - 7 pm; daily; 17 June to 23 July. And by appointment.
Admission fee Adults £2; Children free.

There was little except a few old trees and a 30m waterfall when the Nelsons came to Coiltie in 1980 and took on the neglected and overgrown Victorian garden. They decided not to reconstruct it, but to lay a new informal one on the sloping site, and planted it with trees (100+), hedges, shrubs, climbers, herbaceous plants and lots of roses. Below is a steep ravine with ancient woodlands.

roses; trees; mixed borders.

Owned by Mr & Mrs David Nelson
Number of gardeners 1
Size 1.6ha (4 acres)

DUNROBIN CASTLE GARDENS
Golspie, Sutherland KW10 6SF

Tel: 01408 633177 **Fax:** 01408 634081
www.great-houses-scotland.co.uk
Location 1 mile north of Golspie on A9.
Opening hours Castle & gardens: 10.30 am - 5.30 pm (4.30 pm in April, May & October); 1 April to 15 October. Last admissions 30 minutes before closing.
Admission fee Castle & Gardens: Adults £6.60; OAPs £5.70; Children £4.70. Reductions for groups. RHS members free. Gardens free in winter.

The grand terraced gardens at Dunrobin were laid out in 1850 by Sir Charles Barry, architect of the Houses of Parliament. Their formal style, striding down to the Dornoch Forth, is appropriate to the enormous French-style *château*. Three immensely grand parterres surround the fountains, two traditionally bedded out (but brilliantly and colourfully done) and one planted with hardy geraniums and *Ceratostigma willmottianum*, underplanted with tulips and lilies. One of the parterres was substantially made in recent years, and thereby much improved: some 20 wooden pyramids have been planted with clematis and climbing roses in a modern reinterpretation of 19th-century grandeur.

Elsewhere are lots of interesting plants: *Akebia quinata*; huge clumps of gunneras; tall fuchsias (including *F.* 'Dunrobin Bedder'); *Ceanothus thyrsiflorus* with eccremocarpus threading through it; huge maples, limes and horse-chestnuts (much taller than one might expect so far north); a long herbaceous border where plants grow unusually tall; and extensive rhododendron woodlands. New for 2006 is a *potager* which seeks to combine lilies and roses with a display of colourful and useful vegetables.

woodland garden; topiary; roses (mainly modern); good herbaceous borders; formal gardens; gift shop; tea-room in castle.

Owned by The Sutherland Trust
Number of gardeners 3
Size 2ha (5 acres)

THE HYDROPONICUM
Achiltibuie, Ullapool IV26 2YG

Tel: 01854 622202 **Fax:** 01854 622201
www.thehydroponicum.com
Location Signed off A835, 25 miles north of Ullapool.
Opening hours 10 am - 6 pm; daily; 3 April to 30 September. Guided tours on the hour (last one at 5 pm). Plus tours at 12 noon & 2 pm from Monday - Friday in October (open 11.30 am - 3.30 pm). SGS open days: 14 May & 20 August.
Admission fee Adults £4.95; Concessions £3.95; Children £2.95.

The Hydroponicum has three growing houses (one heated, two unheated), each featuring plants from different climatic zones. Salads, herbs and tree fruits grow in the 'cottage garden' house. Tomatoes, citrus fruit and olives fill the 'South of France' house. And the 'Canary Island zone' is planted with vines, figs, tamarillos and bananas. 'Planted' is not quite the right word: hydroponics are all about soilless cultivation – essential in places like

Saudi Arabia but a small miracle here in the north-west of Scotland.

hydroponic culture; fruit under glass; café.

Owned by Viscount Gough
Number of gardeners 2
Size 0.1ha (¼ acre) of kederhouses & 0.8ha (2 acres) of grounds

INVEREWE
Poolewe, Ross and Cromarty IV22 2LG

Tel: 01445 781200 **Fax:** 01445 781497
www.nts.org.uk
Location On A832, 6 miles north-east of Gairloch.
Opening hours 9.30 am - 9 pm (4 pm from November to March); daily; all year.
Admission fee Adults £8; Concessions £5.25; Children £1.

Inverewe is one of the wonders of the horticultural world, a sub-tropical garden in the north-west Highlands. Its position on a sheltered peninsular, warmed by the Gulf Stream, explains the luxuriance of its plantings. It is also the reason why, even so far north, it has much to interest the plantsman at every time of the year. The garden owes its origins to Osgood Mackenzie, who from 1862 to 1922 planted windbreaks to protect more delicate exotics within. Spectacular large-leaved Himalayan rhododendrons, magnolias, eucalyptus, tree ferns, palms and tender rarities are underplanted with drifts of blue poppies and candelabra primulas. Among Inverewe's record trees are specimens of *Eucalyptus cordata* and *Salix magnifica*, neither of which would be fully hardy in the home counties of England. Inverewe is exceptionally well maintained, though perhaps best on a sunny, dry day in May, before the midges breed.

tallest *Eucalyptus cordata* (30m) in the British Isles, and three further record trees; large shop; plant centre; excellent new restaurant.

Owned by The National Trust for Scotland
Number of gardeners 8
Size 20ha (50 acres)
NCCPG National Collections *Olearia*,
Brachyglottis, *Rhododendron* (Barbatum, Glischra
& Maculifera sections)

JACK DRAKE

Inshriach Alpine Nursery, Aviemore,
Inverness-shire PH22 1QS

Tel: 01540 651287 **Fax:** 01540 651656
www.drakesalpines.com
Location 4 miles south of Aviemore. Take B970
to Inverdruie. Turn right, ¾ mile after the Spey
Bridge.
Opening hours 10 am - 5 pm; daily; March to
October.
Admission fee Free. Donations welcome.

P WC 🌱 ⊏

For more than 60 years this famous
Highland nursery has been a Mecca for
devotees of alpine and rock garden plants.
It offers a large number of selected or
collected forms. True alpines rub shoulders
with herbaceous plants for wild and bog
gardens. The nursery is laid out with
demonstration gardens – screes, peat walls,
wild gardens and bog gardens. A new
woodland walk is under development.
Scotland's premier alpine nursery;
primulas; meconopsis; gentians;
heathers; tea-room.

Owned by John & Gunnbjørg Borrowman
Size 0.8ha (2 acres)

LECKMELM ARBORETUM

by Ullapool IV23 2RH

Location 3 miles south of Ullapool on A835.
Opening hours 10 am - 6 pm; daily; April to
October.
Admission fee Adults £2.50; Children free.

P ⊲

The Leckmelm Arboretum was laid out in
the 1870s, and it is from those days that
many of the finest rhododendron species
and trees date – wellingtonias, cedars,
monkey puzzles and a huge weeping beech
(*Fagus sylvatica* 'Pendula'). Some of the
trees are record-breakers, including an
Abies amabilis 40m high, a good
Chamaecyparis lawsoniana 'Wisselii', a
Thujopsis dolabrata and a *Kalopanax pictus*,
whose presence at such a northerly point
may be explained by the mild climate. The
Troughtons have taken advantage of the
arboretum's position on the shores of Loch
Broom to make new plantings in recent
years: they have put in such large-leaved
rhododendrons as *R. sinogrande* and *R.
macabeanum*, and even a selection of
dicksonias and palms.
ancient trees; good rhododendrons.

Owned by Mr & Mrs Peter Troughton
Number of gardeners 1
Size 5ha (12½ acres)

LOCHALSH WOODLAND GARDEN

Balmacara, By Kyle of Lochalsh, Ross
IV40 8DN

Tel: 01599 566325 **Fax:** 01599 566359
www.nts.org.uk
Location On A87, 3 miles east of Kyle.
Opening hours 9 am - sunset; daily; all year.
Admission fee Adults £2. Honesty box.

P ⊲ WC ♿ 🌱 🌰

This woodland garden is becoming much
better known, and deservedly. The
structure is about 100 years old – tall pines,
oaks and larches with ornamental
underplantings started in the late 1960s.
Rhododendrons from Euan Cox at
Glendoick came first: newer plantings
include collections of hardy ferns,
bamboos, fuchsias, hydrangeas and
Maddenia rhododendrons, as well as plants
from Tasmania and New Zealand. The
season of interest extends from early spring
well into autumn.

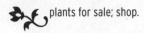 plants for sale; shop.

Owned by The National Trust for Scotland
Number of gardeners 1
Size 5.2ha (13 acres)

THE CASTLE OF MEY
Thurso, Caithness KW14 8XH

Tel: 01808 851473 **Fax:** 01808 521475
www.castleofmey.org.uk
Location On A836 between Thurso & John
O'Groats.
Opening hours 10.30 am - 4 pm; Saturday -
Thursday; 13 May to 27 July & 9 August to 28
September.
Admission fee Adults £3; Concessions £2.50;
Children free.

The Castle of Mey was Queen Elizabeth the Queen Mother's summer home and is planted largely for late-summer enjoyment, but full of interest at all seasons. The main attraction is the kitchen garden, enclosed by 12ft walls and protected by lots of internal hedges of thorn and flowering currant. Here are areas for soft fruit, vegetables, sweet peas and dahlias. On the walls are trained apples and pears – and currants, too. A long herb border has recently been planted and there are borders devoted to *Primula florindae* and astilbes. Best of all are the spectacular glasshouses, crammed with colour. But do not overlook the primulas in the East Garden.

flowers borders; kitchen garden; plants & produce for sale.

Owned by The Queen Elizabeth Castle of Mey Trust

LOTHIAN

BINNY PLANTS
Ecclesmachan Road, Broxburn EH52 6NL

Tel: 01506 858931 **Fax:** 01506 858155
www.binnyplants.co.uk
Location 2 miles north of Uphall on B8046.
Opening hours 10 am - 5 pm; daily; all year. Phone first in winter months.
Admission fee Free.
P WC ✤

This nursery has an expanding range and claims to have Scotland's largest selection of ornamental grasses and a massive range of hardy ferns and other plants for the shady garden, as well as hundreds of perennials and shrubs. Its irises (100+ cultivars), peonies (200+ cultivars), astilbes (50+ cultivars), euphorbias, geraniums, hostas and small shrubs are especially noteworthy.
Owned by Billy Carruthers
Number of gardeners 4

DALMENY HOUSE
Rosebery Estates, South Queensferry
EH30 9TQ

Tel: 0131 331 1888 **Fax:** 0131 331 1788
www.dalmeny.co.uk
Location B924 off A90.
Opening hours 2 pm - 5.30 pm; Sunday - Tuesday; July & August. And for SGS in snowdrop time.
Admission fee Grounds only: free.
P WC ⅋ ✤ ⇩

Visitors to Dalmeny are encouraged to see the valley walk with rhododendrons, wellingtonias and other conifers. But the estate concentrates upon the house and its remarkable collections rather than promoting the gardens and grounds.
✤⚘ woodland garden; snowdrops; mature conifers; rhododendrons & azaleas; wellingtonias; refreshments.
Owned by The Earl of Rosebery

INVERESK LODGE
24 Inveresk Village, Musselburgh
EH21 7TE

Tel: 01721 722502
www.nts.org.uk
Location A6124 south of Musselburgh, 6 miles east of Edinburgh.
Opening hours 10 am - 6 pm; daily; all year.
Admission fee Adults £3; Concessions £2. Honesty box.
P WC ⅋

The modern plantings in this terraced, Victorian garden have much of horticultural interest. In the fine Edwardian conservatory are an aviary and some tree ferns. Elsewhere are good herbaceous borders and interesting climbing plants. Graham Stuart Thomas designed the rose borders.
Owned by The National Trust for Scotland
Number of gardeners 1
Size 5.2ha (13 acres)
NCCPG National Collections *Tropaeolum* species

INWOOD GARDEN
Carberry, Musselburgh EH21 8PZ

Tel: 0131 665 4550
www.inwoodgarden.com
Location In Carberry Towers estate, signed from A6124.
Opening hours 2 pm - 5 pm; Tuesdays, Thursdays & Saturdays; April to September. For SGS: 28 May.
Admission fee Adults £2; Children free. RHS members free (only at some times).
P WC ⅋ ✤ ⇩

This is an immaculately maintained plantsman's garden and full of interest throughout the season. It has a large number of island beds and many different plant communities: trilliums, orchids, tricyrtis and primulas in the woodland parts; ferns, giant lilies and candelabra primulas in the bog

garden; stunning bananas (*Ensete ventricosum* 'Maurelii' and *Musa basjoo*, which is left in the ground in winter), cannas and hedychiums in the exotic jungle garden. All has been made since 1984. There will be an RHS Special Event at Inwood Garden in 2006; details from 020 7821 3408.
Owned by Mr & Mrs Irvine Morrison
Number of gardeners owners only
Size 0.5ha (1¼ acres)

LAURISTON CASTLE
2A Cramond Road South, Davidsons Mains, Edinburgh EH4 5QD

Tel: 0131 336 2060 **Fax:** 0131 312 7165
Location 3 miles from city centre; take Queensferry Road (A90) to Davidsons Mains.
Opening hours 8 am - dusk; daily; all year.
Admission fee Free.
P WC &

Lauriston Castle has an historic 30-acre garden but the main attraction is the new Japanese garden, the largest in Britain, made to celebrate the twinning of Kyoto Prefecture with Edinburgh. Highlights include a magnificent view across the Firth of Forth, cherry trees in spring, and spring-flowering bulbs.
Owned by Lauriston Castle Trust
Number of gardeners 2
Size 12ha (30 acres)

MALLENY HOUSE GARDEN
Balerno EH14 7AF

Tel: 0131 449 2283
www.nts.org.uk
Location South-west of Edinburgh, off A70.
Opening hours 10 am - 6 pm (or dusk, if earlier); daily; all year.
Admission fee Adults £3; Concessions £2. Honesty box.
WC &

Malleny is one of the National Trust for Scotland's best gardens, much praised for its 'personal' quality. The 19th-century shrub roses are richly underplanted with herbaceous plants which carry the display through into the autumn: there is a sense of opulence about the garden throughout the summer and autumn. The magnificent conservatory creates quite another dimension, as do the huge cones of yew topiary, relics of a 17th-century formal garden. It is, above all, a very peaceful garden – and far too little visited.
Owned by The National Trust for Scotland
Number of gardeners 1
Size 1.2ha (3 acres)
NCCPG National Collections *Rosa* (19th-century shrubs)

SUNTRAP GARDEN
43 Gogarbank, Edinburgh EH12 9BY

Tel: 0131 339 7283
www.oatridge.ac.uk
Location 1 mile west of Edinburgh bypass, between A8 & A71.
Opening hours 10 am - 6 pm (4 pm in winter); daily; all year, but with limited facilities at weekends.
Admission fee Adults £1; Children free.
P ⇔ WC & ❦

Suntrap has three acres of demonstration gardens attached to Oatridge College: it is one of the best places in Lothian to learn how to be a better gardener. It has been developed as a life-long learning centre, with courses and events throughout the year. The features include island beds, a rock garden, a peat garden, sculptures, vegetable plots, a sensory garden, annual borders – and much more.

woodland garden; vegetables; roses (mainly modern); plants under glass; daffodils; good herbaceous borders; alpine plants; 'Italian' garden; peat walls.

Owned by Oatridge College
Number of gardeners 2
Size 1.2ha (3 acres)

ROYAL BOTANIC GARDEN EDINBURGH

20A Inverleith Row, Edinburgh EH3 5LR

Tel: 0131 552 7171 **Fax:** 0131 248 2901
www.rbge.org.uk
Location 1 mile north of Princes Street. Entrances off Inverleith Row & Arboretum Place.
Opening hours 10 am - 7 pm; daily; all year. Closes at 6 pm in March & October, 4 pm from November to February. Closed 1 January & 25 December. Glasshouses close at 5 pm (3.30 pm from November to February).
Admission fee Gardens: free. Guided tours available (£3) at 11 am & 2 pm, daily, from April to September. Glasshouses: Adults £3.50; Concessions £3; Children £1; Family £8.

P WC & 🌱 🌰 ✕ ⇩

The Royal Botanic Garden Edinburgh has an important amenity function for both tourists and local people, but is principally a collection of plants of scientific and educational importance. It is internationally renowned for its collection of plants from temperate and tropical regions around the world, including: plants from the Himalayas and west China; the rhododendron collection – the best in the world; the collection of orchids from South-East Asia; alpines; and the flora of Arabia. So far as possible, these have been displayed within the gardens in a naturalistic setting which hints at their native habitats. The landscaping in the glasshouses is particularly good and recreates a whole series of different environments from arid deserts to humid tropics. The newly restored Temperate Palm House, built in 1852, is still the tallest in Britain at 23m high. It goes without saying that everything is extremely well labelled and the standard of maintenance is among the highest in any garden anywhere in the world. The members of staff are also invariably courteous and helpful. The rock garden is over two acres in extent and composed of many different microhabitats, most of them helped by the naturally light sandy soil and low rainfall. More than 5,000 species (from areas as different as high mountains, the Arctic regions and the Mediterranean) flourish in the mounds and gullies of sandstone and conglomerate alongside the stream and in the screes. The heath garden has recently been restored as a Scottish moorland complete with Landrover tracks. The arboretum has nearly 2,000 different trees, many of them seldom seen in cultivation – the sort that visitors consider attractive but are then disappointed to find unavailable commercially. There are also extensive areas dedicated to azaleas and to systematic demonstration gardens. A must for any visitor to Scotland. The Queen Mother Memorial Garden will open in summer 2006.

🌿 woodland garden; sub-tropical plants; roses (ancient & modern); rock garden; rhododendrons & azaleas; herbs; plants under glass; mature conifers; good herbaceous borders; fine collection of trees; alpine plants; peat beds; 45 UK record-breaking trees, more than any other Scottish garden; shop; plant centre; licensed café.

Owned by Board of Trustees
Size 29ha (72 acres)

STRATHCLYDE

ACHAMORE GARDENS
Isle of Gigha PA41 7AD

Tel: 01583 505390 **Fax:** 01583 505394
www.gigha.org.uk
Location Take Gigha ferry from Tainloan (20 mins) then easy walking for 1½ miles.
Opening hours Dawn - dusk; daily; all year.
Admission fee Adults £3.50; Children £1.

🅿 ⏦ WC 🌷

Achamore is one of the best rhododendron gardens in the British Isles, and started as recently as 1944. Despite such a short existence (many rhododendron gardens date well back into the 19th century) Achamore has also had its fair share of ups and downs. It was largely planted by Sir James Horlick, with advice from Jim Russell. It has about 20 distinct areas cut out of the woodland (overgrown with *R. ponticum*) but they all have rhododendrons in common: their names include the Loderi Garden, Thomson Garden and Macabeanum Wood. Camellias, eucalyptus and nothofagus also grow well here, as do many of the Surrey-type trees recommended by Russell – flowering cherries, sorbus and birches. And there are good herbaceous plantings, too, from daffodils through to pulmonarias and primulas.

🌿 woodland garden; sub-tropical plants; rhododendrons; azaleas; biggest *Larix gmelinii* in the British Isles.

Owned by Isle of Gigha Heritage Trust
Number of gardeners 3
Size 16ha (40 acres)

ACHNACLOICH
Connel, Oban PA37 1PR

Tel: 01631 710796 (office hours) **Fax:** 01631 710796
Location On A85, 3 miles east of Connel.
Opening hours 10 am - 6 pm; daily; 25 March to 31 October.
Admission fee Adults £2; OAPs £1; Children free.

🅿 ⏦ WC 🌷 🌳

Achnacloich is a substantial woodland garden, made in three stages. First there were the Scots pine and European larch, which have grown to great heights. Then came the large-scale plantings of rhododendrons, particularly the *triflora* species which have begun to naturalise. The latest stage has been the creation of a plantsman's garden using the tender shrubs and trees which flourish on the west coast of Argyll. Some of the embothriums are taller than the native oaks.

🌿 woodland garden; rhododendrons & azaleas; good shrubs; plants for sale.

Owned by Mrs J. Nelson
Number of gardeners 1
Size 14ha (35 acres)

AN CALA
Isle of Seil PA34 4RF

Tel & Fax: 01852 300237
www.gardens-of-argyll.co.uk
Location In village of Easdale, 16 miles south of Oban on A816.
Opening hours 10 am - 6 pm; daily; April to October.
Admission fee Adults £2.50; Children free.

🅿 ⏦ WC 🌷

This sheltered garden on the wild West Coast was designed by Thomas Mawson and planted by the actress Faith Celli: it still has a 1930s feel to it. There is a natural rock garden and several streams which have been dammed and planted with moisture-loving species. Mrs Downie has recently completed a rustic temple decorated with a mosaic of cones from all over the world. A flock of Rupert Till wire-sculpted sheep complements the straying real ones outside the garden. But the overall effect is of a garden of great lushness with splendid views across the islets of the Inner Hebrides.

rock garden; wild garden; bog garden; waterfalls & streams.

Owned by Mrs T. Downie
Number of gardeners 1
Size 2ha (5 acres)

ANGUS GARDEN
Barguillean, Taynuilt PA35 1HY

Tel: 01866 822335 **Fax:** 01866 822539
www.barguillean.co.uk
Location Turn south off A85 at Taynuilt (signed Glen Lonan): 3 miles on right.
Opening hours Dawn - dusk; daily; all year.
Admission fee Adults £2; Children free.

This garden in a beautiful setting on the shores of Loch Angus has a particularly fine collection of modern rhododendrons in light oak woodland. It doubles up as a test ground for new hybrids introduced by Barguillean Nurseries from the USA. It has recently be acquired by the Josephine Marshall Trust, whose trustees have plans for a substantial expansion of the gardens to create more summer and autumn interest.

woodland garden; rhododendrons & azaleas; newly installed Peace Bell.

Owned by Josephine Marshall Trust
Number of gardeners 1
Size 4.4ha (11 acres) plus 6-ha (15-acre) lake

ARDANAISEIG HOTEL GARDEN
Ardanaiseig, Kilchrenan, by Taynuilt PA35 1HE

Tel: 01866 833333 **Fax:** 01866 833222
www.ardanaiseig.com
Location On Loch Awe, 4 miles up from Kilchrenan.
Opening hours 9 am - 5 pm; daily; all year.
Admission fee Adults £2; Children free.

Ardanaiseig has a fine woodland garden with an important collection of rhododendrons and azaleas. Most were planted about 100 years ago. The hotel is in a stunning position on a promontory. The 19th-century walled garden is now undergoing restoration.

woodland garden; rhododendrons & azaleas; daffodils; good herbaceous borders; bluebells; maples; magnolias; hotel open to garden visitors.

Owned by Bennie Gray
Number of gardeners 1
Size 2ha (5 acres)

ARDCHATTAN PRIORY
Connel, Oban PA37 1RQ

Tel: 01796 481355 **Fax:** 01796 481211
www.gardens-of-argyll.co.uk
Location 5 miles east of Connel Bridge, on the north shore of Loch Etive.
Opening hours 9 am - 6 pm; daily; April to October.
Admission fee Adults £2.50; Children free.

Daffodils, rock plants and azaleas are the main attraction in spring, but Ardchattan is also planted for high summer, with an emphasis on roses and herbaceous borders. The garden is good in late summer and autumn, too: late-flowering *Eucryphia glutinosa* and hydrangeas are complemented by fine leaf-colour from the *Sorbus* species and *Cornus kousa*.

roses (mainly old-fashioned); daffodils; good herbaceous borders; good collection of *Sorbus* species; huge *Hebe* bushes.

Owned by Mrs Sarah Troughton
Number of gardeners 1½
Size 1.6ha (4 acres)

ARDKINGLAS WOODLAND GARDEN
Cairndow PA26 8BH

Tel: 01499 600261 **Fax:** 01499 600241
www.ardkinglas.com
Location Just off A83 at Cairndow, 8 miles north of Inveraray.
Opening hours Daylight hours; daily; all year.
Admission fee Adults £3; Children free.

P ⟲ WC ●

Formerly known as Strone Gardens, Ardkinglas is famous for its magnificent conifers and its fine Lorimer house. As well as one of the tallest trees in Britain, it has the 'mightiest conifer in Europe', a specimen of *Abies alba* with a huge girth. The garden has been substantially improved by recent restoration and new plantings: these include a gazebo, a lochan, an extension to the woodland garden itself and a new bridge across the River Kinglas to a 17th-century mill. The bluebells are spectacular. Among the rhododendrons are many hybrids bred by Michael Noble, Lord Glenkinglas, when he was Secretary of State for Scotland. The nearby Tree Shop, run by the Ardkinglas Estate, is a nursery specialising in trees and shrubs – especially rhododendrons. It is open seven days a week and has a handsome list of unusual plants.

woodland garden; rhododendrons & azaleas; mature conifers; one of the tallest trees, *Abies grandis* (63m), in the British Isles; the mightiest conifer, *Abies alba*, in Europe; and many other champion trees; excellent nursery.

Owned by Ardkinglas Estate
Number of gardeners 1
Size 10ha (25 acres)
NCCPG National Collections *Abies, Picea*

ARDUAINE GARDEN
Arduaine, by Oban, Argyll PA34 4XQ

Tel & Fax: 01852 200366
www.nts.org.uk
Location On A816 between Oban & Lochgilphead.
Opening hours 9.30 am - sunset; daily; all year.
Admission fee Adults £4; Concessions £3.

P WC & ● ⟐

Arduaine is a luxuriant woodland garden in a sheltered, south-facing situation at the edge of the sea. Stout conifers and 12m thickets of *Griselinia* protect the spectacular rhododendrons which two nurserymen planted in the 1970s. *Primula denticulata* and *Narcissus cyclamineus* have naturalised in grassy glades. *Cardiocrinum giganteum* and *Myosotidium hortensia* grow vigorously. There are several outsize and champion trees, including *Eucryphia glutinosa*, *Gevuina avellana*, *Trochodendron aralioides* and the upright form of the tulip tree known as *Liriodendron tulipifera* 'Fastigiatum'. Some of the giant rhododendrons (*R. arboreum* subsp. *zeylanicum*) are 100 years old: the plant of *R. griffithianum*, too, must be one of the largest in existence. But the sheer variety of the plantings is an education, while the whole garden is handsomely maintained.

tallest *Nothofagus antarctica* (26m) in the British Isles and six further records; reception centre April to September; no refreshments in the garden, but Loch Melfort Hotel is next door.

Owned by The National Trust for Scotland
Number of gardeners 3
Size 8ha (20 acres)

BARWINNOCK HERBS
Barrhill, Girvan KA26 0RB

Tel & Fax: 01465 821338
www.barwinnock.com
Location Off B7207, 12 miles north-west of
Newton Stewart.
Opening hours 10 am - 5 pm; daily, except
Wednesdays ; Easter to end of September.
Admission fee Free.

P ✿

Although not far from such tourist
destinations as Galloway Forest Park,
Barwinnock Herbs is set among
wonderfully wild scenery, which forms a
spectacular backdrop to this beautifully
laid out nursery. Primarily a nursery which
specialises in organically grown culinary,
medicinal and aromatic herbs, there is a
small garden, too, in which these plants
are prettily displayed. The plant yard itself
is most attractive, with the pots arranged
on rustic tables amidst a collection of
agricultural bygones. There is a small rural
museum attached, with some local
produce and seed on sale and, for those
who want to venture further afield, there
are some enticing walks mapped out from
the nursery. If you do not want to take
your purchases with you, they are happy
to post them for you.
Owned by Dave & Mon Holtom
Number of gardeners 1

BENMORE BOTANIC GARDEN
Dunoon PA23 8QU

Tel: 01369 706261 **Fax:** 01369 706369
www.rbge.org.uk
Location 7 miles north of Dunoon on A815.
Opening hours 10 am - 6 pm; daily; March to
October. Closes at 5 pm in March & October.
Admission fee Adults £3.50; Concessions £3;
Children £1; Family £8.

P ◁ WC ♿ ✿ ❀ ✕ ☞

Benmore Botanic Garden has been a
regional annexe of the Royal Botanic
Garden Edinburgh since 1929, having
been given to the nation a few years
earlier by the brewer Harry Younger. The
stupendous redwood avenue which greets
the visitor at the entrance dates from
1863 and was the start of a systematic
programme of planting conifers on the
estate, into which the Youngers
introduced ornamental trees and shrubs.
The mild, wet climate makes possible the
cultivation of tender plants from the
lower altitudes of the Sino-Himalaya,
Bhutan, China and the New World.
Benmore is a living textbook of the genus
Rhododendron: over 400 species and sub-
species grow here, and hundreds of hybrids
and cultivars. Their background is of
conifers planted early in the 19th century,
perhaps the best collection in Scotland.
The conifers are at the heart of Royal
Botanic Garden Edinburgh's conservation
programme and have been supplemented
by recent ecological plantings including a
Bhutanese glade and a Chilean glade. But
the whole garden is spacious, educational
and beautifully maintained.

✿ woodland garden; mature conifers;
fine collection of trees; giant redwood
avenue planted in 1863; rhododendrons; ferns;
new Chilean plant collection; ten record-
breaking trees, including *Nothofagus betuloides*
at over 20m; gift shop; café.

Owned by Board of Trustees/Royal Botanic
Garden, Edinburgh
Size 60ha (150 acres)

BIGGAR PARK
Biggar ML12 6JS

Tel: 01899 221085
Location ¼ mile south-west of Biggar on A702:
black iron gates & lodge on the north side.
Opening hours For SGS: 12 noon - 5.30 pm on 4
June (Grand Fête). And by appointment for
groups, May to August.
Admission fee Adults £3; Children £1.

P WC ♿ ✿

Biggar Park garden is a mixture of woodland (formal and informal), spacious lawns, and unusual trees, shrubs and rhododendrons. It is 225m above sea-level, so somewhat susceptible to late-spring frosts. In the traditional working walled garden are fine herbaceous borders, vegetables, fruit trees and a greenhouse. Shrub roses are a special interest: there are good collections of both old and modern cultivars. The gardens also have a good collection of meconopsis. A small Japanese garden is in the process of development. Several ornamental ponds are landscaped into the garden.

herbaceous borders; spring bulbs, especially fritillaries; rhododendrons & azaleas; meconopsis; old roses; good collection of shrubs and trees.

Owned by Captain & Mrs David Barnes
Number of gardeners 1, plus owners
Size 4ha (10 acres)

BRODICK CASTLE
Isle of Arran KA27 8HY

Tel: 01770 302202 **Fax:** 01770 302312
www.nts.org.uk
Location Ferry from Ardrossan to Brodick; follows signs.
Opening hours Park: 9.30 am – sunset; daily; all year. Walled garden: 10 am – 4.30 pm; daily; Good Friday to 31 October. 10 am – 3.30 pm; Friday – Sunday; 1 November to 21 December.
Admission fee Adults £4; Concessions £3.

This lush rhododendron garden was begun by Molly, Duchess of Montrose, in 1923. The climate at Brodick is mild and wet: the sloping hillside is almost frost-free. Some of the Duchess's plantings are now record-breakers, including *Embothrium coccineum* at more than 20m, the seldom-seen *Euonymus tingens*, the wild form of *Leptospermum scoparium* more than 10m high, and the rare *Nothofagus nervosa* which is over 30m high. In the woodland are fine magnolias, camellias, crinodendrons and olearias, too, but none of these plantings is a match for the rhododendrons, many of which were grown from collectors' seed. The work of collectors Forrest, Ludlow and Kingdon Ward are all represented here. The walled garden has a late-Victorian layout, but the plantings take advantage of the mild climate. For those with longer to dally, Brodick also has a fine park with further features including a restored ice house.

tallest *Drimys winteri* (21m) and *Embothrium coccineum* (20m) in the British Isles (& three further records); NTS shop; plant centre; restaurant & tea rooms.

Owned by The National Trust for Scotland
Number of gardeners 6, plus 2 part-time
Size 32ha (80 acres)
NCCPG National Collections *Rhododendron* (subsections Falconera, Grandia and Maddenia)

COLZIUM WALLED GARDEN
off Stirling Road, Kilsyth, Glasgow G65 0PY

Tel: 01236 828150 **Fax:** 01236 826322
Location Signed from Kilsyth on B803.
Opening hours 12 noon – 7 pm; daily; Easter to mid-September. 12 noon – 4 pm; Saturdays & Sundays; rest of year.
Admission fee Free.

Colzium Walled Garden is an up-and-coming young garden, which the Council has developed on an ancient site since 1976. A wide range of plants is grown within the protection of high walls, particularly conifers, rhododendrons and ornamental trees and shrubs of dwarf habit. They are intended to offer colour and interest throughout the year. The standards of maintenance and labelling are excellent.

snowdrops; over 100 different *Galanthus* cultivars.

Owned by North Lanarkshire Council
Size 0.2ha (½ acre)

CRARAE GARDENS
Crarae, by Inveraray PA32 8YA

Tel: & Fax: 01546 886614
Location South of Inveraray on A83.
Opening hours 9.30 am – sunset; daily; all year.
Admission fee Adults £4; Concessions £3;
Children £2.

P WC Y

Crarae was finally saved for the nation by
the National Trust for Scotland, which
took possession in April 2002. There are
plans for extensive restoration to these
fifty acres of romantic woodland, centred
on a steep glen spanned by wooden
bridges. The long, narrow climb up the
glen is a pilgrim's progress for plantsmen,
past all manner of exotic plants displayed
for effect, but especially large-leaved
rhododendrons. Best in the morning, and
in late May.

woodland garden; camellias;
rhododendrons; autumn colour; tallest
Acer pensylvanicum in the British Isles (and
twelve further tree records); visitor centre
(open April to September); light refreshments.

Owned by The National Trust for Scotland
Number of gardeners 2½
Size 20ha (50 acres)
NCCPG National Collections *Nothofagus*

CULZEAN CASTLE &
COUNTRY PARK
Maybole, Ayrshire KA19 8LE

Tel: 01655 884455 **Fax:** 01655 884503
www.culzeancastle.net
Location Off A719, west of Maybole & south of
Ayr.
Opening hours Walled garden: 10.30 am – 5 pm
(last admission 4 pm); daily; Good Friday to 31
October. Park: 9.30 am – sunset; daily; all year.
Admission fee Adults £5; Concessions £3.75;

Children £1.

P WC

Culzean is the flagship of the National
Trust for Scotland, thoroughly restored
and seriously open to the public (more
than 400,000 visitors a year). The gardens
are important and include a deer park, a
ruined arch, a viaduct, an ice house, a
beautiful Gothic camellia house, gazebos,
a pagoda and a vinery. The three areas of
horticultural interest are the walled
garden, the fountain court and 'Happy
Valley', which is a woodland garden with
fine specimen trees. Record-breakers
include an upright Irish yew (*Taxus
baccata* 'Fastigiata') at 20m, and the rare
southern Japanese hemlock *Tsuga sieboldii*
at 25m.

tallest Irish yew *Taxus baccata*
'Fastigiata' (20m) in the British Isles
(plus two further tree records); current holder
of the Sandford Award; good shops; plant
centre; restaurant; coffee shop.

Owned by The National Trust for Scotland
Number of gardeners 7, plus 4 groundsmen
Size 50ha (125 acres)

FINLAYSTONE COUNTRY
ESTATE
Langbank PA14 6TJ

Tel: 01475 540505
www.finlaystone.co.uk
Location On A8, 10 mins west of Glasgow
Airport.
Opening hours 10 am – 5 pm; daily; all year.
Admission fee Adults £3.50; OAPs & Children
£2.50.

P WC

Much of the garden at Finlaystone was
laid out in 1900. The formal gardens
date from this period: the walled garden,
the knot garden and the sunken garden.
All were set within a natural landscape
of ornamental trees and shrubs. The
sunken garden is enclosed within a yew
hedge which was castellated by 'an

enthusiastic family governess and a French aunt' in about 1918. But much of today's imaginative and beautiful garden is more recent, including the long, winding herbaceous border. The wooded areas are thick with azaleas, as well as rhododendrons, bluebells and snowdrops. Celtic themes have inspired the MacMillans to construct two new features. The Celtic paving has an intricate pattern set into grass, using a design in the Book of Kells. In the walled garden is a 'garden oasis' in the form of a Celtic cross with a pool at its centre but all enclosed by a circular brick pergola. There is also a garden of scented plants for blind visitors which is sometimes known as the 'Fragrant Garden' and on other occasions as the 'Smelly Garden'. The 'New Garden' dates from 1959: the banks of a burn are lined with *Darmera peltata*, spectacular in autumn. The rhododendrons and azaleas merge into the wilder woods on the far bank.

rhododendrons & azaleas; daffodils; bluebells; gift shop; good play areas; light meals, 11 am - 5 pm, April to September.

Owned by Arthur Macmillan
Number of gardeners 1, plus family members
Size 4ha (10 acres)

GEILSTON GARDEN
Cardross, Dumbarton G82 5HD

Tel: 01389 849187 **Fax:** 01389 849189
Location On A814, at western end of Cardross.
Opening hours 9.30 am - 5 pm; daily; Good Friday to 31 October.
Admission fee Adults £4; Concessions £3. RHS members free.

P WC &

Geilston is a nice example of the many small country houses, villas and estates which were put together by successful Glasgow industrialists along the banks of the Clyde. The garden retains a sense of being a private space in which the visitor is an invited guest. The many attractive features include a fruit and vegetable garden with a central 'dipping pond', a walled garden with traditional glasshouses and a burn which winds through the wooded glen.

Owned by The National Trust for Scotland
Number of gardeners 1
Size 2.8ha (7 acres)

GLASGOW BOTANIC GARDEN
730 Great Western Road, Glasgow G12 0UE

Tel: 0141 334 2422 **Fax:** 0141 339 6964
Location On A82, 2 miles from city centre.
Opening hours Grounds: 7 am - dusk; daily; all year. Glasshouses & Kibble Palace: 10 am - 4.45 pm (4.15 pm in winter); daily; all year.
Admission fee Free.

◁ᐅ WC &

Most of the elements of the traditional botanic garden are here, including chronological beds, but the glory of Glasgow is its two glasshouses – the Kibble Palace and the Main Range. The spectacular Main Range – all its eleven sections – reopened last year (2005) and looks as it did when new. Restoration continues on the Kibble Palace which is scheduled to reopen in July this year (2006). There are interesting new gardens outside, too: a fine rose garden, a herb garden, vegetable beds and the long, scented border.

roses (ancient & modern); herbs; plants under glass; mature conifers; good herbaceous borders; fine collection of trees; beautiful glasshouse (the 'Kibble Palace').

Owned by Glasgow City Council
Number of gardeners 14, plus apprentices
Size 10.7ha (27 acres)
NCCPG National Collections *Begonia*, *Dendrobium*, *Dicksoniaceae*

GLENARN
Rhu, Helensburgh G84 8LL

Tel: 01436 820493 **Fax:** 0141 221 8450
www.gardens-of-argyll.co.uk
Location Turn up Pier Road at Rhu Marina, first right is Glenarn Road.
Opening hours Dawn - dusk; daily; 21 March to 21 September.
Admission fee Adults £3; OAPs & Children £1.50.
Guided tours for groups.

⊲⊳ ﴾ ❀ ⴵ

Glenarn's ten acres of woodland garden has at least one venerable old rhododendron dating from Joseph Hooker's Himalayan expedition (1849-51) and many species from the 1930s trips of Kingdon Ward and Ludlow and Sheriff. The garden owes its present outline to the Gibson family who owned it from 1927 to 1982, and many of their own rhododendron hybrids still flourish here, though there are plenty of magnolias, camellias, pieris, and other good plants, too. *Magnolia campbellii* var. *mollicomata* is 12m tall, and *Magnolia sprengeri* var. *diva* has made 10m so far. Other plants which date back to the Gibsons are the rare climbing gesneriad *Asterantha ovata* and the swarms of *Primula pulverulenta* which are such a splendid feature in early summer. The Thornleys took over in 1983 – both of them professional architects whose gardening was moulded by the formal gardens of Italy – but their commitment to the woodland nature of the garden is remarkable. They have relaid the steps, recut the paths, restored the vegetable garden and added a pond with a water chute. Work is still progressing in the rock garden, where the owners have completed excavating and restoring the quarry face. Meanwhile they have also propagated the unique plants, renewed the plantings, created spaces, and maintained the balance between individual specimens. It is a remarkable achievement and worth a visit at any season, though especially in spring. There will be a special opening on 1 May for Scotland's Gardens Scheme.

🌿 rock garden; plantsman's collection of plants; mature conifers; rhododendrons; embothriums; refreshments may be booked in advance for groups.

Owned by Mr & Mrs Michael Thornley
Number of gardeners owners only
Size 4ha (10 acres)

GREENBANK GARDEN
Flenders Road, Clarkston, Glasgow
G76 8RB

Tel: 0141 616 5126
www.nts.org.uk
Location 1 mile along Mearns Road from Clarkston Toll, take first left.
Opening hours Garden: 9.30 am - sunset; daily; all year.
Admission fee Adults £4; Concessions £3; Children £2.

🅿 �🆆🅲 ﴾ ❀ ﴾ ⴵ

Greenbank is a demonstration garden: it was left to the National Trust for Scotland in 1976 on condition that it was developed as a teaching resource for people with small gardens. The walled garden has therefore been divided into a great number of sections which represent different interests and skills: a rock garden, fruit garden, dried flower plot, raised beds, winter garden, and so on.

🌿 woodland garden; rock garden; fruit in the walled garden; good herbaceous borders; a garden for the disabled; roses of every kind; NTS gift shop; plant sales; tea-room.

Owned by The National Trust for Scotland
Number of gardeners 3
Size 1-ha (2½-acre) walled garden; 6ha (15 acres) of policies
NCCPG National Collections Bergenia

MOUNT STUART
Isle of Bute PA20 9LR

Tel: 01700 503877 **Fax:** 01700 505313
www.mountstuart.com
Location 5 miles south of Rothesay.
Opening hours 10 am – 6 pm; daily; 1 May to 30 September. Plus 14 to 17 April.
Admission fee Adults £3.50; OAPs £3; Children £2.

P WC & ⚘ ● ⬠

Mount Stuart has a vast and fascinating garden to accompany the sumptuous house. Its 300 acres include: a mature Victorian pinetum; a two-acre rock garden designed by Thomas Mawson and thickly planted with rare collected plants; a 'wee' garden of five acres, planted with tender exotics from Australia and New Zealand; and a kitchen garden redesigned by the late Lord Bute with help from Rosemary Verey. Add in the relics of an 18th-century landscape, a tropical greenhouse, acres of bluebells and established rhododendrons, and you have the measure of a long and fascinating visit.

🌿 woodland garden; rhododendrons & azaleas; plants under glass; mature conifers; bluebells; important rock garden; tender plants; fine new visitor centre; restaurant & café.

Owned by The Mount Stuart Trust
Number of gardeners 9
Size 120ha (300 acres)

TOROSAY CASTLE & GARDENS
Craignure, Isle of Mull PA65 6AY

Tel: 01680 812421 **Fax:** 01680 812470
www.torosay.com
Location 1½ miles from Craignure on A849 to Iona.
Opening hours Gardens: 9 am – dusk; daily; all year.
Admission fee Adults £5.50; Concessions £5; Children £2.25 (castle and gardens). RHS members free (gardens only).

P WC & ⚘ ● ⬠

The best feature of the gardens at Torosay is the Italian Statue Walk, lined with 19 figures by Antonio Bonazza. The formal terraces (attributed to Lorimer) are covered with rambling roses, other climbers and perennials. The oriental garden, bog garden, greenhouses and rock garden add to the sheer variety. The woodland garden is stuffed with interesting specimens: *Eucryphia*, *Embothrium* and *Crinodendron* among many Chilean plants, underplanted with old daffodil cultivars, meconopsis and primulas. There will a RHS lecture on rhododendrons at Torosay on 13 May 2006.

🌿 rock garden; water garden; *Eucalyptus* walk; new conservation plantings with conifers from Royal Botanic Garden Edinburgh; eucalyptus walk; shop; tea-room (April – October) with light lunches.

Owned by Mr C. James
Number of gardeners 1½, plus seasonal extras & volunteers
Size 5ha (12½ acres)

TAYSIDE

BELL'S CHERRYBANK CENTRE
Cherrybank, Perth PH2 0PF

Tel: 01738 472800 **Fax:** 01738 472805
Location Just off A93 Glasgow Road, Perth, between Broxden roundabout & city centre.
Opening hours 10 am (12 noon on Sundays) – 5 pm (4 pm in November & December); daily; April to December.
Admission fee Adults £3.75; Children £2.50. RHS members free.

These immaculately maintained show gardens make good use of water and incorporate some striking modern sculptures. They are best known for their collection of heaths and heathers, the most comprehensive in the British Isles with over 900 cultivars. The National Heather Collection is part of a proposal by Scotland's Garden Trust to create a 45-acre garden of national importance on adjacent land.
heathers; gift shop; light refreshments & drinks.

Owned by Scotland's Garden Trust
Number of gardeners 2
Size 2.6ha (6½ acres)
NCCPG National Collections *Erica*

BLAIR CASTLE
Blair Atholl, Pitlochry PH18 5TH

Tel: 01796 481207 **Fax:** 01796 481487
www.blair-castle.co.uk
Location Signed from A9.
Opening hours 9.30 am – 6 pm; daily; 1 April to 27 October.
Admission fee Adults £2.30; Children £1.20.

The landscaping around Blair Castle is some of Scotland's finest. The Hercules Garden was first laid out by the 2nd Duke of Atholl in 1744 and includes a formal water tank, 1 ha (2.5 acres) in extent, and extensive herbaceous borders. Nearby is Diana's Grove where axial paths and avenues radiate out from a statue of Diana. The fine conifers date from the 19th century and include the tallest Japanese larch in the United Kingdom (44m).

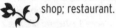 shop; restaurant.

Owned by The Blair Charitable Trust
Number of gardeners 2
Size 3.8ha (9½ acres)

BOLFRACKS GARDEN
Aberfeldy PH15 2EX

Tel: 01887 820344 **Fax:** 01887 829522
www.bolfracks.com
Location 2 miles west of Aberfeldy on A827.
Opening hours 10 am – 6 pm; daily; April to October.
Admission fee Adults £2.50; Children free.

Bolfracks is a plantsman's garden, unusual among Scottish gardens for having a good display of flowers throughout the year. There are rhododendrons and azaleas, of course, but they are principally dwarf species and hybrids, and joined by a large number of daphnes, phyllodoces, pieris, quinces and berberis. Midsummer sees the shrub roses, of which there is a good collection, with everything from Gallicas through to modern shrub roses. But Bolfracks is particularly good for its herbaceous borders: the perennials make an effective display by June and continue through until autumn, when gentians, cyclamen and colchicums take over.

herbaceous plants; roses; lots of plants at every season.

Owned by R.A. Price
Number of gardeners 1
Size 1.2ha (3 acres)

BRANKLYN GARDEN
116 Dundee Road, Perth PH2 7BB

Tel: 01738 625535
www.branklyngarden.org.uk
Location Off Dundee Road, on eastern edge of Perth, ½ mile from Queen's Bridge.
Opening hours 10 am – 5 pm; daily; Good Friday to 30 October.
Admission fee Adults £5; Concessions £4; Children £2. RHS Members free.

The apotheosis of Scottish rock gardening, Branklyn is a suburban garden absolutely crammed with rare plants growing in a series of artificial microhabitats. This is a garden to go round slowly, looking at all the plants – small rhododendrons, alpines, herbaceous plants and peat-lovers. It was built up between 1922 and 1967 by John and Dorothy Renton, who bequeathed it to the National Trust for Scotland. This sort of garden depends for its success upon the understanding and plantsmanship of the gardeners who work in it, and the Trust has been fortunate with their employees at Branklyn since they took it on.

small NTS gift shop; plant sales.

Owned by The National Trust for Scotland
Number of gardeners 2
Size 0.8ha (2 acres)
NCCPG National Collections *Cassiope*; *Lilium*

CHRISTIE'S NURSERY
Downfield, Westmuir, Kirriemuir DD5 8LP

Tel & Fax: 01575 572977
www.christiealpines.co.uk
Location On A926 1 mile west of Kirriemuir.
Opening hours By appointment from March to October. Groups welcome.
Admission fee Free.

This alpine nursery has an impressive list, particularly strong on gentians, hardy orchids, meconopsis, corydalis and lewisias. The owners expect to have about 1,000 different items in stock at any time, and about 2,000 growing in their pretty display garden. There will be two RHS Special Events at Christie's Nursery in 2006; details from 020 7821 3408.

meconopsis; trilliums; lilies; limestone scree garden; refreshments by arrangement.

Owned by Ian & Ann Christie
Size 0.6ha (1½ acres)
NCCPG National Collections *Gentiana*

CLUNY HOUSE
by Aberfeldy, Perthshire PH15 2JT

Tel: 01887 820795
Location 3½ miles from Aberfeldy, on Weem to Strathtay road.
Opening hours 10 am – 6 pm; daily; March to October.
Admission fee Adults £3.50; Children (under 16) free. Season ticket £6.

Cluny is a plantsman's garden, largely made in the 1950s by Mrs Mattingley's father, who subscribed to the Ludlow and Sherriff expeditions. Some older trees date from the 19th century – notably two vast wellingtonias – and the Mattingleys have continued to develop the garden since they took it over in 1987. It is very much a woodland garden, with a natural appearance, except that the canopy is now of rhododendrons, acers, sorbus, euonymus, and birches. It has superb rhododendrons and many other ornamental trees and shrubs from the Himalayas and North America, as well as an underplanting of meconopsis, trilliums, gentians, nomocharis, cardiocrinums, erythroniums, lilies, arisaema and hellebores. But it is memorable, above all, for primulas, of which the Mattingleys used to have a National Collection. The annual display starts with the early-flowering petiolarid species – *P. whitei*, *P. tanneri*, *P. sonchifolia* and *P. nana*, for example. Then come sheets of candelabra species: the first is yellow *P. chungensis*, followed by purple *P. pulverulenta*, the dark pink and white forms of *P. japonica*, purple *P. beesiana*, orange *P. bulleyana*, yellow *P. sikkimensis* and yellow *P. florindae* – as well as naturally occurring hybrids between them. Many exotic species – and not just primulas – seed and regenerate freely in the acid, humus-rich soil. Cluny has lots to excite the visitor throughout the season: bulbs in April, followed by primulas in May to June, lilies in July and excellent autumn interest. The whole garden is hand-weeded and chemical-free: promising seedlings are thereby spotted and protected.

plantsman's collection of plants; fine collection of trees; meconopsis; primulas; cardiocrinums; wellingtonia (*Sequoiadendron giganteum*) with the widest girth in the British Isles.

Owned by Mr J. & Mrs W. Mattingley
Number of gardeners 1 full-time, 3 part-time
Size 2.4ha (6 acres)

DRUMMOND CASTLE GARDENS
Muthill, Crieff PH7 4HZ

Tel: 01764 681433 **Fax:** 01764 681642
www.drummondcastlegardens.co.uk
Location South of Crieff on A822.
Opening hours 1 pm – 6 pm; daily; Easter weekend, then from May to October.
Admission fee Adults £4; OAPs £3; Children £1.50. RHS members free (only at some times).

Drummond has probably the most important formal garden in Scotland, laid out in about 1830 as a St Andrew's cross, with complex parterres filled since the 1950s with roses, statues, clipped cones, herbaceous plants, gravel and lots more besides. The ongoing programme of renovation has already restored much of the garden to a very high standard. The result is order, shape, structure, mass, profusion and colour. There is also a copper beech planted by Queen Victoria to commemorate her visit in 1842. Parts of the film *Rob Roy* were shot in the gardens.

fruit; important formal garden.

Owned by Grimsthorpe & Drummond Castle Trust Ltd
Number of gardeners 5
Size 6ha (15 acres)

DUNDEE BOTANIC GARDEN
Riverside Drive, Dundee DD2 1QH

Tel: 01382 647190 **Fax:** 01382 640574
www.dundeebotanicgarden.co.uk
Location Signed from Riverside Drive (A85), near its junction with Perth Road.
Opening hours 10 am – 4.30 pm (3.30 pm from November to February); daily; all year. Closed 1 & 2 January, 25 & 26 December.
Admission fee Adults £2; OAPs & Children £1. RHS members free.

Dundee has a fine modern Botanic Garden which caters well for visitors: its gentle south-facing slopes are just above the banks of the River Tay. Founded in 1971, it can boast fine collections of conifers and broad-leaved trees, good shrubs, tropical and temperate glasshouses, a water garden and a herb garden. There is a whole series of native plant communities from montane to coastal habitats. These include a collection of *Sorbus* species native to Britain. These are also plant groupings which demonstrate adaptations for survival, such as drought resistance (the Mediterranean garden) and specialised pollination. Among the more surprising collections are *Nothofagus* species from South America and a large number of *Eucalyptus* trees from Australia. There will be two RHS Special Events at Dundee Botanic Garden in 2006; details from 020 7821 3408.

sub-tropical plants; herbs; plants under glass; mature conifers; drought-resistant plants; carnivorous plants; shop; plant centre; café.

Owned by The University of Dundee
Number of gardeners 3
Size 9.2ha (23 acres)

EDZELL CASTLE
Edzell, Angus DD9 7VE

Tel & Fax: 01356 648631
www.historic-scotland.gov.uk
Location On B966 to Edzell village, then signed for 1 mile.
Opening hours 9.30 am – 6.30 pm; daily; April to September. 9 am – 4 pm; Saturday – Wednesday; October to March.
Admission fee Adults £3.30; OAPs £2.50; Children £1.30.

Edzell has a 1930s formal garden in the 17th-century style, designed to be seen from the ruined keep. It is shaped like a quincunx of sorts, with yew bobbles, box edging and roses in the beds. The four main segments have the mottos of the Lindsay family *DUM SPIRO SPERO* ('While I breathe, I hope') and *ENDURE FORT* ('Endure with Strength') cut round their edges in box. In summer, niches in the garden walls are planted with lobelia and alyssum to form a *fess chequy* representing the Lindsay arms. It is a garden of considerable historic importance as the only complete 'pleasaunce' in Scotland but, once you have seen the parterre, Edzell is not a garden to linger in.

topiary; bedding; formal garden; shop.

Owned by Historic Scotland
Number of gardeners 1
Size 0.4ha (1 acre)

GLENDOICK GARDENS
Glendoick, Perth PH2 7NS

Tel: 01738 860205 **Fax:** 01738 860630
www.glendoick.com
Location A90 between Perth & Dundee.
Opening hours 10 am – 4 pm; Monday – Friday; mid-April to mid-June. Buy tickets at garden centre. For SGS: 2 pm – 5 pm; 7 & 21 May. And pre-booked parties of 20+ between mid-April and mid-June.
Admission fee Adults £3; Children free.

Everyone knows of the Glendoick nursery, but the garden is even more important. Started by Farrer's friend Euan Cox in the 1920s, it has one of the best collections of plants, especially rhododendron species, forms and hybrids, in the British Isles. The nursery propagates all its stock on-site. Peter Cox has specialised in breeding low-growing rhododendrons for small gardens: his successes include such well-known cultivars as 'Curlew', 'Razorbill' and 'Egret', as well as evergreen azaleas like 'Panda'. He has also continued to hunt for plants in China, as his father did before him. His own son Kenneth has made ten expeditions to Tibet and Arunachal

Pradesh. There is a good demonstration garden in the garden centre which is open all year. The website is very good indeed.

woodland garden; fine trees; plantsman's collection of plants; primulas; meconopsis; lilies; famous garden centre attached; restaurant.

Owned by Mr & Mrs Peter A. Cox & Kenneth Cox
Number of gardeners owners, with (very) part-time help
Size 4ha (10 acres), including nursery
NCCPG National Collections *Rhododendron* (subsections Campylogyna, Glauca & Uniflora; section Pogonanthum; Cox hybrids)

HOUSE OF DUN
Montrose, Angus DD10 9LQ

Tel: 01674 810264 **Fax:** 01674 810722
www.nts.org.uk
Location On A395, halfway between Montrose & Brechin.
Opening hours 9.30 am – sunset; daily; all year.
Admission fee £2. Honesty box.

🅿 ♿ WC ♿ 🌿 🐝 ▱

The first thing you notice at House of Dun, particularly in winter, is the magnificent line of mature wellingtonias, but there are also sheets of spring bulbs, a Victorian rose garden for summer, a border of *Nerine bowdenii* over 100m long, and a collection of old fruit trees of interest in autumn. The walled garden (next to the house) has been restored as it might have been in the late 19th century and planted with cultivars that date back to the 1880s.

NTS shop; restaurant, open with house.

Owned by The National Trust for Scotland
Number of gardeners 1
Size 18ha (45 acres)

HOUSE OF PITMUIES
Guthrie, by Forfar, Angus DD8 2SN

Tel & Fax: 01241 828245
www.pitmuies.com
Location Signed off A932 Forfar to Arbroath road.
Opening hours 10 am – 5 pm; daily; March to October. And by appointment.
Admission fee Adults £2.50; Children free.

🅿 ♿ WC ♿ 🌿 🐝

House of Pitmuies is one of the most beautiful modern gardens in Scotland, and still expanding. Laid out and planted in the Hidcote style, Pitmuies has wonderful shrub roses in mixed plantings, clever colour schemes, and innumerable different gardens within the garden: a delphinium border, a cherry walk, an alpine meadow for wildflowers, rhododendron glades, vast hollies, a superb *Acer griseum* and splendid trees inherited from Victorian times – and earlier, for there are 400-year-old Spanish chestnuts on the lawn. Enchanted and enchanting. The spring bulbs, hellebores and the alpine meadow, studded with purple and white crocus, are a great joy when the garden opens in March.

roses (ancient & modern); plants under glass; fruit; good herbaceous borders; alpine meadow; ferns; colour schemes; tallest *Ilex aquifolium* 'Argenteomarginata' in the British Isles; home-raised plants & produce in season.

Owned by Mrs Farquhar Ogilvie
Number of gardeners 1, plus 1 groundsman
Size 10.3ha (26 acres)

KINROSS HOUSE
Kinross KY13 8ET

Tel: 01577 862900 **Fax:** 01577 863372
www.kinrosshouse.com
Location M90, Jct 6 into Kinross, right at mini-
roundabout, first left.
Opening hours 10 am - 7 pm; daily; April to
September.
Admission fee Adults £2.50; OAPs £1.50; Children
free.

Many consider Kinross the most beautiful
house in Scotland, and its views across
Loch Leven are extensive. It is approached
along a magnificent avenue of lime trees.
The elegant walled garden has herbaceous
borders and roses and, above all, a 17th-
century sense of proportion. It is one of the
few Scottish gardens which are genuinely
at their best in July and August. The
website is excellent.

 walled garden; mixed borders; lime
avenue.

Owned by James Montgomery
Number of gardeners 4
Size 4ha (10 acres) of walled garden

SCONE PALACE
Perth PH2 6BD

Tel: 0845 126 1060 **Fax:** 01738 552588
www.scone-palace.co.uk
Location Signed from A93, 1½ miles north of
Perth.
Opening hours 9.30 am - 5 .30 pm; daily; April to
October.
Admission fee Gardens only: Adults £3.80; OAPs
£3.50; Children £2.50. RHS members free.

Scone is best known for its large pinetum
and for the Douglas firs (*Pseudotsuga
menziesii*) grown from original seed sent
back by their discoverer David Douglas,
who was born on the estate. Lord
Mansfield has the largest private collection
of orchids in the country. A selection is
always on view in the state rooms.

established pinetum; woodland walks;
rhododendrons & azaleas; daffodils;
new 'Murray' maze; tallest *Tilia platyphyllos*
(37m) in the British Isles and three other record
trees; handsome Douglas firs; largest private
collection of orchid hybrids in Britain; gift shop;
restaurant in old servants' hall.

Owned by The Earl of Mansfield
Number of gardeners 5
Size 40ha (100 acres)

WALES

Most of the best-known gardens of Wales are close to the sea – as, indeed, are most of its larger centres of population. This gives the principality a reputation for being able to grow tender plants that would not be hardy – say – in Surrey. There is some truth in this, though no Welsh garden is truly sub-tropical in the way that Tresco and Inverewe are. The National Gardens Scheme offers gardens to visit in every part of Wales, and in respectable numbers. The RHS has negotiated free access for its members, for some or all of the year, to some of the principality's finest gardens, including Bodnant, the National Botanic Garden of Wales and Picton Castle.

This book lists gardens in Wales under the old 1974 counties, rather than the historic counties or the present administrative units. The 1974 counties are a useful size for the purpose of this book, and their names are readily recognised.

Wales has many historic gardens, made mainly in the 18th and 19th centuries and usually in the styles that were fashionable in England at the time. The National Trust has played an important part in preserving and restoring some of the finest. Bodnant, Plas Newydd and Powis Castle are gardens of the utmost international importance. By and large, however, they share with other Welsh gardens the characteristic of having acquired their horticultural importance during the 20th century: the same is true of other classic Welsh gardens like Portmeirion and Dyffryn. Much of that horticultural input came from England and there was until quite recently a sense among some that gardening was a hobby either for very rich anglicised Welshmen or for the English who came to live in Wales. Despite its troubles, and although it cannot rival such

major botanic gardens as Kew and Edinburgh, the new National Botanic Garden of Wales does give a new focus to Welsh horticulture.

Wales's historic gardens are well supported by the Welsh Historic Gardens Trust. Comparatively few historic gardens in Wales are open to the public, but CADW, the Welsh Historic Monuments Commission in Cardiff, publishes a Register of Parks and Gardens of Special Historic Interest in Wales. This is the work of Elisabeth Whittle who wrote the standard modern work on the subject *The Historic Gardens of Wales* (HMSO, 1992). The Register is modelled on English Heritage's list for England and the criteria for selection and grading gardens are comparable.

The best collection of trees in Wales is at Bodnant, which has a large number of rarities and some 20 champions among them. There are good tree collections also at Dyffryn and Margam in Glamorgan. Wales has comparatively few top-class nurseries, and practically none in South Wales near Cardiff or Swansea. However, the outstanding examples elsewhere in the principality are among Britain's best. Celyn Vale has a unique list of Australasian trees; Dibleys Nurseries is the leading nursery for Streptocarpus and other house plants; and Crûg Farm Plants is a true plantsman's nursery which introduces more new collected plants into cultivation than any other in Britain.

The two principal horticultural colleges are at opposite ends of Wales. Both the Welsh College of Horticulture at Mold (Tel: 01352 841000) and Pencoed College at Bridgend (Tel: 01656 302600) are RHS Partner Colleges with a good number of public lectures and workshops throughout the year.

CLWYD

ABERCONWY NURSERY
Graig, Glan Conwy, Colwyn Bay
LL28 5TL

Tel: 01492 580875
Location South of Glan Conwy, 2nd right off A470. Right at top of hill: nursery is on right.
Opening hours 10 am – 5 pm; Tuesday – Sunday; mid-February to mid-October.

P WC & ※

This nursery is best known as one of the leading nurseries for alpine plants and a steady introducer of new cultivars, especially autumn-flowering gentians. But it also offers unusual shrubs, and herbaceous and woodland plants, including many dwarf rhododendrons and small ericaceous plants. Other specialities are cistus, primulas, small ferns and hybrids of *Helleborus niger*.
Owned by Keith Lever

BODRHYDDAN
Rhuddlan LL18 5SB

Tel: 01745 590414 **Fax:** 01745 590155
Location On A5151, midway between Dyserth & Rhuddlan.
Opening hours 2 pm – 5.30 pm; Tuesdays & Thursdays; June to September. And by appointment; special openings for groups.
Admission fee Adults £2; Children £1.

P ⤳ WC & ⊘

The house and garden at Bodrhyddan date back to mediaeval times – the ancient oaks alongside the parterre are reckoned to be over 500 years old – but most of what we see today was opulently laid out in the 1870s and restored in the 1980s. There is also an avenue of Monterey pines (*Pinus radiata*) dating from 1928, which leads to another avenue of limes (*Tilia platyphyllos*) planted in 1957. William Andrews Nesfield designed the long parterre, which was planted with vegetables when the present Lord Langford returned from World War II, but is now absolutely stunning with seasonal bedding. The Pleasance – abandoned since 1939 – was recreated in 1982 as a woodland garden; it has extensive shrub plantings around four ponds. It is good to see such a distinguished garden on the up again.

 teas.

Owned by Lord Langford O.B.E., D.L.
Number of gardeners 2
Size 2.4ha (6 acres)

CELYN VALE NURSERIES
Allt-y-Celyn, Carrog, Corwen LL21 9LD

Tel & Fax: 01490 430671
www.eucalyptus.co.uk
Location 3 miles east of Corwen & 1 mile from Carrog, near A5.
Opening hours 9 am – 4 pm; Monday – Friday; January to November.
Admission fee Free.

P WC ※

Specialist growers of eucalyptus and acacias: they use seed from high altitude specimens to maximise hardiness and will advise also on suitable species for coppicing, poor drainage, alkaline soils, hedging, salt tolerance and so on. They say that the hardiest gum trees are *E. archeri*, *E. coccifera*, *E. pauciflora* subsp. *debeuzevillei*, *E. pauciflora* subsp. *niphophila*, *E. parvifolia*, *E. perriniana* and *E. subcrenulata*.

Eucalyptus.

Owned by Andrew McConnell

BODNANT GARDEN
Tal-y-Cafn, Colwyn Bay LL28 5RE

Tel: 01492 650460 **Fax:** 01492 650448
www.bodnantgarden.co.uk
Location 8 miles south of Llandudno & Colwyn Bay on A470. Entrance ½ mile along Eglwysbach Road.
Opening hours 10 am - 5 pm; daily; 11 March to 7 November.
Admission fee Adults £6; Children £3. RHS members free.

P WC ♿ 🌱 🍴 ✗ ▯

Two Lords Aberconway, both past Presidents of the Royal Horticultural Society, and three successive generations of the Puddle family, as Managers and Head Gardeners, have made Bodnant compulsory visiting. From its position above the valley of the River Conwy, Bodnant combines dramatic formal terraces with extensive woodland plantings on the grandest of scales. A deep herbaceous border, backing onto a high wall, is instantly striking, with mature, often tender climbers rampant above bold, warm plantings. Although this is North Wales, and the views from the lawns are across the valley to the Carneddau Mountains, parts of the garden feel distinctly Italianate. Beside the house, two enormous cedars overshadow a formal lily pond, on the third of five terraces, where hydrangeas abound. A crisply shaved yew hedge curves above a mezzanine rose pergola, and there are specimens of *Magnolia grandiflora* everywhere. Below is a stately gazebo from the early 18th century, and the Pin Mill, which looks across a flat pool to a grassy stage at the opposite end of its terrace, edged with cut cubes of yew topiary. Plantings of pencil-thin cypresses, and *Cistus* and *Potentilla* cultivars, help to create an intensely Mediterranean feel on clear summer days. Behind the Pin Mill, the mood changes, as the valley fills with tall specimen trees, marching beside a fast-flowing mill stream and a stern old mill. Along the stream there are hostas, bergenias and meconopsis. Some of the massive *Sequoiadendron* specimens bear planting plaques which show them to be in their second century. Winding back in an extended arc towards the house, there are gentler woodland plantings, with shrubby borders, and smaller trees growing in grass. There is a magnificent collection of magnolias, rhododendrons and camellias. Other good plantings include *Viburnum* x *bodnantense*, hybrid camellias, huge rhododendrons, white wisterias, a vast *Arbutus* x *andrachnoides*, flaming embothriums and the famous laburnum tunnel. The garden is admirably maintained, and popular with visitors, too. The walled plant centre (not National Trust) is strong on many of the tender climbers from the garden, and reasonably priced.

🌿 tallest Californian redwood *Sequoia sempervirens* (47m) in the British Isles and 18 further record-breaking tree species - more than any other garden in Wales; plant centre; light lunches, teas, refreshments (11 am - 5 pm).

Owned by The National Trust
Number of gardeners 18
Size 32ha (80 acres)
NCCPG National Collections *Embothrium; Eucryphia; Magnolia* (spp.); *Rhododendron forrestii*

CHIRK CASTLE
Chirk LL14 5AF

Tel: 01691 777701 **Fax:** 01691 774706
www.nationaltrust.org.uk
Location 1½ miles west of Chirk off A5.
Opening hours 10 am – 6 pm (5 pm in October);
Wednesday – Sunday, plus Tuesdays in July &
August; 25 March to 29 October.
Admission fee Adults £4.50; Children £2.50.

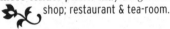

Chirk has a fine 18th-century landscape
by William Emes and handsome 19th-
century formal gardens, with yew hedges
and billowing topiary. Part is planted with
roses. There is also a good 1930s
collection of trees and shrubs, the relics of
a garden by Norah Lindsay. Elsewhere are
a rock garden, a 1950s mixed border, a
lime avenue and drifts of daffodils in
spring. The National Trust has done much
to provide shelter from the wind, so that
more tender plants may be grown.

shop; restaurant & tea-room.

Owned by The National Trust
Number of gardeners 3
Size 2.2ha (5½ acres)

DIBLEYS NURSERIES
Llanelidan, Ruthin LL15 2LG

Tel: 01978 790677 **Fax:** 01978 790668
www.dibleys.com
Location 6 miles south of Ruthin: follow brown
tourist signs from A525.
Opening hours 10 am – 5 pm; daily; April to
September. Plus weekdays in March & October.
Admission fee Garden: £2.50; Glasshouses: free.

Dibleys is the leading British nursery for
gesneriads – especially streptocarpus, of
which they have a comprehensive
collection of cultivars, from 'Constant
Nymph' to the latest modern hybrids like
the ever-blooming 'Crystal Ice'. They will
be introducing new cultivars again this
year (2006). Dibleys have made a great
impact on RHS flower shows in recent
years, and won 16 consecutive gold
medals at Chelsea. They also have a long
list of other gesneriads like *Kohleria* and
Columnea, and a good line in foliage
begonias. An excellent nursery, in top
form. The garden has a wide range of trees
and shrubs, and extensive views over the
Vale of Clwyd. There will be two RHS
Special Events at Dibleys Nurseries in
2006; details from 020 7821 3408.

 café.

Owned by The Dibley family
Size 0.4ha (1 acre) of glasshouses; 4-ha (10-
acre) garden
NCCPG National Collections *Streptocarpus*

ERDDIG
Wrexham LL13 0YT

Tel: 01978 355314 **Fax:** 01978 313333
www.nationaltrust.org.uk
Location Signed from A483 & A525.
Opening hours 11 am – 6 pm; Saturday –
Wednesday, plus Thursdays in July & August; 25
March to 29 October. Opens at 10 am in July &
August; closes at 5 pm in October. Plus Saturdays
& Sundays from 4 November to 17 December.
Admission fee Gardens only: Adults £5; Children
£2.50.

More of a re-creation than a restoration,
Erddig today majors on domestic life in the
early 18th century. There are old-fashioned
fruit trees (an excellent collection of apples,
plums, pears and cherries, beautifully
trained), an avenue of pleached limes, and
a long canal to frame the house, but all are
slightly awed by the Victorian overlay –
avenues of monkey puzzles and
wellingtonias.

restaurant; tea-room.

Owned by The National Trust

Number of gardeners 4
Size 5.2ha (13 acres)
NCCPG National Collections *Hedera*

THE GARDEN HOUSE
Erbistock, Wrexham LL13 0DL

Tel: 01978 781149 **Fax:** 01978 781144
Location Signed in village.
Opening hours 10 am (11 am on Saturdays and 2 pm on Sundays) - 5 pm; daily; all year.

Admission fee Adults £3; Children free. RHS members free from Tuesday to Friday.
🅿

The Garden House features shrub and herbaceous borders in various colour schemes, rose pergolas, a lily pond in the Monet style (complete with bridge) and a Jekyll-style colour-circle.

Owned by The Wingett family
Size 2ha (5 acres)
NCCPG National Collections *Hydrangea*

DYFED

ABERGLASNEY GARDENS
Llangathen SA32 8QH

Tel & Fax: 01558 668998
www.aberglasney.org
Location 4 miles west of Landeilo, signed from A40.
Opening hours 10 am – 6 pm; daily; April to September. 10.30 am – 4 pm; daily; October to March. Coaches by appointment only.
Admission fee Adults £6; OAPs £5; Children £3. RHS members free (only at some times).

P WC & ☀ ◑ ☞

Aberglasney has a garden that lay dormant for about 400 years, until plans were made to restore it in the style of the 16th and 17th centuries. The structure remains fairly intact from that time, including a cloister right at the heart of the layout and a (very rare) parapet walk. Reproduction gardens have been inserted within that framework. There are six in all, including three walled gardens. Hal Moggridge and Penelope Hobhouse have both been involved with the project: work continues – and has cost £4.5m to date. The modern plantings, for year-round interest, include meconopsis, primulas, trilliums and lilies. The dense yew tunnel dates from about 1700. There will be two RHS Special Events at Aberglasney in 2006; details from 020 7821 3408.

❧ important historic garden; yew tunnel; pool garden; new winter garden (2005); shop; café.

Owned by Aberglasney Restoration Trust
Number of gardeners 3
Size 4ha (10 acres)

BRO-MEIGAN GARDENS
Boncath SA37 0JE

Tel: 01239 841232
Location On B4332 between Boncath & Eglwyswrw.
Opening hours 11 am – 6 pm; daily, except Mondays & Tuesdays; 22 March to 29 October. Open Bank Holiday Mondays.
Admission fee Adults £3.50; OAPs £3.25; Children £2. RHS members free in April & October.

P WC & ☀ ☞

There are many gardens within the garden at Bro-Meigan: a turf maze, a lime tree avenue, a cottage garden, a primrose patch, a herb garden and an oriental garden. All have been made since 1986 and are held together by the owners' plantsmanship, which ensures that there is always interest at every season. Bro-Meigan is organically maintained.

❧ tea-room.

Owned by Yvonne & David Gillett
Number of gardeners 2
Size 2.6ha (6½ acres)

CAE HIR
Cribyn, Lampeter SA48 7NG

Tel: 01570 470839
www.caehirgardens.ws
Location In village.
Opening hours 1 pm – 6 pm; daily, except Sundays; April to October.
Admission fee Adults £4.50; OAPs £4; Children 50p. RHS members free.

P ◑ WC ☀ ☞

This vigorous and expanding garden was begun in 1985 and has already been featured many times on television. It is also a RHS Partner garden. Mr Akkermans's energy and achievement are an inspiration. He has taken six acres from the surrounding meadows and made them into a series of beautiful colour-co-ordinated gardens. All different types of plants are here: trees, shrubs and herbaceous plants, often used in original ways. Mr Akkermans is now experimenting with half-hardy trees and shrubs, allowing wildflowers to mix with cultivated ones in some parts of his immaculately tidy garden. Elsewhere are collections of bonsai and cacti, and a water garden fed by natural ponds and a stream. There will be an RHS Special Event at Cae Hir in 2006; details from 020 7821 3408.

colour gardens; bonsai; mature ornamental trees; bog garden; light refreshments.

Owned by Wil Akkermans
Number of gardeners owner only
Size 2.6ha (6½ acres)

COLBY WOODLAND GARDEN
Amroth, Narberth SA67 8PP

Tel: 01834 811885
www.nationaltrust.org.uk
Location Signed from A477.
Opening hours 10 am – 5 pm; daily; 28 March to 29 October. Walled garden opens at 11 am.
Admission fee Adults £4; Children £2.

Colby is an attractive woodland garden, best in late spring and early summer when the rhododendrons and azaleas are in full flower. Among the 19th-century plantings are vast cryptomerias, clumps of *Embothrium coccineum* and a huge specimen of *Rhododendron falconeri* subsp. *eximium*, planted in 1883. In the walled garden, a rill runs down from the *trompe l'oeil* gazebo to a pool. There have been many new plantings recently throughout the garden.

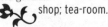 shop; tea-room.

Owned by The National Trust
Number of gardeners 2
Size 11.1ha (28 acres)

MOORLAND COTTAGE PLANTS
Rhyd-y-Groes, Brynberian, Crymych SA41 3TT

Tel: 01239 891363
www.moorlandcottageplants.co.uk
Location On B4329, 12 miles south-west of Cardigan & 7 miles west of Crymych.
Opening hours 10.30 am – 5.30 pm; daily, except Wednesdays; mid-May to mid-September. Nursery opens 1 March.
Admission fee Adults £1.50; Children free. For NGS.

This is a promising young nursery, attached to a charming display garden. It is high up in the Pembrokeshire Coast National Park, and surrounded by hills. Perennials are the main speciality, especially geraniums, campanulas, crocosmias, geums and potentillas. Grasses and groundcover plants are also offered in a wide variety. The garden is open and windy, though now more sheltered as the early plantings grow up; its areas include a grasses garden, a cottage garden and fine mixed borders.

Owned by Jennifer Matthews
Number of gardeners 1 part-time

THE NATIONAL BOTANIC GARDEN OF WALES
Middleton Hall, Llanarthne, Carmarthen SA32 8HG

Tel: 01558 668768 **Fax:** 01558 668933
www.gardenofwales.org.uk
Location 7 miles east of Carmarthen, off A48.
Opening hours 10 am – 6 pm (4.30 pm during British Winter Time); daily, except Christmas Day.
Admission fee Adults £7; Concessions £5; Children £3.50. RHS members free in January & February.

The landscaped park and gardens of the

original 18th-century Middleton Hall estate are the setting for this new national botanic garden which opened to the public in 2000 amid great public acclamation. Near the entrance to the garden is a 'Welsh landscape' with native meadows and woodlands. Then comes the Broadwalk, 220m long, with a rill which runs down through a geological display of Welsh rocks. The garden's collection of herbaceous plants is planted along its edges, with narrow paths leading into the plantings to facilitate access. There is also a Japanese garden and a herb garden, named after the Physicians of Myddfai, with an ethnobotanical collection of native pharmacological Welsh plants. However, it is the Great Glasshouse which has received most of the adulation, and rightly so, because it is a stunning piece of architecture – the largest single-span glasshouse in the world. It concentrates upon the Mediterranean floras of the world – cheaper to maintain than tropical floras – including Chile, California, south-west Australia, South Africa, the Mediterranean basin and the Canary Isles. There will be five RHS Special Events at the National Botanic Garden of Wales in 2006; details from 020 7821 3408.

good glasshouses; herbaceous plants; herbs; shop; plant sales; café; restaurant.

Owned by The National Botanic Garden of Wales
Number of gardeners 8, plus 22 students & 40 volunteers
Size 40ha (100 acres)

PICTON CASTLE
Picton, Haverfordwest, Pembrokeshire
SA62 4AS

Tel & Fax: 01437 751326
www.pictoncastle.co.uk
Location 4 miles east of Haverfordwest off A40.
Opening hours 10.30 am – 5 pm; Tuesday – Sunday & Bank Holiday Mondays; April to October. For NGS: 9 May & 18 July.
Admission fee Adults £4.95; OAPs £4.75; Children £2.50. RHS members free from April to September.

This 13th-century castle has been the home of the Philipps family for some 400 years, and the 40 acres of grounds include fine collections of rhododendrons, azaleas, magnolias, camellias, myrtles, embothriums and eucryphias, some of which have been bred by the castle gardeners. Older specimens like a vast multi-trunked *Abies alba* have been joined by new plantings of recent introductions – *Taiwania cryptomerioides* and *Calocedrus formosana* among them. The climate is mild, and supports normally tender plants like *Pittosporum tobira* 'Variegatum' and *Vestia foetida*. The display is at its best in May to June: summer and autumn bring woodland walks among the massive oaks and giant redwoods. Recent additions include a fern walk and a collection of bamboos. The walled garden has a fish pond, an indoor fernery, rose beds, herbaceous borders and a fountain in the centre. Four RHS Special Events will take place at Picton Castle during 2006; details from 020 7821 3408.

woodland garden; rhododendrons & azaleas; camellias; garden shop selling surplus garden produce; restaurant.

Owned by Picton Castle Trust
Number of gardeners 4, plus 2 part-time
Size 16ha (40 acres)

GLAMORGAN

CLYNE GARDENS
Mill Lane, Blackpill, Swansea SA3 5BD

Tel: 01792 298637/401737 **Fax:** 01792 297394
www.swansea.gov.uk/clyne
Location 3 miles west of Swansea on A4067 coast road.
Opening hours Dawn - dusk; daily; all year.
Admission fee Free. Tours available by prior arrangement.

🅿 ⬩ wc ♿ 🛈

Clyne is a stupendous woodland garden, the best in South Wales, well cared for by enthusiastic and knowledgeable staff. It is supreme as a magic rhododendron valley in May, but the range of rare and tender plants provides interest all year. Bluebells, lysichitons and gunneras are among its other features. It was planted between 1921 and 1952 by a local landowner called Algernon Walker-Heneage-Vivian, who subscribed to many of the Himalayan and Chinese plant-hunting expeditions of the day. The forms and hybrids of *Rhododendron niveum* which the head gardener brought to the RHS flower shows in the 1990s are still remembered by the London rhododendron fraternity. The mild climate means that *R. fragrantissimum* grows happily outside, and there is a group of *R.* 'Loderi King George' 16m high. The carpark is small, and tends to fill up early in the day. During May, the gardens celebrate the Clyne in Bloom Festival with guided walks, band concerts, children's entertainments and plant sales.

🌿 woodland garden; rhododendrons & azaleas; good herbaceous borders; occasional light refreshments.

Owned by City & County of Swansea
Number of gardeners 5
Size 19.6ha (49 acres)
NCCPG National Collections *Pieris; Enkianthus; Rhododendron* (Triflora & Falconera subsections)

DYFFRYN GARDEN
St Nicholas, Cardiff CF5 6SU

Tel: 029 2059 3328 **Fax:** 029 2059 1966
www.dyffryngardens.org.uk
Location M4, Jct 33 on A48 then follow signs.
Opening hours 10 am - 6 pm (5 pm in October and 4 pm in winter); daily; all year. No facilities from November to March.
Admission fee Adults £3.50; OAPs & Children £2.50. RHS members free from Easter to October.

🅿 ⬩ wc ♿ 🌼 🍂 🛈

Dyffryn's sumptuous gardens were designed by Thomas Mawson for Reginald Cory around an Edwardian prodigy house. They are now being restored with a chunky £3.23m millennium grant. Originally intended partly for display – there is even a Roman garden with a temple and fountain – and partly for the Corys' own pleasure, Dyffryn has a huge collection of good plants built up in the early years of the 20th century. Watch it revive over the next year or so: the garden as a status symbol. There will be four RHS Special Events at Dyffryn Gardens in 2006; details from 020 7821 3408.

🌿 woodland garden; roses (mainly modern); rhododendrons & azaleas; good herbaceous borders; spring bulbs; summer bedding; tallest purple birch *Betula pendula* 'Purpurea' in the British Isles (and ten other record trees); plants sales area; tea-rooms; visitor centre.

Owned by Vale of Glamorgan Council
Size 22ha (55 acres)

MARGAM COUNTRY PARK
Port Talbot SA13 2TJ

Tel: 01639 881635 **Fax:** 01639 895897
www.npt.gov.uk/margampark
Location Follow directions from M4, Jct 38.
Opening hours 10 am – 5 pm; daily; March to
September. Closes at 4.30 pm from October to
February. Opens at 1 pm on Monday & Tuesday in
winter.
Admission fee People free. Cars £2.75.

P ◁ WC ᵫ ❀ ☞

Margam is a popular country park with lots
to interest the garden historian and
plantsman. The setting is a 1,000-acre park
with lakes, woodlands and herds of red,
fallow and Père David deer – the best
collection of deer in Wales. Within it is a
wonderful range of conservatories and
glasshouses, including the orangery for
which Margam is famous, a Japanese
garden, rare trees and rhododendrons (some
grown from Kingdon Ward's seed), and
cheerful bedding out. The orangery gardens
(early 17th-century) have just been
completely restored, using some of the large
grant which the garden has received from
the European Regional Fund. The mature
trees here are especially impressive and
include several large tulip trees, a cork oak
and an enormous cut-leaved beech. Recent
additions include Tudor and monastic
gardens and a new pergola 410m (450
yards) long: further work is promised.

🌿 roses (mainly modern); fine collection
of trees; bedding out; daffodils;
rhododendrons; orangery; tallest bay tree *Laurus
nobilis* (21m) in the British Isles; gift shop;
restaurant & light refreshments.

Owned by Neath Port Talbot County Borough
Council
Number of gardeners 4
Size 24ha (60 acres)

PLANTASIA
Parc Tawe, Swansea SA1 2AL

Tel: 01792 474555 **Fax:** 01792 652588
www.plantasia.org
Location Off main eastern approach to
Swansea.
Opening hours 10 am – 5 pm; Tuesdays –
Sundays & Bank Holidays; all year. Closed 1
January, 25 & 26 December.
Admission fee Adults £3.15; Concessions £2.20.

P WC ᵫ ❦ ❀ ☞

Plantasia is a large glasshouse with three
climatic zones – arid, tropical and
rainforest. Each is full with colourful
exotic plants – palms, strelitzias, tree
ferns, nepenthes, cacti and such economic
plants as giant bamboos, bananas,
coconuts and pineapples. The authorities
say that some of the 5,000 plants
represent species which are actually
extinct in the wild. It is the perfect goal
for a winter expedition, provided you like
the insects, birds, monkeys and reptiles as
well as the flowers.

🌿 tropical & arid glasshouses; good
collection of exotic plants; educational
facilities; gift shop; coffee shop.

Owned by City & County of Swansea
Number of gardeners 2
Size 0.4ha (1 acre)

SINGLETON PARK & SWANSEA BOTANICAL GARDENS
Oystermouth Road, Swansea SA2 8QD

Tel: 01792 298637 **Fax:** 01792 297394
www.swansea.gov.uk/botanics
Location Signed from main A4067 coast road,
west of Swansea.
Opening hours Daily; all year. Closes at 6 pm
from Easter to July, 8 pm in August and 4.30 pm
at other times.
Admission fee Free.

WC ᵫ ❀

Singleton Park was once part of Lord

Swansea's estate, but has been a public park since 1919. The Swansea Botanical Gardens are in the top end of the park, best entered from Sketty Road and through the green gates in the high wall. The spectacular herbaceous border inside the entrance, first planted in 1921, makes good use of seasonal bedding. Elsewhere are a rose terrace, a bog garden, a sunny herb garden (lots of Mediterranean plants), and display beds with collections of irises, dahlias, chrysanthemums, sweet peas, carnations, asters, delphiniums and penstemons. In the part known as the Ornamental Gardens are a rock garden, archery lawn and excellent rhododendron collection. The glasshouses are good, too: the Cactus House, the Temperate House, the Tropical House (orchids, bromeliads, epiphytes and tillandsias), and the Economics House (economic plants like sugar cane, olives, rice, coffee and coconut palms).

good herbaceous borders; interesting greenhouse plants.

Owned by City & County of Swansea
Number of gardeners 7, plus 2 trainees
Size 4ha (10 acres)
NCCPG National Collections *Rhododendron* (part)

GWENT

PENPERGWM LODGE
Abergavenny NP7 9AS

Tel & Fax: 01873 840208
www.penplants.com
Location 3 miles from Abergavenny on B4598, opposite King of Prussia pub.
Opening hours 2 pm – 6 pm; Thursday – Sunday; end of March to end of September.
Admission fee Adults £3; Children free. RHS members free.

P ⬧ wc ♿ ⚘ ❀

Catriona Boyle has developed the garden at Penpergwm over the last 20 years, based on the structure created when the house was built in Edwardian times – mature trees, open lawns, some formal areas and old hedges. She has added two exuberant terraces, each planted to a colour theme and linked by an Italianate parterre and a pillared vine walk. There is also a new *Malus* avenue centred on the house. Recent developments include an octagonal brick Golden Jubilee folly and a new summerhouse at the top of the garden: both have excellent views. The pre-war kitchen garden has been completely overhauled with new terracing and a broad, central canal. The nursery has lots of home-propagated plants, mostly unusual herbaceous plants, bulbs, climbers and shrubs, but also half-hardy perennials which flower late into autumn. Specialities include *Aconitum*, euphorbias, cistus, clematis, loniceras, camassias, erythroniums, *Melianthus major* and salvias. Mrs Boyle runs a well-regarded garden school.

🌿 colour borders; good plants; nursery for unusual plants.

Owned by Mrs C. Boyle
Number of gardeners 1
Size 1.6ha (4 acres)

TREDEGAR HOUSE COUNTRY PARK
Newport NP10 8YW

Tel: 01633 815880 **Fax:** 01633 815895
Location M4, Jct 28.
Opening hours Park 9 am – dusk; daily; all year.
Admission fee Park & Gardens free.

P ⬧ wc ♿ 🏷

Tredegar is one of the great historic houses of South Wales, with a park and gardens to match. Much was lost to neglect in the mid-20th century, but the new owners have restored the walled formal gardens, the sunken garden and the orangery with parterres and espaliered fruit trees.

🌿 modern parterres; amenity parkland; refreshments in season.

Owned by Newport City Council
Number of gardeners 2
Size 8.7ha (22 acres)

GWYNEDD

BODYSGALLEN HALL
Llandudno LL30 1RS

Tel: 01492 584466 **Fax:** 01492 582519
www.bodysgallen.com
Location On right, off A470 to Llandudno.
Opening hours Daily; all year.
Admission fee Open only to hotel guests.
Children over 6 welcome.

P WC ら ✗ ♉

Bodysgallen Hall is a top hotel, and the
gardens live up to its high standards. They
include a parterre divided into eight
segments, an extremely busy kitchen
garden, woodland walks, a cascade garden
with a lily pond and white floribundas in
the old walled garden. And it is handy for
Bodnant, too. There will be three RHS
Special Events at Bodysgallen Hall in
2006; details from 020 7821 3408.

woodland garden; roses (mainly old-
fashioned); rock garden; herbs; fruit;
knot garden; parterres; refreshments at hotel.

Owned by Historic House Hotels Ltd
Number of gardeners 4
Size 87ha (220 acres), including parkland

CRÛG FARM PLANTS
Griffith's Crossing, Caernarfon LL55 1TU

Tel & Fax: 01248 670232
www.crug-farm.co.uk
Location 2 miles north-east of Caernarfon, off
A487; follow signs to Bethel.
Opening hours 10 am – 6 pm; Thursday – Sunday &
Bank Holidays; 26 February to 25 September.
Garden open for NGS: 4 June.
Admission fee Nursery free. Garden £1.50 for NGS.

P ❀

Crûg Farm is unusual in specialising in
plants for shade: perennials, shrubs and
climbers. The range is extensive and

interesting. The selection of hardy
geraniums equals many specialists in the
genera. The owners' collecting expeditions
to Korea, Sikkim, Japan, China, Vietnam,
Laos, the Philippines and Taiwan are
making an impact on the gardens of many
discerning plantsmen: new-to-science names
aplenty. The display garden and private
garden are worth seeing when they are open
for the National Gardens Scheme. There
will be two RHS Special Events at Crûg
Farm in 2006; details from 020 7821 3408.
Owned by Bleddyn & Sue Wynn-Jones
Number of gardeners 1
Size 1.2ha (3 acres)
NCCPG National Collections *Coriaria; Paris;
Polygonatum*

PENRHYN CASTLE
Bangor LL57 4HN

Tel: 01248 353084 **Fax:** 01248 371281
www.nationaltrust.org.uk
Location 2 miles east of Bangor on A5122, signed
from A55 – A5 junction.
Opening hours 11 am – 5 pm; daily, except
Tuesdays; 25 March to 29 October. Open at 10 am
in July & August. Last admissions 4.30 pm.
Admission fee Adults £5.40; Children £2.70.

◁ WC ら ❀ ✗ ♉

Penrhyn is a neo-Norman castle with a
distant walled garden of parterres and
terraces merging into slopes of
rhododendrons and camellias. There is
much of dendrological interest (ancient
conifers, holm oaks, champion eucryphias
and naturalised arbutus trees) and a
'dinosaur landscape' of tree ferns, gunneras
and aralias. The snowdrops are spectacular
in February.

light lunches in licensed tea-room.

Owned by The National Trust
Number of gardeners 3
Size 19ha (47 acres)

PLAS BRONDANW GARDENS
Llanfrothen, Panrhyndeudraeth
LL48 6SW

Tel: 01743 241181 **Fax:** 01743 242300
Location On Croesor road off A4085.
Opening hours 9 am - 5 pm; daily; all year.
Admission fee Adult £3 (further Adults £2);
Children free. RHS members free from October
to April.
P WC

Plas Brondanw is the highly original and
architectural Edwardian garden laid out by
Sir Clough Williams-Ellis 17 years before
he began Portmeirion, and now
assiduously restored by his granddaughter
Menna. It is one of the best-kept secrets
in North Wales, full of slate stonework
and such original design ideas as the
arbour of four red-twigged limes. The
garden rooms are inward-looking and
almost cottagey in their planting, but the
mountain peaks are ever present.
Arts & Crafts garden; topiary; follies.

Owned by Trustees of the Second Portmeirion
Foundation
Number of gardeners 2

PLAS NEWYDD
Llanfairpwll, Anglesey LL61 6DQ

Tel: 01248 714795 **Fax:** 01248 713673
www.nationaltrust.org.uk
Location 2 miles south-west of Llanfairpwll on
A4080.
Opening hours 11 am - 5.30 pm; Saturday -
Wednesday; 1 April to 1 November. For NGS: 14
April.
Admission fee Adults £4; Children £2.
P WC ♿ 🌱 ● ✕ ☕

Plas Newydd has a grand collection of
rhododendrons (plus azaleas, magnolias
and acers) within a Repton landscape on
a spectacular site above the Menai Straits.
Its many other horticultural attractions
include an avenue of *Chamaecyparis
pisifera* 'Squarrosa' running down to the
sea, large plantings of hydrangeas for late
colour and an arboretum of Australasian
plants (lots of eucalyptus and nothofagus).
Some of the rhododendrons came as a
wedding present to Lord and Lady
Anglesey from Lord Aberconway at
Bodnant: many others followed. Many
tender species are of considerable size,
including a *R. montroseanum* which is
probably the largest in Britain. Late-
flowering hybrids like 'Polar Bear' extend
the season well into July. The fine
Italianate garden below the house, with
its 'hot and cold' borders, is 1920s –
most surprising.
National Trust shop; tea-room.

Owned by The National Trust
Number of gardeners 4
Size 12.3ha (31 acres)

PLAS-YN-RHIW
Rhiw, Pwllheli LL53 8AB

Tel & Fax: 01758 780219
www.nationaltrust.org.uk
Location 16 miles from Pwllheli. Turn off B4413
at Botwnnog and follow signs along lanes &
through village.
Opening hours 12 noon - 5 pm; Thursday -
Monday; 1 April to 30 September. Plus
Wednesdays from 31 May to 30 September. Also
12 noon - 4 pm; 1, 7, 8, 14, 15 & 21 to 29 October.
Admission fee Adults £2.20; Children £1.10.
£2.20 for snowdrops in February (telephone for
exact times & dates).
P WC 🌱 ●

This pretty garden is small and fairly
formal: it is divided into a series of rooms
which are hedged with cherry laurel and

bay to protect them from the sea-gales. Box-edged parterres are filled with rambling roses and billowing cottage garden flowers. Tender trees and shrubs flourish in the mild coastal climate.

 gift shop.

Owned by The National Trust
Number of gardeners 1, plus 1 trainee
Size 0.4ha (1 acre)

PORTMEIRION
Penrhyndeudraeth LL48 6ET

Tel: 01766 770000 **Fax:** 01766 771331
www.portmeirion-village.com
Location Signed from A487 at Minffordd, between Penrhyndeudraeth & Porthmadog.
Opening hours 9.30 am – 5.30 pm; daily; all year.
Admission fee Adults £6.50; OAPs £5; Children £3.50. RHS members free from October to April.

Portmeirion is where the architect Sir Clough Williams-Ellis worked out his Italianate fantasies. The television series *The Prisoner* was filmed here. The gardens are carved out of a rhododendron woodland but are formal, with a mixture of Mediterranean plants and exotic palms, and full of architectural bric-a-brac of every period. Other attractions include tree ferns, gunneras, phormiums, ginkgos and holm oaks. Williams-Ellis began to lay out the garden at Portmeirion as soon as he made his first purchase of land along the coastline of north-west Wales in 1926. He bought up further estates in later years, by which he acquired one of the chief attractions of the gardens at Portmeirion today – the collection of rhododendrons and azaleas which is known as the Gwyllt gardens.
Rhododendron arboreum has grown to enormous size and in parts of the garden is still impenetrable. The peak display comes in May: the mainstay of late summer and autumn is thousands of hydrangeas throughout the Portmeirion estate. The gardens have been further developed in the last 20 years, taking advantage of the mild climate. One garden – almost at the furthest end of the estate and planted with a background of eucalyptus trees – is known as the 'ghost garden' because of the way the wind whistles in the leaves. There will be five RHS Special Events at Portmeirion in 2006; details from 020 7821 3408.

woodland garden; sub-tropical plants; rhododendrons & azaleas; giant yuccas; exuberant summer bedding; tallest *Maytenus boaria* (18m) in the British Isles; several shops; refreshments; hotel.

Owned by Portmeirion Ltd
Number of gardeners 11
Size 28ha (70 acres)

POWYS

ASHFORD HOUSE
Talybont-on-Usk, Brecon LD3 7YR

Tel: 01874 676271
Location 1 mile east of Talybont along B4588.
Opening hours 2 pm - 6 pm; Tuesdays; April to September. And by appointment (please telephone).
Admission fee Adults £2.50; Children free.

P ◁ WC & ✿ ☕

There are two parts to the garden at Ashford: both have been made by the Andersons. First there is the walled garden, about an acre in extent, with raised beds (lots of alpines), and a plantsman's collection of plants of every kind in fine mixed borders. Then there is the woodland garden, which the Andersons have underplanted with suitable shrubs, especially rhododendrons, camellias and bulbs.

🌿 alpines; woodland with rhododendrons; tea, coffee & biscuits.

Owned by Mr & Mrs D.A. Anderson
Number of gardeners 1 part-time
Size 1.4ha (3½ acres)

THE DINGLE
Welshpool SY21 9JD

Tel: 01938 555145 **Fax:** 01938 555778
www.dinglenurseries.co.uk
Location Turn left to nurseries off A490 to Llanfyllin.
Opening hours 9 am (2 pm on Tuesdays) - 5 pm; daily; all year, except Christmas week.
Admission fee Adults £2.50; Children free. RHS members free.

P ◁ WC & ✿ 🌰 ☕

This steep garden attached to a successful nursery is essentially a plantsman's private garden. It is mainly made up of unusual trees and shrubs, but it has some herbaceous plantings, too. The beds are put together with carefully co-ordinated colour mixtures and designed to look good all through the year.

🌿 south-facing bank; pool; north-facing woodland garden; unusual trees & shrubs; first-rate nursery attached; light refreshments.

Owned by Mr & Mrs D. Hamer
Number of gardeners 2
Size 1.6ha (4 acres)

DOLWEN
Cefn Coch, Llanrhaeadr-ym-Mochnant SY10 0BU

Tel & Fax: 01691 780411
Location Right opposite The Plough Inn, ¾ mile up narrow lane.
Opening hours 2 pm - 4.30 pm; Fridays, plus last Sunday of month; May to August. And by appointment. For NGS: 28 May & 25 June.
Admission fee Adults £2.50; Children free.

P ◁ WC ✿ ☕

This plantsman's garden on a steep site has a stupendous setting in the foothills of the Berwyn Mountains, but blends into its surroundings rather than imposing on them. It has been designed to take advantage of a number of different plant habitats: shade-lovers thrive in the woodland garden, three large ponds (fed by natural springs and connected by waterfalls) favour damp-loving plants, and more open areas are used for climbing roses and wisterias. The many interesting design features include granite boulders, slate bridges and a prospect mount. Dolwen remains one of the best modern gardens in Wales, of ever-growing interest.

woodland garden; roses (mainly old-fashioned); plantsman's collection of plants; good herbaceous borders; water features; tea-room.

Owned by Bob Yarwood & Jeny Marriott
Number of gardeners 3 part-time
Size 1ha (2½ acres)

GLANSEVERN GARDENS
Glansevern, Berriew, Welshpool
SY21 8AH

Tel: 01686 640644 **Fax:** 01686 640829
www.glansevern.co.uk
Location On A483, 4 miles south-west of Welshpool.
Opening hours 12 noon – 6 pm; 14, 15 & 17 April, then Thursday – Saturday & Bank Holiday Mondays from 20 April to 30 September. And parties by appointment on any day of the week.
Admission fee Adults £3.50; OAPs £3; Children free.

The handsome Greek-revival house at Glansevern sits in a landscaped park (1802), complete with its lake and water garden fed by innumerable streams. There is a vast 1840s rock garden which incorporates a spooky grotto. The 'Smoker's Walk' runs down through woodland to the banks of the River Severn with a circular folly perched on a promontory. Splendid Victorian conifers are everywhere, but it is the modern planting which really distinguishes Glansevern: island beds around the house, herbaceous borders on either side of the orangery and an acre of garden rooms in the walled gardens.

rock garden and grotto; roses (mainly modern); water garden; lake; good herbaceous borders; good trees; plants for sale; licensed café.

Owned by Gerran & Meriel Thomas
Number of gardeners 3
Size 8ha (20 acres)

POWIS CASTLE & GARDEN
Welshpool SY21 8RF

Tel: 01938 551920 **Fax:** 01938 554336
www.nationaltrust.org.uk
Location 1 mile south of Welshpool off A483.
Opening hours 11 am – 6 pm; Thursday – Monday; 6 April to 29 October. Plus 11 am – 5 pm on 25 & 26 March and 1 & 2 April. Closes at 5 pm after 17 September.
Admission fee Adults £6.60; Children £3.30.

The hanging terraces draped with bulky overgrown yews and exuberant summer bedding are famous. If you visit Powis in summer or early autumn, you will be completely distracted by the rare and tender plants on the walls – they include Banksian roses, hoherias and a hefty *Acca sellowiana* – and by the containers brilliantly planted with annuals and tender plants. At other times it is the structure which impresses: the 17th-century terraces, lead statues, planters and clipped yews. The views are always a big draw, but especially when the rhododendrons and azaleas are in flower on the ridge opposite the castle. There is much wonderfully rich colour planting and in early autumn the maples colour the lower slopes, as does an Edwardian garden of roses and hollyhocks in summer. The aspect is south-east, so Powis is best seen in the morning light: photographers please note.

plant shop & gift shop; restaurant for light lunches & teas.

Owned by The National Trust
Number of gardeners 8
Size 9.6ha (24 acres)
NCCPG National Collections *Aralia; Laburnum*

CHANNEL ISLANDS

JUDITH QUÉRÉE'S GARDEN

Creux Baillot Cottage, Le Chemin des Garennes, St. Ouen, Jersey JE3 2FE

Tel & Fax: 01534 482191
www.judithqueree.com
Location Directions given when bookings made.
Opening hours Pre-booked guided tours only: 11 am or 2 pm Tuesdays, Wednesdays & Thursdays; May to September.
Admission fee £5, to include guided tour.

Judith Quérée started her garden in 1977: seldom have such good design and so many plants been used together so effectively. It has a true plantsman's collection of rarities – collections of tender salvias, clematis and bog plants, for example – but cultivated with great skill and assembled with artistic sensibility. The design is full of decorative details, and structural innovation like the raised wooden walkway from which you view the bog garden. Every corner has something of interest at every season. Wildlife is respected, too. It is Jersey's most original modern garden: other gardeners on the island talk of it with nothing but reverence.

 some unusual plants for sale.

Owned by Judith & Nigel Quérée
Number of gardeners owners only
Size 0.4ha (1 acre)

SAUSMAREZ MANOR

St Martin, Guernsey GY4 6SG

Tel: 01481 235571 **Fax:** 01481 235572
Location Well signed, off main road between St Peter Port & St Martin.
Opening hours Daily; 1 March to 23 December.
Admission fee Adults £4.50; OAPs, Students & Children £3.50. RHS members free during first week of every month.

The main attraction at Sausmarez is the extensive collection of sculptures of every sort displayed for sale in the grounds. Although there may be as many as 200 around at a time, they are never intrusive. There is a lot more to see in the garden, especially in the thick, woodland jungle around the lake – 50 different bamboos, 8 species of palm, young tree ferns, 320 camellias, giant echiums, tree fuchsias, hydrangeas, hedychiums, gunneras and *Geranium maderense*.

sculptures; tender plants; jungly woodland; café from Easter to October.

Owned by Peter de Sausmarez
Number of gardeners 1
Size 0.5ha (1.2 acres)

NORTHERN IRELAND

Northern Ireland has some fine historic landscapes dating back to the 18th century: Florence Court in Co. Fermanagh and Castle Ward in Co. Down are two that we list. However, there is no doubt that the two best gardens in Northern Ireland are the 20th-century masterpieces – Mount Stewart and Rowallane. Both are in the care of the National Trust, which has maintained them as major tourist attractions. It is a pity that so few people from Britain know them at first hand. Given good weather, they are among the most enchanting and extensive gardens anywhere in the British Isles – and especially lovely in late spring.

Many trees and shrubs flourish in the mild, damp climate of Co. Down and Co. Antrim. The National Arboretum at Castlewellan has a very fine collection of mature trees: 34 of them are record-breakers. Nevertheless, it is fair to say that gardening and garden-visiting are not such popular activities in Northern Ireland as on the mainland of the United Kingdom.

The most comprehensive list of historic parks, gardens and demesnes in Northern Ireland was written by Belinda Jupp and published in 1992 as *The Heritage Gardens Survey*. The Northern Ireland Gardens Committee is keen to complete a more formal register.

The Ulster Gardens Scheme raises funds every year for work in National Trust gardens which would not otherwise be possible. The scheme is run by the Northern Ireland region of the National Trust at Rowallane. The gardens tend to be small and private ones made by the present owners: the Ulster Gardens Scheme also issues a second list of gardens which are open only for group visits by appointment.

Northern Ireland has a few gardening clubs and societies of its own: there is, for example, the Northern Ireland Daffodil Group and the Rose Society of Northern Ireland. Daffodils have for long been a Northern Irish speciality: Brian Duncan and Carncairn Daffodils are two of the world's leading breeders, and their owners follow in the footsteps of other great Ulster daffodil men like Sir Frank Harrison and Guy Wilson. Roses are very popular: the roses in the Sir Thomas & Lady Dixon Park in south Belfast are a great draw in summer and the Dickson rose nursery – now mainly wholesale – has been at Newtownards for over 100 years. Since the closure of the Slieve Donard nursery, there has been no outstanding plantsman's nursery in Northern Ireland, though Gary Dunlop at Ballyrogan comes close to it, and Patrick Ford at Seaforde is a particularly good source of rare trees and shrubs. There are seven National Collections in Northern Ireland, most of them held by corporate owners like the National Trust.

Northern Ireland's only horticultural college is Greenmount College of Agriculture & Horticulture in Co. Antrim, which is a RHS Partner College. RHS members also have free access to a number of gardens in Northern Ireland during the summer, most notably Benvarden Garden and Carnfunnock Country Park in Co. Antrim.

ANNESLEY GARDENS & CASTLEWELLAN NATIONAL ARBORETUM
Castlewellan, Co. Down BT31 9BU

Tel: 028 4377 8664 **Fax:** 028 4377 1762
www.forestserviceni.gov.uk/arboretum.htm
Location 30 miles south of Belfast, 4 miles
west of Newcastle.
Opening hours 9 am – dusk; daily; all year.
Admission fee £4 per car.

P ⚓ WC ♿ ⬇

Castlewellan means trees: 18 oldest
existing specimens in the British Isles,
49 champion trees of the British Isles,
and 86 champion trees of Ireland. The
heart of the collection is in a 12-acre
walled garden, interplanted with
rhododendrons and other shrubs. The
central path has mixed borders at the
top: dwarf rhododendrons are prominent
even here.

Much has been restored in recent years:
the two fountains have been repaired and
lost views of the Mountains of Mourne
reopened. Labelling is good, both here
and in the adjoining six-acre woodland
garden, and the standard of maintenance
high. There are plans to make the
collections of *Podocarpus* and *Eucryphia*
comprehensive. In the Forest Park is the
newly planted 'Peace Maze' which
represents the journey to peace in
Northern Ireland. It is the longest and
largest hedge-maze in the world.

🌿 woodland garden; mature
conifers; fine collection of trees;
autumn colours; embothriums; eucryphias;
tallest *Chamaecyparis nootkatensis* 'Lutea'
(22m) in the British Isles, plus 33 other tree
records; new 'fragrant garden' around a
Lutyensesque tea-house; light refreshments
at peak times.

Owned by Dept of Agriculture & Rural
Development, Forest Service
Number of gardeners 3
Size 40ha (100 acres)

BENVARDEN GARDEN & GROUNDS
Benvarden, Dervock, Ballymoney,
Co. Antrim BT53 6NN

Tel: 028 2074 1331 **Fax:** 028 2074 1955
www.benvarden.com
Location Follow brown tourist signs on B67
Coleraine to Ballycastle road. 8 miles from
Giants Causeway.
Opening hours 12 noon – 5.30 pm; Tuesday –
Sunday & Bank Holiday Mondays; June to
September. And by appointment.
Admission fee Adults £3.50; Children free. RHS
members free from June to August.

P WC ♿ 💐 ✕ ⬇

The main feature of the 0.8ha walled
garden is a spectacular curved red brick
wall, nearly 4m high, dating from
approximately 1780. Around the walls are
espalier-trained apple and pear trees. Other
features include a splendid rose garden,
several herbaceous borders, a new box
parterre, and a fully working kitchen
garden. There are also walks around a small
lake planted with rhododendrons, azaleas,
magnolias and fine trees. A splendid cast-
iron bridge, 36.5m (120ft) long and built in
1870, spans the River Bush.

🌿 roses; herbaceous plants; kitchen
garden; rhododendrons & azaleas;
tea-room.

Owned by Mr & Mrs Hugh Montgomery
Number of gardeners 2
Size 2ha (5 acres)

CARNFUNNOCK COUNTRY PARK
Drains Bay, Coast Road, Larne,
Co. Antrim BT40 2QG

Tel: 028 2827 0541/028 28260
Fax: 028 2827 0852
www.larne.gov.uk/carnfunnock.html
Location On Antrim Coast Road (A2), 3½ miles
north of Larne.
Opening hours 9 am – dusk (9 pm in summer);

daily; all year. Closed 1 January & 25 December.
Admission fee Parking fees apply. Free for RHS
members in July & August.

🅿 🆆 ♿ ✖ ⌷

The walled garden is set within
Carnfunnock Country Park on the
Antrim Coast, an Area of Outstanding
Natural Beauty. It was originally the
cottage garden of Cairncastle Lodge, until
purchased by Sir Thomas and Lady Dixon,
who owned the neighbouring Cairndhu
estate. The gardens contain a wide
collection of plants from all over the
world and enjoy a microclimate which
allows plants such as eucalyptus to
flourish. The gardens are themed to
include a flower garden, butterfly garden,
scented walkway, herbaceous border,
heather garden, rock garden and water
garden. They also boast an amphitheatre,
while one of the central features to the
walled garden is a unique collection of
sundials tracing the history of time. The
park has a hornbeam maze in the shape of
Northern Ireland. A new biodiversity trail
will open this year (2006).

🌿 rhododendrons & azaleas; tender
plants; coffee shop (Easter to
September).

Owned by Larne Borough Council
Number of gardeners 3
Size 0.6-ha (1½-acre) garden, 190-ha
(473-acre) park

CASTLE WARD
Strangford, Downpatrick, Co. Down
BT30 7LS

Tel: 028 4488 1204 **Fax:** 028 4488 1729
www.ntni.org.uk
Location On A25, 7 miles from Downpatrick &
1½ miles from Strangford.
Opening hours 10 am - 4 pm (8 pm from May to
September); daily; all year.
Admission fee Adults £3.80; Children £1.80;
Family £9.40.

🅿 ⏏ 🆆 ♿ ☕ ⌷

It is the position of the house at Castle
Ward which makes it so special – set
among rolling parkland with stupendous
views across Strangford Lough – while the
house itself intrigues the visitor by having
one façade in the Georgian style and the
other in Gothic. There are fine trees in
the park, including embothriums and an
avenue of ancient limes. In the walled
garden are stately cordylines, dwarf palms,
pittosporums and the rare *Mitraria
coccinea*. Elsewhere are yew terraces, a
Victorian rock garden, a pinetum, and
Temple Water, which is claimed to be
Northern Ireland's largest ornamental
garden feature, dating from 300 years ago.
🌿 shop; tea-room.

Owned by The National Trust
Number of gardeners 1, plus volunteers
Size 16ha (40 acres), plus 334ha (840 acres) of
parkland

FLORENCE COURT
Enniskillen, Co. Fermanagh BT92 1DB

Tel: 028 6634 8249 **Fax:** 028 6634 8873
www.nationaltrust.org.uk
Location 8 miles south-west of Enniskillen.
Opening hours Grounds: 10 am - 8 pm (4 pm
from 30 October to 31 March); daily; all year.
Admission fee £3 per car.

🅿 ⏏ 🆆 ♿ 🌱 🌳 ⌷

Florence Court has an 18th-century
parkland, with superb views of the
surrounding mountains and some
magnificent trees. These include the
original 'Irish Yew' (*Taxus baccata*
'Fastigiata') in the adjoining Forest Park
and many specimens of a beautiful form of
weeping beech with a broad curving crown.
The rhododendrons are, for the most part,
huge ancient hybrids of *R. arboreum*, but
there has been much new planting in
recent years and the horticultural interest is
now considerable. The roses in the walled
garden are especially attractive.

MOUNT STEWART
Grey Abbey, Newtownards, Co. Down BT22 2AD

Tel: 028 4278 8387 **Fax:** 028 4278 8569
www.nationaltrust.org.uk
Location East of Belfast on A20.
Opening hours Lakeside gardens & walks:
10 am – sunset; daily; all year. Formal gardens;
10 am – 8 pm; daily; April to October, and at
weekends only in March. Gardens close at 4 pm
in March, and at 6 pm in April & October.
Admission fee Adults £4.50; Children £2.40;
Family £11.40.

P ◁ WC ⏦ ✿

Mount Stewart is the greatest garden in
Northern Ireland, arguably in all
Ireland. There are two factors which have
made this possible: the exceptional climate
which allows plants to thrive that would
not survive in all but the mildest parts of
the British Isles; and the willingness of the
garden's principal maker, Edith,
Marchioness of Londonderry, to spend
money on a large scale on design, plants
and staff. The formal garden in front of the
house is grandly laid out with all manner of
inventive details: best known are the stone
carvings of animals known as the 'dodo
terrace'. Beyond the formal garden is a
sunken Spanish garden and off to one side
is the shamrock garden where a bed
designed by Lady Londonderry to represent
the Red Hand of Ulster has been
surrounded in these more politically
correct times by a green shamrock. The
rare plants begin on the walls of the house

itself: *Rosa gigantea* covers a large area and
there are huge plants of *Magnolia
grandiflora*. Nearby are the wonderfully
flowing beds of the lily wood where exotic
myrtles, pittosporums and phormiums are
underplanted with primulas, cyclamen,
narcissi and lilies, but here – as in every
part of the garden – one is never far from
amazing large-leaved rhododendrons,
cordylines and tree ferns. Better still is the
walk around the lake, where
rhododendrons flood the woodlands: for
many visitors in spring it is the highlight of
a tour of Mount Stewart. The views across
the lake are dominated by the mausoleum
and the exceptional collection of
rhododendrons is interplanted with rare
shrubs like mimosas, clianthus,
prostantheras, pittosporums and grevilleas.
They are underplanted in places with
meconopsis and candelabra primulas and,
at one point, you catch a glimpse of a
white stag in a glade. The outstanding area
is the Jubilee Glade where plants in shades
of red, white and blue provide colour all
through the year. For design, variety, plants
and plantings, Mount Stewart is a place of
miracles. Allow lots of time for your visit.
Owned by The National Trust
Number of gardeners 8, plus volunteers
Size 31ha (77 acres)
NCCPG National Collections *Phormium,
Dianella, Libertia*

ROWALLANE GARDEN
Saintfield, Ballynahinch, Co. Down BT24 7LH

Tel: 028 9751 0131 **Fax:** 028 9751 1242
www.nationaltrust.org.uk
Location One mile south of Saintfield on A7.
Opening hours 10 am - 8 pm (4 pm from 18 September to 13 April); daily; all year. Closed 1 January, 25 & 26 December.
Admission fee Adults £3.80; Children £1.80. (Subject to review.)

P ⬧ WC ♿ ❀ ▯

The extensive gardens at Rowallane can be dated back to 1903, when Hugh Armytage Moore inherited the estate from his uncle John Moore. Uncle John had planted some of the larger trees – wellingtonias, beeches and rhododendrons – but everything else you see today dates from the 20th century. Hugh Armytage Moore was a great plantsman – not just a collector of horticultural curiosities, but a selector of good forms. As his appetite for plants grew, so the garden expanded into the little fields which pattern the estate. The seedlings grew and needed to be planted. The hedges and walls which surround these enclosures remain as the boundary features of each compartment, so that you still have the impression of walking from field to field although each is thickly planted with ornamental trees and shrubs. Moore subscribed to the plant-collecting expeditions of E.H. Wilson and Frank Kingdon Ward. It is to those expeditions that the vast collection of rhododendrons owes its origins. No garden can match it on a sunny day in April or May, as you amble from a glade of *R. augustinii* forms to a line of *R. macabeanum* or back through *R. yakushimanum* hybrids: the large-leaved species are particularly prominent. Because of the mild climate, many other good plants flourish here which are rare elsewhere – *Lomatia ferruginea*, *Grevillea rosmarinifolia* and *Nothofagus cunninghamii*, for example. Rowallane has also given us some good garden hybrids (e.g. *Hypericum* 'Rowallane') and selected forms (e.g. *Viburnum plicatum* 'Rowallane'). Another notable feature is the rock garden – an outcrop of natural whinstone rock which actually has few plants growing in it, but many around the base of the boulders, including the striking candelabra primula 'Rowallane Rose'. And the walled garden, too, is a treasure-house of rare plants, including the National Collection of *Penstemon* species, which gives colour long after the rhododendrons have faded. But it is still the rhododendrons and azaleas for which the garden is best remembered.

tallest *Cupressus duclouxiana* (14m) in the British Isles and three other record trees; light refreshments.

Owned by The National Trust
Number of gardeners 5, plus volunteers
Size 21ha (52 acres)
NCCPG National Collections *Penstemon*

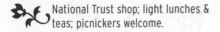 National Trust shop; light lunches & teas; picnickers welcome.

Owned by The National Trust
Number of gardeners 1, plus volunteers
Size 6.4ha (16 acres)

GUY WILSON DAFFODIL GARDEN
University of Ulster, Coleraine, Co. Derry
BT52 1SA

Tel: 028 7044 4141
Location Signed from sports centre, or entry via Portstewart Road.
Opening hours Dawn – dusk; daily; all year. Peak flowering time: mid-March to mid-April.
Admission fee Free.

P WC &

The name says it all – this is both a celebration of Guy Wilson as a daffodil breeder and a museum of his hybrids. Drifts of his cultivars, and others of Irish raising, sweep through the university gardens – more than 1,800 cultivars. Best in April.

 Exceptional collection of daffodils, best in second half of April.

Owned by The University of Ulster at Coleraine
NCCPG National Collections *Narcissus*

SEAFORDE GARDENS
Seaforde, Downpatrick, Co. Down
BT30 8PG

Tel: 028 4481 1225 **Fax:** 028 4481 1370
www.seafordegardens.com
Location Between Belfast & Newcastle.
Opening hours 10 am – 5 pm; Monday – Saturday; 1 pm – 6 pm; Sundays; mid-March to late October. Plus weekdays in winter.
Admission fee Adults £3; Children £2.

WC & ❀ ☕

Seaforde is a leading nursery for trees and shrubs, including Irish specialities (*Eucryphia* x *intermedia* 'Rostrevor') and tender taxa. The list now includes a growing number of rhododendrons grown from Patrick Forde's own collecting expeditions to Bhutan, Yunnan, Tibet and Vietnam. The gardens – open all year – are extensive and important: they have drifts of primulas, camassias and bluebells, as well as both pink forms of *Eucryphia lucida*. In the tropical butterfly house is a fascinating collection of tree ferns.

rare trees; eucryphias; lots of interesting plants; tea-rooms.

Owned by Patrick Forde
Number of gardeners 2
Size 2ha (5 acres)
NCCPG National Collections *Eucryphia*

REPUBLIC OF IRELAND

Until quite recently, gardens were widely thought of in Ireland as part of the culture of the Anglo-Irish: real Irishmen possessed neither the resources nor the cultural points of reference to occupy themselves with horticulture. There was a grain of truth in this: one of the consequences of the Troubles and the land reforms has been the disappearance of many of the historic gardens, parks and demesnes which accompanied the houses of the landed gentry. It is a problem of which the Irish are acutely aware and where such groups as the Irish Georgian Society have done much to change people's perceptions. The new wealth and confidence which Ireland has found within the European Union have helped to dispel the notion that gardens are yet another manifestation of British superiority: now they are seen as something which the Irish can seize upon and adapt to their own cultural styles, traditions, needs and conditions.

The old order is still there, of course. Most of the big gardens attached to big houses and open to the public date back to the 19th century – examples are Lismore, Derreen, Tullynally and Powerscourt. But a number were also made in the middle of the 20th century, often with English pounds (Birr and Malahide) or American dollars (Glenveagh and Mount Congreve). And the best modern gardens in Ireland have most certainly been made by Irishmen.

Ireland is well supplied with garden centres, but has few specialist nurseries. Good garden plants are more difficult to come by. Irish gardeners sometimes say that their best herbaceous plants tend to come from Britain and are then more widely distributed through an informal system of gifting. The NCCPG is represented by the Irish Garden Plant Society: there are only three National Collections in the country – *Garrya* and *Potentilla fruticosa* (cvs.) at National Botanic Gardens, Glasnevin, and *Olearia* in the care of Fingal County Council at Malahide Castle. It is also to be hoped that the new Irish interest in gardening will benefit the Royal Horticultural Society of Ireland, whose 'Royal' title hints at its ties to the United Kingdom but which has fewer than 2,000 members.

Garden restoration is a growth industry in Ireland today. During the last ten years the Heritage Service has helped to rescue the Lutyens gardens at Heywood in Co. Laois and taken over the administration of Fota. Private enterprise has come to the rescue of other gardens: Nicholas and Susan Mosse have made a grand job of restoring the romantic landscape garden at Kilfane in Co. Kilkenny while Benedictine nuns have started to restore the high Victorian gardens at Kylemore Abbey in Connemara. But perhaps the greatest measure of the popularity of gardening in Ireland today is the success of Helen Dillon as a garden-owner, horticultural guru and media star – a success which is very well deserved, for her Dublin garden is an inspiration and her ability to communicate by the written and spoken word is legendary.

ALTAMONT GARDEN
Altamont, Tullow, Co. Carlow

Tel: 00 353 059 91 59444
Fax: 00 353 059 91 59510
www.heritageireland.ie
Location Signed from N80 & N81.
Opening hours All year. Phone for opening times.
Admission fee Adults €2.75; OAPs €2; Children €1.25.

P WC & ⚘ ⚜

Altamont is a charming and romantic woodland garden, full of rare plants, together with lakes, islands, a bog garden and a shady glen. A new double herbaceous border, 75m long within the walled garden, was opened in 2000 with a plant sales area next to it. The woodland garden is a place of contemplation and wonder, and very olde-worlde Irish.

🌿 woodland garden; rhododendrons & azaleas; cyclamen; plant centre.

Owned by Office of Public Works
Number of gardeners 4, plus students
Size 16ha (40 acres)

ANNES GROVE GARDENS
Castletownroche, Mallow, Co. Cork

Tel & Fax: 00 353 22 26145
www.annesgrovegardens.com
Location 1 mile north of Castletownroche on N72.
Opening hours 10 am – 5 pm, Monday – Saturday; 1 pm – 6 pm, Sundays; mid-March to 30 September.
Admission fee Adults €6; OAPs & Students €4; Children €2.

P ⚐ WC 🌿

Annes Grove has long been famous for its 30-acre garden, begun in 1907: 'Robinsonian' is the word most often used to describe it. The walled garden is a flower garden, with a 17th-century mount and a Victorian Gothic summerhouse on top. The river garden is lushly wild with lysichiton, gunnera and candelabra primulas around the pools. In the glen garden lies a wonderfully dense collection of rhododendrons and azaleas, many from Kingdon Ward's seed.

🌿 woodland garden; plantsman's collection of plants; good herbaceous borders; rhododendrons from wild seeds; rare trees; tallest *Azara microphylla* (11m) in the British Isles.

Owned by Patrick Annesley
Number of gardeners 4
Size 12ha (30 acres)

ARDGILLAN PARK
Balbriggan, Co. Dublin

Tel: 00 353 1 890 5629 **Fax:** 00 353 1 890 5649
www.fingalcoco.ie/LeisureandTourism/
Location Off coast road between Skerries & Balbriggan in Co. Dublin. Signed from N1/M1.
Opening hours 10 am – dusk; daily; all year. Guided tours of the walled garden: Thursdays at 3 pm (€4). Groups by appointment only.
Admission fee Free.

P WC & 🌿 ⟱

Ardgillan is a large country house with castellated embellishments, first built in 1738. The original gardens were almost lost, but restored by the Council and opened to the public as a Regional Park in 1985. To the west of the house are the formal rose gardens, where modern roses are planted in the traditional way with one cultivar per bed. Climbing roses on rope swags run down the central avenue. The Victorian conservatory at the end has also been restored: it was originally constructed at Malahide in the 1880s by the Scottish firm McKenzie & Moncur. Nearby, the shrubby *Potentilla* collection is beautifully displayed for learning. The formal walled garden has been restored to its layout on the Ordnance Survey map of 1865. Four demonstration areas are devoted to herbs, vegetables, fruit (trained trees and soft fruit) and flowers. Along the walls are many interesting tender shrubs – crinodendrons, clianthus and huge echiums. And everywhere at Ardgillan you will find very high levels of horticultural interest and a good standard of maintenance.

🌿 roses (ancient & modern); potentillas (nearly 200 cvs.); walled garden; herb garden; *potager*; good herbaceous borders; ice house; 200-year-old yew walk; Victorian conservatory; tea-rooms (closed on Mondays).

Owned by Fingal County Council
Number of gardeners 1
Size 1.6ha (4 acres)
NCCPG National Collections *Potentilla* (shrubby)

ARDNAMONA
Lough Eske, Co. Donegal

Tel: 00 353 74 97 22650 **Fax:** 00 353 74 97 22819
www.ardnamona.com
Location On Lough Eske, 5 miles north-east of Donegal.
Opening hours 10 am – 5 pm; daily; all year.
Admission fee Adults €5; Children free.
🅿 ⬥ ☕

Ardnamona is a masterpiece of huge arborescent rhododendrons, some as much as 20m high, like a Himalayan forest on the lower slopes of the Blue Stack Mountains. A few date back to the introductions of Sir Joseph Hooker in the 1860s. Others were brought by Sir Arthur Wallace as seeds or cuttings from the imperial gardens in Peking and the palace gardens in Kathmandu. All are covered in moss and ferns that revel in the soft climate. Rocky outcrops add to the sense of awesome wilderness, but reclamation and replanting are well under way: the owners have made a big impact on the 40 acres of *Rhododendron ponticum*.

🌿 woodland garden; mature conifers; ancient rhododendrons; B & B offered.

Owned by Mr & Mrs Kieran Clarke
Number of gardeners 1
Size 16ha (40 acres)

BALLYMALOE COOKERY SCHOOL GARDEN
Ballymaloe, Shanagarry, Co. Cork

Tel: 00 353 21 4646785 **Fax:** 00 353 21 4646909
www.cookingisfun.ie
Location Signed from Castlemartyr & Shanagarry.
Opening hours 10 am – 6 pm; daily; 1 April to 1 October.
Admission fee Adults €5; OAPs €2.50; Children €2.50.
🅿 🚻 ♣ ✕

The garden attached to the famous Ballymaloe Cookery School is full of unusual fruit, vegetables and herbs. Seldom is a functional garden so stylishly designed and planted, or so extensive. And it is organic.

🌿 vegetables; roses (mainly old-fashioned); fruit; good herbaceous borders; magnificent formal parterres for herbs; Celtic maze; shell house; garden shop.

Owned by Tim & Darina Allen
Number of gardeners 3
Size 1.2ha (3 acres)

BALLYNACOURTY
Ballysteen, Co. Limerick

Tel: 00 353 61 396409 **Fax:** 00 353 61 396733
Location 3 miles from Askeaton, on River Shannon.
Opening hours By appointment.
Admission fee €5.
🅿 🚻 ♿

Ballynacourty is a fine modern family garden: six densely planted acres won from open farmland. It is interesting for its selection of lime-tolerant trees and shrubs and to see how a garden of this size may be maintained with a minimum amount of help.

🌿 shrub roses (mainly old-fashioned); herbaceous borders.

Owned by George & Michelina Stacpoole
Number of gardeners 1 part-time
Size 2.4ha (6 acres)

BIRR CASTLE DEMESNE
Birr, Co. Offaly

Tel: 00 353 509 20336 **Fax:** 00 353 509 21583
www.birrcastle.com
Location Rosse Row in Birr, Co. Offaly.
Opening hours 9 am - 6 pm; daily; all year.
Admission fee Adults €9; OAPs €7; Children €5.
(Subject to review.)

The best garden in the Irish Midlands, Birr has a huge collection of trees and shrubs, a spacious river walk, a large park with wildflowers, a reedy lake and a good woodland garden. Many of the plants were grown from original collectors' material: some were collected in the wild by the owner's parents, Michael and Anne Rosse. The best bit is the formal garden designed by Anne Rosse in 1935 within the old walled garden. Here is a cloister of arched hornbeams, a lilac avenue, crinums, peonies, Irish yews, two rose gardens (*Rosa roxburghii* 5m high), and the tallest box hedges in the world, extraordinarily slender. Good plants are everywhere and the garden merits a long visit, though parts are now somewhat overrun by Irish melancholy and neglect.
roses (mainly old-fashioned); plantsman's collection of plants; fine collection of trees; *Paeonia* 'Anne Rosse'; *Magnolia* 'Anne Rosse'; tallest *Acer monspessulanum* (15m) and boxwood *Buxus sempervirens* (12m) in the British Isles, plus 49 other record species; craft shop; garden centre; café.

Owned by Earl of Rosse
Number of gardeners 5
Size 52ha (130 acres)

CURRAGHMORE
Portlaw, Co. Waterford

Tel: 00 353 51 387102 **Fax:** 00 353 51 387481
Location 14 miles west of Waterford: enter by Portlaw gate.
Opening hours 2 pm - 5 pm; Thursdays & Bank Holidays; Easter to mid-October. Also (jointly with House): 9 am - 1 pm; Monday - Friday; January, May & June. Other times by prior appointment.
Admission fee Garden & Shell House: €4. House: €6. Combined Ticket: €10.

Lord Waterford's family has lived at Curraghmore since 1170, which is a long time even by Irish standards. It has fine terraced gardens with balustrades and an excellent collection of trees and shrubs, dating mainly from the 19th and early 20th centuries. The outstanding feature is the Shell Grotto which was built in 1754 by the heiress to the property, Catherine Poer, Countess of Tyrone. She personally decorated the interior walls with shells which were collected from all round the world. Curraghmore is a magnificent estate which deserves to be better known. The best time for a visit is from early May to mid-June, but there is much to enjoy at every season.
fine collection of trees; landscaped park.

Owned by The Marquess of Waterford

DERREEN
Lauragh, Killarney, Co. Kerry

Tel: 00 353 64 83588
Location 15 miles from Kenmare on the Castletown road.
Opening hours 10 am - 6 pm; daily; April to October. Closed Monday - Wednesday in August.
Admission fee Adults €5; Children €2.

Derreen is quite extraordinary. The rocky outcrops come right to the front door, but the fast, lush growth of its trees and shrubs is boundless. Tree ferns *Dicksonia antarctica* and myrtles *Luma apiculata* have gone native, and seed themselves everywhere. Moss, lichen and ferns abound. Large-leaved rhododendrons grow to great heights. It is a place of wonder on a sunny day in late April. Great for children, too.

woodland garden; sub-tropical plants; tree ferns; rhododendrons; tea-room.

Owned by Charlie Bigham
Number of gardeners 2
Size 24ha (60 acres)

THE DILLON GARDEN
Ranelagh, Dublin 6, Co. Dublin

Tel: 00 353 1 4971308 **Fax:** 00 353 1 4971308
www.dillongarden.com
Location 45 Sandford Road (behind trees, near junction of Sandford Road & Marlborough Road).
Opening hours 2 pm – 6 pm; daily; March, July & August. Sundays only: April to June, & September. Groups by appointment.
Admission fee Adults €5.
[wc] &

This much-acclaimed plantsman's garden offers a fantastic range of rarities, from snowdrops and hellebores in spring, to tropaeolums in autumn. Unlike some collectors' gardens, this one is immaculately maintained, strictly planted according to colour and beautifully designed as a series of garden rooms. It is also constantly changing. In 2000, she replaced the main lawn with a canal with formal beds and small cascades set in limestone paving. In 2003, she took out the second lawn. In 2005, the front garden was completely renewed. This must be the most intensively gardened garden in the British Isles – a source of constant admiration and inspiration.

plantsman's collection of plants; excellent design; good herbaceous borders.

Owned by Helen & Val Dillon
Number of gardeners 1
Size 0.2ha (½ acre)

FERNHILL
Sandyford, Dublin 18, Co. Dublin

Tel: & Fax: 00 353 1 295 4257
www.gardensireland.com/fernhill-gardens.html

Location 10 miles south of central Dublin on R117 Enniskerry Road, between Lambs Cross & Stepaside.
Opening hours 11 am – 5 pm (2 pm – 5 pm on Sundays); Tuesday – Sunday & Bank Holidays; all year.
Admission fee Adults €5; OAPs €4; Children €2. RHS members €4.
[P] [wc]

This popular garden on the outskirts of Dublin has a good collection of rhododendrons and other woodland plants and some magnificent trees 150 years old. There are steep woodland walks, an enclosed 19th-century garden and an excellent nursery which now sells plants all the year round.

woodland garden; rock garden; good herbaceous borders; fine collection of trees; sculpture exhibitions; rhododendrons; new fern plantings.

Owned by Mrs Sally Walker
Number of gardeners 2
Size 16ha (40 acres)

FOTA ARBORETUM & GARDEN
Fota Estate, Carrigtwohill, Co. Cork

Tel & Fax: 00 353 21 4812728
www.heritageireland.ie
Location 14 miles from Cork city. Take N25 eastbound and turn off for Cobh (R624).
Opening hours Arboretum: 9 am – 6 pm (5 pm from November to March); daily; all year. Walled Gardens: 9 am – 6 pm; Monday – Friday; April to October. Plus some Sundays (ring for times & dates). Closed for Christmas holidays. Tours by prior appointment; ring 00 353 87 7907299.
Admission fee Free. Cars €2.
[P] [wc] &

Fota is famous above all for its trees, most of them planted by the Smith-Barry family towards the end of the 19th century. As well as a fine collection of Victorian conifers (huge redwoods and wellingtonias), the garden and arboretum are notable for the collection of flowering mimosas (*Acacia*), a beautiful *Styrax japonica*, a magnificent collection of mature magnolias, and a spectacular specimen of *Phoenix canariensis* which was planted out over 100 years ago. Some of the record-breaking trees have been lost in recent years but many of Fota's very rare trees still survive, including *Dacrycarpus dacrydioides* and *Phyllocladus tricomanoides*. The garden and arboretum were transferred to the State in 1996 and have since undergone much restoration, regeneration and improvement. New plants have been added, often as part of international conservation programmes. The old walled kitchen garden has been converted to a formal rose garden, with themed borders of monocots, shade-loving and South American plants, a large selection of climbers on the walls, and a collection of Irish-bred daffodils. The Victorian orangery was restored in 2000 and displays a fine collection of contemporary plants. The original formal gardens, known as the 'pleasure gardens', have also been made good – especially the Italian garden.

🌿 woodland garden; mature conifers; 160 Irish-bred daffodil cultivars.

Owned by Office of Public Works
Number of gardeners 5
Size 11ha (27 acres)

GASH GARDENS
Gash, Castletown, Portlaoise, Co. Laois

Tel: 00 353 502 32247
Location ½ mile from N7 at Castletown.
Opening hours 10 am – 5 pm; Monday – Saturday; May to September. At other times by appointment.
Admission fee €5. Group rates by appointment. Not suitable for children.

🅿 ♿ 🌿 🏵

Nothing outside the garden gates suggests the length, extent or beauty of this extraordinary garden, tucked in along the edges of a dairy farm. It was initially laid out and developed by Noël Keenan in 1984 as a complement to his nursery business: his daughter Mary (who trained at UCD and taught at Glasnevin) is continuing to develop and maintain it. You open the high gates, and walk straight into a vast rock garden stuffed with interesting alpines and well-grown rhododendrons, where great artistry is shown in the choice and positioning of plants. Next comes a long narrow garden like a grassy glade with specimen trees and flowing island beds on either side, a bog garden with an island in the middle, foliage borders with phormiums, gunneras and brilliant contrasts of colour and shape, and a laburnum tunnel at the end. Every part is full of unusual plants and maintained to a very high standard. Open a small gate beyond the laburnum tunnel, and a long narrow walk, sometimes in shade, sometimes in the open, runs down alongside a planted stream until finally you reach the River Nore right at the bottom. Here is a long, looped river walk, planted with poplars and larches, beautiful, simple and ingenious. The beauty, the ingenuity and the horticultural interest of the gardens at Gash are incomparable.

🌿 herbaceous perennials; rock garden; rhododendrons; plantsman's collection of plants; nursery at entrance, open all year.

Owned by Mary Keenan & Ross Doyle
Number of gardeners owner, plus part-time help
Size 1.6ha (4 acres)

GLENVEAGH CASTLE
Churchill, Letterkenny, Co. Donegal

Tel: 00 353 74 9137090 **Fax:** 00 353 74 9137072
www.heritageireland.ie
Location 14 miles north-west of Letterkenny on R251.
Opening hours 10 am – 6.30 pm; daily; mid-March to early November.
Admission fee Free. Shuttle bus to garden €2.

🅿 ♿ ⬦ 🚻

Glenveagh was built for its view down the rocky slopes of Lough Veagh: nowhere in Ireland can boast such a contrast between the wild and rugged landscape of a National Park and its carefully nurtured gardens. Part of the gardens is known as the View Garden. Elsewhere is a series of outdoor rooms, each with a different character. The two-acre lawn in the Pleasure Grounds is fringed with rhododendron shrubberies, tree ferns and eucryphias, with massed underplantings of hostas, rodgersias and astilbes. Within the oak woods grow scented rhododendrons, rare trees and tender shrubs: Jim Russell advised on the planting. Paths lead to terraced enclosures furnished with Italian statuary and massive terracotta pots. The unusual shrubs are magnificent: tree-like griselinias and *Michelia doltsopa*, for instance. The *Jardin Potager* is bounded by herbaceous borders and planted with heritage vegetables, Irish apple cultivars and the rare *Dahlia* 'Matt Armour'. Prepare for a long and fascinating visit.

sub-tropical plants; roses (mainly old-fashioned); plantsman's collection of plants; Italianate features; fine collection of trees; restaurant at visitor centre; tea-room at castle.

Owned by The Heritage Service
Number of gardeners 4
Size 11ha (27 acres)

GLIN CASTLE
Glin, Co. Limerick

Tel: 00 353 68 34173 **Fax:** 00 353 68 34364
www.glincastle.com
Location On N69, 32 miles west of Limerick.
Opening hours By appointment.
Admission fee Adults€7.

Simple formal gardens run down towards the park and merge with the surrounding woodland. The walled kitchen garden has recently received a make-over: cutting borders, herbs, herbaceous borders and

such vegetables as sea-kale and asparagus. In the pleasure gardens are some fine ornamental trees – dogwoods, magnolias, cherries and parrotias, as well as rhododendrons and camellias. Taken with the Gothicised castle and its magnificent position on the Shannon estuary, Glin is a place of rare enchantment.

vegetables; sub-tropical plants; rhododendrons & azaleas; daffodils; camellias; bluebells.

Owned by Desmond Fitzgerald, Knight of Glin
Number of gardeners 2
Size 2ha (5 acres)

HEYWOOD GARDENS
Ballinakill, Co. Laois

Tel: 00 353 502 33563
Location In grounds of Ballinakill College.
Opening hours Dawn - dusk; daily; all year. Guided tours by arrangement.
Admission fee Free.

Heywood House disappeared in the Troubles (replaced by a hideous modern Salesian college) but fragments remain of the formal gardens designed by Lutyens in 1912 for Sir Hutcheson Poë. Three small terraced gardens enclosed by yew hedges – one is a herb garden – lead down to the spacious oval garden with ragstone walls and oval portholes. It was boldly replanted in the 1990s with advice from Graham Stuart Thomas. A short formal lime avenue leads towards the other end of the terrace where a classical, arcaded pergola looks down a steep slope to a long lake full of water lilies and up across the countryside to the distant hills. The stonework is impressive; in its heyday it must have been stunning. Imagine what an Edwardian garden looked like when newly made.

Lutyens garden; Graham Thomas plantings; woodland garden.

Owned by Office of Public Works

HILLSIDE
Annmount, Glounthane, Co. Cork

Tel & Fax: 00 353 21 4353119
Location From Cork, turn left at Glounthane Church, up hill, under bridge, 100 yards on right.
Opening hours By appointment between May & September.
Admission fee €5.

P WC

This is an intensely cultivated plantsman's garden in a setting of mature trees (beech and pines) and rhododendrons, azaleas, pieris and woodland plants. It burgeons with alpine plants in every part – stone troughs, a scree bed and gravel areas. It also won the 'Top Garden in Ireland' award in 1996 and 2000 for its all-season attractions. And it is forever changing and improving. rhododendrons & azaleas; plantsman's collection of plants; alpine plants; woodland plants.

Owned by Mrs Mary Byrne
Number of gardeners owner only
Size 1.6ha (4 acres)

ILNACULLIN
Garinish Island, Glengariff, Bantry, Co. Cork

Tel: 00 353 276 3040 **Fax:** 00 353 276 3149
Location 1 mile by boat from Glengariff.
Opening hours 10 am – 6.30 pm; Monday - Saturday; March to October. Opens at 9.30 am in July & August; closes at 4.30 pm in March & October. Plus 11 am – 6.30 pm on Sundays (1 pm – 5 pm in March & October; 1 pm – 6.30 pm in April).
Admission fee Adults €3.50 (in 2005). Plus boat fare (€10 return in 2005).

WC

Ilnacullin is famous for its *casita*, a pavilion built by Harold Peto in 1910. It looks over an Italianate pool lined with Japanese bonsai in elegant pots. Elsewhere are a Grecian temple, a genuine Martello tower and a woodland of exotic trees and shrubs known as Happy Valley. Tree ferns,

dacrydiums, and *Schima wallichii* subsp. *wallichii* var. *khasiana* are some of the best-known plants. The scent of *Rhododendron fragrantissimum* pervades the whole island in spring. coffee shop.

Owned by Heritage Ireland
Size 15ha (37 acres)

JAPANESE GARDENS & ST FIACRA'S GARDEN
Tully, Kildare Town, Co. Kildare

Tel: 00 353 45 521617 **Fax:** 00 353 45 522964
www.irish-national-stud.ie
Location Signed in Kildare.
Opening hours 9.30 am – 6 pm; daily; 12 February to 12 November.
Admission fee Adults €9; OAPs €7; Children €4.50.

P WC

The Japanese garden is a sequence which symbolises Man's journey through life. It was made for Lord Wavertree by Japanese gardeners in the early years of the 20th century and contains some handsome old bonsai and cloud-clipped trees. That said, the garden is planted and maintained in a very Irish style – especially pretty in late spring when the wisteria and water irises are in flower. The standard of maintenance is excellent. Elsewhere on the estate is a very substantial new garden, dedicated to St Fiacre, the patron saint of gardeners, which provides a grand contrast. It has little of horticultural interest, but is very evocative of the Irish landscape as it developed in the 6th and 7th centuries. The unusual design, with its strange pseudo-outcrops of weathered limestone, has a strong spiritual quality which perfectly complements the oriental intellectualism of the Japanese garden. famous Japanese garden; souvenir shop; light refreshments.

Owned by Irish National Stud
Number of gardeners 3
Size 1.6ha (4 acres) in all

JOHN F. KENNEDY ARBORETUM
New Ross, Co. Wexford

Tel: 00 353 51 388171 **Fax:** 00 353 51 388172
Location 8 miles south of New Ross off R733.
Opening hours 10 am - 8 pm; May to August.
10 am - 6.30 pm; April & September. 10 am - 5 pm;
October to March. Closed Good Friday & Christmas
Day.
Admission fee Adults €2.90; OAPs €2.10;
Children & Students €1.30; Family €7.40.

P ⬧ WC ⬧ ⬧ ⬧

This is a memorial arboretum founded in
1968 (with financial help from
Irish/American citizens) on 623 acres
near the Kennedy homestead. Thirty
years on, the statistics are impressive:
4,500 types of trees and shrubs arranged
taxonomically, and 200 plots arranged
by geographical distribution. All are
meticulously labelled, and planted with
artistry. There is one circuit for broadleaves
and another for conifers, interwoven at
times to improve the overall appearance of
the collection. Special features include an
'ericaceous garden' with 500 different
rhododendrons, and many varieties of
azaleas and heathers. There is also a
slow-growing conifer collection, a
hedge collection, a display of groundcover
plants and a selection of climbing plants
on a series of stone and timber shelters.
In summer a miniature railway runs
through plantings that represent each
continent.
mature conifers; fine collection of trees;
eight different tree records for the
British Isles; souvenirs; cafeteria for teas/
refreshments in summer.

Owned by Office of Public Works
Number of gardeners 14
Size 252ha (623 acres)

JOHNSTOWN CASTLE GARDENS
Wexford, Co. Wexford

Tel: 00 353 53 42888 **Fax:** 00 353 53 42213
Location 4 miles south-west of Wexford.
Opening hours 9 am - 5 pm; daily; all year, except
Christmas day.
Admission fee €4 car and passengers.

P ⬧ WC ⬧ ⬧

Johnstown Castle has 50 acres of
ornamental grounds with good trees, tall
cordylines, three lakes and the Irish
Agricultural Museum. There is a section in
the museum devoted to old lawn mowers
and antique garden equipment. The
collection of 19th-century conifers in the
park is exceptional, as is a huge
Rhododendron arboreum nearby.
woodland garden; mature conifers;
walled gardens; ornamental lakes;
tallest *Cupressus macrocarpa* (40m) in the British
Isles; coffee shop with snacks (July and August
only).

Owned by TEAGASC (Food & Agriculture
Development Authority)
Number of gardeners 5
Size 20ha (50 acres)

KILFANE GLEN & WATERFALL
Thomastown, Co. Kilkenny

Tel: 00 353 56 24558 **Fax:** 00 353 56 27491
Location Off N9, 2 miles north of Thomastown.
Opening hours 11 am - 6 pm; daily; July & August.
Admission fee Adults €5.50; OAPs €5; Children
€4.50.

P WC ⬧ ⬧

A romantic landscape garden laid out in
the 1790s and vigorously restored by the
present owners. Sit in the tiny *cottage ornée*,
admire the exquisite form of the waterfall
across the ravine, and dream of Rousseau.
woodland garden; bluebells; excellent
modern art pieces; teas by
arrangement.

Owned by Nicholas & Susan Mosse
Number of gardeners 2
Size 8ha (20 acres)

LISMORE CASTLE
Lismore, Co. Waterford

Tel: 00 353 58 54424 **Fax:** 00 353 58 54896
www.lismorecastle.com
Location Centre of Lismore.
Opening hours 1.45 pm - 4.45 pm; daily; 15 April to 1
October. Opens at 11 am in high season.
Admission fee Adults €6; Children €3.

Lismore is best for the castellated house: the
gardens are interesting rather than
exceptional, but there is a pretty grove of
camellias and a double yew walk planted in
1707. The upper enclosure is even older, a
Jacobean survivor. The herbaceous border
aligned on the cathedral spire has recently
been replanted to give colour throughout the
summer. Contemporary sculptures include
one by Anthony Gormley. Visit the walled
garden for some fine traditional kitchen
gardening: the vinery was designed by Paxton
– this is the Irish Chatsworth.
woodland garden; roses (mainly old-
fashioned); magnolias; spring bulbs;
interesting modern sculptures (including Anthony
Gormley).

Owned by Lismore Estates
Number of gardeners 4
Size 2.8ha (7 acres)

LODGE PARK WALLED GARDEN
Straffan, Co. Kildare

Tel: 00 353 1 628 8412 **Fax:** 00 353 1 627 3477
www.steam-museum.ie
Location Follow signs to Steam Museum Straffan
from Maynooth & Kill.
Opening hours 2 pm - 6 pm; Wednesday - Sunday &
Bank Holidays; June to August. Visits in May &
September by appointment.

Admission fee €7.50. Price includes Museum.
Groups (20+) €5 each.

As it did in the 18th century, the walled
garden at Lodge Park continues to produce
fruit and vegetables with much more besides.
The edible crops grow alongside an ever-
increasing collection of lesser-known
ornamental plants. Coloured borders of
white, blue and yellow greet the visitor and a
pink border begins the main walk of the
garden, near a collection of peonies. Behind
a new classical entrance, the original cold
greenhouse allows semi-tender plants to be
displayed. A more modern heated
greenhouse gives protection for such plants as
cymbidiums and brugmansias. The main walk
of the garden is lined with box hedges,
interrupted by topiary yews: behind the box
lies a south-facing border of shrubs and
perennials. In the centre is new area of lawn
and wide flower borders, with vegetables
planted decoratively behind. The main
herbaceous border has a backdrop of roses
and is spectacular in July. The rose garden
includes a circular iron structure clad in
climbing roses topped by a copper rosebud.
The north-facing border allows for a
collection of shade-loving plants, especially
hellebores and pulmonarias.
roses; good herbaceous borders; gift
shop at museum; tea-room.

Owned by Mr & Mrs Robert Guinness
Number of gardeners 1½
Size 0.8ha (2 acres)

MOUNT USHER GARDENS
Ashford, Co. Wicklow

Tel: 00 353 404 40205 **Fax:** 00 353 404 40116
www.mount-usher-gardens.com
Location Ashford, 30 miles south of Dublin off N11.
Opening hours 10.30 am - 6 pm; daily; 10 March to
31 October.
Admission fee Adults €6.50; OAPs & Children
€5.50. Guided tours for pre-booked groups
available (€40 extra).

P WC & 🐝 ☞

These twenty acres of garden have the River Vartry running through their middle: both sides of the river are crowded with unusual trees and shrubs – 5,000 different species and cultivars, some of them *very* rare. The self-sown *Pinus montezumae* are justly famous. The collection of 100ft eucalyptus trees growing from a sea of bluebells is breathtaking. The *Nothofagus dombeyi* is the largest in Ireland. There are good herbaceous plants, too, and lilies in July. It is a truly remarkable plantsman's garden made in the Robinsonian style by four generations of Walpoles from 1868 to 1980 and extensively restored by the present owner.

🌿 woodland garden; sub-tropical plants; plantsman's collection of plants; mature conifers; fine trees; spring bulbs; pretty bridges across the river; tallest *Cornus capitata* (18m) in the British Isles, plus 28 other record tree species; shopping courtyard; tea-room with home-baked food.

Owned by Mrs Madelaine Jay
Number of gardeners 5
Size 8ha (20 acres)

MUCKROSS HOUSE & GARDENS
Muckross, Killarney, Co. Kerry

Tel: 00 353 64 31440 **Fax:** 00 353 64 33926
www.muckross-house.ie
Location 4 miles south of Killarney on N71.
Opening hours Dawn – dusk; daily; all year, except one week at Christmas.
Admission fee Free.

P ⋘ WC & 🐝 ☞

Killarney National Park provides a most beautiful setting for the gardens and ancient parkland of Muckross House. The walled garden has recently been restored, as has the range of Richardson greenhouses. There is a young arboretum (now fully open to visitors) and some enormous old rhododendrons, but the woodland is of oak, yew, Scots pines and arbutus trees and, even more exciting for a

garden-visitor, the rock garden is a natural one, of carboniferous limestone. Well maintained.

🌿 woodland garden; rock garden; mature conifers; fine collection of trees; rhododendrons; azaleas; greenhouse collection; extensive young conifer plantings in arboretum; craft shop; lunches, hot & cold snacks daily.

Owned by Dept of Environment, Heritage & Local Government
Size 6ha (15 acres), plus 10-ha (25-acre) arboretum

NATIONAL BOTANIC GARDENS
Glasnevin, Dublin 9, Co. Dublin

Tel: 00 353 1 804 0300 **Fax:** 00 353 1 836 0080
www.botanicgardens.ie
Location 3 miles north of city centre between N1 & N2: exit from M50 to City Centre at Junction X or Y.
Opening hours 9 am – 6 pm (10 am – 4.30 pm in winter); daily, except 25 December. Open at 10 am on Sundays.
Admission fee Free.

P WC & ☞

Glasnevin was founded in 1795 to promote a scientific approach to the practice of agriculture: education remains a priority at the gardens which have a flourishing school of horticulture. The design of the botanic gardens is classically Victorian, laid out as a beautiful public park in undulating ground on the south bank of the River Tolka: plants are comprehensively documented, labelled and classified. Notable trees include a magnificent *Zelkova carpinifolia* near the new Herbarium building, good specimens of *Tetradium daniellii*, *Gymnocladus dioica* and *Davidia involucrata* and notable plants of a prostrate form of maidenhair tree (*Ginkgo biloba*) and the weeping Atlantic cedar (*Cedrus atlantica* 'Pendula'). Recent years have seen a dramatic programme of restoration and renewal. The elegant curvilinear range of glasshouses, built by Richard Turner between 1843 and 1868, has been magnificently restored. It has – among many tropical plants – a good collection of cycads. The great palm house (1882) has just been restored, too; its collection is very strong on tropical plants from Central America. The cactus and fern houses – the borders around them are planted with arum lilies and white watsonias – each have extensive collections, including a 400-year-old tree fern presented by the Melbourne Botanic Garden in the 1890s. The gardens are a focal point for horticulture and plant conservation in Ireland. New education and visitor facilities have recently been added and it remains the finest collection of plants in Ireland. Allow a full day to do justice to the garden and its attractions.

large collection of trees including conifers; plant families collection; rock garden and alpine yard; rose garden; vegetable garden; native plants; arboretum; herbaceous borders; seasonal bedding and displays; serpentine pond and heather garden; four ranges of public glasshouses; tropical water lilies; succulents; tender conifers and cycads; Vireya rhododendrons; house plants; palms; orchids; tallest variegated Plane tree *Platanus* x *hispanica* 'Suttneri' (21m) in the British Isles, plus 25 other tree records; tea-rooms.

Owned by Office of Public Works
Number of gardeners 40
Size 20ha (50 acres)
NCCPG National Collections *Garrya*

NATIONAL GARDEN EXHIBITION CENTRE
Kilquade, Kilpedder, Co. Wicklow

Tel: 00 353 1 2819890 **Fax:** 00 353 1 2810359
www.clubi.ie/calumet
Location Signed from N11, 7 miles south of Bray.
Opening hours 10 am (1 pm on Sundays) - 6 pm (dusk in winter); daily; all year.

Admission fee Adults €4.50; OAPs €3.50; Groups (10+) €5 (with guided tour) or €3.50 (without guided tour).

This is a permanent exhibition of contemporary style attached to a garden centre. It has 20 linked but distinct gardens: the Herb Garden; 'Oriental Reflections'; 'Shady Secrets'; the Contemplative Garden; the Celtic Garden; the 'Sensory Garden', and so on. Each was made by a different designer and construction team. It all adds up to the best of modern Irish design for small gardens: a shop window for ideas on style, plants and materials.

model gardens; garden centre; restaurant.

Owned by Tim & Suzanne Wallis

POWERSCOURT GARDENS
Powerscourt Estate, Enniskerry, Co. Wicklow

Tel: 00 353 1 204 6000 **Fax:** 00 353 1 204 6900
www.powerscourt.ie
Location 12 miles south of Dublin off N11.
Opening hours 9.30 am - 5.30 pm (dusk in winter); daily, except 25 & 26 December; all year.
Admission fee Gardens only: Adults €7; OAPs €6; Children €4.

Powerscourt is a wonderful mixture of awesome grandeur and sheer fun. It is also extremely well organised for visitors. The main Italianate garden, dominated by a stately 1860s staircase down to a lake, has the Great Sugarloaf Mountain as an off-centre backdrop. It is lined with bedding plants, statues and urns (look out for the sulky cherubs). To one side is the Japanese garden – not strongly Japanese – but full of twists and hummocks. In the arboretum are many rare trees. Powerscourt is busy in summer, but you can escape into solitude along the avenue of monkey puzzles. The magnificent house is now open to visitors again.

woodland garden; mature conifers; fine collection of trees; much recent restoration, including the Bamberg gates, and a remodelling of the Japanese garden; tallest *Abies spectabilis* (32m) in the British Isles, plus 10 other record tree specimens; garden centre; terrace café with lunches.

Owned by Powerscourt Estate
Number of gardeners 6
Size 19ha (47 acres)

PRIMROSE HILL
Primrose Lane, Lucan, Co. Dublin

Tel: 00 353 1 6280373
Location Lucan village, at top of Primrose Lane, through black iron gates.
Opening hours 2 pm - 6 pm; daily; February, then June to the beginning of August. And by appointment.
Admission fee Adults €5; Children €2.
P WC

Primrose Hill is a plantsman's garden, particularly interesting for its rare forms of herbaceous plants and its snowdrops. The planting continues, and includes a small arboretum, but this is a garden which gets better every year.

snowdrops; plantsman's collection of plants; good herbaceous borders.

Owned by Robin Hall
Number of gardeners owner only
Size 2.4ha (6 acres)

TALBOT BOTANIC GARDENS
Malahide Castle, Malahide, Co. Dublin

Tel: 00 353 1 8160014/8462456
Fax: 00 353 1 8169910/8463620
www.fingalcoco.ie/LeisureandTourism
Location 10 miles north of Dublin off R107 Malahide Road.
Opening hours 2 pm - 5 pm (or by appointment); daily; May to September. Groups by arrangement.

Admission fee Adults €4.50; Groups €4.
P WC

The Talbot Botanic Gardens at Malahide Demesne were the work of Milo Talbot, a passionate amateur botanist with a particular interest in southern hemisphere plants, notably the flora of Tasmania and Chile. He built up a collection of 5,000 different taxa and, since the soil is limey, they are mostly calcicole plants. The gardens consist of an 18-acre woodland garden and a four-acre walled garden, divided into seven distinct areas which give the impression of a series of secret gardens, each with its own particular range of plants. It is in this walled garden that the rarer and tender species will be found. There are seven small glasshouses including a Victorian conservatory at the end of the central path – a prominent focal point. Each house is very different in its style and in its plantings. The smallest has a collection of *Primula auricula* cultivars, while the Victorian house has a collection of Australasian plants. There are extensive collections of escallonias, *Syringa*, philadelphus, nothofagus and pittosporum as well as the National Collection of *Olearia*. Malahide is best visited at 2 pm on Wednesday afternoons when guided tours are offered of the walled garden (not otherwise open).

woodland garden; plantsman's collection of plants; mature conifers; fine collection of trees; alpine plants; Tasmanian plants; restaurant.

Owned by Fingal County Council
Size 8.7ha (22 acres)
NCCPG National Collections *Olearia*

TRINITY COLLEGE BOTANIC GARDEN
Palmerston Park, Dartry, Dublin 6, Co. Dublin

Tel: 00 353 1 4972070 **Fax:** 00 353 1 6081147
Location 3 miles south of city centre, near Ranelagh, opposite Municipal Park.
Opening hours 9 am – 5 pm; Monday – Friday; by prior arrangement only.
Admission fee Free.
[wc]

This is essentially a teaching garden, with an emphasis upon conservation biology, taxonomy, physiological ecology and plant response to climate change. It also has a good collection of plants, including a systematic garden, an arboretum, seven greenhouses and the Irish Rare and Threatened Plant Genebank. It has acquired a considerable patina of horticultural charm since moving here from central Dublin in 1967.
Owned by Trinity College

TULLYNALLY CASTLE
Castlepollard, Co. Westmeath

Tel: 00 353 44 61159 **Fax:** 00 353 44 61856
www.tullynallycastle.com
Location Signposted from Castlepollard. 12 miles from Mullingar.
Opening hours 2 pm - 6 pm; daily; June to August. Plus weekends & Bank Holidays in May. Groups at other times by arrangement.
Admission fee Adults €6; Children €3.

Tullynally has a romantic Loudonesque garden for a rambling Gothic Revival house. Formal terraces overlook the park and lead to the woodland gardens, enriched with recent plantings of maples and magnolias. A fine avenue of Irish yews is the centrepiece of the walled garden: they are thought to be about 200 years old and thus among the oldest in existence. The owner Thomas Pakenham has now followed up his acclaimed *Meetings with Remarkable Trees*, some of whose photographs were taken at Tullynally, with *Remarkable Trees of the World* (Weidenfeld, 2002). And he has introduced some interesting exotics to Tullynally from his travels abroad.

woodland garden; grotto; lake; new Chinese & Tibetan gardens; plants collected by owners; several of the largest beech trees *Fagus sylvatica* in the British Isles; shop; tea-room.

Owned by Mr & Mrs Thomas Pakenham
Number of gardeners 2
Size 10ha (25 acres)

PLANT-
LOVERS'
GUIDES

NCCPG NATIONAL COLLECTIONS

ABIES
Ardkinglas Woodland Garden
Strathclyde, Scotland

ACACIA
Tresco Abbey
Cornwall, England

ACANTHUS
Hillview Hardy Plants
Shropshire, England

ACER
Hergest Croft Gardens
Herefordshire, England

ACER (Japanese cvs.)
**Westonbirt The National
Arboretum**
Gloucestershire, England

ACHILLEA
Capel Manor
London, England

ADIANTUM
Tatton Park
Cheshire, England

AESCULUS
West Dean Gardens
West Sussex, England

ALCHEMILLA
**Cambridge University Botanic
Garden**
Cambridgeshire, England

ANEMONE
(Japanese anemones)
Heathlands
Hampshire, England
Broadview Gardens
Kent, England

ANEMONE NEMOROSA
Kingston Lacy
Dorset, England

ANTHEMIS
**Winterbourne Botanic Garden,
University of Birmingham**
West Midlands, England

AQUILEGIA
Hardwicke House
Cambridgeshire, England

ARALIA
Powis Castle & Garden
Powys, Wales

ARALIACEAE
Meon Orchard
Hampshire, England

ARBUTUS
Dunster Castle
Somerset, England

ARTEMISIA
Elsworth Herbs
Cambridgeshire, England

**ASPLENIUM
SCOLOPENDRIUM**
Sizergh Castle
Cumbria, England

ASTER
Temple Newsam Park
West Yorkshire, England
Upton House & Gardens
Warwickshire, England

ASTER
(autumn-flowering)
The Picton Garden
Herefordshire, England

ASTILBE
Holehird Gardens
Cumbria, England
Marwood Hill Gardens
Devon, England

ASTRANTIA
Warren Hills Cottage
Leicestershire, England

AUBRIETA
**University of Leicester Botanic
Garden**
Leicestershire, England

AZARA
Exeter University Gardens
Devon, England
Trelissick Garden
Cornwall, England

BEGONIA
Glasgow Botanic Garden
Strathclyde, Scotland

BERBERIS
Mill Hill Plants
Nottinghamshire, England
Sherwood
Devon, England

BERGENIA
Greenbank Garden
Strathclyde, Scotland

BERGENIA
(species & primary hybrids)
**Cambridge University Botanic
Garden**
Cambridgeshire, England

BETULA
Hergest Croft Gardens
Herefordshire, England

Wakehurst Place
West Sussex, England

BONSAI
**Birmingham Botanical Gardens
& Glasshouses**
West Midlands, England

BRACHYGLOTTIS
Inverewe
Highland, Scotland

BUDDLEJA
Longstock Water Gardens
Hampshire, England

BUDDLEJA
**Paignton Zoo & Botanical
Gardens**
Devon, England

BUXUS
Ickworth
Suffolk, England
Langley Boxwood Nursery
Hampshire, England

CALLUNA VULGARIS
RHS Garden Wisley
Surrey, England

CALTHA
Rowden Gardens
Devon, England

CAMELLIA
Mount Edgcumbe Gardens
Cornwall, England

CAMELLIA JAPONICA
Antony Woodland Garden
Cornwall, England

CAMELLIA X *WILLIAMSII*
Wentworth Castle Gardens
South Yorkshire, England

CAMPANULA
**Burton Agnes Hall
Gardens**
East Yorkshire, England

Lingen Nursery and Gardens
Shropshire, England

CARPINUS
**The Sir Harold Hillier
Gardens**
Hampshire, England

CARPINUS BETULUS
**(cvs.)
Beale Arboretum**
London, England

CASSIOPE
Branklyn Garden
Tayside, Scotland

CATALPA
Cliveden
Buckinghamshire, England

*CEANOTHUS
(DECIDUOUS)*
Knoll Gardens
Dorset, England

CELMISIA
St Luke's Cottage
Northumberland and
Tyne & Wear, England

CENTAUREA
Bide-a-Wee Cottage
Northumberland and
Tyne & Wear, England

*CHAMAECYPARIS
LAWSONIANA*
**University of Leicester
Botanic Garden**
Leicestershire, England

*CHAMAECYPARIS
LAWSONIANA* **(cvs.)**
Bedgebury National Pinetum
Kent, England

CHRYSANTHEMUM
**(Charms & Cascade)
Temple Newsam Park**
West Yorkshire, England

CITRUS
**Hales Hall Gardens &
Reads Nursery**
Norfolk, England

CLEMATIS
Burford House Gardens
Shropshire, England

CLEMATIS VITICELLA
Longstock Water Gardens
Hampshire, England

COLCHICUM
Felbrigg Hall
Norfolk, England

CONOPHYTUM
Abbey Brook Cactus Nursery
Derbyshire, England

CONVALLARIA
Kingston Lacy
Dorset, England

COPROSMA
County Park Nursery
Essex, England

CORIARIA
Crûg Farm Plants
Gwynedd, Wales

CORNUS
RHS Garden Rosemoor
Devon, England
The Sir Harold Hillier Gardens
Hampshire, England

CORNUS **(not C. florida cvs.)
Newby Hall**
North Yorkshire, England

CORYLUS
The Sir Harold Hillier Gardens
Hampshire, England

*CORYLUS (COBNUTS &
FILBERTS)*
Brogdale
Kent, England

COTONEASTER
The Sir Harold Hillier Gardens
Hampshire, England

COX HYBRIDS
Glendoick Gardens
Tayside, Scotland

CROCUS
RHS Garden Wisley
Surrey, England

x CUPRESSOCYPARIS
Bedgebury National Pinetum
Kent, England

CYDONIA OBLONGA
Norton Priory Museum & Gardens
Cheshire, England

CYSTOPTERIS
Sizergh Castle
Cumbria, England

DABOECIA
RHS Garden Wisley
Surrey, England

DAPHNE
Brandy Mount House
Hampshire, England

DELPHINIUM
Rougham Hall Nurseries
Suffolk, England
Temple Newsam Park
West Yorkshire, England

DENDROBIUM
Glasgow Botanic Garden
Strathclyde, Scotland

DEUTZIA
The Hollies Park
West Yorkshire, England

DIANELLA
Mount Stewart
Co. Down, Northern Ireland

DIANTHUS
Kingstone Cottage Plants
Herefordshire, England

DIANTHUS
(MALMAISON CARNATIONS)
Crathes Castle
Grampian, Scotland

DICKSONIACEAE
Glasgow Botanic Garden
Strathclyde, Scotland

DIERVILLA
Sheffield Botanical Gardens
South Yorkshire, England

DIGITALIS
The Botanic Nursery
Wiltshire, England

DRYOPTERIS
RHS Garden Harlow Carr
North Yorkshire, England
Sizergh Castle
Cumbria, England

DWARF &
SLOW-GROWING CONIFERS
Savill Garden
Surrey, England
Valley Gardens
Surrey, England

ECHINOPSIS HYBRIDS
Abbey Brook Cactus Nursery
Derbyshire, England

ELAEAGNUS
Beale Arboretum
London, England

EMBOTHRIUM
Bodnant Gardens
Clwyd, Wales

ENKIANTHUS
Clyne Gardens
Glamorgan, Wales

EPIMEDIUM
Lilliesleaf Nursery
Borders, Scotland
RHS Garden Wisley
Surrey, England

ERICA
Bell's Cherrybank Centre
Tayside, Scotland
RHS Garden Wisley
Surrey, England

ERYTHRONIUM
Greencombe Gardens
Somerset, England
R.V. Roger Ltd
North Yorkshire, England

EUCALYPTUS
Meon Orchard
Hampshire, England

EUCRYPHIA
Bodnant Gardens
Clwyd, Wales
Seaforde Gardens
Co. Down, Northern Ireland

EUPHORBIA
Oxford Botanic Garden
Oxfordshire, England

FAGUS
Kirkley Hall Gardens
Northumberland and Tyne & Wear, England

FERNS
Savill Garden
Surrey, England
Valley Gardens
Surrey, England

FICUS
Hales Hall Gardens & Reads Nursery
Norfolk, England

FRAXINUS
The Quinta
Cheshire, England

Thorp Perrow Arboretum &
Woodland Garden
North Yorkshire, England

FRITILLARIA
(European)
**Cambridge University Botanic
Garden**
Cambridgeshire, England

FUCHSIA
**University of Leicester
Botanic Garden**
Leicestershire, England

FUCHSIA (hardy)
**Croxteth Hall &
Country Park**
Lancashire, Greater Manchester
& Merseyside, England
Kathleen Muncaster Fuchsias
Lincolnshire, England

*FUCHSIA SECTION
QUELUSIA*
RHS Garden Harlow Carr
North Yorkshire, England

GALANTHUS
Brandy Mount House
Hampshire, England
RHS Garden Wisley
Surrey, England

GARRYA
National Botanic Gardens
Co. Dublin, Republic of Ireland

GAULTHERIA
Greencombe Gardens
Somerset, England

GENTIANA
Christie's Nursery
Tayside, Scotland

GERANIUM
(species & primary hybrids)
**Cambridge University Botanic
Garden**
Cambridgeshire, England

GREVILLEA
Pine Lodge Gardens & Nursery
Cornwall, England

GYMNOCALYCIUM
Abbey Brook Cactus Nursery
Derbyshire, England

HAMAMELIS
Swallow Hayes
Shropshire, England
The Sir Harold Hillier Gardens
Hampshire, England

HAWORTHIA
Abbey Brook Cactus Nursery
Derbyshire, England

HEDERA
Erddig
Clwyd, Wales
Fibrex Nurseries Ltd
Warwickshire, England

HELIOTROPIUM
Hampton Court Palace
London, England

HELLEBORUS
Broadview Gardens
Kent, England

HELLEBORUS (part)
White Windows
Hampshire, England

HEMEROCALLIS
Antony
Cornwall, England

HEMEROCALLIS (Coe hybrids)
The Hollies Park
West Yorkshire, England

HEMEROCALLIS (cvs. post-1970)
Rosewood Daylilies
Kent, England

'*HILLIER*' *PLANTS*
The Sir Harold Hillier Gardens
Hampshire, England

HOHERIA
**Abbotsbury Sub-Tropical
Gardens**
Dorset, England

HOSTA
(large leaved)
The Hollies Park
West Yorkshire, England

HOSTA
(modern hybrids)
Ann & Roger Bowden
Devon, England

HYACINTHUS ORIENTALIS
Ripley Castle Gardens
North Yorkshire, England

HYDRANGEA
Holehird Gardens
Cumbria, England
The Garden House
Clwyd, Wales

HYPERICUM
Wakehurst Place
West Sussex, England

ILEX
RHS Garden Rosemoor
Devon, England
Savill Garden
Surrey, England
Valley Gardens
Surrey, England

INULA
**Bluebell Cottage Gardens &
Lodge Lane Nursery**
Cheshire, England

IRIS
Myddelton House
London, England

IRIS
(fulva, pseudacorus, versicolor,
virginica & laevigata cvs.)
Rowden Gardens
Devon, England

IRIS
(species)
The Harris Garden
Berkshire, England

IRIS ENSATA
Marwood Hill Gardens
Devon, England

IRIS SIBIRICA
Lingen Nursery and Gardens
Shropshire, England

IRIS SPURIA
Belsay Hall
Northumberland and
Tyne & Wear, England

IRIS UNGUICULARIS
(provisional)
**Winterbourne Botanic
Garden, University of
Birmingham**
West Midlands, England

JUGLANS
**Thorp Perrow Arboretum &
Woodland Garden**
North Yorkshire, England
Wimpole Hall
Cambridgeshire, England

JUNIPERUS
**Bedgebury National
Pinetum**
Kent, England

KNIPHOFIA
Barton Manor
Isle of Wight, England

LABURNUM
Powis Castle & Garden
Powys, Wales
**Thorp Perrow Arboretum &
Woodland Garden**
North Yorkshire, England

LAVANDULA
Downderry Nursery
Kent, England

LEWISIA
Ashwood Nurseries Ltd
Staffordshire, England

LIBERTIA
Mount Stewart
Co. Down, Northern Ireland

LIGUSTRUM
The Sir Harold Hillier Gardens
Hampshire, England

LILIUM
Branklyn Garden
Tayside, Scotland

LIRIODENDRON
West Dean Gardens
West Sussex, England

LITHOCARPUS
The Sir Harold Hillier Gardens
Hampshire, England

LITHOPS
Abbey Brook Cactus Nursery
Derbyshire, England

LONICERA (shrubby species &
primary hybrids)
**Cambridge University Botanic
Garden**
Cambridgeshire, England

LUPINUS (Russell strains)
Swallow Hayes
Shropshire, England

LYSIMACHIA
Cotswold Garden Flowers
Worcestershire, England

MAGNOLIA
Caerhays Castle Gardens
Cornwall, England
Savill Garden
Surrey, England
Sherwood
Devon, England
Valley Gardens
Surrey, England

MAGNOLIA (spp.)
Bodnant Gardens
Clwyd, Wales

MAGNOLIA
(species)
Wentworth Castle Gardens
South Yorkshire, England

MAHONIA
Savill Garden
Surrey, England
Valley Gardens
Surrey, England

MALUS
Granada Arboretum
Cheshire, England

MALUS
(apples, ornamental cvs. &
cider apples)
Brogdale
Kent, England

MAMMILLARIA
Abbey Brook Cactus Nursery
Derbyshire, England

MENTHA
Iden Croft Herbs
Kent, England

MISCANTHUS
Bressingham Gardens
Norfolk, England

MONARDA
Leeds Castle
Kent, England

NARCISSUS
Brodie Castle
Grampian, Scotland
Guy Wilson Daffodil Garden
Co. Derry, Northern Ireland

NARCISSUS
(miniature)
Broadleigh Gardens
Somerset, England

NEPETA
Iden Croft Herbs
Kent, England

NERIUM OLEANDER
Elsworth Herbs
Cambridgeshire, England

NOTHOFAGUS
Crarae Gardens
Strathclyde, Scotland
Wakehurst Place
West Sussex, England

NYMPHAEA
Bennetts Water Lily Farm
Dorset, England
Burnby Hall Gardens
East Yorkshire, England
Kenchester Water Gardens
Herefordshire, England
Stapeley Water Gardens
Cheshire, England

OENOTHERA
Old Vicarage
Wiltshire, England

OLEARIA
Inverewe
Highland, Scotland
Talbot Botanic Gardens
Co. Dublin, Republic of Ireland

ORIGANUM
Chesters Walled Garden
Northumberland and
Tyne & Wear, England
Iden Croft Herbs
Kent, England

OSMUNDA
Sizergh Castle
Cumbria, England

PAEONIA LACTIFLORA
Kelways Ltd
Somerset, England

PAPAVER ORIENTALE
Water Meadow Nursery and

Herb Farm
Hampshire, England

PARIS
Crûg Farm Plants
Gwynedd, Wales

PELARGONIUM
Fibrex Nurseries Ltd
Warwickshire, England

PENNISETUM
Knoll Gardens
Dorset, England

PENSTEMON
Kingston Maurward Gardens
Dorset, England
Pershore College
Worcestershire, England
Rowallane Garden
Co. Down, Northern Ireland

PERNETTYA
Savill Garden Surrey, England
Valley Gardens
Surrey, England

PHILADELPHUS
Pershore College
Worcestershire, England
The Hollies Park
West Yorkshire, England

PHLOX PANICULATA
Temple Newsam Park
West Yorkshire, England

PHORMIUM
Mount Stewart
Co. Down, Northern Ireland

PHOTINIA
The Sir Harold Hillier Gardens
Hampshire, England
Trelissick Garden
Cornwall, England

PHYGELIUS
Knoll Gardens
Dorset, England

PICEA
Ardkinglas Woodland Garden
Strathclyde, Scotland

PIERIS
Clyne Gardens
Glamorgan, Wales

PINUS
The Quinta
Cheshire, England

PINUS **(excl. dwarf cvs.)**
The Sir Harold Hillier Gardens
Hampshire, England

PLANTS INTRODUCED
BY SIR FREDERICK STERN
Highdown
West Sussex, England

PLATANUS
Mottisfont Abbey
Hampshire, England

PODOCARPACEAE
Meon Orchard
Hampshire, England

POLYGONATUM
Crûg Farm Plants
Gwynedd, Wales

POLYGONUM **(i.e. Fagopyrum,**
Fallopia & Persicaria)
Rowden Gardens
Devon, England

POLYPODIUM
RHS Garden Harlow Carr
North Yorkshire, England

POLYSTICHUM
Greencombe Gardens
Somerset, England
Holehird Gardens
Cumbria, England

POPULUS
Lackham Country Park
Wiltshire, England

POTENTILLA (shrubby)
Ardgillan Park
Co. Dublin, Republic of Ireland

POTENTILLA FRUTICOSA (cvs.)
Webbs of Wychbold
Worcestershire, England

PRIMULA (Cortusoides section)
Plant World Botanic Gardens
Devon, England

PRIMULA AURICULA
Golden Acre Park
West Yorkshire, England

PRUNUS (cherries)
Brogdale
Kent, England

PRUNUS (plums)
Brogdale
Kent, England

PULMONARIA
Stillingfleet Lodge Nurseries
North Yorkshire, England

PYRUS
Brogdale
Kent, England

QUERCUS
The Sir Harold Hillier Gardens
Hampshire, England

RANUNCULUS FICARIA
Rowden Gardens
Devon, England

RHEUM (culinary)
RHS Garden Wisley
Surrey, England

RHEUM (viewable on request)
RHS Garden Harlow Carr
North Yorkshire, England

RHODODENDRON FORRESTII
Bodnant Gardens
Clwyd, Wales

RHODODENDRON (Barbatum, Glischra & Maculifera sections)
Inverewe
Highland, Scotland

RHODODENDRON (Ghent azaleas)
Sheffield Park Garden
East Sussex, England

RHODODENDRON (Knap Hill azaleas)
Sherwood
Devon, England

RHODODENDRON (Kurume azaleas, the Wilson 50)
Isabella Plantation
London, England

RHODODENDRON (part)
Singleton Park & Swansea Botanical Gardens
Glamorgan, Wales

RHODODENDRON (species & Glenn Dale azaleas)
Savill Garden
Surrey, England
Valley Gardens
Surrey, England

RHODODENDRON (subsections Campylogyna, Glauca, Uniflora)
Glendoick Gardens
Tayside, Scotland

RHODODENDRON (subsections Falconera, Grandia and Maddenia)
Brodick Castle
Strathclyde, Scotland

RHODODENDRON (Triflora & Falconera subsections)
Clyne Gardens
Glamorgan, Wales

RHODODENDRON species
Wentworth Castle Gardens
South Yorkshire, England

RIBES (species & primary hybrids)
Cambridge University Botanic Garden
Cambridgeshire, England

RIBES GROSSULARIA (gooseberries)
Brogdale
Kent, England
Rougham Hall Nurseries
Suffolk, England

RIBES NIGRUM (blackcurrants)
Brogdale
Kent, England

RIBES SATIVUM (currants other than blackcurrants)
Brogdale
Kent, England

RODGERSIA
Hadspen Garden
Somerset, England

ROSA
Mottisfont Abbey
Hampshire, England

ROSA (19th-century shrubs)
Malleny House Garden
Lothian, Scotland

ROSA ('English Rose' cultivars)
David Austin Roses
Shropshire, England

ROSA (History of European roses)
Winterbourne Botanic Garden, University of Birmingham
West Midlands, England

ROSA (species & cultivars)
The Gardens of the Rose
Hertfordshire, England

ROSA (species)
Peter Beales Roses
Norfolk, England

ROSMARINUS
Downderry Nursery
Kent, England

RUSCUS
**Cambridge University Botanic
Garden**
Cambridgeshire, England

SALIX
**Westonbirt The National
Arboretum**
Gloucestershire, England

SALVIA
Kingston Maurward Gardens
Dorset, England

SAMBUCUS
Wallington
Northumberland and
Tyne & Wear, England

SARCOCOCCA
Capel Manor
London, England

SAXIFRAGA
Waterperry Gardens
Oxfordshire, England

SAXIFRAGA
**(European species)
Cambridge University Botanic
Garden**
Cambridgeshire, England

SECTION POGONANTHUM
Glendoick Gardens
Tayside, Scotland

SKIMMIA
**University of Leicester Botanic
Garden**
Leicestershire, England
Wakehurst Place
West Sussex, England

SOLENOSTEMON
Temple Newsam Park
West Yorkshire, England

SORBUS
**East Durham & Houghall
Community College**
Co. Durham, England
Granada Arboretum
Cheshire, England

SORBUS
**(Aria & Micromeles)
Winkworth Arboretum**
Surrey, England

STEWARTIA
High Beeches
West Sussex, England

STREPTOCARPUS
Dibleys Nurseries
Clwyd, Wales

STYRACACEAE
**(incl. Halesia,
Pterostyrax, Styrax,
Sinojackia)
Holker Hall**
Cumbria, England

SYRINGA
Golden Acre Park
West Yorkshire, England
The Hollies Park
West Yorkshire, England

TAXUS
Bedgebury National Pinetum
Kent, England

THUJA
Bedgebury National Pinetum
Kent, England

THYMUS
Chesters Walled Garden
Northumberland and
Tyne & Wear, England

TILIA
**Thorp Perrow
Arboretum & Woodland
Garden**
North Yorkshire, England

TRADESCANTIA
**(Andersoniana Group)
Kayes Garden Nursery**
Leicestershire, England

TROPAEOLUM (species)
Inveresk Lodge
Lothian, Scotland

TULBAGHIA
Marwood Hill Gardens
Devon, England

TULIPA (species & primary
hybrids)
**Cambridge University Botanic
Garden**
Cambridgeshire, England

VACCINIUM
Greencombe Gardens
Somerset, England

VIBURNUM
RHS Garden Hyde Hall
Essex, England

VIOLA ODORATA (cvs.)
C. W. Groves & Son
Dorset, England

VITIS VINIFERA (grapes)
Brogdale
Kent, England

VITIS VINIFERA (grapes)
**Hales Hall Gardens & Reads
Nursery**
Norfolk, England

WEIGELA
Sheffield Botanical Gardens
South Yorkshire, England

YUCCA
Renishaw Hall
Derbyshire, England

ZELKOVA
Hergest Croft Gardens
Herefordshire, England

WHERE TO SEE...

ALPINES

Brandy Mount House
Hampshire, England

Cambridge University Botanic Garden
Cambridgeshire, England

Glen Chantry
Essex, England

Hillside
Co. Cork, Republic of Ireland

W.E.Th. Ingwersen Ltd
West Sussex, England

Jack Drake
Highland, Scotland

National Botanic Gardens
Co. Dublin, Republic of Ireland

Pershore College
Worcestershire, England

Pottertons Nursery
Lincolnshire, England

RHS Garden Wisley
Surrey, England

Royal Botanic Garden Edinburgh
Lothian, Scotland

Royal Botanic Gardens, Kew
London, England

St Luke's Cottage
Northumberland and Tyne & Wear, England

University of Leicester Botanic Garden
Leicestershire, England

ARBORETA

Abbotsbury Sub-Tropical Gardens
Dorset, England

Antony
Cornwall, England

Arley Arboretum
Worcestershire, England

Bath Botanic Gardens
Somerset, England

Batsford Arboretum
Gloucestershire, England

Bicton Park Gardens
Devon, England

Bluebell Arboretum & Nursery
Derbyshire, England

Bodenham Arboretum
Worcestershire, England

Caerhays Castle Gardens
Cornwall, England

Cambridge University Botanic Garden
Cambridgeshire, England

Chatsworth
Derbyshire, England

Chyverton
Cornwall, England

Cowdray Park
West Sussex, England

Cruickshank Botanic Garden
Grampian, Scotland

Dawyck Botanic Garden
Borders, Scotland

East Bergholt Place
Suffolk, England

Exbury Gardens
Hampshire, England

Exeter University Gardens
Devon, England

Fota Arboretum & Garden
Co. Cork, Republic of Ireland

Golden Acre Park
West Yorkshire, England

Granada Arboretum
Cheshire, England

Hergest Croft Gardens
Herefordshire, England

Highclere Castle
Hampshire, England

Landford Trees
Wiltshire, England

Lynford Arboretum
Norfolk, England

Marwood Hill Gardens
Devon, England

National Botanic Gardens
Co. Dublin, Republic of Ireland

Nymans
West Sussex, England

Pencarrow
Cornwall, England

Pershore College
Worcestershire, England

RHS Garden Wisley
Surrey, England

RHS Garden Hyde Hall
Essex, England

RHS Garden Rosemoor
Devon, England

Rowallane Garden
Co. Down, Northern Ireland

Royal Botanic Garden Edinburgh
Lothian, Scotland

Royal Botanic Gardens, Kew
London, England

Saling Hall
Essex, England

Seaforde Gardens
Co. Down, Northern Ireland

Sheffield Park Garden
East Sussex, England

Talbot Botanic Gardens
Co. Dublin, Republic of Ireland

Tatton Park
Cheshire, England

Thorp Perrow Arboretum & Woodland Garden
North Yorkshire, England

Torosay Castle & Gardens
Strathclyde, Scotland

Westonbirt The National Arboretum
Gloucestershire, England

Whitfield
Herefordshire, England

Winkworth Arboretum
Surrey, England

Woburn Abbey
Bedfordshire, England

BEGONIA

Blackmore & Langdon
Somerset, England

Glasgow Botanic Garden
Strathclyde, Scotland

BLUEBELLS

Ardkinglas Woodland Garden
Strathclyde, Scotland
Emmetts Garden
Kent, England
**Fairhaven Woodland & Water
Garden**
Norfolk, England
Furzey Gardens
Hampshire, England
Galloway House Gardens
Dumfries & Galloway, Scotland
Haughley Park
Suffolk, England
High Beeches
West Sussex, England
Hole Park
Kent, England
Killerton
Devon, England
Lanhydrock
Cornwall, England
Leonardslee Lakes & Gardens
West Sussex, England
Lydney Park Gardens
Gloucestershire, England
Royal Botanic Gardens, Kew
London, England
Sheffield Park Garden
East Sussex, England
Stourhead
Wiltshire, England
**Thorp Perrow Arboretum &
Woodland Garden**
North Yorkshire, England
Wakehurst Place
West Sussex, England
Winkworth Arboretum
Surrey, England

BORDER AND HERBACEOUS PLANTS

Arley Hall
Cheshire, England
Barrington Court
Somerset, England
Beningbrough Hall & Gardens
North Yorkshire, England
Beth Chatto Gardens
Essex, England
Bressingham Gardens
Norfolk, England

Buscot Park
Oxfordshire, England
Castle Drogo
Devon, England
Clare College Fellows' Garden
Cambridgeshire, England
Cottesbrooke Hall
Northamptonshire, England
The Courts Garden
Wiltshire, England
East Ruston Old Vicarage
Norfolk, England
Felley Priory
Nottinghamshire, England
Forde Abbey
Dorset, England
Garsington Manor
Oxfordshire, England
Goodnestone Park
Kent, England
Great Dixter
East Sussex, England
Hatfield House
Hertfordshire, England
Helmingham Hall
Suffolk, England
Hestercombe Gardens
Somerset, England
Hinton Ampner House
Hampshire, England
Hoveton Hall
Norfolk, England
Kingston Maurward Gardens
Dorset, England
Leeds Castle
Kent, England
**The National Botanic Garden
of Wales**
Dyfed, Wales
National Botanic Gardens
Co. Dublin, Republic of Ireland
Ness Botanic Gardens
Cheshire, England
Newby Hall
North Yorkshire, England
Nymans
West Sussex, England
Packwood House
Warwickshire, England
Parham
West Sussex, England

Pashley Manor Gardens
East Sussex, England
Pershore College
Worcestershire, England
RHS Garden Wisley
Surrey, England
RHS Garden Hyde Hall
Essex, England
Rodmarton Manor
Gloucestershire, England
Royal Botanic Gardens, Kew
London, England
Sandringham House
Norfolk, England
Savill Garden
Surrey, England
Tintinhull House
Somerset, England
Upton House & Gardens
Warwickshire, England
Wallington
Northumberland and Tyne &
Wear, England
White Windows
Hampshire, England

CACTI

Abbey Brook Cactus Nursery
Derbyshire, England
**Birmingham Botanical Gardens
& Glasshouses**
West Midlands, England
**Cambridge University Botanic
Garden**
Cambridgeshire, England
Holly Gate Cactus Nursery
West Sussex, England
National Botanic Gardens
Co. Dublin, Republic of Ireland
RHS Garden Wisley
Surrey, England
**Royal Botanic Garden
Edinburgh**
Lothian, Scotland
Royal Botanic Gardens, Kew
London, England
**University of Durham Botanic
Garden**
Co. Durham, England

CAMELLIAS

Bodnant Gardens
Clwyd, Wales

Burncoose Gardens & Nurseries
Cornwall, England

Coleton Fishacre Garden
Devon, England

Galloway House Gardens
Dumfries & Galloway, Scotland

Glendurgan
Cornwall, England

Greenway
Devon, England

Lydney Park Gardens
Gloucestershire, England

Marwood Hill Gardens
Devon, England

Mount Edgcumbe Gardens
Cornwall, England

RHS Garden Wisley
Surrey, England

Savill Garden
Surrey, England

Trehane Camellia Nursery
Dorset, England

Trewidden Gardens
Cornwall, England

Wentworth Castle Gardens
South Yorkshire, England

Crathes Castle
Grampian, Scotland

RHS Garden Wisley
Surrey, England

CHRYSANTHEMUMS

Halls of Heddon
Northumberland and
Tyne & Wear, England

RHS Garden Wisley
Surrey, England

CLEMATIS

Burford House Gardens
Shropshire, England

Elworthy Cottage Plants
Somerset, England

Helmsley Walled Garden
North Yorkshire, England

Kelmscott Manor
Oxfordshire, England

Thorncroft Clematis Nursery
Norfolk, England

CONIFERS

Ardkinglas Woodland Garden
Strathclyde, Scotland

Ascott
Buckinghamshire, England

Benmore Botanic Garden
Strathclyde, Scotland

Bressingham Gardens
Norfolk, England

Brodsworth Hall & Gardens
South Yorkshire, England

Chatsworth
Derbyshire, England

Clumber Park
Nottinghamshire, England

Cragside
Northumberland and Tyne &
Wear, England

Dawyck Botanic Garden
Borders, Scotland

Eastnor Castle
Herefordshire, England

Elvaston Castle
Derbyshire, England

Fota Arboretum & Garden
Co. Cork, Republic of Ireland

Great Comp
Kent, England

Hergest Croft Gardens
Herefordshire, England

Kingston Lacy
Dorset, England

Mount Stuart
Strathclyde, Scotland

National Botanic Gardens
Co. Dublin, Republic of Ireland

Nymans
West Sussex, England

Pencarrow
Cornwall, England

RHS Garden Wisley
Surrey, England

Royal Botanic Gardens, Kew
London, England

Scone Palace
Tayside, Scotland

Sheffield Park Garden
East Sussex, England

Thorp Perrow Arboretum & Woodland Garden
North Yorkshire, England

Trelissick Garden
Cornwall, England

Wakehurst Place
West Sussex, England

Westonbirt The National Arboretum
Gloucestershire, England

Winkworth Arboretum
Surrey, England

CYCLAMEN

Ashwood Nurseries Ltd
Staffordshire, England

Cadenza
Surrey, England

Foxgrove
Berkshire, England

RHS Garden Wisley
Surrey, England

Tile Barn Nursery
Kent, England

DAFFODILS

Acorn Bank Garden
Cumbria, England

Broadleigh Gardens
Somerset, England

Brodie Castle
Grampian, Scotland

Chenies Manor
Buckinghamshire, England

Clandon Park
Surrey, England

Docton Mill
Devon, England

Erddig
Clwyd, Wales

Escot
Devon, England

Felley Priory
Nottinghamshire, England

Fota Arboretum & Garden
Co. Cork, Republic of Ireland

Guy Wilson Daffodil Garden
Co. Derry, Northern Ireland

Hever Castle
Kent, England

Overbury Court
Worcestershire, England

Petworth House
West Sussex, England

RHS Garden Wisley
Surrey, England

Springfields Show Gardens
Lincolnshire, England
Stourhead
Wiltshire, England
Thorp Perrow Arboretum &
Woodland Garden
North Yorkshire, England
Threave Garden
Dumfries & Galloway, Scotland

DAHLIAS
Anglesey Abbey
Cambridgeshire, England
Biddulph Grange Gardens
Staffordshire, England
Halls of Heddon
Northumberland and Tyne &
Wear, England
Hever Castle
Kent, England
Orchid Paradise
Devon, England
Port Lympne
Kent, England
Savill Garden
Surrey, England
Valley Gardens
North Yorkshire, England

DELPHINIUM
8 Dunstarn Lane
West Yorkshire, England
Blackmore & Langdon
Somerset, England
Cambridge University Botanic
Garden
Cambridgeshire, England
Falkland Palace
Fife, Scotland
Godinton Park
Kent, England
Haddon Hall
Derbyshire, England
RHS Garden Wisley
Surrey, England
Rougham Hall Nurseries
Suffolk, England

FERNS
Abbey Cottage
Hampshire, England
The Abbey House
Wiltshire, England

Brodsworth Hall & Gardens
South Yorkshire, England
Fibrex Nurseries Ltd
Warwickshire, England
Glasgow Botanic Garden
Strathclyde, Scotland
National Botanic Gardens
Co. Dublin, Republic of Ireland
RHS Garden Harlow Carr
North Yorkshire, England
Royal Botanic Garden
Edinburgh
Lothian, Scotland
Royal Botanic Gardens, Kew
London, England
Sherborne Garden
Somerset, England
Sizergh Castle
Cumbria, England

FRUIT
Beningbrough Hall & Gardens
North Yorkshire, England
Berrington Hall
Herefordshire, England
Blackthorn Nursery
Hampshire, England
Brogdale
Kent, England
Broughton House Gardens
Dumfries & Galloway, Scotland
Croxteth Hall & Country Park
Lancashire, Greater Manchester
& Merseyside, England
Deacon's Nursery
Isle of Wight, England
Erddig
Clwyd, Wales
Felbrigg Hall
Norfolk, England
Garden Organic Ryton
Warwickshire, England
Hales Hall Gardens & Reads
Nursery
Norfolk, England
Heligan Gardens
Cornwall, England
Osborne House
Isle of Wight, England
Pershore College
Worcestershire, England

Reaseheath College
Cheshire, England
RHS Garden Wisley
Surrey, England
Rougham Hall Nurseries
Suffolk, England
Thornhayes Nursery Ltd.
Devon, England
Upton House & Gardens
Warwickshire, England
West Dean Gardens
West Sussex, England
Westbury Court
Gloucestershire, England

FUCHSIAS
Duchy of Cornwall Nursery
Cornwall, England
Green Island
Essex, England
Margam Country Park
Glamorgan, Wales
The Vernon Geranium
Nursery
Surrey, England

GLADIOLI
RHS Garden Wisley
Surrey, England

GLASSHOUSES
Bicton Park Gardens
Devon, England
Birmingham Botanical Gardens
& Glasshouses
West Midlands, England
Cambridge University Botanic
Garden
Cambridgeshire, England
Duthie Park
Grampian, Scotland
The Eden Project
Cornwall, England
Houghton Lodge
Hampshire, England
The Living Rainforest
Berkshire, England
The National Botanic Garden
of Wales
Dyfed, Wales
National Botanic Gardens
Co. Dublin, Republic of Ireland

Ness Botanic Gardens
Cheshire, England
Oxford Botanic Garden
Oxfordshire, England
Plantasia
Glamorgan, Wales
RHS Garden Wisley
Surrey, England
Roundhay Park & Tropical World
West Yorkshire, England
Royal Botanic Garden
Edinburgh
Lothian, Scotland
Royal Botanic Gardens, Kew
London, England
Singleton Park & Swansea Botanical Gardens
Glamorgan, Wales
Sir George Staunton Country Park
Hampshire, England
Stapeley Water Gardens
Cheshire, England
Stowell Park
Gloucestershire, England
University of Durham Botanic Garden
Co. Durham, England
University of Leicester Botanic Garden
Leicestershire, England
Wentworth Castle Gardens
South Yorkshire, England

HEATHERS
The Abbey House
Wiltshire, England
The Bannut
Herefordshire, England
Bell's Cherrybank Centre
Tayside, Scotland
Champs Hill
West Sussex, England
Exeter University Gardens
Devon, England
Furzey Gardens
Hampshire, England
Jack Drake
Highland, Scotland
Ness Botanic Gardens
Cheshire, England

Royal Botanic Garden
Edinburgh
Lothian, Scotland
Threave Garden
Dumfries & Galloway, Scotland
Valley Gardens
Surrey, England

HEBES
University of Bristol Botanic Garden
Gloucestershire, England

HEMEROCALLIS
Apple Court
Hampshire, England
Ann & Roger Bowden
Devon, England
Goldbrook Plants
Suffolk, England
Rosewood Daylilies
Kent, England

HERBS
The Abbey House
Wiltshire, England
Acorn Bank Garden
Cumbria, England
Buckland Abbey
Devon, England
Chesters Walled Garden
Northumberland and Tyne & Wear, England
Downderry Nursery
Kent, England
Garden Organic Ryton
Warwickshire, England
Iden Croft Herbs
Kent, England
The National Botanic Garden of Wales
Dyfed, Wales
RHS Garden Wisley
Surrey, England
RHS Garden Rosemoor
Devon, England
Royal Botanic Gardens, Kew
London, England
Salley Gardens
Nottinghamshire, England
University of Leicester Botanic Garden
Leicestershire, England

The Walled Garden
Worcestershire, England
York Gate
West Yorkshire, England

HOSTAS
Apple Court
Hampshire, England
Ann & Roger Bowden
Devon, England
Goldbrook Plants
Suffolk, England
Mill Hill Plants
Nottinghamshire, England
Park Green Nurseries
Suffolk, England
Rushfields of Ledbury
Herefordshire, England

IRISES
The Abbey House
Wiltshire, England
Broadleigh Gardens
Somerset, England
Kelways Ltd
Somerset, England
Lingen Nursery and Gardens
Shropshire, England
Marwood Hill Gardens
Devon, England
Mill Hill Plants
Nottinghamshire, England
Myddelton House
London, England
Rowden Gardens
Devon, England
Wakehurst Place
West Sussex, England

LILIES
Wakehurst Place
West Sussex, England

MAGNOLIAS
Bodnant Gardens
Clwyd, Wales
Caerhays Castle Gardens
Cornwall, England
Chyverton
Cornwall, England
Glendurgan
Cornwall, England
Lanhydrock
Cornwall, England

Marwood Hill Gardens
Devon, England
Millais Nurseries
Surrey, England
RHS Garden Wisley
Surrey, England
Savill Garden
Surrey, England
Sherwood
Devon, England
Trewidden Gardens
Cornwall, England
Trewithen
Cornwall, England
Valley Gardens
Surrey, England
Wentworth Castle Gardens
South Yorkshire, England

ORCHIDS
Glasgow Botanic Garden
Strathclyde, Scotland
Kelways Ltd
Somerset, England
RHS Garden Wisley
Surrey, England
Royal Botanic Garden
Edinburgh
Lothian, Scotland
Royal Botanic Gardens, Kew
London, England
Scone Palace
Tayside, Scotland

PLANTSMAN'S GARDENS
Antony
Cornwall, England
Beth Chatto Gardens
Essex, England
Biddulph Grange Gardens
Staffordshire, England
Birkheads Cottage Garden
Nursery
Northumberland and Tyne &
Wear, England
Bishop Burton Botanic Garden
East Yorkshire, England
Bluebell Cottage Gardens &
Lodge Lane Nursery
Cheshire, England
The Botanic Nursery
Wiltshire, England

Bressingham Gardens
Norfolk, England
Brook Cottage
Oxfordshire, England
Cally Gardens
Dumfries & Galloway, Scotland
Cambridge University Botanic
Garden
Cambridgeshire, England
Cannington College Heritage
Garden
Somerset, England
Capel Manor
London, England
Castle Howard
North Yorkshire, England
Chelsea Physic Garden
London, England
Chyverton
Cornwall, England
Coleton Fishacre Garden
Devon, England
Copton Ash Gardens
Kent, England
Cotswold Garden Flowers
Worcestershire, England
The Courts Garden
Wiltshire, England
Crûg Farm Plants
Gwynedd, Wales
Cruickshank Botanic Garden
Grampian, Scotland
The Dillon Garden
Co. Dublin, Republic of Ireland
Dundee Botanic Garden
Tayside, Scotland
East Ruston Old Vicarage
Norfolk, England
The Garden House
Devon, England
Glen Chantry
Essex, England
Gravetye Manor Hotel
West Sussex, England
Great Dixter
East Sussex, England
Greencombe Gardens
Somerset, England
The Harris Garden
Berkshire, England
Heathlands
Hampshire, England

Herterton House Gardens &
Nursery
Northumberland and Tyne &
Wear, England
Hidcote Manor Garden
Gloucestershire, England
High Beeches
West Sussex, England
Highdown
West Sussex, England
Hinton Ampner House
Hampshire, England
Hodnet Hall Gardens
Shropshire, England
Holbrook Garden
Devon, England
Holehird Gardens
Cumbria, England
Home Covert Garden &
Arboretum
Wiltshire, England
Howick Hall
Northumberland and Tyne &
Wear, England
Hunts Court
Gloucestershire, England
W.E.Th. Ingwersen Ltd
West Sussex, England
Kiftsgate Court
Gloucestershire, England
Killerton
Devon, England
Lackham Country Park
Wiltshire, England
Lamorran House
Cornwall, England
Leonardslee Lakes & Gardens
West Sussex, England
Longstock Water Gardens
Hampshire, England
Marwood Hill Gardens
Devon, England
Meon Orchard
Hampshire, England
Myddelton House
London, England
National Botanic Gardens
Co. Dublin, Republic of Ireland
Newby Hall
North Yorkshire, England
North Court
Isle of Wight, England

Nymans
West Sussex, England
Old Vicarage
Wiltshire, England
Oxford Botanic Garden
Oxfordshire, England
Plant World Botanic Gardens
Devon, England
Ramster
Surrey, England
RHS Garden Wisley
Surrey, England
RHS Garden Harlow Carr
North Yorkshire, England
RHS Garden Hyde Hall
Essex, England
RHS Garden Rosemoor
Devon, England
Rock Farm
Kent, England
Rowallane Garden
Co. Down, Northern Ireland
**Royal Botanic Garden
Edinburgh**
Lothian, Scotland
Royal Botanic Gardens, Kew
London, England
Saling Hall
Essex, England
Sausmarez Manor
Guernsey, Channel Islands
Savill Garden
Surrey, England
Scotney Castle Garden
Kent, England
Sheffield Park Garden
East Sussex, England
Sherborne Garden
Somerset, England
Snape Cottage
Dorset, England
Spetchley Park
Worcestershire, England
Spinners
Hampshire, England
St Andrews Botanic Garden
Fife, Scotland
Sticky Wicket
Dorset, England
Stillingfleet Lodge Nurseries
North Yorkshire, England

Stone House Cottage Garden
Worcestershire, England
Talbot Botanic Gardens
Co. Dublin, Republic of Ireland
Trebah Garden Trust
Cornwall, England
Tregrehan
Cornwall, England
Trelissick Garden
Cornwall, England
Trengwainton Garden
Cornwall, England
Tresco Abbey
Cornwall, England
Trewithen
Cornwall, England
**University of Durham Botanic
Garden**
Co. Durham, England
**University of Leicester Botanic
Garden**
Leicestershire, England
Valley Gardens
Surrey, England
Ventnor Botanic Garden
Isle of Wight, England
Wakehurst Place
West Sussex, England
Waterperry Gardens
Oxfordshire, England
West Dean Gardens
West Sussex, England
White Hall Plants
Suffolk, England
**Winterbourne Botanic Garden,
University of Birmingham**
West Midlands, England

PRIMROSES
Edrom Nurseries
Borders, Scotland

RHODODENRONS AND AZALEAS
Achamore Gardens
Strathclyde, Scotland
Angus Garden
Strathclyde, Scotland
Benmore Botanic Garden
Strathclyde, Scotland
Blackhills
Grampian, Scotland

Bodnant Gardens
Clwyd, Wales
Borde Hill Garden
West Sussex, England
Bosahan
Cornwall, England
Brodick Castle
Strathclyde, Scotland
Cannizaro Park
London, England
Chyverton
Cornwall, England
Clyne Gardens
Glamorgan, Wales
Cragside
Northumberland and Tyne &
Wear, England
Crarae Gardens
Strathclyde, Scotland
Dawyck Botanic Garden
Borders, Scotland
Dorothy Clive Garden
Staffordshire, England
Exbury Gardens
Hampshire, England
Furzey Gardens
Hampshire, England
Glenarn
Strathclyde, Scotland
Glendoick Gardens
Tayside, Scotland
Glendurgan
Cornwall, England
Glenveagh Castle
Co. Donegal, Republic of
Ireland
Gresgarth Hall
Lancashire, Greater Manchester
& Merseyside, England
Hergest Croft Gardens
Herefordshire, England
High Beeches
West Sussex, England
Highclere Castle
Hampshire, England
Higher Knowle
Devon, England
Hodnet Hall Gardens
Shropshire, England
Hydon Nurseries
Surrey, England

Isabella Plantation
London, England
Lanhydrock
Cornwall, England
Lea Gardens
Derbyshire, England
Leonardslee Lakes & Gardens
West Sussex, England
Logan House
Dumfries & Galloway, Scotland
Lukesland
Devon, England
Lydney Park Gardens
Gloucestershire, England
Marwood Hill Gardens
Devon, England
Millais Nurseries
Surrey, England
Minterne
Dorset, England
Mount Stewart
Co. Down, Northern Ireland
Muncaster Castle
Cumbria, England
National Botanic Gardens
Co. Dublin, Republic of Ireland
Ness Botanic Gardens
Cheshire, England
Nymans
West Sussex, England
The Old Glebe
Devon, England
Plas Newydd
Gwynedd, Wales
Ramster
Surrey, England
RHS Garden Wisley
Surrey, England
Rowallane Garden
Co. Down, Northern Ireland
Royal Botanic Gardens, Kew
London, England
Savill Garden
Surrey, England
Scotney Castle Garden
Kent, England
Sheffield Park Garden
East Sussex, England
Sheringham Park
Norfolk, England
Sherwood
Devon, England

Singleton Park & Swansea Botanical Gardens
Glamorgan, Wales
Stourhead
Wiltshire, England
Trengwainton Garden
Cornwall, England
Trewithen
Cornwall, England
Valley Gardens
Surrey, England
Wakehurst Place
West Sussex, England
Wentworth Castle Gardens
South Yorkshire, England

ROCK GARDENS
Cambridge University Botanic Garden
Cambridgeshire, England
Cruickshank Botanic Garden
Grampian, Scotland
Dorothy Clive Garden
Staffordshire, England
Mount Ephraim
Kent, England
Mount Stuart
Strathclyde, Scotland
National Botanic Gardens
Co. Dublin, Republic of Ireland
Ness Botanic Gardens
Cheshire, England
RHS Garden Wisley
Surrey, England
Royal Botanic Garden Edinburgh
Lothian, Scotland
Royal Botanic Gardens, Kew
London, England

ROSES, MODERN
The Abbey House
Wiltshire, England
The Alnwick Garden
Northumberland and Tyne & Wear, England
Benvarden Garden & Grounds
Co. Antrim, Northern Ireland
Chartwell
Kent, England
David Austin Roses
Shropshire, England

The Gardens of the Rose
Hertfordshire, England
Hever Castle
Kent, England
Longleat House
Wiltshire, England
Mattocks Roses
Oxfordshire, England
Nunwell House
Isle of Wight, England
Polesden Lacey
Surrey, England
Queen Mary's Gardens
London, England
Ragley Hall
Warwickshire, England
RHS Garden Wisley
Surrey, England
RHS Garden Hyde Hall
Essex, England
RHS Garden Rosemoor
Devon, England
Royal Botanic Gardens, Kew
London, England
Savill Garden
Surrey, England
Sledmere House
East Yorkshire, England
Winterbourne Botanic Garden, University of Birmingham
West Midlands, England

ROSES, OLD
Arley Hall
Cheshire, England
Castle Howard
North Yorkshire, England
Coton Manor
Northamptonshire, England
Cruickshank Botanic Garden
Grampian, Scotland
David Austin Roses
Shropshire, England
Drum Castle
Grampian, Scotland
Felley Priory
Nottinghamshire, England
The Gardens of the Rose
Hertfordshire, England
Hardwick Hall
Derbyshire, England

Helmingham Hall
Suffolk, England
Highnam Court
Gloucestershire, England
The Hiller Garden
Warwickshire, England
Hunts Court
Gloucestershire, England
Kiftsgate Court
Gloucestershire, England
Lackham Country Park
Wiltshire, England
Mannington Gardens
Norfolk, England
Mottisfont Abbey
Hampshire, England
Myddelton House
London, England
Nymans
West Sussex, England
Peter Beales Roses
Norfolk, England
RHS Garden Rosemoor
Devon, England
Royal Botanic Gardens, Kew
London, England
Westbury Court
Gloucestershire, England
Winterbourne Botanic Garden, University of Birmingham
West Midlands, England

Snowdrops
Anglesey Abbey
Cambridgeshire, England
Attingham Park
Shropshire, England
Benington Lordship
Hertfordshire, England
Berrington Hall
Herefordshire, England
Birr Castle Demesne
Co. Offaly, Republic of Ireland
Brandy Mount House
Hampshire, England
Cambo Gardens
Fife, Scotland
Colzium Walled Garden
Strathclyde, Scotland
East Lambrook Manor
Somerset, England

Easton Walled Gardens
Lincolnshire, England
Fairhaven Woodland & Water Garden
Norfolk, England
Foxgrove
Berkshire, England
Galloway House Gardens
Dumfries & Galloway, Scotland
Heale House Garden
Wiltshire, England
Hever Castle
Kent, England
Hodsock Priory
Nottinghamshire, England
Kailzie Gardens
Borders, Scotland
Lacock Abbey
Wiltshire, England
Monksilver Nursery
Cambridgeshire, England
Myddelton House
London, England
Painswick Rococo Garden
Gloucestershire, England
Penrhyn Castle
Gwynedd, Wales
Plas-yn-Rhiw
Gwynedd, Wales
Polesden Lacey
Surrey, England
Rode Hall
Cheshire, England
Rodmarton Manor
Gloucestershire, England
Snape Cottage
Dorset, England
Studley Royal
North Yorkshire, England

Sub-tropical Plants
Abbotsbury Sub-Tropical Gardens
Dorset, England
Achamore Gardens
Strathclyde, Scotland
Antony
Cornwall, England
Bosahan
Cornwall, England
Coleton Fishacre Garden
Devon, England

Derreen
Co. Kerry, Republic of Ireland
Dunster Castle
Somerset, England
East Ruston Old Vicarage
Norfolk, England
The Eden Project
Cornwall, England
Exeter University Gardens
Devon, England
Fota Arboretum & Garden
Co. Cork, Republic of Ireland
Glendurgan
Cornwall, England
Greenway
Devon, England
Greenways
Oxfordshire, England
Knoll Gardens
Dorset, England
Lamorran House
Cornwall, England
Logan Botanic Garden
Dumfries & Galloway, Scotland
Meon Orchard
Hampshire, England
Mount Stewart
Co. Down, Northern Ireland
Mount Stuart
Strathclyde, Scotland
North Court
Isle of Wight, England
Overbeck's Museum & Garden
Devon, England
The Palm Centre
London, England
Penrhyn Castle
Gwynedd, Wales
Rowallane Garden
Co. Down, Northern Ireland
Royal Botanic Gardens, Kew
London, England
Sausmarez Manor
Guernsey, Channel Islands
Talbot Botanic Gardens
Co. Dublin, Republic of Ireland
Torosay Castle & Gardens
Strathclyde, Scotland
Trebah Garden Trust
Cornwall, England
Trelissick Garden
Cornwall, England

Trengwainton Garden
Cornwall, England
Tresco Abbey
Cornwall, England
University of Bristol Botanic
Garden
Gloucestershire, England
Ventnor Botanic Garden
Isle of Wight, England
Westdale Nurseries
Wiltshire, England

TOPIARY
Abbotsford
Borders, Scotland
Athelhampton
Dorset, England
Avebury Manor Garden
Wiltshire, England
Brodsworth Hall & Gardens
South Yorkshire, England
Burton Agnes Hall Gardens
East Yorkshire, England
Chirk Castle
Clwyd, Wales
Cliveden
Buckinghamshire, England
Drummond Castle Gardens
Tayside, Scotland
Elvaston Castle
Derbyshire, England
Garsington Manor
Oxfordshire, England
Graythwaite Hall
Cumbria, England
Hatfield House
Hertfordshire, England
Herterton House Gardens &
Nursery
Northumberland and Tyne &
Wear, England
Hutton-in-the-Forest
Cumbria, England
Langley Boxwood Nursery
Hampshire, England
Levens Hall
Cumbria, England
Mount Ephraim
Kent, England
Packwood House
Warwickshire, England

Pitmedden
Grampian, Scotland
Renishaw Hall
Derbyshire, England
The Romantic Garden Nursery
Norfolk, England

VEGETABLES
Beningbrough Hall & Gardens
North Yorkshire, England
Croxteth Hall & Country Park
Lancashire, Greater Manchester
& Merseyside, England
Felbrigg Hall
Norfolk, England
Garden Organic Ryton
Warwickshire, England
Heligan Gardens
Cornwall, England
Le Manoir aux Quat'Saisons
Oxfordshire, England
Mertoun Gardens
Borders, Scotland
Pershore College
Worcestershire, England
Reaseheath College
Cheshire, England
RHS Garden Wisley
Surrey, England
RHS Garden Rosemoor
Devon, England
Upton House & Gardens
Warwickshire, England
West Dean Gardens
West Sussex, England
West Green House
Hampshire, England

VIOLAS
Elizabeth MacGregor
Dumfries & Galloway, Scotland
C. W. Groves & Son
Dorset, England

WILDFLOWERS
The Garden House
Devon, England
Naturescape
Nottinghamshire, England

WOODLAND GARDENS
Broadleas
Wiltshire, England

Heligan Gardens
Cornwall, England
High Beeches
West Sussex, England
Hodnet Hall Gardens
Shropshire, England
Home Covert Garden &
Arboretum
Wiltshire, England
Leonardslee Lakes & Gardens
West Sussex, England
Mount Stewart
Co. Down, Northern Ireland
Muncaster Castle
Cumbria, England
RHS Garden Wisley
Surrey, England
Rowallane Garden
Co. Down, Northern Ireland
Savill Garden
Surrey, England
Trebah Garden Trust
Cornwall, England
Trelissick Garden
Cornwall, England
Trengwainton Garden
Cornwall, England
Trewithen
Cornwall, England
Valley Gardens
Surrey, England
Wakehurst Place
West Sussex, England
Westonbirt The National
Arboretum
Gloucestershire, England

UNITED KINGDOM & REPUBLIC OF IRELAND

SCOTLAND

MAP 20

MAP 19

NORTHERN IRELAND

MAP 18

MAP 22

MAP 17

MAP 16

ENGLAND

REPUBLIC OF IRELAND

MAP 15

MAP 12 MAP 13

MAP 14

MAP 21

MAP 11

WALES

MAP 8

MAP 10

MAP 9

MAP 7

MAP 5

MAP 6

MAP 4

MAP 2

MAP 3

MAP 1

N

100km

100miles

Key To Garden Location Maps

——— Coastline	M5 Motorway	✳ Garden location
International border	A30 Dual carriageway	
Regional border	A39 Main road	
County border	Urban area	

Maps © JP Map Graphics Ltd, based on XYZ Digital Map Company data

MAP 2   CORNWALL   **449**

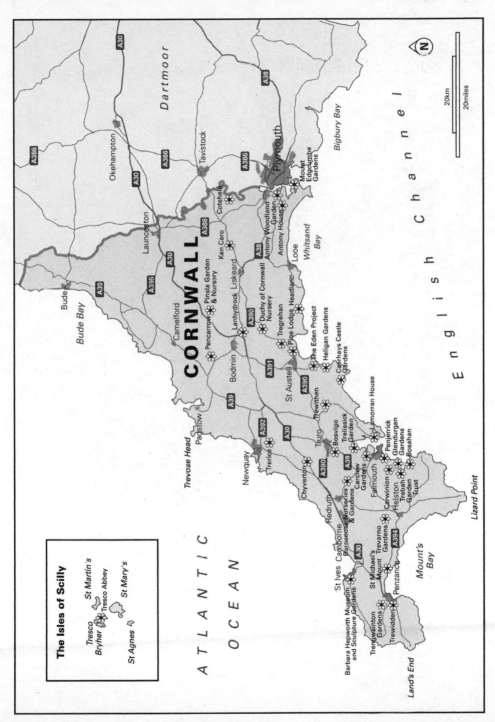

The Isles of Scilly

Tresco   St Martin's
Bryher   Tresco Abbey
         St Mary's
St Agnes

ATLANTIC

OCEAN

English Channel

Bigbury Bay

N

20km
20miles

Dartmoor

A30

A386

Okehampton

A30

A386

Tavistock

A386

Plymouth

A38

Mount
Edgcumbe
Gardens

Launceston

A388

Cotehele

Antony Woodland
Garden
Antony House

Whitsand
Bay

CORNWALL

Ken Caro

Pencarrow   Pinsla Garden
            & Nursery

Camelford   Lanhydrock   Liskeard

A30

A395

A39

Bude

Bude Bay

A390

A38

Looe

Duchy of Cornwall
Nursery

Tregrehan

Pipe Lodge, Headland

The Eden Project

Bodmin

Padstow

A391

St Austell

Heligan Gardens

Caerhays Castle
Gardens

Trevose Head

A390

Trewithen

Newquay

A392

Trerice

A30

Truro   Boswigo

Lamorran House

Trelissick
Garden

Penjerrick
Glendurgan
Gardens
Bosahan

Chyverton

A390

A39

Carclew
Gardens

Redruth

Burncoose Nurseries
& Gardens

Falmouth

Carwinion   Treban
Helston   Garden
Glendurgan Trust

St Ives   Camborne

A30

St Michael's
Mount   Trevarno
Gardens

Mount's
Bay

Barbara Hepworth Museum
and Sculpture Gardens

Penzance

A394

Trengwainton
Gardens

Trewidden

Land's End

Lizard Point

E
n
g
l
i
s
h

C
h
a
n
n
e
l

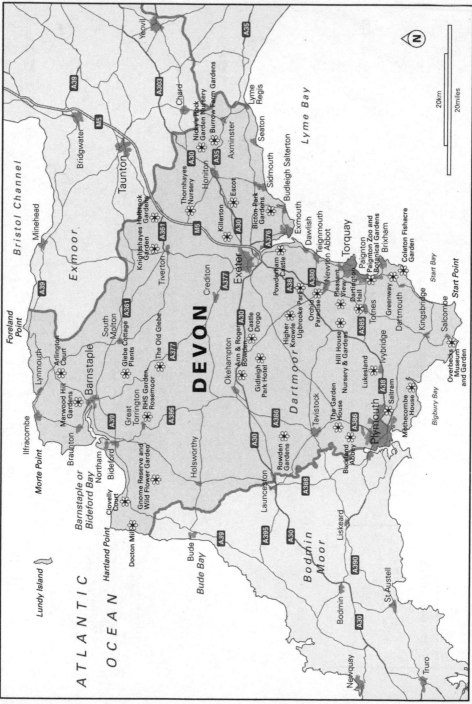

ATLANTIC OCEAN

Lundy Island

Bristol Channel

Foreland Point

Minehead

Bridgwater

Yeovil

A39

A303

A35

M5

Lyme Bay

Chard

Nickys Rock Garden Nursery

Burrow Farm Gardens

Lyme Regis

Seaton

Axminster

Honiton

A30

A35

Sidmouth

Budleigh Salterton

Thornhayes Nursery

Escot

Bicton Park Gardens

Exmouth

Killerton

A376

Dawlish

Teignmouth

Torquay

Paignton

Paignton Zoo and Botanical Gardens

Brixham

Coleton Fishacre Garden

Start Bay

Start Point

Exmoor

Lynmouth

Lynton

A39

Knightshayes Holnicott Garden

A361

M5

Tiverton

Crediton

A377

Exeter

Powderham Castle

A38

A380

Newton Abbot

Pleasant View

Dartington Hall

Totnes

A385

Greenway

Dartmouth

Kingsbridge

Salcombe

Ilfracombe

Morte Point

Braunton

South Molton

Arlington Court

Marwood Hill Gardens

Barnstaple

Glebe Cottage Plants

A361

The Old Glebe

A377

DEVON

Okehampton

Ann & Roger Bowden

Castle Drogo

Gidleigh Park Hotel

Higher Knowle

Ugbrooke Park

Orchid Paradise

Hill House Nursery & Gardens

Lukesland

Ivybridge

A38

Saltram

Modbury

Overbecks Museum and Garden

Bigbury Bay

RHS Garden Rosemoor

Great Torrington

A386

Dartmoor

Tavistock

The Garden House

A386

Plymouth

Mothecombe House

Barnstaple or Bideford Bay

Northam

Bideford

A39

Holsworthy

A30

Rowden Gardens

Buckland Abbey

A388

Clovelly Coast

Gnome Reserve and Wild Flower Garden

Docton Mill

Hartland Point

Bude

Bude Bay

Launceston

A395

A30

Bodmin Moor

Liskeard

A390

Bodmin

St Austell

Newquay

Truro

A30

N

20km

20miles

MAP 4   DORSET & HAMPSHIRE   **451**

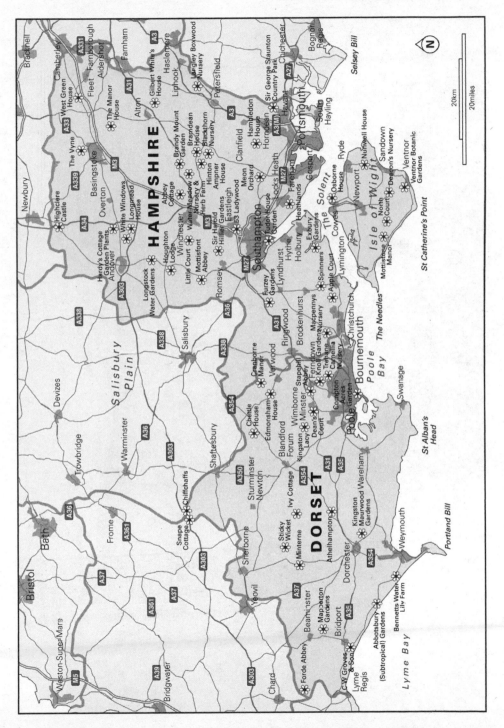

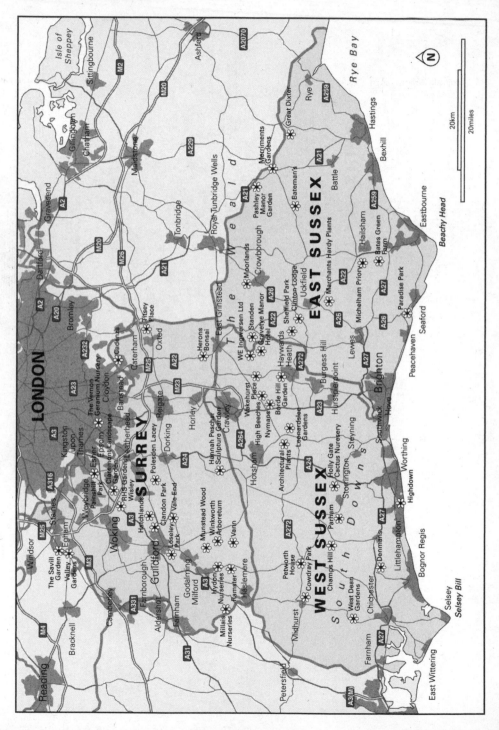

MAP 6 KENT **453**

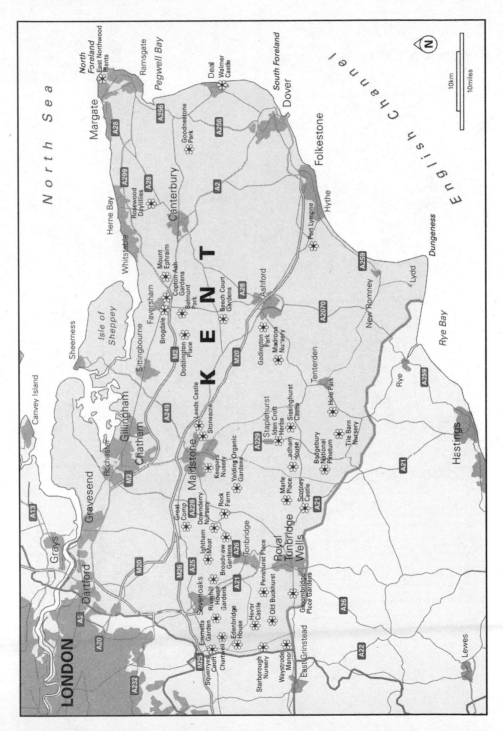

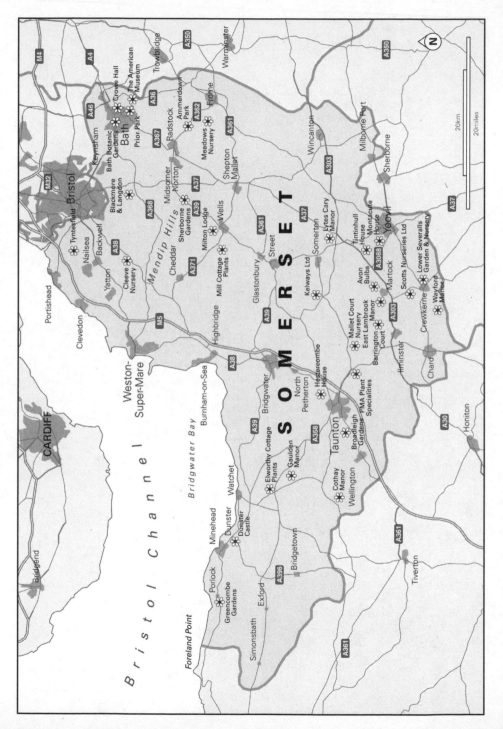

N

20km
20miles

M4

A4

A46

Keynsham

M32

Bristol

Portishead

Clevedon

CARDIFF

Weston-Super-Mare

Bridgend

Bristol Channel

Bridgwater Bay

Foreland Point

Porlock

Minehead

Dunster

Dunster Castle

Bridgetown

Simonsbath

Exford

Greencombe Gardens

A396

A350

Trowbridge

Warminster

Grove Hall

The American Museum

Bath

Prior Park

Bath Botanic Gardens

A36

Amerdown Park

A362

Frome

A361

Radstock

A367

Meadows Nursery

Shepton Mallet

Wincanton

Milborne Port

Sherborne

A37

A303

Tyntesfield

Backwell

Nailsea

A38

Yatton

Cleeve Nursery

Blackmore & Langdon

A368

Midsomer Norton

Mendip Hills

Sherborne Gardens

A39

Milton Lodge

Cheddar

A371

Wells

Mill Cottage Plants

Highbridge

M5

Glastonbury

Street

A361

Somerton

Kelways Ltd

Lytes Cary Manor

A37

Tintinhull House

Montacute House

Yeovil

A3088

Martock

Scotts Nurseries Ltd

Lower Severalls Garden & Nursery

Crewkerne

Wayford Manor

A303

Avon Bulbs

Mallet Court Nursery

East Lambrook Manor

Barrington Court

A39

Burnham-on-Sea

A38

Bridgwater

North Petherton

Hestercombe House

PMA Plant Specialities

Broadleigh Gardens

Taunton

A358

Watchet

A39

Elworthy Cottage Plants

Gaulden Manor

Cothay Manor

Wellington

S O M E R S E T

Ilminster

Chard

A30

Honiton

A361

Tiverton

A37

A350

MAP 8   WILTSHIRE   **455**

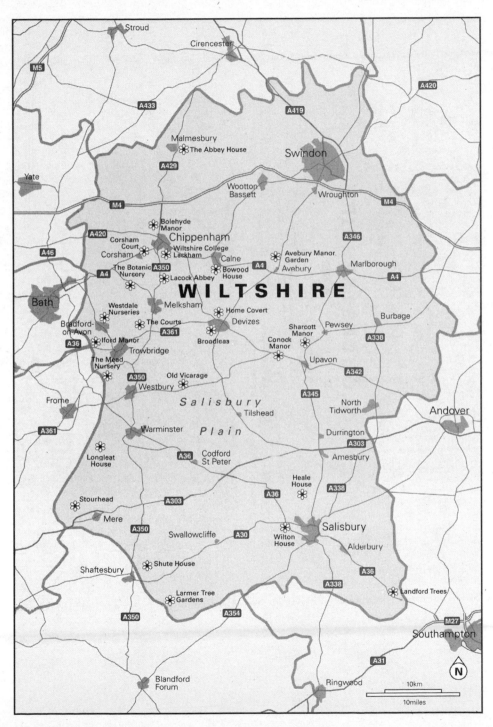

Stroud

Cirencester

M5

A420

A433

A419

Malmesbury
The Abbey House

Swindon

A429

Yate

Wootton
Bassett

Wroughton

M4

M4

A346

A420

Bolehyde
Manor

Corsham
Court

Wiltshire College
Lackham

Chippenham

Avebury Manor
Garden

Marlborough

A46

Corsham

The Botanic
Nursery

A350

Calne

A4

Avebury

A4

Bowood
House

Lacock Abbey

WILTSHIRE

A4

Bath

Westdale
Nurseries

Melksham

Home Covert

Bradford-
on-Avon

The Courts

A361

Devizes

Sharcott
Manor

Pewsey

Burbage

A36

Iford Manor

Trowbridge

Broadleas

Conock
Manor

A338

The Mead
Nursery

A350

Old Vicarage

Upavon

A342

Frome

Westbury

Salisbury

A345

North
Tidworth

Andover

A361

Warminster

Plain

Tilshead

Longleat
House

A36

Codford
St Peter

Durrington

Amesbury

A303

Stourhead

A303

A36

Heale
House

A338

Mere

A350

Swallowcliffe

A30

Wilton
House

Salisbury

Alderbury

Shaftesbury

Shute House

A338

A36

Larmer Tree
Gardens

Landford Trees

A350

A354

M27

Southampton

A31

Blandford
Forum

Ringwood

N

10km

10miles

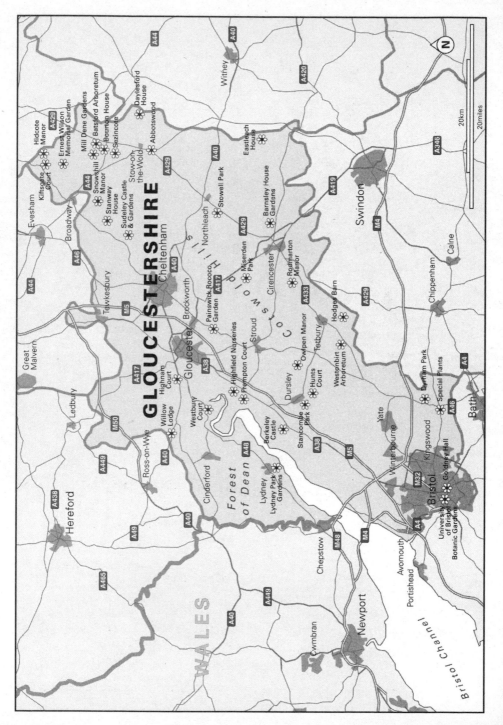

N

20km
20miles

GLOUCESTERSHIRE

WALES

Forest of Dean

Bristol Channel

A44
A40
A429
A420
A346
A429
A44
A46
A417
M5
A40
A38
A417
A429
A433
A419
M4
A4
A16
A46
A4
M48
M4
A32
A41
A38
A48
A449
A40
A40
A465
A138
A449
A49

Hidcote Manor
Kiftsgate Court
Ernest Wilson Memorial Garden
Mill Dene Gardens
Batsford Arboretum
Bourton House
Sezincote
Daylesford House
Abbotswood
Withey
Eastleach House
Snowshill Manor
Stanway House
Sudeley Castle & Gardens
Stow-on-the-Wold
Stowell Park
Barnsley House Gardens
Evesham
Broadway
Tewkesbury
Cheltenham
Northleach
Miserden Park
Rodmarton Manor
Swindon
Calne
Chippenham
Great Malvern
Ledbury
Highnam Court
Gloucester
Brockworth
Painswick Rococo Garden
Cirencester
Stroud
Hodges Barn
Dunham Park
Special Plants
A4
Ross-on-Wye
Willow Lodge
Westbury Court
Highfield Nurseries
Frampton Court
Dursley
Owlpen Manor
Hunts Court
Tetbury
Westonbirt Arboretum
Yate
Bath
Hereford
Cinderford
Berkeley Castle
Stancombe Park
Winterbourne
Kingswood
Goldney Hall
Bristol
Lydney
Lydney Park Gardens
University of Bristol Botanic Gardens
Chepstow
Avonmouth
Portishead
Cwmbran
Newport

MAP 10 OXFORDSHIRE / BUCKINGHAMSHIRE / BERKSHIRE **457**

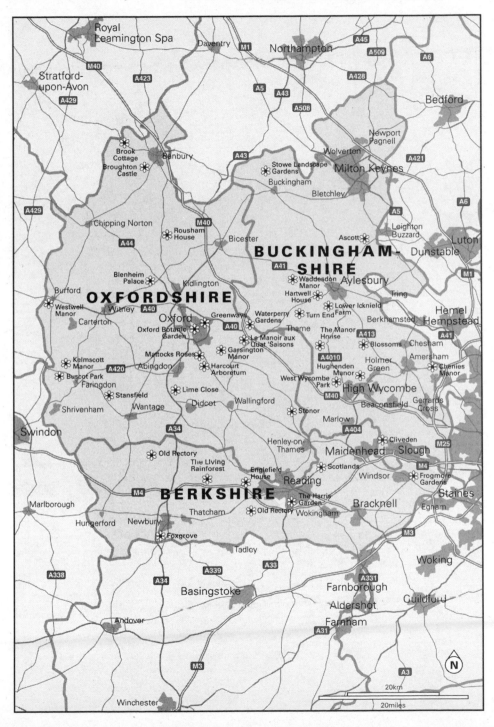

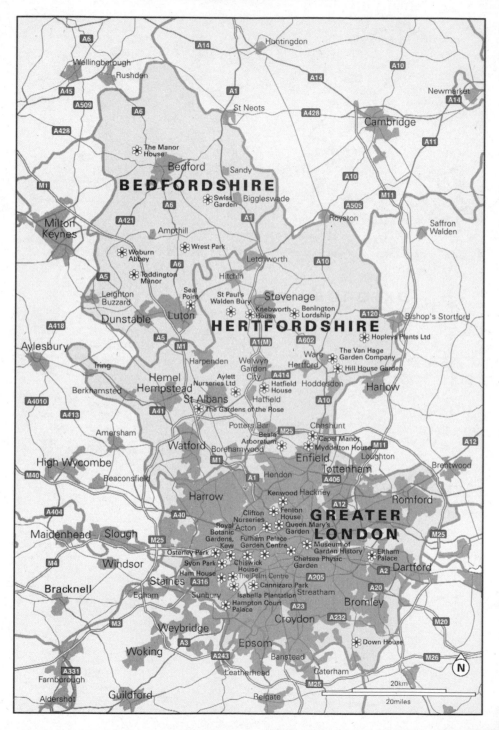

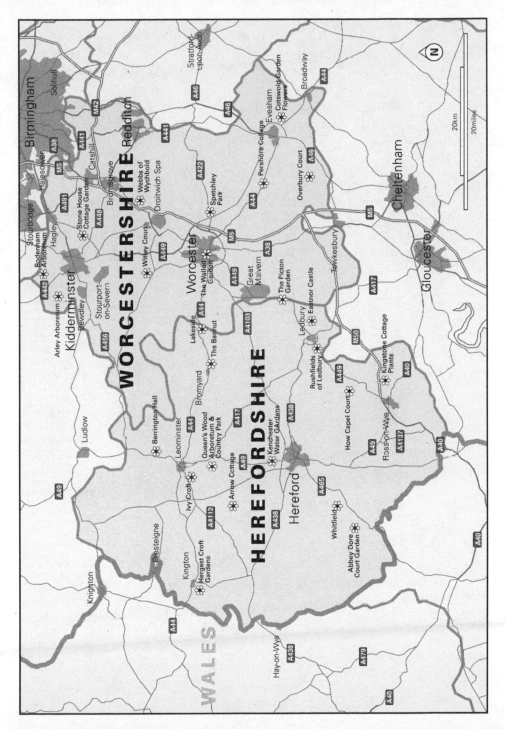

MAP 12 WORCESTERSHIRE & HEREFORDSHIRE 459

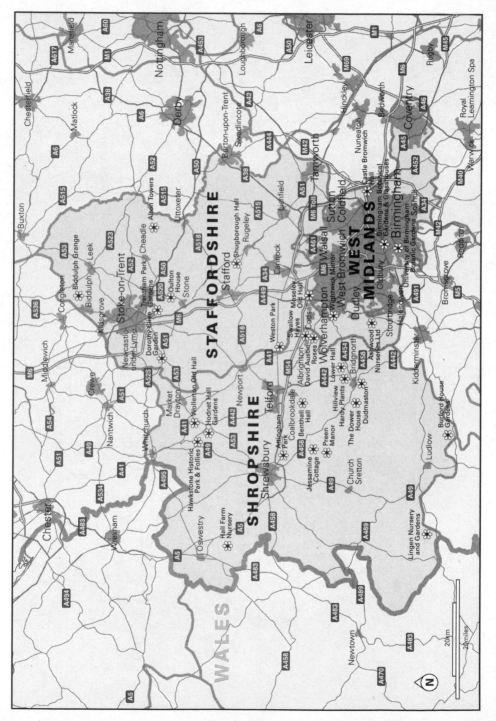

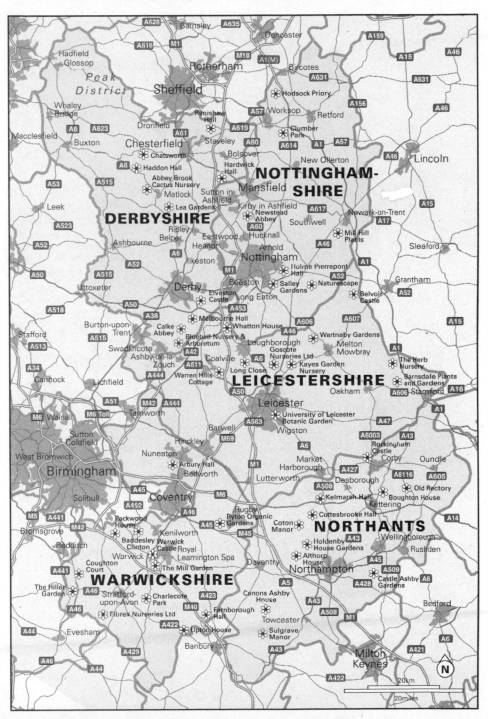

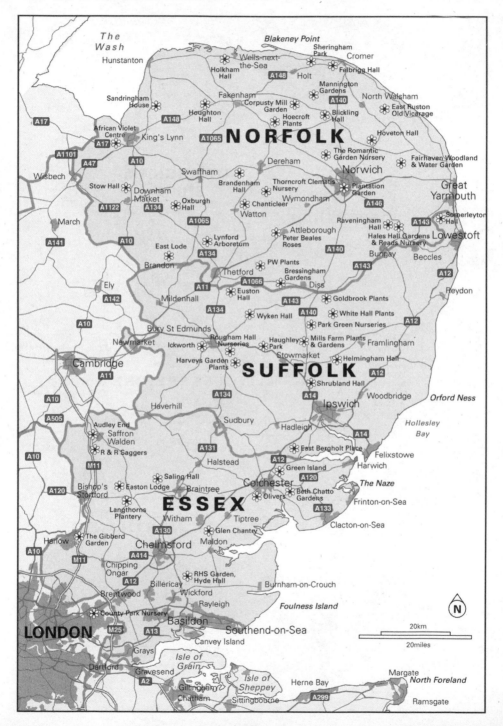

The Wash

Blakeney Point

Hunstanton

Sheringham Park

Cromer

Wells-next-the-Sea

Holkham Hall

Holt

Felbrigg Hall

A148

Mannington Gardens

North Walsham

East Ruston Old Vicarage

Sandringham House

Fakenham

Corpusty Mill Garden

A140

Blickling Hall

Houghton Hall

Hoecroft Plants

African Violet Centre

King's Lynn

A1065

NORFOLK

Hoveton Hall

A17

A17

A148

The Romantic Garden Nursery

Fairhaven Woodland & Water Garden

A1101

A10

Dereham

Norwich

A47

Wisbech

Swaffham

Great Yarmouth

Stow Hall

Brandenham Hall

Thorncroft Clematis Nursery

Plantation Garden

Downham Market

Oxburgh Hall

Chanticleer

Wymondham

A146

A1122

A134

Watton

Raveningham Hall

Somerleyton Hall

March

A1065

Attleborough

Hales Hall Gardens & Reads Nursery

A143

Lowestoft

Lynford Arboretum

Peter Beales Roses

A140

Bungay

Beccles

East Lode

A10

A134

Brandon

PW Plants

Bressingham Gardens

A143

A12

Ely

Thetford

Diss

Reydon

A142

A11

Euston Hall

Goldbrook Plants

A143

Mildenhall

A134

Wyken Hall

A140

White Hall Plants

A12

Bury St Edmunds

Rougham Hall Nurseries

Haughley Park

Park Green Nurseries

Mills Farm Plants & Gardens

Newmarket

Ickworth

Framlingham

Harveys Garden Plants

Stowmarket

Helmingham Hall

Cambridge

SUFFOLK

A12

A11

A134

Shrubland Hall

Woodbridge

Orford Ness

Haverhill

A14

Ipswich

A10

Sudbury

A505

Hadleigh

Hollesley Bay

Audley End

Saffron Walden

A14

R & R Saggers

A131

East Bergholt Place

Felixstowe

M11

Halstead

A12

Green Island

Harwich

A10

Saling Hall

Colchester

A120

The Naze

Easton Lodge

Braintree

Olivers

Beth Chatto Gardens

A120

Bishop's Stortford

ESSEX

Frinton-on-Sea

Langthorns Plantery

Witham

Tiptree

A133

A130

Clacton-on-Sea

M11

The Gibberd Garden

Glen Chantry

Harlow

Chelmsford

Maldon

A10

A414

Chipping Ongar

RHS Garden, Hyde Hall

Burnham-on-Crouch

A12

Billericay

Wickford

Brentwood

Rayleigh

Foulness Island

County Park Nursery

Basildon

M25

Southend-on-Sea

LONDON

A13

Canvey Island

Grays

Isle of Grain

Dartford

Gravesend

Isle of Sheppey

Herne Bay

Margate

North Foreland

A2

Gillingham

Chatham

Sittingbourne

A299

Ramsgate

N

20km

20miles

MAP 16 LINCOLNSHIRE & CAMBRIDGESHIRE **463**

M62

Barton-upon-Humber

Normanby Hall Country Park

A15

Immingham

Grimsby

Spurn Head

N O R T H

M180

M181

Scunthorpe

Cleethorpes

S E A

M18

Doncaster

Pottertons Nursery

A46

A18

A159

A15

Hippopottering Nursery

A46

Kathleen Muncaster Fuchsias

Martin Nest Nurseries

Market Rasen

Louth

A1(M)

A631

A631

Hall Farm & Nursery

Mablethorpe

Gainsborough

A156

Worksop

A1

A57

Alford

A614

Doddington Hall

A158

Horncastle

A1028

Gunby Hall

A1

A46

Lincoln

Skegness

LINCOLNSHIRE

Gibraltar Point

Newark-on-Trent

A617

A15

A16

A52

A6097

A46

Nottingham

A52

A1

Sleaford

A17

Boston

The Wash

Belton House

Grantham

A52

Donington

A52

A15

A16

A607

Easton Walled Gardens

Springfields Show Gardens

A17

Holbeach

Long Sutton

A148

Grimsthorpe Castle

Baytree Nurseries

Sutton Bridge

A46

Melton Mowbray

A1

Bourne

Spalding

King's Lynn

A606

A16

A1101

A47

A10

Market Deeping

Peckover House

Wisbech

Leicester

Stamford

A16

A15

A47

A47

Peterborough

A1122

A134

A1065

A6003

A43

Whittlesey

March

A6

Elton Hall

A141

A10

Corby

Yaxley

A427

A605

A1(M)

Chatteris

Littleport

Kettering

CAMBRIDGESHIRE

Abbots Ripton Hall

Warboys

Ely

A508

A43

A45

A14

Huntingdon

Sutton

A142

A11

Wellingborough

Rushden

A14

St Ives

A10

Soham

Netherhall Manor

Monksilver Nursery

A14

Northampton

A1

Elsworth Herbs

Anglesey Abbey

Newmarket

St Neots

Clare College Fellows' Garden

Hardwicke House

A428

A6

Cambridge

Docwra's Manor

Cambridge University Botanic Garden

A11

A43

Bedford

Wimpole Hall

Great Shelford

Sawston

Crossing House Garden

A10

Melbourn

N

Royston

M11

20km

20miles

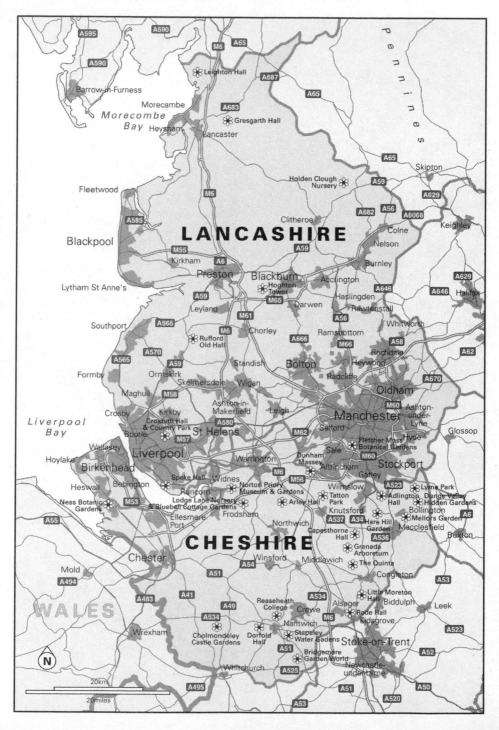

Pennines

A595
A590
M6
A65
Barrow-in-Furness
A590
Leighton Hall
A687
Morecambe
A683
Morecombe Bay
Heysham
Gresgarth Hall
Lancaster
A65
Fleetwood
Skipton
Holden Clough Nursery
A59
A629
A585
Clitheroe
A682
A56
A6068
Keighley
Blackpool
LANCASHIRE
Colne
Nelson
M55
Kirkham
A6
A59
Burnley
A629
Preston
Blackburn
Accrington
A646
A646
Halifax
Houghton Tower
Lytham St Anne's
A59
Leyland
M65
Darwen
Haslingden
Rawtenstall
Southport
A565
M61
Chorley
A56
Whitworth
A62
M6
Ramsbottom
A565
A570
Rufford Old Hall
A666
M66
Rochdale
A59
Standish
Bolton
Heywood
A58
Formby
Ormskirk
Radcliffe
A670
Maghull
Skelmersdale
Wigan
Oldham
M58
Crosby
Kirkby
Ashton-in-Makerfield
Leigh
M60
Ashton-under-Lyne
Croxteth Hall & Country Park
A580
Manchester
Glossop
Bootle
St Helens
Salford
Hyde
Liverpool Bay
M57
Fletcher Moss Botanical Gardens
Hoylake
Wallasey
Warrington
M62
Sale
M60
Stockport
Liverpool
Dunham Massey
Altrincham
Gatley
Heswall
Birkenhead
Speke Hall
Widnes
M6
M56
Wilmslow
A523
Lyme Park
Bebington
Norton Priory Museum & Gardens
Tatton Park
Adlington Hall
Dunge Valley Hidden Gardens
Ness Botanic Gardens
M53
Runcorn
Arley Hall
A537
A34
Bollington
A6
Lodge Lane Nursery & Bluebell Cottage Gardens
Knutsford
Hare Hill Garden
Mellors Garden
A55
Ellesmere Port
Frodsham
Northwich
Capesthorne Hall
Macclesfield
Buxton
Granada Arboretum
A536
Chester
CHESHIRE
Winsford
Middlewich
The Quinta
Congleton
A53
Mold
A51
A54
Little Moreton Hall
A494
Biddulph
Leek
A483
A41
A534
Alsager
Reaseheath College
Rode Hall
A49
Crewe
M6
Kidsgrove
A523
WALES
A534
Nantwich
Stapeley Water Gardens
Stoke-on-Trent
Wrexham
Cholmondeley Castle Gardens
Dorfold Hall
A51
A52
Bridgemere Garden World
Newcastle-under-Lyme
Whitchurch
A525
A50
N
A495
A51
A520
20km
A53
20miles

MAP 18 YORKSHIRE **465**

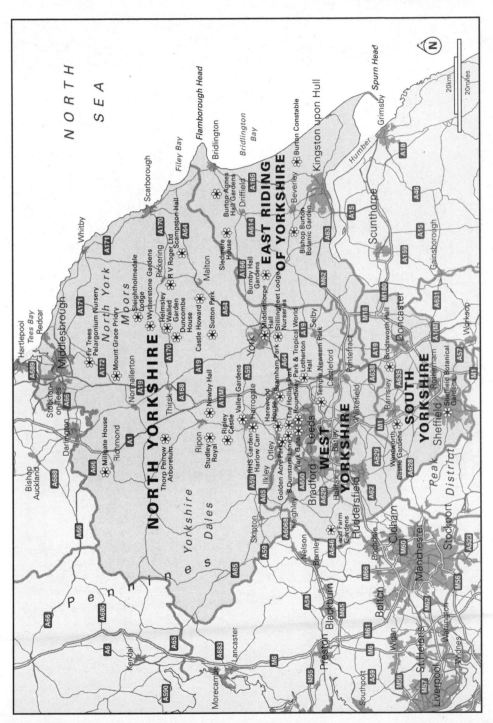

NORTH SEA

20km
20miles

Spurn Head

Grimsby

Humber

Kingston upon Hull

Burton Constable

Flamborough Head

Filey Bay

Bridlington

Bridlington Bay

Beverley

Bishop Burton Botanic Garden

EAST RIDING OF YORKSHIRE

A15

A46

A18

Scunthorpe

A15

Gainsborough

A159

A63

Whitby

Scarborough

A171

A171

Fir Trees Pelargonium Nursery

Mount Grace Priory

Sleightholmedale Lodge

Witherstone Gardens

R V Roger Ltd

Helmsley Walled Garden

Pickering

Scampston Hall

A170

A170

A64

Malton

Duncombe House

Castle Howard

Sutton Park

A64

Sledmere House

Burton Agnes Hall Gardens

Driffield

A614

A166

Burnby Hall Gardens

A165

North York Moors

York

Middlethorpe Hall

Stillingfleet Lodge Nurseries

A19

A62

M180

M18

Doncaster

Brodsworth Hall

A1(M)

A57

Worksop

A19

A638

A635

Barnsley

Wentworth Castle Gardens

Wortley

SOUTH YORKSHIRE

Rotherham

M1

Sheffield

Sheffield Botanical Gardens

Peak District

A523

Stockport

M56

M62

Warrington

Widnes

Liverpool

St Helens

M57

M58

Southport

A59

M55

Preston

Blackburn

M65

M66

Burnley

Nelson

A646

A6068

Keighley

Skipton

A59

A65

Lancaster

A683

Morecambe

A590

Kendal

A6

A65

A66

A685

A66

Pennines

Yorkshire Dales

Richmond

Millgate House

A66

A6

Darlington

Bishop Auckland

A688

Stockton on Tees

A66

A67

Middlesbrough

A689

Hartlepool

Tees Bay

Redcar

A172

Northallerton

A19

A168

Thirsk

A19

Ripon

Thorp Perrow Arboretum

Studley Royal

Newby Hall

A1(M)

Ripley Castle

Harlow Carr

RHS Garden Harlow Carr

Valley Gardens

Harrogate

A59

A658

Otley

Ilkley

B-Dunstan Lane

Golden Acre

York Gate

Leeds

Bradford

A650

A657

A62

A629

A638

A628

Halifax

Huddersfield

WEST YORKSHIRE

Wakefield

A61

Castleford

Pontefract

Temple Newsam Park

Roundhay Park

The Hollies

Lotherton Hall

Selby

A63

M62

Bramham Park

Harewood House

Land Farm Gardens

Oldham

M60

Manchester

Rochdale

Bolton

M61

M6

Wigan

A6

NORTH YORKSHIRE

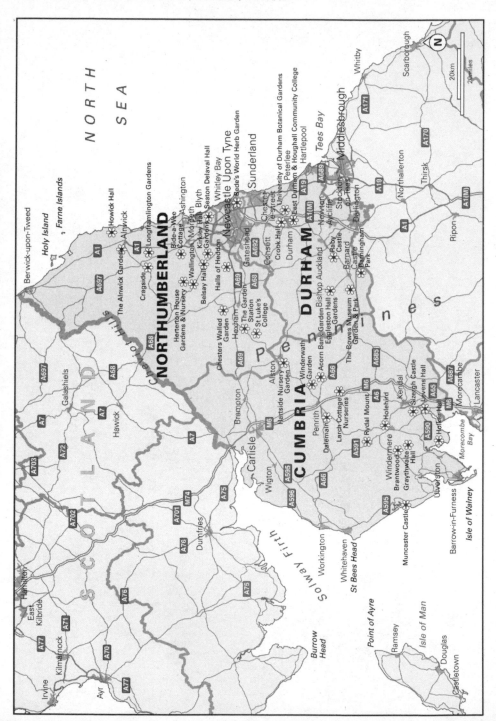

N O R T H

S E A

N

20km

20 miles

Scarborough

Whitby

Middlesbrough

Tees Bay

A171

A170

Northallerton

Thirsk

Ripon

A19

A1(M)

A1

A19

A1(M)

Hartlepool

Stockton-on-Tees

Darlington

Newton Aycliffe

East Durham & Houghall Community College

Peterlee

University of Durham Botanical Gardens

Bede's World Herb Garden

Sunderland

Whitley Bay

Seaton Delaval Hall

Blyth

Newcastle Upon Tyne

Gateshead

Chester-le-Street

Consett

Crook Hall

DURHAM

Durham

A692

A68

A69

Bishop Auckland

Raby Castle

Barnard Castle

Bedburn

Park

The Bowes Museum Garden & Park

Eggleston Hall Gardens

Acorn Bank Garden

A685

A66

A6

M6

Winderwath Garden

Alston

Hartside Nursery Garden

Brampton

Carlisle

M6

Penrith

Dalemain

Larch Cottage Nurseries

A591

Rydal Mount

Holehird

Kendal

Sizergh Castle

Levens Hall

A590

Holker Hall

A6

A65

A684

A683

A687

Morecambe

Lancaster

Morecambe Bay

Ulverston

Windermere

Brantwood

Graythwaite Hall

A595

Muncaster Castle

Barrow-in-Furness

Isle of Walney

CUMBRIA

A595

A596

A66

Wigton

A75

Whitehaven

St Bees Head

Workington

Burrow Head

Point of Ayre

Solway Firth

Dumfries

M74

A701

A76

A75

A7

A703

A702

A72

A697

S C O T L A N D

Galashiels

Hawick

A7

A7

A68

A68

C h e v i o t   H i l l s

A697

A1

A1

Berwick-upon-Tweed

Holy Island

Farne Islands

Howick Hall

Alnwick

The Alnwick Gardens

Cragside

Longframlington Gardens

NORTHUMBERLAND

Herterton House Gardens & Nursery

Bide-a-Wee Cottage

Ashington

Wallington

Morpeth

Belsay Hall

Kirkley Hall Gardens

Halls of Heddon

Hexham

The Garden Station

St Luke's College

Chesters Walled Garden

A69

A58

A69

P e n n i n e s

East Kilbride

Hamilton

Kilmarnock

Irvine

Ayr

A77

A71

A70

A77

A76

Isle of Man

Ramsey

Douglas

Castletown

MAP 20 SOUTHERN SCOTLAND **467**

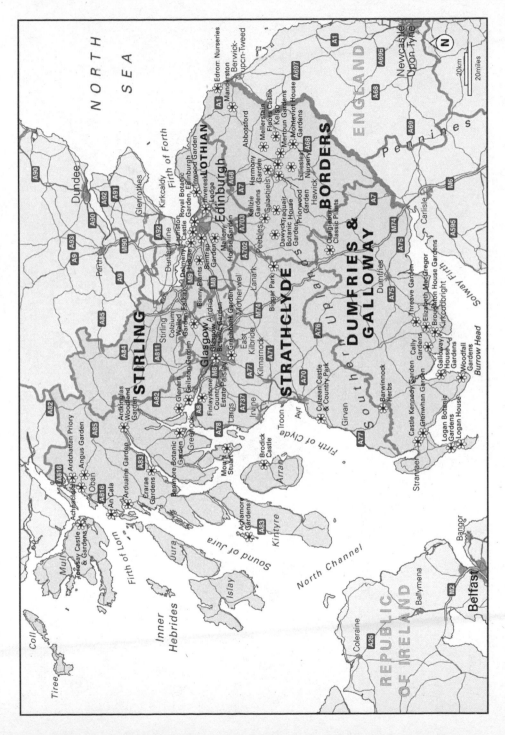

NORTH SEA

ENGLAND

Pennines

Newcastle-Upon-Tyne

Berwick-upon-Tweed

Edror Nurseries

Manderston

Abbotsford

Mellerstain
Floors Castle
Kelso
Mertoun Gardens
Monteviot House Gardens

BORDERS

Kirkcaldy
Firth of Forth

Inveresk Lodge

Dunfermline
Harriston
Dalmeny Garden
Royal Botanic Garden, Edinburgh
Linwood Garden

LOTHIAN

Edinburgh

Dawyck Botanic Garden

Harmony Garden
Priorwood Gardens
Hawick
Lilliesleaf Nursery
Kailzie Gardens
Traquair House Garden
Peebles

Hallmeny House Garden
Malleny Garden
Bimtrap

Binny Plants

Stirling
Colzium Walled Garden
Glenarn
Geilston Garden

Falkirk

Glasgow
Aubrie
Botanic Garden
Greenbank Garden

Lanark

Biggar Park

Outgerston Classic Plants
Galashiels

DUMFRIES & GALLOWAY

Dumfries

Motherwell
East Kilbride
Kilmarnock
Irvine

STRATHCLYDE

STIRLING

Finlaystone Country Estate
Greenock
Largs

Kilmarnock

Ayr

Troon

Brodick Castle

Arran

Firth of Clyde

Culzean Castle & Country Park

Girvan

Barwinnock Herbs

Castle Kennedy Gardens
Glenwhan Garden

Logan Botanic Gardens
Logan House

Stranraer

Threave Garden
Elizabeth MacGregor
Broughton House Gardens
Kirkcudbright

Galloway House Gardens
Woodfall Gardens

Cally Gardens

Burrow Head

Southern Upland

Solway Firth
Carlisle

A74
A75
A7
M6
M74
M75
A595

A697
A68
A69
A696
A1

Ardkinglas Woodland Garden

Ardchattan Priory
Angus Garden
Achnacloich
Oban
An Cala
Arduaine Garden
Crarae Gardens
Torosay Castle & Gardens

Benmore Botanic Garden

Mount Stuart

Achamore Gardens

Kintyre

Inner Hebrides

Mull
Coll
Tiree

Jura
Islay
Sound of Jura
Firth of Lorn

North Channel

REPUBLIC OF IRELAND

Belfast
Bangor
Ballymena
Coleraine

M2
A26

Dundee
Perth
Glenrothes

A90
A91
A92
A93
A9
A85
A84
A82
A83
A81
A77
A78
A70
A71
A73
A76
A7
A702
A703
A8
A9
A68

20km
20miles

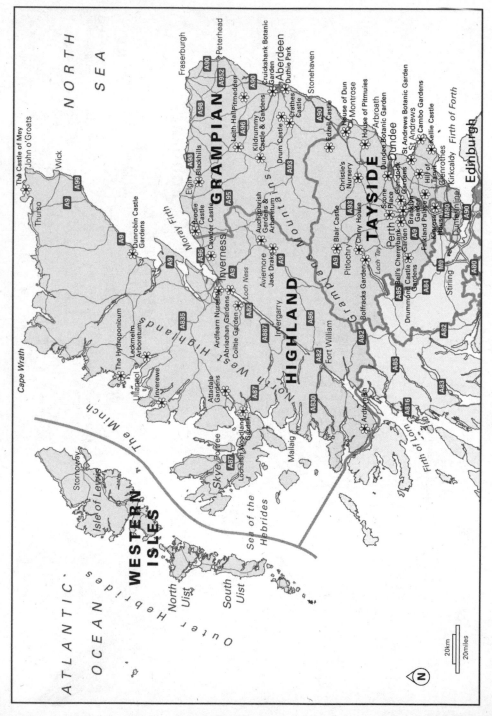

MAP 22 WALES **469**

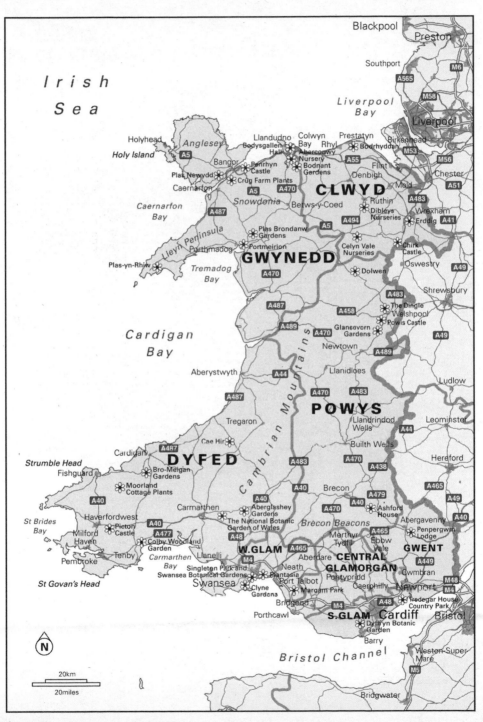

Blackpool

Preston

Southport

M6

Liverpool
Bay

M58

Liverpool

*Irish
Sea*

Holyhead

Holy Island

Prestatyn

Colwyn
Llandudno Bay Rhyl
Bodysgallen
Hall Aberconwy
Nursery
Bodnant
Gardens

Birkenhead

Bodrhyddan

M53

M56

Chester

Anglesey

A5

Bangor

Penrhyn
Castle

Plas Newydd

Crûg Farm Plants

Caernarfon

A5

Flint

A55

Denbigh

Mold

A51

A483

CLWYD

*Caernarfon
Bay*

A487

Snowdonia

Betws-y-Coed

Ruthin

Dibleys
Nurseries

Wrexham

Erddig

A41

Lleyn Peninsula

Plas Brondanw
Gardens

Plas-yn-Rhiw

Porthmadog

Portmeirion

GWYNEDD

A470

A487

*Tremadog
Bay*

Celyn Vale
Nurseries

A494

A5

Chirk
Castle

Oswestry

A49

Dolwen

A483

Shrewsbury

The Dingle
Welshpool
Powis Castle

Glansevorn
Gardens

A470

Newtown

A489

*Cardigan
Bay*

Aberystwyth

A487

A44

Llanidloes

A470

A483

Ludlow

POWYS

Leominster

Tregaron

Cae Hir

Llandrindod
Wells

A44

Builth Wells

Cardigan

A487

DYFED

A483

A470

A438

Hereford

Strumble Head

Fishguard

Bro-Meigan
Gardens

Moorland
Cottage Plants

Brecon

A40

A479

Ashford
House

A465

A49

*St Brides
Bay*

A40

Haverfordwest

Carmarthen

A40

Aberglashey
Gardens

A470

A40

Abergavenny

A40

Picton
Castle

A477

The National Botanic
Garden of Wales

Brecon Beacons

A465

Penpergwm
Lodge

Milford
Haven

Colby Woodland
Garden

A48

Merthyr
Tydfil

Ebbw
Vale

GWENT

Pembroke

Tenby

*Carmarthen
Bay*

Llanelli

W.GLAM

A465

Aberdare

**CENTRAL
GLAMORGAN**

A449

Cwmbran

St Govan's Head

Singleton Park and
Swansea Botanical Gardens

Plantasia

Neath

Port Talbot

Pontypridd

Caerphilly

M48

M4

Newport

Swansea

Clyne
Gardens

Margam Park

Bridgend

M4

Bristol

S.GLAM

A48

Tredegar House
Country Park

M4

Porthcawl

S.GLAM Cardiff

Dyffryn Botanic
Garden

Barry

Weston-Super-
Mare

M5

Bristol Channel

Bridgwater

N

20km

20miles

ATLANTIC

OCEAN

Islay

Kintyre *Arran*

Glenveagh
Castle

Coleraine

Guy Wilson
Daffodil Garden
Benvarden Garden
& Grounds

Londonderry

A2

A6

A26

Ardnamona

N15

NORTHERN
IRELAND

Carnfunnock
Country Park

*Donegal
Bay*

N15

*Lower
Lough Erne*

A5

Omagh

*Lough
Neagh*

A2

M2

Belfast

Mount
Stewart

A32

Enniskillen

A29

Portadown

Lisburn

Rowallane
Garden

N16

Sligo

A4

Armagh

A3

Annesley Gardens
Castlewellan National
Arboretum

Castle
Ward

Florence
Court

Seaforde
Gardens

N17

N4

*Lough
Conn*

Newry

A1

N2

N5

Dundalk

Castlebar

N3

Ardee

M1

Drogheda

*Lough
Mask*

REPUBLIC OF

Longford

N4

Tullynally
Castle

Roscommon

*Lough
Corrib*

IRELAND

*Lough
Ree*

Ardgillan Park

N17

Mullingar

N2

Irish

Galway

Athlone

N6

N4

National
Botanic
Gardens

Talbot Botanic
Gardens

Sea

Galway Bay

N6

Primrose Hill

The Dillon Garden

Aran Islands

Lodge Park Walled Garden

M7

Fernhill

DUBLIN

Japanese
Gardens

N18

*Lough
Derg*

Birr Castle
Demesne

N9

Powerscourt Gardens
National Garden
Exhibition Centre
Wicklow

N7

Gash Gardens

Heywood
Gardens

Mount Usher
Gardens

N8

Carlow

Altamont
Garden

N11

Limerick

Kilkenny

Ballynacourty

N10

Kilfane Glen
& Waterfall

Glin Castle

N24

New
Ross

Enniscorthy

N21

N20

Clonmel

John F Kennedy Arboretum

Annes Grove
Gardens

N8

N9

Curraghmore

Wexford

N22

Killarney

Lismore
Castle

N25

Waterford

Johnstown Castle
Gardens

Muckross House
& Gardens

N20

N8

Derreen

N22

Hillside

Cork

Fota Arboretum & Garden

Ilnacullin

Ballymaloe Cookery
School Garden

Bantry Bay

St George's Channel

Celtic   Sea

N

50km

50miles

INDEX

The entries in **bold** refer to main entries

YOUR COMPLETE GUIDE TO GARDENING TOOLS & SUPPLIES

THE Gardener's COMPANION

INDEX

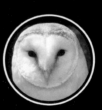

fig. 1

Introducing the range of gardener's boots the RHS *does* give a fig about...

A playfully chic exterior, but seriously hard wearing underneath – these boots were made for digging. A metal shank makes light work of even the toughest earth-turning, while the soft cushioned insoles and silky cotton linings ensure a comfort and fit hitherto unheard of on the gardener's grapevine. Constructed of strong natural rubber, they'll provide many seasons of horticultural happiness. Soon everything in your garden will be coming up roses – and sunflowers, and holly...

rhswellies.com

The RHS Digger boot by

HUNTER

The Hunter Rubber Company Limited, Edinburgh Road, Dumfries, DG1 1QA, Scotland, UK. Telephone: +44 (0) 1387 269 591 www.rhs.org.uk

ALL UK & OVERSEAS

SPECIALIST WATER FEATURES
Relaxing Naturalistic Landscapes
10%/20% off season discount March Only.
For more information see ad under Water Gardening in classifieds.
This is my style whether acres or your tiny backyard !
Paul Dyer, RHS Gold Medal + 12 Chelsea's since 92 !
View 1000+ on www.waterfeatures.co.uk
0800 91 98 33   7 days 8 to 8

HOLKER HALL

HOLKER HALL ESTATE & GARDENS

THE HALL & GARDENS
A sense of history

**FOOD HALL, GIFT SHOP
& COURTYARD CAFÉ**
A sense of taste

**LAKELAND
MOTOR MUSEUM**
A sense of adventure

A feast for all the senses

Whether you're enjoying the breathtaking Cumbrian parkland,
walking through the stunning gardens, shopping for
gourmet treats in the celebrated Food Hall, soaking up history
in the famous Lakeland Motor Museum or relaxing
in the alfresco delights of the Courtyard Café, a visit to the
Holker Estate is always a feast…for all the senses.

FOR FULL DETAILS OF ALL OPENING HOURS VISIT
www.holker-hall.co.uk

HOLKER HALL, CARK-IN-CARTMEL, GRANGE-OVER-SANDS, CUMBRIA LA11 7PL
TEL 015395 58328   FAX 015395 58378
EMAIL publicopening@holker.co.uk   WEB www.holker-hall.co.uk

FREE
PARKING

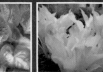

THE
Gardener's
COMPANION

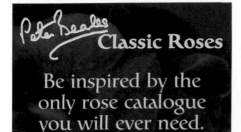

sooth & stroll & unwind

In the 17th Century, tulips were considered so desirable that a single bulb was traded for 2 loads of wheat, 4 loads of rye, 4 fat oxen, 8 fat swine, 12 fat sheep, 2 hogsheads of wine, 4 barrels of beer, 2 barrels of butter, 1,000 lb of cheese, one complete bed, one suit of clothes and one silver tankard. And a large field. There is no better place to appreciate the mesmerising properties of this irresistible flower than in Pashley Manor Gardens where they hold a 'Tulip Festival' every April/May with over 14,000 bulbs and more than 85 different varieties...

Experience more at
www.visithastings.com/soothstrollunwind

Hastings & 1066 Country

Visit the South East's historic coast and countryside where high emotions, extraordinary sensations and unforgettable experiences await you.

Battle o Bexhill o Hastings o Pevensey o Rye
www.1066country.com

ABOUT THINK BOOKS

If you have enjoyed *RHS Garden Finder*, why not try some of these other publications from Think Books.

Wildlife Gardening for Everyone

A collection of need-to-know answers to over 101 questions about cultivating wildlife in your garden. Published in association with the Royal Horticultural Society, The Wildlife Trusts and their co-produced website www.wildaboutgardens.org £12.99

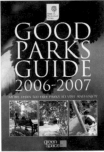

Good Parks Guide

The ultimate compendium of over 500 of the best public, countryside, urban and historic parks in the UK, complete with contact details and maps. Published in association with the Royal Horticultural Society and GreenSpace £12.99

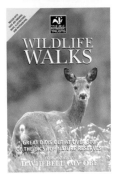

Wildlife Walks

A unique walking guide to over 500 of the most beautiful nature reserves in the UK, complete with contact details, over 100 colour maps, and wildlife guides. Published in association with The Wildlife Trusts £12.99

The Gardener's Companion

For anyone who has ever put on a pair of gloves, picked up a spade and gone out into the garden in search of flowers, beauty and inspiration. Whether you're a gardener or a garden lover, a veggie planter or an orchid painter, *The Gardener's Companion* is the perfect pocket filler £9.99

Think Books, Think Publishing, The Pall Mall Deposit, 124-128 Barlby Road, London W10 6BL
020 8962 3020 www.think-books.com

RHS GARDEN FINDER 2007-2008

Order your copy of *RHS Garden Finder 2007-2008* today.

To order:

Full Name: ....

Address: ....

....

Telephone: ....

E-mail: ....

Credit Card Number: ....

Expiry: ....

Start Date (if applicable): ....

Issue (if applicable): ....

Signature of Card Holder: ....

Or send a cheque for £12.99 made payable to Think Publishing to the address below.

Ref: G62

Send to: RHS Garden Finder Offer, Think Publishing, Pall Mall Deposit, 124-128 Barlby Road, London W10 6BL.